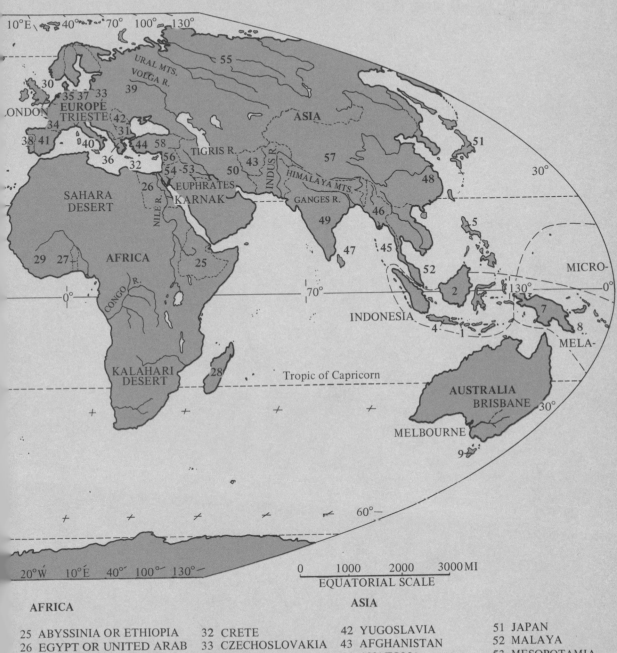

10°E 40° 70° 100° 130°

URAL MTS.
VOLGA R.

55

30

35 37 33   39
LONDON   EUROPE
          TRIESTE   42
34   31
38 41   40
       36   32
             54 53
       26   EUPHRATES
            KARNAK

ASIA

TIGRIS R.   58
      56
             43   57
  INDUS R.
       50   HIMALAYA MTS.
                GANGES R.

51

48

30°

SAHARA
DESERT

NILE R.

5

AFRICA
29 27   25
                49   47   45
CONGO R.
                         52
0°   70°   2   130°
           INDONESIA   4   1

MICRO-

7

0°

8

MELA-

KALAHARI
DESERT   28   Tropic of Capricorn

AUSTRALIA
BRISBANE   30°

MELBOURNE

9

60°

20°W   10°E   40°   100°   130°

0   1000   2000   3000 MI
EQUATORIAL SCALE

AFRICA

25 ABYSSINIA OR ETHIOPIA
26 EGYPT OR UNITED ARAB
         REPUBLIC
27 DAHOMEY
28 MADAGASCAR
29 MALI

EUROPE

30 BRITISH ISLES
31 BULGARIA

32 CRETE
33 CZECHOSLOVAKIA
34 FRANCE
35 GERMANY
36 GREECE
37 POLAND
38 PORTUGAL
39 SOVIET UNION
40 SICILY
41 SPAIN

ASIA

42 YUGOSLAVIA
43 AFGHANISTAN
44 ANATOLIA
45 ANDAMAN ISLANDS
46 BURMA
47 CEYLON
48 CHINA
49 INDIA
50 IRAN OR PERSIA

51 JAPAN
52 MALAYA
53 MESOPOTAMIA
      OR IRAQ
54 PALESTINE
55 SIBERIA
56 SYRIA
57 TIBET
58 TURKEY

An Introduction to
Anthropology

An Introduction to

Ralph L. Beals
Harry Hoijer
Alan R. Beals

Anthropology

5th edition

Macmillan Publishing Co., Inc.
NEW YORK

Collier Macmillan Publishers
LONDON

Harry Hoijer, who contributed so much to this and previous editions of *An Introduction to Anthropology*, died March 4, 1976, following a prolonged illness. He is survived by his wife, Dorothy Hoijer, who worked long and hard removing errors of spelling, grammar, and fact from this edition as she had from previous editions.   A.R.B.

Macmillan Publishing Co., Inc.
866 Third Avenue, New York, New York 10022

Collier Macmillan Canada, Ltd.

Library of Congress Cataloging in Publication Data

Beals, Ralph Leon, (date)
   An introduction to anthropology.

   Includes bibliographies and index.
   1. Anthropology.   I. Hoijer, Harry, (date)
joint author.   II. Beals, Alan R., joint author.
III. Title.
GN25.B42   1977   301.2   75-40279
ISBN 0-02-307450-7

Printing: 1 2 3 4 5 6 7 8   Year: 7 8 9 0 1 2 3

Preface

An Introduction to Anthropology is primarily a book about culture. It provides information about the ways in which the concept of culture has been defined; it explores the expressions of culture found among different peoples; it considers the various methods by means of which anthropologists study culture; it presents current thought and information about the development of culture, and it outlines major findings on each of the principal aspects of culture. Because culture is primarily a property of human beings that exists only in attenuated form, if at all, among other animal species, this is also a book about human beings. It considers the biological properties of human beings that are relevant to their possession and development of culture, and it examines the fossil and archaeological records with a view toward tracing the origin and development of culture and its impact upon the development of humanity.

Chapter 1 describes anthropology as a discipline and discusses the manner in which each of its four branches — biological anthropology, cultural-social anthropology, archaeology, and linguistics — contributes to our ongoing investigations of the nature of culture and humanity. Chapter 2 presents a variety of understandings and definitions of culture, and Chapter 3 considers the various kinds of data available to the anthropologist and the principal methods that are used in collecting and analyzing it. Chapters 4 and 5 deal with biological anthropology as a means of understanding the origins and nature of the human capacity for culture and as a means of tracing the interplay between culture and biology in the processes of human evolution.

Following these introductory chapters concerning the basic nature of anthropology, humanity, and culture, Chapters 6 through 9 provide a survey of the major ecological adaptations of human groups using the materials provided by archaeology and cultural anthropology. These chapters cover the development of culture from its earliest beginnings, discuss the origins in time of each of the major human adaptations, and illustrate each of the major forms of adaptation with descriptions of recent or modern peoples.

The major part of the book, Chapters 10 through 19, describes each of the important aspects of culture — economics, marriage and kinship, social organization, religion, language, art, psychology, and change — and presents our current understandings of the development, nature, and contribution of each of them. Chapters 20 and 21, which deal with applied anthropology and urban anthropology, present some of the ways in which the findings of anthropology have found relevance in dealing with current human problems. Finally, Chapter 22, which has been left unchanged from the previous edition, presents Ralph Beals' and Harry Hoijer's thoughtful conclusions concerning the intellectual and practical contributions that anthropology can make to the modern world.

Because a variety of simplified and specialized textbooks of anthropology and cultural anthropology are available, I have not tried to abbreviate or simplify the present work. This means that in many cases instructors will not wish to require their students to read every page or every chapter. Nevertheless those chapters that are not required reading in the introductory course are available to the student, and the text itself will serve as a useful resource long after the student has completed the introductory course. The primary advantage of a more or less encyclopedic textbook, such as *An Introduction to Anthropology,* is that it provides both teacher and student with a broad universe of general information within which they can freely pursue their own special interests.

In preparing this revision of the Fourth Edition, I have been constantly aware — indeed Ralph Beals has persistently reminded me of it — that *An Introduction to Anthropology* has consistently asserted the unity of anthropology and the strong interconnectedness of its branches throughout long and arid decades during which the different branches seemed to be developing into independent and essentially unrelated disciplines. Teachers and textbook writers in the field of cultural anthropology have argued persuasively that discussions of human biology, language, and archaeology should have no place in a textbook of cultural anthropology. Frequently, the attempt to integrate the different branches of anthropology into a single presentation has been regarded as characteristic of a distant period when the separate branches were closer together and a single individual might be regarded as a specialist in all four.

In recent years the idea that an integrated approach to the study of anthropology and culture was old-fashioned or obsolete has been increasingly abandoned. As biological anthropologists have specialized more and more in the study of the genetics of small populations or in the investigation of primate societies, the lines dividing biological and cultural anthropology have become blurred. Biological and cultural anthropologists now share a common theoretical base organized around such general concepts as adaptation, ecology, communication, and social organization.

With the development of what has been called the "new archaeology," archaeologists have turned away from purely historical interests toward serious attempts to contribute to developing theoretical insights concerning evolution, cultural change, and adaptation. In many contexts archaeologists and cultural anthropologists have joined hands in the construction of general theoretical frameworks that each can explore through the use of his or her own unique approach and methodology. In the same way linguistics, which at one time seemed to be taking on a separate life of its own almost totally apart from cultural anthropology, has moved away from its preoccupations with structure and grammar toward a broader study of the uses of language and its impacts upon communication. With the destruction of the barriers between language and behavior, linguistics has again become a part of cultural anthropology, and it is no longer possible to determine whether such specializations as sociolinguistics, ethnoscience, or cognition belong to linguistics or to cultural anthropology.

We find now that the concept of "general" anthropology, kept alive in *An Introduction to Anthropology* and in a very few other textbooks, is central to the pursuit of almost all of the "hot" research approaches that have developed over the past few years. All of the branches of anthropology are engaged in the study of humanity and culture. Progress in the field seems increasingly to be achieved only when the different branches are brought together by their shared theoretical orientations toward the study of such master concepts as adaptation, change, ecology, cognition, and communication.

The above discussion may serve to explain why, although I am separated by a generation gap from Ralph Beals and Harry Hoijer—one my father and the other my first anthropology teacher—I have not encountered very many difficulties in reconciling their approaches to my own. Although I have rearranged a few chapters, the present edition is essentially similar in form to the first. My main intent has been to make changes where they were mandated by recent developments in the field and to leave things much as they were where the coverage was already adequate. Nearly every chapter has been completely or partially rewritten, and new concepts, illustrations, and approaches have been introduced where relevant. The chapters that have been changed least are those dealing with language, the arts, and urban anthropology. Although there have been important research contributions in each of these three fields, most of them have been of a technical nature unsuitable for presentation in an elementary textbook. In the language chapter, for example, there was a temptation to introduce a discussion of the modern controversy concerning the nature of the phoneme, but this would have required a chapter in itself. Again, a discussion of transformational grammar and of the new grammars, which according to at least one linguist have rendered transformational grammar obsolete, would have introduced alarming complication. In the end, it seemed that both linguists and students would be most satisfied with the chapter if it remained, as in the previous edition, within the still valid general outline provided by Sapir, Bloomfield, and, of course, Hoijer.

In several chapters fairly radical revisions were undertaken in order to accommodate recent changes in our views of culture and of the role of the individual within it. Chapter 2, "The Nature of Culture," was almost totally rewritten, and this made necessary radical change in the social organization chapters to accommodate the many recent studies of political process and decision making. Many of the same considerations led to a thorough recasting of the chapter on religion. Chapter 18, "Culture and the Individual," was modified considerably to reflect recent work concerning education, cognition, and mental illness. The chapters dealing with human evolution, ecology, and adaptation, Chapters 5 through 9, have been altered to take into account new findings and new perspectives on human adaptations, but their overall structure remains substantially the same. The chapters on economics, marriage, and kinship contain some new examples and new approaches, but much of these chapters remains unchanged.

Although this revision contains much of the previous work done by Ralph Beals and Harry Hoijer, the various changes from the Fourth Edition are all my own responsibility. Both senior authors evidently felt that they had contributed sufficiently in the past and, therefore, with audible sighs of relief, excused themselves from any responsibility for the Fifth Edition. I was, however, able to prevail upon Ralph Beals to comment upon the chapters as they were finished. His comments were the most penetrating and useful of the editorial suggestions I received.

My colleagues and students at the University of California, Riverside, also contributed helpfully to this edition. David Kronenfeld and Alan Fix made useful comments on the chapters that concerned them. David Kronenfeld, Sylvia Broadbent, Lynn Thomas, Ed Plummer, Francine Marshall, and Clay and Carole Robarchek were kind enough to contribute photographic illustrations. Sherry Washburn of the University of California, Berkeley, was also generous and helpful in contributing illustrations. Judy Solter, Mary Jo Cittadino, Kathy Smith, and Alberta Brose were most helpful in collecting information, searching for bibliographic references, and straightening out footnotes. The work of Joye Sage, Sandi Stout, and Marilyn Davis in typing the manuscript deserves special gratitude.

Finally, I should like to apologize in advance for the various errors and omissions that may have been introduced as I struggled with a manuscript of unaccustomed length and complexity. It is not easy to fill the shoes of Ralph Beals and Harry Hoijer, and I would certainly appreciate any advice or suggestions that readers of this book might give with regard to possible future editions.

Alan R. Beals
University of California, Riverside

Concerning
Illustrations and Maps

The fifth edition of *An Introduction to Anthropology* retains many of the line drawings and photographs used in earlier editions. Although some of the photographs and drawings illustrate the text only in a general way, an effort has been made to find and select photographs which would illustrate statements made in the text or which would provide additional information about points made in the text. In these cases, a careful reading of the picture captions is advisable.

Many of the maps used in the text are derived from the third edition and were especially drawn by John Carthey, then departmental cartographer to the Department of Geography, University of California, Los Angeles. As a base for these maps, Mr. Carthey developed an entirely new rendition of the Flat-Polar Quartic Projection originally developed and published by the Bureau of the Census for world statistical maps by F. Webster McBryde and Paul D. Thomas.[1]

An important requirement of world maps of the distribution of anthropological data is that they possess the quality of equivalence or equal area. In a standard rectangular

[1] F. Webster McBryde and Paul D. Thomas, "Equal-Area Projections for World Statistical Maps," United States Department of Commerce, Coast and Geodetic Survey, Special Publication No. 245 (Washington, D.C.: U.S. Government Printing Office, 1949).

map, regions in northern or southern latitudes will tend to be represented by an area much larger than they, in fact, occupy. Equal area maps, on the other hand, tend to distort the shapes of land masses, especially near the polar regions.

The Flat-Polar Quartic Projection offers an unbroken network of meridians and parallels that at the same time suggests a round world. To minimize the distortion of land masses, Mr. Carthey has used 20 degrees west longitude as the central meridian on the map, thus insuring that most distortion will cover bodies of water or unimportant land masses. This also permits division of the map into Old World and New World sections. The shape of Alaska is improved over other renditions of this projection, and the Bering Strait, the probable migration route of the American Indian, shows plainly. New Zealand also appears in proper relationship with the rest of Polynesia, although its shape has lost some character.

Contents

1/ The Nature and Scope of Anthropology

1. What Is Anthropology?

Anthropology is the study of the origin, development, and nature of the human species. The word *anthropology* is a combined form derived from the Greek terms *anthrōpos* (human being) and *logos* (word) and can be translated as "the study of humanity." Its subject matter includes the earliest fossilized bones of humanlike creatures, the artifacts and material traces left in the earth by our ancestors, and all of the living or historically described peoples of the earth. Through the systematic analysis and comparison of all that can be discovered about humanity, anthropology seeks to develop increasingly profound and useful knowledge about the human condition.

The four major branches of anthropology are biological anthropology, cultural-social anthropology, archaeology, and linguistics. Biological anthropologists use the techniques of the biological sciences in the study of fossil and living human beings. Cultural-social anthropology uses techniques of historical research, observation, and interview in the study of recent and living peoples. Archaeology uses techniques of excavation and historical research to reconstruct the ways of life of vanished peoples. Linguistics uses the same techniques as cultural-social anthropology for the analysis of human languages.

Although the four branches of anthropology use different techniques and examine somewhat different subject matters, they all share the goal of understanding humanity, and they all make use of a single theoretical concept, the idea of culture. The idea of culture, which represents one of the great scientific discoveries of the nineteenth and twentieth centuries, is that human behavior, unlike that of any other animal species, is uniquely influenced and determined by cultural traditions that are transmitted among groups of human beings primarily by means of language. Each of the peoples of the earth possesses its own distinctive way of life including its own ways of doing things and its own ways of speaking. In a word, each people has its own culture. Anthropology is not just the study of human beings. It is the study of human beings living in societies and following distinctive ways of life labeled "culture." Even the study of human biological evolution requires understanding of relationships between biological processes and emerging cultural forms.

This introduction to anthropology weaves together the findings of biological anthropology, cultural-social anthropology, archaeology, and linguistics to provide an explanation of the development and nature of human cultures. Because any general statements about human beings are relevant to living peoples, the principal emphasis of this book is upon cultural-social anthropology. We rely upon biological anthropology for understandings of the biological evolution of humanity and for understandings of the biological foundations that underlie all human cultures. Because archaeology and linguistics represent studies of particular aspects of culture, these two subdisciplines can be regarded as specialized branches of cultural-social anthropology. To this book, archaeology contributes its knowledge of the evolution and development of human culture across the millennia, and linguistics contributes its knowledge of the development of language and its use in the transmission of culture and the organization of human activities.

2. The Aims of Anthropological Research

The central problem of anthropology is the explanation of humanity. Anthropologists seek to understand the origin and development of the species, the manner in which humans form groups and develop distinctive ways of life, and the various limitations and potentials inherent in humanity. Anthropology is concerned with all human beings, past and present, and with all of their works and activities.

There are many other disciplines that deal with humanity. In the biological sciences, anatomy is concerned with the physical structure of human beings, both in itself and in contrast to that of other animals. Physiology, embryology, and medicine all shed light on particular aspects of the human condition. All of the social sciences study aspects of human activity. Art, music, literature, drama, and all the other humanistic disciplines examine the works of humanity.

Anthropology's special role among the many disciplines concerned with people lies in its unique combination of holistic, historical, and comparative methods. The holistic method involves the study of human beings or groups of human beings in terms of the entire pattern of their lives. Thus, even when anthropologists specialize in particular fields such as biology, social relationships, economics, or art, they tend to consider those fields in terms of their relationships to all other aspects of humanity and human endeavor. The basic proposition underlying holism in anthropology is that human behavior arises out of complex interactions taking place within a cultural system. The nature of cultural systems is discussed in greater detail in Chapter 2.

The historical method in anthropology involves both the attempt to describe the entire course of human biological and cultural evolution and the attempt to place each way of life in historical perspective. Thus archaeology and ethnohistory attempt to reconstruct the origins, development, and interrelationships among the various peoples of the earth, whereas cultural anthropology interprets the cultures of existing peoples in terms of historical influences on their present ways of life and on their probable future development. Once holistic and historical methods have been used to obtain understandings of ancient and modern peoples, comparative methods are used as a means of explaining the similarities and differences among the various peoples of the earth. Comparative methods can be used in a limited way to construct explanations of variations within single political units or among closely related peoples. They can also be used in broad comparative studies designed to test broad, general propositions and theories concerning the nature of human beings and the cultures they construct.

Anthropological explanations are not limited to any particular group of human beings or to any single period of history. The anthropologist is as interested in the earliest forms of humanity as in contemporary forms. The biological evolution of the human species and the development of human ways of life are studied from the earliest times for which any record survives to the present. In studying contemporary humanity, the anthropologist is as interested in small distant human populations as in those that are large and close. The comparative study of the human species centers its attention upon the differences and similarities that separate and unite all of the peoples of the earth. It attempts to isolate and define the laws and principles that account for the development and perpetuation of such differences and similarities.

From the time of the earliest human attempts to discover the place of humanity within the natural world, it has been concluded that human beings are unique in the animal kingdom. Although there are many anatomical similarities between human beings and other animals, human beings possess a number of bodily attributes that are rarely or never present even among closely related animals. The brain of the human being is more complex than that of any other animal. Human beings walk and stand in a completely erect position. This is made possible by the possession of a distinctive foot structure, a broader and shallower pelvis than that of other animals, legs that are relatively long in proportion to body and arm length, and an S-shaped rather than a straight or bow-shaped backbone.

In the field of behavior human beings possess a complicated variety of tools and constructed objects, specialized techniques for obtaining and processing food, a division of labor in terms of arbitrary principles, a social and political organization, a system of religious belief and rituals, and the ability to communicate with others by means of a spoken language. Except in rudimentary form in a few exceptional cases, these cultural characteristics are lacking in other animals. Only human beings possess in developed and completed form the ongoing and flexible modes of behavior that anthropologists call culture.

To some extent the uniqueness of the human species rests upon the fact that it possesses all, rather than some, of the characteristics listed above. Taken individually, most human characteristics can be found in at least rudimentary form among other animal species. Bees and ants display a complicated division of labor, but it is based upon biological differences rather than upon arbitrary principles. Chickens possess a rudimentary form of social hierarchy. Wild chimpanzees have been observed to make and use crude sorts of tools. Monkeys in Japan, with some assistance from human beings, have been observed to invent new modes of behavior and pass them on to their offspring and their contemporaries. In the laboratory, chimpanzees have been trained to duplicate a wide range of human activities including the use of simple "languages" based on gestures or tokens and involving vocabularies of a few hundred "words."

The development of most animal species has taken place in connection with processes of adaptation to particular environmental circumstances. This has usually involved development from simple and generalized forms to increasingly complex and specialized forms. With the development of complex and specialized adaptations, most animal species tend to be restricted in range to particular environments or environmental niches within which their special adaptations are effective. Human beings, in contrast, appear to have remained relatively unspecialized. Such apparent specializations as exist—the complex brain, the flexible hand, the erect posture—seem to have been instrumental in permitting human beings to function in an unspecialized way in a wide range of contrasting environments.

Most important, as Julian Huxley puts it, human beings have developed the capacity to have culture, that is, the capacity to invent and learn new forms of behavior and to transmit them to other members of the species. This particular ability permits human beings, within limits, to construct their own environments and therefore to adapt to new situations without the necessity of a long period of biological change. Where the climate is unsuited to human biological adaptations (*Homo sapiens*, like the closely related apes, is of tropical origin), human beings have learned to make clothing and build shelters capable of maintaining an immediate environment resembling that of the tropics even in the Arctic. Where available foodstuffs are unfit for consumption in a raw state, people have developed ways of making them edible. In hundreds of other details human beings have discovered ways of extending and supplementing their physical powers and of adjusting to environments or shaping them to meet human needs. Because human beings are social animals living in groups and communities, the various sorts of adaptations mentioned above are generally the property of groups rather than individuals. Human adaptation, perhaps more than that of any other social animal, depends upon cooperation and exchange among the members of the group.

The capacity to have culture exists primarily as a consequence of the human ability to use language. Language enables human beings to achieve close and effective cooperation, and it permits the transmission of knowledge and experience from one individual to another. Human beings, unlike other animals, are not obliged to learn all that they know by direct experience or by observing and imitating the actions of others. They gain most of their knowledge through the medium of the spoken or written word. Although the written word permits the preservation of detailed records of past experience, cultures that lack written records may nevertheless preserve an ever-growing heritage of traditional knowledge that is passed across the generations from older to younger members. Language permits individuals to share the experiences, not only of their contemporaries, but of their ancestors as well. Within all human cultures the inventions and discoveries of long-past generations are handed down, often with successive improvements or modifications, to those who succeed them.

The fact that human beings have so freed themselves from environmental limitations as to permit their occupation of a large part of the land surface of the earth has had a profound influence on the development of human physique, behavior, and culture. Modern human beings, although all belong to the same species, are far more divergent in physical form than are the individual representatives of most other species. Although all human cultures and languages share broad similarities, differences in environmental adaptation, in the nature and amount of communication with other human groups, and in the historical experience of each group have brought about cultural and linguistic diversity.

It is probable that the first unquestionably human beings came into existence as *Homo erectus* more than a million years ago in the tropical regions of Asia and Africa after a period of development lasting at least four million years. These humans, possessing at least a rudimentary language and culture, spread over the Old World, gradually adapting, through the medium of culture, to a variety of environments ranging from Africa to the British Isles and from northern China to the island of Java. Some or all of these far-flung human beings ultimately developed into our own species, and for the last 50,000 years, a single genus with only one species (*Homo sapiens*) has existed. Today all varieties of humanity belong to this species.

The record of cultural and linguistic development is less complete. The stone and bone tools representing the surviving traces of ancient cultures show a progressive increase in sophistication and complexity. Existing human languages and cultures reveal differences so wide and so numerous that they must have had their origins far in the past. Because many of the unique biological features of the human species seem to reflect a pattern of evolution and adaptation characterized by the presence of culture, including the use of tools and language, it seems fair to conclude that a capacity to have culture and language developed in conjunction with the use of tools.

Because human beings develop cultures and, equally, develop within cultures, it follows that any explanation of humanity must take into account the presence of culture. Understandings of human biological evolution and of existing human biological properties require consideration of the cultural settings within which human beings evolve and survive. Understandings of human social relationships require knowledge of the patterns of behavior and of the beliefs and experiences handed down in the form of culture. All of the things that people say and do reflect the impress of the cutural settings within which they carry out their daily life.

The search for explanations of humanity is in large part a search for explanations of human culture, for it is culture that sets human beings apart from all other animal species. The central problem of anthropology is not, then, simply the explanation of humanity, for there cannot be an explanation of humanity without an explanation of culture. In examining widely varying cultures, anthropology seeks explanations of the similarities and differences among them. It asks questions like these:

What is the nature of culture?
How do cultures affect the personalities of the individuals contained within them?
How do individuals respond to the goals and ideals set by their cultures?
How does culture influence those forces of selection and reproduction which affect human biological evolution?
What directions is cultural evolution taking?
How do cultures moderate the relationships between human beings and the natural environment?

A search for the answers to these and related questions constitutes the central theme of anthropological research. Solutions to such problems require intensive study and comparison of many kinds of human beings and human cultures. The world of today and the fragmentary remains of its past are the sources of data for anthropological research.

A great many different approaches are required for the understanding of humanity in culture. Each of these approaches requires the development of its own specific methods. Anthropology, therefore, like many other disciplines, is divided into branches and subbranches, each having to do with some specialized aspect of the field.

3. Biological Anthropology

Biological, or physical, anthropology is the anthropological counterpart of the various biological sciences that deal with human beings. Because it studies human beings living in diverse cultures and examines the role of culture in the evolution of the species, it is properly set apart from those disciplines that regard human bones and bodies in strictly biological terms. Over the last twenty-five years, in response to revolutionary changes in biological science, biological anthropology has undergone change in the complexity and variety of the problems it studies and in the sophistication of the techniques it employs. In an earlier period much of physical anthropology involved increasingly standardized measurements of human skeletal materials or bodily characteristics. Detailed measurements of head shape and other bodily measurements were taken, and individuals, sometimes even from the same population, were assigned to a variety of racial or other categories on the basis of artificially constructed ideal types or by means of averages which often concealed large degrees of variation. The biological training of the physical anthropologist was limited to comparative anatomy and physiology, paleontology (the study of fossil forms), and simple Mendelian genetics.

Today, depending on the thrust of his or her research, the biological anthropologist may rely upon molecular biology and such techniques as electrophoresis, used for the analysis of hemoglobins, or computer simulations, used in population genetics. Although the use of specialized methodologies derived from a variety of biological sciences has created many highly technical subfields within biological anthropology, the discipline remains primarily concerned with human evolution within the context of culture or the emergence of culture. Evidence concerning human evolution can be obtained by the examination of surviving closely related animals, through the study of human and humanlike fossils, and through consideration of biological variation within existing human populations. The three main subfields of biological anthropology, then, are the study of Primates (primatology), the study of fossil humans, and the study of living human populations.

Although biological anthropologists share the study of living primates with the established biological discipline of primatology, the biological anthropologist is specifically concerned with the similarities and differences between human beings and other primates. This involves investigation of the kinds of environmental factors or life circumstances which might have led our early ancestors to assume an erect posture, to use tools, to hunt, to organize themselves into societies, and to develop language and culture. Often, very much like cultural anthropologists, who live with the people they study, biological anthropologists live in close association with wild monkeys or apes, observing their behavior and considering the nature of social relationships within and between troops.

The study of fossil humans and hominoids deals mainly with bone materials that have somehow survived the normal processes of decay and transformation. Although all recent human fossils represent the single species *Homo sapiens,* more ancient fossils seem to belong to different species which were either ancestral to *Homo sapiens* or represent evolutionary side branches that became extinct. Further back in time fossils appear to be less and less human and more and more apelike. Some are believed to represent common ancestors of apes and human beings, and some may be simply apes.

Biological anthropologists compare the scattered fossil evidence of human evolution, attempt to reconstruct the environments within which human beings evolved, and try to develop explanations of the patterns of development they find. Although the possession of culture, including the use of language and tools, marks the divide between true human beings and their cousins and ancestors, many fossils are not found in association with tools. Even when they are, the tools may not seem to be tools and, of course, most other evidences of language and culture have disappeared. Biological anthropologists then consider the size of the brain cavity or the shape of fossil hands, teeth, and other bones and try to estimate the humanity of their finds. In recent years, sophisticated chemical analyses have made it possible to compare the molecular composition of different fossils with that of modern human beings. Such chemical analyses are in the early stages of development, and the meaning of molecular resemblances between fossils is not completely understood.

In studying populations of living human beings, the biological anthropologist is primarily interested in observing the processes of evolution that are taking place within human populations at the present time. Here cultural factors affecting the determination of group boundaries and the selection of spouses and sexual partners exert a strong influence both in defining groups of people that interbreed and in influencing the survival of different individuals and of the genes they carry. The genetic composition of different human populations may be directly affected by adaptations to high and low altitude or to particular extremes of climate. Different technologies and different ways of living are likely to encourage the survival of some biological characteristics at the expense of others. Patterns of warfare, trade, or migration may alter population boundaries and create new populations that differ from the previous populations out of which they emerged. Examination of the biological similarities and differences between populations may then shed light on historical relationships between different peoples or on the impact of particular environments and ways of life upon the ongoing evolution of the human species.

In addition to these general questions about the relationships of human beings to other primates or about past and present human evolution, the biological anthropologist is deeply concerned with the question of the extent to which biological factors exert influence upon the nature, behavior, and potentialities of human individuals and populations. Although these questions are sometimes approached by means of attempts to draw a distinction between human traits that result from heredity and those that result from environment or culture, more meaningful approaches have to do with the relative contribution of heredity and environment or with patterns of interaction between hereditary and environmental influences. The human ability to develop languages and cultures is rooted in human biology, but it is not yet clear whether this is a general sort of ability or one that places highly specific limitations on the kinds of languages and cultures that human beings may develop. All human behaviors have a biological basis, to the extent that they are made possible by such biological things as the human hand or brain, and a cultural basis, to the extent that they are encouraged or forbidden within particular cultural settings. The task of explaining the complex interplay between biological and cultural factors is one of the challenges facing all of the subdisciplines of anthropology.

4. Cultural and Social Anthropology

Because human beings always possess culture and always live in societies, there is a broad sense in which all of anthropology can be considered to be cultural-social anthropology. Within anthropology those concerned primarily with the ways of life of people living in recent or existing cultures and societies generally refer to themselves as cultural anthropologists. When a distinction is made between cultural and social anthropology, cultural anthropologists are generally regarded as those who emphasize cultural traditions and their content, whereas social anthropologists are regarded as those who emphasize behavior and social interaction. Because human social interaction always takes place with reference to cultural traditions, society is generally regarded as an aspect of culture, and social anthropologists are often regarded as a variety of cultural anthropologist. In this book the term *culture* is used inclusively to refer to both societies (people interacting) and to the cultural traditions that influence their interaction.

Cultural anthropologists are interested in the description and comparison of all human cultures, and they search out and describe diverse cultures wherever they may be found: on Arctic coastlines, in the deserts and grasslands of Africa, on islands in the South Pacific, or in densely populated towns and cities. Because the predatory expansion of urban and industrialized cultures has threatened the existence of many of the world's small and technologically uncomplicated peoples, much of the research effort in cultural anthropology has involved a kind of desperate, last-minute attempt to describe the lifeways of broken and vanishing peoples. Although this emphasis has sometimes led to the description of cultural anthropology as the study of "primitive," tribal, or "nonliterate" cultures, the goals of cultural anthropology have always been to describe the entire range of human behavior and to develop explanations of the similarities and differences among cultures. Cultural anthropologists have, among other things, studied industrialized agriculture in the central valley of California and in Israel, cities in Japan and Massachusetts, and rural communities in France and Mexico.

Because people are many and cultural anthropologists few, anthropologists have only begun to comprehend the enormous range and diversity of human cultures and to devise systematic ways of comparing them. To describe even the simplest of human cultures, the cultural anthropologist must spend many months interviewing, observing, and participating. Even so, it is impossible to attain a complete description. For this reason most cultural anthropologists attempt to describe the most important or most basic attributes of the cultures they study and then to pursue some selected aspect or aspects of the culture in greater depth.

The tendency to emphasize particular aspects of culture has given rise to a variety of subfields with cultural anthropology. *Ecological anthropologists* emphasize relationships between cultures and their environments. *Cultural historians* examine the beliefs that people hold about their past history and test them against existing historical documents in order to reconstruct the course of development of their culture. *Economic anthropologists* consider the manner in which goods are produced, the systems of trade or exchange by means of which they are distributed, and the ways in which they are consumed. *Social anthropologists* consider the kinds of groupings and subdivisions that exist among the members of a culture and the kinds of relationships and interactions that take place between them. *Psychological anthropologists* consider the relationships between individuals and their cultures. Other specialists study religion, cultural change, conflict, medicine, education, law, art, play, music, and literature. Students of world view and ethnoscience consider the ideas people have concerning the nature of things and the various ways in which they classify the kinds of things they believe to exist.

Because both the study of language and of ancient culture require highly specialized techniques, linguistics and archaeology will be discussed separately. Language is, however, a part of culture — some whould say the most important part — and it follows that there must be a close connection between explanations of language and explanations of culture. *Archaeologists* deal for the most part with the material remains of formerly existing cultures and can be regarded as cultural anthropologists working under the handicap of restricted information about the cultures they study. The archaeologist enjoys the special advantage of being able to consider cultural evolution and change over periods of thousands of years.

5. Archaeology

Archaeology attempts to reconstruct the cultural forms of the past and to trace their growth and development in time. In this, historians, culture historians, and archaeologists share the same objectives. History, in the sense of written history, is based upon written documents describing aspects of life in former times. Unfortunately such written documents cover only the last 5,000 years, and only those cultures that possessed writing. Very often surviving written documents give an inadequate picture of former cultures, and it is necessary to supplement written history with archaeology.

In most cases the archaeologist must reconstruct the cultures of the past from material remains alone. Tracing clues provided by the smoke-blackened walls of caves, unusual variations in the soil, or pieces of chipped stone excavated by gophers, the archaeologist locates the campsites, villages, or towns of bygone cultures. Highly specialized techniques are used to remove carefully, layer by layer, the various traces left behind by unknown peoples. Skeletons of the ancient dead are found along with the ornaments they once wore and the tools they once carried. The archaeologist finds ancient house floors, bits of pottery, and objects of stone and imperishable metals — only that which does not rot or wash away.

From bits of bone and pollen hidden in the dirt, the archaeologist, with the assistance of biologists and other natural scientists, can reconstruct the natural environment and reach conclusions about the foods consumed by ancient peoples. From the charcoal left behind by ancient fires, or from other organic materials, the archaeologist can obtain estimates of the time period during which people lived at the site being excavated. By examining human bones found in the site, guesses can be made about the number of people present, their age and sex, and the causes of their deaths. Pottery figurines and other works of art may provide information about the appearance of the people, their dress, and sometimes their social life. Grains of wheat pressed into baked clay or surviving as the carbonized remnants of a burnt dinner may suggest the presence of agriculture.

The archaeologist's reconstruction of the past provides the major outlines of the passage of humanity through time. Archaeologists have discovered the tool-like objects used by earliest human beings, and have traced the movement of humanity across the world. The archaeological record shows us the human occupation of new environments and the slow development within each of specialized techniques of adaptation and survival. Some cultures, isolated from the mainstream, lacking access to materials, or protected from the challenges that have forced other cultures to change rapidly, have developed relatively slowly, so that many peoples of the present or recent past follow a hunting and collecting way of life not unlike that of the ancients.

Elsewhere, cultural evolution led to new technologies, to the replacement of hunting and collecting by agriculture, to the development of new techniques of food processing, or to the exploitation of particularly abundant natural resources. Such technological development was related to increases in population and to the development of increasingly complicated forms of social organization. As the archaeologist reconstructs the history of each of the regions of the world, evidence accumulates concerning patterns of change and stability in human affairs. Working with the cultural anthropologist, the archaeologist considers the various factors that contribute to the development of new inventions, to their diffusion across cultural boundaries, and to their impact upon the cultures into which they are introduced.

6. Anthropological Linguistics

Although language is a part of culture, and the linguist may be regarded as a kind of cultural anthropologist, the study of language requires highly specialized techniques for the recording, description, and comparison of languages. Linguists study and describe the languages spoken by tiny bands of Indians in the rain forests of the Amazon; they examine Greek, Roman, and Sanskrit literature in order to reconstruct languages spoken in the past. They stand by with their notebooks or tape recorders to record the dialects spoken in different parts of the United States or in the slums and upper-class suburbs of modern cities. Unlike the practical linguist or polyglot who speaks and understands several languages, and unlike the student of literature and the philologist who are primarily interested in the relationships between language and literature, the linguist studies the origins, development, and structure of language, and its relationship to other aspects of culture.

Through the application of highly technical methods, the linguist reconstructs the history of particular languages and uncovers the historical relationships that exist among languages. This is done, not simply as a means of reconstructing history, but as a means of arriving at broad generalizations concerning the processes that lead to the origin and development of human languages. The systematic comparison of unrelated or apparently unrelated languages leads to understandings of the universal properties of all human languages.

The linguist is also interested in the many relationships between language and other aspects of culture, including study of the ways in which the language spoken by a group of people is related to their status or social position. Rich and poor, men and women, old and young, even thieves and physicists, all speak specialized dialects that confirm and sometimes maintain their place in society. Studies of the meaning and use of particular words and phrases serve as a means of understanding the ways in which people in different cultures visualize the various objects and settings that surround them. Special linguistic symbols used in religious rites and ceremonies or on other important occasions provide insights into the things that people in different cultures consider most important or significant. As cultures change or borrow new concepts from other cultures, the changes tend to be reflected in new words and phrases. Thus the linguist can contribute to the cultural anthropologist's understandings of the nature and direction of cultural change. The study of the manner in which children learn language and of the processes by which language is transmitted from one generation to another leads to understandings of the way ideas are transmitted within cultures and of the ways beliefs, ideals, and traditions are perpetuated. The linguist tries to understand the role of language in human life and the part it has played in the emergence and development of humanity.

7. The Historical Background of Anthropology

A concern with the nature of humanity and with the variety of human cultures seems almost universal among human beings. Often this interest is expressed in myths and legends describing the creation of human beings, their wanderings in search of a homeland, and the discovery or acquisition of such things as fire, useful tools, and domesticated plants and animals. Surviving materials from the ancient literary traditions of China, India, and the Mediterranean region reflect these interests and in some cases also reflect earnest attempts to describe strange peoples and to arrive at explanations of their differentness. Herodotus, a Greek historian of the fifth century B.C., described, among others, the Scythians and the Egyptians, and proposed a hypothesis concerning the original language of mankind.

Although there was extensive trade and visiting among the ancient literate civilizations of Europe and Asia, the merchants and voyagers of that time seem to have had little interest in preserving detailed records of the ways of life of other peoples. Even when they speculated about human origins and human diversity, their conclusions were more likely to be based upon imagination than upon careful consideration of the facts.

After the fifteenth century, as the peoples of western Europe commenced extensive voyages of exploration and discovery, a body of anthropological data began to accumulate. The sudden emergence of this interest in other peoples is not easily explained. The introduction of the printing press, the gradual development of a scientific method somewhat separated from religious and philosophical speculation, and an awareness of culture created by rapid change may all have contributed. Although many of the early documents provided by travelers, soldiers, and missionaries were fanciful or likely to omit many details as "too repugnant to be described," there now came into existence for the first time in history a body of literature that was broadly descriptive of human beings.

Somewhat later, during the first half of the nineteenth century, a number of European scholars began to study flint implements and skeletal remains of ancient peoples. This study was stimulated by and depended upon the advance of geological and paleontological research revealing the considerable age of the earth and of the plants and animals that populated it. Boucher de Perthes, a French scholar, found stone tools in the Somme Valley gravels as early as 1830 and later (1847–1864) published his discoveries in a series of monographs. The first direct evidence of fossil man, recognized as such, was the discovery of Neanderthal man in Germany in 1856. With the gradual and reluctant acceptance of the antiquity of stone tools and human fossils, it became possible to visualize for the first time the long processes of cultural and biological evolution which led to the development of present-day humanity.

Increased knowledge of the nonliterate peoples of the world and the rapid growth of archaeological data led, during the second half of the nineteenth century, to the emergence of anthropology as an independent scientific discipline. In England, Edward B. Tylor's *Primitive Culture*[1] provided the first generally acceptable definition of culture and marked the development of methods of comparison designed to establish the pattern of human cultural evolution and to explain the similarities and differences between cultures. Lewis H. Morgan in the United States carried out an ambitious study of kinship systems[2] and used his findings to develop an evolutionary classification of human cultures published in 1877 under the title *Ancient Society.*[3]

[1] Edward Burnett Tylor, *Primitive Culture, Researches into the Development of Mythology, Philosophy, Religion, Art, and Custom.* (London: John Murray, 1871).

[2] Lewis Henry Morgan, *Systems of Consanguinity and Affinity of the Human Family* (U.S. Smithsonian Institute. Smithsonian Contributions to Knowledge, Vol. XVII, Art. 2, Smithsonian Institution Publication 218, 1870).

[3] Lewis Henry Morgan, *Ancient Society* (New York: Holt, Rinehart and Winston, 1877).

Because anthropology did not exist as a separate academic discipline, Tylor, Morgan, and the many other important contributors to nineteenth-century anthropology came into anthropology from a variety of other fields. The lack of anthropology departments and programs of anthropological training meant that nineteenth-century anthropologists often lacked the critical standards required for the verification of data or the systematic development of theoretical propositions.

Modern anthropology developed during the early part of the twentieth century in response to the teachings of Edward Burnett Tylor (1832–1917) in England; Friedrich Ratzel (1844–1904), the geographer, in Germany; Lewis Henry Morgan (1818–1881) in the United States; and Emile Durkheim (1858–1917) in France. Franz Boas (1858–1942), who might well be called the stepfather, rather than the father, of American anthropology, was a physicist who studied under Ratzel and later founded the first department of anthropology in the United States at Clark University.[4] Under the influence of Boas, American anthropology came to combine the critical standards of German science with the data- and artifact-collecting traditions of L. H. Morgan and the many explorers and museum workers who had supplied the United States government with information about the American Indian since the time of Thomas Jefferson.

Anthropology today is recognized as an important scholarly discipline in Europe, North America, Japan, India, and in much of Africa and Latin America. To date, its major contributions consist of its accumulating understandings of the growth and development of humanity and of the range and variety of human lifeways. Anthropology has challenged traditional concepts linking race and culture and has developed fresh understandings of human biological evolution and cultural diversity. Together, the subdisciplines of anthropology have refined and extended our understandings of the nature of culture, developed systematic ways of describing other languages and cultures, and worked out increasingly rigorous criteria for the cross-cultural testing of social science theory.

8. Anthropology and Other Disciplines

Anthropology is commonly classified as a social science, related to such disciplines as sociology, psychology, geography, economics, and political science. Through biological anthropology, it is closely connected to such fields as anatomy, physiology, embryology, and genetics. Biological anthropology, archaeology, and cultural anthropology, all exchange points of view with the more general biological sciences of ecology and ethology. Archaeologists,

---

[4] A. I. Hallowell, "The Beginnings of Anthropology in America," in *Selected Papers from the American Anthropologist 1888–1920*, ed. Frederica deLaguna (Evanston, Ill.: Row, Peterson, 1960), pp. 1–96.

seeking new methods of dating or new ways of analyzing archaeological sites and their contents, are often closely linked to geologists, paleontologists, soil chemists, and physicists. Linguists, archaeologists, and cultural anthropologists maintain a close liaison with such humanistic disciplines as history, literature, art, and music. For almost all scientific and humanistic disciplines, anthropology provides a view of the past and a constant remembrance of human diversity.

The principal contribution of anthropology to other disciplines stems from its role in the development of the concept of culture. Of particular importance, here, are the facts that culture is learned, that the parts of any culture tend to be interrelated in a systematic way, that the various rules and laws that govern human conduct tend to reflect human endeavor rather than natural or divine law, and that perceptions of truth, beauty, goodness, and wisdom are deeply influenced by the cultural traditions to which the individual has been exposed.

For the humanistic disciplines the concept of culture carries the implication that styles of art, music, and literature are based upon arbitrary criteria characteristic of individual cultural traditions. Although particular kinds of images or particular kinds of sounds may have a universal appeal among human beings, the findings of anthropology demonstrate that there is no kind of song, picture, or story that everyone must automatically consider beautiful or worthy of attention. Because anthropologists are the only academic specialists who are routinely trained in the art of studying and understanding cultures other than their own, anthropologists have willy-nilly become authorities on the art, music, and literature of most of the peoples of the world. Just as the student of language must turn to the anthropological linguist for information about the languages of the world, so the student of the humanities must turn to the cultural anthropologist for knowledge about the artistic creations of other cultures.

Because anthropologists rarely possess the specialized knowledge acquired by specialists in the humanities, anthropologists, for their part, must turn to the humanities for information about the methods to be used in describing and analyzing art styles, or literary and philosophical traditions.

Specialists trained in the social sciences, like specialists in the humanities, tend to emphasize the study of their own or closely related cultures. If they are to make wide-ranging generalizations about human psychology, politics, or economics, social scientists must depend upon anthropologists and the data they have collected in order to demonstrate the general importance of their findings. If a sociologist studying Chicago discovers that city people are less religious than country people, he or she must often depend upon the anthropologist to discover whether the same thing holds true in Timbuktu or Samarkand. The psychologist who has discovered interesting differences in ability or personality between male and female college students cannot generalize the findings to all human males and females until similar information has been obtained from other cultures. Within anthropology such specializations as social anthropology, psychological anthropology, economic anthropology, and political anthropology have the task of maintaining liaison with other social science fields and of testing the general applicability of their findings. Anthropologists also borrow research methods and theoretical approaches from the more specialized disciplines.

Although the force of gravity or the proper growing conditions for asparagus are generally unaffected by anthropological findings, ways of perceiving gravitational forces and ways of cultivating asparagus are strongly influenced by culture. Anthropological understandings of the influence of culture upon human perception may thus help to free the physicist or engineer from his own cultural biases concerning the nature of things.

Because biologists and anthropologists are united in the study of living things, there is a continuing exchange of information and point of view between anthropology and the biological sciences. Biologists who are directly concerned with the study of human beings must depend upon anthropology for much of their information about human beings living in different cultures. In the field of nutrition, information about the requirements of the human animal can often be verified by consideration of the varied diets characteristic of people living in different cultures. The anthropologist often approaches physical scientists, biologists, and mathematicians with due humility hoping for answers concerning the age of some particular archaeological site, the identification of crop plants utilized by the Ashanti of Africa, or for the proper method of analyzing the numeral system of the Pomo Indians of California.

Because anthropologists tend to think in holistic terms, both about humanity in general and societies and cultures in particular, anthropology has an important role to play in integrating the findings of more specialized disciplines into more general and holistic explanations of human behavior. Anthropology has brought to the less global sciences a special sort of objectivity and relativity of point of view. The anthropologist's ability to compare modernized societies with other quite different societies tends to highlight unusual features of modern society and modern thought. In the process of asking why it is that the Bushmen do the things that they do, we are inevitably brought to question why it is that we do the things that we do. In every field of thought, from literary criticism to atomic physics, the asking of this hard question about traditional ways of doing things is a fertile source of consternation and of change.

9. The Uses of Anthropology

Like physics, anthropology has generally regarded itself as a basic science dedicated to the discovery of basic principles that might later find application. Even today the practical value of anthropology lies not so much in the general principles it has discovered as in the data it collects and in the methods it has developed for collecting such data. For many students the discovery of anthropology is the discovery of the possibility of an objective and dispassionate view of humanity. Through the lens of the archaeologist or cultural anthropologist it is possible to see one's own society as a mere episode in the millions of years of human history and as a single instance, no better and no worse, of the many different societies that exist today or have existed in the past. In coming to understand the Eskimo, the Hopi Indians, or the Arunta of Australia as they really are or recently were, the individual discovers a kinship with humanity. If these other peoples believe and act as they do because they have learned some particular cultural tradition, then we, ourselves, can perceive the impact of our own cultural tradition upon the things that we believe in and act upon. Anthropology provides the means of discovering new ways of doing things and new ways of seeing things.

Although practical persons have argued that education should be limited to that special training which will enable the individual to find a job and pay taxes, anthropology remains a stronghold of liberal education. Courses in linguistics, archaeology, and biological anthropology provide more than a taste of scientific method, while courses in the art, literature, and religion of other peoples provide background in the humanities. On the whole, anthropology is not so much a means of preparing for life as a means of enjoying and understanding it.

Most of the jobs available to anthropologists are teaching jobs in universities. Such jobs require a Ph.D. and the Ph.D requires five or six years of graduate training. A master's degree in anthropology, although it may sometimes be useful in obtaining jobs in junior colleges or museums, is mainly useful in conjunction with other more practical disciplines. A bachelor's degree in anthropology, combined with an appropriate selection of other courses, may sometimes be useful in securing admission to schools of law, social welfare, education, or business administration. Some knowledge of anthropology is likely to be useful in almost any career in the teaching or helping professions, or in the humanities or social sciences. Students considering further study in anthropology should consult one of the two student handbooks by Charles Frantz and Morton H. Fried.[5]

One of the problems in the development of an applied cultural anthropology is that those in government or industry who can afford to support applied anthropologists are often concerned with the manipulation of subject peoples, employees, or client groups in ways that individual anthropologists consider unethical. The fact that "he who pays the piper, calls the tune" is a problem common to all sciences, from the physicists who build atomic bombs to the marine biologists who discover more effective ways of killing fish. Nevertheless the emergence of anthropology was in part based on the need of colonial governments to discover ways of governing or controlling their sometimes unwilling subjects. French, British, Dutch, and other colonial governments at one time made extensive use of anthropology as a means of understanding tribal peoples who had come under their control. At best such anthropological collaboration with governmental agencies produced vast improvements in otherwise intolerable situations. James Mooney, who was asked by the United States government to investigate the ghost dance of the American Indians and

[5] Morton H. Fried, *The Study of Anthropology* (New York: T. Y. Crowell, 1972); Charles Frantz, *The Student Anthropologist's Handbook: A Guide to Research, Training, and Career* (Cambridge, Mass.: Schenkman, 1972).

the circumstances surrounding the massacre of the Sioux Indians at Wounded Knee Creek, brought in a ringing condemnation of American policy toward the Sioux which may, in fact, have influenced government policy.[6] In India, Christoph von Fürer-Haimendorf's study of the Chenchu tribe in Hyderabad led him to formulate a policy for protection of the tribe which may have prevented their extermination.[7] In other cases the record is not so clear, and it is sometimes argued that anthropologists helped to support obsolete colonial regimes. Such a charge could not, however, be laid at the door of Jomo Kenyatta, a Cambridge M.A. in anthropology, now considered the father of independent Kenya, nor could it be well applied to the many German anthropologists who were killed or forced into exile by Adolf Hitler or to the many South African anthropologists who have resisted racist policies there.

In recent years cultural anthropologists interested in applying their knowledge in practical situations have become increasingly cautious, and the main thrust of their interests now centers upon four fields: community development, urban anthropology, medical anthropology, and educational anthropology. In community development the anthropologist's role is generally that of developing an overall picture of the community or communities to be developed and attempting to propose courses of action that will bring about improvements desired by members of the developing communities. Although anthropologists work with medical personnel in a variety of ways, the main thrust of their efforts has to do with understanding folk categories of disease and methods of diagnosis and proposing ways of improving the delivery of medical care. In educational anthropology the impact of anthropology is generally in the direction of modifying teaching methods and bureaucratic policies in ways that will make education more generally available to members of minority ethnic groups or to populations that are being offered, or having forced upon them, a modern educational system. The usefulness of cultural anthropology in the preparation of environmental impact studies or in the solution of other pressing social problems has only been sporadically recognized.

Surprising as it may seem, the practical utility of archaeology is far more widely recognized than is that of cultural anthropology. In the United States, many states subsidize the recovery and exhibition of archaeological remains, and the importance of preserving archaeological sites from careless excavation or ruthless bulldozing is generally recognized by law. In countries like Mexico, Italy, Egypt, and India substantial tourist income is derived from the exhibition of archaeological sites that are preserved and maintained by large and influential government departments.

Linguistics, perhaps the most developed of the four subdisciplines of anthropology, has for years served the practical purpose of improving instruction in language. Linguistic research into the special dialects spoken by various ethnic groups in the United States has facilitated teaching and com-

---

[6] James Mooney, *The Ghost Dance Religion and the Sioux Outbreak of 1890*, edited and abridged by Anthony F. C. Wallace (Chicago: University of Chicago Press, 1965).

[7] Christoph von Fürer-Haimendorf, *The Aboriginal Tribes of Hyderabad* (London: Macmillan and Co., Ltd., 1943).

munication in interethnic situations. The ability of linguists to teach a variety of languages using native speakers as teaching assistants has made possible an expansion in language teaching, so that many universities now offer training in as many as thirty or forty different languages including such languages as Hindi, Tamil, Ewe, Swahili, and Thai.

Biological anthropology, from its beginnings as a method of measuring human bodily dimensions, has contributed to the better design of machines, furniture, clothing, artificial limbs, and other equipment that must be closely matched to human bodily dimensions. It contributes to the solution of many medical and legal problems ranging from the identification of bone materials to genetic counseling for those who fear their children may inherit possible genetic defects.

Despite the highly specific and practical value of particular specializations in archaeology, linguistics, and biological anthropology, it seems probable that the true use of anthropology will always arise out of the understandings of cultural similarities and differences that it provides. A knowledge of the ways in which other peoples have planned their buildings, educated their children, developed new art styles, handled their population problems, or settled their conflicts will always be of value to those who are concerned with the improvement of the human condition.

10. Summary

Anthropology is the study of the origin, development, and nature of the human species through the use of specialized methods employed by four closely cooperating subfields: biological anthropology, cultural-social anthropology, archaeology, and linguistics. The central concept linking the four subfields is the idea of culture. Research in anthropology involves a concern with all human beings, past and present, and with all of their works and activities. Although there are many disciplines that deal with human beings, anthropology occupies a special role because it involves a combination of holistic, historical, and comparative methods. The ultimate goal of anthropological research is the explanation of the similarities and differences among all of the past and present peoples of the earth. Anthropology requires the use of special research methods, not used in the study of other animal species, because human beings differ in a number of important ways from other animals. These differences are most notable in the development of tools, language, and culture among human beings. Although most distinctively human characteristics exist in one form or another among other species of animals, they are all found together only among human beings. Human adaptations to the environment have been made largely in terms of culture. This has permitted human beings to remain relatively unspecialized from a biological point of view and therefore adaptable to a wide range of environments. The human culture-building capacity is closely associated with the ability to invent and use language and therefore to develop an ever-growing heritage of traditional knowledge.

Although the archaeological record demonstrates the development of a human, or humanlike, tradition of tool manufacture and use over a period of at least five million years, there is little evidence concerning the development of language or the nonmaterial aspects of culture. A conservative guess is that language and culture were well, if not fully, developed with the emergence of *Homo erectus* some one million years ago. The presence of tools, and probably of rudimentary forms of language and culture, during the several million years of evolution in the human direction suggests that human biological evolution was in part a reflex of human cultural evolution. The presence of culture, then, is a part of the human condition, and it follows that an explanation of humanity involves an explanation of culture. The basic research questions in anthropology have to do with culture and its relationships to human evolution, to environmental relationships, and to the human personalities who paradoxically create cultures, yet are themselves created by culture.

Among the subdisciplines of anthropology, biological anthropology is most concerned with the biological nature of humanity. It differs from other biological sciences dealing with humanity because it uses the concept of culture to define the groups that it studies and as a means of developing understandings of human biological evolution. Although the recent and explosive development of the biological sciences has created a variety of specialized subfields within physical anthropology, the main subfields continue to be defined in terms of the study of primates, of fossil remains, and of living populations.

Although there is a sense in which all of anthropology can be regarded as cultural anthropology, the terms *cultural anthropology* or *social anthropology* generally apply to those who specialize in the study of the ways of life of recent or existing peoples. The goals of cultural anthropology include the description of the entire range of human behavior and the development of explanations of the similarities and differences among cultures. Cultural anthropologists tend to emphasize selected aspects of culture and this has led to the emergence of a wide variety of subfields ranging from ecological and economic anthropology to the anthropology of art.

In a sense archaeologists are cultural anthropologists who work under the handicap of dealing only with the material remains of former cultures, but with the advantage of being able to consider variation and change over periods of thousands of years. Because written history began only about 5,000 years ago and is often lacking in details concerning everyday life, archaeology is the only means of providing historical information concerning cultures lacking written history or possessing inadequate written histories. Archaeology, then, is the means by which the human past is reconstructed and the major outlines of cultural evolution described.

Like the archaeologist, the linguist can be regarded as a specialized kind of cultural anthropologist. The linguist, using a highly sophisticated set of methods, prepares descriptions of existing or surviving languages. These descriptions are used to establish historical relationships among languages and to elucidate the processes involved in the origin and development of language. They also permit the development of understandings of human thought and communication and of the relationships among language and other aspects of culture.

The discipline of anthropology arose comparatively recently with the accumulation of systematic information concerning non-Western peoples. The early anthropologists, such as Edward B. Tylor and Lewis H. Morgan, were trained in other disciplines, and formal training in anthropology developed only after initial steps in the definition of culture and in the development of anthropological theory were completed. To date, the major contributions of anthropology include the development of systematic ways of describing other languages and cultures, the working out of the implications of the concept of culture, the understanding of the complicated relationships between biology and culture, and the formulation of increasingly rigorous criteria for the cross-cultural testing of social science theory.

Although generally classified as a social science, anthropology maintains important relationships with the humanities and biological sciences. Anthropology provides a wide range of scholarly disciplines with the cross-cultural information required for the development of truly universal interpretations of human beings and the world about them. Anthropology, in turn, relies upon more specialized disciplines for the methods needed for the understanding of particular aspects of culture. For all human beings, developing anthropological understandings of the nature of culture provides a fresh means for the reevaluation of traditional ways of doing things.

Collateral Reading

Boas, Franz. "Anthropology," *Encyclopedia of the Social Sciences*, Vol. II. New York: Macmillan Publishing Co., Inc., 1930, pp. 73–110.

Fried, Morton H. *The Study of Anthropology*. New York: Thomas Y. Crowell Company, 1972.

Frantz, Charles. *The Student Anthropologist's Handbook: A Guide to Research, Training, and Career*. Cambridge, Mass.: Schenkman Publishing Co., Inc., 1972.

Hallowell, A. I. "The Beginnings of Anthropology in America," *Selected Papers from the American Anthropologist, 1888–1920*, ed. Frederica deLaguna. Evanston, Ill.: Row, Peterson & Company, Inc. 1960.

Hays, Hoffman Reynolds. *From Ape to Angel: An Informal History of Anthropology*. New York: Alfred A. Knopf, Inc., 1958.

Kardiner, Abram, and Edward Preble. *They Studied Man*. New York: New American Library of World Literature, Inc., 1963. Informal sketches of early anthropologists and their work.

Langness, L. L. *The Study of Culture*. San Francisco: Chandler and Sharp Publishers, Inc., 1974. A concise discussion of major anthropological points of view in historical perspective.

Ethnographic References

Apache: Opler, 1941.
Eskimo: Balikci, 1970; Chance, 1966; Oswalt, 1969.
Quechua (Inca): Means, 1931; Murdock, 1935, Chapter XIV.
United States: Keiser, 1969; Leibow, 1967; Whyte, 1955.
   Dunkard: West, 1945.

2/The Nature of Culture

1. The Diversity of Human Behavior

Although representatives of many animal species are capable of learning and of transmitting learned behavior to other members of the flock or herd, individual animal species do not generally exhibit the diversity of behavior that characterizes humanity. Animal behavior can generally be explained in terms of biologically inherited and species-specific characteristics combined with direct and simple adaptations to problems posed by specific environments. The human species, in contrast to other animal species, exhibits a high degree of biological uniformity and a high degree of behavioral variation at the same time.

The diversity of human behavior may be illustrated in almost every activity in which human beings engage. Food habits vary endlessly. The Eskimos of the Arctic traditionally lived almost exclusively upon meat and fish, in contrast to many Mexican Indian peoples, whose diet is still based primarily upon cereals and vegetables. Milk and its products are regarded as luxury foods among the Baganda of East Africa, while many Chinese regard milk as a poisonous substance.[1] Fish is used as a food by most

---

[1] Milk may in fact be poisonous to most Chinese and to many other people as well. See Robert D. McCracken, "Lactase Deficiency: An Example of Dietary Evolution," *Current Anthropology,* **12**: 479–517 (1971).

American Indian tribes, but many Navajos and Apaches of New Mexico and Arizona still consider it nauseating and unfit for human consumption. Many peoples eat dog meat (in former times, some groups of Mexican Indians bred dogs especially for eating), but there are many others who, like ourselves, find the idea of eating dog meat disgusting.

There are variations in the manner in which foods may be combined. Orthodox Jews do not combine meat and dairy products in the same meal, but take them separately. A similar custom obtains among the Eskimos, who require that seafoods be kept apart from foods obtained from land animals and served in different containers. Special observances of this sort may extend to the very processes of eating: witness not only the Polynesian custom of reserving certain utensils for the eating of human flesh, but also the rigid formality of our own table etiquette with respect to the proper use of knives, forks, and spoons.

Habits of dress and ornament are similarly variable. Many peoples — for example, the aboriginal Australians and the Indians of Tierra del Fuego — virtually dispensed with clothing altogether. Other peoples, for example, the Baganda of East Africa, must be fully clothed from neck to ankles. Ornamentation of the body may include earrings, nose and lip plugs, and combs and other articles worn in the hair. The body may be decorated with paint or clay, or tattooed in intricate designs. Some peoples make designs on their bodies by raising long scars.

There is also great divergence in the ways in which people relate to each other. Among the Navajos of the American Southwest, a man was not supposed to speak to or even look at his wife's mother. Among the Crow Indians of the North American Plains, a man was required to joke with certain of his relatives and was not supposed to show anger when these relatives humiliated him in public. In northwestern India, married older brothers were not expected to exhibit jealousy when younger brothers slept with their brides. Among the Hopi Indians of the American Southwest, the father's sister was expected to initiate a young man into the mysteries of sex. The Trobriand Islanders of Melanesia traditionally did not require a man to support, educate, or discipline his children; these functions belonged to the mother's brother. Among the Kariera of Australia, a man was ideally supposed to marry a cross-cousin, that is, a cousin related through the mother's brother or the father's sister.

The catalog of behavioral differences among the various peoples of the world is a long one, and one that will be examined more systematically in later chapters. The examples given here illustrate the fact that human variation in behavior is too great to be explained in terms of biological inheritance or in terms of any simple sorts of relationship to the environment.

2. The Idea of Culture

When members of a group are asked to explain why they practice cross-cousin marriage or why they avoid speaking to their mothers-in-law — in a word, why they do things differently from other people — they are rarely at a loss for an explanation. Perhaps an ancient lawgiver acting under divine inspiration established the patterns of their life; perhaps the ancestors, acting out of a wisdom greater than their descendants now possess, laid down the rules of life; perhaps the gods themselves ordered their followers to behave in certain ways. In Mexico people say, "es costumbre" (it is the custom); in India they say, "It is coming from time immemorial." In some cases peoples who attach that special importance to themselves that anthropologists call ethnocentrism find that their own way of life obeys divine commands that the other foolish people of the world have neglected or failed to hear. In Europe and the United States people tend to suggest that they do things because it is right to do them and that everyone else is doing it wrong.

During the nineteenth century, when anthropology was first beginning to develop as a science, a number of separate theories concerning human variation were in existence. Some, for example, still believed that there had once been a golden age and that all modern peoples represented degenerate and inferior descendants of that time. Certain peoples had degenerated more than others and therefore exhibited more animal-like, less human, behavior. Opposed to this idea, and based upon the nineteenth-century experience of rapid change and modernization, was the idea of progress. According to this theory some peoples, often believed to be biologically superior, progressed at a faster rate than others. During the later half of the nineteenth century, ideas of progress and evolution led to the development of explicitly evolutionary theories in biology and social science. Theories of biological evolution firmly and definitively placed human beings among the animals, and this led some to conclude that differences between groups of human beings could be explained in strictly biological terms. Peoples possessing a simple technology and living in small groups were sometimes thought of as having a primitive mentality, like that of the first or primal human beings. Peoples living in cities and possessing a more complicated technology were regarded as further evolved in a biological sense and therefore capable of developing a more elaborate way of life.

During the 1850s this general line of thinking coalesced into a body of theory somewhat loosely called "classical evolutionism." In anthropology the major representatives of this approach were Lewis Henry Morgan in the United States and Edward B. Tylor in England. Although most classical evolutionists recognized the unity of the human species and the basic similarity of human thought processes (Tylor used the term *psychic unity*), their overall tendency was to assume that those human beings whom they regarded as civilized were further evolved in a biological sense than those they regarded as primitive. Very often they assumed that with proper care and protection, perhaps that provided by a reservation or by a colonial government, the "less advanced" peoples would eventually evolve biologically to a point where they could cope with the complexities of civilization.

Classical social evolutionists, and some biological evolutionists as well, often interpreted the progression of species and the development of peoples in terms of a divine plan. Human beings stood at the pinnacle of biological evolution, and French, German, and/or English and American civilization stood at the pinnacle of human evolution. All other peoples and biological species were "living fossils" representing stages that the "advanced" species or peoples had already passed through and completed. The goal of anthropology, then, was seen as collecting information about the "plan" of human evolution and using such information to help all peoples to pass on to higher stages of civilization.

Perhaps more than any other classical evolutionist, Tylor was aware of some discrepancies in the theory. He knew that many otherwise "primitive" peoples possessed "advanced" characteristics and that many "civilized" peoples possessed what were called survivals. It was also evident that some peoples had bypassed important evolutionary stages. Many of these discrepancies could be explained away by the diffusion of ideas from "advanced" peoples to those less "advanced," but in many cases it seemed that people had independently invented characteristics they now shared with peoples otherwise placed in a higher evolutionary stage. Although Tylor truly believed that some peoples were biologically inferior to others, he also enunciated the doctrine of psychic unity arguing that if ideas could diffuse or if they could be independently invented, surely it could be taken as evidence of the "like working of men's minds."[2]

One U.S. anthropologist, Daniel G. Brinton, resolved the problem of diffusion by denying its existence. Most classical evolutionists ignored the problem, perhaps because they clung to the idea, usually attributed to Lamarck, that changes in biological heredity could be induced by education or by other environmental effects. Until the end of the nineteenth century, scientists could use the term *race* without necessarily implying any stable or relatively permanent condition. For most nineteenth-century writers the distinction between behaviors acquired as a result of biological inheritance and behaviors acquired as a result of learning or experience was not considered important. The terms *ethnology* and *ethnography*, which anthropologists now use to describe the comparison and description of ways of life acquired by learning and experience, are derived from a Greek word meaning "race" or "people." Terms like the *French race* or the *Anglo-Saxon race* continued in common usage until quite recently.

As mechanisms of biological heredity became better understood, *race* began to acquire a specific and technical biological meaning, and it became increasingly evident that the larger part of human behavior could not be

---

[2] Edward B. Tylor, *Researches into the Early History of Mankind and the Development of Civilization.* Edited and abridged with an introduction by Paul Bohannon (edited from 3d ed., rev.). (Chicago: University of Chicago Press, 1964), p. 3.

explained in biological terms. Even the first attempts to describe biological differences between different peoples revealed a lack of connection between biological factors and the characteristic behaviors exhibited by the members of human groups. During the later part of the nineteenth century the term *culture*, with its implications of growth, training, and cultivation, gradually replaced all other terms as a means of referring to the characteristic behaviors of groups of people.

The first important definition of culture was provided by Tylor: "Culture . . . is that complex whole which includes knowledge, belief, art, law, morals, custom, and any other capabilities and habits acquired by man as a member of society."[3] Tylor's definition is silent concerning the means by which culture is acquired and, in fact, leaves open the possibility that culture is totally or partly acquired through mechanisms of biological heredity. Although Tylor specifically attributes culture to human beings, his definition does not eliminate the possibility that animals might also transmit capabilities and habits by social means.

The important point is that people learn what to do from other members of their group. Most of what they learn is transmitted by means of language. Like other animals, people learn by experience or by observing the actions of others, but the use of language permits every member of the group to gain access to the experience and knowledge of every other member. Even more important, it permits the transmission and accumulation of information across time, so that every human being has access to the accumulated wisdom and experience of remote ancestors.

A culture emerges when a set of individuals come together to form a group and consciously or unconsciously make decisions affecting some sort of common enterprise. Culture is most visible as the characteristic behaviors of some particular group of people, but it also exists in the form of the ideas, plans, and common understandings that are acknowledged by the membership. One of the characteristic behaviors of traditional Eskimos was the hunting of seals and walruses. They hunted seals and walruses in a distinctively Eskimo fashion, and they also dressed, talked, moved their bodies, and built their houses in a characteristically Eskimo way. In addition to these characteristic and easily observable Eskimo patterns, there was the sort of knowledge and information that permitted each Eskimo individual to know how to behave like an Eskimo. Culture, then, exists obviously as characteristic ways of doing things and subtly as ideas and understandings that must be inferred rather than directly observed.

Once it is understood that any human being can learn to act and think like an Eskimo, and that an Eskimo can learn to think and act like the members of any other human group, then we can understand Eskimo culture as the Eskimo themselves understand it. It is a pattern for living handed down

---

[3] Tylor, *Primitive Culture, Researches into the Development of Mythology, Philosophy, Religion, Art, and Custom.* (London: John Murray, 1871), p. 1.

through speech and example from the ancestors. *A culture is a set of learned ways of thinking and acting that characterizes any decision-making human group.*

3. Meanings of Culture

Although many different anthropologists have attempted to arrive at definitions of the term *culture* that would be at once rigorous and widely useful, the fact of the matter is that master concepts like culture, life, or democracy tend to refer not so much to a particular class of things as to a particular direction of travel. In very general terms the concept of culture has to do with the human capacity to use language and with related capacities for learning and for the transmission of ideas and ways of behaving.

Very often *culture* is used as a synonym for such terms as *society, sociocultural system, nation, tribe,* or *cultural system.* Everyone knows what is meant by *Navajo society* or *Navajo culture* and to most people the two statements mean the same thing. On the other hand, because sociology and anthropology are separate disciplines, one studying society and one studying culture, many scholars have attempted to define the two terms in quite different ways.

Informally, anthropologists frequently apply the term *culture* to entities both larger and smaller than a single cultural system. On the Plains of North America, after the introduction of the horse and gun facilitated buffalo hunting, there lived no fewer than thirty-one American Indian tribes. Each of these had its own name, such as Crow, Cheyenne, or Omaha, each had its characteristic culture and language, and each was politically independent. Nevertheless the thirty-one or so Plains cultures did have a large number of common characteristics. In all the tribes, buffalo were hunted for food; dwellings (called *tipis*) were built of poles covered with skins; the dog (and later the horse) was used as a pack animal and to pull a kind of land sledge (*travois*) made of two trailing poles; clothing was made of buffalo hide and deer skin; hides were worked with artistry and skill; artworks with geometric designs were common; men were organized into "military" societies; dwellings were usually set up in a distinctive order called the camp circle; a complex ritual (the sun dance) was practiced; and men were graded in terms of their success in warfare according to a well-defined scoring system. These ways of behaving, together with others, are collectively called *Plains culture* to distinguish them from similarly broad complexes of cultural items found among other groups of American Indian tribes, such as those of the Eastern Woodlands, the Pacific Northwest, or California.

In terms such as *Plains culture, European culture, West African culture,* or *Circumpolar culture,* the term *culture* applies to ways of behaving common to a number of societies, and not to one alone. Societies that share certain characteristic behaviors in this way are presumably linked by common origins or geographic nearness, so that certain aspects of culture have spread beyond the borders of a single culture and have become the common possession of a number of different groups. Usually such regional cultures occur in environmental areas that favor the same ecological adaptations in different parts of the area. By extension, it is possible to speak of Protestant culture, urban culture, or the culture of poverty.

In large and complicated cultural systems, it is often possible to speak of subcultures or subcultural systems that are restricted to some particular portion of the membership. The Inca Empire was a predominantly Quechua-speaking society which centered in ancient times in Peru and included at its height up to six million people, who were divided into three major classes. At the top were the Incas, an aristocratic class composed of individuals related by blood and common interest to the emperor's family. Next came a class of provincial nobility, the Curaca, composed for the most part of kings, chiefs, and other officials of conquered nations and tribes. The great mass of common people made up the third and largest class.

Differences in culture between these classes were marked. The Incas were expected to wear clothing of the finest fabrics; to ornament themselves with gold, silver, feathers, and precious stones made into symbols distinctive of their class; to occupy massive dwellings of stone or adobe; to educate their children at a special college in Cuzco, the capital city; to take over top positions in the government, army, and priesthood; and to employ their own special language. The Curaca class shared some of these ways of behaving, but not all. Their clothing and ornaments were supposed to be less elaborate, their positions in the army and government were not so near the top of the hierarchy, and they probably did not share in the religious rituals peculiar to the Incas, nor in the special Inca language. Commoners were supposed to wear only coarse garments of wool and were forbidden all ornaments. They were expected to till the soil and do other menial labor, but owned no land and occupied no positions of significance in either the government or the army. It is quite probable that they spoke a variety of languages and dialects and that their religious beliefs and practices were not only different from those of the Inca and Curaca classes but also different from region to region.

In Quechua society, then, we find at least three subcultures dependent upon class affiliation, and probably a number of others dependent upon local variation. This division of larger societies into subgroups and subcultures is a common phenomenon, and in most modern societies we may speak of regional and class subcultures as well as of sexual, ethnic, occupational, and even recreational subcultures. It is possible to speak of upper-class culture, the culture of women, the culture of loggers, the culture of skiers, or Jones family culture. In each case the term *culture* refers to a particular set of people in a particular environment who exhibit certain characteristic behaviors with the aid of a particular material culture, and in reference to a particular cultural tradition.

The use of *culture* to refer to human culture, to regional cultures, to national and tribal cultures, and to a wide range of subcultures becomes confusing only when we lose sight of the particular set of people being discussed or the particular environments in which they exhibit their characteristic behaviors.

4. Cultures, Societies, and Cultural Systems

When we speak of *Navajo society* or *Navajo culture,* we refer, of course, to the group of people who call themselves Navajo and who exhibit to one degree or another such characteristic Navajo behaviors as speaking the Navajo language, participating in tribal government, or simply presenting themselves to outsiders as Navajo. Because the term *society* conveys an emphasis upon individual Navajo and their relationships to each other, whereas the term *culture* may convey an emphasis upon the beliefs and behaviors characteristic of the Navajo, neither term really seems to encompass what is meant when we speak of *the Navajo.* To avoid confusion in technical usage, many anthropologists and sociologists prefer to use such terms as *sociocultural system* or *cultural system.* These terms imply the same things implied by *society* or *culture,* but they imply also a concern with the entire set of relationships that exist among the Navajo and between the Navajo and the environment. Use of the term *system* implies a theoretical point of view that sees human behavior as an outcome of complex interactions among a variety of biological, psychological, historical, and environmental factors that are perceived and organized in terms of their relevance to shared understandings and experiences constituting a cultural tradition.

The major components of cultural systems are as follows:

1. A *group or society* consisting of a set of members. Members are individuals who exhibit behaviors characteristic of the group and who participate in or are affected by decisions concerning the relevance or appropriateness of particular behaviors to the group. A group or society exists by virtue of the fact that it possesses the capacity of reaching decisions that are influential or binding upon its membership.
2. An *environment* within which the membership carries out its characteristic activities.
3. A *material culture* consisting of the equipment and artifacts used by the membership and including the permanent and tangible effects that past and present memberships have had upon the environment.
4. A *cultural tradition* representing the historically accumulated decisions of the membership or its representatives. Such decisions have to do with understandings concerning the nature of the group and its setting and material culture and with the appropriateness and desirability of particular behaviors, circumstances, and outcomes.
5. Human *activities and behaviors* emerging out of complex interactions among the membership, the environment, the material culture, and the cultural tradition.

The exact meanings given to such terms as *group, environment, material culture, cultural tradition and behavior* tend to vary somewhat depending upon the nature of the cultural system studied and the point of view of the individual carrying out the study. Although we may think of a society as a unit within which all the processes of the human life cycle are carried out and of the group as some sort of subdivision of the membership of a society, there are nonetheless some regions in which marriage takes place between distinct and sometimes hostile groups. In many parts of the world clans and clubs, which are certainly groups and not societies, may draw their membership from individuals belonging to a number of distinct societies. A society is generally thought to be a political entity, but some societies are so loosely organized that it is difficult to determine whether they should count as single societies or as clusters of similar societies.

Human groups may be formed in a variety of different ways, and a single individual may belong to a variety of different groups. In the case of a Boy Scout troop, it is easy to obtain a list of the members and to determine which members are paying dues and regularly attending meetings. In the case of informal groups that lack membership lists and even any fixed criteria of membership, it may be difficult to determine where the boundaries of the group are. The Tiwi tribe, which traditionally occupied Melville and Bathurst Islands off the northern coast of Australia, was divided into a number of separate bands, but because of constant visiting and exchange of membership among the bands, ethnographers have found it almost impossible to determine who belonged to which band. In the same way, street-corner groups in urban slums, such as those described by Liebow,[4] often have such fluid memberships that it is difficult or impossible to apply the concept of group at all.

Although with corner groups it is easy to define the environment and difficult to define the group, that is not the case with all cultural systems. Groups of hunters and gatherers often place their campsites on the boundaries between two or more quite distinct ecological zones. Near San Francisco Bay archaeological sites are usually located near sources of fresh water and in a transition zone between oak parkland and estuaries that give access to the bay. Although the territory of such a band or tribe may be fairly sharply defined, it is never easy to determine just which parts of the environment are actually occupied or in use. It is also difficult to determine which parts of the environment exert actual influence upon the group. Other peoples in the environment, possessing similar or different cultures, may be regarded as an aspect of the environment, but they may at the same time be borderline members of the group.

Because material culture is defined as material largely by virtue of the fact that it tends to persist in the environment in material form, it is often hard to determine what should be regarded as material culture and what should be regarded as part of the environment. Items of equipment in daily use are clearly part of material culture, but what of subtle changes in vegetation, animal populations, or soils that were initiated centuries before, perhaps by members of a totally different group? In most parts of the world centuries of

---

[4] Elliot Liebow, *Tally's Corner: A Study of Negro Streetcorner Men* (Boston, Toronto: Little, Brown, 1967).

human occupation have produced major changes in the environment, so that it is generally impossible to say whether particular groups are reacting to the "natural" environment or to the environment they themselves created.

The cultural traditions of neighboring peoples are never completely different and sometimes they are so similar as to lead to the conclusion that two neighboring societies possess the same culture. Even where neighboring societies occupy quite different environments and exhibit striking differences in behavior, it can sometimes be argued that this represents different expressions of the same cultural tradition in response to different environments. In complex situations, individuals may be familiar with several different cultural traditions in addition to that of some identified group, and this may accentuate the always present contrast between actual behavior and what members describe as the proper or traditional way of doing things.

Perhaps the simplest way of defining the activities and behaviors generated by the membership of a particular cultural system is to regard everything done by the members as part of the behavior characteristic of the cultural system. It might be said, for example, that Navajo behavior consists of what Navajos do. On the other hand, a great many Navajos do things that are not done by other Navajos and that are not in any way distinctly Navajo. One of the problems in defining cultural systems, then, is to develop ways of making distinctions between behaviors that are meaningful to the membership and relevant to the operation of the cultural system and behaviors that are meaningless and irrelevant to it.

These and many more problems encountered in the process of defining a cultural system as the object of a particular study reflect the fact that sharp boundaries between objects rarely occur in nature. The anthropologist is helped when people make sharp distinctions between themselves and others. When they do not, arbitrary distinctions must be made with the understanding that the results of research will be meaningful only if reasonable distinctions have been made.

5. Culture as Behavior

When anthropologists speak of the culture of a particular group of people, whether it be the Eskimo of Baffinland, the Vice-lords of Chicago, or the Dunkards of Plainville, they are expressing a generalization derived from an examination of behavior or of the results of behavior. A study of any particular culture or subculture involves talking to people, observing their activities, examining the settings within which activities take place, keeping track of the material artifacts such as tools, containers, works of art that people make and use, and examining the various impacts of human activities upon the settings within which they operate. Ideally a description of the Kariera culture of Australia is a series of generalizations derived from a close observation of the manner in which many different individual Kariera behave under particular sorts of conditions.

Some of the problems involved in describing another culture are illustrated by Morris Opler's study of the Chiricahua Apache.[5] The Chiricahuas were then a society of some 600 people living in eastern New Mexico. One of them recounted the following incident which took place when, as a young unmarried man, he went to visit an old lady, the grandmother of a marriageable girl.

> I went to her place that night. I had heard the old lady had some *tiswin* [a fermented liquor made of corn]. When I got there she told me to have a drink. As we talked she told me that I was single and needed a wife. She mentioned this girl [her grandchild] and said it was worth two horses to get her. I had never seen the girl before. When I got home I started to think about it seriously. I talked it over with my relatives. An uncle of mine gave me a mule, and a cousin gave me a horse.
>
> The next day I went to the home of a certain woman, a middle-aged woman. She was eating when I arrived. I called her outside and hired her to speak for me to this girl's grandmother. This woman lived just on the other side of a stream from the girl and her grandmother. The next day my go-between went to the old woman and asked her to give me the girl. The old woman demanded two good horses. My go-between thanked the grandmother and came to tell me what had been said. I gave her the horse and the mule to lead to the old woman, and the next day I went to the girl.[6]

In the course of his work among the Chiricahuas, Opler collected numerous incidents like the above that had to do with getting a wife. Here, because it is difficult to actually observe the process of getting a wife, the anthropologist must reconstruct the actual process from events remembered by individuals that have observed it. When all of the incidents are brought together and organized, it is possible to abstract from them common procedures relating to the arrangement of marriages. In the case of the Chiricahua Apache, there seems to have been no hard-and-fast rule concerning the initiation of the procedure. The initiative in proposing marriage could be taken by the girl's relatives as in the example above, the boy's relatives, or, less often, by the young people themselves. A generalization derived from this might be that any concerned party can take the initiative in proposing marriage. Such a generalization is, of course, a predictive statement. If we visited the Chiricahuas, we should not expect to see perfect strangers initiating marital proposals.

Another generalization formulated by Opler is that once a young man decides to marry he must consult his relatives to gain their consent to the marriage and their help in raising the necessary bride price, a gift made by the boy's family to that of the girl. This is what happened in the example quoted. Once permission has been granted and the bride price obtained, a go-between must be selected to make the necessary arrangements for the marriage. It is improper for the individual to arrange his or her own marriage. The

---

[5] The past tense is used in ethnographic examples in reference to the times at which the groups were studied. Many cultures, like that of the Chiricahua, or our own, have changed dramatically but still survive.

[6] Morris E. Opler, *An Apache Life-Way* (Chicago: University of Chicago Press, 1941), p. 157.

go-between was usually an older relative or friend, preferably one known for ability in matters of this sort. All of these generalizations hold true in the example given and presumably in all or most of the other incidents collected by Opler. It is important to note here that the generalizations constituting a description of a culture can range from vague statements, such as a concerned party must propose the marriage, to relatively specific statements, such as a go-between must be selected.

In one sense, then, culture is a set of statements about a group of people that is useful in predicting some aspects of their behavior. Such a set of statements is not, of course, identical to actual behavior, and so we may always wonder whether or not culture as seen by the anthropologist is quite the same as whatever mysterious force may be involved in coordinating the behaviors of a group of people. Although some writers have made much of the principles that no one can really know what goes on inside of people's heads and that skepticism must be maintained concerning the anthropologist's interpretations of culture, there is some comfort in the fact that physicists and chemists cannot communicate at all with the particles and molecules they study.

6. Patterns of Culture

Anthropological generalizations about the culture of any group or society do not precisely describe the behavior of any one individual. Put another way, every individual has unique experiences and unique interpretations of what is supposed to be done. In our society, when a man passes a woman acquaintance on the street, he customarily makes some gesture of greeting. If he is wearing a hat, and has a high regard for traditional ways of doing things, he is likely to lift it, tip it, or touch it with his hand. If the man is not wearing a hat or is uninfluenced by the genteel traditions of the past, he is likely to nod his head or raise and move his right hand in some fashion. These gestures are in addition to any verbal greetings. Each individual, in performing these rituals of greeting, reveals an idiosyncratic interpretation of a custom or cultural rule which says, in effect, thou shalt not pass an acquaintance on the street without exhibiting one of several possible gestures symbolizing recognition. Another way of saying this is that cultural rules permit each individual to generate appropriate actions in a unique way. Although all cultures have rituals of greeting, not all cultures make provision for the greeting of women acquaintances in public, and, of course, different cultures have different rituals of greeting. We might say, then, that all human beings engage in rituals of greeting and we might even suspect that rituals of greeting have some sort of biological basis, but the actual details of the ritual are the result of the unique individual's interpretation of what are conceived to be the rules of proper behavior.

The term *pattern* refers to the socially recognized limits within which such individual variation takes place. A ritual greeting pattern consists of the various rules and limits that seem to govern the process of greeting. Cultural patterns differ among each other in several ways. The script of a play, for example, can be a pattern that governs the verbal and nonverbal behavior of the actors in great detail. The rules of a game place certain limitations upon the players and at the same time set aside wide areas where the players can do and say anything they like within the rules. In either a play or a game it is generally understood that the patterns provided by the script or by the rules must be closely adhered to. Other sorts of rules are less likely to be obeyed.

An observation "on the behavior of 1,541 automobile drivers in the presence of [a] boulevard stop sign," made by Fearing and Krise,[7] gave the following results: 5.1 percent actually stopped their cars at or beyond the stop line, 11.5 percent slowed to one to three miles per hour, 45.1 percent slowed to six plus miles per hour, and 3.2 percent ignored the signal entirely. Here, a cultural pattern so sacred as to be dignified by the term *law* is seen to have far less impact on behavior than might have been expected. This illustration points up the difference between traditional or ideal patterns of behavior and actual or observed patterns of behavior. Ideal patterns such as *thou shalt stop at stop signs* or *thou shalt not covet thy neighbor's wife* exert an influence on behavior, but complete conformity to them is generally expected only of saints, schoolteachers, and ministers of the church. Ideal patterns represent the official cultural tradition and are generally responses to questions dealing with propriety such as, "What is the right way to drive?" or "What is the best way of doing X?" Actual patterns must be estimated on the basis of observed behavior or may sometimes be elicited by questions such as "How do people usually do X?"

Among the Chiricahuas a man who discovers that his wife is unfaithful is expected to take drastic action:

> A wronged husband who does not show some rancor is considered unmanly. . . . The woman, since she is close at hand, is likely to be the first to feel the husband's wrath. A beating is the least punishment she suffers. If there is no one to intercede for her, her very life may be forfeit, or she may be subjected to mutilation. . . . The husband is just as insistent that the man who has disrupted his home be punished: [quoting an Apache] "After the husband has punished or killed his wife, he will go after the man and kill him."[8]

Actual examples of infidelity reveal that affronted husbands do not always take such extreme steps. In one account given by Opler the husband, though he pretended great fury, "didn't care. He married right away to a Comanche."[9] Here, the effect of the ideal pattern is probably that of discouraging adultery because the wife and her lover can never be quite certain of what will happen when the husband finds out. The actual pattern, in which the husband shows great fury but rarely takes any further action, has the effect of preventing the uncontrolled violence that would result in the event of absolute conformity to traditional patterns of proper behavior.

[7] Franklin Fearing and E. M. Krise, "Conforming Behavior and the J-Curve Hypothesis," *Journal of Social Psychology,* **14**: 109–118 (1941).

[8] Opler, *An Apache Life-Way,* op. cit., pp. 409–410.

[9] Ibid., p. 409.

The difference between ideal and actual patterns of behavior was originally thought to be almost exclusively a result of cultural change. Thus one interpretation of the Apache traditional rules for dealing with infidelity is that they were once applied scrupulously, but were then rendered obsolete by changing social circumstances. Eventually, it could be argued, the rules would be changed to reflect the actual behavior, and the distinction between ideal and actual behavior would then disappear. Perhaps a more useful way of looking at the distinction is that the ideal pattern often influences rather than determines behavior. The existence of the law, with attached penalities, that everyone must stop at stop signs does influence behavior in the direction of exercising caution in the vicinity of stop signs. Similarly the Apache ideal pattern of vengeance emphasizes a need to take action against the adulterers and may have a deterrent effect.

The fact that people formulate rules that are not intended to be followed or that are not actually followed in practice creates discrepancies between behavior sanctioned by tradition and behavior that actually takes place. A cultural tradition is not a folk description of what happens; it is much more often a folk description of what ought to happen. Because what ought to happen very often does happen, there are many cases where anthropological generalizations concerning a culture conform quite closely to traditional understandings. Cultural systems are composed of individuals who generally find it convenient to do what they are supposed to do, but who are quite willing to do something else if it is more convenient or if they feel they can escape the anxiety, ridicule, or other punishment that so often accompanies the breaking of rules.

Both ideal and actual patterns vary in terms of the people to whom they are applied and in the extent to which they provide one or several different ways of behaving. Clyde Kluckhohn (1905–1960) has suggested that patterns can be classified in terms of the following five categories:[10]

1. Compulsory, where the culture provides but one acceptable means of meeting certain situations.
2. Preferred, where several ways of behaving are accepted, but one is more highly valued than the rest.
3. Typical, where several ways of behaving are more or less equally acceptable, but one is more often expressed than the rest.
4. Alternative, where several ways of behaving are acceptable, and there is no difference either in value or frequency of expression.
5. Restricted, where certain ways of behaving are acceptable only for some members of a society, not for the society as a whole.

Some of these differences are illustrated by avoidance relationships in Chiracahua society. Among the Chiricahua, when a man marries he must establish certain well-defined relations with his wife's relatives. There are three possible relationships: (1) total avoidance, which means that the man and his

[10] Clyde Kluckhohn, "Patterning in Navajo Culture," *Language, Culture and Personality*, ed. Leslie Spier (Menasha, Wis.: Sapir Memorial Publication Fund, 1941), pp. 109–130.

in-laws may have no direct contact; (2) partial avoidance, where direct contact may occur, but only in a highly formalized manner; and (3) no avoidance, where the man and his in-laws ignore all special usages.

Total avoidance is obligatory between a man and his wife's mother, father, mother's mother, and mother's father. "With these persons," writes Opler, "[total] avoidance is the unalterable rule and no choice is permitted."[11] The sisters of the wife's mother have a choice between total and partial avoidance of the husband. Total avoidance is preferred, especially when the relative concerned takes a lively interest in her niece. Partial avoidance is not so highly valued and would only be chosen by an aunt who had little contact with her niece and so was not directly concerned with her marriage.

Male relatives of the wife, excepting those for whom total avoidance is obligatory, typically follow a policy of partial avoidance but may also follow total or zero avoidance without fear of criticism. Most female cousins of the wife, and sometimes her sisters as well, find all three alternatives equally acceptable. The above patterns—compulsory, preferred, typical, and alternative—are all *restricted* in the sense that they apply only to the wife's relatives and only to certain categories of relatives.

Another sort of restricted pattern occurs in hierarchical societies where different patterns apply to different social levels or classes. In Peru, before the Spanish Conquest, a sharp distinction was made between the ruling Inca and Curaca classes and the common people (the Purics or householders) over whom they exercised sovereignty. This distinction was marked by ideal patterns that defined ways of behaving that were proper to the rulers alone. Members of the ruling classes wore clothing made of fine fabrics, whose use was prohibited to the Purics. Only Incas and Curacas could be army officers, government officials, church dignitaries, and *amautas,* wise men or teachers. The Puric was limited to such humbler occupations as farming, herding, mining, army service in the ranks, and common labor. An Inca or Curaca could have more than one wife and take concubines from the Puric class, but a Puric was restricted to one wife, who was also a Puric. In effect the restricted pattern says: "If you are an Inca or a Curaca, you should behave as follows; if you are a Puric, you should behave in a different way."

To summarize, patterns are the models or guidelines that people follow when they organize and plan their behavior. Ideal patterns tend to suggest behaviors that only an ideal or perfect individual can follow, while actual patterns approximate the working models that guide the everyday behavior of ordinary people. There may be little difference between ideal and actual patterns (if you are making a soufflé, it is wise to follow the recipe fairly closely), or the difference may be quite substantial. Even when the difference between ideal and actual patterns is substantial, the actual pattern is almost always influenced by the ideal. People actually do stop at stop signs some of the time, and if they do covet their neighbors' wives, they are likely to do so discreetly and with the knowledge that it is not an approved practice.

Because individuals like to present themselves as conforming fairly closely

---

[11] Opler, *An Apache Life-Way,* op. cit., p. 164.

to ideal patterns of behavior, interview techniques, no matter how carefully worked out, tend to produce accounts of ideal patterns. Individuals often seem to be unaware of the actual patterns that form the basis of their day-to-day behavior. Thus an actual pattern is likely to be a construct based upon behavior. Such an actual pattern predicts behavior to the extent that it calls for highly specific actions. For example, knowledge of the actual pattern allows us to predict that all Chiricahua weddings of the traditional sort will involve go-betweens. Other actual patterns may predict some aspects of the go-between's behavior, but much of the behavior will be idiosyncratic and unpredictable in detail. In effect knowledge of an actual pattern provides a prediction of culturally relevant or meaningful behavior but it does not predict everything that an individual will do in a given situation.

7. The Integration of Culture

In their totality the various patterns constituting a culture form a more or less integrated whole. Such activities as planting crops, conducting rituals, or fighting wars have to be orchestrated so that one activity does not interfere with another. Similarly what people learn in one situation should not be totally opposed to what they learn in another. A Maya Indian of Yucatán performs certain rituals before he clears his field or plants his crop. Superficially the ritual activity and the agricultural activity seem to be quite separate and quite different. But the success or failure of the maize crop is dependent upon the amount and timing of the rainfall, and, according to Maya culture, the rainfall is controlled by supernatural beings who must be appealed to by rituals of a certian sort. There is a single convincing explanation that integrates both ritual and agricultural activities.

One of the key problems in anthropology has always revolved around the question of the precise manner in which cultures are integrated. In other words, what are the parts and how are the parts related to each other? E. B. Tylor, despite the fact that he defined culture as a "complex whole," did not go much beyond a listing of the various parts a culture might have. Even today many ethnographies or descriptions of cultures consist of little more than a listing of cultural patterns crudely organized into such major categories as economics, child training, the life cycle, social organization, religion, art, play, and cultural change. Headings such as these make it relatively easy for workers from other disciplines to find the materials that concern them, but it does little to convey a sense of how the cultural system operates; that is to say, how the behavior of its membership is orchestrated. A rain-making ritual may be placed under religion, despite the fact that the membership considers it essential for crop production, while the group that performs the ritual is likely to be discussed under social organization. A description of agriculture may have to do with the size of fields, the number of seeds planted per acre, and the reliability of the harvests without ever saying very much about who does it or why, or what they do about the problem of unpredictable rainfall. Assuming that agriculture is one of the major activities of the group described, there are likely to be concrete effects of agriculture upon every aspect of group life.

Because agriculture requires forethought and planning, we should expect agriculture to have strong effects upon the way people think and feel about the world. It should have effects upon the size of the group and the distribution of the group in relationship to other groups. It should even affect such things as the structure of the family and the kinds of relationships that develop between families or between individuals. One of the key questions for anthropology has to do with the manner in which different kinds of activities and patterns affect each other and the manner in which they contribute to the overall operation or functioning of the cultural system.

One of the early approaches to this problem was made by the French social scientist Émile Durkheim, who drew a parallel between cultural systems and biological organisms. In his view, the different aspects of any one culture persisted because they were "true," in the sense that they contributed to the integration of society and therefore to its survival. Things that were not "true" or adaptive, things that were in error, would sooner or later encounter obstacles and, therefore, cease to survive. The expression of the unity of a cultural system was to be found in "collective representations" that were mobilized in the carrying out of religious and ritual actions. Durkheim's argument that there existed a kind of collective consciousness which stood above the individual and which generated collective representations controlling the actions of the individual ran counter to important developments in psychological theory and to the developing cult of the individual, which was nowhere stronger than in the United States. Although most scholars were willing to accept the value of an organic analogy that stressed certain similarities between organisms and cultural systems, Durkheim's concept of a "group mind" seemed too much to bear. From some points of view it does seem that the concept of collective consciousness, and sometimes even the concept of culture, reduces the individual to the role of a cell in an organism blindly obedient to the dictates of the group mind or of the cultural tradition. From another point of view, it could be argued that Durkheim's collective representations are nothing more than sacred symbols, like motherhood, the flag, apple pie, and individualism, which stand for and reinforce the individual's loyalty and commitment to the principles of the group. At the turn of the century, when Durkheim wrote, there seemed to be no easy way to answer such a question as, "Is culture the slave of the individual or is the individual the slave of culture?" We know now that this was the wrong question. Like nature or nurture and most other either/or questions, it is irrelevant to the complexities of real life.

Durkheim's organic analogy, largely shorn of its emphasis on collective representations, was taken up in England by Alfred Reginald Radcliffe-Brown (1881–1955) and Bronislaw Malinowski (1884–1942). In Radcliffe-Brown's view the essence of a cultural system was a *social structure*, a set of relationships between individuals and collections of individuals. Economic activities, religious rituals, and other patterns of behavior, then, had the *function* of maintaining the integrity of the social structure. Child training and other forms of cultural transmission had the function of preparing the individual to take a place within the social structure. Economic activities had the function of ensuring that goods and services were obtained and distributed in such a way as to maintain the social structure. Religious rituals had the function of promoting the integration of the individual into the social structure.

Although Malinowski also made use of Durkheim's organic analogy, his general line of argument was that all human beings have biologically derived needs which must be filled by the cultural system if the cultural system is to survive. Malinowski, then, saw cultural systems as consisting of a series of institutions each of which had the *function* of satisfying some particular human need. Where Radcliffe-Brown attempted to assign a priority to social structure, Malinowski was perhaps the first theorist to visualize cultural systems as systems in which each of the parts was equally important, each playing a role in the final outcome. To simplify matters a bit, Radcliffe-Brown tended to see social structure as being causally responsible for such things as economics and religion, whereas Malinowski tended to see all institutions, whether economic or social or religious, as more or less equally important.

For most anthropologists the idea of function introduced a need to think about the contribution that each aspect of culture made to the functioning of the cultural system as a whole. Unfortunately few anthropologists even today are fully aware of the need to demonstrate the existence of particular functions. For the United States it is easy to say that the rituals of Thanksgiving and Christmas have such functions as promoting social integration or strengthening family ties, but it is difficult, perhaps impossible, to demonstrate that such functions actually exist. Perhaps the only effective demonstration of the function of Christmas would be to abolish it and see if it made a difference. The main advantage of thinking in terms of the functional relationship of the parts of a cultural system is that it permits a consistent and organized picture of the whole that is far easier to grasp than a mere listing of cultural traits or patterns.

The idea that everything people do must in some way contribute to the functioning of the cultural system and hence to its survival is useful in the same way that the idea that all of the pieces of a jigsaw puzzle are present contributes to persistence in finishing the puzzle. Carried to an extreme, the idea of function leads us to the conclusion that people never make mistakes, that all wars and conflicts serve useful functions, and that everything is for the best. But if everything in a cultural system is ideally arranged to maximize survival, it becomes rather difficult to explain why cultures change or to justify any change in existing culture. Durkheim once argued, for example, that criminals exist because society needs criminals in order to function. This may well be the case in certain circumstances, but it is also possible to imagine that some societies might manage to survive a sharp reduction in the crime rate. In politics functionalism has been used in support of things as they are, sometimes as an argument against forcing unwanted changes upon subject peoples, sometimes as an argument in support of existing colonial regimes.

Although most anthropologists in the United States were receptive to functionalist concepts to some extent, they found it difficult to reconcile func-

tionalist ideas with their strong interests in American Indian cultures.
Although many retained a historical interest in the reconstruction of traditional societies, others became interested in the processes of American Indian
adaptation to English and Spanish-speaking neighbors and conquerors. These
studies, which usually went under the name of *acculturation*, were difficult to
interpret in terms of such concepts as maintenance of the social structure or
the preservation of an equilibrium or steady state. Under the influence of
Franz Boas, many anthropologists in the United States felt that, in any case,
intelligent theories about the nature of cultural systems could only be developed after large quantities of information about them had been collected.

Until after World War II many anthropologists in both the United States
and Europe found ample justification for regarding their task as being limited
either to ethnographic reconstruction of traditional cultures or to ethnographic description of patterns of acculturation. There was no recognition
of the fact that each such description was, in itself, a theory of culture. A few
anthropologists, Robert Redfield (1897–1958), for example, applied simple
evolutionary frameworks to their data in the hope that the transition from folk
to urban or from traditional to modern could be explained in terms of the
acquisition of particular diagnostic traits. Although some important generalizations can be made about the differences between small and large communities, such things as the discovery that cities have larger and more diverse
populations than villages were hardly exciting.

Most anthropologists, then, had a tendency to focus upon the unique aspects of the groups they studied and to raise questions about why different
tribes or villages underwent different patterns of acculturation or modernization. This question might have been answered, and indeed sometimes was
answered, in terms of different environmental influences, as implied by the
distinction between forced and voluntary acculturation. On the other hand, the
idea that environmental or economic forces might play a role in determining
the nature of culture smacked dangerously of Marxist economic determinism
and materialism. Anthropology's vigorous support of biological evolution and
its equally vigorous attacks on racism had already brought the new science
under suspicion of radicalism in a number of quarters. Had these views been
combined with ideas of economic or environmental causation, the political
repercussions might have been catastrophic. Marxism in any literal sense was
anathema to most anthropologists because it seemed to represent just another
version of nineteenth-century classical evolutionism elevated to the position of
a political dogma.

In any event theories of cultural integration in the United States gradually
came to take the form of functionalist theories in which the functioning of the
cultural system had the effect of preserving particular sorts of personalities or
particular views of life. This approach was first developed, surprisingly
enough in view of the repudiation of cultural integration in her doctoral dis-
sertation, by Ruth Benedict (1887–1948) in *Patterns of Culture*.[12] Benedict
suggested that some cultures could be described in terms of a set of character-

---

[12] Ruth Benedict, *Patterns of Culture* (Boston: Houghton Mifflin, 1934).

istic purposes not necessarily shared by other societies. The Zuñi and neighboring Pueblo Indians of New Mexico seemed to her to follow an Apollonian ideal, emphasizing order and restraint. The Pueblos, for example, sought supernatural power through membership in a cult group. Such membership is purchased and requires only that the candidate learn an extensive ritual. The Plains Indians, on the other hand, were Dionysian. They sought supernatural power through visions induced by fasting, self-torture, and the use of drugs. Similar distinctions permeated all aspects of the two cultures and gave each its characteristic unity and configuration.

The idea of Apollonian and Dionysian cultures, like most simple dichotomies, leaves a great deal to be explained. Nevertheless the concept of a cultural core or focus was taken up by a number of anthropologists interested in acculturation and, in many cases, it has been possible to demonstrate the maintenance of particular personality orientations or particular cultural patterns in the face of major changes in technology or in other aspects of culture. A developing culture and personality school, heavily influenced by Freud and other psychoanalysts, came to place an increasing emphasis on the role of early childhood training in the development of a national character or basic personality type. Working with Ralph Linton (1893–   ), Cora Du Bois (1903–   ), and other anthropologists, the psychoanalyst Abram Kardiner (1891–   )[13] developed an explanation of cultural integration in which many aspects of religion and ideology were regarded as projections of a basic personality type formed by uniform practices of child training. Although few would doubt that some aspects of personality, especially in small-scale societies, are widely distributed within the population, the notion that people in the same society share the same personality does not always jibe with the wide personality variations encountered almost everywhere. Logically it would appear reasonable to suppose that even the smallest group benefits by the presence of a variety of distinct personalities. At times the idea of national character leads to gross generalizations about particular peoples that seem hardly different, once the psychoanalytic jargon has been penetrated, from vulgar prejudice. Early studies of national character generally assumed that personality, as established in childhood, was relatively fixed and that child-training practices or childhood experiences would therefore be predictive of adult behavior. Although this is true in many cases, it assumes that human beings are slaves of habit who are unlikely to change their behavior when confronted with new situations. An important, and not yet completely resolved question, then, has to do with the conditions under which behavior is determined by situations and the conditions under which it is determined by personality or by past experience.

Another related approach to an understanding of cultural integration lies in the idea that people in different cultures pursue somewhat different goals and hold somewhat different beliefs about the nature of things. Their behavior, then, is partly dependent upon the particular values they choose to pursue

[13] Abram Kardiner, ed., *The Individual and His Society* (New York: Columbia University Press, 1939); *The Psychological Frontiers of Society,* with the collaboration of Ralph Linton, Cora Du Bois, and James West (pseud.) (New York: Columbia University Press, 1945, 1950).

and the particular postulates about the nature of things that they hold to be important. As Morris Opler (1903–   )[14] has pointed out, many cultures, perhaps a majority, are not dominated by a central summative principle. He suggests that most societies have a number of such principles, which he calls themes. As an example, one theme for Chiricahua Apache culture is that men are superior to women physically, mentally, and morally. Opler demonstrates the existence of this theme by citing a number of examples: A lively fetus is assumed to be male. Women are said to be unstable and excitable, have less willpower, and are more apt to be tempted into sorcery or irregular sexual conduct. Men always take precedence over women socially and hold all important political positions. Women are barred from a number of ceremonial and recreational activities.

Such a theme is not all-pervasive. Other themes may reinforce or limit any particular theme. Thus, although the importance of long life and old age is a major theme of Chiricahua culture, it is limited by another theme that position must be validated by participation. When an old man can no longer participate in significant aspects of male activities, his leadership is diminished or vanishes. In Ralph Linton's words, every culture has a set of "things that make life worth living."[15] The integration of culture, then, derives from those special hierarchies of value and belief that define the important things of life and set in motion a variety of activities designed to maximize those things.

Another view of integration, developed by the French anthropologist Claude Lévi-Strauss (1908–   ),[16] argues that human thought is organized in terms of basic oppositions between such things as male and female and culture and nature. These basic oppositions underlie all behavior and serve to explain why such diverse activities as agriculture and art fit together to form a single integrated culture. Modern students of cognitive anthropology, influenced by linguistics, and especially by the work of Noam Chomsky (1928–   ),[17] have accepted Lévi-Strauss's basic concept of an underlying cognitive order, but have been deeply dissatisfied with the manner in which Lévi-Strauss demonstrates his findings. Cognitive anthropologists tend to interpret culture as consisting of a set of basic paradigms or patterns, very much like the rules of a grammar, which permit the generation of appropriate behavior which nevertheless bears the stamp of the individual's own style or personality. In this view a cultural tradition consists of a set of rules and definitions which determine the nature of the individual's perceptions of the environment and which account for the behavior generated in response to those perceptions.

[14] Morris E. Opler, "Themes as Dynamic Forces in Culture," *American Journal of Sociology,* **51:** 198–206 (1945); "An Application of the Theory of Themes in Culture," *Journal of the Washington Academy of Sciences,* **36:** 137–166 (1946).

[15] Ralph Linton, *The Study of Man* (New York: Appleton-Century-Crofts, 1936).

[16] Claude Lévi-Strauss, *Structural Anthropology,* trans. C. Jacobson (New York: Basic Books, 1963).

[17] Noam Chomsky, *Language and Mind,* Enlarged Edition (New York: Harcourt Brace Jovanovich, 1972).

8. Culture as an Adaptive Mechanism

When cultural systems are thought of as devices for maintaining a particular social system, a particular personality type, or a particular arrangement of values and concepts, it is easy to drift away from the more fundamental idea that cultural systems represent the means by which the human animal adapts to the environment. "Man cannot live by bread alone" does not mean that people can do without bread. No matter how intriguing the social system, how interesting the personalities, or how exciting the cognitions characteristic of a particular group of people, their survival still depends upon the set of relationships that they maintain with their environment. If all goes well, it is these relationships that permit the members of a cultural system to obtain and distribute the energy and resources required for its continuation.

Early attempts to relate cultural systems to their environments in causal terms were largely unsuccessful because cultural systems in quite similar environments turned out to be quite different. It was this that led to the conclusion that environment was not really very important in determining the characteristics of a cultural system and to a search for an explanation of similarities and differences in terms of historical factors, such as diffusion, or in terms of such things as social structure or cognition. Statements about the relationships that hold between members of a cultural system or about the ideas they hold in their heads, do not, however, provide an explanation of how things got that way in the first place. Minor changes in such things can sometimes be explained in terms of a working out of inconsistencies or in terms of a kind of variation from one state to another, but there is no way of explaining major changes.

Because the environment is the only thing that can vary independently of the cultural system, it was inevitable that anthropologists would eventually return to the environment as a source of explanations of the origin and development of cultural systems. Fresh consideration of the importance of adaptation to environmental circumstances in influencing the nature of cultural system was made possible by the development of new ways of understanding environments in terms of ecological relationships. Where early views of the relationships between environment and culture were essentially simpleminded and often attributed cultural variation to a small number of environmental variables such as temperature or type of vegetation, modern students of anthropological ecology view the environment as consisting of a variety of complex relationships that can be understood only through detailed study of such things as the food chain or the transfer of energy and resources among the various species inhabiting the environment.

Early approaches to ecological explanations of cultural systems generally interpreted basic features of cultural systems as being directly caused by environmental forces, and they generally emphasized the importance of the natural environment and gave scant consideration to the importance of neighboring peoples who were part of the environment. Julian Steward, for example, in his early studies of the Paiute Indians of Nevada and California suggested that a series of particular environmental features such as the presence of large game animals gave rise to a number of characteristic patterns of social organization. He anticipated that similar patterns of social organization would arise wherever hunters with simple technologies lived in environments characterized by those particular features. Going a step further, Marvin Harris (1927–   ) has argued that the nature of cultural systems is *determined* by the interaction between technology and environment. People entering a new environment bring with them or develop a technology suited for survival in that environment. The nature of the technology that they develop, according to Harris, then determines the overall pattern of their social relationships and this in turn determines the various ideas they have about the nature of things.

In the biological sciences it is a commonplace that species can adapt to the environment in a variety of different ways; for example, they may become specialized or generalized in their pattern of adaptation. In the same way, human beings entering upon a new environment generally have a variety of alternative means of adapting to it. Their choice of adaptive technology is likely to be based, in part, upon the concepts of social organization and the other ideas and perceptions which they brought with them to the environment. They are likely, then, to select means of adaptation which permit them in some degree to retain and continue the social arrangements and ways of thinking which they brought with them from their previous environment. An imaginary environment so harsh and limiting as to permit one and only one pattern of adaptation to survive would of course exert a determining effect upon the social arrangements and ways of thinking of any group that managed to survive within it. A lush environment, by contrast, might have virtually no influence upon people moving into it because almost anything the people chose to do would be adaptive. In such a strictly hypothetical case the determining effect of the environment would be close to zero.

Peoples having similar technologies and living in similar environments may have quite different social arrangements and quite different ideas about the nature of things. Despite these differences, which a strict environmentalist might label superficial, we would expect to find broad similarities arising out of the fact that when environment and technology are held constant, the possible range of variation in other aspects of the cultural system is reduced. It is therefore possible to identify broad similarities among hunter-gatherers or among agricultural peoples living in similar environments.

Cultural systems survive in particular environments because they are adapted to them. In essence this means that the members of the cultural system are able to survive and reproduce by translating into action the various beliefs and policies contained in the cultural tradition. To do this, the members must share the general belief that the cultural tradition provides the best possible or the best available guidelines for surviving and carrying out the good life. In other words, the survival of a cultural system is based upon what might be called the loyalty of its membership as well as upon its ability to provide solutions to the problems of adaptation.

The human species differs from other animal species in the extent to which individuals and populations within the species are capable of learning and exhibiting diverse forms of behavior. This is illustrated by the diversity of food habits, patterns of dress and ornament, and styles of human relationship among the different peoples of the world. The existing diversity cannot be explained in terms of biological inheritance or in terms of any simple relationships to the environment.

Although most peoples have some sort of explanation for the unique aspects of their own behavior, the first attempt at a scientific explanation of the phenomenon was a form of evolutionism, "classical evolution," that developed during the 1850s. The essential argument of this theory was that existing peoples represented a series of stages in a ladderlike progression toward an end-state called civilization which all peoples would achieve in time. Early classical evolutionists often failed to make any clear distinction between behaviors acquired by biological evolution and behaviors acquired through learning. As anthropological scholars became increasingly aware of the limitations upon a purely biological explanation of human diversity, increasing emphasis came to be placed upon the concept of culture. Beginning with Tylor's early definition of culture, more and more importance came to be attached to the human ability to form cultural traditions in which knowledge and experience were transmitted and accumulated through the use of language.

Culture can now be seen as an emergent property of human groups that begins to take form as soon as decisions are made concerning the conduct of common enterprises. Culture is visible as the characteristic behaviors of a group of people, but it also exists in the form of plans and common understandings that are acknowledged by a membership. A culture is a set of learned ways of thinking and acting that characterizes any decision-making human group. In general terms, culture has to do with the human capacity to use language and with related capacities for learning and for the transmission of ideas and ways of behaving. *Culture* can be used broadly to refer to sociocultural systems such as the Navajo Tribe or to regional uniformities such as Plains culture or Western culture. *Culture* can also be used in reference to such subcultural entities as upper-class culture or Jones family culture. Because *culture* is often used in a restricted sense to refer to cultural tradition, while *society* may refer solely to individuals and their relationships to each other, many anthropologists and sociologists prefer to use such terms as *sociocultural system* or *cultural system* to refer to the entire set of relationships that characterize any particular people or group. The major components of a cultural system include a group, an environment, a material culture, a cultural tradition, and human activities and behaviors.

Because a large part of culture consists of plans and ideas invisibly stored within the heads of some or all of the membership, information about any particular culture depends upon talking to people and observing their activities and the contexts within which their activities take place. Essentially, an anthropologist's description of any particular cultural system consists of a set of inferences or educated guesses about the nature of the forces that influence or determine actual behavior and speech. Because every individual is unique, all human behavior emerges out of individualistic interpretations of what can and should be done in any particular situation. Cultural patterns provide sets of rules and alternatives that set limits upon the varieties of behavior that are approved or permissible. Important distinctions can be made between ideal and actual cultural patterns or in terms of the extent to which any particular pattern sets limits on and therefore serves as a predictor for particular kinds of behavior.

The various patterns constituting a culture form a more or less integrated whole. Questions regarding the exact nature of cultural patterns and the precise nature of their integration have been a basic concern of anthropological thinkers. The somewhat different approaches to these problems developed by Durkheim, Radcliffe-Brown, and Malinowski have influenced many anthropologists in the United States, but others encountered difficulties in reconciling such functionalist theories to the dynamic changes then taking place in the American Indian groups they were studying. Consequently, American anthropologists often avoided theoretical interpretations and concentrated upon largely descriptive tasks. Theories of cultural integration that did develop generally took the form, under the leadership of Ruth Benedict, of an identification of basic psychological attitudes or fundamental interests — "the things that make life worth living" — that tended to persist even when overwhelming changes in outward behaviors were taking place. Modern theories of cultural integration are similar to the older theories except that they tend to point to an underlying cognitive or intellectual order rather than to an underlying emotional order — not the things that make life worth living, but the way things are "spozed" to be.

Recent theories concerning the nature of culture have also placed an increasing emphasis on the environment — the way things are — and on the character of cultural systems as adaptive or problem-solving devices. The return to environmentally based interpretations of cultural systems and of their adaptive strategies depended upon the development of increasingly sophisticated interpretations of environmental forces provided by the development of ecological points of view in the biological sciences. The early ecological interpretations in anthropology were biased by an excessive concern with the biological and physical aspects of the environment and a failure to consider the influence of neighboring peoples. The modern, developing interpretation of cultural systems emphasizes concepts of feedback and interaction in which outcomes are interpreted as a result of a complex interplay of forces rather than in terms of simple causation.

Collateral Readings

Geertz, Clifford. *The Interpretation of Cultures; Selected Essays.* New York: Basic Books, Inc., 1973.

Goodenough, Ward H. *Culture, Language and Society*. Reading, Mass.: Addison-Wesley Publishing company, 1971. Key concepts defined in relationship to each other.

Harris, Marvin. *The Rise of Anthropological Theory: A History of Theories of Culture*. New York: Thomas Y. Crowell Company, 1968. An extensive discussion written from the viewpoint of a "technoenvironmental" determinist.

Kaplan, David, and Robert A. Manners. *Culture Theory*. Englewood Cliffs, N.J.: Prentice-Hall, Inc., 1972. Compact overview of anthropological theory.

Keesing, Roger M. "Theories of Culture," *Annual Review of Anthropology*, **3**:73–97 (1974). A recent review of works dealing with the culture concept.

Kluckhohn, Clyde, and William Kelly. "The Concept of Culture," *The Science of Man in the World Crisis*, ed. Ralph Linton. New York: Columbia University Press, 1945, pp. 78–106. A brief analysis of the culture concept.

Kroeber, Alfred L. *Anthropology: Culture Patterns and Processes*. New York and Burlingame: Harcourt Brace Jovanovich, 1963. Selections from a classic textbook.

Kroeber, Alfred L., and Clyde Kluckhohn. "Culture: A Critical Review of Concepts and Definitions." Cambridge, Mass.: Harvard University. *Papers of the Peabody Museum of American Archaeology and Ethnology*, Vol. 47, 1952.

Opler, Morris E. "Some Recently Developed Concepts Relating to Culture," *Southwestern Journal of Anthropology*, **4**:107–122 (1948). Progress as of 1948.

White, Leslie A. "The Concept of Culture," *American Anthropologist*, **61**:227–251 (1959).

Ethnographic References

Australian aborigine: Hart and Pilling, 1960; Kaberry, 1970; Meggitt, 1962; Radcliffe-Brown, 1931.

Eskimo: Birket-Smith, 1936; Coon, 1948, Chapter 4; Rasmussen, 1908, 1931.

United States: Keiser, 1969; Whyte, 1955.
  Dunkard: West, 1945.

3/Strategies and Methods in the Study of Culture

1. The Data of the Anthropologist

The preceding chapter identified culture as the central concept of anthropology and presented some general views on its nature. Another approach to an understanding of culture is to consider the kinds of data involved in describing culture and the methods used in collecting it. In broad terms the data of anthropology consist of human beings living in groups and their products and behavior. Because anthropologists seek to understand cultures of the past, as well as of the present, there is a grand methodological divide between anthropologists who study modern or recent cultures and those who study past cultures. Students of modern cultures are in a position to observe behavior as it takes place, to interview persons familiar with the culture, or to analyze any written records that might exist. Students of past cultures, although they may sometimes benefit from written records that have been preserved in various ways, are unable to observe behavior or to interview the people they study. The reconstruction of past ways of life is largely dependent upon the examination of such relatively indestructible remains as skeletal materials, buildings, and stone and bone tools.

The two methods of studying culture can be referred to as the ethnographic method, used by cultural anthropologists, and the archaeological method. Linguists generally use highly specialized forms of ethnographic method, whereas biological anthropologists, depending upon their interests, use either method in combination with appropriate methods derived from biology. Ethnographic and archaeological methods are quite general. All human beings use crude ethnographic methods in the course of attempts to learn their own cultures. All of the social sciences and the humanities are dependent upon ethnographic methods for the collection of the specialized information required by their own particular disciplines. Geologists, paleontologists, historians, and others interested in the past make use of many of the same techniques as archaeologists. Ethnographers and archaeologists do not have a monopoly on the methods they use. Most of their methods are, in fact, shared with other disciplines. To the extent that anthropological methods differ from those of other disciplines, they differ in the direction of simplicity and generality. On the whole they are methods that can be applied readily and with a minimum of complicated equipment or preparation to a wide variety of past and present cultures. The basic equipment of the archaeologist consists of a tape measure and a shovel; the basic equipment of the ethnographer is a pen and notebook.

Civilized people, that is to say people who live in cities, are generally contemptuous of those who are unfamiliar with the latest happenings at the capitol or at the theater. "Where it's at" is here and now. As a famous economist once remarked to an anthropologist who came to him for advice, "People who earn less than seventy dollars per year are of no significance." The ethnographer who leaves the city, perhaps the country as well, for the purpose of studying the lifeways of obscure peoples like the Bushmen of the Kalahari desert or the fishermen of Malaya is likely to be cursed in newspaper editorials that enquire, "Why spend ten thousand dollars to study the Hottentot when we have all of these serious problems at home?" The archaeologist who studies *dead* Bushmen or *dead* fishermen is likely to be doubly cursed, perhaps even by ethnographers who see more urgent priorities among the living.

Early anthropologists justified the conduct of ethnographic and archaeological research on the grounds that the ills of modern society could be attributed to the accidental survival of ancient ways of doing things. By identifying such survivals of uncivilized ways of life, they felt that they could weed them out and thus move human society that much closer to ultimate civilization. In the same vein modern anthropologists argue that a full knowledge of the range of possible human behaviors combined with an understanding of the general course of human development will increase the range of problem-solving techniques available to modern society and provide a general understanding of the possible lines of future human development. For any culture the archaeological and historical record tells us how long it has been the way it is and the direction in which it is developing. Were it not for the existence of archaeological and historical estimates of the size of past human populations, the world would still be unaware of the population problem that now threatens the quality of human life. The persons (or cultures) that don't know where they've been, probably don't know where they're going.

2. The Collection of Archaeological Data

The major goals of archaeology are to reconstruct the lifeways or cultures of the past as fully as possible, to interpret and relate these cultures to general anthropological problems and theories, and to test such hypotheses as are possible given the nature of archaeological materials. In the past archaeology was devoted to the classification of artifacts and to the study of their distribution in space and their ordering in time. Although these tasks remain important, contemporary archaeology, with the development of improved methods, has focused more and more on the problem of reconstructing in as much detail as possible the overall way of life of those whose garbage pits and living sites they study. Although the archaeologist cannot deal directly with human behavior, it is assumed that all evidences of former human presence are the product of human behavior and that the actual behavior can be inferred from a general knowledge of the nature of humanity.

In its simplest form "archaeology as such is simply a technique (essentially digging holes in the ground or stooping over to pick up objects)," [1] but there are some complex ways of performing these tasks. A handbook dealing with techniques of field research lists 1,250 items in its bibliography, but reviewers have criticized it for failing to deal in sufficient depth with research planning and sampling problems. There is no single way to undertake an archaeological field study. Each region or area and each site presents special problems that must be worked out before investigations are begun. Field archaeology is more than the recovery of tools and works of art; it calls for the investigation of every possible bit of evidence concerning those who occupied the region or site and their activities. A piece of charcoal may yield a date by tree-ring or by carbon-14 analysis; the date is meaningless unless it can be shown that the charcoal is the product of human activity and related to other evidences of human presence. The arrangement of stones may tell something about cooking methods or house construction. Animal bones tell something about economic activities, so too may analysis of soil samples. Differences in house construction or in the things buried with the dead may indicate status or class differences; the burials also may suggest some aspects of religious belief. Locations of settlements indicate relations of the inhabitants and their culture to present or past landscapes, natural resources, or human' neighbors. Although some information may come from rock drawings or engravings, quarries, or evidence of trails, most basic archaeological data are the remains of dwellings or campsites and the abandoned tools and debris people have left.

Ideally the first step in exploring a new area is a survey to locate all the places or sites showing evidence of human habitation on the surface of the ground. (See Figure 3–1.) These are mapped, and a representative sample of artifacts located on the surface are collected and their relations to natural fea-

---

[1] Albert C. Spaulding, "Explanation in Archeology," *New Perspectives in Archaeology*, ed. S. R. Binford and L. R. Binford (Chicago: Aldine, 1968), p. 38.

University of California

ARCHAEOLOGICAL SITE SURVEY RECORD

1. Site _____ 2. Map _____ 3. County _____

4. Twp. _____ Range _____ 1/4 of _____ 1/4 of Sec. _____

5. Location _____

_____

_____ 6. On contour elevation _____

7. Previous designations for site _____

8. Owner _____ 9. Address _____

10. Previous owners, dates _____

11. Present tenant _____

12. Attitude toward excavation _____

13. Description of site _____

_____

14. Area _____ 15. Depth _____ 16. Height _____

17. Vegetation _____ 18. Nearest water _____

19. Soil of site _____ 20. Surrounding soil type _____

21. Previous excavation _____

22. Cultivation _____ 23. Erosion _____

24. Buildings, roads, etc. _____

25. Possibility of destruction _____

26. House pits _____

27. Other features _____

28. Burials _____

29. Artifacts _____

_____

_____

30. Remarks _____

31. Published references _____

32.   Accession No. _____ 33. Sketch map _____

34. Date _____ 35. Recorded by _____ 36. Photos _____

Figure 3–1 A site survey record form. Systematic survey records are essential in arranging for the preservation of existing sites and in making decisions about future excavation. (Courtesy of Archaeological Survey, UCLA.)

tures noted. On large sites the area should be divided in sections and the artifacts from each section kept separately. Analysis may show significant differences between parts of the site. Often the survey will indicate the number of different cultures that have existed in the area (although the later discovery of a completely buried culture is sometimes a happy surprise), something of their complexity, and the way the environment was utilized. Relative ages of these cultures often can be established. The location of all sites of a given type above an ancient beach line, for example, suggests that they are older than sites of another type located below the beach line.

Not only may the variations in the artifacts collected from the surface of different sites show the presence of different cultures, but analysis may suggest their sequence in time. An early example of this is afforded by Leslie Spier's survey of the region of Zuñi pueblo in New Mexico, published in 1917.[2] Up to that time the archaeological cultures of the Southwestern United States were usually considered to be a single prehistoric culture. Spier collected a large number of pottery samples from Zuñi and surrounding prehistoric sites and classified them according to shape, color, and design elements. He then counted the numbers of the various types established and analyzed them statistically. Although the statistical treatment today would be considered unsophisticated, it was one of the very first applications of statistics to archaeological material. As a result of his studies, Spier suggested that there were several time periods in Southwestern archaeology reflected in changing styles and percentages of pottery found on different sites. His conclusions were almost simultaneously verified by the first stratigraphic excavations done in the Southwest by N. C. Nelson.[3] Spier's use of statistics and the survey approach was later refined and expanded by the use of better analysis and more sophisticated statistical techniques, including today the use of computers.

The survey may be used to give preliminary information about differences in culture, possible time sequences, culture change, settlement patterns, and ecological relations. If the existence of a culture has already been established by excavation at a key site, the survey may show the limits of its distribution in space or the distribution of special elements in the culture. Perhaps the most important use of the survey, however, is to determine which sites should be excavated thoroughly and which should merely be sampled. It is rarely possible to excavate completely or even partially all sites in a region. It is important, therefore, that those sites excavated should be as representative as possible, and most apt to supply data to test hypotheses and answer problems. It may, for example, be desirable to excavate not only large and imposing sites but smaller sites and workshops. Systematic sample excavation on a number of sites may also be indicated to determine whether the artifacts collected in a surface survey are representative of the artifacts underneath the ground in the various sites surveyed.

[2] Leslie Spier, "Outline of Chronology of the Zuñi Ruins," *American Museum of Natural History—Anthropological Papers*, **18**:209–331 (1917).

[3] N. C. Nelson, "Chronology of the Tano Ruins," *American Anthropologist*, **18**:159–180 (1916).

Partially excavated site of gathering culture; circular house floor is in center. Inland Gabrieleño area, California, Site LAN-162. (Courtesy of Archaeological Survey, UCLA.)

The selection of sites for excavation involves a number of problems over which the archaeologist may not always have control. Sites are often threatened with destruction by road or pipeline construction, quarrying, dam building, leveling land for irrigation, or urban expansion. There is considerable pressure to excavate at least some of these sites before they are destroyed. Such salvage archaeology is increasingly recognized by governments and even corporations constructing pipelines in the United States, and many archaeologists have been employed in such activities. In other cases sites may be excavated and restored to create tourist attractions, because they are large and imposing or because they promise large numbers of art objects for museums or private collectors. The careful removal and rebuilding of the temples at Abu Simbel in Egyptian Nubia to raise them above the lake created by building the Aswan dam is perhaps the most spectacular example. In this case international interest was aroused and some millions of dollars spent in preserving a monument which contributed little to archaeological knowledge, for the temples already had been studied. The preservation of the Abu Simbel temples cost several times the annual world budget for archaeological research. Salvage archaeology certainly is justified, but it often diverts funds and the attention of archaeologists from sites that are much more likely to contribute to the solving of archaeological problems. Other special-interest excavation may be rapidly and carelessly done, destroying data useful for broader interpretations.

Once a site has been selected for excavation, the archaeologist still has numerous problems before beginning work. Costs must be estimated and the necessary funds raised. Permission of the landowners or of local and national government agencies must be secured. If the site is in another country, special requirements may have to be met. If the site is on an Indian reservation in the United States, permission of the tribal council may have to be secured. Agreements must be reached about the final disposition of the artifacts recovered and the condition in which the site is to be left when excavation is complete. In the case of imposing architectural remains, the buildings may have to be restored as far as possible. Usually the archaeologist must refill pits or trenches to prevent animals from falling in or to restore the surface for agricul-

Excavating a village farming site in the United States Southwest. Surviving wall features are being excavated. The earth removed is screened to locate small artifacts and other materials of interest. (Courtesy of the Field Museum of Natural History.)

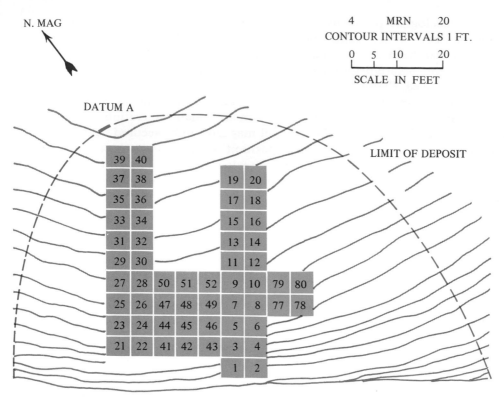

Figure 3–2 Preparing to excavate. Contour map of an archaeological site, showing one method of laying out numbered squares and reference points. [Courtesy of D. J. McGeem and W. C. Mueller (*American Antiquity*, **21,** No. 1 (1955), 53).] Another method is to lay out two coordinates at right angles, one with lettered intervals, the other with numbered intervals. Stakes or squares are then identified as A1, A2, B1, B2, and so on.

ture. When these preliminaries are finished, there are often problems of housing, supplies and equipment, and transportation. Finally, there is the problem of recruiting a labor force. Local labor may be unobtainable because the people are all engaged in critical farm activities. On the other hand, there may be opposition to bringing in outsiders. Wage rates must be negotiated and sometimes unions dealt with. Local languages must be learned or good interpreters found to direct workers. National or local pride and fears that the archaeologist is "stealing" some of the local cultural heritage must be assuaged; this may require diplomatic handling of the press. The late Wendell Bennett often maintained that anyone who could successfully organize and carry out an archaeological project in Peru was thoroughly prepared to undertake ethnographic research as well.

Once the preliminaries are completed, the archaeologist must select from a wide variety of techniques those most suited to the site. Often these must be adapted to special circumstances. Some of these techniques are derived from

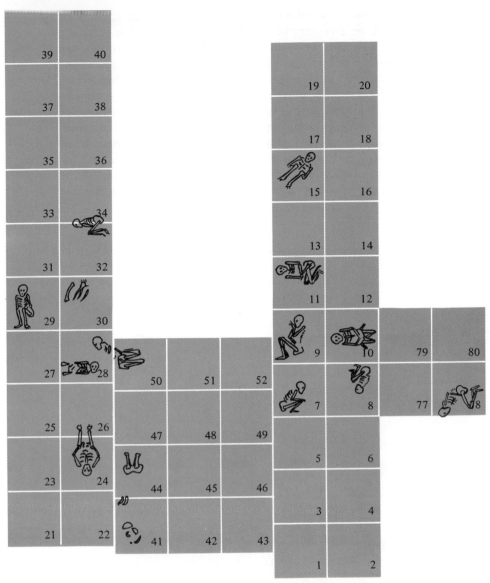

Figure 3–3 Locating features horizontally on the site. Illustration of method of locating burials in numbered squares. [Courtesy of D. J. McGeem and W. C. Mueller (*American Antiquity*, **21**, No. 1 (1955), 58).]

those of the geologist and paleontologist: stratification and association. Things found more deeply buried are older than things closer to the surface, if there has been no disturbance of the deposits. Things found associated together presumably existed at the same time and were used by the same people. Careful excavation and record keeping are basic to the understanding of the remains of the past.

A common method of the archaeologist is to lay out a site in squares of convenient size, usually 1 or 2 meters to a side. Either a surveyor must be employed or the archaeologist must learn to use surveying instruments. Stakes at each corner give reference points for the squares and the elevation of the points. Each square is excavated in layers of perhaps 3 to 12 inches (depending on the character of the site), and the earth is passed through a wire screen to recover all small artifacts not seen during excavation. However, every effort is made to locate artifacts in place, where they are photographed and their location and depth in the square are plotted. Hence the trowel and the brush often are more useful than the shovel. Each artifact or "lot" of artifacts is numbered, and the number is entered in a catalog with all pertinent information. If the excavation and recording are properly done, the archaeologist should be able

Figure 3–4   Stratigraphy: The Vertical Record. Composite drawing of a trench wall showing natural stratigraphy in Danger Cave, Utah. [Courtesy of Jesse D. Jennings (Memoir 14, Society for American Archaeology, 72).] If natural stratigraphy is absent, excavation is conducted in horizontal layers of arbitrary depth.

DEPTH FT.

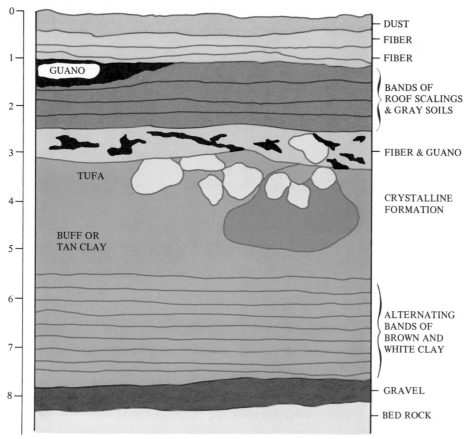

Excavating a room in a village farming site in the United States Southwest. The walls have been exposed outside the room and the accumulated materials inside the room are being excavated in layers. (Courtesy of the Field Museum of Natural History.)

substantially to reconstruct the site, with each artifact, architectural feature, and so on, in its proper place.

Sites often show natural stratigraphy; that is, layers or strata of differing color or texture. (See Figure 3–4.) In such cases, instead of excavating each square in arbitrarily fixed layers, each stratum is followed and removed. Whichever method is followed, a careful watch must be kept for architectural features such as walls, floors, postholes, and fireplaces. Each of these must be traced and recorded. Photography is an essential tool. Burials are especially important, for not only do they give us knowledge of the physical characteristics of the inhabitants of a site, but frequently articles are buried with the corpse. Such a collection is usually fairly certain evidence that all the kinds of articles found were in use simultaneously. Animal bones, evidences of textiles (often found through impressions in clay), and pieces of charcoal useful for dating must be watched for. Soil samples may, through chemical analysis or pollen content, give approximate ages or tell something about the environment.

Today many archaeologists are not satisfied with excavations which permit only the establishment of typologies and chronologies or time dating. Instead they wish to extend archaeological inference to its limits, and this frequently

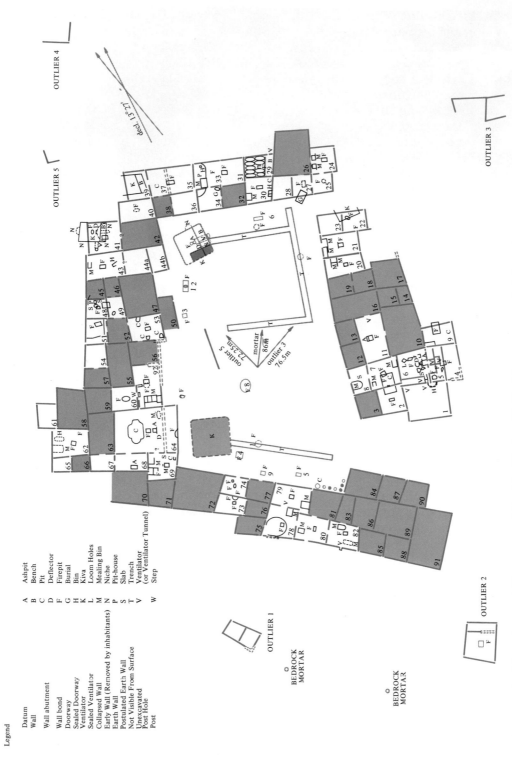

Legend

Datum		A	Ashpit
Wall		B	Bench
Wall abutment		C	Pit
Wall bond		D	Deflector
Doorway		F	Firepit
Sealed Doorway		G	Burial
Ventilator		H	Bin
Sealed Ventilator		K	Kiva
Collapsed Wall		L	Loom Holes
Early Wall (Removed by inhabitants)		M	Mealing Bin
Earth Wall		N	Niche
Postulated Earth Wall		P	Pit-house
Not Visible From Surface		S	Slab
Unexcavated		T	Trench
Post Hole		V	Ventilator (or Ventilator Tunnel)
Post		W	Step

Figure 3–5   Map of a partially excavated Pueblo (Broken K. Pueblo, east central Arizona) showing surface features and excavated portions. (Courtesy of James Hill.)

means total excavation of the site. Properly done, this may reveal whether the occupation was permanent or seasonal, permit estimates about population sizes and their fluctuation in time, and establish differences in productive activity between different parts of the site, suggesting specialization or permitting inferences about some aspects of the social organization such as the size and probable composition of hearth or household groups.

An example of such excavation is provided by Hallam L. Movius, Jr., in his excavation in the Abri Pataud, a site within the village of Les Eyzies in the Dordogne, France, a region famous for its Paleolithic sites. Here Movius undertook careful stratigraphic excavation of large contiguous areas. He established the existence of fourteen different occupation levels. In six of these levels he found a number of fire hearths with associated features such as river stones and in some cases upright stone slabs. By careful analysis of the size and distribution of the hearths and the associated features, he has established at least a strong probability that the users of these hearths were organized in four different kinds of residential units related to particular levels.[4] As more data of this kind are accumulated and ecological relationships investigated, it may be possible to extend our knowledge of prehistoric social organization.

Once the excavation is complete, the task of analysis begins. In the laboratory the artifacts are classified according to type, and their depths, locations, and associations are plotted. These data and the records of architecture and other features are collated and interpreted. (See Figures 3–6 and 3–7.) In all this it is the information rather than the artifact that is of primary importance, and without it the artifact is useless. Enthusiastic but poorly informed amateurs and collectors have destroyed more evidence about the human past than archaeologists have been able to recover.

Once the data from a given site have been analyzed, the archaeologist must attempt to relate the site to others and to its specific environment. Sites that show the same general assemblage of artifacts are assumed to represent the same culture, or, depending on the nature of the differences, a variant caused by differences in time or environment. Special kinds of artifacts, such as those representing a distinctive pottery type, may occur in several cultures of about the same age and so give relative dating from one place to another. Stratification in one or more sites may show one culture to be superposed over another, giving relative dating, or show changes through time within a single culture. More precise dating may be possible through the use of carbon 14, a radioactive form of carbon accumulated by living organisms, whose age can then be determined by the decline in radioactivity since the death of the organism. In some places, such as the United States Southwest, timbers may be dated by counting the annual growth rings and comparing the intervals to those on a master chart. In Scandinavia materials have been dated through their position in glacial clays. These clays are deposited in annual layers, and by counting back from the present, the age of the materials may be determined. None of these methods as yet permits us to go back more than a few thousand years

---

[4] Hallam L. Movius, Jr., "The Hearths of the Upper Perigordian and Aurignacian Horizons at the Abri Pataud, Les Eyzies (Dordogne), and Their Possible Significance," *American Anthropologist*, **68**:296–325, No. 2, Part 2 (1966).

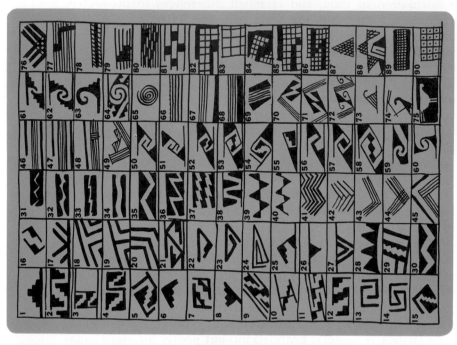

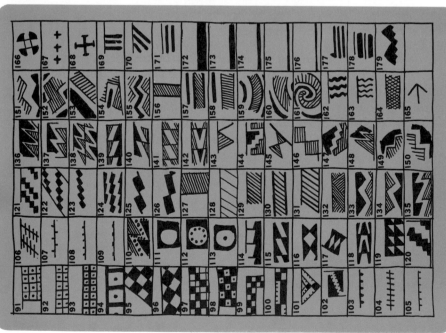

Figure 3–6   Catalogue of design elements on ceramics from Broken K. Pueblo, east central Arizona. Data on occurrence of each design element are fed into a computer. (Courtesy of James Hill.)

BK SITE DESIGN ELEM STUDY FREQS VAR MIN 10 OBS MIN 5

CORRELATION COEFFICIENTS

		1 6B	2 19B	3 20B	4 29B	5 31B	6 39B	7 45B	8 46B	9 50-51B	10 65B	11 67B	12 82B	13 84B	14 89B	15 90-94B
1	6B	1.000														
2	19B	-0.156	1.000													
3	20B	-0.092	0.103	1.000												
4	29B	-0.048	-0.063	0.291	1.000											
5	31B	-0.050	-0.093	0.312	0.225	1.000										
6	39B	-0.094	-0.177	-0.159	-0.023	0.220	1.000									
7	45B	0.581	-0.112	-0.237	-0.102	0.002	-0.145	1.000								
8	46B	0.679	-0.023	-0.050	-0.101	0.030	-0.131	0.855	1.000							
9	50-51B	0.766	-0.088	-0.049	-0.113	-0.071	-0.118	0.508	0.666	1.000						
10	65B	0.682	0.070	-0.119	0.022	-0.092	-0.116	0.575	0.679	0.613	1.000					
11	67B	0.036	-0.107	0.272	0.300	0.695	-0.123	-0.038	-0.042	-0.145	-0.092	1.000				
12	82B	0.600	0.216	0.093	0.147	0.354	0.140	0.504	0.603	0.580	0.689	0.207	1.000			
13	84B	-0.139	0.513	-0.038	0.414	-0.095	-0.011	-0.095	0.102	0.092	0.169	-0.098	-0.203	1.000		
14	89B	-0.016	-0.062	0.359	0.291	-0.106	-0.183	-0.008	0.033	-0.024	-0.036	-0.113	0.286	-0.095	1.000	
15	90-94B	-0.123	-0.034	0.076	0.210	0.181	0.000	0.054	0.070	0.126	0.027	-0.016	0.024	0.116	0.111	1.000
16	95-99B	-0.146	-0.100	0.191	0.101	0.394	0.100	0.142	0.004	-0.173	-0.157	0.288	0.049	0.006	-0.107	0.113
17	110B	-0.132	-0.140	0.250	-0.235	-0.045	-0.015	-0.004	-0.010	-0.089	-0.015	-0.031	-0.011	0.203	-0.028	-0.020
18	115B	-0.039	-0.091	0.253	-0.028	0.045	-0.151	0.025	0.178	-0.070	-0.064	-0.241	-0.135	-0.177	0.141	-0.105
19	127B	-0.002	0.055	0.406	0.227	0.297	-0.048	0.037	0.154	-0.019	0.002	0.172	0.067	0.227	0.458	0.277
20	127K	-0.018	-0.105	0.223	0.304	-0.018	-0.161	0.216	0.279	0.062	-0.036	-0.166	0.008	0.337	0.275	0.265
21	130B	-0.899	-0.096	-0.133	-0.119	-0.056	-0.092	-0.715	0.794	0.796	0.768	-0.013	0.642	-0.086	-0.105	-0.127
22	131B	-0.089	0.228	-0.083	0.095	-0.082	-0.039	0.176	-0.008	-0.143	0.091	0.081	0.143	0.174	-0.221	-0.139
23	133B	0.654	0.098	0.111	0.059	-0.142	0.075	0.400	0.611	0.656	0.681	-0.139	0.608	0.089	0.040	-0.053
24	133R	-0.027	-0.062	0.002	0.182	-0.097	0.055	0.053	0.116	-0.132	0.154	0.144	-0.017	0.279	0.141	0.048
25	134B	-0.065	-0.139	0.080	0.177	-0.039	0.209	0.254	0.179	-0.041	0.091	0.048	0.091	0.298	0.019	0.069
26	134R	-0.145	-0.148	-0.054	-0.021	0.152	-0.051	0.396	0.288	-0.144	0.013	-0.007	0.058	0.193	-0.113	-0.032
27	135B	-0.111	-0.266	0.061	0.287	0.268	0.073	0.372	0.237	-0.148	0.011	0.113	0.122	0.172	-0.258	-0.000
28	146B	-0.108	0.023	-0.168	0.002	0.053	-0.043	0.590	0.383	-0.103	0.170	-0.038	0.147	0.336	-0.015	0.189
29	148B	0.018	-0.121	-0.200	0.171	-0.022	-0.093	0.166	0.081	-0.081	0.150	0.256	0.022	-0.007	-0.125	0.118
30	153B	0.110	-0.214	-0.108	-0.092	0.225	0.017	0.027	-0.110	-0.077	-0.123	-0.123	-0.056	-0.223	-0.183	-0.169
31	155B	-0.049	-0.040	-0.137	0.016	0.081	-0.049	-0.629	0.446	-0.086	0.136	-0.029	0.170	0.367	-0.085	0.125
32	156B	-0.071	-0.110	-0.094	0.403	-0.109	-0.239	-0.131	-0.137	0.291	-0.112	-0.106	0.121	0.376	-0.161	0.159
33	158B	0.767	-0.043	-0.082	-0.020	-0.108	-0.137	0.601	0.779	0.725	0.626	-0.004	0.497	-0.006	-0.066	-0.066
34	158R	-0.102	-0.084	0.142	0.018	0.085	-0.152	0.442	0.347	-0.133	0.129	0.081	0.068	0.288	-0.066	0.108
35	159B	-0.108	0.202	0.176	0.408	0.119	-0.128	0.072	0.049	0.044	0.076	0.127	0.096	0.451	0.011	0.265
36	160B	0.106	0.070	0.159	0.117	-0.126	-0.020	-0.114	-0.043	-0.038	-0.069	-0.037	-0.094	0.121	0.240	0.080
37	160R	-0.188	-0.163	0.191	0.013	-0.046	-0.256	0.021	0.057	-0.145	-0.008	-0.151	-0.158	-0.086	0.210	0.141
38	164B	-0.019	-0.182	0.310	0.397	0.181	-0.081	0.073	0.114	-0.025	0.050	0.066	0.062	0.072	0.380	0.165
39	169B	0.559	-0.042	0.136	0.099	0.579	0.027	0.372	0.481	0.409	0.393	0.554	0.606	-0.163	-0.171	-0.000
40	174B	-0.037	-0.187	0.153	0.312	0.319	0.050	0.216	0.134	-0.085	-0.006	0.310	0.084	0.080	-0.204	0.132
41	175B	0.447	0.038	0.256	0.421	0.316	-0.100	0.590	0.652	0.359	0.525	0.296	0.604	0.269	0.208	-0.000
42	176B	0.027	-0.042	0.413	0.591	0.386	-0.022	-0.112	-0.028	-0.025	0.160	0.320	0.161	0.131	0.437	0.231
43	177B	0.015	-0.110	0.637	0.304	0.340	-0.075	-0.159	0.017	-0.014	0.027	0.269	0.096	-0.078	0.468	0.265
44	14/R	0.718	0.151	-0.116	-0.114	-0.087	-0.160	0.685	0.699	0.632	0.791	-0.133	0.687	0.099	-0.069	-0.056

----SAMPLE SIZE = 38----   ----NULL ERROR = 0.164----

Figure 3–7 Beginning of a computer readout showing correlations between each design element in Figure 3–6 with every other element. On the basis of this and other computer operations it is possible to infer matrilocal residence and family preferences in designs. (Courtesy of James Hill.)

Exposed floor of a room in a village farming site in the United States Southwest. Arrow shows north; the divisions on arrow and rod give dimensions. Note mealing bins and enclosed central fireplace. The continuous walls indicate entry was probably from the roof, as in some modern Pueblos. (Courtesy of the Field Museum of Natural History.)

(about 50,000 to 60,000 for carbon 14 and about 2,000 for tree rings). For very long reaches of early human history we still have only relative dating; that is, determining through stratigraphy which of two assemblages of artifacts is the older. Potassium-argon dating and neutron-decay or fission-track dating of uranium, thorium, and other radioactive substances are proving useful for longer-term dating. Unfortunately the margin of error is so great that the method is of little use for periods more recent than 0.5 million years. Obsidian hydration analysis and an increasing number of chemical tests are useful within limited areas to determine the relative age of specimens. Thermoluminescence may aid in dating pottery.[5]

[5] A good summary of dating methods is Joseph W. Michels' "Dating Methods," in *Annual Review of Anthropology*, ed. Bernard J. Siegel, Alan R. Beals, and Stephen A. Tyler, **1**:113–126 (1972).

The archaeologist also must attempt to determine the function of artifacts and explain their variation both within and between sites. If the occurrence of artifacts is nonrandom, with higher concentrations in one part of a site, explanations must be sought. Thus, if artifacts generally associated with male activities show little variation in different parts of the site and artifacts associated with female activities show consistent variation from one living cluster or house to another, matrilocal residence with men going to live in the household of their wives is strongly suggested. Matrilocal residence brings together groups of related females and allows the transmission of idiosyncratic variations in family lines.

Even when the task of the archaeologist is completed, the information provided has limitations. When the archaeologist's work is well done the relationships between humans and their environment can be defined. The key to this is reconstruction of the economy, what Graham Clark calls the "hinge" between the environment and the way people satisfy the needs inherent in their culture.[6] Thus according to Clark much of what prehistory is about is, in modern idiom, the study of rising standards of living. Even so, only under rare favorable circumstances can we discover much about the perishable materials they used or made. We can often tell what weapons and tools were used, but only rarely what containers or clothing. Animal bones reveal what animals were eaten, but it is hard to determine what berries or seeds were collected. Pollens preserved in a site may show what types of vegetation existed but not what plants were used. From burials, cult objects, or the presence of shrines or temples we may infer something of the system of religious specialists. From the character of shelters and their numbers we may establish the size and pattern of settlements and infer the general character of the social organization, but not such specific features as the presence or absence of clans. And many of these inferences can be made only because of the ethnologist's knowledge of the cultures of peoples still existing who lead a similar life to those of the past. The archaeologist may not hope to reconstruct all aspects of a culture, but he or she can, however, achieve a series of statements about the probable culture and social organization of the people who produced the evidence being studied.

Not all archaeology has been done with such goals. Many archaeological sites have been excavated solely to recover specimens suitable for museum display or for private collections. Others have emphasized interest in the history of art or of architecture. The rich harvest of information available from refined excavation techniques often is ignored. Archaeology, more than most disciplines, usually destroys its basic data in the process of collecting it. The archaeologist thus has a special obligation to be thorough in methods of data collection. This cannot be done fully unless the archaeologist is not only familiar with the technical problems of data collection, but very familiar with various kinds of theoretical problems to which archaeology may contribute.

Despite these limitations the work of the archaeologist is essential to our

---

[6] Graham Clark, "Review of Karl W. Butzer's *Environment and Archaeology: An Introduction to Pleistocene Geography*," *American Anthropologist*, **67**:1332 (1965). (Chicago: Aldine, 1964).

understanding of culture. We gain a humbling perspective of the enormous time it took humans to accumulate the essential basic controls over nature that have made our own recent extraordinary advances possible. The archaeologist also reveals the innate adaptability and tenacity that let humanity occupy such a wide range of environments and survive under such difficult conditions. At the same time the archaeologist shows our common humanity by demonstrating, on the one hand, how in all times and places people have faced similar problems and, on the other, the ingenuity with which they have produced varied solutions. More important, the archaeologist has helped us identify not the causes, perhaps, but the preconditions for a number of the great expansions of human knowledge and culture. With present broader and more intensive methods, the archaeologist contributes to understanding of cultural variability and cultural change and tests hypotheses leading toward the development of more soundly based theories of culture.

3. The Collection of Ethnographic Data

Ethnography, the study of the cultures of living peoples, provides most of the raw data of the cultural anthropologist. In the past, anthropological field studies centered upon tribal or peasant peoples in nonliterate societies outside the influence of Western culture or only marginally influenced by it. Most of the special research methods, interests, and points of view of anthropology developed in the study of such societies, but they are now being widely applied to the study of subcultures in industrialized societies. The experience of studying peoples of different cultures is widely viewed as an essential part of the training of most professional cultural anthropologists. Sometimes disparaged as the "mystique" of anthropology, the study of peoples of different cultures broadens one's ability to understand the research of others, sharpens insight into one's own culture, and serves as a source of self-knowledge.

The anthropological fieldworker must undergo specific preparation and make an intelligent selection of the location of a field site. This requires an adequate general background in anthropology, including both the kinds of data and the kinds of problems with which it deals. At one time the fact that they were relatively unknown was enough to justify the study of a people. Today the main types and varieties of cultures have been established and the selection of a location for field study should involve the preliminary identification of problems and a plan of study. This requires a thorough knowledge of the literature already published about the area, including that in other languages. The researcher must find out what other researchers have worked or are working in the area and what they have studied. Again this includes not only scholars in the United States but those of other countries. It is important to learn about the scholars in the country to be visited, make contact with them, and seek their advice. A considerable number of students are drawn into anthropology by essentially romantic notions that it would be fun to travel and live among exotic peoples. Today the student must be prepared to justify the choice and ask the question whether the problems to be investigated require or justify undertaking a long and expensive sojourn abroad. The student must also face the fact that in some countries or areas foreigners may not be welcome, or restrictions may exist which interfere with the integrity of research. In such cases the researcher may well need to ask whether the research can be carried out just as well in some other place.

Part of the preparation of the field researcher, once a general or specific location has been selected, is to learn the requirements for entry into the area. In some countries investigators must register with a specific agency or have their research sponsored by some local institution. Sometimes the ethnographer may be dependent on a missionary group or government administrative agency for housing and the logistics of supplies and equipment, and there may already be in the locality all the anthropologists that can be accommodated. Can the researcher go alone or must there be servants or assistants? Health problems should be evaluated and preparations made. Is malaria still common? Are typhus, typhoid, yellow fever, cholera, or less familiar diseases such as bilharzia, onchocercosis, yaws, or others a problem? What protective measures should be used? His the researcher adequate medicines to deal with the dysenteries that will be contracted? Can local sources be depended on for food or must food be carried or sent in? Can the ethnographer cook? Will it be possible to live with a local family or rent a house, or must the first task be to build a house? A sick, hungry, or extremely uncomfortable anthropologist cannot perform at high efficiency. Here, the advice of persons living in or familiar with the area usually is essential. For some areas field guides exist and should be consulted.

Once field plans are made, most field researchers must seek financing for the proposed research. This involves identifying organizations granting funds or fellowships for the type of research planned and preparing applications in a form acceptable to the fund-granting organizations. Care must be taken not to seek or accept funds from organizations that may be in bad repute in the country of study; special care must be taken not to accept any obligations which involve collection of secret information for nonscientific purposes. At least one anthropologist has been murdered because he was suspected of spying. The field researcher must have no source of funding or purposes that cannot be revealed.

On arrival in the country, the researcher may have to deal with divergent social or political groups. As a researcher in one African country commented, officials in the capital are unwilling to have people study the villagers for fear it will reveal how little grass-roots support there is for the government; local officials are fearful that their superiors may learn of the amount of graft or mistreatment they inflict on local people; numbers of the local community are fearful that information may lead to taxation or repression by government. Missionaries may resent inquiries into aboriginal religion, as this may undercut their efforts. Where there are class or caste differences local officials, traders, landlords, and others will identify the researcher with their group. Researchers who live with or ally themselves with the lower class may be seen as deviants or threats to the existing class structure.

When the researcher arrives in the field, "culture shock" may be encountered. Entry into a new culture always is accompanied by psychological stress; this is particularly acute when one is isolated in a new culture. The student is confronted with an environment whose dangers are imperfectly known. Is this strange insect dangerous; will that strange plant cause a painful rash? Adjustment must be made to unfamiliar foods and sometimes to completely different eating patterns. Where does one bathe or relieve oneself if there are no bathrooms, toilets, or privies? And even more difficult, how does one relate to the people among whom one finds oneself? Initially the ethnographer's language is inadequate for much communication; linguistic or behavioral cues cannot be interpreted, and those of the ethnographer are not understood. Should attention be paid to small children or will this create fear of the evil eye? How does the ethnographer's sex affect communication and interaction?

Most difficult of all perhaps is adjusting to the role of stranger, of being part of an ethnic minority, often a minority of one, in situations where it is always the ethnographer who must adjust, not the others. Under these and similar circumstances the individual often becomes emotionally disturbed, apprehensive or fearful, afflicted with compulsive handwashing, unable to eat available food, inclined to excessive drinking, and so on. In time most individuals adjust, but loneliness often continues and grows. Awareness of the problem helps some in the recovery. Some individuals can never adequately adjust and are not suited for field research. Rather than follow the early custom of turning people loose on their own for their first field trip, graduate schools in the United States increasingly emphasize a brief period of supervised field training, not only to help students to adjust to fieldwork problems, but to identify those who are temperamentally unsuited for the field situation.

The field investigator must develop understanding of the people studied. Without empathy, the ability to project oneself into the feelings of others, success is unlikely. The fieldworker also must develop a high tolerance for ambiguity, accepting the fact that many things do not make sense at first and refusing to make early judgments or conclusions. The ethnographer must be tolerant of behaviors, attitudes, and values found repugnant; the job is not to change or condemn, but to understand. Most cultural behavior has a reason or is consonant with established value structures. The investigator at the same time is a product of a culture. Usually total abandonment of one's own values is not expected and may even be repugnant to the people studied. Too great an involvement may warp judgment or impede research. In a classical example in the last century, F. H. Cushing finally came to be one of the six high priests of Zuñi in New Mexico; in this role he was pledged to secrecy and was no longer able to function as an anthropologist.

Aside from problems of personal adjustment, how does the researcher proceed? Precise rules are difficult to give, for the field procedures must be modified in terms of the personality of the researcher, the nature of the culture, the behavioral characteristics of the group studied, and the particular research problems. Three initial approaches are common: participant observation, unstructured interviews, and the use of the key informant. Participant observation simply is to observe and record as much behavior that seems relevant as is possible, and to take part or participate in as many activities as opportunity affords. In some open societies one may be invited immediately on arrival to be present at some event such as a christening or naming ceremony, a wedding, or a ritual feast. Acceptance of such invitations usually is imperative, but they are often very disturbing. One is plunged immediately into the problems of what to eat or drink, how to behave, how to interpret the behavior of others toward oneself. Usually the researcher cannot take notes but must try to remember and record all observations as soon as possible, with the knowledge that probably many significant things have not been observed. In a naming ceremony, for example, who does what, with whom, and why usually must be reserved for later questioning.

The unstructured interview involves preparing a series of possibly significant questions to ask whenever opportunity offers. The purpose is not primarily to secure answers to the questions but to stimulate the subject to talk, in the hope of learning what the subject thinks is important. The key informant is a person who has a good knowledge of the culture and is interested in talking about it. Frequently one can find an individual with a basically philosophical bent of mind who readily understands the purpose of the research. The key informant can give a systematic preliminary outline of the culture and identify the most fruitful problems for more intensive research. Only if one is very lucky can a key informant be located immediately; even then, the investigator must proceed with caution, for the key informant may well be a deviant personality or be involved deeply in factional disputes. In the latter case too close identification with one person may antagonize important individuals or groups. For this reason the investigator should try to "hang loose," talking briefly with as many people as possible in the early stages. At a later stage a variant of the key informant, a person with special knowledge of an occupation or technique or of ritual, politics, or law may be useful.

In the early stages the researcher must seek to develop an acceptable role in the group. Initially the people being studied will place the researcher in the role of stranger, and some of their first reactions will depend upon the definition of "strangers" and how they normally react to them; these may vary from hostility to hospitality and generosity. In both cases curiosity will usually be intense. Charles Wagley reports that among one Amazonian tribe the attitudes quickly changed to pity; he was seen as a person ignorant of most of the basic knowledge necessary for survival, who must be taught everything. Participant observation, thus, was the dominant technique. Whatever the attitudes and initial role definition, the researcher must try to develop or modify the role definition to one which will allow the greatest acceptance and freedom of action, to become a friend rather than a stranger. Above all, the researcher must explain openly her or his purposes in terms that the people can understand. Often this explanation can develop and expand through time; initially expressed interest in language or customs may be enough.

Other techniques used are the genealogical method and the census (see Figure 3–8); often these can be combined. At a fairly early point it usually is possible to make an informal census of households, building up lists of people who live together, their main occupations, and data about the house and its

HOUSEHOLD CENSUS FORM

House Number

_____

Name of Informant

_____

Name of Head

_____

Date

_____

Village Name

_____

Interviewer's Name

| Land Tax | Number living in House | Cows | Water Buffaloes | Bullocks |

Number of children in School   Languages spoken in house

1. Persons living in house including those gone less than six months.

Name and Father's Name	Sex	Relation to Head	Age	Relation to Husband	Birthplace
Head:					
Others:					

Figure 3–8 Household census form. English translation of a census form used in South Indian villages. Occupation was omitted because it was always given as "farmer." The question about relation to husband was designed to record the existing high proportion of marriages to close relatives. Questions about land tax paid and livestock owned were designed to provide an indication of comparative wealth.

equipment. At the same time the relationships of household members can be recorded; this can be extended to record relationships with individuals in other households, to create a series of genealogies. When the census approach is impossible, friendly informants can be used to construct extensive genealogies. This can be done while the ostensible task is learning language. Kinship terms may be elicited and their true meaning determined through discovering the way they are applied to biologically determined relatives and to nonrelatives or to classes of people in the society. Along with this, information can be elicited concerning the residence, occupation, and social roles of each individual, thus constructing a census indirectly. The genealogical approach is especially useful in small, simple societies where kinship is the dominant organizing principle. It must, however, not be allowed to obscure the existence of alternative organizing principles, such as territoriality, associations and clubs, religious organizations, and various achieved-status positions. One must also avoid the trap into which many early workers fell of attempting direct translations of kin terms. The term *father* in English normally refers to the progenitor of the speaker; in many kinship systems the kinship term applied to the progenitor includes him in a class of individuals; in some cultures the class may include entirely unrelated individuals. In any case, genealogical methods may permit identification of differing roles and the distribution of economic, political, and religious functions in the group. In some circumstances, then, the informal census may be the best way to collect information about kinship and its functions; in others the genealogical approach may provide the first data for a census.

A formal and detailed census, however desirable, may be impossible. Undertaken too early, it may arouse more apprehensions than it is worth. The important questions to be included in a census often are not apparent in the early stages of field work, neither are the sensitive areas for which indirect methods must be used. Often peasants hide information about landholdings or crop production, either because they fear envy or tax collectors or because they actually do not know the answer in quantitative terms. In any case, answers obtained through a census must often be checked by asking people about their neighbors. Where secrecy is enjoined either by fear or by cultural prohibitions, a variety of indirect methods is necessary. Beliefs in witchcraft are frequently difficult to discover; practitioners normally will not admit to their activities, whereas others may fear to arouse the enmity of witches. Yet witchcraft may be very important in the functioning of a culture and reveal much about the interpersonal tensions in a society. In most cases the use of indirect methods raises ethical questions which must be carefully considered before the methods are used or the results published.

An important aspect of fieldwork is often the systematic accumulation of quantitative data. This involves counting the numbers engaged in activities, the production of food or craft items, days spent in ritual activities, and similar problems. This should be started immediately, with the reservation that often one does not know at first what should be counted. Increasingly, anthropologists are also using structured interviews, interview schedules, or questionnaires. Usually these can best be used in the later phases of fieldwork. Considerable time and experience are necessary to frame questions so that they will have the same meaning for the interviewer and the respondent or so that they cover the most important problems. Generally, the main purpose of a schedule or formal interview is to correct impressions and biases formed by the investigator from intensive interviews of a relatively few people and to permit quantification of answers to key questions. It is not enough to say a group is endogamous (within the group). Is this always true? Is it true in 90 percent of marriages, 75 percent, or 51 percent?

The use of schedules and questionnaires requires careful attention to sampling. In small groups it may be possible to interview every person or every household head. In most cases this is not true. The sampling method may vary, but it should be explicit. The investigator may decide that some figure, such as 10 percent, is adequate, but to interview the first 10 percent of individuals encountered may produce a very biased sample. The persons interviewed may be from the same part of the village, represent a single class group, or be merely those friendly to the interviewer. Sampling accidents are possible with the most careful methods; a sample of households in the village of Nayon, Ecuador, was drawn by applying a table of random numbers. The sample included three times the percentage of households headed by women that actually existed when measured by a complete household census.

Although some formal sampling method is essential to collecting any data that are to be analyzed statistically, the problem exists in concealed form for most ethnographic data collection. The basic problem, regardless of the methods of data collection, is whether the information collected is representative of the total culture. Even with participant observation or nonstructured interviews, the field researcher makes some decisions about representativeness. Often these decisions are intuitive, based upon the researcher's knowledge of the group. Sometimes the law of diminishing returns operates; additional observations and interviews produce no new data and the researcher concludes that the data are complete. It is best, however, that decisions be conscious and explicit.

It is, of course, impossible to record all the behavior of a group of people or even of an individual. The anthropologist therefore is selective in recording data. This selection is made in terms of the researcher's assumptions and theoretical biases or preferences. It is important that the anthropologist constantly test these biases and assumptions while collecting data. The unique quality of the anthropological method is that the anthropologist is both the primary recorder of raw data and its analyst. In the course of field research, the ethnographer should constantly make preliminary analyses, check these against data, and return to sources for further data when necessary.

An important technique in anthropological field studies is the widest possible use of the local language. Claims that researchers have mastered the local language may be true for some aspects of daily life, but understanding of the more subtle and conceptual parts of life requires years of experience. For these the use of interpreters or a common second language is necessary as checks. In any case technical vocabularies should be developed. Names of things, positions or roles, institutions, and concepts should be recorded systematically and used in interviews and conversations. The ability to understand conversations or to engage in simple discussions is usually an attainable goal and is productive of many insights and information.

An important part of the use of linguistic tools in research is to discover the ways in which the people being studied see and categorize their own experience. The anthropologist, as we have noted, brings certain theoretical biases and assumptions to research. On the basis of these the anthropologist selects, organizes, and categorizes data. The categories formed and the linkages seen between phenomena may not, however, be the same as those of the people studied. In recent years some scholars have elevated this concern to a formal method they call ethnoscience. Drawing heavily upon some linguistic methods, they suggest that the main direction of anthropological field studies should be to concentrate upon the ways the people studied organize and categorize their culture. Actually the dangers of imposing external categories upon ethnographic data have long been recognized. The ethnoscientists have introduced refinements of method and have produced some very detailed analyses of some aspects of particular cultures. These studies spell out in unusual detail the underlying logic involved.

An important tool of the anthropologist often is the life history. One use is perhaps more humanistic than scientific; good life histories illuminate what it means to be a person living in the culture under study. Life histories also reveal much of the way the total culture is articulated as a system. Life histories also reveal values, problems, and concerns that the interviewer may otherwise completely miss simply because the researcher, trapped in his or her own biases and presuppositions, never asks the right questions. A good life history, however, takes a long time and is never the product of a single set of interviews. Non-Western peoples often have a different sense of time; the life story emerges in episodes, often apparently without order, and stimulated by a variety of questions.

Increasingly, anthropologists also make use of nonverbal psychological tests. Perhaps the most common are the Rorschach and Thematic Apperception tests. Rorschach tests involve a set of standardized ink blots; the subject is asked through standardized questions to report what is perceived in the blots. The Thematic Apperception Test consists of a set of pictures and the subject is asked to tell a story suggested by the picture. Both tests call for some training in their administration and a great deal of preparation for their full interpretation. The TAT, however, can be useful at fairly unsophisticated levels and may be adapted to the local culture. In his study of the Ulithi atoll in the Pacific, William Lessa introduced one picture of a man leering from behind a coconut palm at an attractive, scantily clad young woman with a tray of fruit. In the United States this produced stories involving some sexual advance or attack; in Ulithi almost invariably the story involved no sexual advances, but the theft and eating of the fruit. This difference underlines the fact that in Ulithi there are few inhibitions or frustrations about sex, but food often is scarce and people are often hungry.

Anthropologists frequently are asked how they know their informants are telling the truth. In fact, systematic liars are rare. In any case misinformation

BOMBAY VISITORS—RETURNEES

(We want to write about the kinds of experiences people have in Bombay. Where they live there, what their complaints are, etc.)

1. Tell us about Bombay.
   (Ask this first to get general answers, then use probes given below to obtain any details omitted.)

PROBES

1. How long did you live in Bombay?

2. Did you work the whole time? What did you do when you were unemployed?

3. How much were you paid? Were you asked to send money home?

4. What kind of work did you do? How was the work done?

5. What sort of people did you work with?

6. Do you remember any interesting happenings on the job?

7. Where did you live? Did you move much?

8. What people did you live with? Were they from here? What sort of cooking and sleeping arrangements did you have?

9. What were your usual expenses for housing, food, recreation, clothing, cinema, etc.?

10. What kinds of things happened to you in Bombay?

11. Did you learn anything useful that made you wiser or better able to earn a living?

12. Is there anything else we should know about Bombay?

13. Can you give us addresses of anyone in Bombay who might answer questions if we called on him?

Figure 3–9 Bombay visitors–returnees. English translation of an informal questionnaire used in South India. Questionnaires of this sort are used to obtain as much information as possible by asking as few questions as possible, the idea being that questions may bias the responses in the direction of the interviewer's interests. In this questionnaire, although a few possible biases are introduced at the beginning, additional questions are introduced only after the informant has had the opportunity to state his own impressions of Bombay in his own way.

can be quite as revealing as truth. Individuals may not understand the question, the question may touch on sensitivities, the individual may wish to enhance or conceal personal status or present one side of a controversial issue, or simply wish to give the answer believed to please the investigator. The solutions to this are several. The reliability of a particular informant may be tested by going over the same subject matter at a later time. Several different people may be asked the same questions; this is important to check not only the reliability of information but its representativeness. A final check is whether the information is congruent with other aspects of the culture. The sensitive observer rather quickly becomes aware of the systematic aspect of the culture being studied. Inconsistencies may genuinely exist; both they and contradictions in data must be investigated and often open up aspects of the culture that have been overlooked because the researcher did not know the right questions to ask. Differences between ideal and actual behavior may emerge. Frequently the problem lies in the fact that even in simple cultures, no individual knows all of the culture or views it in the same way as others. This is especially common between the sexes.

4. The Analysis of Ethnographic Data

Once the researcher returns from the field, there is an obligation to analyze and interpret materials and make the results available to others. Research is essentially a cooperative enterprise. Any particular research undertaken draws upon the existing body of knowledge and the methods and techniques developed by others. In turn it should contribute to the growth and refinement of knowledge. The frequent charge that teachers in universities must "publish or perish" to retain their positions springs from a misunderstanding of the nature of research and of universities. A university, as distinguished from an undergraduate college, is designed not only to teach but to enlarge knowledge, and class hours required of faculty are adjusted with this in view. The faculty member who performs research, usually supported at considerable cost by the university or outside agencies, fails to meet obligations to the institution or the discipline if results are not made available to others, normally by publication.

It is not appropriate in an introductory volume to examine the methods of analysis in detail. A few of the kinds of analysis should nevertheless be mentioned. In the preceding section we pointed out that the researcher in anthropology is somewhat unique in that he or she typically carries out initial analysis while still collecting the data. On returning from the field, the researcher must complete the analysis and interpret the data. This may involve several levels.

At the lowest level field data are organized to give the reader the most accurate possible understanding of the specific nature of the culture studied. The data should be presented so that they will be useful for others to use for more complex analysis. At a second level the data should be given theoretical significance by explaining how the data support, modifiy, or contradict various general theories and points of view in anthropology or other social sciences. At yet another level structural relations between various aspects of the culture studied are considered.

In another kind of analysis, common to all cultural anthropologists, there is an attempt to explain the variety of phenomena discovered. Because cultures in part represent traditions, historical events may be examined which may account for some of the characteristics of the culture. In so doing the ethnographer may invoke diffusion, the process of borrowing elements from some other culture. At its best the historical approach may tell us much about what happened. By itself, however, it does little to explain why things happened or why a culture persists in its present form.

The ecological approach, which may of course be combined with the historical approach, seeks to explain a culture in terms of responses or adaptations to its environmental situation. It is sometimes possible, especially when comparative studies are made, to show that certain types of social organization or institutions are impossible under specific ecological conditions. Thus in a limited environment cultures with a restricted hunting and gathering technology do not require, and frequently could not support, some types of social institutions or arrangements, such as occupational or class structures, permanent settlements, or elaborate economic or political machinery.

A most important aspect of anthropology is its comparative approach. Like other approaches, this may be misused. Many early comparative studies were undertaken to bolster a particular ideological or theoretical position. The authors surveyed the ethnographic literature and culled from it examples which supported the theoretical points of view, ignoring data which did not fit. Progress of comparative studies was also hampered by the enormous diversity of cultures. Only with the analysis of function and structure did it become apparent that uniformities underlay some of this diversity. Quite different behavior patterns or institutions on analysis prove to have the same or quite similar functions. On the other hand, identifiable functions, it also became recognized, could be carried out in a variety of ways. The problem then became one of discovering the limits to the ways a given function or end could be accomplished, and the variety of ends a given set of behaviors or institutions could serve. Comparative analysis of structure further suggested that there were some invariant or frequent relations between different kinds of behaviors and institutions.

One type of comparative study began fairly early in anthropology with E. B. Tylor,[7] who attempted to show by statistical means that certain types of marriage and descent rules tend to be associated with one another. This he did by comparing a number of cultures for the presence or absence of various kinds of marriage and descent rules and showing statistically that there was a high correlation between some and a negative correlation between others. This at-

[7] E. B. Tylor, "On a Method of Investigating the Development of Institutions: Applies to the Laws of Marriage and Descent," *Journal of the Royal Anthropological Institute of Great Britain and Ireland,* **18**:245–272 (1889).

tempt was severely criticized because in many cases it appeared that some of the tribes he selected were so close together and so similar in culture that they should be regarded as a single case.

For many years this approach was neglected, to be revived mainly by George P. Murdock, whose efforts were partly stimulated by the Human Relations Area Files, an effort systematically to collect and organize data from a large, worldwide sample of cultures. The Files help the researcher to bring together for statistical treatment a large number of examples of possibly interrelated phenomena. These efforts potentially present the same sampling problems involved in Tylor's earlier attempt. Are the examples independent of one another or do they represent a single historically related case? Various attempts to meet this objection have been undertaken and still continue.

Statistically demonstrated correlations or associations of cultural phenomena do not, of course, explain the reasons for the associations. These require analysis beyond the statistical manipulation. Murdock has done some interesting work on this problem. He has, for example, shown that certain types of kinship terminologies may develop out of other types but that the reverse could not occur. This is a step in showing necessary sequences in the development of culture, a goal sought by Julian Steward using other approaches.

Another and perhaps most fruitful approach is the method of controlled comparison. This method, whose best formal description has been given by Fred Eggan,[8] involves examining a number of cultures that have selected features in common but that otherwise may be divergent. Each culture is then analyzed to discover what variables exist in each that may account for the similarities.

Related to this approach is what Julian Steward has called cultural ecology, a modern form of evolutionary explanation. Steward and others have sought to identify irreversible sequences in cultural development. In his principal effort Steward analyzed large-scale irrigation systems in various parts of the world to show that they involved not only population increases associated with increased productivity but also the development of a central authority in order to maintain and manage the water supply.

This and a number of the preceding analytical approaches involve the identification of associations between a group of cultural phenomena and the formulation of hypotheses to explain the associations. The associations may be either simultaneous or, where historical data are available, sequential. This is accompanied by efforts to locate the factors or variables involved. The goal is to establish empirical generalizations about some body of cultural phenomena and ultimately to formulate theories that will explain them. Anthropological theory in the past suffered from its early association with nineteenth-century physical sciences, which emphasized immutable and universal laws. In the present century the physical sciences deal less with immutable laws and more with statements of probability. The great variability and complexity of cultural phenomena made the formulation of "laws" virtually impossible so

[8] Fred Eggan, "Social Anthropology and the Method of Controlled Comparison," *American Anthropologist,* **56**:743 (1954).

long as any exception was held to destroy the "law." Now that it is recognized that most general statements are probable and that the exceptions are to be explained by the existence of unique variables or factors, a new growth of theory is possible.

5. Summary

The data of the cultural anthropologist are human behavior and the products of this behavior. These data are collected by the detailed study of the behavior of members of particular cultures. The anthropologist's primary interest is culturally determined behaviors; to identify these behaviors and understand their significance requires the study of their variations in space and time.

Ethnohistory provides some data about past cultures, but for most of human history archaeology is the main source of information. The archaeologist cannot observe behavior directly, but only those of its products which have been preserved. These products are not only artifacts but evidence of shelters, foodstuffs, refuse accumulations, and other signs of human presence. The location of these indications in space and their associations with each other and with the natural landscape are more important than the objects themselves.

The two main field methods, involving complex techniques, are the survey and excavation of sites with evidence of human presence. Early archaeology emphasized the establishment of typologies and their distribution in space and time. Another goal which has become increasingly important is, through inferences and analytical interpretations, to reconstruct the past culture as fully as possible. The archaeologist's task involves not only field surveys and excavations but laboratory analysis. Archaeology can be especially fruitful in providing evidence for cultural variation and change and in testing some kinds of anthropological theories and hypotheses. Today archaeology demands a closer relation between theory and hypothesis and the field excavations and sophisticated use of sampling methods and statistical analysis.

Ethnography is the study of the cultures of living peoples through direct and indirect observation of behavior. The selection of peoples and preparation for their study involves careful preparation and planning. Most early ethnography was exploratory and descriptive; today the ranges of cultural variation are fairly well known and much contemporary field research is related to specific problems. Ethnography calls for the use of a wide variety of techniques of observation and recording. Ecological and psychological approaches aid in cultural interpretation. The anthropologist, more than most social scientists, both collects and analyzes data, and part of this is done in the field. Much, however, must be done later.

Besides the collection and analysis of field data about specific cultures, the anthropologist also attempts to understand culture in general. Various kinds of comparative analysis aid in the search for general statements which will help not only to understand culture as a whole but to cast light on specific cultures.

As Albert Spaulding remarks, "there is abundant evidence that social systems are not closed systems. Instead they are articulated at almost every point with biological and environmentally oriented behavior. . . . Cultural ecology and cross-cultural investigations of associations between social and technological behavior are the necessary link between the poles of archaeology and social anthropology, between artifacts and behavior."[9]

Collateral Reading

American Anthropological Association. *Professional Ethics, Statements and Procedures of the American Anthropological Association.* Washington, D.C.: American Anthropological Association, 1973. Required reading for anyone intending to do anthropological research.

Beals, Ralph L. *Politics of Social Research.* Chicago: Aldine Publishing Company, 1969. The funding of research and the ethics of field investigation.

Beattie, John. *Understanding an African Kingdom: Bunyoro.* New York: Holt, Rinehart and Winston, Inc., 1965.

Binford, Sally R., and Lewis R. Binford (eds.). *New Perspectives in Archaeology.* Chicago: Aldine Publishing Company, 1968. Lucid statement of archaeology as a scientific discipline.

Brim, John A., and David H. Spain. *Research Design in Anthropology: Paradigms and Pragmatics in the Testing of Hypotheses.* New York: Holt, Rinehart and Winston, Inc., 1974. Discussion of hypothesis testing in relation to specific anthropological problems.

Brown, Robert. *Explanation in Social Science.* Chicago: Aldine Publishing Company, 1963. Discusses the nature of scientific explanation and its problems as applied to social science.

Casagrande, J. B. (ed.). *In the Company of Man.* New York: Harper & Row, Inc., 1960. Exceptionally well-written series of accounts of outstanding informants by anthropologists.

Chagnon, Napoleon A. *Studying the Yanomamö.* New York: Holt, Rinehart and Winston, Inc., 1974. Describes personal experiences and methods of analysis.

Chang, K. C. (ed.). *Settlement Archaeology.* Palo Alto, Calif.: The National Press, 1968. A useful contribution to understanding the "newer" archaeology.

Collier, John, Jr. *Visual Anthropology: Photography as a Research Method.* New York: Holt, Rinehart and Winston, Inc., 1967. Exceptionally useful.

Epstein T. S. (ed.). *The Craft of Social Anthropology.* London and New York: Tavistock Publications, 1967.

Freilich, Morris (ed.). *Marginal Natives: Anthropologists at Work.* New York: Harper & Row, Inc., 1969. Studies of anthropologists in the field.

Golde, Peggy (ed.). *Women in the Field: Anthropological Experiences.* Chicago: Aldine Publishing Company, 1969. Accounts of field experiences by women.

---

[9] Spaulding, op. cit. p. 39.

Heizer, Robert F., and John A. Graham. *Guide to Field Methods in Archeology*, New rev. ed. Original title *Guide to Archaeological Field Methods*, Palo Alto, Ca.: National Pr., 1967, 1969.

Jongmans, D. G., and P. C. W. Gutkind (eds.). *Anthropologists in the Field*. Assen, Holland: Van Gorcum and Company, 1967. Essays on actual field experiences and methods.

Langness, L. L. *The Life History in Anthropological Science*. New York: Holt, Rinehart and Winston, Inc., 1965. Review of literature, theoretical context, and procedures.

Levine, Robert M. *Brazil: Field Research Guide in the Social Sciences*. New York: Institute of Latin American Studies, Columbia University Press, 1966. Problems of field research in Brazil; probably outdated by recent political events.

Malinowski, Bronislaw. *Argonauts of the Western Pacific*. New York: E. P. Dutton & Co., Inc., 1922. The first clear statement of basic field methods.

Meighan, Clement W. *The Archaeologist's Note Book*. San Francisco: Chandler Publishing Co., 1961. A useful field manual.

Middleton, John. *The Study of the Lugbara: Expectation and Paradox in Anthropological Research*. New York: Holt, Rinehart and Winston, Inc., 1970. Role of alien fieldworker studying an African culture.

Naroll, Raoul, and Ronald Cohen (eds.). *A Handbook of Method in Cultural Anthropology*. Garden City, N.Y.: The Natural History Press; reissued by Columbia University Press (1973), 1970. Articles on methods in general use.

National Academy of Sciences-National Research Council. *Field Guides Prepared by the Committee on International Anthropology*, Division of Anthropology and Sociology, Washington, D.C. Alan Beals, John Hitchcock (and Mary Jean Kennedy): *India (and Pakistan)*, Publication 716, 1959; Richard E. Beardsley: *Japan*, Publication 704, 1959; H. W. Hutchinson: *Brazil*, Publication 908, 1960; Felix M. Keesing: *Oceania*, Publication 701, 1959. Alvin W. Wolfe: *West and Central Africa*, Publication 702, 1959. Although outdated to some extent, many basic suggestions are still sound.

Pelto, Pertti J. *Anthropological Research: The Structure of Inquiry*. New York: Harper & Row, Inc., 1970. A useful overview of research problems and basic methods.

Pitt, David C. *Using Historical Sources in Anthropology and Sociology*. New York: Holt, Rinehart and Winston, Inc., 1972.

Powdermaker, Hortense. *Stranger and Friend: The Way of an Anthropologist*. New York: W. W. Norton & Company, Inc., 1966. A detailed account of problems of fieldwork.

Schusky, Ernest L. *Manual for Kinship Analysis*, 2d ed. New York: Holt, Rinehart and Winston, Inc., 1972.

Spier, Robert F. G. *Surveying and Mapping: A Manual of Simplified Techniques*. New York: Holt, Rinehart and Winston, Inc., 1970.

Spindler, George D. (ed.). *Being an Anthropologist: Field Work in Eleven Cultures*. New York: Holt, Rinehart and Winston, Inc., 1970. Anthropologists record their experiences in collecting field data.

Spradley, James P., and David W. McCurdy. *The Cultural Experience: Ethnography in Complex Society*. Chicago: Science Research Associates, 1972. Ethnographic research in familiar settings for undergraduate students.

Thomas, David Hurst. *Predicting the Past: An Introduction to Anthropological Archaeology*. New York: Holt, Rinehart and Winston, Inc., 1974.

Trigger, Bruce G. *Beyond History: The Methods of Prehistory*. New York: Holt, Rinehart and Winston, Inc., 1968.

Watson, Patty Jo, et al. *Explanation in Archeology.* New York: Columbia University Press, 1971. Good review of the scientific method and its specific utilization in archaeology.

Wax, Rosalie. *Doing Fieldwork: Warnings and Advice.* Chicago and London: University of Chicago Press, 1971.

Willey, Gordon, and Phillip Phillips. *Method and Theory in American Archaeology.* Chicago: University of Chicago Press, 1958. To be read by any student committed to a career in archaeology.

Williams, Thomas Rhys. *Field Methods in the Study of Culture.* New York: Holt, Rinehart and Winston, Inc., 1967.

4/Human Biological Variation

1. The Basis of Heredity and Variation

Each living organism is the product of a complex process of development involving an interaction between the potentials for growth inherent in the individual's biological makeup and a variety of external or environmental influences that affect the growth or development of the individual from the moment of conception. In species that can survive only under relatively fixed and invariable environmental circumstances, variation tends to be determined primarily by internal biological factors inherited at the time of conception. In species, like *Homo sapiens,* which tolerate considerable environmental variation, the role played by environment in influencing development is correspondingly greater. Because human beings live in groups and develop technologies that enable them to influence and control the environments in which they live, human growth and development tend also to be influenced by the artifactual or constructed environments characteristic of particular ways of life. The role of cultures or ways of life in influencing human variation forms the subject of most of the chapters in this book. Because variation involves the interaction of inherited biological factors and environmental factors, it is useful, before considering the role of culture in human variation, to consider sources of variation that are internal to the organism. This chapter, then, deals mainly with biological or genetic inheritance and the manner in which it sets the stage for culturally induced variation among human beings.

Understandings of the biological processes involved in variation within and between species were first organized in scientific form with the publication of Charles Darwin's *Origin of Species* in 1859.[1] The theory of the origin of species developed by Darwin (1809–1882) accepted the fact of variation within species as a "given" and sought to explain the development of new species as a consequence of selection leading to increased adaptation. Within any particular environment some members of a species survive and reproduce, while others do not. Among a set of varying individuals, those individuals whose unique qualities make them most capable of surviving and reproducing are those who determine the biological makeup of their descendants. *Adaptation* is the capacity to survive and reproduce. *Selection* refers to those environmental factors that permit some to survive and reproduce, while others do not. In differing environments different sorts of individuals are "selected" to survive and reproduce. Over a period of time members of the same species living in different environments will be subjected to different patterns of selection leading to the formation of separate species.

Although the concepts of adaptation and selection explain how a single species can evolve into two different species, they do not explain how the original variation developed. Part of the explanation was available four years before Darwin published the *Origin of Species* in a paper published in 1866 by Gregor Mendel (1822–1884).[2] The significance of Mendel's paper was not recognized until his results were independently rediscovered in 1900. Mendel, working mainly with obvious contrasting characters, such as green-yellow or smooth-wrinkled peas, showed that such characters were inherited according to regular patterns. To explain these patterns Mendel postulated the existence of two independent particles or factors (now called genes), one inherited from each parent. In the processes of reproduction only one of the two parental genes would be transmitted to the offspring. Mendel established that the two genes present in each parent each had an equal chance of being replicated in the offspring. For the kinds of simple contrasting characteristics studied by Mendel, the offspring receives one out of two genes, at random, from each parent. This, Mendel's first law, is called *the principle of independent segregation*. Mendel's second law, *the principle of independent assortment*, was based on the fact that different pairs of genes were usually inherited independently of each other. Thus a pea might inherit its wrinkles from one parent and its yellow color from the other. In the process of reproduction the individual inherits an absolutely unique set of genes drawn from both parents. Except in the case of identical twins, each individual is genetically unique. Sexual recombination is an important biological mechanism for ensuring variation within the species.

[1] Charles Darwin, *On the Origin of Species by Means of Natural Selection, or the Preservation of Favoured Races in the Struggle for Life* (London: John Murray, 1859).

[2] Gregor Mendel, *Experiments in Plant-Hybridisation* (Cambridge, Mass.: Harvard University Press, 1950; first published in German in 1866).

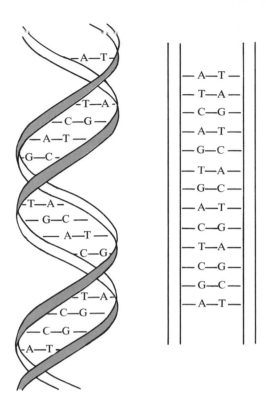

Figure 4–1 Diagram of section of DNA molecule. Unwound, it would resemble ladder on right. The Adenine-Guanine and Cytosine-Thymine pairs are spaced equally and the sides of the molecule are equidistant throughout. When the message is "read" by mechanisms within the cell, the base molecules are interpreted in groups of three.

Mendel arrived at his conclusions by observing the effects achieved by breeding plants, but he and other early students of genetics did not understand the precise mechanisms involved. This came later, during the twentieth century, with the development of increasingly refined understandings of the structure of cells and the mechanisms involved in their division and reproduction. The structure of the gene itself has been understood only during the last thirty years.[3] It is now known that the gene is a chemical molecule called deoxyribonucleic acid, or DNA. DNA is a long molecule consisting of phosphoric acid, deoxyribose (a sugar), and four nitrogenous ring compounds or bases called adenine (A), guanine (G), cytosine (C), and thymine (T). The phosphoric acid and the sugar usually form a double helix, a two-stranded rope fastened together by pairs of the four base compounds (see Figure 4–1). The base compound pairs are always made up either of adenine and thymine or of guanine and cytosine. Because these two basic pairs can be attached to either side of the helix, each side of the helix may possess any of the four base compounds.

If we compare this with the Morse code, in which each letter of the alphabet is represented by dots and dashes, it is apparent that complicated messages could be transmitted by arranging the bases along the strands of the

[3] James D. Watson, *The Double Helix: A Personal Account of the Discovery of the Structure of DNA* (New York: Atheneum, 1968).

helix in different orders. A single strand of DNA, representing one or more genes, may contain up to 200,000 nucleotides or units of three bases. Although it oversimplifies both the Morse code and the genetic code, we can think of the Morse code as consisting of a two-letter alphabet (dots and dashes), whereas the genetic code consists of a four-letter alphabet (the four bases).

In the process of reproduction the two strands of the double helix unwind, separating each of the pairs of bases. (See Figure 4–2.) By the time the process of unwinding is completed or shortly thereafter, the separated bases on each strand acquire the complementary base required to complete the pair. If the separated base is adenine (A), it acquires a fresh molecule of thymine (T); if it is cytosine (C), it acquires a fresh molecule of guanine (G), and so on. When the process is complete, two identical large molecules of DNA have been created out of the separated strands of the original molecule. There now exist two copies of the information originally contained in the single molecule of DNA.

In most living cells DNA molecules are linked together to form even larger molecules called chromosomes. Each human cell contains 46 chromosomes arranged in 23 pairs. In the process of normal cell division, or *mitosis,* each of the 46 chromosomes and each of the DNA molecules of which it is composed divide in such a way as to produce two sets each composed of 46 new chromosomes. The new chromosomes separate, and the cell itself then divides

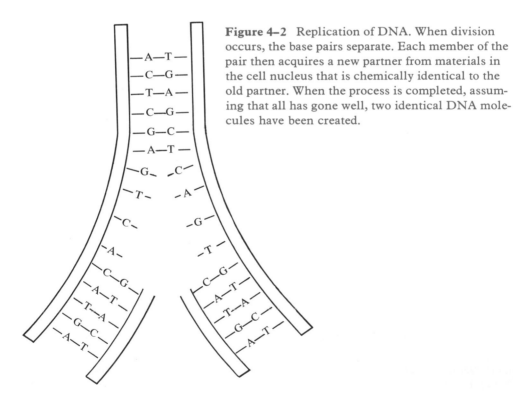

Figure 4–2 Replication of DNA. When division occurs, the base pairs separate. Each member of the pair then acquires a new partner from materials in the cell nucleus that is chemically identical to the old partner. When the process is completed, assuming that all has gone well, two identical DNA molecules have been created.

Figure 4-3   Stages in ordinary cell division (mitosis). The chromosomes become arranged linearly and then divide, each chromosome producing two identical daughter chromosomes. The new chromosomes move apart and the cell divides to produce two identical daughter cells.

producing two new cells each containing the identical genetic information contained in the original cell (see Figure 4–3). In the process of sexual reproduction sex cells, or gametes, are formed through a process called *meiosis* (see Figure 4–4). In this process the 23 pairs of chromosomes separate, and two new cells are formed each containing 23 chromosomes instead of the normal 46. When a female sex cell or ovum is fertilized by a male sex cell or sperm, a new cell called a *zygote* is created. The 23 chromosomes in the egg and in the sperm now form 23 pairs of chromosomes giving the zygote the full normal complement of chromosomes. The zygote now begins to reproduce itself by the normal pattern of mitosis and, if the environment is suitable, forms a human being.

Although the chromosome pairs are generally formed out of identically shaped chromosomes, there is one exception which occurs in all males. In males the 23rd pair of chromosomes consists of one large chromosome, the X-chromosome, and one small chromosome, the Y-chromosome. In females the 23rd pair consists of two X-chromosomes. As the egg, containing one of the mother's two chromosomes, is fertilized, it acquires either the X-chromosome or the Y-chromosome from the male parent. If it acquires the X-chromosome, it will contain a single pair of X-chromosomes and will be a female. If it acquires the Y-chromosome, it will contain one X-chromosome and one Y-chromosome and it will be a male. At the time of their formation exactly half of the sperm contain Y-chromosomes and half contain X-chromosomes. Assuming that they also have equal opportunities to fertilize egg cells, there is a fifty:fifty chance that the resulting zygote will be male or female.

The individual can be considered to be formed in response to the action of matched pairs of genes located on the 23 paired chromosomes. Each pair of genes and each pair of chromosomes contains one member received from the male parent through the sperm and one member received from the female parent through the egg. Except for the Y-chromosome, the genetic contribution of the mother and father to the child is absolutely equal. By the same token each of the four grandparents contributes one-fourth of the genetic materials and each of the eight great-grandparents contributes one-eighth. Because each ancestor's genetic contribution to the zygote is made through the chance assortment of chromosomes, there is no way of foretelling which genetic materials will be transmitted. Each individual contains an absolutely

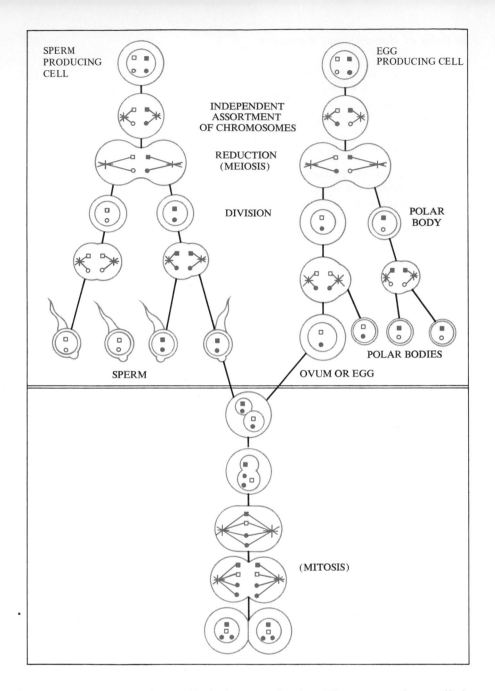

Figure 4–4 Formation of sex cells during reproduction. The sperm and egg cells in this drawing each contain two pairs of chromosomes. Each of the chromosome pairs is represented by a light figure and a dark figure indicating that each of the chromosomes contains different alleles at some gene locations. As the cells divide, the chromosomes separate and one member of each pair is drawn at random to each of the daughter cells. The process of reduction-division creates daughter cells having half the normal complement of chromosomes. These daughter cells then divide again to produce four sperm or one egg and three polar bodies. When the sperm is united with the egg, a cell containing the normal complement of chromosomes is created and begins to form an organism through the process of mitosis, or normal cell division.

unique assortment of genetic materials. No other individual, except an identical twin descended from the same fertilized egg, is likely to have the same genetic makeup. In the normal course of events, if the zygote is not altered by radiation or other forms of stress, genetic inheritance is completely determined at the time the ovum is fertilized by the sperm. Alteration of the genetic message at a later stage in life can be ruled out for all practical purposes because through the process of mitosis the genetic message has been copied or replicated in every cell of the body.

The effect of the various processes of cell division and reproduction is the transmission of information contained within molecules of DNA from parent organisms to their offspring. Among species that reproduce solely by mitosis or asexual reproduction, the genetic materials contained within the offspring will normally be identical to those contained within the parent. Barring various sorts of environmental disturbance, the form, capabilities, and behaviors of the offspring will be identical to those of the parent. A species reproducing asexually will possess relatively little within species variation, with the result that selection would have relatively little impact upon the genetic makeup of the species. There would be, in effect, no easy way of rewriting the genetic message.

In human beings, and other sexually reproducing plants and animals, each member of the species contains slightly different genetic information. If environmental circumstances change, there is always the chance that some individuals will be more fit to survive and reproduce than others. In such a case the process of natural selection has the effect of editing the genetic message to the extent that some individuals reproduce, and others do not. In the absence of selective pressures, all individuals in a population would have an equal chance of reproducing, and the genetic message would remain relatively unchanged.

Genetically unique individuals are created through sexual reproduction only when the parents contain somewhat different genetic materials. If the paired parental chromosomes and genes were identical, there could be no variation between individuals except that resulting from differing environmental pressures. What is needed, then, are some mechanisms that would permit the development of variation in the hereditary materials. There are, in fact, a number of ways in which mutations or changes can occur. Although molecules of DNA are protected from most sorts of environmental disturbance by the membranes of the cell, they may still be altered by various forms of physical and chemical interference of which radiation is the obvious example. Thus a part of the coded message may be cut away, the order of the base pairs may be changed, or one base pair may be substituted for another. If such a disturbance of the DNA molecule is drastic, the fertilized egg or the infant produced from it may fail to survive. In the case of minor disturbances the resulting new gene may be inherited. If it confers an adaptive advantage, those who carry it will be more likely to reproduce, and the chance of its spread throughout the population will be increased. Changes in the hereditary materials may also occur as molecules of DNA are replicated or as chromosomes divide. Molecules of DNA can break and come together in different ways, and the same sorts of things can happen to chromosomes. These sorts of mutations are strictly analogous to the kinds of things that happen when a manuscript is sent to the printer. There are bound to be a few typographical errors which don't change the meaning very much, but it is also possible that whole paragraphs or pages will get out of order or even that chapters (chromosomes) will get rearranged in various ways. In most cases such errors are not adaptive — they detract from the value of the book; in a few cases the changing of a word or reordering of chapters may have no noticeable effect; and in a small number of cases it may be a definite asset.

When a new gene comes into being, it is likely to occupy the same position in the chromosome as the old gene of which it represents an altered form. Genes occupying the same locus or position on the same chromosome are called *alleles*. Obvious contrasting characters of the type used by Mendel are usually considered the product of sets of alleles. Thus green-yellow or smooth-wrinkled peas are considered to result from sets of alleles that determine the color or smoothness of peas. Because the individual receives one gene from each parent, any inherited characteristic must be understood in terms of the relationship between genes derived from each parent. If the individual receives the same allele from each parent, for example, the alleles for smoothness in peas, the individual pea will be smooth. (See Figure 4–5.) When the individual pea acquires an allele for smoothness from one parent and an allele for wrinkledness from the other parent, the resulting pea is also smooth. This is the phenomenon known as *dominance*. The allele for

Figure 4–5 The classical Mendelian experiment. When pure strains of round and wrinkled peas are crossed, a mixture of round and wrinkled peas are produced in the ratio of 4:1. Genetically, the ratio is 1:2:1 as demonstrated in the second generation when one of the round peas breeds true, but the two others each produce one wrinkled pea. Because of the independent assortment of chromosomes, crossing two hybrid peas produces the same result as crossing the pure strains. Because the peas appear round, even when they are hybrid, roundness is said to be dominant over wrinkledness.

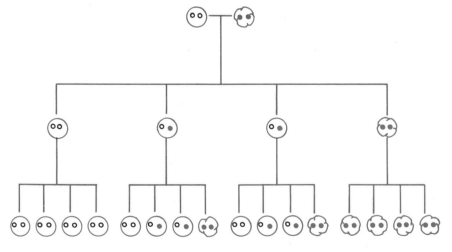

smoothness is dominant over the allele for wrinkledness and prevents its expression. The gene for wrinkledness is said to be *recessive.*

The importance of this discovery is that it means that the genes possessed by an individual cannot always be definitely identified by an examination of the characteristics exhibited. A smooth pea could contain two alleles for smoothness, or it could contain one allele for smoothness and one allele for wrinkledness. In such a case a distinction has to be made between the *phenotype,* or the external appearance of a life form, and its *genotype,* or genetic makeup. Because the gene for wrinkledness in peas is recessive, it follows, assuming that only two alleles are involved, that a wrinkled pea always contains two alleles for wrinkledness. In the case of a wrinkled pea the genotype can be identified on the basis of the phenotype. When the individual receives the same allele from both parents, it is said to be *homozygous;* when it receives a different allele from each parent it is said to be *heterozygous.* Although the presence or absence of some recessive genes can be identified by special techniques, the traditional method of identifying the genotype is through a program of crossbreeding. Thus it is possible to develop a strain of smooth peas which is homozygous for the trait of smoothness. If a pea known to be homozygous for smoothness is bred with a wrinkled pea, the next or F_2 generation is produced in the Mendelian ratio of three smooth peas to one wrinkled pea. Genotypically the Mendelian ratio would of course be one homozygous smooth pea, two heterozygous smooth peas, and one homozygous wrinkled pea.

In many cases the alleles received from each parent express themselves in one degree or another. Pink four-o'clocks, for example, are known to be the offspring of red and white four-o'clocks. In this case the presence of an allele for whiteness and an allele for redness result in phenotypic pinkness. Red four-o'clocks are homozygous for redness, white four-o'clocks are homozygous for whiteness, and pink four-o'clocks are heterozygous.

Although any plant or animal, including human beings, has characteristics that are inherited by means of sets of alleles having the same locus on the chromosome, many characteristics are not inherited in such straightforward fashion. Instead of inheritance being determined by alleles or different genes at the same locus or position on the chromosomes, it may be *polygenic* in character involving several different genes occupying different locations on the chromosome, or even different chromosomes. For human beings simple traits inherited monogenically through systems of alleles can sometimes be identified by the examination of genealogies; traits inherited polygenically are inherited in a much more unpredictable fashion. The inheritance of human eye, skin, and hair color, for example, is not well understood because the color is determined polygenically. To the extent that human intelligence, personality, stature, or other complex characteristics or talents might be inherited, all seem to be inherited polygenically. Although some blood types, some kinds of genetic disease, and some minor bodily characteristics of human beings are predictably inherited in simple Mendelian fashion, most of the characteristics that human beings care about and talk about are inherited polygenically in ways that are as yet poorly understood.

Members of the same population, in this case the Fanti of Ghana, may be quite similar in some respects, quite different in others.

Fanti men (Ghana) repairing fishnet. (Kindness of David Kronenfeld.)

Opposite: A fanti man (Ghana) making crosspiece for canoe with an adze. (Kindness of David Kronenfeld.)

Opposite left: Fanti man (Ghana) with embroidered shawl. (Kindness of David Kronenfeld.)

Opposite right: Fanti man (Ghana). (Kindness of David Kronenfeld.)

Above and opposite above: Fanti women (Ghana).
(Kindness of David Kronenfeld.)

Opposite Fanti women (Ghana). (Kindness of Earl Plumm

Even if the nature of human genetic inheritance were perfectly understood, there would still be obstacles in the path of any program that would predict the nature of the offspring from a knowledge of its parental genotypes. Here it will be recalled that the genetic message is essentially a blueprint or plan. The gene itself acts by producing complex chemicals that have an impact upon the growth and behavior of the organism. From the earliest stages the chemicals produced by genes must interact with substances produced in the environment. In the case of recessive alleles the presence of a dominant allele in its immediate environment prevents its expression. In the case of polygenic inheritance other genes within the cell may prevent or encourage the expression of any particular gene. Substances that penetrate the cell wall may also prevent or encourage the expression of any particular gene. If the environment is deficient in substances required for the normal growth of the organism, the action of many genes will be suppressed or altered. An environment that is optimal for the expression of some genes will probably not be optimal for the expression of others. A knowledge of the individual organism's genetic potential, like knowledge of the novel upon which a film has been based, tells us a great deal of what might have been, but it permits us to predict the final nature of the organism or film only when environmental influences upon the original design have been understood.

2. The Nature of Human Variation

The fundamental concept required for an understanding of human biological variation is that of the *breeding population*. This is the set of people that interbreed with each other relatively more frequently than they do with other people. More loosely defined, a breeding population is any set of human beings whose pattern of interbreeding leads to the development of measurable biological differences between the interbreeding set and other neighboring populations. Although the members of a breeding population interact in the process of interbreeding and can therefore be said to form a group, the group formed by interbreeding is not necessarily the same as the groups formed by other sorts of communication or interaction. Although villages, tribes, nations, and other sorts of linguistic or cultural units may form breeding populations, linguistic and cultural differences do not always serve as barriers to interbreeding or intermarriage. People sharing the same language or culture do not always interbreed or intermarry. A breeding population may include several linguistic or cultural units, or, conversely, a single linguistic or cultural unit may include several breeding populations.

For example, a village in India forms a well-defined social group consisting of individuals who interact more frequently with each other than with any other set of individuals. Especially in North Indian villages, interbreeding rarely takes place within the village, with the result that the breeding population must involve several different villages. If the village is near a linguistic boundary, the breeding population is likely to include individuals speaking two different languages. Because most Indian villages are subdivided into castes that rarely interbreed, each village is likely to contain members of several different breeding populations. On a larger scale all speakers of English or all citizens of the United States do not interbreed and therefore do not form a breeding population.

The development of significant biological differences between breeding populations depends upon the extent to which they are reproductively isolated. When interbreeding takes place between adjacent breeding populations, the resulting transfer of genetic materials between the two populations will tend to reduce the extent of the biological differences between them. Generally the development of biologically distinctive subspecies or varieties within a single species requires that the species be divided, often by geographical barriers, into several reproductively isolated breeding populations. When a new breeding population is formed by individuals who differ biologically from the other members of their original breeding population, the result is a kind of instant biological variation, which has been described as the *founder effect*. For example, if an isolated village or tribe is formed by a single family or lineage drawn from a larger breeding population, the genes represented in the newly formed village or tribe will be only those carried by the original founders and may therefore be quite different from the selection of genes present in the larger breeding population. The modern population of Pitcairn's Island consists largely of the descendants of English mutineers and the Tahitian men and women they brought with them to the island.[4] Such a population is quite different biologically from either of the parent populations, both because it represents a mixture of two parent populations and because neither the mutineers nor the Tahitians were completely typical of Englishmen or Tahitians.

Once a breeding population has been established in a new environment, other mechanisms may cause further biological differentiation to occur. Genes that were adaptive in the old environment may prove to be maladaptive in the new environment, with the result that processes of selection may cause them to become less frequent in the population or to vanish altogether. Mutations or genetic changes that occur in the new breeding populations are not likely to occur simultaneously in the old breeding population, with the result that some new genes, absent in the parent population, may, if they are adaptive, become quite common in the new population. When breeding populations are quite small, chance factors may result in the disappearance of some genes and in increases in the frequency of other genes. If a population contains only five women of reproductive age and one of them is infertile, any unique genes possessed by the infertile woman will vanish forever. In a large population the chances are that any single gene will be shared by several people, and such chances or accidents as infertility will have relatively little effect on the frequency of different genes in the *gene pool* of the population. Accidental or chance variations in gene frequency are described by the term *genetic drift*.

---

[4] Most studies of molecular evolution have emphasized the role of genes. A number of new approaches emphasizing changes in the manner in which genes are regulated or in the number and arrangement of chromosomes are described in Gina Bari Kolata, "Evolution of DNA: Changes in Gene Regulation," *Science,* **189**:446–447. (August 1975).

Men and woman of Gopalpur, South India. Similarities of dress and gesture and shared phenotypic characteristics may create impression of biological similarity. Careful examination reveals striking variations within the same community. (Photos by Alan Beals.)

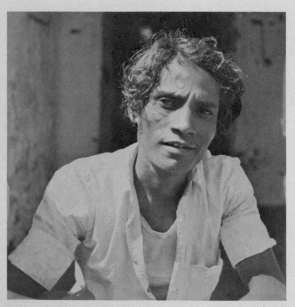 

Because a single human generation covers a period of twenty to thirty years, changes in human populations resulting from selection, mutation, and genetic drift usually take a long time to occur. In the normal course of events the development of significant biological differences between human populations, other than those caused by founder effect, requires periods of reproductive isolation lasting for many thousands of years. Because the development and worldwide spread of *Homo sapiens* is a comparatively recent phenomenon, even relatively isolated populations, such as the Australian aborigines, have not been isolated for a long enough period of time to permit the development of separate species.

In most of the world human breeding populations have not been reproductively isolated for very long periods of time. Some degree of interbreeding with neighboring populations is characteristic of almost all known human breeding populations. Because the ability to identify and recognize close relatives appears to have been absolutely essential for the early development of the human species, it seems probable that such recognition, along with the development of incest taboos forbidding interbreeding within family, lineage, or other sets of close relatives, led in very early times to the development of systematic practices involving the exchange of marital partners between different local groups. Among human beings, then, the development of distinctive subspecies or varieties seems always to have been held in check by the flow of genetic materials across population boundaries.

When populations are isolated for long periods of time, processes of selection and genetic drift would eventually decrease biological variability within the population. Selection would tend to increase the frequencies of the most adaptive genes and decrease the frequency of maladaptive genes, while genetic drift would tend to cause the accidental loss of genes that were present in low frequencies. When populations are not isolated, the continuing introduction of new genetic materials would result in increased individual variability. Although it would seem to be advantageous to have populations in which all individuals possessed only genes that were highly adaptive, such a turn of events would be adaptive in the long run only if the environment were held constant and only if a lack of individual variation made possible the formation of the most efficient sort of human group. A population containing many alternative possibilities within its gene pool would be much more capable of surviving changing conditions than would one that produced adults of the same type, all adapted to the same environmental circumstances. Similarly a human group composed of many different kinds of people, each possessing somewhat different sorts of abilities, might well be more capable of handling the day-to-day challenges, even of a constant environment, than would a group that was genetically homogeneous.

Whether the cause be intermarriage, the adaptive value of variety, or both, human populations are highly variable. Species, such as *Homo sapiens*, that are characterized by a high degree of individual variation are called *polymorphic*. In terms of visible biological characteristics this means that the members of any human population are likely to vary widely in stature, skin color, hair form, eye color, nose shape, body weight, head shape, and so on. Although visible biological characteristics are the result of interaction between inherited potentialities and environmental circumstances and so do not necessarily reflect the presence or absence of particular genes, almost all known human genetic characteristics follow the same general pattern as the visible biological characteristics. Different human populations tend to possess the same genes, but they tend to be present in different frequencies. Although some populations, especially if they are from geographically distant places, possess visible biological characteristics or genetic characteristics that other populations do not possess, most differences between human populations must be expressed in terms of average differences or in terms of differing percentages of the same traits. In terms of stature, for example, average differences between populations are usually a matter of a few inches. Because each of the populations is highly variable, the frequency distributions of the two groups would overlap to a considerable degree, as illustrated in Figure 4–6. On the average the English are taller than the Japanese, but there are many Japanese and English who are of the same stature. Similarly, where one population has a high frequency of blood group gene A and another population has a low frequency of the same gene, there would ordinarily be substantial numbers of individuals in both populations who possessed gene A.

Figure 4–6 Normal curves of distribution. Comparisons between populations are often given in terms of the mean or average difference between them. When people say, for example, that the Greens average five inches shorter than the Blues, the impression is left that all Greens are shorter than all Blues. In real life, there is a range of variation around the mean in each population. Thus some Greens would, in fact, be taller than some Blues. In the diagram below, Population A and Population B have substantially different mean scores, but most people in both populations are indistinguishable in terms of their scores on the measure.

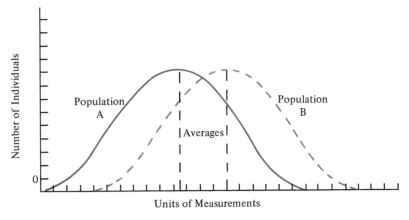

3. The Distribution of Biological Characteristics

Differences in the average frequency or percentage of both visible and genetic characteristics tend to increase as the geographical distance between human populations increases. For the most part the geographical distribution of particular characteristics follows a clinal pattern.[5] A characteristic that exists with high frequency in one part of the world tends to decline gradually with geographical distance. This is the pattern we should expect if a characteristic developed a high frequency in one place, perhaps during a period of reproductive isolation, and then spread outward as a result of resumed interbreeding with neighboring populations. A clinal pattern would also result if strong selective factors favored a high frequency in one place, and interbreeding led to its diffusion to other places where it possessed little adaptive significance. The existence of clinal variation makes it difficult to draw sharp lines between neighboring groups and thus interposes a formidable obstacle to any attempt to divide the human species into different varieties or biological types. Although significant biological differences can be found between geographically distant human populations and a classificatory distinction might be made, perhaps separating very tall populations from very short populations, most human beings would tend to fall between the two extremes. Such a classification, into which most human beings would not fit, would be useful only for highly specialized purposes.

Another property of the distribution of visible and genetic characteristics is that the distributions of different characteristics tend not to be isomorphic — different characteristics follow different patterns of geographical distribution. The observed pattern of such distributions is what we should expect if each individual characteristic developed in some particular part of the world and then spread in response to whatever geographical or selective factors may have influenced its distribution. If there were clusters of biological characteristics that shared the same pattern of distribution, that is, that were isomorphically distributed, the task of dividing the human species into subtypes would be relatively easy. The absence of clusters of isomorphically distributed characteristics places grave obstacles in the way of any division of the species in terms of large geographical areas. We may speak of an American, an African, or a European variety of *Homo sapiens,* but only with the knowledge that there are very few characteristics whose patterns of distribution match the boundaries of these geographical areas.

To illustrate the problems of clinal variation and of the absence of isomorphic distributions, consider the distributions of those visible biological characteristics that tend to form the basis of folk classifications of human beings. Skin color in the Old World, but not in the New, tends to get darker in the warmer latitudes of the Northern Hemisphere. People with dark skins are found in parts of Africa, India, New Guinea, and Australia. Peoples with

[5] H. L. Shapiro, *The Heritage of the Bounty* (Garden City, N.Y.: Natural History Library, 1962).

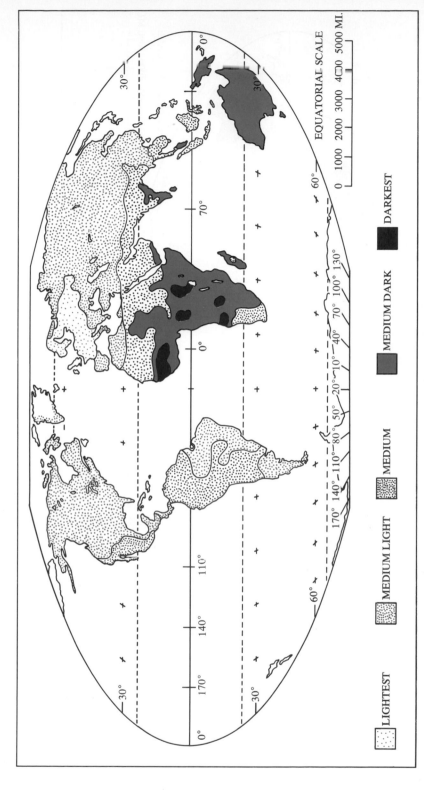

Figure 4-7 Variation in human skin color. Maps of this sort attempting to reconstruct the situation as it existed before the great population movements of the last several hundred years are crude approximations which suppress a great deal of local variation. Especially in the Old World, there is rough association between tropical residence and dark skin color. (After Brace and Montagu.)

LIGHTEST

MEDIUM LIGHT

MEDIUM

MEDIUM DARK

DARKEST

EQUATORIAL SCALE

0   1000   2000   3000   4000   5000 MI.

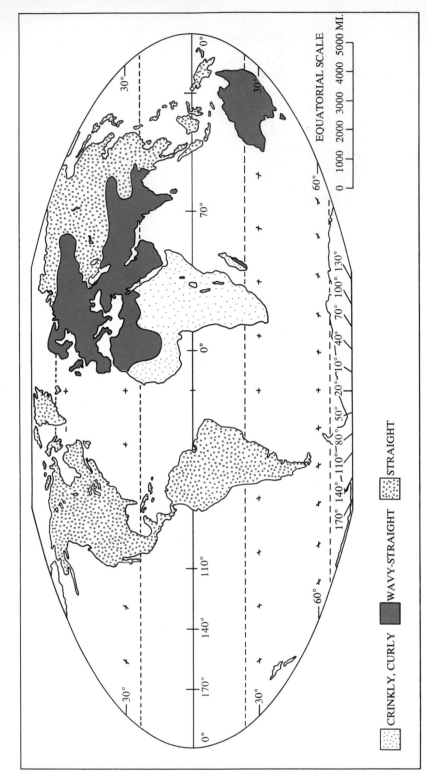

Figure 4–8 Variation in human hair form. (After Brace and Montagu.)

CRINKLY, CURLY   WAVY-STRAIGHT   STRAIGHT

EQUATORIAL SCALE

0   1000   2000   3000   4000   5000 MI.

extremely light skins are found in northern Europe, whereas most of the peoples of Asia and the New World are of intermediate skin color. (See Figure 4–7.) Differences in skin color are, of course, average differences, and many populations contain both dark and light individuals. Although there are possibilities that dark skin is adaptive in warm climates because it inhibits sunburning or that light skin may be adaptive in cold climates because it facilitates the manufacture of vitamin D, the adaptive value of skin color has not been demonstrated in such a way as to generate any very broad agreement among biological anthropologists.

Hair form overlaps the distribution of skin color in some places but not in others. (See Figure 4–8.) Crinkly or very curly hair is common throughout Africa south of the Sahara and in New Guinea. Wavy hair is common from Europe, through India, clear over to Australia. Straight hair is the common hair form in Eastern Asia and in the New World. In Africa the most tightly curled hair is found among the Bushmen of the Kalahari Desert in South

Figure 4–9 Average statures in and near Europe (after Coon). Maps of this sort permit a better understanding of the extent of local variation. A comparison with Figures 4–10 and 4–11 illustrates the difficulties involved in attempting to identify racial types.

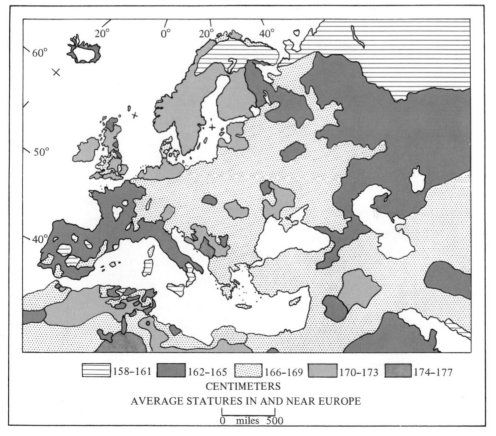

| | 158–161 | | 162–165 | | 166–169 | | 170–173 | | 174–177 |

CENTIMETERS
AVERAGE STATURES IN AND NEAR EUROPE

0   miles   500

Africa, but their skin color is about the same as that of the straight-haired peoples of Eastern Asia and the New World. In South India, where some breeding populations are extremely dark, hair form is generally indistinguishable from that of Europeans. On the whole many people with crinkly hair have dark skins, many people with straight hair have intermediate skin color, and many people with wavy hair have light skin color—but there are also many exceptions to these tendencies. In particular there seems to be little correlation between wavy hair and skin color. Figures 4–9, 4–10, and 4–11 illustrate the problems involved in defining a European race of tall, blue-eyed blondes.

The ABO blood group system, consisting of at least four alleles—O, A$_1$, A$_2$, and B—has a quite different pattern of distribution. (See Figure 4–12.) Allele A has a high frequency, over 50 percent, among the Blackfoot Indians of western North America and then drops in the northern part of North America to a frequency of 10 to 20 per cent. The frequency rises again to 20 to 30 per cent among the peoples of the North American Arctic. Moving south,

Figure 4–10   Percentage frequencies of light hair in and near Europe (after Hulse). The highest percentage occurs in parts of Scandinavia with a decline in percentages at increasing distances from the center.

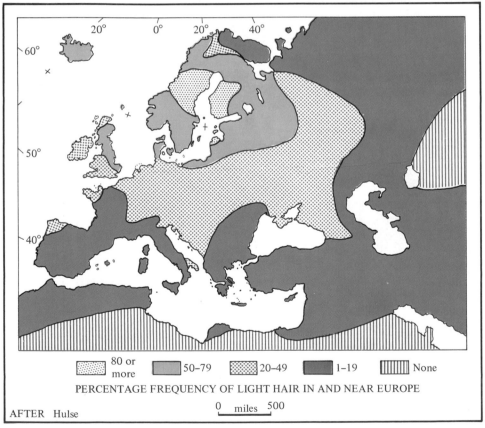

PERCENTAGE FREQUENCY OF LIGHT HAIR IN AND NEAR EUROPE

80 or more   50–79   20–49   1–19   None

AFTER Hulse

0   miles   500

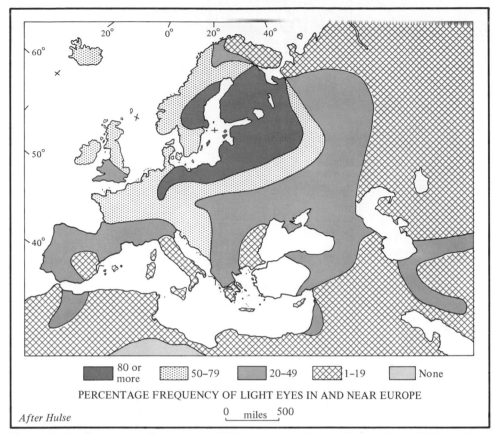

80 or more   50-79   20-49   1-19   None

PERCENTAGE FREQUENCY OF LIGHT EYES IN AND NEAR EUROPE

After Hulse

0   miles   500

Figure 4–11   Percentage frequency of light eyes in and near Europe (after Hulse). The distribution of light eyes and light hair follow a crudely similar pattern, but it would be hard to draw a boundary defining a light-haired and light-eyed population that would include more than a small percentage of existing light-haired and light-eyed people.

most of the pre-Colombian peoples of the United States and Latin America seem to have had frequencies of less than 5 per cent. In Eurasia high frequencies of A are found in Scandinavia and Australia, while relatively low frequencies are found in Africa and northeastern Asia and in parts of Australia. The B allele is almost absent in the New World and in Australia, but reaches frequencies as high as 25 percent in parts of Asia. In Europe, in Africa, and in northeastern Asia, frequencies of B range between 5 and 15 per cent. The allele M of the M,NSs blood group system ranges up to 80 or 90 per cent in the New World, but has frequencies of less than 50 per cent in parts of Scandinavia, in Africa, and in Australia, while ranging between 50 and 70 per cent in most of the Old World. (See Figure 4–13.) A classification based on these blood groups would be quite different from one based on hair form and skin color.

The distributions of visible and genetic human biological characteristics are too various to permit the development of any very useful subclassifications

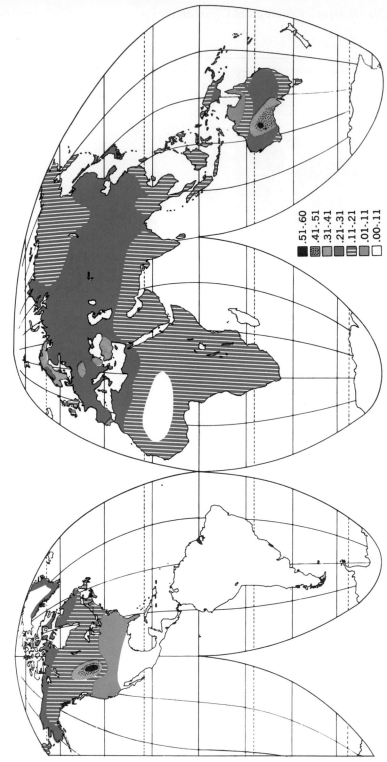

Figure 4–12 Percentage frequencies for the distribution of allele A₁ of the A,B,O blood group. Such gene maps are averages which tend to obscure local variation. Apparent patterns may also shift considerably depending upon the percentage intervals chosen. Compare with the distributions of other phenotypic and genotypic characteristics.

.51-.60
.41-.51
.31-.41
.21-.31
.11-.21
.01-.11
.00-.11

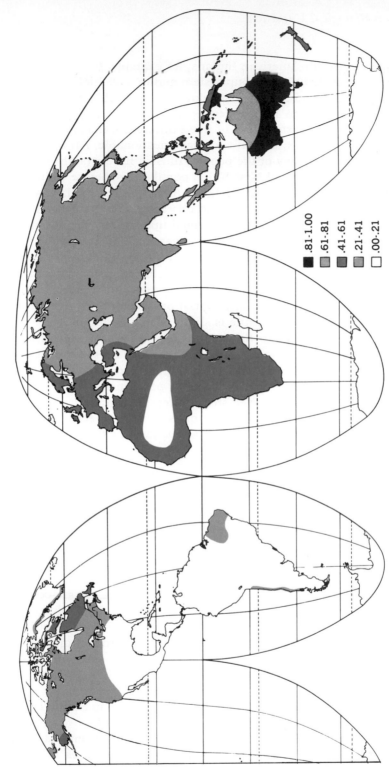

Figure 4–13 Percentage frequencies for the distribution of Allele N of the M,N blood group. Compare with Figure 4–12.

of the human species. South American Indians, for example, tend to lack both A and B alleles of the A,B,O blood group system and to have high frequencies of allele M, straight hair, and intermediate skin color. On this basis it might be argued that South American Indians represent a distinctive type of human being. When the worldwide distribution of these different traits is considered, the significance of such a classification becomes questionable. All of the peoples of the New World and many of the peoples of Asia have straight hair and intermediate skin color. Almost all New World populations, before Columbus, seem to have had high frequencies of allele M. Although hundreds of visible human characteristics and dozens of genetic characteristics have been identified and elaborate statistical analyses performed upon them, the absence of isomorphic distributions of such characteristics has made it impossible to arrive at any consistent or widely acceptable division of the human species into subcategories or biological types. On the whole, biological differences within human populations are more important than biological differences between them, and most of the observed biological variation seems to involve superficial characteristics whose adaptive value is slight or undetermined.

The available evidence leads to the conclusion that *Homo sapiens* represents a single, unified biological species, all of whose members share the same basic biological adaptations. Any normally functioning human being can learn any language or perform any task that is routinely performed by the members of any human population. The observed sharp differences in the behavior and daily activity of the members of different groups represent learned patterns transmitted within each society by means of language and example.

4. Culture and Human Biology

The best-known and best-documented example of the interaction between culture and human genetics is provided by the distribution of the sickle-cell gene in parts of Africa and the Old World. Individuals who are homozygous with respect to the sickle-cell gene, having inherited one sickle-cell gene from each parent, tend to suffer from a disease called sickle-cell anemia. Sickle-cell anemia is an often fatal disease characterized by the presence of defective sickle-shaped red blood corpuscles unable to function properly. Because victims of sickle-cell anemia tend to die before reaching the age of reproduction, it might be expected that normal processes of natural selection would cause the gene to exist at comparatively low frequencies or to die out altogether. In fact this is the case throughout most of the world. However, high frequencies of the sickle-cell gene have been found to exist in India, in Greece, in South Turkey, and across a wide section of tropical Africa. (See Figure 4–14.)

Populations with a high incidence of the sickle-cell gene tend to have a high incidence of the malaria *Plasmodium falciparum*. Research on this interesting coincidence has led to the discovery that individuals who are heterozygous with regard to the sickle-cell gene, having one sickle-cell gene and one normal gene, are relatively, if not completely, immune to falciparum

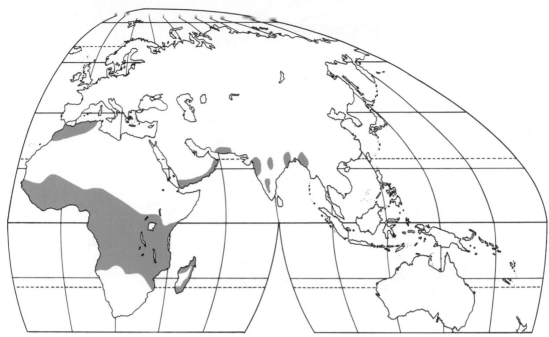

Figure 4–14 Presence of high frequencies of the sickle-cell trait in the Old World in recent times. Compare with Figure 4–15.

malaria. Because falciparum malaria is the most deadly of the malarias, capable of causing very high rates of infant mortality, it follows that it exerts a very powerful selective pressure against any population affected by it. In such populations, Livingstone has suggested that people who are heterozygous with regard to the sickle-cell gene tend to survive, while those who are homozygous with regard to either normal genes or sickle-cell genes are strongly selected against either by malaria or by sickle-cell anemia.[6]

Plasmodium falciparum, considered the most deadly and the most recently developed of the malarias, is carried by the mosquito *Anopheles gambiae*. *A. gambiae* clusters about human habitations, often resting on thatched roofs. It tends to breed in clear water lacking strong currents. In the tropical rain forests, which formerly covered most of the region now occupied by *Plasmodium falciparum*, sunlit pools of clear water are virtually nonexistent. When human beings cut down the forest, sunlight is admitted to existing ponds and swamps, creating breeding places for *A. gambiae*. Figure 4–15 illustrates the distribution of falciparum malaria in Old World rain forests and tropical agriculture regions. Agricultural and house-building activities create additional freshwater ponds and puddles. Finally, the introduction of irrigated agriculture, especially rice agriculture, creates an environment filled with ideal breeding places for the mosquito. Thus human cultural practices seem to have

[6] F. B. Livingstone, "Natural Selection, Disease, and Ongoing Human Evolution, as illustrated by the ABO Blood Groups," *Human Biology*, **32**:17–27 (1960).

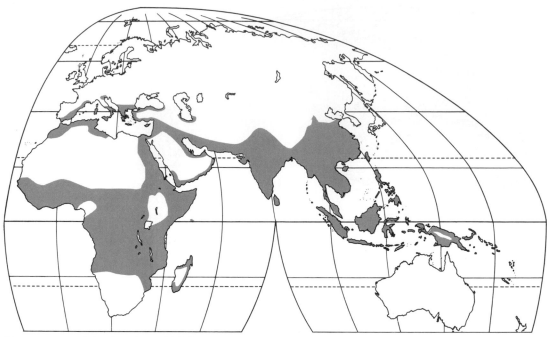

Figure 4–15   Distribution of falciparum malaria in the Old World in recent times. Assuming some recent population movement and a recent spread of falciparum malaria in some regions, the correlation between the presence of sickle-cell trait and the presence of falciparum malaria is quite high.

modified the environment in such a way as to encourage a disease that was one of the most deadly threats to human survival in all of history and, at the same time, to produce one of the most deadly and widespread genetic diseases affecting humanity.

Few other cases of the interaction between culture and biology are as well understood as that of the sickle-cell trait. Such dramatic examples can exist only when a very high rate of selective pressure creates extremely rapid biological evolution. As noted in Chapter 5, the biological evolution of the human species has always been strongly affected by the human use of tools and by the development of culture. With the development of agriculture and later of industrial and urban societies, there is every reason to believe that human culture has exercised an increasing influence upon processes of biological evolution. In modern societies, where newly developed medical techniques have sharply reduced the mortality of children and adolescents, the principal thrust of "natural" selection is provided by those largely social factors that cause some individuals to produce many more children and grandchildren than others.

Several scholars have in fact become alarmed over the prospect that improved medical care might lead to the survival of genetic characteristics that might otherwise have been weeded out by "natural" selection. The case of the sickle-cell gene and other genes conferring immunity to malaria is instructive here because the survival value of such genes may be largely dependent upon the presence or absence of malaria. Current programs for the elimination of the sickle-cell gene through selective breeding seem advantageous in terms of present cultural and environmental circumstances in which malaria has ceased to be a threat to human survival. If, however, we predict the destruction of civilization and/or the return of *Plasmodium falciparum,* the elimination of the sickle-cell gene will clearly have been a mistake. Should civilization be further destroyed to the point where agriculture ceases to be practiced, the reforestation of large areas would create a situation in which the incidence of malaria declined and the sickle-cell gene would again become a liability.

New possibilities for identifying particular genes in individuals and employing genetic counseling to eliminate such genes from the human population permit the influence of cultural factors upon human evolution to be sharply increased. Such consciously planned biological evolution cannot be very useful without some foreknowledge of the kinds of selective pressures that might affect the species in the distant future. Modern medicine allows individuals to survive and reproduce who possess genetic characteristics that would not have permitted survival and reproduction under former conditions. Although such unintended change in the biological makeup of the species deserves careful consideration, it is worth remembering that the only possible index of adaptive value is the individual's present capacity to survive and reproduce. The individuals who survive and reproduce today are precisely those individuals most fitted to survive and reproduce in the environment in which they find themselves.

In addition to creating specific environmental conditions that favor the development of particular genetic characteristics, culture exerts influence upon human biological makeup by creating patterns of social relationship which significantly alter existing gene pools. In Australia, according to Joseph Birdsell,[7] the division of the population into small and relatively isolated tribal groups has resulted in the creation of breeding populations favoring rapid biological evolution. The twenty-eight Australian tribes considered by Birdsell show a range of genetic variability as great as that existing between such geographical "races" as the Caucasoids and Mongoloids.

Studies such as those conducted in Venezuela by Neel[8] and in Malaya by Fix[9] suggest that marriage rules, patterns of residence following marriage, or patterns for the fission and fusion of residential groups may have striking effects upon the distribution of genetic factors within the population considered. In the industrialized world the slave trade and patterns of migration within and between nations and continents have created massive genetic intermixture and led to the development of increasingly large breeding populations. The White, Black, Brown, Yellow, and Red ethnic groups in the United States rep-

[7] J. B. Birdsell, *Human Evolution: An Introduction to the New Physical Anthropology* (Skokie, Ill.: Rand McNally, 1972), pp. 453–454.

[8] J. Neel et al., "Studies on the Yanomama Indians," *Human Genetics Proc., IV. Int. Congr. Human Genetics* (Paris, Amsterdam: Excerpta Medici, 1972), 96–111.

[9] Alan Fix, "Fission-Fusion and Lineal Effect: Aspects of the Population Structure of the Semai Senoi of Malaysia," *American Journal of Physical Anthro.,* **43,** No. 2 (September, 1975).

Phenotypic variation among African men.

Left: Cabrais man from village near Lama-Kara, Togoland. (Courtesy of the United Nations.)

Left below: Young Masai (Tanganyika). (Courtesy of the United Nations.)

Below: A Watusi man from Ruanda-Urundi; the outstretched arms represent cattle horns. (Courtesy of the United Nations.)

resent mixtures of diverse breeding populations from their respective continents of origin as well as extensive genetic mixture between the ethnic groups. Although such ethnic groups are clearly not races in any strict biological sense, among other things the degree of biological variation within each of the groups is probably greater than that which exists between them, such conglomerations of the descendants of diverse breeding populations are quite unique from a biological point of view. Similar ethnic groups in India and in other parts of the world have a much longer history, and some Indian castes seem to be much more homogeneous biologically than newly formed ethnic groups in many other modern nations.

Although considerable attention has been devoted to the systematic study of similarities and differences within and between ethnic groups, the results of such research have not yet led to any generally significant findings. The development of increasingly sophisticated understandings of human genetics has, however, provided new means of tracing the influence of social arrangements upon human evolutionary tendencies. Thus the general problem of the influence of culture and society upon human biology should lead to increasingly interesting results in the near future. For the present, there seems little doubt that human social and cultural arrangements have been a factor in biological evolution over the past several million years. The division of the species into social groups with corresponding patterns of fission, fusion, intermarriage, and migration has almost certainly played a role in accelerating human evolution to a degree not normally to be expected in more or less randomly interbreeding populations characteristic of most other species.

5. Biology and Culture

Questions about the influence of biological heredity upon human behavior are often framed in terms of the rather senseless assumption that there exists some kind of sharp dividing line between "nature," or heredity, and nurture, or environment. Is kissing, diabetes, arrogance, sex, intelligence, pulse rate, or mother-in-law avoidance to be regarded as something that is caused by genetic inheritance or something that is caused by training and experience? The best answer to this question is, "Yes." All of these things—everything that is characteristic of human beings—are caused by nature and nurture working together. The action of any single gene is deeply influenced by a genetic environment consisting of the other genes present in the cell. The action of the cell is deeply influenced by surrounding cells and the availability of particular chemicals in the environment of the cell. From the time an egg cell is fertilized until the time of birth, its development is influenced by an intrauterine environment that is influenced in turn by the culturally inspired activities, diets, and medications of the mother. There is no point in time at which the genetic message operates independently of the environment. Heredity and environment always work together in the development of the individual.

Nothing is determined by heredity, nothing is determined by environment; everything is determined by the interaction of heredity and environment. Serious questions about heredity and environment have to do with the manner in which the two forces interact and the extent to which either may constrain or shape the potentialities of the other. The genetic message sets up possibilities and limitations within which a biological individual may develop. The environment sets up a different set of possibilities and limitations. Processes of selection and adaptation ensure that most individuals contain genetic messages capable of reaching viable expression within the environment. Each species, because it must be different from other species, contains within its genetic messages certain fixed elements which determine what are called *species-specific characteristics.*

Phenotypic variation among Indian and Ladino women from the Americas.

Ladino woman, El Salvador, Central America. (Courtesy of the United Nations.)

Peasant woman from Colombia. (Kindness of Sylvia Broadbent.)

For human beings, the ability to develop cultures based on the use of tools and language is a species-specific characteristic. Many details of human physiology—the shape of head, heart, and hand—are also species-specific. We know that the ability to develop culture is species-specific because we know that no other species has quite the same potential. We do not know exactly what biological mechanisms provide us with this potential. It is possible, for example, that the capacity for culture is simply a minor by-product of progressive increase in the size of the human brain. It is also possible that the capacity for culture involves some highly specific biograms or biological programs that exert powerful influence upon language, technology, interpersonal relationships, religion, and many other universal or near-universal aspects of culture. Whether the capacity for culture is a relatively narrow set of options

Indian woman (Guatemala) grinding corn. (Courtesy of the United Nations.)

Crow Indian woman (United States). (From the Morrow Collection. Courtesy W. H. Over Museum.)

sharply restricted by biological limitations or a broad set of options exercised within very broad biological limitations is a question for future research.

The answer to this question and to other less global questions connected with it is of the greatest practical importance. For example, we know that human beings have lived in small communities characterized by strongly knit family organizations during most of human history. Today we observe that small communities are rapidly disappearing and that family organizations have become increasingly fragile. If small communities and families are biologically necessary for mental health or for the maintenance of culture, the human species must be added to the list of species threatened by the expansion of civilization. If the nature of the community or the existence of the family is biologically irrelevant, we have nothing to worry about. If aggression and warfare develop in response to currently unchangeable biological programming, an ultimate war of mutual extermination seems inevitable. On the other hand, if aggression and warfare are just things that people have learned to do and that they can learn not to do, the chances of peace in our time are enhanced. The question even extends to esthetics, for if there are certain combinations of sound or forms of art that have an innate appeal, then it is possible to establish universal standards of art and beauty. Although these questions are all framed in nature–nurture terms, the answers to them will always involve some weighting of the relative contributions of nature and nurture.

Attempts to find solutions to questions of these kinds involve (1) the comparison of humanity with other animal species, (2) studies of the variability of the human species, and (3) studies of the impact of various kinds of environments upon human individuals or groups. All of these methods of solution are somewhat indirect and inconclusive. The only absolute way of knowing what the human genetic message contains is to decode it. This can be done in some degree with traits that follow simple Mendelian patterns of inheritance. A more general deciphering may someday result from current advances in molecular genetics.

The emphasis in comparisons of humanity with other species has inevitably been placed upon various closely related primate species. Because human beings are primates, it follows that biological characteristics shared by other primates, constituting what has been called a primate biogram, are likely to be shared by human beings as well. The search for evidence of culture or protoculture among primates has centered upon such close relatives as the chimpanzee. Wild chimpanzees, although they possess nothing as complicated as a human culture, have been observed to make use of simple tools and to maintain a rather complex set of social relationships both within and between groups. Although early efforts to raise chimpanzees with human infants were successful in some respects, chimpanzees tended to fall behind their adopted human siblings when the human children began to learn language. Although chimpanzees make a number of calls or meaningful sounds in the wild, attempts to teach chimpanzees to talk like human beings drew an almost complete blank. Later research, in which chimpanzees were trained to use gesture languages or special codes based on tokens, have proved much more successful and have shown that chimpanzees are capable of grasping some, perhaps all, of the basic principles upon which languages are based. With the natural enthusiasm of animal lovers everywhere, scholars responsible for this dramatically successful communication with chimpanzees have sometimes exaggerated the cleverness of their subjects. So far, laboratory-trained chimpanzees have had rather small vocabularies, and their dialogue is considerably less interesting than that of two-year-old human beings. It is apparent, however, that the evolutionary gap between humans and chimpanzees is much smaller than had previously been believed and that many of the differences are more quantitative than qualitative. Chimpanzees naturally use tools and can be trained to use gesture languages, but human beings do both things in much greater detail and much more frequently.

The systematic study of primates living in the wild or under naturalistic circumstances by ethologists and biological anthropologists has led to a host of interesting speculations about the biological bases of human behavior. Popular interpretations of early studies, especially of baboons, have created an extensive mythology concerning various supposedly biologically based forms of human behavior. Because baboons seemed to defend particular territories against invasion by other baboons, it was immediately assumed that baboons and human beings universally possessed an instinct or biogram for the defense of territory and that this provided the explanation for human warfare. When it was observed that baboon males exerted considerable dominance over baboon females, it was immediately concluded that subservience of the human female was biologically decreed.

As more and more studies of a variety of different primate species were completed and as research techniques became increasingly sophisticated, primatologists have displayed an increasing reluctance to leap to conclusions about the primate biogram. Differences in the extent of male dominance, in patterns of leadership, in techniques of child care, and in patterns of territoriality and aggression have been shown to exist not only between different species but within the same species under different environmental circumstances. In fact many forms of behavior that were initially thought to be manifestations of an inherited biogram have now been shown to be learned and transmitted within the troop by imitation. The evidence now points to the conclusion that the primate biogram lacks detailed specification, so that primate behavior including human behavior is primarily determined by learning and experience.[10]

A second approach to the development of hypotheses concerning the influence of biological factors upon culture is the comparison of a wide range of different cultures with a view to identifying universal characteristics. For example, Joseph Greenberg[11] has developed a series of characteristics of language that appear to be universal, and Noam Chomsky[12] has postulated the

---

[10] Hans Kummer, *Primate Societies: Group Techniques of Ecological Adaptation* (Chicago, New York: Aldine-Atherton, 1971).

[11] Joseph H. Greenberg, *Language Universals: With Special Reference to Feature Hierarchies* (The Hague: Mouton, 1966).

[12] Noam Chomsky, *Language and Mind*, Enlarged Edition (New York: Harcourt Brace Jovanovich, 1972).

existence of a basic biological format that underlies all language. George Peter Murdock[13] and other scholars have argued that the nuclear family is universal or virtually universal and for that reason probably represents a largely biologically determined optimum arrangement for rearing children or for carrying out economic activities.

Brent Berlin and Paul Kay[14] have examined the human use of color terms and have uncovered certain apparently universal relationships that suggest that our identification of particular colors within the entire spectrum of colors is biologically based. With Dennis Breedlove, Berlin has also identified certain common patterns that characterize all forms of human classifications of plants and animals.[15]Following the child psychologist Piaget, many anthropologists believe that the development of the child's abilities to think and to conceptualize may follow an orderly and universal pattern that is biological in origin. The universal tendency of human beings to divide labor and to organize societies in terms of age and sex has obvious biological implications, as do such closely related things as age at menstruation, length of pregnancy, frequency of births, and length of human generations. All of these things are, of course, affected by culture, but within limits set by species-specific biological characteristics. Incest taboos and exogamous rules affecting sexual relationships and patterns of intermarriage between brother and sister, father and daughter, or mother and son are virtually universal and are also believed by some to reflect biological predispositions.

The various aspects of culture including such broad headings as language, technology, social organization, politics, religion, art, play, and many narrower headings are also often considered to be universal and to reflect biological influences. Many universal aspects of culture may, however, be simply properties of culture having only indirect connections with any kind of biological programming. The incest taboo, for example, might reflect a specific biologically based abhorrence of sexual relationships with close relatives, but it might also reflect purely social advantages gained by sharply differentiating relatives and lovers or by compelling individuals to marry outside the family.

There are at least four ways in which a particular practice or behavior can come to be universal. It can be universal because it reflects some degree of biological programming, because it is part of or strongly implied by something else, because it represents the only possible solution to some particular and universal sort of adaptive problem, or because it represents an early and useful invention, such as the use of fire, that has spread among, or has been preserved within, most human cultures. A universal characteristic may become universal as a result of several or even all of the above factors. Inadequate data collection or misleading terminology—ethnographic error—can make things seem

---

[13] George P. Murdock, *Social Structure* (New York: Free Press, 1949).

[14] Brent Berlin and Paul Kay, *Basic Color Terms: Their Universality and Evolution* (Berkeley: University of California Press, 1969).

[15] B. Berlin, D. E. Breedlove, and P. H. Raven, "Folk Taxonomies and Biological Classifications," in S. A. Tyler (ed.), *Cognitive Anthropology* (New York: Holt, Rinehart and Winston, 1969), pp. 60–66.

universal that aren't, or make things seem not to be universal when they really are.

All of the universals listed in the above paragraphs exist because they are biologically possible. We cannot speak without mouths or make tools without hands. The question is, does any given universal reflect biological necessity or biological programming and if so in how much detail? The ability of chimpanzees to make use of systems of communication strongly resembling language strengthens the case for a biological predisposition toward the development and use of language, but at the same time, it weakens the case for the biological necessity of language: chimpanzees have the ability, but they never made the invention. Children reared in isolation by presumably psychotic parents often lose the ability to learn language, and it is conceivable that a group of human beings reared in isolation from infancy might never develop any sort of language. Even if they did develop a language resembling other languages in many details, we would have to consider the possibility that the development of language represents an adaptive solution to survival problems that is of biological origin only in the sense that it is possible. Isolated and uncultured individuals lacking any biological equipment for cutting or pounding would almost certainly develop cutting and pounding tools strongly resembling those used by other human beings. This, not necessarily because of any inherited predisposition to make such tools, but because they could hardly survive without them.

Traits, such as the sickle-cell gene, which can be demonstrated to be heritable and to be the source of serious human disease, can be reduced in importance by education and genetic counseling. Where traits are believed to be largely biological in origin, but where evidence is lacking concerning the means by which they are inherited, genetic counseling is likely to be an ineffective means of dealing with them. Granted the current state of our knowledge, a decision that a particular human characteristic is biologically programmed often amounts to a decision to do nothing about it. If sexual intercourse is biologically programmed, then sexual education is not needed. If war is biologically inevitable, then our only hope is to try to survive the next one. The error of deciding that a given human characteristic is biological in origin when in reality it is strongly affected by environmental factors is dangerous because it renders irremediable something that can be remedied. The error of assuming that a human characteristic is cultural in origin when it is really biological in origin may also have serious consequences in some cases. In most cases it merely leads to the application of unsuccessful remedies. Insofar as the question of maximizing human survival is concerned, the safest course would be to assume that the ills of humanity are mostly of cultural rather than of biological origin while agreeing that most human characteristics represent a combination of biological and cultural factors.

For example, although biological predispositions are undoubtedly factors in any kind of illness, many illnesses such as diabetes, heart disease, cancer, and stomach ulcer, once thought to be inherited, have now been shown to be strongly affected by environmental and cultural factors such as diet, exercise, and air pollution. Millions have died unnecessarily because inadequate consideration was given to the impact of environmental and cultural factors. For complex behavioral traits such as criminality, drug addiction, aggressiveness, poverty, and poor school performance, the assumption—without basis in fact—of overriding biological causation is equally dangerous and immoral.

6. Biology and Ability

It is a biological and social truism that some individuals do not perform the tasks of ordinary life as efficiently, as rapidly, or as neatly as others. Individuals who perform some tasks well may perform other tasks poorly. Even in the smallest and most isolated of human societies, different people are expected to perform different tasks, and products of their labors are not equally distributed among them. To some extent in all societies, the division of labor and the distribution of goods are connected with ability to perform but are also associated with such apparently arbitrary criteria as sex, age, or descent. In all human societies the task of explaining why some individuals receive the rewards of life, whereas other individuals do not, receives considerable attention.

Menangkabau men (Sumatra). (Courtesy of Lynn Thomas.)

Few of those charged with the responsibility of explaining the injustices of life are as honest as the Englishman who wrote, "Whatever happens we have got the gatling gun and they have not." Traditional societies, lacking the benefits of modern science, have generally justified things as they are by means of appeals to the supernatural. Inequitable distribution of food, work, or other resources and opportunities thus becomes a part of a divine plan laid down by the ancestors or by the deities. Because policies of fairness to all individuals and all classes are easier to speak about than to enforce, it follows that all societies require strong mythologies that explain the existence of unfairness and/or the necessity for it. If those who perform unpleasant tasks or receive proportionately small rewards are not convinced of the appropriateness of their position, serious trouble is likely to ensue.

In modern societies, as the religious bases of our social mythologies have been whittled away, there has been an inevitable tendency to develop scientific mythologies that would rationalize the unequal distribution of opportunities and resources. In the United States this has involved attempts to demonstrate that particular abilities are biologically inherited and that they are the characteristic properties of particular classes defined in terms of sex, age, or ethnic group.

Of course, there can be no argument about the fact that some abilities and disabilities are biologically inherited. Geneticists and biological anthropologists have successfully identified a substantial number of diseases and disabilities causing everything from slow death to color blindness which are inherited in simple Mendelian fashion. Abilities and disabilities inherited polygenically, that is, by several different genes acting together, are much harder to identify and much more likely to have their action modified or suppressed by environmental forces. Although particular small groups or breeding populations may sometimes be especially afflicted with particular genetic diseases, the overall distribution of genetic disease has not provided a firm basis for social discrimination. Genetic disease afflicts the rich and the poor. It is, in fact, one of the ironies of history that Queen Victoria possessed an X-chromosome containing a gene capable of causing hemophilia, or failure of the blood to clot. When this chromosome was passed on to her male descendants, it exerted a dominant influence because there was no opposing gene on the Y-chromosome, and therefore they suffered from hemophilia.

Although the quite general distribution of genetic disabilities, to say nothing of other known genetic characteristics, among the population of the world might lead some to abandon the search for a biological basis for social inequalities, a few unsophisticated researchers have attempted to discover real differences between social groups or classes and then to attempt to demonstrate that such differences are of biological origin. In its simplest and most naive form, this is accomplished by assuming that position in society provides a direct measure of biological ability. Thus the president of the company must be biologically superior to the janitor because otherwise their roles would be reversed. The assumption here is that life experience and training have nothing to do with achievement, and that both the president and the janitor had equal opportunities from the start.

With the development of psychological tests that could be used with some effectiveness to predict the individual's success in school or in particular kinds of jobs, it became possible to measure, at least roughly, the individual's capacity to perform certain tasks. The classic means of constructing such a test is to find a series of problems or questions that are solved or answered most readily by those who are skilled at some particular task. A test of the ability to play the bagpipe, for example, might include questions about the Loch Ness monster or the differences between a kilt and a tartan. Some might argue that persons scoring high on the test had a high natural or biological ability to play the bagpipe; others might argue that the test was primarily a test of Scottishness, the bagpipe being a Scottish instrument.

The intelligence test is a test that is relatively effective in predicting school grades and some other achievements. Exactly why it is called an intelligence test is one of the mysteries, but there are a great many people who believe that it measures intelligence and that intelligence is some kind of property that human beings and other animals possess. Because people who do well in school generally do well in a number of other phases of life, an intelligence test provides a means of identifying persons likely to do well in everything they attempt. Thus intelligence could be considered to be the capacity to do well in the sense of achieving the official goals of society. Just as in the case of the company president and the janitor, the assumption that the capacity to achieve a high intelligence test score is an inborn biological capacity requires a willing suspension of any belief in the effects of education or life experience.

Many scholars believe that the ability to score high on intelligence tests is an indication that the individual's life experience and education resemble that of the middle-class whites upon whom the tests were standardized. It is, of course, a simple task to construct tests upon which poor people or Hopi Indians score much higher than college students with high grade point averages. In many school districts in the United States Southwest, Spanish-speaking students have been routinely assigned to classes for the mentally retarded because of their low scores on English language intelligence tests. Such children perform quite adequately on Spanish language tests which their English-speaking classmates would be unable to read.

When intelligence tests or other measures of ability are applied in comparisons between ethnic groups, there are likely to be substantial average differences between groups. The average American black scores about fifteen points below the average American white on tests of intelligence designed for whites. Although these differences have been taken to imply a difference in inherited ability between the two ethnic groups, it can be explained as a result of cultural bias in the tests and as an expression of the different environments and life circumstances affecting the two ethnic groups.[16] A critical test of the hypothesis that the difference reflects a difference in inherited abilities would

[16] Jane Mercer, "Latent Functions of Intelligence Testing in the Public Schools," in L. T. Miller (ed.), *The Testing of Black Students* (Englewood Cliffs, N.J.: Prentice-Hall, 1974); S. Scarr-Salapatek, "Race, Social Class, and IQ," *Science,* **174**:1285–1295 (1971); Walter F. Bodmer and Luigi Luca Cavalli-Sforza, "Intelligence and Race," *Scientific American,* **223**:19–29 No. 4 (October 1970).

involve rearing large numbers of individuals from both groups under precisely equal environmental circumstances. Such a test cannot be performed under existing social conditions and would be immoral and unethical in any case.

The existence of any sort of average difference between two ethnic groups implies a considerable degree of overlap between them. Many blacks score higher on white intelligence tests than the average white. The argument that all blacks should receive special treatment because the average black scores lower than the average white on a white intelligence test is illogical. Even if white intelligence tests were measures of inherited ability—which they are not—special treatment should be accorded to all persons scoring low rather than to blacks regardless of whether they score high or low. If there were some characteristic upon which all blacks differed from all whites, knowledge of the individual's ethnic group membership might be useful. If possession of a low test score is the fact that justifies such actions as genocide, genetic counseling, special schools, denial of medical care, or special admissions policies,

Bukuria or Watende girls (Kenya and Tanganyika). (Courtesy of the United Nations.)

then the cures need to be applied to all who possess low test scores.[17] Within this context the issue of ethnic group membership is totally irrelevant, comparable to telling a 7-foot woman that she can't play basketball because females are too short to play.

The source of this particular sort of irrelevancy is the belief that ethnic groups are homogeneous biological entities whose members uniformly share particular characteristics. Studies of gene frequencies and distributions demonstrate that American ethnic groups, and even such groups as the aborigines of Australia, display a high degree of genetic variability quite comparable to that displayed by the species as a whole.

[17] For example, Jensen's arguments that intelligence test scores reflect inherited differences in ability have been used to argue in favor of the creation of special segregated schools for all Black children.

Afghan man exhibiting grapes (Afghanistan). (Courtesy of the United Nations.)

Anthropologist Clay Robarchek and Semai man (Malaysia). Individual representatives of widely separated populations may differ strikingly on such dimensions as stature. Differences in stature are strongly affected by such environmental influences as nutrition. Even if they were not, it would be difficult to classify human beings on such a basis because most human beings would fall between these two extremes. (Kindness of Clay and Carole Robarchek.)

In view of the history of racism and various other kinds of social discrimination, it is small wonder that most anthropologists regard with the greatest skepticism the repeated and persistent attempts to place labels of inferiority or disability on large segments of the world's population. None of these attempts have withstood the test of time and many of them have led to both systematic and unsystematic attempts at genocide and repression including the involuntary sterilization of teen-age black mothers of illegitimate children in some hospitals, the wholesale killing of subject populations in many modern states, and the denial of food and assistance to countries suffering from famine.

As pointed out previously, our existing knowledge of the role of biological factors in the development of the human individual deals primarily with traits inherited in simple Mendelian fashion. These traits, especially when they have to do with genetic diseases of various kinds, may have sweeping consequences for the comparatively small proportions of most populations that are affected by them. Polygenetic characteristics, those that are not inherited in simple Mendelian fashion, are much more common. The patterns of interrelationship between heredity and environment that determine the expression of such polygenetic traits are not understood, and there is no generally acceptable scientific methodology that permits even an approximate determination of the

relative contribution of heredity and environment in the development of socially valued abilities or performances. Until such a methodology has been
developed, all statements attributing genetic inferiority to groups of people
selected on the basis of sex, ethnic group identity, or nationality must be
regarded as unwarranted speculation.

The present state of our knowledge permits the conclusion that most
complex human abilities and performances are strongly influenced by environmental factors. For diseases, such as sickle-cell anemia, whose hereditary
basis is clearly understood, genetic counseling is a possible solution; for more
complex human characteristics environmental manipulations, such as providing improved diet, medical care, or education, are likely to provide workable solutions in most cases. Human abilities and performances, whether they
represent genetic or cultural inheritance or a combination of both, are often
the result of adaptations to particular environmental circumstances. Because
any of these characteristics is likely to be of adaptive significance in the future,
a strong case can be presented in favor of preserving and even increasing the
genetic and cultural variability of the human species.

7. Summary

Variation among human groups and individuals is the result of complex interactions between biological and environmental factors. In this chapter emphasis has been placed upon the role of biological factors in stimulating
human variation. Darwin's concepts of selection and adaptation combined
with Mendel's discovery of genetic inheritance form the basis of our understandings of the biological contribution to human variability. Mendel's principles of independent segregation and independent assortment provide the basic
explanation of individual biological uniqueness. Recent research on the structure of the gene has shown it to consist of a molecule of DNA capable of con-
veying complex messages by means of arrangements of the bases—adenine,
thymine, cytosine, and guanine. Because these bases are arranged in pairs connecting the twisted strands of the DNA molecule, separation of the strands
leads to replication of the DNA molecule as each base attaches itself to a fresh
complementary base. This is the basic mechanism of reproduction.

DNA molecules are generally linked together to form chromosomes. In
normal cell division, or mitosis, the chromosomes reproduce themselves, and
two new cells are formed each containing chromosomes identical to those
contained in the parent cell. In meiosis, or sexual reproduction, the number of
chromosomes in each of the two new cells is reduced by half. When two such
cells—an ovum and a sperm—combine, the result is a zygote possessing the
normal complement of chromosomes. Females are formed by the combination
of an X- and a Y-chromosome. The individual is formed by the normal cell
division of the zygote in response to the action of the matched pairs of genes
located on the 23 paired chromosomes. The individual derives half of his
genes from each parent, the selection of genes from each parent being deter-

mined by random assortment of the chromosomes. Thus it is impossible to predict which genes the individual will acquire from each parent.

The selective advantage conveyed by sexual reproduction appears to lie in the fact that the offspring are different from the parents and the population is therefore more variable than would be possible under vegetative or mitotic reproduction. The resulting variation permits change in the genetic message, as processes of selection permit some and not others to survive and reproduce. Changes or mutations in the genetic message resulting from environmental disturbance or faulty replication of genes, chromosomes, or cells serve as the original source of variation upon which selection operates. When a new gene is formed, it is likely to occupy the same position on the chromosome as the old gene from which it was derived. Alleles, or alternative genes on the same chromosome locus, may be dominant or recessive. Because a dominant gene can obscure the presence of a recessive gene, a distinction has to be made between an individual's genotype, or genetic makeup, and the phenotype, or external appearance. When the individual receives the same allele from each parent, it is homozygous; when it receives different alleles, it is heterozygous. Although many characteristics are inherited by means of alleles, other characteristics are inherited polygenically as the result of the action of several genes located on different chromosomes or on different locations on the same chromosome. Most human characteristics, especially those considered socially important, are inherited polygenically. This means that the inheritance of particular characteristics tends to be unpredictable. This unpredictability is enhanced by the fact that the expression of each gene may be deeply influenced by environmental factors.

One fundamental unit of human biology is the breeding population. Breeding populations have no necessary connection with populations that speak the same language, share the same cultural tradition, or belong to the same social group. Biological differences between human breeding populations depend upon the extent to which they are reproductively isolated. The founder effect is observed when individuals, possibly representing a single family or lineage in a larger breeding population, form a new and reproductively isolated population. Once a new population has been formed, processes of mutation, selection, and genetic drift will increase the contrasts between the new population and the ancestral population. Among human beings the length of the generation and the tendency to avoid total reproductive isolation have prevented the development of strong biological differences between human populations while enhancing the variability of individuals within populations. Thus the human species is said to be polymorphic, or possessing many shapes.

Differences between human populations generally have to be expressed in terms of differences in the frequency of particular phenotypic or genetic characteristics. The geographical distribution of most human traits follows a clinal pattern. Where they do not, the distributions of different genes are generally not isomorphic. As a result there are formidable obstacles in the way of any attempt to subdivide the human population into races, varieties, or other biological units larger than the breeding population. *Homo sapiens* represents a single, unified biological species, all of whose members share the same basic biological adaptations. Observed differences in the behavior and daily activity of the members of different human groups represent learned patterns transmitted within each society by means of language and example—in a word, culture.

The best documented example of the interaction between human culture and human biology is found in the relationships among the sickle-cell gene, falciparum malaria, and agricultural practices that encourage the multiplication of malarial mosquitoes. The length of human generations, the comparatively recent emergence of *Homo sapiens*, and the comparatively recent development of agriculture and industrialization, all conspire to obscure the exact relationships between human biological evolution and human cultural evolution. Nevertheless there is every reason to believe that cultural factors are exerting ever-increasing influence upon human biology and they may eventually lead to the emergence of consciously planned biological evolution and "genetic engineering." For the present it is apparent that marriage rules, patterns of migration, and other cultural factors have always had an impressive influence upon the biological makeup of human breeding populations and have played an important role in the acceleration of human biological evolution.

There is no sharp dividing line between nature and nurture, or heredity and environment. Both work together to produce the individual. Scientific research concerning heredity and environment is concerned with the manner in which they interact in order to do so. One such topic of research has to do with the identification of the biological factors that lead to the development of species-specific characteristics among human beings. Although several strategies are available for identifying human species-specific characteristics, all of them lead to results that are somewhat inconclusive. Studies of closely related primates have led to a number of speculations concerning the existence of a primate biogram, but the extreme variation even among nonhuman primates seems to suggest that the primate biogram lacks detailed specification. In the same way, comparison of existing human societies has led to the identification of a number of universals, but it is not known how closely these universals are linked to biological factors because there are other ways in which a human characteristic can become universal. The assumption that any human characteristic is completely or largely biological in origin may have dangerous social consequences. In most cases, where action must be taken to solve human problems, it is safest to proceed under the assumption that a remedy lies in the manipulation of environmental and cultural factors.

Within any society individuals differ in their ability to perform particular tasks. The distribution of material goods and other rewards is often associated with this fact, but it may also be associated with such arbitrary criteria as sex, age, or descent. The existence of social injustice or unequal distribution means that in most societies mythologies are developed to explain it. In the United States inequitable distribution is often justified in terms of mythologies concerning the biological inheritance of particular abilities or disabilities. Because known and identified genetic disabilities are rarely distributed in an appropriate manner that would explain existing inequalities, there has been a tendency to identify differences between social groups or classes and then to attempt to explain them in biological terms. This tendency has been accelerated by the development of psychological tests, particularly "intelligence" tests, and the assumption that such tests measure biologically derived abilities. Most scholars now believe that such tests reflect cultural differences far more than they reflect biological differences. There is no generally acceptable scientific methodology that permits even an approximate determination of the relative contribution of heredity and environment in the development of socially valued abilities or performances. Statements attributing genetic inferiority to groups of people selected on the basis of sex, ethnic group identity, or nationality represent unwarranted and malicious speculation.

Collateral Readings

Asimov, Isaac. *The Genetic Code.* New York: The New American Library, Inc., 1962. A popular version by a fine writer.

Birdsell, Joseph B. *Human Evolution, An Introduction to the New Physical Anthropology,* 2d ed. Skokie, Ill.: Rand McNally & Co., 1975. An outstanding textbook.

Boas, Franz. *Race, Language, and Culture.* New York: Macmillan Publishing Co., Inc., 1940. Collected articles by the "father" of American Anthropology.

Brace, C. Loring, Geroge R. Gamble, and James T. Bond (eds.). *Race and Intelligence.* Washington, D.C.: American Anthropological Association, 1971.

Buettner-Janusch, John. *Physical Anthropology: A Perspective.* New York: John Wiley & Sons, Inc. A major textbook.

Clarke, Bryan. "The Causes of Biological Diversity," *Scientific American* (August 1975), pp. 50–60. Summarizes recent findings.

DeVore, Irven (ed.). *Primate Behavior: Field Studies of Monkeys and Apes.* New York: Holt, Rinehart and Winston, Inc., 1965. Relatively new perspectives on behavior in natural settings.

Dobzhansky, Theodosius G. *Genetic Diversity and Human Equality.* New York: Basic Books, Inc., 1973. Popular discussion of race, heredity, etc.

Dolhinow, Phyllis, and Vincent M. Sarich. *Background for Man, Readings in Physical Anthropology.* Boston: Little, Brown and Company, 1971. A good, basic reader.

Katz, Solomon H. *Biological Anthropology, Readings from Scientific American.* San Francisco: W. H. Freeman and Co., 1975. Well and popularly written articles by the giants in the field.

Lerner, I. Michael. *Heredity, Evolution, and Society.* San Francisco: W. H. Freeman and Co., 1968. A biologist's lucid explanation of genetics and human genetics.

Mourant, A. E., et al. *The Distribution of Human Blood Groups and Other Polymorphisms,* 2d ed. (Oxford Monographs on Medical Genetics) New York: Oxford University Press, 1974.

Sayre, Anne. *Rosalind Franklin & DNA.* New York: W. W. Norton & Company, Inc., 1975. Argues for recognition of Franklin's contribution to discovering the structure of DNA.

Stocking, George W., Jr. *Race, Culture and Evolution: Essays in the History of Anthropology.* New York: The Free Press, 1968. A study of changing anthropological views of race.

Watson, James D. *The Double Helix, A Personal Account of the Discovery of the Structure of DNA.* New York: The New American Library, Inc., 1969. An innocent abroad in the laboratory.

Watson, James D. *Molecular Biology of the Gene,* 2d ed. New York and Amsterdam: W. A. Benjamin, Inc., 1970. A clear and useful summary.

5/ The Evolution of Humanity

1. Humans as Biological Organisms

Two major themes of biological anthropology are basic to anthropology as a whole. The first, discussed in the preceding chapter, has to do with the contribution of human biological variability to human variability in general. The second, which forms the subject of this chapter, has to do with the evolution of the human bodily form and the development of biological predispositions toward the use of language and culture. The origin and history of human beings as biological organisms can be partly understood through a knowledge of the place of human beings in the biological scheme of things. The place of human beings within the standard scheme of biological classification is as follows:

(1) The animal kingdom divides into two grades: Protozoa, or single-celled animals, and Metazoa, or many-celled animals. Human beings belong to the Metazoa.

(2) Within the Metazoa, human beings belong to the phylum Chordata and the subphylum Vertebrata. The chordata, or chordates, are animals whose nervous systems are organized by a long chord running lengthwise. Among the Vertebrata, or vertebrates, the chord has a bony covering.

Figure 5–1

Man's place in nature summarized:

Kingdom	Animalia
Phylum	Chordata
Class	Mammalia
Order	Primates
Family	Hominidae
Genus	Homo
species	sapiens

(3) Within the Vertebrata, human beings belong to the class Mammalia, characterized in part by the possession of mammary glands for suckling the young, and to the subclass Eutheria or placental mammals, who possess an internal structure designed to nourish the fetus between conception and birth.

(4) Within the Eutheria, human beings belong to the Primate order, most easily distinguished from other closely related orders by the possession of flat fingernails and toenails. The Primate order includes all of the apes and monkeys, as well as such animals as lemurs, tarsiers, and lorises who are thought to be precursors of the monkeys or simians and are assigned to the suborder Prosimii. Human beings, along with monkeys and apes, belong to the suborder Anthropoidea.

(5) Within the Anthropoidea, human beings are assigned to the superfamily Hominoidea, which includes the apes. Old World monkeys belong to the superfamily Cercopithicoidea; New World monkeys belong to the Ceboidea.

(6) Within the Hominoidea, human beings belong to the Hominidae, which includes modern human beings as well as a number of extinct forms resembling human beings. The great apes, such as the orangutan, gorilla, and chimpanzee, belong to the family Pongidae; the smaller gibbon is usually placed in a third family.

(7) Within the Hominidae, or human family, all modern human beings are classified as members of the genus *Homo*. Some scholars regard most extinct humanlike forms as early representatives of the genus *Homo;* others believe that there have been several genera of Hominidae, all but *Homo* having become extinct.

(8) Within the genus *Homo*, modern human beings and their ancestors for at least the past 50,000 years or so belong to the single species *sapiens*.

(9) Within the species *sapiens*, human beings are sometimes divided into races or varieties. There is no generally accepted or consistent classification of such subdivisions of *Homo sapiens* into racial types or varieties.

The foregoing classification was originally intended as a means of arranging all animals in such a way as to indicate the fundamental resemblances between them. Monkeys, apes, and humans are classed together as Anthropoidea, because they resemble each other more closely than they resemble dogs, cats, or horses, which belong to other orders and suborders. For evolu-

Ring-tailed lemur, *Lemur catta*. Modern lemurs resemble early primate forms. Babies must achieve ability to cling to mother's fur soon after birth. (San Diego Zoo photo by Ron Garrison.)

Figure 5–2 Primate forms. Similarities among the different primate families suggest their common origin from early generalized forms perhaps resembling the lemur or tarsius.

Mindanao tarsier, *Tarsius syrichta carbonarius*. A modern form of an early type of primate. Six-day-old baby can already cling to branch. (San Diego Zoo photo.)

Orangutan (Bornean), *Pongo pygmaens pygamaens*. (San Diego Zoo photo.)

tionary purposes, it is assumed that the animals in each order, family, genus, or species share a common ancestral species from which they evolved through processes of biological evolution.

2. Key Problems in Evolution

Evolutionary theory is a means of accounting for the diversity of living forms and the emergence of new species and varieties. It seeks to understand the means through which an ancestral species can give rise to new forms and is based upon the idea that biological variation can be largely accounted for in terms of the impact of selection upon the mechanisms of biological inheritance.

Speaking of biological inheritance, it is a commonsense observation that like produces like. Cats give birth to cats, and birds produce birds. Close ob-

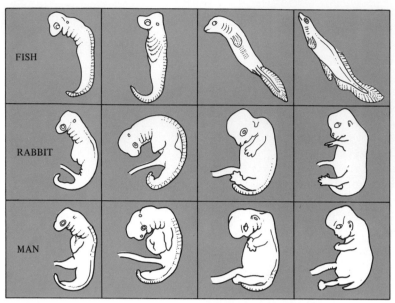

Figure 5–3 Comparison of embryological development of fish, rabbit, and man. Note similarity in early stages and progressive divergence in later stages. Such similarities are considered evidence of a common evolutionary origin.

servation reveals that cats and kittens or hens and chickens do not precisely resemble each other. Each living organism is unique, just as every snowflake is unique. Cats resemble other cats more closely than they resemble any other living thing, but each cat is also a unique individual. This fact of variation within limits is inherent in the basic processes of sexual reproduction. The way in which reproduction leads to variation was discussed in Chapter 4. The important point here is the fact of *continuous variability* within species.

Another commonsense observation is that in order to survive, any organism must be able to gain food and energy from its environment and to withstand such threats as extremes of moisture and temperature, or attack by predators. Species and individuals within species differ in their ability to use the environment or to defend themselves from its threats to their survival. Some organisms can survive in a variety of environments; some organisms are specialized to survive in particular environments or on particular kinds of food. Species are adapted to particular environments and are equipped to use only particular parts of the environment. On a smaller scale, the same is true of individual plants and animals.

Those species whose members are better adapted to the environment in which they live than are members of competing species are more likely to survive and multiply. When species occupy stable or unchanging environments, they are likely to achieve adaptations that permit them to survive with little change over many millions of years. Although some of the one-celled animals, or Protozoans, presumably represent the earliest animal forms, their adaptations were evidently sufficient to permit their long-term survival without embarking upon such daring experiments as multicellularity.

When the environment changes or when individual members of a species find themselves confronted with a new and different environment, those individuals who manage to survive and produce offspring are likely to be quite different from those individuals who failed to do so. Species that adopt or have forced upon them the strategy of occupying a single unchanging environment and using its resources in a particular way are generally described as *specialized*. Species that adopt the strategy of occupying a variety of environments and/or using their resources in a number of ways are described as *generalized*. Generalized species are more capable of surviving environmental changes than are specialized species, but specialized species are usually more capable of surviving in unchanging environments. Some species may be generalized in some respects and specialized in others. Human beings are usually regarded as generalized animals because they occupy a wide variety of environments and because they possess relatively few specialized organs. The concepts of gener-

Baboons, like human beings, spend most of their time on the ground. Also, like human beings, they make use of their tree-climbing adaptation when faced with danger. (Kindness of S. L. Washburn.)

alization and specialization need not have much to do with the relative complexity of organs. The primate brain, most particularly the human brain, is large and complex but it tends to be used for generalized rather than specialized adaptations. The fossil record suggests that the general trend of evolution has been from very simple and generalized forms in the oldest geological periods towards more complex and specialized forms in recent times (see Figure 5–7). Human beings are presumably an exception to this tendency, for although they are complex, they are generalized.

The view of human beings as generalized animals pertains, however, to an exclusively physiological view of the species. The human biological ability to develop culture as a means of adapting to particular environments means that in behavioral terms human beings should be regarded as highly specialized. The difference between human specializations and the specializations characteristic of physiologically specialized animals is that human beings are capable of rapidly altering their specializations to suit changing environmental circumstances. The development of culture resolves the ancient contrast between

Early human beings are thought to have evolved in close association with other animals. Ungulates have acute senses of smell and hearing, and primates have acute vision. Thus predators are unlikely to escape detection. (Kindness of S. L. Washburn.)

A feature of baboon adaptation is a complex social organization. Note juvenile in front while two males guard mother and child. (Kindness of S. L. Washburn.)

generalized animals that can live in many environments and specialized animals that can survive in only one. The generalized human being simply adopts new cultural specializations as he moves from one environment to another. The human pattern of adapting through learning rather than through genetic change is evident in the other primates as well. The more typical pattern of adaptation through increasing biological specialization is illustrated by the evolution of the horse.

The horse evolved more or less at the same time as the primates (see Figure 5–4). The ancestors of the horse in the Eocene, which ended about fifty million years ago, were small animals that ran on their toes. Horses gradually grew larger and became increasingly specialized in the consumption of grasses and similar plants and in the use of speed to escape predators. Accompanying

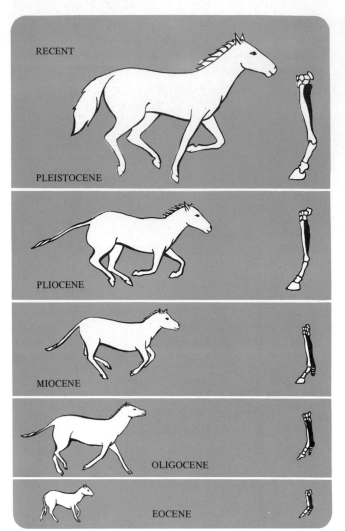

RECENT

PLEISTOCENE

PLIOCENE

MIOCENE

OLIGOCENE

EOCENE

Figure 5–4 Evolution of the horse from a small forerunner. On right, the sequence of changes in the limbs with the development of hooves.

these changes were modifications of the teeth for cutting and grinding rather than tearing food and modifications of the original five-toed feet to a large central toe with the claw or nail characteristic of most mammals modified into a hoof and the other toes reduced to insignificance.

New species can be formed either when an entire species responds to changes in the environment or when individual members of a species find themselves in a new environment and begin to acquire adaptations not shared with the remainder of their species. Both of these processes of species formation depend upon changes or mutations that affect the genetic code governing the development and reproduction of the organism. Although various accidents and statistical variations can produce differences between groups of animals belonging to the same species, the major cause of species formation lies in the fact that any particular environment encourages the survival of some individuals, their offspring, and their genes more than it encourages the survival of others. When a species has a geographically limited distribution or is sufficiently mobile so that interbreeding leads to a widespread distribution of new adaptations, a series of cumulative genetic variations may lead to progressive change in the entire species. In such a case, when an entire species gradually changes into another species over time, both species are usually described as *temporal* species.

When individual members of a species are reproductively isolated from other members of the species, especially when they occupy a different and more difficult environment, they are likely to develop more rapidly and along different lines from those followed by the members of their original species. In time, accumulating variations may make interbreeding between the isolated group and the original species impossible. At this point, sometimes even sooner, the isolated group is generally considered to form a new and separate species. Such a new species may spread out from its original location through what is called *adaptive radiation* and ultimately replace the parent species, or, if it has become adapted to a radically different environmental niche, it and its parent species may both continue to exist. Similar species rarely coexist in the same environment because they are likely to be in competition for the same resources.

Many of these key problems in evolution have a particular relevance for the human species. For example, human beings display a great deal of individual variation. Important questions have to do with how long this has been the case and whether such variation allows the setting up of classifications within the species in terms of race or variety. Because human evolution took place quite rapidly, we are faced with the problem of trying to identify environmental circumstances that might explain such rapid biological change. Although human beings display many characteristics of generalized animals, they are nevertheless highly specialized in some ways. Interesting questions revolve around the nature of these specializations and the extent to which they can be interpreted in the same way as specializations characteristic of other animals. Finally, although it is generally believed that human evolution involved a succession of temporal species, it is also considered possible that a variety of different geographical species or even genera of humanlike forms existed at certain periods of time. There is some suspicion that closely related species of human beings coexisted during some time periods, and that some geographical species underwent adaptive radiation and replaced other species which then became extinct.

3. Aspects of Human Evolution

Although human beings are generalized in terms of their ability to adapt to a wide variety of environments, many of the adaptations that set human beings apart from other animals are connected with the development of complex

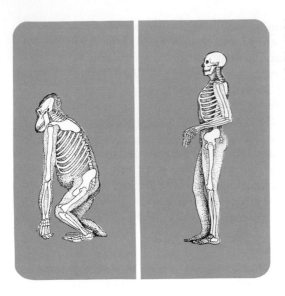

Figure 5–5 A generalized ape and human being, showing differences in posture, limb proportions, other skeletal differences, and the different distribution of the fleshy parts of the body.

organs. Humans are the only mammals that characteristically stand and walk (bipedal locomotion) in an upright posture (Figure 5–5). The adoption of an upright posture has been accompanied by specialized changes in the structure of human feet, legs, spinal chord, and head. In the skull the *foramen magnum*, or entryway for nerves leading from the spinal chord into the skull, has moved from the back of the skull to its base, while the face has shifted forward (Figure 5–6). The development of bipedal locomotion was presumably synchronous with increased use of the hands for the manipulation of objects. The adaptive advantages of skillful manipulation appear to have led to the development of an opposable thumb. The thumb permits utilization of a precision grip that gives humans a greater capacity for fine manipulations than other primates.

Figure 5–6 Chimpanzee and human, showing difference in the form of skull and position of the foramen magnum and differences in eyebrow ridges, face, and relations of the jaw. Shaded areas suggest fleshy parts.

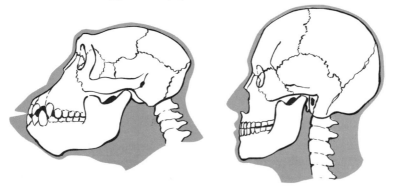

Baboon mother carrying her dead child. Strong maternal sentiments are an important factor in the survival of comparatively helpless human infants. Even among nonhuman primates, there is some evidence that such sentiments are aquired through the mother's own experience of maternal care. (Courtesy S. L. Washburn.)

A human baby is incapable of holding on. As among many other primates, baby can be "mothered" by other members of group, in this case an older sister. Gopalpur, South India. (Photo by Alan Beals.)

The most significant of the human adaptations involved the development of a large and complex brain. Increasing brain size and complexity seem to be a characteristic of primate evolution and may have been stimulated by the need for maintaining complex social relationships within the primate troop. Ultimately, in human beings, the increasing ability to remember and calculate led to the development of the ability to symbolize, that is, to invent and share arbitrarily established meanings that form the basis of language and of human social interaction.

The ancestors of humanity appear to have been erect bipedal primates having a long period of gestation or pregnancy and whose young were born singly and in a relatively helpless state. Where primate babies are typically able to cling to their mother's fur, the human, and presumably protohuman baby, had to be carried either because it was too weak to hang on or there was no fur for it to hang on to. The need to care for the baby and its mother probably increased the necessity for social living and for the development of new forms of cooperation which were enhanced by an improved capacity to communicate and remember.

The structure of the human shoulders and arms, ideally designed for swinging from branches (brachiating), serves as a reminder of a primate, tree-dwelling past. Many primates, such as baboons and probably the early forms of humanity, developed adaptations to grassland and parkland regions. Human bipedal locomotion may well be an adaptation to such regions, while the relative hairlessness and other complicated properties of the human skin

Baboons, wildebeeste, and zebra at water hold in Tanzania, East Africa. Australopithecines may have evolved in an environment similar to this. (Kindness of S. L. Washburn.)

Chimpanzee, *Pan troglodytes*. The ability to brachiate is shared by human beings. Note position of thumb. (San Diego Zoo photo.)

may have been an adaptation to the heat of tropical grasslands. Adaptation to a plains environment, perhaps some nine to fifteen million years ago, may also have marked the separation of the hominids from their close pongid relatives, the gorillas and chimpanzees, who either remained in the forests or much later retreated from the plains in the face of hominid competition.

4. When Is a Human?

Because the evolution of a new species involves a slow process of gradual modification, it has always been difficult to identify the point in time at which the hominid and pongid lines separated. It is equally difficult to assign a point in time for the emergence of the genus *Homo* or the species *sapiens*. Recently the general pattern of hominid evolution has been clarified by the discovery of

ERA	MILLIONS OF YEARS AGO	PERIOD	IMPORTANT EVENTS
CENOZOIC	0 3 65	Quaternary	Evolution of Genus *Homo*
		Tertiary	Expansion of mammals
MESOZOIC	135 180 225	Cretaceous	Dinosaurs dominant; placental mammals and flowering plants appear
		Jurassic	Dinosaurs dominant; first birds; first mammals
		Triassic	First dinosaurs and mammal-like reptiles; conifers abundant
PALEAOZOIC	270 350 400 440 500 600	Permian	Primitive reptiles become increasingly dominant
		Carboniferous	Amphibians dominant; extensive forests; first reptiles and trees
		Devonian	Fish dominant; first amphibians
		Silurian	Sea scorpions; primitive fish; invasion of land by plants and arthropods. Terrestrial species
		Ordovician	First vertebrates; invertebrates dominate seas
		Cambrian	All invertebrate phyla present. Abundant record of marine life
PRECAMBRIAN			First fossils by 3.3 billion years ago

Figure 5–7 Geological Time Scale Showing Major Eras and Periods.

Figure 5–8 Geological Time Scale for the Cenozoic Era. (Dates from William A. Berggren, "A Cenozoic Time Scale – Some Implications for Regional Geology and Paleography, "*Lethaia* 5:195–215.)

PERIOD	MILLIONS OF YEARS AGO	EPOCH	IMPORTANT EVENTS
Quaternary	00.01 3.0	Recent	Modern animals and Homo sapiens
		Pleistocene	Giant mammals, now extinct; and evolution of Genus Homo
Tertiary	12.0 22.5 37.5 53.5 65	Pliocene	Large carnivores, pomgids, and hominids
		Miocene	Dryopithecus; abundant grazing mammals
		Oligocene	Large running mammals
		Eocene	Modern types of mammals
		Paleocene	Diversified hoofed mammals

148

Lowland gorilla (juvenile), *Gorilla gorilla.* An erect posture makes it possible to carry objects in the hands. The gorilla's curving spine and feet designed for grasping make the position somewhat awkward. (San Diego Zoo photo.)

additional fossil materials and by the development of increasingly exact ways of dating such finds. The issues mentioned above concerning the precise temporal boundaries between apelike and humanlike, as well as the possibility that particular fossils represented side branches that became extinct and not directly ancestral forms, will never be completely resolved. Nature, on the whole, is not as neatly compartmented as human beings would like it to be.

Most students of fossil humans believe that the ancestor of the Hominoidea was a species of *Dryopithecus,* a varied genus that lived in Asia, in Africa, and in Europe from the Miocene well into the Pliocene. Although the evidence concerning *Dryopithecus* consists mainly of teeth and incomplete jawbones, the teeth, especially their crowns, have a hominoid form. This,

Lowland gorilla (juvenile). A faster and more comfortable way of getting around, but the hands must remain empty. (San Diego Zoo photo by Ron Garrison.)

combined with the fact that there are no other serious contenders for the position, has led scholars to conclude that the *Dryopithecus* genus is most probably ancestral to present-day apes and humans.

Two finds from India and Africa, considered to be between nine and fifteen million years old, seem to fall in a transitional zone between the dryopithecines and the hominids and pongids. The oldest of these finds, currently labeled *Ramapithecus wickeri*, was found in Kenya. Although, like most dryopithecines, it is represented mainly by teeth and jawbones, the teeth display a number of features such as greatly reduced canine teeth that are more humanoid than apelike. *Ramapithecus punjabicus*, found in Northwestern India, is believed to be between nine and fourteen million years old. This second version of Ramapithecus, probably more recent than the first, has teeth and jawbones that seem even more humanoid than those of *Ramapithecus wickeri*.

Some scholars have felt that *Ramapithecus* was too recent to serve as an ancestor for the hominids and have accordingly searched without much result for older and more suitable ancestors; others have come to feel that *Ramapithecus*

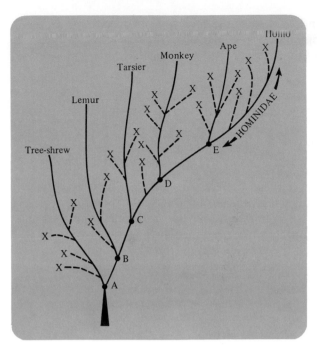

Figure 5–9 Probable ancestral development of the family *Hominoidea* and their living primate relatives. The capital letters represent points of divergence or probable common ancestral form; the broken lines ending in X's suggest the former existence of collateral lines that became extinct and have no living descendants.

is not recent enough. This last view derives in part from a "molecular" time scale based upon the presumably steady rate of evolution of proteins. Comparing the proteins in blood serum albumin and the genetic material known as DNA (see Chapter 4, §1) from humans and other living primates, Wilson and Sarich have discovered close similarities among the chimpanzee and modern human beings.[1] On the basis of knowledge of the length of time required for the development of differences between the protein molecules of different species, Wilson and Sarich argue that the separation of pongids and hominids must have occurred less than five million years ago. Recent studies of chimpanzee abilities in the learning of languagelike codes and in the use of tools also suggest a closer affinity between human beings and gorillas and chimpanzees than had been thought to exist. One possibility is that chimpanzees and gorillas represent late adaptations to forest environments and that their ancestors might have been much more like hominids than the modern forms. Although current opinion favors the idea that *Ramapithecus* is ancestral to the hominids and not to the pongids, the possibility that he is ancestral to both cannot be neglected.

Although *Ramapithecus'* unique possession of a humanoid set of teeth is enough to create the suspicion that he belongs somewhere in our ancestry, most of us would prefer that an ancestor displayed signs of intelligence and behavior resembling our own. Ideally a human ancestor would demonstrate humanity by occupying a comparatively large part of the earth's surface, by

[1] A. C. Wilson and V. M. Sarich, "A Molecular Time Scale for Human Evolution," *Proc. Nat. Acad. Sci.*, Washington, **63**:1088–1093 (1969).

using tools or something like tools, and by displaying evidence of the possession of something like culture and language. In the past years the existence of such an ancestor has become increasingly evident.

5. The Toolmaking Australopithicinae

When the first *Australopithecus* fossil was found in 1925 by Raymond Dart (1893–   ) of Johannesburg, South Africa, it was viewed as an ape with some humanlike characteristics. Subsequent finds made by Dart and by R. Broom (1866–1951) of the Transvaal Museum suggested there were two main types, *Australopithecus africanus*, a small form weighing perhaps 50 to 60 pounds, and a large form that weighed about twice as much. As new australopithecines were found in other parts of Africa a number of different genus names were applied to them. Recent reviews of the evidence concerning the australopithecines by Tobias and Campbell[2] suggest an emerging consensus that there was

[2] Phillip V. Tobias, "New Developments in Hominid Paleontology in South and East Africa," *Annual Review of Anthropology,* **2:**311–334 (1974); Bernard J. Campbell, "Conceptual Progress in Physical Anthropology: Fossil Man," *Annual Review of Anthropology,* **1:**27–54 (1972).

Adult male chimpanzee skull and jaw. Note low vault to skull, heavy jaw and eyebrow ridges, absence of projecting nasal bones, massive canine teeth, and forward projection of the upper jaw. (Courtesy CGM: General Biological, Inc., Chicago.)

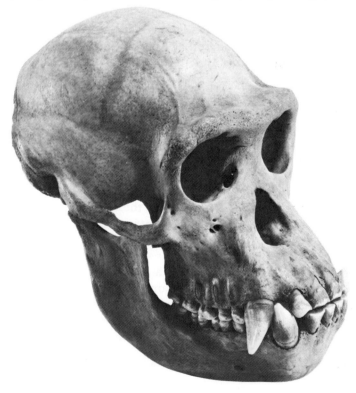

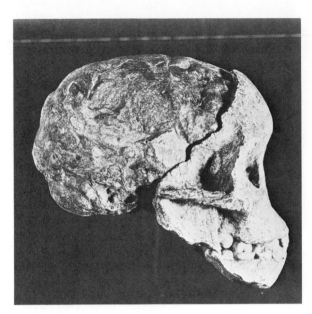

Skull and jaw of *Australopithecus africanus*. Note rounded forehead, absence of brow ridges, relatively light jaw without projecting canines, and some projection of nasal region but with projection of jaw region and absence of chin. (Courtesy of the American Museum of Natural History.)

probably only one genus of australopithecine, divided into two or three species. Of these species, *africanus* resembles later hominid fossils sufficiently to permit the conclusion that it is directly ancestral to humanity. Because substantial numbers of *africanus* fossils have been found including many critical parts of the skeleton, such as hands, long bones, pelvises, jaws and skulls, *africanus'* status as a human ancestor is unlikely to change.

Australopithecus africanus was an erect bipedal creature. In such critical features as the form of the foot and hand, the shape of the pelvis, the nature of the teeth, and the shape of the skull, *africanus* is more human than apelike. The relatively recent dates assigned to some *africanus* fossils and the relatively small size of most *africanus* brains originally created some doubt concerning the correctness of the conclusion that *africanus* was ancestral to humanity. The early belief that *africanus* lived too recently to qualify as a human ancestor has now been modified. New and more reliable dating techniques now place the most recent *africanus* finds at some 2.5 million years ago instead of 0.5 million years. *Africanus* is now thought to have existed and, of course, to have evolved over a period stretching from 5.0 to 2.5 million years ago and is, thus, considerably more recent than *Ramapithecus*. The size of *africanus'* brain, recently calculated at an average of 442 cubic centimeters, is, if body size is taken into account, relatively large for a small animal. Recent research also indicates that the australopithecine brain possessed hominid features uncharacteristic of the pongids.[3] It is also suspected that *africanus* and other australopithecine species made use of crude tools, but the evidence for this is somewhat tentative.

[3] Ralph L. Holloway, "The Casts of Fossil Hominid Brains," *Scientific American*, **231**:106–115, No. 1 (July 1974).

Figure 5–10 Skull of *Zinjanthropus* (now classed as *Australopithecus*). Note the small crest at top, heaviness of eye orbits, massive jaw, and thick skull.

Information concerning the use of tools either by australopithecines or by early humans stems largely from excavations conducted by L. S. B. (1903–1972) and Mary Leakey (1913–   ) and their associates in the Olduvai Gorge in Tanzania (Figure 5–12). On July 17, 1959, Mary Leakey found a fragment of a skull (Figure 5–10) resting on what proved to be a definite living floor; that is, a clearly identifiable level bearing signs of occupation including tools and the bones of animals used as food. Later, remains of several additional individuals were found at about the same level.

The Leakeys named their first find *Zinjanthropus boisei* on the grounds that it differed significantly from previously known australopithecines. Some

Figure 5–11 Australopithecine skull and pelvis. In total configuration, both are more human than apelike.

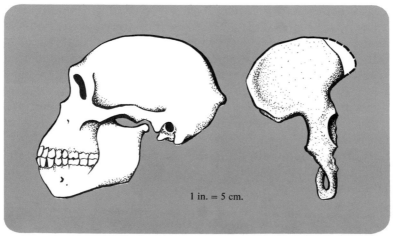

1 in. = 5 cm.

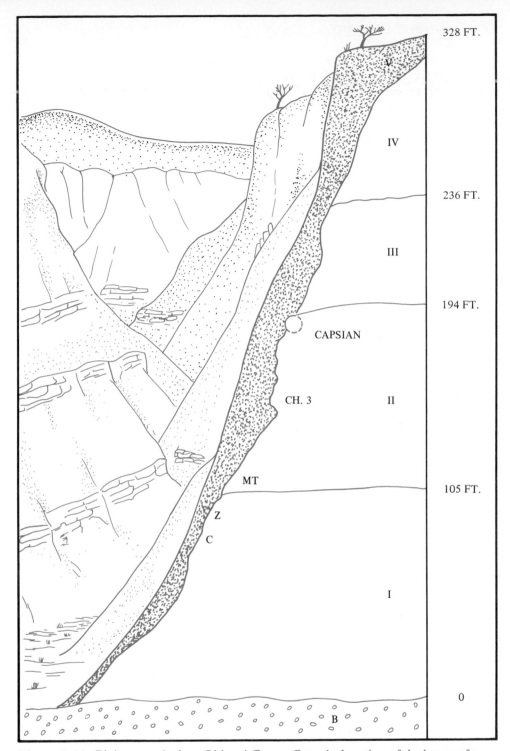

Figure 5–12 Pleistocene beds at Olduvai Gorge. C marks location of the bones of a child; Z, the Zinjanthropus skull; MT, two humanlike milk teeth; CH. 3, the Chellean 3 skull, now considered *Homo erectus;* and *Capsian,* a complete skeleton of Capsian age found in bed V by Hans Beck. (After Coon and Aroumberg.) Evidence of a living floor with stones piled into a crude wall formation have been found at the lowest level and are dated at about 1.8 million years ago.

155

subsequent finds were also assigned to the same genus. Other finds were believed to belong to an early example of the genus *Homo* and were assigned the name *Homo habilis*. As a result of revisions in the classification of the australopithecines, *Zinjanthropus* is now called *Australopithecus boisei*. The Leakeys' original belief that *habilis* and *boisei* coexisted raised a storm of controversy because it violated the expectation that similar species could not exploit the same environment. One possibility is that *habilis* and *boisei* exploited the environment in quite different ways. *Boisei's* dentition suggests an adaptation to a diet of raw grain, while the diet of *habilis* seems to have been less specialized and less vegetarian. Although the possibility that *habilis* ate *boisei* would explain the presence of the bones of both species in the same place, there is really no satisfactory evidence concerning the relationships between the two species. Considering the great variability of the hominids, some scholars believe that *habilis* and *boisei* belong to the same species.

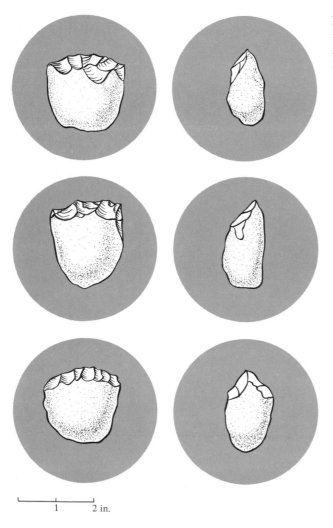

Figure 5–13 Pebble tools of Oldowan type, believed to be associated with the australopithecines or with *Homo habilis* at Olduvai.

1   2 in.

In her latest report on Olduvai Gorge, Mary Leakey has concluded that the tools found in the lowest level were definitely made by *habilis*.[4] These tools, of a type called Oldowan, are made of pebbles or rock fragments roughly shaped on one side to provide a cutting edge (Figure 5–13). Other tools include disk-shaped choppers, hammer stones, bashers, and stone flakes that had been utilized or retrimmed. Some of the materials found at Olduvai appear to have been transported forty-five or fifty miles.

The use of several different kinds of tools, including tools used to make tools, suggests that *habilis* should be classified as a member of the genus *Homo*. The existence of living floors that may have been more or less permanent campsites also suggests an essentially human pattern of life. On the whole, *habilis* appears to be an intermediate species that could equally be classified as australopithecine, or human. It is probable that *habilis* evolved from *africanus* to *erectus* during a period of 2.5 million to 1.3 million years ago.

In South Africa, during roughly the same period, a relatively robust hominid resembling *africanus, habilis,* and *boisei* in varying degrees appears to have existed. This fossil, usually labeled *Australopithecus robustus,* has aroused considerable controversy because a good case can be made for either its separate status as an independent species or for its being simply a local variant of one of the other species. According to Campbell[5] there is no evidence that *robustus* ever coexisted with another hominid species. Mary Leakey has examined the few tools found in association with *robustus* and concluded that they resemble those found at Olduvai.

6. Homo Erectus

As the name implies, *Homo erectus* is a definitely human species of the same genus as ourselves. One of the earliest fossil finds, *Homo erectus* was discovered by a Dutch physician, Dr. Eugene Dubois (1858–1940), in Java in 1891. At first the specimen was considered a humanlike ape and was named *Pithecanthropus erectus*. Additional finds in Java, and similar fossils in China, first identified as *Sinanthropus pekinensis,* suggested a widespread and rather variable hominid (Figure 5–14). Other specimens have now been found in Africa, including several on higher levels than the *habilis* remains in Olduvai Gorge. A massive but humanlike jaw from near Heidelberg, Germany, once known as *Homo heidelbergensis,* and several other African finds are now classified as *Homo erectus*. A human occipital bone, indicating a brain as large as that of modern humans, and some milk teeth found in Hungary in 1965 are also classified as examples of *erectus*.

In age the *erectus* fossils range from more than 1 million years ago to roughly 300,000 years ago. The dating, the physical characteristics involved,

[4] Mary Douglas Leakey, *Olduvai Gorge.* Vol. 3: *Excavations in Beds I and II, 1960–63* (London: Cambridge University Press, 1971).

[5] Campbell, op. cit., p. 45.

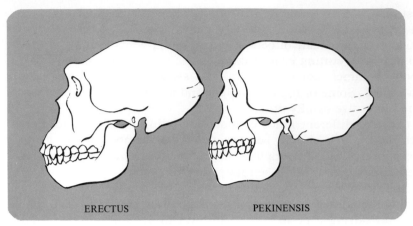

ERECTUS   PEKINENSIS

Figure 5–14 *Homo erectus* skulls from Java (left) and China. The Java form is more primitive in the teeth and jaw and in the possession of heavy brow ridges and a slightly smaller skull.

and the tools and cultural remains associated with many of the *erectus* finds all support the conclusion that *erectus* evolved from *Homo habilis* and, in turn, gave rise to *Homo sapiens*.

The tools associated with *Homo erectus* in Africa include a bifaced hand ax and a cleaver made by flaking over the entire surface of a pebble or rock fragment using a technique known as percussion flaking. Tools of these sorts, representing the Acheulian tool tradition, are also found in southwestern Europe and southwestern Asia perhaps as far as India. Cruder tools, representing refinements of the partially flaked pebbles characteristic of the Oldowan tool tradition, remain common in eastern Asia and eastern Europe. Other types of tools lack the widespread distribution of these "typical" tool traditions and thus reflect the emergence of local cultures within the widespread *Homo erectus* species.

Equally important is the evidence that at least some of the *Homo erectus* groups made use of fire for cooking and warmth. This is best established for the Chinese finds which occur in cave deposits at a latitude with extremely cold winters. Such caves would have been uninhabitable without fire even if some use of skin clothing was known. The use of fire to soften tough foods probably increased the available food supply and may well have contributed to the continuing diminution of the human tooth and jawbone.

The australopithecines ate meat when they could get it and probably hunted small game. *Homo erectus*, or rather some groups and cultures of *Homo erectus*, appear to have routinely killed quite large animals, including elephants, by means of organized hunting expeditions. The spread of the single species, *erectus*, over much of the world and its differentiation into separate cultures rather than separate species is part of the evidence that *erectus* was fully human. Because the separate tool traditions characteristic of *erectus* could not possibly be transmitted genetically and are probably too complicated to have been handed down on the basis of pure imitation, it is hard to escape the conclusion that they were handed down by means of an early form of language. Similarly the coordination required for the cooperative hunting of big game and the dividing of the kill may have required language, although wild dogs hunt cooperatively without it. The rapid development of specialized tools and techniques required for big game hunting in some environments also suggests the presence of at least rudimentary language and culture.

7. Homo Sapiens

The transition from *Homo erectus* to *Homo sapiens* is still inadequately known. The best-known early examples of the species are the Steinheim skull from Germany and the Swanscombe skull fragments from England both identified as belonging to the end of the Holstein interglacial period, about 350,000 years ago. One skull, found recently at Arago in France and dating from the Holstein interglacial, shows resemblances to *Homo erectus* fossils. Somewhat later, during the Eem interglacial, the so-called Neanderthal type appeared in Europe, with a massive masticatory apparatus little smaller than that of *Homo erectus* and with heavy brow ridges and nuchal area (the back part of the skull in the neck region). Despite this the Neanderthal skulls were larger brained on the average than are those of modern human beings. Although other evidence is required to demonstrate Neanderthal's intelligence, the large skull is an indication that Neanderthal's brain was somewhat heavier than that of modern humans on the average. About fifty thousand years ago, Neanderthal is rather suddenly replaced by *Homo sapiens sapiens*. The best known of these are the Cro-Magnons (Figure 5–15), who do not differ significantly from their modern descendants.

Homo erectus, the Neanderthals, and modern human beings all share the characteristics of being widely distributed and highly variable. Under these circumstances it is always difficult to make meaningful statements about the biological differences between them. For example, the Swanscombe skull fragments were first thought to represent an early species of modern humanity. After the Steinheim skull, together with a face and lower jaw, was found, it became increasingly evident that although Swanscombe's brain was of modern size his other features were more reminiscent of *erectus* than of *sapiens*.

Excavations in two caves at Mt. Carmel in Israel have brought to light two distinct populations. The oldest occupied cave appears to have been inhabited by Neanderthals, perhaps displaying a few modern characteristics. The more recently occupied cave seems to have been occupied by modern humans displaying a few Neanderthal characteristics. Many scholars feel that this is evidence of interbreeding between *sapiens* and Neanderthal populations. If so, there would be some justification for assigning subspecies status to Neanderthal, who then becomes *Homo sapiens neandertalensis*, while we become *Homo sapiens sapiens*. On the other hand, what seems to have held true at Mt.

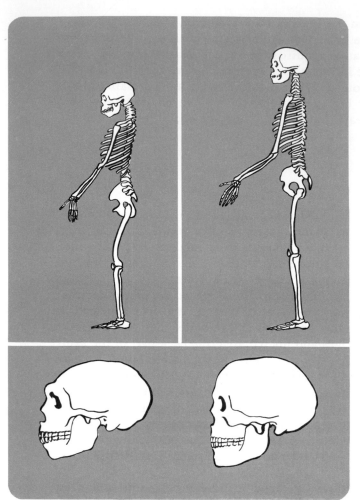

Figure 5–15 Classical European Neanderthal (left) and Cro-Magnon compared. Note heavier jaw and brow ridges of Neanderthal and slightly curved thigh bone. Both have larger skull capacities than the average for modern human beings.

Carmel did not necessarily hold true elsewhere or at a later time. Thus it is conceivable that Neanderthals in southwestern Europe belonged to separate species incapable of interbreeding with *Homo sapiens.*

The replacement of *habilis* by *erectus, erectus* by *neandertalensis,* and *neandertalensis* by *sapiens* was probably accomplished in some regions simply by the transformation of the one into the other. Because all four species displayed great geographic mobility, it is probable that genetic changes, as they occurred, spread over considerable distances. Because *neandertalensis* and *sapiens* both occupied wider geographical areas than their predecessors, it is unlikely that populations of *erectus* or *neandertalensis* were left isolated for a sufficient period to permit them to lose the capacity for interbreeding with slightly more advanced types. If and where interbreeding between successive human species became impossible or difficult — and there is no evidence that it did — then the principle that similar species could not long survive in the same environment almost certainly operated. Here, romantic as it may seem, it is not necessary to imagine that the more successful species engaged in wars of extermination or extensive cannibalism in order to rid itself of its competitor. More likely, the unsuccessful species was simply driven away from the more productive sources of food and water ultimately to die out as a result of malnutrition and hardship.

The theory that successive species of human beings exterminated their predecessors is essentially a cataclysmic theory based on the now discredited idea that species develop as a result of sudden genetic mutations. Evolution,

Erect posture in hominids. Left to right, australopithecines, Neanderthal, and modern *Homo sapiens*. Such reconstructions are highly speculative; controversy still surrounds the posture of Neanderthal and the australopithecines. (Courtesy of the American Museum of Natural History.)

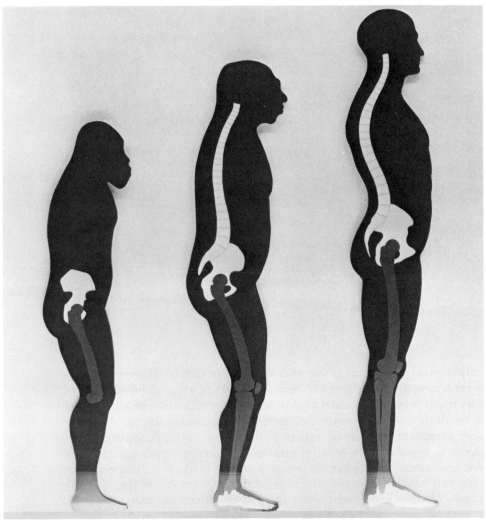

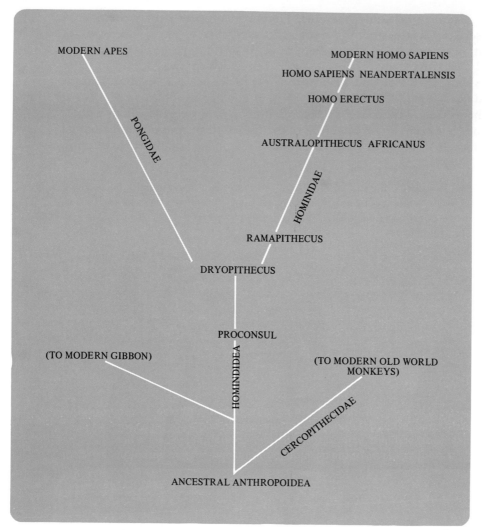

Figure 5–16 Most probable phylogenetic relationships of the *Anthropoidea*. The point of separation of the *Pongidae* and the Hominidae is currently in dispute; some think *Ramapithecus* is ancestral to both.

even very rapid evolution, takes place over many generations allowing plenty of time for each new genetic change to spread over wide areas. The absence of a continuous fossil record of human evolution and the relatively small number of fossils contribute to an appearance of sudden evolutionary leaps.

The more abundant remains of human tools and artifacts, described in detail in Chapter 6, show a much more continuous pattern of development. The various tool traditions that began to be identifiable with the emergence of *Homo erectus* can be distinguished at times by the appearance of significantly different kinds of new implements, but the old traditions do not disappear.

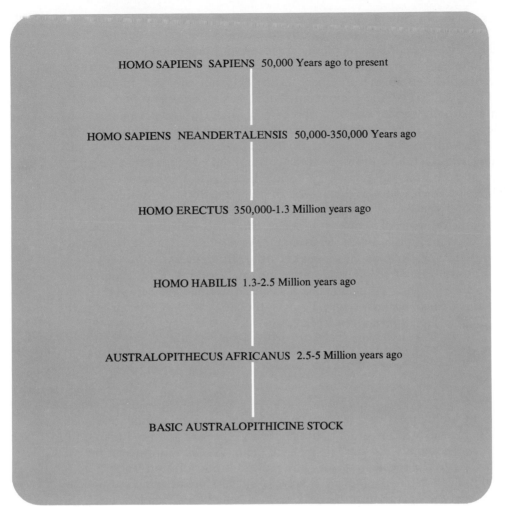

HOMO SAPIENS SAPIENS 50,000 Years ago to present

HOMO SAPIENS NEANDERTALENSIS 50,000-350,000 Years ago

HOMO ERECTUS 350,000-1.3 Million years ago

HOMO HABILIS 1.3-2.5 Million years ago

AUSTRALOPITHECUS AFRICANUS 2.5-5 Million years ago

BASIC AUSTRALOPITHICINE STOCK

Figure 5–17 A lumper's view of the development of *Homo sapiens* through a series of chrono-species. Most scholars believe that separate geographical species of *Australopithecus*, *Erectus*, and *Neandertalensis* developed and were then replaced by more progressive types. As yet, there is not enough evidence to resolve such questions.

Flake tools appeared before the emergence of the Neanderthals, but they were usually crude and fewer in number than tools made from pebble cores such as hand axes or cleavers. Flake tools became much more common among the Neanderthals and are based upon somewhat improved techniques, but the bifaced core tools still persist. In some regions of the world, perhaps for environmental reasons, bifaced core tools persist right into modern times and flake tools remain relatively rare. The cultural record does show abrupt discontinuities in certain parts of the world. In European Russia a glamorous cultural tradition attributed to *Homo sapiens* and characterized by artistic figurines replaced a much more humdrum tradition attributed to Neanderthal after a break of only 5,000 years.[6] While this might suggest to some a sharp intellectual difference, there are plenty of present-day peoples that create fewer and less interesting imperishable tools than did the Russian Neanderthals. Further, despite the apparently sharp break between the tool tradition attributed to Neanderthal and the one attributed to *Homo sapiens,* both peoples lived in essentially similar dwellings presumably made of hides stretched over a wooden frame, weighed at the bottom with mammoth bones, and heated with a fire. Although in the absence of information many theories are equally acceptable, the essential continuity of the cultural record lends some weight to the idea of continuity in human evolution from *Australopithecus africanus* through *Homo erectus,* to *neandertalensis* and *sapiens.* Because these are essentially temporal species representing a more or less continuous development over time, the drawing of genus and species lines between them must always be a somewhat arbitrary process. *Habilis* and *neandertalensis,* in particular, are difficult to classify. In practice, it makes little difference whether *habilis* is regarded as the last of the australopithecines or the first of the humans or whether *neandertalensis* is regarded as a species intermediate between *erectus* and *sapiens* (*Homo neandertalensis*) or as the first of the wise or sapient humans (*Homo sapiens neandertalensis*).

8. Summary

In terms of biological classification, human beings are placental mammals belonging to the primate order. Human beings belong to the superfamily *Hominoidea,* the family *Hominidae,* and the genus *Homo.* All modern human beings belong to the species *sapiens.* The processes of evolution leading up to the development of *Homo sapiens* involve a succession of temporal species resulting from the operation of the processes of selection dependent upon the continuous variability of the successive species. In contrast to such animals as the horse, human beings appear to become increasingly generalized in a physiological sense. In many ways the need for physiological specializations in order to cope with differing environments was replaced by the ability to develop cultural specializations. Other problems in human evolution have to do with the extent to which particular human populations were reproductively isolated and the degree to which reproductive isolation led to the development of geographical species or varieties. The question of whether human evolution proceeded by a series of adaptive radiations in which newly developed species replaced less progressive competitors or by the development of wide-ranging temporal species which progressed by the wide diffusion of new adaptations has not yet been solved, although it is evident that reproductive isolation and the development of geographical species have become less and less important

---

[6] Richard G. Klein, "Ice-Age Hunters of the Ukraine," *Scientific American,* **230:**96–105, No. 6 (June 1974).

as the human species has evolved. Similarly, the possibility that human evolution has violated the principle of competitive exclusion by permitting the coexistence of similar species raises some interesting questions.

Despite the assertion that human beings are generalized in a physiological sense, human beings possess a number of special, and therefore specialized (?), physiological characteristics. These include erect posture and bipedal locomotion, an opposable thumb permitting a precision grip, a large and complex brain, infant helplessness requiring the development of behavioral patterns for the care of infants and their mothers, and a hairless and specialized skin apparently representing adaptation to a tropical grassland environment. These characteristics almost certainly developed together as part of an organized response to the development of tool use, language, and culture.

The earliest stages of evolution in the human direction may be represented by *Dryopithecus*, whose wide distribution and hominoid teeth suggest an ancestral relationship to apes and humans. *Ramapithecus* could be ancestral to both apes and humans or to humans alone, but more evidence is required

Grooming and child care are thought to be important factors in primate social behavior. (Kindness of S. L. Washburn.)

before the status of *Ramapithecus* can be resolved. The earliest fossils both sufficiently numerous and sufficiently different from the apes to be identified as ancestral to humanity are those of the australopithecines. Although there is debate about whether the australopithecines represent one species or many, there is a general consensus that the history of *Australopithecus africanus* from 5.0 to 2.5 million years ago represents a pattern of evolution in the direction of modern humanity. Between 2.5 and 1.3 million years ago, the transition between *africanus,* the last of the humanlike apes, and *erectus,* the first of the indisputably human fossils, seems to have been accomplished by the tool-using *Homo habilis.* Whether such forms as *boisei* or *robustus* represent separate species (evolutionary side branches) which later died out or simply variant geographical forms of *africanus* or *habilis* which were later absorbed into the mainstream of human evolution remains a matter for debate. An erect posture, a large brain, a widespread distribution, and the use of tools and fire, all support the classification of *erectus* as a human being that existed from 1.3 million to 300,000 years ago. The transition between *erectus* and modern humanity is dominated by *neandertalensis* during a time period of from about 300,000 to 50,000 years ago. It is difficult to say whether *neandertalensis* should be clas-

Human beings may have acquired their taste for meat and their inclination toward hunting by scavenging the kills of predators. However, some predators don't leave much behind. (Kindness of S. L. Washburn.)

Baboon male employing warning gesture. Note contrast with human teeth. (Kindness of S. L. Washburn.)

sified as the first of the modern human beings (*Homo sapiens neandertalensis*) or as a separate species (*Homo neandertalensis*). Although there are many fascinating side issues in the history of the evolution of the human species, the simplest and best substantiated version is in terms of a succession of temporal species: *africanus, (habilis), erectus, (neandertalensis), sapiens.*

Collateral Readings

Alland, Alexander. *Evolution and Human Behavior.* London: Tavistock Publications, 1969.

Birdsell, Joseph B. *Human Evolution, An Introduction to the New Physical Anthropology,* 2d ed. Skokie, Ill., Rand McNally & Co., 1975.

Buettner-Janusch, John. *Physical Anthropology: A Perspective.* New York: John Wiley & Sons, Inc., 1973. An authoritative textbook.

Campbell, Bernard G. "Conceptual Progress in Physical Anthropology: Fossil Man," *Annual Review of Anthropology,* **1**:27–54, ed. Bernard J. Siegel. Palo Alto, Calif.: Annual Reviews Inc., 1972. Bibliography of recent technical literature.

Campbell, Bernard G. *Human Evolution, An Introduction to Man's Adaptations*, 2d ed. Chicago: Aldine Publishing Company, 1974. Brilliant use of ecological and cultural perspectives to weave an integrated point of view.

Campbell, Bernard G. (ed.) *Sexual Selection and the Descent of Man*. Chicago: Aldine Publishing Company, 1972.

Dolhinow, Phyllis (ed.) *Primate Patterns*. New York: Holt, Rinehart and Winston, Inc., 1972. New views of primate characteristics.

Hewes, Gordon W. *The Origin of Man*. Minneapolis: Burgess Publishing Company, 1973. A brief summary.

Jolly, Alison. *The Evolution of Primate Behavior*. The Macmillian Series in Physical Anthropology. New York: Macmillan Publishing Co., Inc., 1972.

Kummer, Hans. *Primate Societies: Group Techniques of Ecological Adaptation*. New York and Chicago: Aldine-Atherton, 1971. Brief but authoritative statement explaining primate variation.

Lancaster, Jane B. *Primate Behavior and the Emergence of Human Culture*. New York: Holt, Rinehard and Winston, Inc., 1975.

LeGros Clark, Sir Wilfred E. *Man-Apes or Ape-Men, the Story of Discoveries in Africa*. New York: Holt, Rinehart and Winston, Inc., 1967. Dated, but useful survey of australopithecines.

Napier, John R. *The Roots of Mankind*. London: Allen & Unwin, 1971.

Pfeiffer, John E. *The Emergence of Man*, 2d ed. New York: Harper & Row, Inc., 1972. A popular account enlivened by romantic and probably erroneous speculations about such things as the role of big-game hunting in human evolution.

Simonds, Paul E. *The Social Primates*. Animal Behavior Series. New York: Harper & Row, Inc., 1974.

Tobias, Phillip V. *The Brain in Hominid Evolution*. New York: Columbia University Press, 1971.

Tobias, Phillip V. "New Developments in Hominid Paleontology in South and East Africa," *Annual Review of Anthropology*, 2:311–334, ed. Bernard J. Siegel. Palo Alto, Calif.: Annual Reviews Inc., 1973. Summarizes recent work.

Washburn, Sherbourne L., and Ruth Moore. *Ape into Man: A Study of Human Evolution*. Boston: Little, Brown and Company, 1974.

6/Culture in the Past

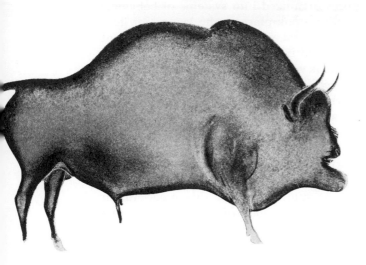

1. The Ecology of Prehistoric Humanity

The great variation and complexity of modern cultures obscure the fact that the origins of culture, the development of its main functional categories, and most of the variable solutions to basic adaptive problems occurred before the dawn of history. The historical record began about 5,000 years ago in Mesopotamia and parts of the eastern Mediterranean. For most of the world the historical record began a few hundred years ago or less. Evidences of culture, on the other hand, extend at least 2.5 million years into the past, covering human evolution from the australopithecines to modern humanity. Most of our knowledge of the development of culture consequently depends upon archaeology.

Most of the archaeological record of past culture is based upon the products of human technology, supplemented by information on settlement patterns, and exploitation of the environment. This record spans the Pleistocene and Holocene (Recent) geological periods, marked by major changes in climate, with accompanying shifts in flora and fauna which required human beings either to shift their residence or to modify their technology, change their diet, and alter their social organizations. The prehistorian may at times appear to be preoccupied with stone tools and the technology which produced them, but interpretations must be based on ecology and an awareness that the archaeological record deals with cultures organized into systems of behavior.

The beginnings and evolution of culture took place in the last major geological epoch, the Quaternary, the same period which saw the evolution of *Homo sapiens*. The Quaternary is subdivided into the Pleistocene and Holocene, or Recent, periods. The latter period is very brief and, compared with the latter part of the Pleistocene, saw relatively little environmental change. The Pleistocene, on the other hand, was marked by drastic changes in climate, particularly in its latter phases, changes that required a number of cultural adaptations or migrations for survival.

Climates of the Pleistocene   The Early Pleistocene occupied from one-half to three-fourths of the time usually assigned to the Pleistocene. It was mainly a period of high rainfall, although recent studies indicate this predominant climate may have been interrupted by several periods of glaciation. As this period drew to a close, the earth began gradually to become cooler. The fall of earth temperatures led in turn to the extension of the polar ice caps and the gradual enlargement of glaciated areas. Eventually large portions of Europe, Asia, and North America were covered by huge glaciers very much like those that cover the interior of Greenland today. The advancing glaciers affected the plant and animal life of the world as well as the rivers, lakes, and sea coasts. Plants and animals in many cases were obliged to migrate because of drastic climatic changes, and in some cases they became extinct. Rivers, lakes, and seas were reduced in volume because of the large amounts of water frozen in the glaciers. The increasing weight of ice on land surfaces and the reduction of weight of ocean waters caused marked changes in the interrelationships of land and sea areas. Areas of rainfall moved in toward the equator so that regions that were formerly deserts became temperate, grassy plains.

Later, the earth became warm again. The glaciers retreated and in many areas disappeared entirely. Rainfall areas shifted northward and southward from the equator. Plants and animals moved back into formerly glaciated regions. Rivers, lakes, and seas rose in volume, and the coastlines of islands and continents took on new forms.

Glacial advances and retreats of this sort took place at least three times during the Pleistocene. In Europe these major advances (there were a number of minor fluctuations as well) are known as the Elster, Saale, and Weichsel, respectively. Corresponding advances in North America are the Kansan, Illinoian, and Wisconsin. Between the successive European glaciations were two warmer periods, the Holstein and Eem interglacials. The corresponding interglacial periods in North America were the Yarmouth and Sangamon. At some time during this postglacial epoch (the precise time varies with the region) the Pleistocene gave way to the geological Recent, or Holocene. (See Figure 6–1.)

The pluvial (wet) and interpluvial (dry) periods in tropical areas still are difficult to correlate precisely with the glacial and interglacial periods of Europe and North America; nevertheless they afford important evidence of the age of some cultural and fossil remains. Changes of sea level also are useful for dating sites in some areas; during some of the glacial periods the sea levels

PERIODS	YEARS AGO	EUROPE	NORTH AMERICA	EVENTS
Holocene	0	Modern Postglacial Climate	Modern Postglacial Climate	Agriculture
Upper Pleistocene	10,000	Weichsel Glaciation	Wisconsin Glaciation	Occupation of New World *Homo Sapiens sapiens*
	75,000	Eem Interglacial	Sangamon Interglacial	
	130,000	Saal Glaciation	Illinoisan Glaciation	*Homo sapiens neandertalensis*
Middle Pleistocene	400,000	Holstein Interglacial	Yarmouth Interglacial	
		Elster Glaciation	Kansan Glaciation	*Homo erectus*
Lower Pleistocene	850,000	Uncertain		*Australopithecus Africanus*
Pliocene	3,000,000			

Figure 6–1 Climatological periods of the Pleistocene. (After Fagan.) European glacial periods are no longer derived solely from Alpine glaciations. Doubt has been cast
on the number and timing of glaciations preceding the Elster-Kansan period.

may have been as much as 300 feet lower than at present, whereas in interglacial periods they may have risen as much as 100 feet above current
levels. (See Figure 6–2.) In Europe and North America some interglacial
periods were much longer than the glacial periods and evidently much warmer
than present climates. It is far from certain that the relatively brief Holocene
period is really a postglacial period or merely an early phase of an interglacial
interlude.

Paleontological Periods   Paleontologists, dealing with the fossil evidence
of plants and animals of the past, customarily divide the Pleistocene into three
major portions called the Lower, Middle, and Upper. This division may
roughly be correlated with modern geological epochs as follows. (See Figure
6–1.)

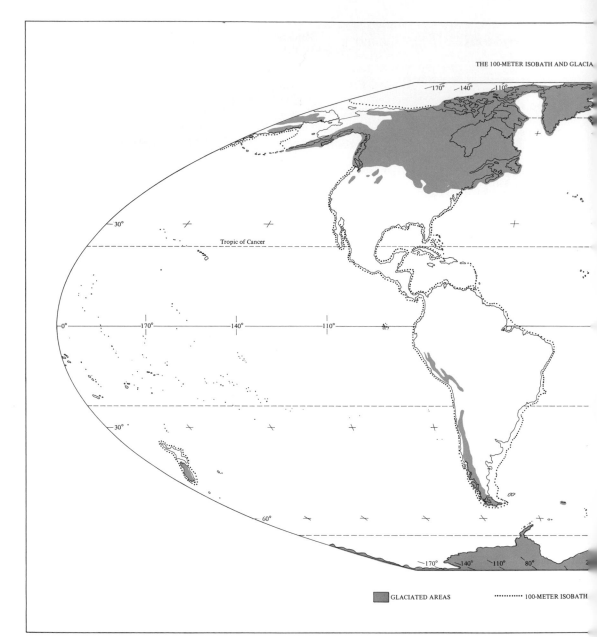

Figure 6–2   Maximum glaciation and sea-level subsidence during the Pleistocene. The shaded area shows the maximum extent of major glaciations. The map does not show the extent of ice coverage for any single glacial period. The dotted line shows the approximate location of the 100-meter depth of the present ocean. This depth is slightly less than the estimated maximum lowering of sea level in Pleistocene times. Of particular interest is the broad land bridge at the Bering Straits connecting Asia and North America and the land bridges between Asia and Australia. For some parts of the world the line is interpolated from the 100-fathom line derived from hydrographic information; for more critical areas—such as Southeast Asia, Europe, and the Bering Strait region—the 100-meter line is derived from various more detailed sources. Scale is 2,500 miles to the inch. Compiled especially for this text.

COVERAGE DURING THE PLEISTOCENE

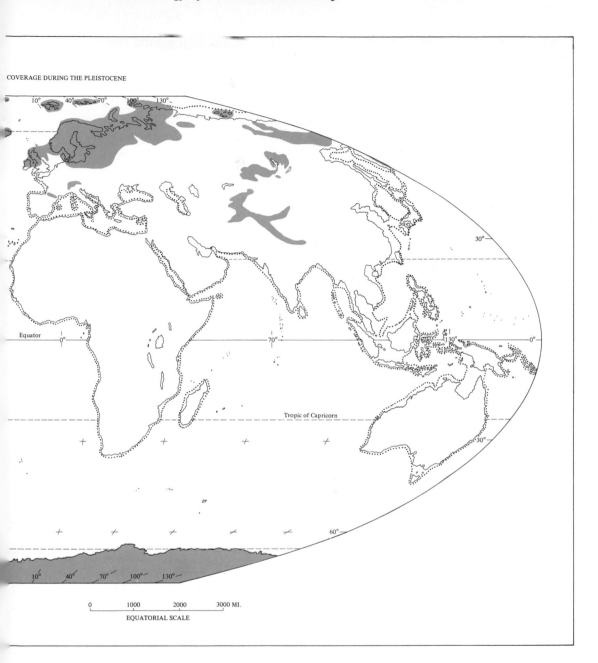

The Lower Pleistocene period includes a large portion of the total time span involved, from approximately 3 million years ago to somewhat before the onset of the Elster glaciation, about 850,000 years ago. It is associated with a major change in animal populations, especially in Europe.

The Middle Pleistocene extends from 850,000 years ago to the end of the Eem glaciation including all of the Holstein interglacial and the Saale glaciation, a period lasting until 75,000 years ago. The Upper Pleistocene extends from the beginning of the Eem interglacial to the end of the Weichsel glaciation or from 75,000 years ago to about 10,000 years ago. In parts of the world some plants and animals characteristic of the Pleistocene persisted for a longer period of time. One of the factors in the extinction of Pleistocene animals was the presence of human beings who are known to have hunted such animals as the mammoth. In tropical regions, where glaciation did not occur, the dating of archaeological sites must often be based upon associated plant and animal remains. Because Pleistocene plants and animals did not all become extinct at the same times and because some survived for longer periods in some regions of the earth, dates assigned to tropical archaeological sites are often debatable. Many Pleistocene species appear to have flourished in North America long after similar forms had become extinct in Europe.

Technology and Material Culture   The ecology of humanity, in contrast to that of other living beings, is heavily influenced by technology and its material products. Technology is the sum total of the techniques possessed by members of a society; that is, the totality of their ways of behaving in respect to collecting raw materials from the environment and processing these to make tools, containers, foods, clothing, shelter, means of transportation, and many other material goods. What is usually called material culture, on the other hand, refers to the sum of the artifacts (manufactured goods and devices of all sorts) resulting from technology. In a strict sense, according to our definition of culture, these material objects are products of culture rather than a part of it. Nevertheless, their careful study is essential to the understanding of human ecology and assists in the abstraction of many patterns and themes that make up culture. The relation of technology and ecology has long been evident for societies with restricted or simple technology; today it is being brought home forcibly to modern complex societies as well. A nonindustrialized society may destroy itself by overhunting, burning forests, or initiating erosion cycles; modern industrial societies add to these mining, pollution of air and water, exhaustion of fossil fuels, or misuse of atomic energy.

Technology has been called a cultural screen that people set up between themselves and their environment. As such it affects the ways in which they may both exploit and modify that environment. Whereas most other animals simply utilize the natural environment as such for food and shelter, changing it relatively little in the process, people alter or transform their environments. They make tools of wood, stone, shell, bone, and metal to increase their efficiency in using the environment; they build shelters and manufacture clothing to protect themselves from the weather; and they frequently cause food plants to grow or keep food animals under domestication to supply their needs. As a result, though people, like the apes, are by nature tropical animals, they are able to live almost anywhere on the earth's surface. Human societies are found in the Arctic, in deserts and semiarid regions, in tropical rain forests, in grasslands and arctic tundras, and in the great temperate zones of the world. In contrast, our closest relatives anatomically, the anthropoid apes, are restricted to the moist, tropical regions of Africa and Asia; lacking our technologies, they cannot survive elsewhere.

A society having a very restricted technology and lacking any means of transportation save human carriers is confined to the resources of a single area, and unless this is unusually rich in easily obtained food plants and animals, the members of the society may achieve only a bare subsistence. There are many examples of such societies, even in recent times—the desert-dwelling Indians of Nevada and southeastern California, the Eskimos of the Arctic coasts, and the Pygmies, tropical forest dwellers of Africa. Restricted technologies are not necessarily simple. The products of Eskimo technology often are ingenious, complex, and highly specialized and require great skill in their manufacture.

Limited technologies also restrict many societies to a limited use of their environment, even though other uses might be made possible by a more sophisticated technology. The Plains Indians of North America, for example, obtained much of their food from the buffalo and other game which also supplied skins for clothing, shelter, and numerous other needs. Buffalo provided robes, but clothing and tent covers were made from deer, elk, and antelope. Lacking efficient devices for cultivation, the Plains Indians made practically no use of the agricultural potential of their environment, part of which today is one of the best farming areas in the world. Even their ability to hunt buffalo was limited until the horse and gun were introduced.

Societies with more advanced technologies exploit their environments more fully; the Iroquois Indians, for example, practiced hunting, fishing, food collecting, and horticulture. In industrialized societies, technological development permits an almost exhaustive exploitation of environmental resources. Further, efficient transportation has made it possible for us to use the resources of many environments, so that even some of our common foods are imported regularly from diverse regions. Conversely, modern technology and transportation enable people to live comfortably even in waterless deserts, or, as many have done recently, on the Antarctic continent, an area that in the winter is almost totally devoid of food resources.

If we examine all existing human societies, we find that certain broad categories of technology are universal. All people have some techniques for the gathering or production of food, for the building of shelters and the making of clothing, for manufacturing tools and containers, and for transporting their belongings. This does not mean of course that these categories are equally developed in all societies. Food gathering and production include techniques as disparate as berry picking and modern agriculture, the latter a series of highly complicated, machine-aided techniques. Toolmaking includes not only the chipping of flint to make arrow or spear points, but also intricate techniques of the modern machine shop. Building techniques show a similarly wide range, from the simplicity of constructing a lean-to to the complexity and multiplicity of techniques involved in the construction of a skyscraper. In short, technologies vary obviously from one culture to another; and the range of variation is great, from the crude stone-tool technology of the contemporary Australian aborigines or the first shaping of stone by our Paleolithic ancestors to the complex industrial technology of modern nations.

The study of technology over time also reveals its cumulative character. Generally, technologies do not disappear unless they cease to be useful or are replaced by more efficient technologies. Further, study of technology over time shows that some changes in technology permitted striking changes in ways of life; for example, the development of farming. The late V. Gordon Childe called these changes revolutionary, but accumulating evidence suggests this was true only in a very special sense, when very long time spans are examined. Farming, for example, was evidently invented in a number of times and places in the past. But the inventors did not suddenly switch from hunting or gathering to farming. In many cases several thousand years elapsed between the first invention of farming and its becoming the primary source of food for the inventors. Only those who borrowed fairly well-developed farming technologies made the transition rapidly.

The rest of this chapter will be devoted to the broad outlines of the development of material culture and technology through time. In later chapters we will deal with some of the cultural and social correlates of different kinds of technologies.

2. Culture History of the Old World: Paleolithic

During the immense span of time from the beginning of the Pleistocene to the present, the interaction of environmental, biological, and cultural processes of change and adaptation gave rise to the technologies and cultures that we know today and that are themselves in the process of further change and development. The culture history of the Old World is traditionally divided into four major epochs: the Paleolithic, or Old Stone Age; the Neolithic, or New Stone Age; the Copper-Bronze Age; and the Iron Age. Although these terms remain in common use, the Neolothic tends to be associated with the development of agriculture rather than with the improvement of stoneworking techniques, whereas the Copper-Bronze Age tends to be associated with the emergence of an urban way of life. Subdivisions within the major epochs are increasingly being based upon such criteria as subsistence base, settlement patterns, land use, and the development of technology in a more general sense. The change is a result of improved research techniques borrowed from the natural sciences which permit the collection of detailed information about ancient environments.

The use of tool types to distinguish the different cultures of the Paleolithic was necessary because, in a great many cases, traditional archaeological techniques permitted identification only of tools. Utilization of new kinds of materials such as pollen and coprolites (dried feces) give new indications concerning diet, disease patterns, parasite infestations, and existing flora, fauna, and climatic conditions. Proper analysis of this evidence, combined with an analysis of tools, reveals additional information concerning the functions served by the tools, the techniques by which the tools were made, the environment and its utilization, and some aspects of the living patterns of the toolmakers.

Paleolithic stone tools were made by chipping or flaking hard siliceous (glasslike) materials such as flint, quartzite, and obsidian, which can be broken into sharply edged and pointed pieces. Techniques for stone chipping and the skill with which the techniques were used varied considerably through time and also from one region to another. The quality of the materials available in different places also affected the quality of the finished product. In general, two major techniques have been employed to produce chipped instruments. One is percussion: striking a piece of suitable material with a hammer stone to knock off flakes. Another is pressure flaking: removing small flakes through

Percussion flaking of stone implements by striking with a hammer stone. (Courtesy of the American Museum of Natural History.)

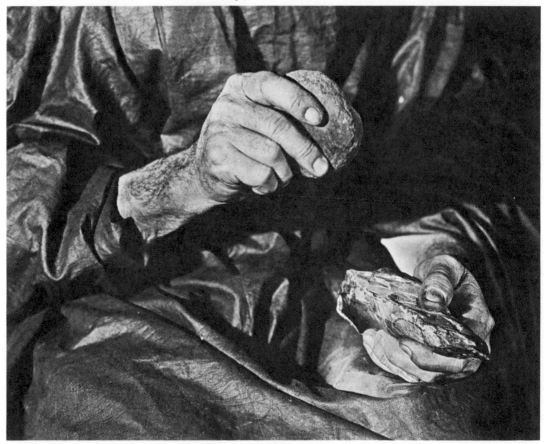

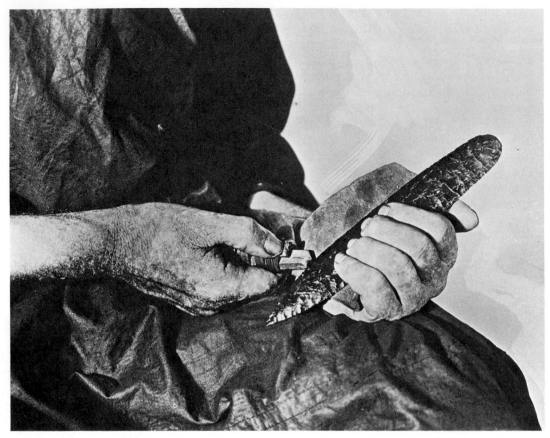

Pressure flaking or chipping of stone implements by applying pressure with a bone or similar instrument. (Courtesy of the American Museum of Natural History.)

the application of pressure, usually with a bone tool either pressed by hand or struck lightly with a hammer stone. The two methods are not mutually exclusive, for percussion is usually employed to prepare large flakes or pieces for subsequent pressure flaking or retouching. Moreover, these two basic techniques may be used in many different ways, depending upon the type of raw material used, the ways of preparing them, and the processes of shaping into a variety of forms.

In describing Paleolithic archaeological materials, it has been traditional to speak of toolmaking traditions rather than cultures. Such traditions are sets of habits associated with the making of certain types of tools. Such toolmaking traditions are sometimes found by themselves, but very often with tools derived from other traditions. Groups of tools of various types found together are usually known as assemblages, or facies. If enough associated data occur, the term *culture* may be applied to an assemblage or to a group of related or similar assemblages. With the acquisition of better information about environmental circumstances, typologies based upon tool traditions are in the process of being replaced by typologies based upon environment and subsistence activities. The following sections present an outline of such a typology.

(1) *Foraging*   This is the period, formerly called the eolithic, during which the transition was made to the systematic manufacture of tools. During this period, the australopithecines lived essentially as other primates, moving from place to place within a limited territory. The australopithecines were primarily vegetarian foragers who gathered plant foods and probably supplemented them with insects, small animals, and perhaps meat scavenged from the kills of the larger predators. Like some of the other primates, they probably picked up and used stones, sticks, and perhaps large bones as they needed them, perhaps with some shaping. The identification of stone tools from this period is difficult or impossible. Only if stones have been given shapes not occurring naturally, are systematically given similar shapes, are found in numbers in or near identifiable living floors, or are found at a significant distance from their place of origin can we assume the use of stones as tools. There must have been a period when human forerunners experimented with stone shaping, but not until standardized techniques and shapes were followed can there be any certainty that a tradition existed. Evidence from Olduvai Gorge, Bed I, indicates that *Australopithecus* was involved only in tool-using, or possibly in the simple shaping of objects, but was not actually using tools to make tools.

The technology of the australopithecines apparently excluded knowledge of clothing or of fire, so that they were restricted to warm or subtropical climates. Their further needs for water and food appear to have prevented them from colonizing desert or dense forest zones. The effects of the australopithecines on wildlife may have been considerably less than that of other major animal predators. "Minor" animal food sources — rodents, insectivores, bats, birds, chameleons, lizards, crabs, fish, and tortoise — appear to have been relatively important in the diet, although occasional remains of large mammals are to be found. One possible technique for hunting large mammals would be to drive them into swampy or shallow water where deep mud or sand restricted their movements and club them to death in a cooperative effort. It is also possible that scavenging the kills of other large carnivores was practiced. The influence of early hominids on plant cover was probably comparable to that of chimpanzees or gorillas today, as their numbers and technology were on a roughly comparable scale.

(2) *Oldowan or Toolmaking Tradition*   Oldowan traditions are distinguished from preceding protocultures largely by the systematic manufacture of stone tools. Although Oldowan cultures involved a good deal of wandering from place to place, there was probably a greater tendency to return repeatedly to the same campsites. Such standardized tools as protocore bifaces, flakes, and choppers appear and are found at a variety of widely distributed sites. The standardization of tools implies that they formed a part of a culturally organized technology which presumably involved the rudiments of specialization in the hunting, gathering, and utilization of particular plant and animal species. Local patterns of subsistence activity associated with these early tools

are not well understood as yet, but the Oldowan tradition was probably the basic tradition from which all subsequent toolmaking derived.

The Oldowan tradition was first identified in Africa. The best-known site is Olduvai, Bed I, where it is found in association with *Homo habilis*. Similar implements have been reported from spots in Asia and more recently from Vértessöllös in western Hungary and other locations in Central Europe.

Oldowan tools are stream bed pebbles, sometimes other rocks, usually ovoid in shape, with a few flakes knocked off on one or both sides to make a cutting edge. Particularly in the earliest period, they are often difficult to distinguish from naturally fractured pebbles; only when a number of "possibles" are found in one location is it certain that intentionally made tools are involved. One of the older sites in the Olduvai Gorge in Tanzania fortunately has a number of pebble tools associated with living surfaces together with flakes struck from them and a number of other smaller and perhaps specialized forms as well as unworked natural stones. Many of these stones must have been transported from locations as much as forty miles away. The number of well-dated pebble tools known is still small, but there is evidence that they changed somewhat through time and that regional styles developed. Throughout there is evidence of some increasing standardization; in other words, the makers shared a technique and envisioned an "ideal" type.

The makers of pebble tools lived long enough in one spot (or else returned repeatedly to the same spot) to leave traces of a living surface. They still were probably predominantly vegetarians, but they also made more use of, and may have hunted, larger animals than did earlier primates. In the Olduvai Gorge, for example, there are significant numbers of bones of larger mammals, and all the marrow bones have been cracked open. We do not know what use they made of perishable materials such as wood or whether they had any cords or containers to transport objects. The probabilities are strong that they lived in groups larger than a single family. With further evidence a clearer picture of the life of the pebble-toolmakers will emerge, but the Oldowan tradition seems to have endured with relatively few changes from about 2.5 million years ago until the end of the Lower Pleistocene, about 850,000 years ago. There is no evidence of the use of fire in early African sites, but recent excavation by Howells of the cave of St. Estève in southern France revealed five distinct hearths in deposits that he believes belong to the very end of the basal Pleistocene. If he is correct, fire was used nearly 1 million years ago. More definite evidence of fire was found in the site of Terra Amata, discovered in 1966 at Nice, France, accompanied by remains of several oval huts, 20 to 50 feet long and 12 to 18 feet wide, probably housing several families. The tool assemblages in general are similar to those found by Clark Howells at Torralba and Ambrona in Spain a little earlier. The evidence for the use of fire in the Spanish sites is less conclusive but they provide a clear picture of big game hunters who killed mammoths and other large game. The tool assemblages are also surprisingly varied, including such things as burins (engraving tools), backed blades, and various types of notched tools. The dating, approximately 300,000 years ago, is much older than that for other early appearances of such specialized tools in Europe.

In south and east Asia the Oldowan tradition seems to have developed into what is called the chopper-chopping tool traditions, such as the Soan (India) and Choukoutienien (China); these were more sophisticated assemblages of tools but still were based largely on the use of pebbles. The evidence is still relatively scanty and the apparent differences from the course of development in Africa, in western Asia, and in Europe may be the result of sampling error.

(3) *Generalized Hunting and Gathering*   With the emergence of *Homo erectus* during the Middle Pleistocene, the geographical range and complexity of human tool kits are vastly increased. This is exactly what should be expected if early forms of language and culture were now making possible cultural rather than biological adaptations to a variety of quite different environments. Tool traditions of Europe are the best understood, largely because Europe has been the site of prolonged and systematic archaeological research. The absence of tropical hardwoods in Europe may also have forced a greater reliance on stone tools that could later be retrieved by the archaeologist.

The best-known Middle Pleistocene or Early Paleolithic tool tradition is the biface tradition, also known as the core, cleaver, hand-ax tradition or the Acheulian. It was first identified in Europe in the first interglacial period, perhaps 500,000 years or more ago. In Africa the beginning date is considerably older and the tradition is continuous. In Olduvai Gorge, and perhaps at Ternafine in North Africa, tools of the biface tradition have been found associated with *Homo erectus* fossils. Elsewhere, at Kanjera (Africa), Swanscombe (England), and Fontechevade (France), Acheulian implements have been found with early Neanderthal fossils. (See Figure 6–3.)

The distribution of tool types and early hominids often overlap. Tool-using *Australopithicus boisei* remains are found alongside toolmaking *Homo habilis* in Bed I at the Olduvai site. Middle and Upper Bed II at Olduvai has also yielded evidence of two dissimilar industrial complexes, the Advanced Oldowan and Acheulian, found under what appear to be identical environmental conditions. The two cultural traditions appear to represent the work of *Homo habilis* and *Homo erectus*, respectively.

The characteristic tool of the biface tradition is made from a nodule of flint or similar material, such as quartzite in East Africa, that has been trimmed by removing flakes, usually over the entire surface, using a percussion technique. The most characteristic form is pear-shaped with a more or less rounded point at one end and cutting edges extending along part of the sides; the larger end is shaped to be held in the hand. Pounders and choppers also appear. An alternative means of making tools is to use flakes removed from unprepared stones and throw away the core from which the flakes were struck. Tools manufactured in this manner are often found in conjunction with biface tools, sometimes alone. Another technique (Levalloisian) involved the careful preparation of a "turtle-shaped" core from which a variety of sizes and shapes of flakes could be struck and either used directly or shaped into more specialized tools.

At one time the use of simple pebble tools, stone cores, flakes, or prepared cores was considered to be an indicator of technological advancement. The frequently overlapping temporal and spatial distributions of these varying

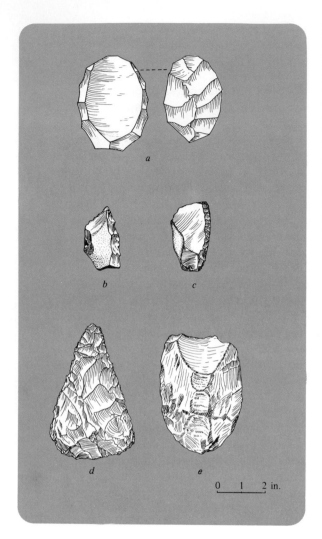

Figure 6–3 Examples of Early Paleo-lithic tools: (a) Levalloisian core and a tool made from a flake from the core (after Bordes); (b) rough flake tool (after Bordes); (c) side scraper (after Oakley); (d) Acheulian hand ax (after Oakley); (e) cleaver (after Oakley). Earlier Abbevillian (Chellean) hand axes differed in being heavier and less finely chipped but were formed on large pebbles or cores. The flake and Levalloisian techniques are more finely worked and involved sets of techniques which occur in a number of cultures of the Lower and Middle Paleo-lithic period.

techniques of manufacture have cast doubt upon the value of a hierarchy of such techniques. Reasonable alternative interpretations would have to do with differences in the use of the different types of tools and with the adaptability of the different techniques to different sorts of raw material.[1]

The producers of Early Paleolithic tools appear to have been active gatherers and hunters living principally in relatively open country, mainly in areas with mild climates. There is no evidence of Early Paleolithic man in Scandinavia, in Russia north of the Caucasus, or in Siberia. Population proba-bly was rather small. Campsites appear not to have been occupied perma-nently, but in some cases they were revisited repeatedly. Generally they are close to water and are associated with bones of many animals, including

[1] Karl W. Butzer, *Environment and Archeology: An Ecological Approach to Prehistory,* 2d ed. (Chicago: Aldine-Atherton, 1971), p. 440.

some quite large types. Some specialized activities are evident in Africa; some locations appear to have been butchering sites, possibly associated with cooperative hunts or drives. Animals were also driven into swamps. Some known locations in the Acheulian seem to have been the scene of intensive toolmaking. One African site (Kalambo Falls) suggests the use of a temporary windbreak or shelter. The heavier tools may have been made rather rapidly and may have been left at campsites rather than carried from one place to another.

Evidence of wooden spears and clubs or throwing sticks also is known from the Early Paleolithic. This evidence is very slight—a spear point from Clacton-on-Sea in England; a complete spear associated with an elephant and Levalloisian industry near Bremen, Germany; and fragments of worked wood from Kalambo Falls, northern Rhodesia. That even this much evidence of such perishable material has survived suggests widespread use of wood for tools. Long bones of animals may have been used as clubs. Indeed, Dart has argued that the australopithecines used such bones as tools before the use of stone, but only one or two pieces of worked bone have been found of comparable age. Although Early Paleolithic peoples undoubtedly hunted more than did the australopithecines, the tool inventory is not very efficient for the taking of large game. Some very large animals certainly were taken, perhaps in pit traps or in marshes, but vegetable foods probably still formed an important part of the diet.

Apparently fish was not an important item of diet in the Early Paleolithic. One late Acheulian site in Africa contains fish bones. Considering the indications of the use of fire in Oldowan sites, evidence for the use of fire in the Early Paleolithic is quite limited. Until recently the earliest unmistakable evidence of fire comes from the upper cave at Choukoutien in China, datable to the time of the Saale glaciation. Elsewhere unquestioned early evidence of the use of fire appears only in Africa. Although direct evidence is lacking as yet, almost certainly techniques were developed to transport food and things beyond carrying them in the hands, techniques basic to the development of the wider range of movement characteristic of the hominid primates.

The Early Paleolithic was, then, a long period in which simultaneously the development of basic toolmaking techniques and the evolution of *Homo sapiens* took place. Human groups were able to exploit a wider range of the animal and vegetable resources of their environment, to cover greater distances in seeking food, and toward the end of the period, to persist in increasingly unfavorable climates.

(4) *Technological Specialization*   The term *Mousterian* is often applied to the cultural remains from the Middle Paleolithic. More properly, the term applies to a new tradition utilizing flakes from disklike cores that often are retouched along the edges by pressure flaking, a new technique for removing small flakes by the skillful application of pressure with a blunt pointed tool, usually of bone. (See Figure 6–4.) Rounded side scrapers, pointed implements, and a variety of other small tools were made by this technique. (See Figure 6–5.)

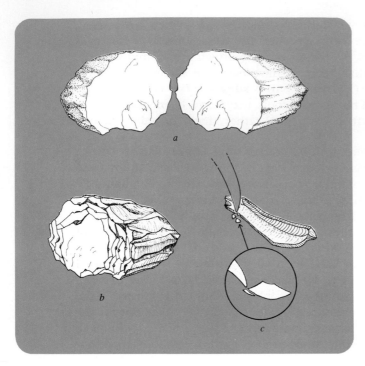

Figure 6–4 Flake tool making: (a) flint nodule broken in half ready to remove flakes; (b) a reconstituted core with flakes reassembled; (c) sharpening flake edge by retouching technique applying pressure with a bone or similar tool. Finding proper materials and obtaining the desired shape requires training and skill. Try it yourself.

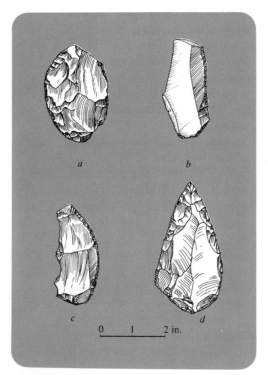

Figure 6–5 Examples of Mousterian or Middle Paleolithic tools: (a) biface scraper (after Bordes); (b) back knife (after Bordes); (c) end scraper (after Bordes); (d) Mousterian point (after Leakey). All are made on flakes, involving pressure flaking rather than percussion techniques in shaping the final cutting edges.

Characteristically, Middle Paleolithic tool kits show varying mixtures of different traditions of tool manufacture. Only recently has some order begun to emerge through the work of François Bordes and Hallam L. Movius, Jr., and their associates and students. Three possible explanations follow: (1) Occupation sites of the same people will differ according to season or purpose. A kill site, a more or less permanent living site, and a workshop for making tools will show different assemblages because different jobs were done at each place. (2) People in various regions developed differing sets of habits; if local movements occurred, occupation sites along the boundaries between groups would show differing successions of tool assemblages. (3) The Middle Paleolithic was a time of relatively rapid fluctuations in climate, with accompanying changes in the predominant animals and plants in any one locality; the kinds of tools needed would also change. Very likely all three of these factors operated. The somewhat confused details of the Middle Paleolithic are still the province of the specialist. Clearly, people had several toolmaking traditions available to them and they used them in different ways; the same problems face the archaeologist in the Upper Paleolithic and later periods.

Through the Early and Middle Paleolithic periods patterns of increasing emphases on big game hunting, specialization and standardization of traditions of tool manufacture, and expansion into new and often colder environments continued. On a more specific level, the Middle Paleolithic can be distinguished from the Early Paleolithic by the increasing differentiation of local traditions. In part, such increased regional differentiation was probably a result of adaptation to such newly occupied environments as European tundras during the Weichsel glaciation and tropical rain forests. Permanent occupation of caves, especially in the colder regions, may also have played its part.

The fossil remains most commonly found associated with Mousterian or Mousterian-like assemblages of classical types are of *Homo sapiens neandertalensis*. There are also some associated fossils which may possibly represent early forerunners of *Homo sapiens sapiens*. In any case the continuity of traditions and tool forms from the Early Paleolithic across the Middle Paleolithic and into the Late Paleolithic argues against associating the development of traditions with any particular type of human being. Often cultural adaptations may have been the cause rather than the result of biological changes.

The main period of the various Mousterian cultures in Europe was the relatively cold time preceding and including the early Weichsel glaciation, roughly from 100,000 to 35,000 years ago. The climate was more severe than at present in Europe, but game was abundant. There were reindeer, Arctic fox, Arctic hare, large bison, horse, mammoth, and hairy rhinoceros, as well as such carnivores as the bear, lion, panther, hyena, and wolf. Mousterian cultures consequently emphasized hunting. Differences in the most common animal bones found may indicate different food preferences or variations in the abundance of different animals at various times and places. Shells in some sites suggest the use of marine resources, but many shoreline sites must have been covered by the rise in sea level following the end of the glaciation. Control of fire permitted human beings to live in caves, and the abundance of game probably permitted fairly stable residence. Bits of red and yellow ochre, used by later peoples as a mineral coloring matter, were collected. Intentional burials with offerings and altarlike assemblages of the skulls of cave bears offer analogies with religious rituals and at the very least suggest increasingly complex ways of thinking and patterns of social life.

Outside Europe the Middle Paleolithic is less well known and no coherent picture has yet emerged. North Africa and Southwest Asia show many similarities to Europe, although with local variations. Flake tools, made by the Levalloisian technique, are widespread in East and South Africa, apparently associated with a variety of local tool assemblages. Mousterian affiliations are less clear-cut, except in North Africa and western Asia. In South Africa core biface tools appear to be earliest, followed by Levalloisian-type flake implements. Some South African traditions appear to have developed directly from the Acheulian tradition and to have persisted after the Mousterian had disappeared.

(5) *Specialized Hunters and Collectors*   By the Upper Paleolithic, subsistence patterns had become relatively specialized and involved selective hunting of particular species and seasonal collecting patterns. Foraging refers to the more or less unplanned harvesting of whatever natural foods were nearby, and the term *collecting* refers to planned and systematic harvesting. The Upper Paleolithic represents the climax of a trend toward the development of increasingly specialized local cultures of hunters and collectors. The period is relatively brief, beginning during the Weichsel glaciation and terminating at the start of postglacial times. Despite this short duration of some 40,000 years, the late Paleolithic is a period of rapid cultural change and substantial regional diversity. Such rapid change may well have been the result of the emergence of a fully developed capacity for the use of language and symbols. All fossil remains associated with the late Paleolithic are assignable to *Homo sapiens* of essentially modern type.

The fauna of the Late Paleolithic in Europe was characteristic of cold climates and included most of the forms of the Middle Paleolithic, although range and proportions varied with climatic changes. Part of the time great herds of horses, bison, oxen, and red deer roamed much of Europe. The reindeer was prominent much of the time, and in cold periods penetrated as far south as central Spain and Italy.

Stone tool types were highly varied. Many Mousterian tools, such as side scrapers and denticulate tools, continued to be made throughout the late Paleolithic. Most tools were made from blades split from carefully prepared cores by means of a blunt bone tool struck with a hammer stone (Figure 6–6). Such blades were often used directly, but many other tools were fashioned from them by shaping and retouching in a variety of ways. Blade tools actually appear in Acheulian times and are fairly common in some Mousterian sites, just as flake tools occur in the later period, emphasizing the continuity of Paleolithic cultures. If one compares the totality of the tool assemblages at typical Middle and Late Paleolithic sites, very great differences are evident, and tools and techniques represented in one type of site may be totally absent

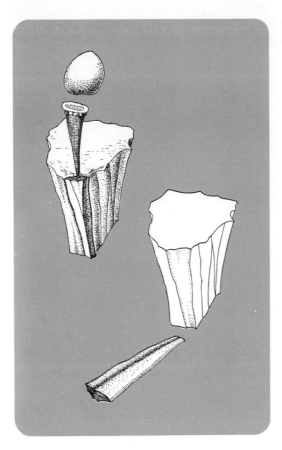

Figure 6–6 Blade tool manufacture. Long flakes are removed from a prepared core by tapping a bone tool with a hammer stone. This technique is very rapid and the blade does not need further shaping if it is to be used as a simple cutting tool.

from the other. At the same time, other tools and techniques are very similar, if not identical.

Eisely offers a measurement of the changing efficiency of stone tool workmanship during the Paleolithic. On Oldowan pebble tools, a point of flint provides about 5 cm of cutting edge; on Acheulian hand axes, 20 cm; on Mousterian tools, 100 cm, on Upper Paleolithic tools, 300 to 1200 cm. This exponential rate of increase in cutting edges provides a rough index of overall technological improvement during the Paleolithic, but it is well to keep in mind that the techniques are not mutually exclusive and that the different techniques produced tools used for different purposes.[2]

Some prehistorians, such as Clark, doubt that the basic Late Paleolithic tradition originated in Europe. An exclusively blade tradition is found at El Dabba, Cyreniaca, in North Africa, datable at about 36,000 B.C. and believed to be intrusive from Southeast Asia. The Emiran of Palestine, a relatively late phase of similar culture, is immediately overlaid by Aurignacian-type deposits.

Among the varied new tools of the Late Paleolithic, scrapers and burins (engraving tools) were common. Multiple tools often were made, such as

[2] Ibid.

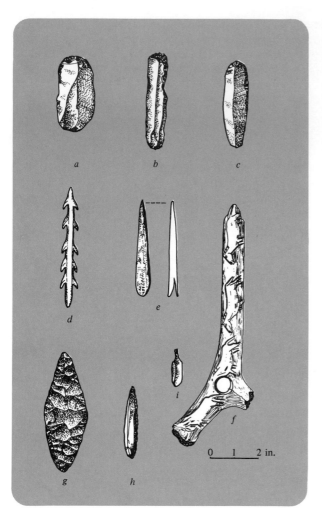

Figure 6–7   Late Paleolithic tools: (a,b,c) end scraper; (d) Magdalenian harpoon (after Bordes); (e) Aurignacian bone point (after Bordes); (f) *baton de commandment* (after Oakley); (g) Solutrean point (after Leakey); (h) backed point (after Oakley); (i) perforator (after Bordes). The stone tools are the product of more complex and refined techniques.

double scrapers, multiple burins and borers, or composite affairs having two tools on the same flake. Work in bone, ivory, and horn likewise became very important and varied. Tools included awls, eyed needles, shaft straighteners, and progressively more elaborate harpoon points. (See Figure 6–7.) Engraving of designs and carving of female figurines are among the early manifestations of the famous Late Paleolithic art. The best artwork known consists of engraved, painted, or modeled representations, mainly of animals, found in caves.

The earliest European Late Paleolithic cultures are the Aurignacian and Perigordian. These two cultures are completely independent, at least in France. The typical tools of one are not found in the other, and tools found in both occur in quite different proportions. The evidence is that the two evolved independently and contemporaneously. They must have shifted territory, however, for in some sites—for example, La Ferrassie in the Dordogne—an early

Perigordian stratum is overlaid by strata representing five successive and different phases of the Aurignacian. These in turn are overlaid by strata containing three phases of evolved or Late Perigordian. It seems clear that Early and Late Perigordian bracketed the Aurignacian in France and Spain. Similar types are found elsewhere in Africa and Asia, but sequences are not yet well understood. In south Russia a tradition called the Gravettian appears well developed and is immediately succeeded by the Solutrean.

Early Perigordian often is found directly overlaying Mousterian deposits. Large curved pointed blades with blunt backs, called Châtelperron points, and blades with steep retouched edges are characteristic. Later phases of the Perigordian are characterized by gravette blades, similar to Châtelperron, but straight rather than curved. Numerous small human sculptures and additional tool types also appear in later phases.

Sites in the Aurignacian tradition are more widely distributed. Thick scrapers and other distinctive stone tools are found in the Aurignacian, but more striking is the extensive use of bone tools, including javelin points, chisels, gouges, and dart-shaft straighteners. Decorated bits of stone, ivory, bone, and pierced teeth and shells probably were worn as necklaces. Female torsos were carved in bone, and profile drawings of various animals were engraved and painted on cave walls.

In many respects the Aurignacian tradition appears to lead directly into the final period of the Late Paleolithic, the Magdalenian, but in much of western Europe the Solutrean intervenes. This tradition apparently developed in central or eastern Europe but spread westward and reached its fullest development in southwestern France and northern Spain during a relatively cold climatic period. The finest flint chipping of the Paleolithic characterizes the Solutrean, utilizing a new technique to remove flat, regular, parallel flakes. The best specimens are laurel-leaf blades, so-called from their shape. Shouldered points are also characteristic. Bone implements are neither distinctive nor of great importance.

At least six identifiable variations of the Magdalenian are also known; the earliest, the proto-Magdalenian, sometimes is succeeded by late Aurignacian deposits. Some of the sequential differences represent progressive elaborations of culture, but others almost certainly represent local ecological adaptations which replaced one another in response to shifting climatic and biotic conditions.

The Magdalenian phase is widespread and is marked by rapid changes. Its most characteristic features are the quantity of bone and horn tools and, especially in France and Spain, its highly developed art. The most extensively used stone implements were long blades, prismatic in cross section, with parallel sides. Few distinctive types occurred, possibly because of the greater attention paid to bone and horn. During the Magdalenian, javelin points developed into simple harpoons, then into more complex forms, first with barbs on one side, then on both. Awls, needles, chisels, and many other tools were made of bone. The first definite "machine" appeared, the spear thrower, a device to extend the arm and give greater leverage in throwing a spear. The first evidence of the bow and arrow also comes from this period.

Magdalenian art involves portable objects and mural decorations on the walls of caves. Stone, bone, ivory, and antlers were delicately engraved and carved or sculptured in the round. Utilitarian objects often were carefully decorated. Realistic, stylized, and geometric decorations all occur. (See Figure 6–8.) Cave painting developed from engraved outlines and single-color painting to elaborate use of several colors with delicate shadings. Perspective in drawing reached a point not duplicated again until the European Renaissance. A high degree of realism is present. (See Figure 6–9.) Most subjects are animals, but there are some masked human figures in what appear to be dancing postures. The subject matter and the fact that most of the known mural art occurs in the deepest parts of caves without evidence of habitation suggest magical or ritual purposes for the art.

Late Paleolithic peoples like those of the Mousterian, were primarily hunters, although in some regions considerable use was made of fish. Both presumably utilized the plant environment for food as well. The coexistence of

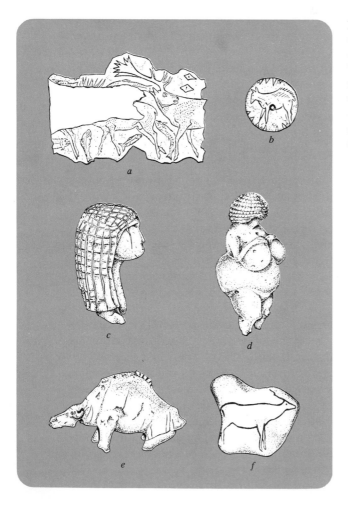

Figure 6–8 Late Paleolithic Art: (a) Magdalenian engraving on horn (after MacCurdy); (b) Magdalenian bone button (after MacCurdy); (c) female head in ivory (after Mac-Curdy); (d) Aurignacian figurine (after MacCurdy); (e) carving of animal (bison?); (f) engraving on stone. (Not to common scale.)

Figure 6-9 Painting of hind from Altamira, Spain. (After Boule and Vallois.)

Polychrome Bison from Font-de-Gaume, Dordogne, France. (Courtesy of the American Museum of Natural History.)

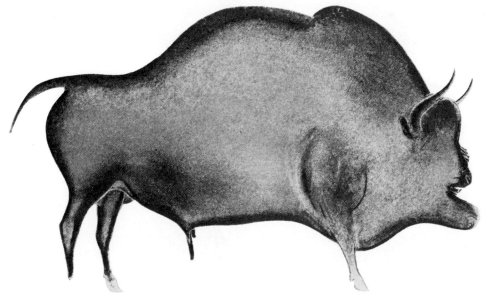

numerous similar neighboring sites suggests delimited tribal hunting territories and a fairly complicated social organization. The cooperative killing of
large animals also suggests well-coordinated activities. Both caves or rock
shelters and open locations were occupied. Some of the latter may have been
seasonal hunting sites, but in Russia remains of pithouses have been found.
Some must have been occupied by several families. The Sungir site in Russia
shows that tailored skin clothing very like that of the modern Eskimo was
worn. Beads, pins, bracelets, and anklets were made of bone, stone, ivory,
amber, fired clay, and shells. The dead were buried with full clothing and their
ornaments. The shells especially provide clear evidence of extensive trade in
articles for conspicuous consumption.

The two most widespread culture types of the Late Paleolithic of Europe
were the Aurignacian and the Magdalenian. Many local and temporal variations existed, and the river Rhine seems to have been a boundary between
eastern and western versions.

Late Paleolithic sequences in Africa and Asia are still unsatisfactorily
known. In North Africa in the very Late Paleolithic, the Aterian, based on a
Late Levalloisian tradition, was succeeded by the Capsian and the Oranian.

Horse and hind from Altamira, Spain. (Courtesy of the American Museum of Natural
History.)

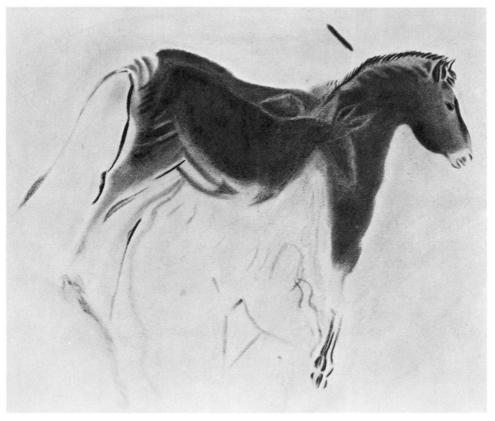

Microliths (very small stone implements) are characteristic of the Capsian, which includes also implements in the Châtelperron–Gravettian tradition characteristic of the French Perigordian. The Oranian, occurring to the west along the coast from Tunis to Morocco, offers relatively crude stone implements with many bone tools.

The Egyptian sequences seem to resemble those of Europe in both flake and core traditions. The Upper Paleolithic here terminates in the Sibelian, characterized by advanced Levalloisian-type tools and, in its late phases, many microliths.

In Uganda, in eastern Africa, a culture resembling the Capsian of North Africa is found. However, it seems to be Middle Pleistocene, much older than the Capsian of North Africa. A local culture related to that known as Stillbay seems to conclude the Upper Paleolithic here.

South Africa seems to have had a number of local cultures in the Late Paleolithic that cannot well be equated with developments elsewhere. The Smithfield culture, marked by the extensive use of shale for tools, seems to be a continuation in this region of the Lower Paleolithic into the recent geological period. It is followed by the Wilton, a culture with typical microliths. This same culture in East Africa is associated with pottery and hence is probably Neolithic.

The Congo region of Africa is little known. Most finds are recent and suggest that the Congo is an area in which early types of implements persisted much later than in other regions. Indeed, some believe the Congo was mostly uninhabitable swamp during much of the Paleolithic.

In western Asia, Late Paleolithic cultures with more or less resemblance to those of Europe are known, in part coexisting with the latest Mousterian sites, in part apparently merging with Mousterian traditions, as in Europe. In other places, as at the Shanidar Cave in Iraq, there is a sharp break between Mousterian and the local Late Paleolithic culture known as Baradostian. In some mountain regions and in Soviet Asia there seem to be no intervening cultures between the Mousterian and the Mesolithic. It seems likely that these areas were not populated during the time of the Weichsel glaciation. Eastern and southern Asia are not well known. As noted earlier, chopper-chopping tool traditions persisted, but other traditions occasionally occur.

In the Middle and Late Paleolithic the accelerating pace of technological development, so apparent in our time, first becomes evident. Although these periods were much shorter than the Lower Paleolithic, evidence appears for whole new categories of activity. New techniques of stoneworking are accompanied by a great increase in specialized types of tools. New uses of wood and bone became prominent. Hafted tools and missile weapons appear, all giving increasing prowess in hunting the larger mammals. Evidence of cannibalism is widespread from China to Europe. Controlled use of fire, construction of shelters, and use of clothing permitted residence in colder climates. Medical knowledge and social concern are indicated by successful amputation at Shanidar Cave and successful trephining operations in Late Paleolithic Europe. Burials with offerings indicate concern for the dead. Interest in esthetic problems is evidenced in Late Paleolithic art, and there is indication that people practiced magic and developed religious beliefs and rituals. Social mechanisms for the organization of small groups probably existed, although we can only guess at their forms. Some specialization of roles and skills, ideas of property, and trade or exchange are evident. During the Late Paleolithic, human beings probably exerted major impact on the environment through the use of fire to remove or regenerate vegetation and through their hunting and possible contribution to the extinction of some Pleistocene mammalian species. Except that they had not yet developed a means of food production but continued to rely upon hunting and collecting of natural products, Paleolithic peoples had laid, in broad outline, the essential base for human civilization.

3. Culture History of the Old World: Mesolithic

As the Weichsel glaciation retreated, environmental conditions changed rapidly. In Europe new areas became habitable; warmer climates were accompanied by the return of the forests to large areas and great changes in the distribution of game animals. In parts of Africa and Asia desert and semidesert areas expanded. In Europe herd hunting was replaced by individual hunting as the reindeer were replaced with deer, elk, aurochs (a relative of domesticated cattle), and wild pig. The bow and arrow came into general use. More extensive use was made of shellfish, fish, and wild fowl. Canoes and, in the far north, skis and sledges provided new means of transportation. The increased powers of cultural adaptation evident in the Late Paleolithic are even more clearly evident.

In western Europe the two major cultures in the southern part are the Azilian of southern France and Spain and the Tardenoisian of England, Germany, and France. In both of these, and to a lesser extent in the closely related local cultures of Spain, Ireland, and Scotland, the dominant stone tools were small, geometric microliths, evidently related to those of the earlier Capsian culture of North Africa. The Azilian is further marked by many pebbles painted in geometric or dot-dash designs in red. The uses of these are unknown, but they represent a dramatic change from the elaborate art forms of the preceding Magdalenian period. Tardenoisian cultures are generally located north of the Azilian, but in some places where both occur, the Tardenoisian is later than the Azilian.

In northern Europe, the Mesolithic is later in time than in the south. Counting of varves or layers in the deposits of glacial clays provide definite datings.

During Period I, from 8300 to 6800 B.C., a series of local cultures characterized by tanged points, reindeer-antler picks or axes, microliths, and a variety of blade and other tools of Upper Paleolithic types spread from Belgium to the Ukraine and up the Norwegian coast. The scarcity of stone axes in these cultures suggests that the forest had not yet spread extensively.

During Period II, 6800 to 5000 B.C., cultures called Maglemosean extended from Britain to Russia. Most of the sites are on the margins of inland waters and swampy places. Subsistence came from hunting forest animals and birds, fishing, and gathering wild plant foods. Wood was used extensively for implements, handles, and dugout canoes. Bone points of specialized types, for use in hunting, fishing, and bird catching, were perhaps the most important implements, but there was as well a wide variety of stone axes and distinctive smaller tools. Barbless fishhooks appear for the first time, as does the domesticated dog.

Period III, 5000 to 2500 B.C., saw the continuation of a variety of cultures based on the Maglemosian, of which the best known is the Ertebolle of Denmark. These cultures are characterized by huge shell middens, indicating a heavy dependence on the sea for food. Some of the points found imply the use of the bow and arrow, known more definitely from cave paintings in Spain. Toward the end of the period, some axes are made by pecking or grinding stone, and some coarse pottery cooking vessels appear. These techniques — stone grinding and pottery making — suggest contact with Neolithic peoples.

The changes mentioned above are essentially modifications of environmental strategies used to meet the altered climatic and hunting conditions that existed in Europe at the close of the Pleistocene. The changes are not of kind but of detail, so that, for Europe and Africa, there seems to be no cultural justification for distinguishing the beginning of the Holocene from the end of the Pleistocene. In southwestern Asia and perhaps a few other favored spots, however, people were experimenting with the domestication of plants and animals.[3] This revolutionary cultural adaptation would later turn most human beings into food producers. The transition from specialized hunting and collecting to food production took place far more quickly than the earlier transition from unspecialized hunting and gathering to specialized hunting and collecting.

The beginning of this adaptation involves the beginnings of plant cultivation and animal domestication and, perforce, took place within or near the natural habitats of potential plant and animal domesticates. One such habitat in Palestine was occupied by a culture called the Natufian. Although many of the tools from Natufian sites are microliths, resembling those of the Capsian culture elsewhere in North Africa, the Natufian sites also contain tools consisting of small blades set in straight handles. These were almost certainly used to cut grass or grain, as they possess a characteristic sheen or polish that develops on stones so used. It is not certain that the Natufians were actually cultivating grain, but they and some of their neighbors, who lived in areas that had become increasingly arid and therefore lacking in game resources, had certainly turned to the use of large seeded grasses for food and may have begun the experimentation that led to the cultivation of these grasses.

[3] Daniel Zohary and Pinhas Spiegel-Roy, "Beginnings of Fruit Growing in the Old World," *Science*, **187**:319–327 (January 31, 1975).

4. Culture History of the Old World: Neolithic

The Neolithic was originally identified primarily in terms of the appearance of stone tools made by polishing and grinding rather than chipping or flaking. Today, however, evidence of the presence of farming is the major criterion of the Neolithic. The reason for this shift is that farming permits an entirely new way of life, whereas it makes little difference to a hunter whether his knives and arrow points are flaked or ground into shape. In Europe polished stone tools appear later than farming, and their appearance sometimes is used to distinguish between the early Neolithic and the later or full Neolithic. In other parts of the world, however, polished stone tools often are found among peoples lacking knowledge of farming.

V. Gordon Childe often called the Neolithic a "revolution," because it opened the door to an entirely new way of life. People began to produce their food and were less dependent upon the vagaries of nature. People also could build more or less permanent villages and live in larger clusters. Moreover, these larger clusters required much less land for survival and hence could be closer together. More people and more contacts led to a faster rate of invention and a much faster rate of diffusion. Finally, as techniques of farming improved in favorable locations, surpluses permitted the support of nonfarming specialists and the carrying on of more trade.

By a revolution Childe did not mean that a sudden, violent change took place in ways of life, but that the practice of farming, once begun, led ultimately to a radical difference in the way people lived. The first farming probably was carried on as a sort of sideline by people for whom hunting and gathering still remained important. The number of cultivated plants was few and farming techniques were relatively unproductive. Initially only a sharpened stick served for cultivating and planting, and grains were cut with crude sickles made by setting small stone blades in wood or baked-clay handles. Even the hoe was not a great improvement, and it was not until the invention of the plow and the use of draft animals that farming really became a successful way of life in many parts of the Old World.

The first stages of farming and of animal domestication are not yet known. The major center probably was in the foothill and upland valleys in the mountains surrounding Mesopotamia, from the Zagros on the east, to the mountains of Lebanon and Palestine. Here wild ancestors of wheat and barley, the earliest grains, still grow. In this region also are found wild relatives of several domestic animals, such as goats, sheep, cattle, and pigs. The earliest farmers probably already were harvesting wild grains. The sickles of the Natufian of Palestine have been mentioned. Hand-milling stones, querns, and possible sickle stones are found in the Shanidar area by about 8000 B.C. A domesticated sheep is dated from this area about 8900 B.C. In this area game was not abundant, but the long, dry summers favored the development of grasses that stored a relatively large amount of nutriment in their seeds. Once it was found that cultivation could increase their yield, even the most primitive farming became rewarding.

In this region also appears one of the oldest known villages of people who definitely were farmers. This is the site of M'lefaat, east of Mosul in Iraq. The site has been only partially excavated, but it shows several architectural levels. Mortars, pestles, querns or grinding stones, and stone axes or hoes are fairly well made, but there appears to be no pottery or evidence of domesticated animals.

Better known is the site of Jarmo, a little farther south. This site was occupied for some time by a population of about 150 people, who built mud-walled cottages having several rooms. They grew barley, pulses, and two different kinds of wheat, which they cut with flint sickles, ground on stone querns, and baked in ovens or ate as porridge out of stone bowls.[4] They kept domesticated goats and possibly some other animals, although the horse, sheep, cattle, dog, and pig bones found may be from wild species. They also ate quantities of land snails. They experimented with modeling in clay, but baked pottery does not appear until the last third of the occupation period, and then in such advanced form that the technique was probably learned from others. That the Jarmo people were not isolated is shown by their use of volcanic glass or obsidian for some of their chipped-stone tools, materials that must have been traded over a distance of at least 300 miles.

The earliest post-Natufian levels at the biblical site of Jericho show similar characteristics, although the architecture is somewhat more complex than at Jarmo. Both these sites represent early but already well-established village life based upon cultivation of cereals and the domesticated goat. The dog and possibly the cat were present at Jericho; the dog was possibly, but not certainly, present at Jarmo. Evidence for the ages of Jarmo and Jericho has been somewhat contradictory, but a date around 6500 B.C. for both is now accepted by Braidwood. Simple agriculture probably began 1,000 or more years earlier.

Jarmo and Jericho are important primarily because they were among the first fully reported sites excavated by modern techniques that illustrate the transition to settled village life based on agriculture and animal husbandry. More recent excavations, as yet incompletely reported, suggest that the Anatolian plateau in Turkey may have been the primary center of development for village life. Sites excavated so far, such as the town of Çatal Hüyük, appear not to be older than Jarmo or Jericho, but the inventory of plants and animals, the size of settlement, and sophistication and complexity of material culture seem considerably more advanced.

According to Protsch and Berger,[5] the earliest evidence of domesticated animals are goat and sheep bones from Asia in West Central Iran. These remains are dated at 8000 B.C. Evidence from Ukrainian sites indicates that the horse was domesticated there between 2000 and 4000 B.C. The primacy of Southwest Asia (traditionally referred to as the Near East) as the center for domestication of animals is challenged by findings in Greek Thessaly which

[4] Daniel Zohary and Maria Hopf, "Domestication of Pulses in the Old World," *Science*, **182**:887–894 (November 30, 1973).

[5] Reiner Protsch and Rainer Berger, "Earliest Radiocarbon Dates for Domesticated Animals," *Science*, **179**:235–239 (January 19, 1973).

indicate that pigs and cattle were domesticated there at around 7000 B.C. The straits of the Bosporus, separating Greece from Southwest Asia, do not represent a significant geographical barrier, and it may be that the whole region was characterized by the same cultural developments.

Although farming in Europe was undoubtedly later than in Southwest Asia, use of new dating techniques has moved the dates of European farming villages beyond 6000 B.C. The major domesticated plants not only are not native to the European area, but had to be adapted from growing in a region of winter rains and dry summers to the rainy summers of much of Europe. The earliest European farmers almost certainly learned to cut and burn the forests and planted in cleared areas, for the grasslands of that area are almost uncultivable with a simple digging stick or even a hoe. Cutting the forests resulted in extending the grasslands, so the early farmers had to move frequently in search of new areas. Southern Scandinavia was the site of agricultural villages and domesticated farm animals by 3500 B.C. By 4000 B.C. such common elements as the cultivation of cereal crops, the domestication of animals, forest clearance with stone axes, and settlements of rectangular houses were widespread throughout temperate Europe. The farming pattern did not totally replace the hunting and collecting way of life; the two continued to coexist for some time.

A third adaptation, swidden agriculture, which involves the planting of mixed crops, often roots and tubers, in temporary forest clearings is not well known archaeologically. Swidden agriculturalists relied heavily upon wooden tools and artifacts, their village sites were often moved, and acid forest soils tended to destroy evidence of their presence. Presumably swidden agriculture is as old as or older than the village farming way of life. Village farmers, specializing in grain crops and domesticated animals, could maintain continuous use of their fields by allowing animals to graze on them during fallow periods or by systematically applying animal manure to them. In many parts of the world, swidden agriculturalists could be replaced by settled agriculturalists only when improved axes or perhaps the action of swidden agriculture itself led to the conversion of forests to grasslands suitable for raising domesticated animals. Similarly in many grassland areas settled agriculture became possible only when plows capable of cutting through the sod were developed.

Farming may have entered Europe in several ways. One major route was probably east of the Black Sea into southern Russia and then westward. Another was across the Bosporus and up the Danube Valley. A third was along the Mediterranean coast, possibly in part by sea. Along each of these routes different cultural adaptations developed. When these met and fused, new patterns emerged. In other parts of the Old World the history seems similar.

Although early farmers in some areas may have moved in search of better farming areas, the spread of farming does not imply widespread migrations, nor should we assume that farming was the invention of a single people in a single area.[6] Although middle-altitude regions of the Near East seem to have

[6] Jack R. Harlan, "Agricultural Origins: Centers and Noncenters," *Science,* **174**:468–474 (October 29, 1971).

Figure 6–10 Reconstructed Neolithic lake shore dwellings in Switzerland. (After MacCurdy and R. R. Schmidt.)

been the scene of the earliest farming experiments around 8000 B.C., other regions were not far behind. Excavations by Chester Gorman at Spirit Cave in Thailand suggest that fruit and root crops were cultivated by about 7000 B.C.,[7] and recent evidence indicates that experiments in Mexico were equally early, with other New World areas not far behind. It seems likely that the changing environments of the postglacial period, with their demands for new ecological adaptations, may have played a part in stimulating people in widely separated areas to experiment with ways of improving the supply of food plants.

The village-farming way of life was accompanied by numerous other innovations. Domestication of animals was begun, probably by early farmers. It is evident that the earliest domesticated animals were kept primarily for their flesh. Early domesticated sheep apparently had no wool, and early cattle could

[7] Chester F. Gorman, "Hoabinhian: A Pebble-Tool Complex with Early Plant Associations in Southeast Asia," *Science,* **163**:671–673 (February 14, 1969).

not effectively be milked. The use of animal fibers and milk, as well as the employment of animals to pull plows and vehicles, seem to be later developments.

Sedentary life also encouraged the use of pottery instead of containers of basketry or leather, although pottery did not completely coincide with the beginnings of agriculture. Some hunting and collecting peoples, such as the Jomon of the Japanese islands, who manufactured clay pots in 8000 B.C., are known to have manufactured and used pottery routinely. Through much of the Neolithic the varied styles of pottery made afford the archaeologist the best evidence of cultural development and relations between cultures (Figure 6–11). Trade, as we have mentioned, continued to expand, and the accumulation of property increased.

The village-farming life of the Neolithic was such a successful new type of adaptation that it spread widely throughout the Old World. The dwellers of the steppes and grasslands in some cases became herders rather than farmers, but only in remote or inhospitable areas did the older hunting and gathering

Figure 6–11 Neolithic pottery from Europe: (a) calciform vase; (b) pot with banded ornamentation; (c) late Neolithic vase with teat-shaped supports; (d) lake village pot; (e) ornamented pot from Mondsee; (f) early Neolithic vessel with stylized human figure. (After MacCurdy.)

life persist. Many arctic dwellers, such as the Lapps, became reindeer herders, but others continued in the older pattern and some desert dwellers, such as the Bushmen, continued to hunt and gather. In the Orient farming penetrated far into the Pacific but did not reach Australia and Tasmania. Finally, in more favored spots, such as the lowlands of Mesopotamia, villages grew into towns, perhaps with attached villages, and in some cases grew into cities, initiating the next great shift, the urban revolution. (See Chapter 8 for fuller treatment of the technology of food production.)

5. Culture History of the Old World: The Urban Revolution

Once towns became large enough, a new way of life was imposed. Country life and town life became increasingly different, for town life required a greater degree of organization and was accompanied by increasing specialization. The number of political and religious functionaries increased, as did the number and kinds of artisans and tradesmen. Moreover, the towns had to establish increasing controls over the sources of food, thus encouraging the formation of larger political units.

The urban revolution was marked by a number of innovations. The invention of smelting, first of copper, then its alloy, bronze, permitted the manufacture of new and better tools and containers. Because the raw materials for metallurgy are unevenly distributed, trade on a larger scale and over longer distances became essential, and this in turn provided mechanisms for the more rapid diffusion of new ideas and techniques. The invention of the wheel facilitated travel and transport. Increased trade called for record keeping and hence probably stimulated the development of writing. In arid regions cultivation could be expanded through irrigation, and large-scale irrigation works were more efficient than small ones. Large-scale irrigation, however, required a higher level of organization, often over larger areas. So the urban revolution was accompanied in most places by the rise of city-states and empires.

All these trends were stimulated by the discovery of iron smelting about 1500 B.C. Not only does iron provide better tools, weapons, and containers, but it is easier to work and the raw materials are more widely distributed and more cheaply extracted and processed. Each of the new innovations seems to have spread more rapidly than the earlier traits. Thus, although it took over 3,000 years for village-farming patterns to spread from the Near East to England, it took less than 1,000 years after its invention for bronze to appear in the latter country at around 1900 or 1800 B.C. Ironworking reached Germany shortly after 750 B.C., and the first iron users appeared in Britain a little before 400 B.C.

The metal ages and the urban revolution are viewed by many as laying the groundwork for the industrial revolution. Until the industrial revolution, most people in all parts of the world still lived essentially as they did in Neolithic times. While it is true that they often had metal tools and certain other technological products associated with the urban revolution, most people were village-dwelling farmers who grew their own food, made most of their own tools, shelter, and clothing, and had little disposable surplus. Whether people lived by slash-burn agriculture in Borneo or southwestern Asia, or were peasants in an ancient farming village in India or Europe, they were closely attached to the land and were little affected by the way of life developed in the city.

Wherever the industrial revolution has been fully developed, however, radical changes have occurred. In such countries as England, Germany, and the United States the majority of people now live in cities and do no farming. Farmers are increasingly affected by the ways of the city. They tend no longer to grow their own food, weave their own cloth, or make many of their own tools, but to grow a crop for the market, sell it for cash and then buy food, clothing, and other items. In such places as Southern California, although there is a large agricultural production, 90 percent of the population is urban, and the way of life of most of the remaining people is almost indistinguishable from that of the urban dweller except for their occupation. A very similar situation is found in the fruit and truck-farming areas of New Jersey and many parts of the Middle West. In recent years the industrial revolution has spread rapidly throughout the world, and we may reasonably anticipate soon a world in which only a minority of people are farmers and that these will share in the lifeways of the city.

This great shift poses many problems, for most of our institutions, habits of thought, and values were developed under the Neolithic way of life (insofar as some of them do not go back to our hunting and gathering ancestors). The Neolithic was a successful type of adaptation, for it led to a great increase in human population and a much more efficient utilization of the environment. It seems clear, however, that the institutions and points of view suitable for a Neolithic pattern are inadequate to an industrial civilization. As Howells has said, "The Neolithic Way of Life was a success, providing we can now grow beyond it." [8]

6. Prehistory of the Americas

The prehistory of the Americas is a complex and fascinating subject. Its main interest in an introductory text is the evidence it affords of a relatively, and perhaps completely, independent series of developments paralleling those of the later prehistory of the Old World. It is thus useful in checking theories about cultural change and development.

Human beings arrived late in the New World as fully developed and relatively modern types of *Homo sapiens;* this places a maximum date of about 50,000 years ago for their first migration. Actually it must have been much

---

[8] William Howells, *Back of History: The Story of Our Own Origins* (Garden City, N.Y.: Doubleday, 1954), p. 223.

later. Every serious student is agreed that the earliest American Indians must have walked across from Asia at a time when lowered sea levels created a land bridge in the Bering Strait area between Asia and Alaska. This agreement is for the simple reason that people evidently were in the Americas before they developed any kind of canoes or boats. Moreover, there is no evidence that humans occupied northeastern Asia before 20,000 years ago. To confuse the issue, there are few resemblances between the known stone implements of northeast Asian cultures and those of the early American Indians.

The dating of the earliest people in America is closely related, then, to the last Wisconsin glaciation and the conditions just before it. People could have entered America just before the full onset of the Wisconsin glaciation; there is no evidence that they did so, and there are good arguments against it. The next possibility was during two interstadial periods in the Wisconsin glaciation, the first 50,000 to 40,000 years ago, the second 27,000 to 8,000 years ago. A number of finds suggest one or both of these possibilities. Unfortunately those sites with reliable dating consist of evidence of fire of problematical origin, while all sites containing human artifacts for which great age has been claimed are quite problematical in their dating. Finally, earlier evidence of humanity in northeastern Asia must be found. Many archaeologists, such as Jennings, intuitively feel that humanity did reach America in this period, but also they are compelled to reject all the evidence so far advanced as not being reliable or proved.

Evidence generally accepted as incontrovertible places humans in North America at around 15,000 B.C.; somewhat less reliable datings extend this to 25,000 B.C.; and evidence accepted by some would give dates of around 50,000 B.P. or even 70,000 B.P.[9] People also had reached the southern part of South America by about 11,000 B.P. and some time must be postulated for travel from the Bering Straits.

Whatever the ultimate resolution of the time element, there is no clear relation between the tool complexes of the early American Indians and those of the Old World. Some crude chopper-scraper complexes suggest derivation from Asiatic chopper-chopping tool traditions; others show Mousteriod similarities, and there is some evidence of blade-tool techniques. Many other widespread complexes, such as those producing the fluted Folsom point, have as yet no Old World counterparts. What does seem clear is the early inhabitants of America were big game hunters, dependent in part in North America upon a number of large extinct species, such as the elephant, camel, horse, giant bison, peccary, and ground sloth.

The period of big game hunters began perhaps as early as 23,000 B.P. and terminated about 5000 B.P. Some, but not all, archaeologists believe that there was an early preprojectile point period characterized by choppers and scrapers. If such a period existed, hunting must have been relatively inefficient. The subsequent period of big game hunters has been called also the Paleo-Indian,

[9] Jeffrey L. Bada, Roy A. Schroeder, and George F. Carter, "New Evidence for the Antiquity of Man in North America Deduced from Aspartic Acid Racemization," *Science*, **184**:791–792 (May 17, 1974).

Paleo-American, Early American Hunter, and Lithic periods. Based primarily upon differences in projectile points it is subdivided in North America into the Llano, Folsom, and Plano periods. The points generally are thin, fine-chipped, and laurel-leaf shaped, differing in outline and in the presence or absence of fluting. (See Figure 6–12.) They are accompanied by a varied assemblage of scrapers, burins, hammer stones, and other cultural remains. Best known from the High Plains of North America, they evidently occurred in regional variants over most of the continent and Mesoamerica, and perhaps into South America. The spear thrower was in use, but not the bow and arrow.

The immigrants who went into the region west of the Rocky Mountains found a large, semiarid-to-desert region of low rainfall. It is true that rainfall was somewhat higher than today, and there were larger lakes and more streams. However, the plant life was not greatly different from that of today, and the amount of game was relatively small. Although the first immigrants

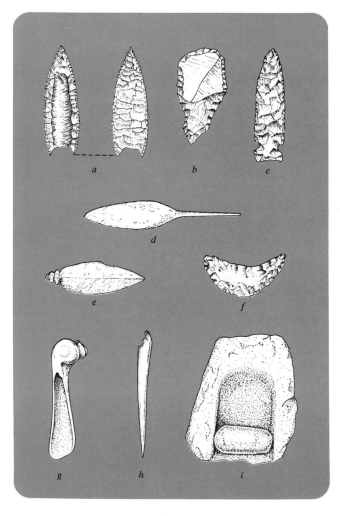

Figure 6–12 Stone, copper, and bone implements (North America): (a) Folsom point, after and before fluting; (b) scraper from a site in Massachusetts; (c) chipped-stone point (Upper Great Lakes area); (d, e) copper implements (Upper Great Lakes area); (f) crescent-shaped stone implement from a Washington site; (g) bone end scraper (Pueblo III); (h) bone awl (Pueblo III); (i) metate (Pueblo I). (After Wormington; not to scale.)

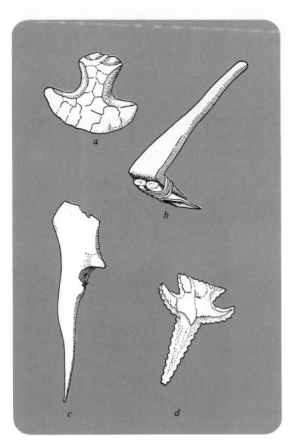

Figure 6–13 Scrapers, awl, and drill from North America: (a) chipped-flake scraper (after Moorehead); (b) hafted elk-rib scraper (after Holling); (c) bone awl (after James); (d) stone drill (after Moorehead). (Not to scale.)

probably were hunters, few confirmed evidences of their presence have so far been found. All that can be said with complete certainty is that people were present in the Great Basin 11,000 years ago and that shortly thereafter had developed an adaptation to arid lands that is possibly unique in human history. Special tools for efficiently gathering and processing a wide variety of seeds, both large and small, were invented. Milling stones for grinding seeds thus appear by 8000 B.C., as early as they are known to have been used in the Old World. Because of the good preservation in dry caves of the region, we also have recovered a wide series of specialized basketry containers such as trays, seed beaters, and watertight containers. Basketry fragments of possibly equal age in the Old World are reported only from Shanidar Cave in Iraq. To a people with few large hides and faced with the problem of collecting and storing small seeds, basketry would be particularly useful.

The desert cultures give abundant evidence that the Paleo-Indian was able to adapt culture rapidly to a new set of conditions and in the Great Basin region to evolve a unique adjustment to an inhospitable area. With increasing dessication, variations of this adaptation spread throughout arid North America, extending far south into Mexico. In some periods of drier climate, the arid-land adaptations certainly spread temporarily through the Plains area and perhaps even farther east.

The western Paleo-Indian traditions proved adaptable to California, where resources, although much more abundant, were primarily the same types of seeds, because of the long, arid summers. The California Indian expanded much more in numbers than was possible in the Great Basin and introduced many more cultural elaborations, but the basic economic pattern and repertory of techniques was not greatly different. Those Paleo-Indians who penetrated to the northern coasts, however, underwent a profound change as they adapted to the abundant resources of the salmon streams and the sea.

In the southern part of the United States, especially from west Texas to Arizona, a series of cultures known as Cochise developed within the general arid American pattern. These persisted with only minor changes for several thousand years. Arid Mexico is as yet much less well known, but there is evidence of similar local cultures extending far to the south. It is possible that, as in the case of the Natufians or their arid-land neighbors of the Old World, followers of the seed-using tradition in Mexico may have initiated the first experiments in the cultivation of the most distinctive New World cultivated grass, maize, or Indian corn.

The basically seed-gathering cultures that earlier appeared in the West either persisted with only moderate change up until recent times or formed the underlying basis for the early farming cultures that succeeded them in parts of the Southwest. The Paleoeastern tradition, on the other hand, appears to have modified into a series of regional cultures known collectively as the Archaic. The oldest cultures of this type may well have come into existence before the extinction of the mastodon in the eastern part of the country. Their most marked common character seems to be that they lie between early cultures, evidently based primarily on hunting, and later pottery-using farming cultures. Although hunting seems to have remained relatively important, the Archaic made much more use of wild vegetable foods and, where appropriate, of fish and shellfish. Many of the large shell mounds along eastern and southeastern rivers and coasts appear to be the product of Archaic cultures. Extensive trading networks developed by the Archaic people handled items as diverse as seashells from the Florida coast and worked copper from the vicinity of Lake Superior.

The final period of the Archaic cultures is still somewhat obscure. New cultures appear, using burial mounds, pottery, and possibly a simple form of nonmaize agriculture. The burial-mound complex and especially much of the pottery are suggestive of Asiatic materials, and many believe the stimulus for the earliest post-Archaic cultures to be part of a late movement of peoples from Asia. The premaize plants cultivated may possibly have been local domestications.

The great change in the eastern, however, as in the southwestern part of the United States, is associated with the introduction of maize agriculture, accompanied evidently by a long-continuing although perhaps intermittent series of influences from Mexico.

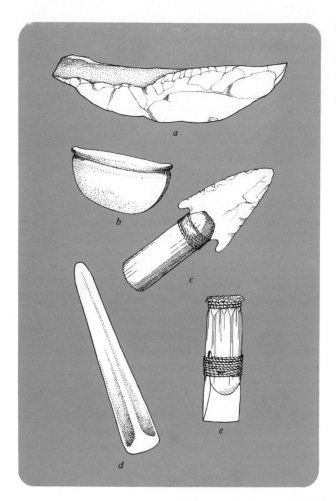

Figure 6–14 Knives and chisels from North America: (a) curved flake knife (after Moorehead); (b) semilunar knife (after Willoughby); (c) hafted flint knife (after Willoughby); (d) copper chisel (after Moorehead); (e) chisel (after Goddard). (Not to scale.)

As in the Old World a major change in human life in parts of the New World was associated with the development of sedentary villages based upon farming practices. This development in the New World probably was associated with the cultivation of maize (see later paragraphs), but this was preceded by a stage of incipient agriculture. Botanical and archaeological evidence indicates four major areas of incipient agriculture in the New World: the eastern United States, central Mexico, Peru, and the tropical forests of South America.

The first is of minor importance, involving cultivation of the sunflower, several varieties of the goosefoot or amaranth (*Chenopodium*), and a variety of the squash (*Cucurbita pepo*). These were cultivated in the Mississippi Valley and to the east as early as 1000 B.C., but probably provided only a small part of the subsistence base. True farming in the eastern United States did not begin until maize cultivation spread from nuclear America.

The second center of importance was in Mexico. In the heartland of Mexico we have as yet little information on premaize agriculture, but from caves in the arid northeast of Mexico, in Tamaulipas, we have the oldest evidence of cultivation in the Americas, where, in what MacNeish calls the Infernillo phase between 7000 and 5000 B.C., there is evidence of domesticated squash (*Cucurbita pepo*) and traces of possibly domesticated peppers, gourds, and small beans. Amaranth varieties probably also were important. Associated with these are flint implements, cordage, and basketry similar to those used by the collecting peoples of arid North America. In the next Ocampo phase, 5000–3000 B.C., cultivated beans are certain. In the succeeding thousand years a small-eared, rather primitive maize was cultivated. Even in this latest period, MacNeish estimates only 9 percent of the food supply was from cultivated plants. Even earlier maize, also of primitive type, has been found at Bat Cave in New Mexico, associated with a Cochise-like culture.

In recent excavations of dry caves in the valley of Tehuacán, south of Puebla, Mexico, MacNeish has exposed a complete sequence from the collection of wild maize, through various stages of domestication, to the emergence of sedentary village farmers. Wild maize was evidently gathered and employed as food by a hunting and gathering people using these caves early in the Coxcatlan phase, dated between 5200 and 3400 B.C. Definitely cultivated maize appears in the Abejas phase between 3400 and 2300 B.C. Wild chili, avocados, and gourds also were early, followed by amaranth, tepary beans, yellow zapotes, and squash (*Cucurbita moschata*), all apparently cultivated. An accidental cross of maize with another grass, a species of *Tripsacum*, probably occurred elsewhere (perhaps the Balsas Valley), giving rise to a series of new hybrids. Evidence of intromission of *Tripsacum* genes occurs in some Abejas-phase specimens. It is also found in most North American corns, including most of the important commercial varieties. Significantly, all original maizes of South America evidently diffused to that continent before the *Tripsacum* cross occurred.

As maize improved under domestication, it became increasingly important in the diet until, as in the Near East, a sedentary village life began, laying the basis for the rapid emergence of more complex civilizations. This change began possibly in the Abejas phase, but it is well established for the Ajalpan phase between 1500 and 960 B.C. These people were full-time farmers, cultivating hybrid corn, three kinds of squash (*mixta, moschata*, and *pepo*), gourds, amaranths, beans, chili, avocados, zapotes, and cotton. A similar and perhaps slightly older sequence has recently been established from the nearby valley of Oaxaca.

In Peru, archaeological evidence from the small river valleys which flow from the Andes to the Pacific indicates that coastal peoples had adopted a subsistence pattern involving the use of marine resources and the cultivation of small gardens between 4200 and 2650 B.C. They cultivated jack and lima beans, gourds, and squashes. Domesticated cotton first appears around 2500 B.C., but the late appearance of maize around 2500 B.C. suggests it is an import from Mesoamerica. The appearance of maize is marked by the development of sedentary villages.

From the interior of Peru, Guitarrero Cave in the valley of Callejón de Huaylas yielded examples of fully domesticated common beans (*Phaseolus vulgaris*) and lima beans (*Phaseolus lunatus*). The beans were found in the portion of stratum II which has a carbon-14 date of 7680 B.C. The early date supports the view that the Peruvian area was an independent center of domestication, distinct from Mesoamerica.

The fourth center of cultivation is not yet substantiated by archaeological evidence but must be postulated to account for the origin of a number of lowland cultivated plants, such as manioc (*Manihot utilisima* and *M. api*), the sweet potato (*Ipomoea batatas*), and the peanut (*Arachis hybogaea*). Some tropical fruits, such as the pineapple, may be associated with this development. The presence of this complex at about 1000 B.C. in lowland Venezuela is inferred from archaeological evidence. An independent village development may have arisen in connection with the lowland tropical cultivation.

Pottery, usually associated with farming, seems to have two, possibly three, independent centers of origin in the Americas. In the United States, pottery making, which may ultimately be of Asiatic origin, occurred in the Northeast perhaps as early as 1500 B.C. and in the Southeast as early as 2000 B.C. The second pottery center in nuclear America appears to have been in northern South America; at least our oldest definitely dated pottery complex (about 2500 B.C.) thus far comes from the Valdivia phase in coastal Ecuador (although some even older pottery is now known from Colombia). Similar pottery from Panama dates about 2100 B.C. These ceramics are simple enough that they may form part of a basic substratum underlying both Peruvian and Mexican pottery, but as yet there is no definite evidence. The oldest known pottery in Mexico is from the Purron phase (2300–1500 B.C.) of the Tehuacán Valley. The oldest known Peruvian pottery is some centuries later. (See Figure 6–15.) A third center of origin, in California, is possible, following the discovery of a group of ceramic objects dated at approximately 6500 B.P.[10]

Shortly after 1000 B.C., in both Mexico and Peru, the sedentary villages were developing into towns having elaborate ceremonial centers. Initially these great ceremonial centers may have served a number of small towns and villages, with only a small population nucleus around the centers themselves. In time they developed into towns such as La Venta in southern Vera Cruz, Mexico, and Chavin in Peru. In Mexico the pre-Classic period was marked by some growth of true urbanism, including the development of an elaborate calendar based on complicated astronomical observations, a rudimentary system of writing, fine stone carving, and the beginnings of stone architecture.

The Classic period was marked by a great efflorescence of the Mexican and Central American cultures, with a considerable degree of cultural uniformity over extensive areas. Cities became large in this period; Teotihuacán, northeast of modern Mexico City, probably reached a population of 100,000 or more. Political unity or empires may have existed, controlling extended areas.

The post-Classic period was evidently one of some confusion and of breakdown of cultural and political unity. Numerous local cultures developed. In turn this was followed by what some have called a militaristic period, in which

[10] Christopher E. Drover, "Seasonal Exploitation of Chione Clams on the Southern California Coast," *The Journal of California Anthropology*, 1:224–232, (Winter 1974).

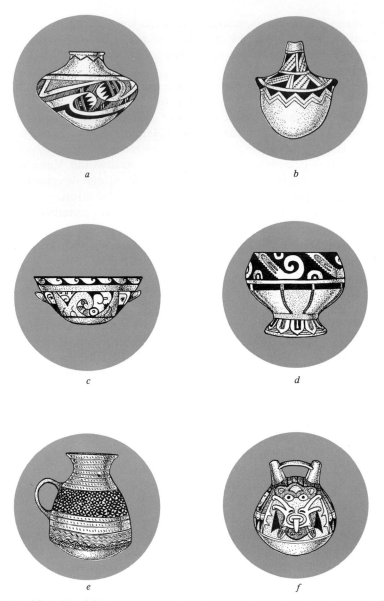

Figure 6-15 New World Pottery: (a, b) jars from ancient Pueblo cultures (after Martin, Quimby, and Collier); (c, d) Aztec pottery (after Vaillant); (e, f) Inca and Nazca pottery (after Bennett and Bird).

extended areas were unified by aggressive military action. This was the situation at the time of the Spanish Conquest, when a league of cities controlled large areas of Mexico in what is generally known as the Aztec Empire. Cities were large and numerous, especially in the highlands, and great public works, extensive commerce, and complex stratified societies were common. (See Figure 6-16.)

In South America the sequence of events was similar. In the Andean region in the Formative period, many local cultures developed. The Classic period, which had greater cultural uniformity, began about 1 A.D., and the post-Classic about 800 A.D., with the spread of highland influence to the coast in the Tiahuanaco phase. This period, in turn, was succeeded by a series of local autonomous cultures, followed by the highly organized state known as the Inca Empire.

Influences from these two great centers spread outward, undergoing local modifications and changes. In the southwestern United States the Anasazi (better known popularly as Pueblo) cultures developed on the plateau area and upper Rio Grande Valley, with primary dependence upon agriculture, elaborate ceramic traditions, and complex ritual and social organizations. However, although settlements varied in size, the Anasazi did not progress much beyond the village tradition. In the Arizona lowlands another tradition, the Hohokam, developed extended irrigation and a distinctive pottery and architecture, but underwent a severe decline before the coming of the Europeans.

Figure 6–16 Model of a Mayan temple, Yucatan, Mexico. (After Vaillant.)

In southern New Mexico and northern Chihuahua, a third tradition, Mogollon, can be distinguished, although this tradition is much influenced by Anasazi and Hohokam in its later phases.

In the eastern and southeastern parts of the United States, a series of phases known in the Mississippi Valley as Adena, Hopewell, and Mississippian succeeded one another. Here the platform mound-building tradition and certain political ideas apparently took root. Although nothing comparable in complexity to the Mexican cultures developed, the major earthen platform mound at Cahokia near St. Louis may have been the largest structure ever built by nonindustrial peoples. Although settlements were mainly of village size, these were linked in elaborate leagues or confederacies.

In South America the influence of the complex cultures of the Andean region at times penetrated into the tropical lowlands. There, however, they were unable to develop effectively, and over most of lowland South America relatively simple village-farming communities persisted into recent times.

The prehistory of the Old and New Worlds, hence, exhibits a rough parallelism. Once cultures at the hunting and gathering level achieved a fairly efficient degree of adaptation to local environment, experiments in the cultivation of plants occurred in a number of areas. Once such relatively high-yield and storable grains as wheat and corn were developed, a village-farming pattern developed. Increased efficiency in farming, especially where irrigation was involved as in Peru, led to the formation of larger settlements and the elaboration of political and social institutions. The Neolithic revolution in both continents led apparently to the urban revolution.

In the New World at this point some divergences appear. Metallurgy seems to have been less significant in the Americas. The technology in the New World remained essentially Stone Age. Even though metal was known and used in Peru before the Christian era, it played only a minor role in providing tools; in Mexico metallurgy did not appear until a few centuries before the coming of the Europeans. The absence of large animals suitable for domestication, the absence of the plow, and the less adequate development of writing severely handicapped New World civilizations, but their achievements are consequently the more remarkable, based as they were on a limited technology.

A recurring problem is the possibility that some of the New World developments were the product of voyagers from Asia. The currently most strongly documented case is in the early pottery from Ecuador.[11] The earliest Valdivia phase pottery from that region shows many specific resemblances to the oldest known Old World pottery from the Jomon period of Japan. The same region also produces early clay models of houses, neck rests, pan pipes, and other items similar to objects occurring from India to Japan. Many of the resemblances are striking. Critics have pointed out that the Jomon period was very long and that the resemblances in ceramics not only come from widely scattered sites separated in time, but that they may be duplicated in simple pottery

[11] Emilio Estrada, Betty J. Meggers, and Clifford Evans, "Possible Transpacific Contact on the Coast of Ecuador," *Science*, **135**:371–372, (February 2, 1962).

The Temple of the Inscriptions at Palenque, an example of Maya architecture. (Kindness of Francine Marshall.)

in other parts of the world. The critics point out that it is unlikely that elements from several sources would all be combined in one period in Ecuador. The assemblage would suggest a considerable number of voyages extended through time, an unlikely situation given the state of navigation in the Jomon period. Accidental voyages probably cannot be ruled out, but the known cases of Asiatic vessels drifting across the Pacific seem all to have arrived on the north Pacific coast of America, whereas the Polynesian Islands show no evidence of settlement until much later. The possibility of occasional trans-Pacific contacts certainly cannot be ruled out, but most anthropologists believe the American developments to have been essentially independent.

7. Summary

The beginnings and evolution of culture took place during the Pleistocene. Although the climates of the Early Pleistocene are difficult to reconstruct, the Pleistocene as a whole appears to have been a period of climatic and environmental change characterized by periodic glacial advances and retreats. Human biological and cultural evolution may be regarded as, in part, a response to rapid environmental changes that contributed to the extinction of other Pleistocene species. Modification or extinction of some species with consequent environmental changes can also be attributed, especially in the Middle and Late Pleistocene, to the activities of human beings.

213

Within this context the possession of culture permitted human beings to develop technologies that could be rapidly modified in response to changing environmental circumstances. Variation in technology from one culture to another is itself an index of the range of specialized adaptations to environmental circumstances made possible by culture. Variation in human technology over time was traditionally discussed in terms of four major epochs: the Paleolithic, the Neolithic, the Copper-Bronze Age, and the Iron Age. The spread of humankind over most of the world took place during the Paleolithic, as did the biological evolution of the human organism.

The earliest human, or rather protohuman, form of ecological adaptation was the foraging pattern characteristic of the australopithecines. It is probable that the australopithecines used tools and other objects which they may have shaped. It is unlikely that the australopithecines used tools to make tools. On the whole their technology is too crude to permit any certain distinctions to be made among tools, objects used as tools, and naturally occurring objects. The australopithecines appear to have lived primarily by foraging for vegetable foods and by hunting such small animals as they could conveniently catch.

The Oldowan or toolmaking tradition appears to be associated with late australopithecines or with *Homo habilis*. Oldowan tools are usually stream bed pebbles with a few flakes knocked off on either side in order to form a cutting edge. Such tools show some evidence of standardization, of improvement through time, and of regional variation. Presumably the possession of such tools permitted the hunting of larger animals and more efficient gathering of vegetable foods. The Oldowan tradition persisted with relatively few changes until the end of the Lower Pleistocene. The relatively unchanging quality of the Oldowan tradition suggests that the intellectual capacity required to make full use of potentialities for language and culture had not yet developed.

With the emergence of *Homo erectus* during the Middle Pleistocene the geographical range and complexity of the human tool kit were vastly increased. The best-known Middle Pleistocene (Early Paleolithic) tradition is the Acheulian tradition in which a nodule of flint or similar material is trimmed through the use of a percussion technique to remove flakes, often from its entire surface. Tools made from flakes or from flakes removed from carefully prepared cores (Levalloisian) were also used. Hunters and gatherers of the Acheulian traditions made effective use of a wide range of plants and animals available within their environments. Like many modern hunters and gatherers, they do not seem to have developed any very highly specialized techniques for exploiting particular species.

The basic pattern of hunting and gathering continues into the Middle Paleolithic where it is associated with *Homo neandertalensis*. During this period, the term *Mousterian* is often applied to a new tradition of tool production involving the use of flake tools made from prepared cores and retouched by the newly developed technique of pressure flaking. It becomes increasingly difficult to identify widespread tool traditions during the Middle Paleolithic. This difficulty is the result of an increasing tendency toward specialized adaptations to particular environments. In Europe the use of fire, the inhabitation of caves, and a relative abundance of large game animals led to the development of specialized hunting cultures in a climate that had until then been too cold for human survival.

During the Upper Paleolithic and with the emergence of *Homo sapiens* the trend toward increasing technological specialization had resulted in the emergence of specialized hunters and collectors in many parts of the world. Tool traditions became increasingly variable from place to place and increased dramatically in complexity. Evidences of art and religion are, however, characteristic of most Upper Paleolithic cultures as they are of all modern and recent cultures. With the retreat of the Weichsel glaciation less than ten thousand years ago, Europe was dominated by Mesolithic cultures which eventually displayed the increasing influence of Neolithic cultures to the south. The reforestation of Europe and the expansion of desert and arid regions elsewhere in the world may have led to an increasing emphasis on fishing during the Mesolithic in Europe, while elsewhere specialized seed gathering leading to incipient agriculture may have been encouraged by the same events. With the development of agriculture, the distribution of cultures took the basic form that it still has today with expanding regions dedicated to intensive agriculture surrounded by zones occupied by incipient or marginal agriculturalists and by surviving specialized hunters and collectors or unspecialized hunters and gatherers, nearly all of whom have been influenced by agricultural peoples. Little is known of the details of the transition from seed collecting or other forms of collecting to incipient agriculture or from incipient agriculture to intensive agriculture and animal domestication. In several parts of the Old World a village farming way of life, perhaps independently invented, had developed perhaps as early as 8000 B.C. The development of new varieties permitting the wide dissemination of the new technology required several thousand years.

In favored spots, such as the lowlands of Mesopotamia, use of the plow and of irrigation led to increasing populations and to the eventual transition from a village way of life to a town and city way of life. This urban revolution was accompanied by the development of the complex economic, political, and religious institutions required for the perpetuation of cities, states, and empires. The urban revolution was accompanied by the development of the wheel, of metallurgy, and ultimately of writing. With the discovery of iron smelting in about 1500 B.C., the urban revolution was essentially complete, and the dominant historical picture became one of the rise and fall of empires. Radical change in a world dominated by peasant farmers and the empires they supported depended upon the discovery of a new source of energy, fossil fuels, and the beginnings of the industrial revolution only a few centuries ago.

In the New World, patterns of cultural evolution were essentially similar to those of the Old World. The first American Indians were specialized hunters. Later, where hunting proved to be a less than successful adaptation, a wide range of specialized hunting and collecting societies emerged. Agriculture developed in the New World almost simultaneously with the development of agriculture in the Old World. Settled farming villages seem to have appeared considerably later, however, in Mexico and Peru, perhaps around 2500 B.C. Towns developed in the same places by about 1000 B.C.; cities were well established, especially in Mexico, by the time of Christ. The lack of large domesticated animals in the New World precluded the development of the plow or the wheel. Similarly, although metallurgy was highly developed, methods for the reduction of iron ore were absent.

Collateral Reading

Allchin, Bridget, and Raymond Allchin. *The Birth of Indian Civilization*. Hammondsworth, Middlesex, England: Penguin Books, 1968.

Bordes, François. *A Tale of Two Caves* (Harper's Case Studies in Archeology). New York: Harper & Row, Inc., 1972.

Bordes, François. *The Old Stone Age*. New York: McGraw-Hill Book Company, 1968. Authoritative review of the evidence with many new interpretations.

Boserup, E. *The Conditions of Agricultural Growth: The Economics of Agrarian Change Under Population Pressure*. Chicago: Aldine Publishing Company, 1965. Did hard times compel the development of agriculture?

Braidwood, Robert J. *Prehistoric Men*, 8th ed. Glenview, Ill.: Scott, Foresman and Company, 1975. A popular and reliable summary.

Chard, Chester S. *Man in Prehistory*, 2d ed. New York: McGraw-Hill Book Company, 1975. A readable summary.

Childe, V. Gordon. *The Dawn of European Civilization*. London: Kegan Paul, 1948. The classical work on the Near Eastern origins of European Neolithic and later cultures.

Clark, J. Desmond (ed.). *Atlas of African Prehistory*. Chicago: University of Chicago Press, 1967.

Culbert, T. Patrick. *The Lost Civilization: The Story of the Classic Maya*. New York: Harper & Row, Inc., 1974. A brief survey.

Fagan, Brian M. *Men of the Earth*. Boston: Little, Brown and Company, 1974. An outstanding textbook.

Fairservis, Walter Ashlin. *The Roots of Ancient India: The Archaeology of Early Indian Civilization*. New York: Macmillan Publishing Co., Inc., 1971.

Gorenstein, Shirley, Richard Forbis, Paul Tolstoy, and Edward Lanning. *Prehistoric America*. New York: St. Martin's Press, Inc., 1974. A recent survey.

Hawkes, Jacquetta. *The First Great Civilizations: Life in Mesopotamia, the Indus Valley, and Egypt*. New York: Alfred A. Knopf, Inc., 1973.

Jennings, Jesse. *Prehistory of North America*. New York: McGraw-Hill Book Company, 1968. A good detailed treatment of North American archaeology.

Movius, Hallam L. *Excavations of the Abri Pataud, Les Eyries (Dondonne)*. (Harvard University American School Res., Bull. No. 30). Boston: Harvard University, Peabody Museum, 1974.

Patterson, Thomas C. *America's Past: A New World Archaeology*. Glenview, Ill., and London: Scott, Foresman and Company, 1973.

Sanders, William T., and Barbara J. Price. *Mesoamerica: The Evolution of a Civilization*. New York: Random House, Inc., 1968.

Sanders, William T., and Joseph Marino. *New World Prehistory: Archaeology of the American Indian*. Englewood Cliffs, N.J.: Prentice-Hall, Inc., 1970.

Stigler, Robert, Ralph Holloway, Ralph Solecki, Dexter Perkins, Jr., and Patricia Daly. *The Old World: Early Man to the Development of Agriculture*. New York: St. Martin's Press, Inc., 1974. A survey.

Thompson, J. Eric. *The Rise and Fall of Maya Civilization*, 2d ed. (Reprint of 1954 edition.) Norman, Okla.: University of Oklahoma Press, 1973.

Treistman, Judith M. *The Prehistory of China*. Garden City, N.Y.: The Natural History Press, 1972.

Weaver, Muriel Porter. *The Aztecs, Maya, and Their Predecessors*. New York: Seminar Press, 1972.

Willey, Gordon R. *An Introduction to American Archaeology, Vol. 1: North America and Middle America*. Englewood Cliffs, N.J.: Prentice-Hall, Inc., 1966.

Willey, Gordon R. *An Introduction to American Archaeology*, Vol. 2: *South America*. Englewood Cliffs, N.J.: Prentice-Hall, Inc., 1971.

7/Hunter-Gatherers

1. Technology and Environment

Although cultural systems emerge out of the complex interactions of many variables, there is general agreement that technology and environment together have powerful effects. If cultural systems are to adapt and survive for a period of time, they must establish relatively stable relationships with their environments. Conceived historically, in terms of the archaeological record, human societies fall into simple technological categories. First, during all except the last 10,000 years, all human beings lived by hunting animals and gathering plant foods. During the early stages of human history most people were generalized hunter-gatherers who exploited a wide variety of plant and animal species within the environment. More recently, during the last 50,000 years or so, in environments dominated by a relatively few species, various groups of highly specialized hunters, fishermen, or collectors developed.

Within the last 10,000 years a few groups, probably of specialized collectors, began the systematic practice of food production and animal domestication. Although such peoples may have started with a relatively small number of domesticated species, they soon developed a generalized agriculture in which each group produced the variety of plants and animals required for home consumption. In a few locations where there were lush environments, where irrigation was a possibility, or where intensive cultivation of a small number of crops resulted in high yields, the development of complex urban societies became possible. Thus the movement from generalized to specialized agriculture roughly parallels the movement from generalized to specialized hunting and gathering. Excluding the industrial revolution of some 300 years ago and the incipient age of atomic power, there were three major technological revolutions in human history: the toolmaking revolution, the food-producing revolution, and the urban revolution. Groups representing each of these adaptations are described in the next three chapters.

Although types of cultural systems can be regarded as concomitant with each of these revolutions, any given cultural system may derive atypical characteristics from special environmental conditions or from unique historical experiences. For example, the fishermen of the Northwest Coast of North America are technologically classified as specialized hunters, yet their extraordinarily successful exploitation of their environment led to dense populations. This has led some anthropologists to classify them as urban. Similarly the Indians of the North American Plains seem at one time to have been specialized and rather unsuccessful hunters of the buffalo. Long before they were adequately described, they had acquired the horse and gun and were involved

The pump drill. Downward push provides power. Wooden disk flywheel stores energy required to rewind string on up stroke. Drill reverses direction with each downstroke. Used for fire making and to drill holes in wood, shell, bone, or stone. The pump drill has a limited distribution, but was used by some hunting peoples, such as the Eskimo. (Courtesy of the American Museum of Natural History.)

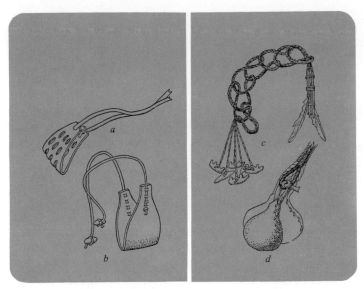

Figure 7–1   Slings and bolas: (a) Navajo sling (after Knight); (b) Ona sling (after Gusinde); (c) Eskimo bird bola, knotted for carrying, with ivory weights shaped like bear, seal, and bird and a quilled handle to guide it in flight (after Nelson); (d) Argentine bola, with weights of clay or stone covered with leather (after Knight).

in a frontier economy that rapidly destroyed the buffalo and radically changed the ecology of the Plains.

Most contemporary primates, as well as the protohominids, are best described as foragers, depending primarily on vegetable foods supplemented by insects, occasional rodents, and other small animals that could be caught with the hands. Foragers are limited to temperate or tropical regions where year-round supplies of vegetable foods are available. Foraging represents a generalized adaptation to the environment, and this implies use of a wide variety of plant and animal species and an absence of specialization in the collection of particular plants or animals. Foraging does not permit the development of any complex or specialized technology: tools must be simple, portable, and useful for a variety of purposes. To take advantage of naturally occurring harvests in tropical environments, where no single natural species is likely to be dominant, foragers must visit different localities each day, and this often means that they must move their campsites as well. Foragers do not store food, and this means that their numbers are limited by the amount of food available during the season of greatest scarcity. Primate foragers, with the possible exception of our own immediate ancestors, usually do not share food. Each individual harvests and consumes his own food. Although foraging may consume considerable amounts of time in some environments or during some seasons, the prevailing pattern is an alternation of periods of foraging and periods of resting. Primate social groups play an important part in the food quest because the older, more experienced animals tend to remember where food has been found on previous occasions and to lead the subordinate members of their

Figure 7–2 Throwing sticks: top, Hopi throwing stick (after Hough); bottom, Baganda throwing stick.

troops to such spots. If we may judge by our primate contemporaries, the earlier forms of humanity consisted of small troops that wandered from place to place within a limited area.

The immediate effects of the toolmaking revolution upon this pattern of foraging are somewhat problematical. With the emergence of *Homo erectus*, toolmaking conferred a sufficient adaptive advantage to permit the occupation of an increased variety of environments and the establishment of regular living sites used, probably seasonally, over periods of years. Such semipermanent campsites may, in fact, have been developed much earlier by *Homo habilis* or by australopithecines at Olduvai Gorge. *Homo sapiens neandertalensis* and early *Homo sapiens sapiens* developed elaborate stone toolmaking traditions considerably more complicated than those of some recently existing peoples.

Recent food-gathering peoples differ, however, in a number of important ways from the specialized hunters who dominated the Late Paleolithic in Europe. Most recent food gatherers have occupied relatively inhospitable environments, very often those that have proved unsuitable for food production.

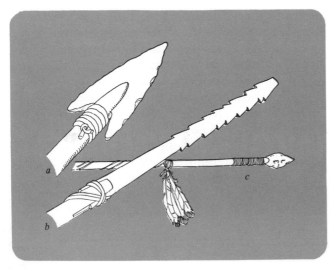

Figure 7–3 Lance points and spearheads. (a) southwest lance point (after Holling); (b) early Aleut spearhead (after Martin et al.); (c) Nez Percé spearhead (after Wissler).

Specialized hunters, who usually inhabited plains regions ideally suited for pastoralism or modern forms of agriculture, largely disappeared soon after the food-producing revolution, and are represented in recent times only in a few regions such as the Arctic, the Northwest Coast of North America, and the North American Plains. Collectors or specialized gatherers have also been largely displaced by agricultural peoples, the most notable exception to this rule being the recently displaced acorn collectors in California. Most recent food-gathering peoples, then, are generalized hunters and gatherers surviving in mountain, desert, or forest regions which are marginal to regions inhabited by agriculturalists. Most have been deeply influenced by neighboring agricultural peoples and many have worked out specialized adaptations involving regular contact with such peoples.

2. Generalized Hunter-Gatherers

Generalized hunter-gatherers, owing to the wide range of often inhospitable environments which they occupy and the different sorts of environmental influences to which they have been exposed, differ from each other in a variety of ways. Their mode of adaptation does place strong limitations upon some aspects of their cultural system, with the result that most share the following characteristics:

(1) *Low population density.* This means that their social arrangements are simple, and group members are mostly known relatives.
(2) *Scarce and widely dispersed food resources.* This requires frequent movement in order to take advantage of seasonal concentrations of food resources, and the development of generalized tools and skills permit-

The fire plow. Heat is produced by rubbing stick back and forth in groove. The fire plow or a stick rotated between the palms were the most common fire-making methods. (Courtesy of the American Museum of Natural History.)

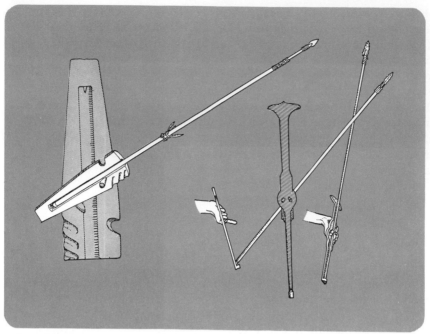

Figure 7–4 Types of spear throwers or atlatls. The spear thrower precedes the bow and arrow in Europe and the Americas. (After Boas and Cushing.)

ting the utilization of a wide variety of plant and animal species. The necessity for frequent movement requires that technology be simple and portable.

(3) *Band organization.* The basic unit of a hunter-gatherer society is a band consisting of a small number of related families. Bands exchange population with neighboring bands in order to maintain a close fit between resources and population. Leadership and band organization tend to be informal and flexible. Groups of related bands sharing basically the same language and culture probably range in size between a few hundred and several thousand people depending upon environmental circumstances.

Most of the hunter-gatherer groups that have survived into recent times were those occupying forbidding environments such as the desert regions of South Africa, Australia, the United States Southwest, and the tropical rain forests of South America. Hunter-gatherers, mostly somewhat influenced by neighboring agricultural peoples, also exist in considerable numbers in hilly or forested regions in South Asia and in the African Congo.

Although the hunter-gatherers of Australia have changed greatly in recent years and very few still survive by hunting and gathering, the isolation of many of these peoples and the different environments they occupy made it possible to study many of them while they were still carrying out their traditional mode of life. A number of small groups, often on reservations, still follow the

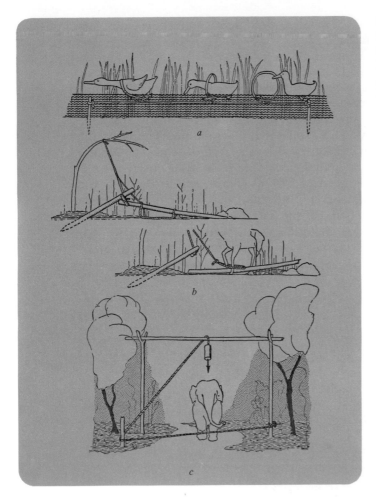

Figure 7–5 Traps and snares are widely used: (a) Eskimo duck snare (after Nelson); (b) Bushman animal trap; (c) East African elephant trap (after Lindblom).

traditional pattern. In the drier parts of Australia population densities were low and resources were dispersed over wide areas. For the Pitjandjara of the Great Western Desert[1] the end of the summer rains created temporary water sources in the desert and led to the dispersal of game. At this time single bands of perhaps ten to twenty people moved out across the desert searching for game and edible plant materials. As the desert water holes began to dry up, the bands moved toward permanent sources of water in the mountains. Because the larger game animals and many species of birds were driven toward the permanent sources of water at the same time, hunters could lie in ambush near the water, and small boys and girls could strike down the birds with sticks. When the summer rains came, animals dispersed, and there was often a period of semistarvation until the new growth of plants provided a source of food. As the "raintime" continued, food became abundant and time was

[1] Norman B. Tindale, "The Pitjandjara," in M. G. Bicchieri (ed.), *Hunters and Gatherers Today* (New York: Holt, Rinehart and Winston, 1972), pp. 217–268.

passed in storytelling, repairing equipment, and loafing. As the cool, dry weather began, the bands again dispersed.

Because of their frequent movement, even modern Australian hunter-gatherers, maintain a very small inventory of material goods. Traditionally, among the Pitjandjara, clothing was minimal and there were few implements. The Pitjandjara made and used stone knives and choppers in 1965. Men fought and hunted with spears and throwing sticks, and also made and used spear throwers (atlatls), wooden dishes, and shields. Women made and used a digging stick. The woman went out for the day in search of food carrying her digging stick and several bolas (weighted ropes used in hunting) nested in her wooden water container. The man carried several spears, a spear thrower, and a stone chisel tucked into his waist belt. The man carried a few valuables—a piece of red ochre or a marine shell—in his hair, along with some kangaroo sinews for repairing his weapons. Both men and women also carried fire sticks. There is other special ceremonial equipment, but this is usually left in

Minmara, a Ngatatjara man, bites off stone flakes to trim adze, Warburton Ranges, West Australia. (Courtesy of the American Museum of Natural History.)

Figure 7–6 Means of transporting water are important to most people. Left, a skin water bottle in a carrying net; right, an elongated gourd container.

hiding places near permanent campsites. Despite the harshness of their environment and the simple and generalized character of their technology, the Australian peoples developed an elaborate pattern of ceremonial life and complex patterns of social relationships.

The Bushmen of the Kalahari Desert in southwest Africa occupy a similar desert environment and resembled the Australian aborigines in their basic patterns of adaptation. They too were wanderers, and they too lived in small bands which came together on relatively rare occasions. In hunting, the Bushmen used the bow and poisoned arrow, rather than the spear thrower. The hunter generally carried, as well as his bow and quiver full of arrows, a prepared ostrich egg slung in a net, cutting tools for butchering game, and a digging stick, which also served as a spear. Food and equipment were carried in net bags made out of cords twisted by rolling fibers against the thigh.

Although the Bushmen exist today under fairly constant pressure from Bantu and European agriculturists living on the fringes of the Kalahari Desert, Lee reported in 1972 the existence of some 45,000 Bushmen, many of whom had taken up agriculture, but some of whom have continued to follow the traditional way of life. The !Kung Bushmen of the Dobe area described by Lee recognized more than 100 species of edible plants and more than 54 species of edible animals.[2] Meat provided between 20 and 50 percent of their diet, depending upon the season, and the remainder consisted of plant foods more than half of which were provided by the *mongongo* nut. The Bushmen followed a seasonal round, not unlike that of the Pitjandjara, living near water holes in the dry season and dispersing throughout the surrounding region when temporary sources of water were available.

Recent studies of the Bushmen, and of other hunter-gatherer groups as well, have shown that the traditional picture of hunter-gatherers as people whose lives are "nasty, brutish, and short" has been considerably overdrawn. The Bushmen used only a part of the resources available to them and they

[2] Richard Borshay Lee, "The !Kung Bushmen of Botswana," in M. G. Bicchieri (ed.), *Hunters and Gatherers Today* (New York: Holt, Rinehart and Winston, 1972), p. 363.

Wagaitj boy carrying fishing spear. Australia. (Courtesy of the American Museum of Natural History.)

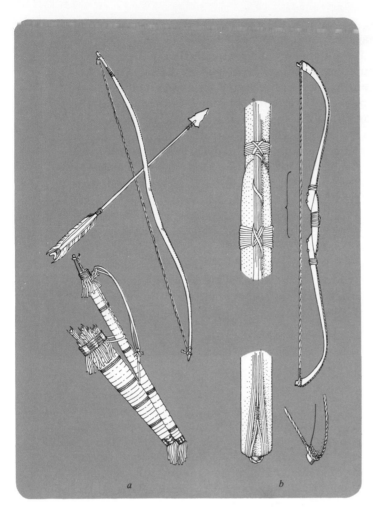

Figure 7–7 Bows, arrows, and quiver: (a) Dakota self-bow and stone-tipped arrow with flaring nock (above), quiver and bow case of dressed buffalo hide (below); (b) Eskimo compound bow backed with sinew. (After Mason.)

rarely spent more than a few hours a day attending to their subsistence needs. Their technology, however, was carried in their heads rather than on their bodies—the hunting equipment, medicine, cosmetics, ornaments, toys, musical instruments, tobacco pipes, and kitchen gear of a family would fit into two leather sacks the size of overnight cases. Should life at the water hole become difficult as a result of conflicts or as a result of a temporary shortage of resources, the family could move easily and quickly to visit relatives at another water hole.

Unlike the Australians, the Bushmen placed little value on warfare, wrestling matches, games of strength, or ordeals. They preferred to meet challenges by melting away into the bush. Although such a pattern is characteristic of hunter-gatherers subject to the oppressive might of neighboring agricultural peoples, it may, in the Bushman case, have had something to do with the constant availability of the poisoned arrow. Homicide was not uncommon. Like the Australians, the Bushmen placed great emphasis on religious ceremony, sometimes holding all-night ritual curing dances as often as two or three times a week. Perhaps because they lacked warfare, and therefore found no need to develop and maintain alliances, the Bushmen had a more casual and less complicated approach to social organization than did the Australians. Life in Australia often involved complicated strategies for the accumulation of wives by older men and the corresponding oppression of the younger men. Hart and Pilling[3] in fact suggest that the optimum household in the Australian ecology was one consisting of an older man with many wives. The nuclear family, organized around one husband and one wife, was the common pattern for the Bushmen. Perhaps, in fact, the young Bushman with his poisoned arrows is a more efficient hunter than the young Australian with his spear thrower, and his greater economic value made possible a relatively early marriage.

Although the Australians and the Bushmen occupied similar environments, had similar technologies, and followed similar patterns of life, there were striking differences between them. Some of these differences can be attributed to real differences in environment and technology; some of them seem more likely to be related to different sorts of contacts with other cultures or alternative adaptive choices made during the development of the two regional cultures.

3. Specialized Hunters

The Crow Indians of the Great Plains of North America were specialized hunters who pursued the buffalo and other large grazing animals with the aid of bows and arrows and a variety of stone, wood, leather, and bone implements. Although we are ignorant of some details of traditional Crow technology, it was far more complex than that of any hunter-gatherers. One of the reasons for this is that although the Crow moved frequently, they possessed large numbers of dogs that were used to transport household equipment. The efficiency of the dogs was often increased through the use of a travois, a primitive sledge consisting of two trailing poles and a platform for the load which were attached to the dog. (See Figure 7-9.)

By 1800 some thirty-three years before the Crow were first seen by the European invaders of North America, the Crow were engaged in the trade of horses secured from Indians to the west and south for guns and metal goods obtained from Indians to the east. In 1833, when visited by Prince Maximilian of Wied-Neuwied, a scientifically trained German, the Crow had already diverged significantly from their earlier way of life. The present account of the Crow derives from the work of Robert H. Lowie, who studied them during the period 1907 to 1931.[4] By 1907 the Crow had abandoned hunting and had

---

[3] C. W. M. Hart and A. Pilling, *The Tiwi of Northern Australia* (New York: Holt, Rinehart and Winston, 1960).

[4] Robert H. Lowie, *The Crow Indians* (New York: Farrar, Straus & Giroux, Inc., 1935).

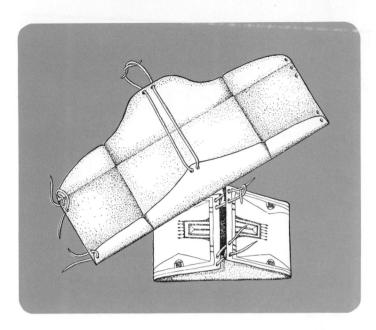

Figure 7–8 Plains Indian parfleche of hide.

turned, perforce, to agriculture. Lowie's account of Crow technology and environmental relationships is based partly on literary research and partly on the memory of living Crow and—Lowie is not always exact on this point—seems to cover the period from 1833 to roughly 1880, including a description of many practices that had survived with little apparent change until 1931.

Until the disappearance of big game from the Plains, the Crow depended primarily upon the meat of large animals, not only for food, but for the con-

Figure 7–9 Plains Indian dog travois and a horse-drawn travois from central Asia. (After Clark.)

Winter quarters, Sioux Indians. Part of group of tipis arranged in a circle in a grove of box elders near the banks of the Missouri River. (From the Morrow Collection. Courtesy of W. H. Over Museum.)

struction of conical skin dwellings (*tipis*), for clothing, and for a wide variety of tools and utensils. In this, they closely resembled the specialized hunters known from archaeological sites in Europe and Asia. Although game might be hunted by individuals or by small groups, communal hunts were of much greater importance. Before the introduction of the horse, communal hunts apparently involved circling around behind a herd of animals and driving them over a cliff or into a corral. To keep the animals running in the right direction, rock piles were erected leading to the cliff or corral, and men and women stood between them waving their hide robes at beasts attempting to escape. Such an animal drive required a level of organization and numbers of people far greater than could be mustered by a band of ordinary hunter-gatherers.

Plains Indian women, Cheyenne tribe, sewing tanned deerskins to make a new tipi cover. Meat drying in background. Meat preservation was essential for Plains Indian tribes to guard against periodic shortages of game. Even without salt, properly dried jerky will last for many months. (From the Morrow Collection. Courtesy of the W. H. Over Museum.)

Figure 7–10 Tailored Plains Indian woman's dress of tanned hides.

Except for the drives, which required the participation of virtually the entire group, hunting was carried out predominantly by young men. Men also manufactured most of the implements used in hunting and warfare, including arrowheads of bone and stone. Arrow shafts and bows were generally manufactured by experts. Bows were made of strips of horn or antler glued together and backed with sinew. Manufacture of a single bow might take as long as three months, including carving, ornamenting, and painting. Equipment for warfare included spears, war clubs, and circular shields.

Because the great herds of bison tended to scatter and break up during the winter season, the tribes of the northern plains also tended to break up during that time. During summer, when the grass was green and the hunting good, families and bands would gather together in great camp circles. At this time large communal hunts would be organized, parties would go forth to steal horses from neighboring tribes or to wreak vengeance on enemies, and grand ceremonials, such as the Sun Dance, would be organized. Such ceremonials provided a focus for the summer's activities and a means of bringing together the entire tribe or subtribe; they also provided a setting in which young men by means of fasting and suffering could attract the pity of supernatural agencies and thus receive power for curing, hunting, or war.

The Plains Indians had begun a process of rapid cultural change long before their way of life had been systematically studied. As a matter of fact, most groups of Plains Indians did not move out into the plains until the horse and gun made it possible to slaughter bison almost at will. Those groups that existed on the plains before the introduction of the horse and gun possessed a way of life that was considerably less glamorous, but probably quite similar in its basic outlines.

Specialized hunters, or rather groups that resemble specialized hunters in some ways, are found elsewhere only in the vicinity of the Arctic Circle. Here the Eskimo, although possessing a highly specialized technology, made use of a wide variety of animal products. The central and eastern Eskimo depended for part of the year upon individual hunting of seal through holes cut in the sea ice; walrus and polar bear were sometimes hunted by organized groups of men. The hunting implements were primarily the harpoon and spear. There were also a variety of cutting, scraping, and graving implements for butchering game, preparing tailored fur clothing, and making various other objects. When the sea ice broke up in the spring, seals and walruses could be hunted from *kayaks*. In some places birds and bird eggs supplemented the diet, and extensive use was made of raw fish, which provided one of the few available sources of vitamin C. The central Eskimo tended to move inland during the summer to hunt migrating herds of caribou. In recent times Eskimo technology and hunting patterns have been deeply influenced by the introduction of modern rifles and modern ways of life, and there is great variation in the extent to

Plains Indian women, Sioux tribe, dressing buffalo hides, showing manner of stretching them. Meat drying in background. Adjustable ventilators on tipi are clearly shown. (From the Morrow Collection. Courtesy of the W. H. Over Museum.)

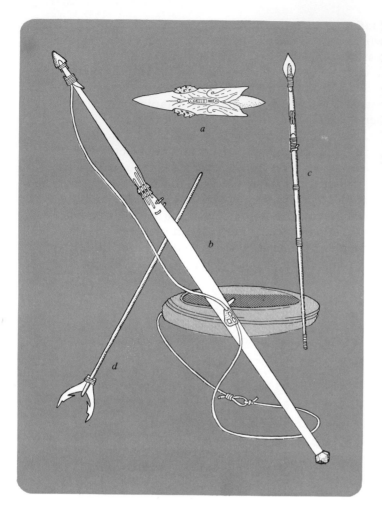

Figure 7–11 Harpoons and fish spear. (a) Decorated harpoon head of ivory with side blades of chipped stone (after Martin et al.); (b) composite harpoon with detachable head and float (after Boas); (c) whale lance (after Holling); (d) California Indian fish spear with prongs of antler (after Martin et al.).

which individual groups of Eskimo have continued or abandoned traditional methods of Arctic survival.

During the summer the Eskimo lived traditionally in skin tents. In the winter they lived in ingeniously designed houses made of stone, or, more rarely, out of blocks of snow. Essential to survival was a seal oil lamp which provided heat and light inside the winter house. Skin-covered boats, both the small *kayak* and the larger woman's boat, or *umiak*, were essential for sea hunting or movement of camp in summer. The dogsled, required for travel in winter and the transportation of game, was also essential, as was a good pair of snowshoes. The dogsled was also used in the European Arctic in early times, but it was used with skiis rather than snowshoes.

Complex skills and elaborate technologies permitted the Eskimo to survive, but the harshness of the environment made it impossible, except in a few favored locations, to develop anything larger than small and widely scattered settlements. Eskimo marriage patterns, like our own, seem always to have

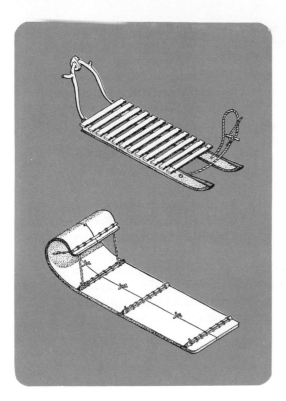

Figure 7–12 Top: Eskimo sled (after Boas); bottom: Indian toboggan (after Mason). The sled with runners is superior for use on ice and hard-packed or crusted snow; the toboggan is better for soft snow.

been simple and flexible. There were no formally appointed chiefs or rulers, proper behavior being ensured by social pressures of a kind possible only in tightly knit and interdependent groupings. When these failed—most often when a violent man or bully terrorized the settlement—a group of men would come together and secretly murder the disruptive individual.

The Eskimo way of life, or at least Eskimo technology, seems fairly close to that of Late Paleolithic specialized hunters of Europe. Some items of equipment, such as the harpoon and the tailored skin clothing, seem almost identical. The great difference between the two peoples was that the Eskimo lived in a much less hospitable environment. Hunters of the Late Paleolithic had to cope with cold weather, but they had more abundant game and better sources of fuel.

4. Specialized Fishers

Hunting and fishing are, of course, essentially similar activities. Many peoples both hunt and fish. Eskimo sea mammal hunting is plainly a borderline case. In most parts of the modern world, fishing and hunting are now carried on in conjunction with agriculture; this was true in most parts of the ancient world as well. In recent history the most striking examples of peoples specialized in the consumption of fish were to be found on the northern Pacific coasts of North America. These coasts receive very heavy rainfall, averaging well over 60 inches per year, with some precipitation each month. Summers are relatively cool and winters relatively mild, although temperatures become quite extreme in inland areas or at higher elevations. Until they were partially destroyed by the woodman's ax, dense coniferous forests stretched from south of San Francisco to Alaska. These forests provided limited food for herbivorous animals, and small quantities of fruits and berries in the summer.

As if to compensate for the lack of resources within the forest, enormous runs of several species of Pacific salmon entered the numerous streams to spawn during the summer period. Pacific halibut, cod, herring, and other fish were abundant the year round in relatively shallow waters. Numerous islands, bays, and inlets, in the northern part of the region, give protection from Pacific storms, and high mountain ranges paralleling the coast and the storm activity itself tend to protect the region from Arctic air in the winter.

Although the different cultures of this rather large area were by no means uniform, each responding to particular features of a complex local ecology, the Haida Indians of Queen Charlotte Islands can be regarded as representative. The salmon harvest took place mainly during the summer months. In season

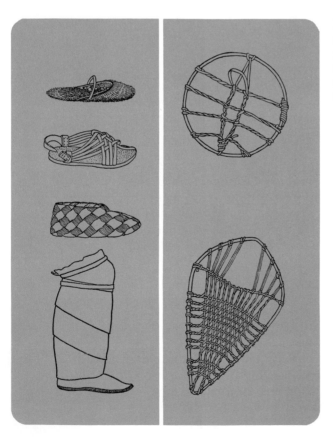

Figure 7–13 Feet need protection in rocky or cold environments and support in soft deep snow. Left: Sandals and mocassins from Peru, Afghanistan, Finland, and Zuñi Indians; right: two types of netted snowshoes.

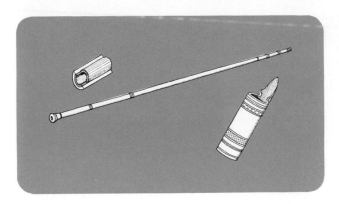

Figure 7–14 Semang (Southeast Asia) blowgun and quiver. Cross section shows composite construction. (After Murdock.)

the Haida traditionally worked up to twenty hours a day catching salmon, cleaning salmon, smoking salmon, and storing salmon in dry places. A few salmon were caught in the open sea, but the principal technique was to spear them as they entered the streams to spawn. When the salmon were not running, fruits and berries were collected from inland regions.

Once the salmon season was over, the Haida led a much more leisurely life. Deep-sea fishing for halibut, cod, and other fish continued throughout the year, weather permitting, and both sea and land mammals were hunted as well. Owing to a lack of land mammals on their island habitat, the Haida had to trade with mainland tribes in order to get hides for clothing and other purposes. The possibility of obtaining and storing large quantities of food enabled the Haida and other Northwest Coast peoples to develop relatively dense populations, often as dense as those characteristic of agricultural regions. The close availability of large numbers of people and enforced periods of leisure when either the salmon were not running or the weather was stormy made it possible for the Haida to develop a complex technology involving elaborate houses and boats. These circumstances also made possible the development of elaborate ceremonials and artistic performances, as well as elaborate expeditions for purposes of trade or warfare.

The Haida possessed the bows and arrows, spears, and other implements found among many hunting peoples; they also had many special devices for fishing, including a variety of fish spears, fishhooks, gigs, lines, and nets. Their dugout canoes ranged from small inshore fishing craft to huge war and trading dugouts capable of carrying forty or fifty men or more and up to 2 tons of cargo. Dried fish and other items were stored in wooden boxes made by bending and sewing cedar planks. Watertight boxes for cooking were filled with water that was heated to a boil by the addition of stones heated in the fire. To protect food stores and people from the weather, the Haida built large gabled houses with walls and roofs of split cedar planks. Such a house involved a major investment in labor, but it had a life of sixty years or more. Entrances were decorated with elaborately carved and painted house posts; similar carved posts, the so-called totem poles, were erected nearby or in cemeteries as a record of the individual's social status and possession of

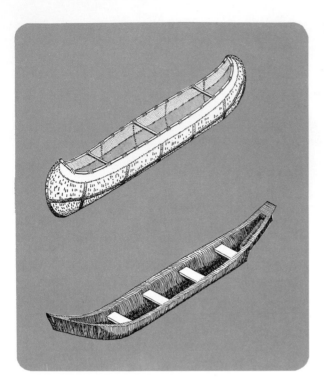

Figure 7–15 Top: American Indian birch bark canoe; bottom: American Indian dugout canoe. (After Martin et al.)

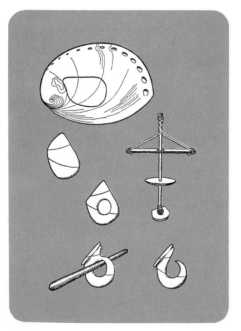

Figure 7–16 California Indian fishhooks, showing steps in manufacture. (Courtesy of Museum of Natural History of Santa Barbara, California.)

rights and privileges. Haida women had an extensive repertoire of basketry techniques used to make headgear, containers for certain goods, and pack baskets for light and convenient transportation. The decorative art of the Haida and of neighboring peoples is famous (see Chapter 17, §3).

Haida village populations often numbered many hundreds, and a single village might remain in one place for many generations. There was an elaborate clan system and a complicated machinery for determining and confirming social position, the ownership of property, and a variety of ceremonial and religious privileges. The Haida way of life was, in fact, more complicated than that of many farming peoples, and their highly successful adaptation to their particular environment marks an exception to the general rule that population densities among agricultural peoples are greater than those among peoples that depend upon hunting, fishing, or gathering.

Haida house. Poles bear representations of family honors and privileges. (Courtesy of the American Museum of Natural History.)

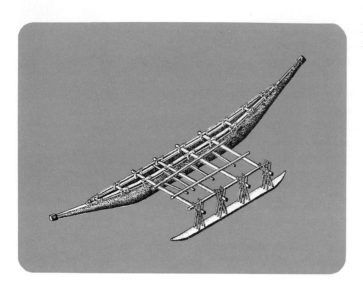

Figure 7–17   A Polynesian outrigger canoe.

Rod and line fishing from large outrigger canoe. Ceylon. (Courtesy of the United Nations.)

Somewhat different sorts of fishing cultures appear to have existed along the Santa Barbara Channel in southern California, although they disappeared too quickly after European contact for our knowledge to be extensive.[5] The various Shoshonean- and Chumash-speaking peoples of this region lacked the abundant forest resources of the northern coast, but made seaworthy boats by sewing planks to the sides of shallow dugout canoes and calking the seams with tar collected along the beach. Such boats permitted regular voyages to the offshore islands and extensive open-sea fishing with hook and line. Fishing with hook and line is of respectable antiquity. In ancient Europe fishhooks appear in Maglemose sites dating about 8000 B.P.

The availability of fish throughout the year as well as abundant sources of shellfish and such vegetable food supplies as the acorn made possible the development of a dense population. Early Spanish records suggest that some settlements contained several thousand people, but some archaeologists feel this was an exaggeration. Steatite, or soapstone, from a quarry on Catalina Island was traded over a considerable length of coast. Steatite cannot be placed on a fire, but may have been used with hot stones for boiling water. Some steatite containers were elaborately decorated.

[5] Alfred L. Kroeber, *Handbook of the Indians of California*, Bulletin 78 (Washington, D.C.: Bureau of American Ethnology, 1925). (Berkeley: California Book Co., reprint.)

Net fishing is often a group enterprise. Ceylon. (Courtesy of the United Nations.)

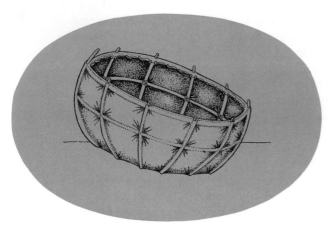

Figure 7–18 One of simplest boats. A Plains Indian coracle of hides stretched over a frame.

The importance of fishing in human history is difficult to estimate. In the archaeological record, relatively few specialized fishing peoples are to be found, even though almost all peoples fish part-time. Evidence of significant use of fish appears only in the Late Paleolithic of Europe, but it is hard to guess what this means because early evidence of fishing may have been destroyed by increases in sea level following the end of the Ice Ages. Extensive use of shellfish, which need only to be collected with a chisel-shaped stick and thrown into a basket or other container, is probably much older than other kinds of fishing and might well be regarded as collecting rather than as fishing. Shellfish, of course, require no storage. Like some tubers, they can be left in place until required for consumption. Where large quantities of shellfish are available, permanent human settlements are possible, with a corresponding development of material culture. For example, the oldest known pottery is found, dating from about 9000 B.P., in the extensive shell mounds of the Jomon period in Japan. Elsewhere, pottery is normally associated with sedentary farming peoples. The possibility of early pottery in California at 6500 B.P. is mentioned in Chapter 6, §6.

Boats or canoes, necessary if any ambitious fishing is to be done, are not known to have existed before the postglacial period around the Baltic Sea in Europe. The boats of the Eskimo, Haida, and Chumash seem quite complicated, and so do those of such peoples as the Malayo-Polynesians who use outriggers or double hulls to maintain stable sailing vessels in the open sea. Simpler sorts of rafts and boats are widely distributed. The Plains Indians made a coracle by stretching hides over a bowl-shaped frame. (See Figure 7–18.) Such craft are still used in Mesopotamia and South India and in many other parts of the world. The word *coracle* is Welsh. Log rafts or rafts made by tying bundles of reeds together are common. In ancient Egypt and on Lake Titicaca in South America, reed boats were large enough to accommodate sails. Wooden rafts of balsa — a very light wood — with centerboards and sails were seen by early visitors to the coasts of Ecuador and Peru. Such rafts were capable of extended sea voyages. Thor Heyerdahl has shown that balsa rafts could cross the eastern Pacific to Polynesia and that reed boats could cross the

Atlantic.[6] The fact that such voyages could be made in modern times does not demonstrate that such voyages were made in the past, and there is no conclusive archaeological evidence of early transoceanic contact between Peru and Polynesia or between Europe and the New World.

5. Collectors

Although collecting is sometimes equated with gathering, there is now a tendency to restrict the use of the term *collecting* to those who use relatively specialized techniques to gather wild plant foods and who gain most of their subsistence by those techniques. Over 50 percent of the Bushman diet comes from the Mongongo nut, but the nut itself requires no special training to find, to process, or to eat. By contrast, collectors (specialized gatherers) have (1) techniques of food processing which render plants inedible in their raw state palatable and nourishing; (2) sufficiently efficient techniques to permit the accumulation of a reserve of storable plant foods; and (3) adequate containers for transport and storage.

In historic times the arid and semiarid lands of western North America extending from eastern Washington and Oregon to Central Mexico and from the coast of California to the Gulf of Mexico were largely occupied by collectors. Throughout this region rainfall is generally limited, and the mountainous topography tends to create a wide range of contrasting environments. Vegetation is relatively sparse and adapted to the characteristic long dry season. This means that the vegetation either grows rapidly and has a short life or it can remain dormant through long dry periods. In either case the plants tend to produce seeds with a high starchy component and a hard outer shell or coating. Numerous members of the cactus family have seeds encased in a pulpy edible envelope protected by formidable spines. In much of the area animal life is limited by scarcity of water or the absence of edible plants.

Collecting in these arid lands appears to have begun before 8000 B.C. when the early hunting cultures were replaced by what have been called the desert cultures of western North America. At one early site, Danger Cave in Utah, over sixty-five species of plants have been identified in the remains, all still existing in the area. Danger Cave and other similar sites have a tool kit resembling that of more recent peoples, including the presence of flat milling stones and grinders (*metates* and *manos*); bone, shell, and wood tools; and a variety of forms of cordage, matting, and basketry.

The Shoshonean people of parts of Nevada and Utah deserts exemplified an adaptation to a region with scant resources.[7] For a portion of the year their

---

[6] Thor Heyerdahl, *American Indians in the Pacific: The Theory Behind the Kon-Tiki Expeditions* (London: Allen & Unwin, 1952).

[7] Julian H. Steward, *Basin-Plateau Aboriginal Socio-Political Groups*, Bulletin 120 (Washington, D.C.: Bureau of American Ethnology, 1938); Isabel Kelley, *Southern Paiute Ethnography*, (Salt Lake City: University of Utah, Department of Anthropology, 1964).

mainstay was small seeds from a large number of plants which grew in small quantities in a variety of localities. The seeds ripen earliest in the lower elevations, so in late spring or early summer the Shoshoneans moved to these spots, migrating slowly into higher elevations following the ripening seeds. As supplies anywhere were limited they moved in small groups, often a single family. Collecting seeds was an individual activity carried on primarily by women; the more women involved, the more rapidly the supply in a given spot was exhausted. While women gathered, the men hunted game, of which rabbits and smaller rodents were the most abundant. Migratory waterfowl were important seasonally; limited water resources resulted in great concentrations of fowl during the migration period. In much of the area the climax of the wild harvest came with the piñon pine nut season. The piñon pine is a prolific producer of large edible nuts, but the various groves have good crops only once in two or three years, so each fall a different grove must be sought.

When the piñon season began, the entire family worked feverishly, bringing down the still green cones before they opened and scattered the nuts, roasting them to force them open, and gathering and storing the nuts. Ordinarily the quantity obtained was limited by the short time the nuts could be harvested; with luck an average family collected about 1,200 pounds of nuts. This was too much to transport any distance along with the other necessary gear, so a fall and winter camp was made in a sheltered spot. The relative abundance of wood for firewood and housing, actually a fairly simple dome-shaped shelter of poles, brush, and perhaps a few hides, compensated for the colder climate at this elevation. During this season the men were particularly active in hunting, but with the best of luck the supply of piñon nuts was exhausted before winter was over; at that time the game resources were also depleted. The Shoshoni then moved toward lower elevations, hunting and collecting edible greens, roots, bulbs, and tubers. At last, after semistarvation through the late winter and spring, the early seeds ripened in the lowlands again. Of the Shoshoneans, Chapple and Coon wrote that "anyone who can walk and use their fingers can collect food if there is any to be collected."[8] This is utterly absurd; anyone who tried to live in the desert with what could be collected with the fingers would speedily starve. Life is possible only with the support of a complex specialized technology. Most desert seeds are very small and many are inedible without processing. The desert people used tightly woven trays to catch the seeds, which were knocked out by a woven beater. (See Figure 7–19.) Many of the seeds were then parched by shaking them together with hot coals on the same or a similar tightly woven tray (tightly woven so the seeds will not fall through). Many seeds must be ground on a flat slab milling stone sufficiently to break the hard outer shells; the resulting meal was usually made into a soup or mush by boiling, which was done by dropping hot rocks into baskets tight enough to hold water. Some seeds must be leached to remove noxious elements. A digging stick must be used to get edible roots, bulbs, and tubers, and one must know the signs to tell where to dig. Even to gather piñon nuts ef-

[8] Elliot Chapple and Carleton Coon, *Principles of Anthropology* (New York: Holt, Rinehart and Winston, 1942), p. 144.

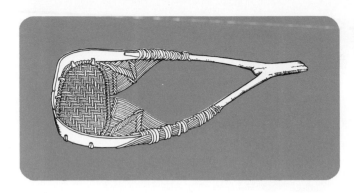

Figure 7–19 Woven seed beater used in collecting small grass seeds.

ficiently a special pole must be shaped with a hook at one end to pull loose the cones from higher branches, and skill must be employed to pull the roasting green cones from the fire at just the right moment before the nuts drop into the fire. For hunting, bows and arrows must be made as well as long nets into which rabbits must be driven. Clothing is essential in winter; because of the scarcity of large game, hide clothing was supplemented by warm blankets ingeniously woven from strips of rabbit fur on a suspended warp loom. Basketry water bottles coated with pine pitch were another essential in most of this arid land.

Because of the scarcity of food the unit of food production was the family. Often families moved by themselves or with two or three other families; only at the piñon groves in fall and winter did larger groups form, to break up when the move to lower elevations began. Only rarely was the winter group composed of the same families in successive years; each family decided which area was going to be most productive. Groups constantly reformed on the basis of kinship, friendships, and expediency. As a result little political activity occurred beyond interfamily relationships. Sometimes a chief was recognized as the leader and mediator of the group, but he had no real authority, nor was the group of his followers constant. His main function usually was to organize cooperative hunts. Similarly most rituals were family affairs concerned with crisis periods, such as birth, puberty, and death. Bands were sometimes recognized on the basis of dialect differences and their common exploitation of a large but poorly defined territory, but the members rarely if ever were all in the same place at the same time. These bands rarely numbered more than a few hundred people. Under pressure of Europeans in the last century some of these bands became more functional for a time, mainly either for protection or to raid the camps or settlements of whites as farming and cattle began to encroach on or destroy traditional food supplies.

Although the Shoshonean desert peoples resembled the Australians and the Bushmen in many ways—and a good case can be made for grouping them together—the oak and the piñon which provided the bulk of the Shoshonean diet required the development of specialized techniques. The harvesting of both natural crops was seasonal; the acorn in particular required extensive processing. Special methods were also required for the storage and transportation of both crops.

Figure 7–20 A California Indian basketry mortar for pounding acorns. The top basket has the bottom removed and is affixed to the shallow stone mortar with pitch and the whole set in a larger basket to catch any spillage. (After Mason.)

In parts of California, using basically the same technology, the greater abundance of seed-bearing plants made a markedly different pattern of life possible. The main difference, though, was the abundance of acorns and, in some places, the salmon runs on the rivers. Acorns may be stored for a year or more, and salmon can be dried. Although acorn crops vary from year to year, they usually are unbelievably abundant. One large valley live oak often can feed a single family for a year. Especially productive trees may be "owned" by a family, but in a good year another family may be given permission to gather from one of the limbs. In the extensive oak parklands of the Kern-Kaweah River deltas in central California, population was between 7 and 11 per square mile, a density approached or exceeded by only a very few fishing or farming peoples north of Mexico.

Although the acorn was relatively easy to gather, it often required tree climbing and the use of poles as well as the services of all the members of the family in the relatively brief harvest season. The harvest was stored either in underground granaries or woven surface granaries and protected from moisture and rodents. To be eaten, the nuts were shelled and the meats pounded in a mortar to produce a coarse flour. (See Figure 7–20.) Basketry trays were used to winnow the flour, returning coarser particles to the mortar for further treatment. The flour was leached by placing it in a basin of basketry or a hollow in the ground and pouring water on it carefully enough that the flour was not washed away. The flour was then formed into cakes and baked in hot ashes or boiled into mush by dropping hot stones into watertight baskets. (See Figure 7–21.)

The acorn took care of the basic diet; not only was it abundant, but it had a high fat and vegetable protein content. Nevertheless, a pure acorn diet was monotonous, and acorns from some oak species taste better than others. To supplement the diet men spent considerable time hunting either alone or in cooperative groups. Deer could be driven past concealed hunters; larger groups had a number of long nets into which rabbits could be driven. Fires could be set to encircle game which if not killed by the fire could be slaughtered as it tried to escape. Women spent a good deal of their time collecting small seeds or digging bulbs and tubers. Goldschmidt[9] describes Nomlaki

[9] Walter Goldschmidt, *Nomlaki Ethnography* (Berkeley: University of California Press, 1951).

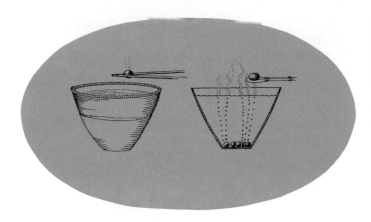

Figure 7–21 Heating water in a cooking basket using hot stones. Note the hinged stick to remove stones from fire and looped stock to remove stones from the basket. The same technique can be used with hide containers or wooden boxes. (After Holmes.)

women spending an arduous day to collect a handful or two of small seeds prized not for their food value but for flavoring. The techniques were basically the same as those used in the deserts to the east.

For parts of the year, at least, the food quest was not all-engrossing. Women not only made the many varieties of basketry needed, but they often embellished them with extensive decoration. The Pomo north of San Francisco Bay are especially noted for small, essentially useless coiled baskets, beautifully decorated with bright feathers and sometimes with stitches as fine

Basketweaving. Among agricultural and industrialized peoples such skills as basketweaving tend to be performed by specialists, such as these members of a basketweaving caste in Gopalpur, South India. (Photo by Alan Beals.)

as coarse pongee silk. Men hunted woodpeckers to gather special feathers to make ornamented bands for ceremonial costumes or to decorate baskets. Not only were there many local ceremonies involving music and dancing, but villages often staged major events to which hundreds of neighboring villagers were invited and lavishly fed.

The basic unit of most California Indian societies was the politically autonomous tribelet consisting of from a few hundred to perhaps 1,500 persons living at least part of the year in a single village or a village with satellite hamlets. The tribes usually referred to in the literature actually were groupings of such tribelets sharing a common language or dialect, a very similar culture, and often with some sense of solidarity as opposed to other "tribes," that is, people of different speech habits. The villages or settlements were occupied a significant part of each year, but, as among the Nisenan, some or even all of the population moved into higher mountains during the summer. In part this migration followed the migrations of the deer herds into higher elevations; in part it was to escape the extreme summer temperatures in most of the interior valleys.

The domestic architecture of these villages consisted of rather impermanent shelters of poles and brush, bark, or mats. The more permanent locus of the settlement was a sizeable subterranean house with an earthen roof supported by posts, rafters, and grass or brush. This structure was used by some of the men or by visitors for sleeping, but its main purpose was for ceremonies. The labor involved and the long life of such a structure militated against frequent relocations of settlements as, in lesser degree, did the labor expenditure in constructing acorn granaries. The tribelets had a fairly strong sense of territoriality, which applied mainly to rights to the resources; mere transit of the territory usually was not resented.

Tribelets had chiefs or headmen, often quasi-hereditary among the Nisenan and others. Such chiefs had little authority but, if popular, often had significant coercive powers. The principal functions of the chief were to compose disputes, advise people about their economic activities; receive and feed visitors, care for the ceremonial house, maintain the major ceremonies and administer such matters as the collection of food and its distribution for major events, and to see that the bodies of persons dying at a distance were brought for burial near their deceased or living relatives. A chief might have a speaker, particularly if he was not a good orator himself. Often he worked closely with the shaman, a powerful and often feared figure; by cooperating, both could enhance their influence. Concepts of wealth existed and were linked with status.

The basic social unit of the Nisenan was the nuclear family, but more extended kin ties were important. Upon these the individual had to depend for protection or redress of wrongs more than upon the chief. Some neighboring groups, such as the Nomlaki,[9] had at least incipient unilineal organizations of kinsfolk; this was absent among the Nisenan. Wives were sometimes from other tribelets; on occasion, if a man lacked relatives or disputes became acute, a family might live with the woman's tribelet instead of the more usual residence in the man's community.

Religious ideas were complex; some groups had rather sophisticated philosophic systems to explain both the natural and supernatural order. Ritual and ceremonial, accordingly, were well developed and involved both family and group activities. Some secret rituals were known only to the initiated, at times organized into secret societies.

In much of California, then, the combination of relatively abundant edible plant resources and a specialized technology permitted gatherers to approximate permanent village life and to develop some aspects of social and ceremonial life ordinarily to be found only among farming peoples. Collectors of the desert, on the other hand, although sharing a very similar basic technology, were forced to lead a significantly different life because of the less abundant food supply.

The collectors of the western United States illustrate the potentialities of basketry techniques. In this region practically every known technique occurred. Earliest specimens are all made by twining, a technique using either rigid or flexible warps tied together with flexible wefts. (See Figure 7–22.) This technique produced soft, flexible containers especially suited for carrying bags. It was early adapted to making other objects, such as matting. Somewhat later, stiff baskets of wicker, a variation of twilling or weaving, in which warps are stiff but the wefts are flexible, were used to make sturdier containers for storage and transportation. (See Figures 7–23 and 7–24.) Coiling also ap-

Figure 7–22 Three major basketry techniques. left: Coiling by sewing bundles of grass (a rod is sometimes used); center: twilling or weaving techniques; right: twining techniques.

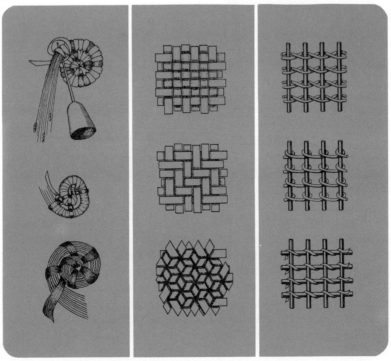

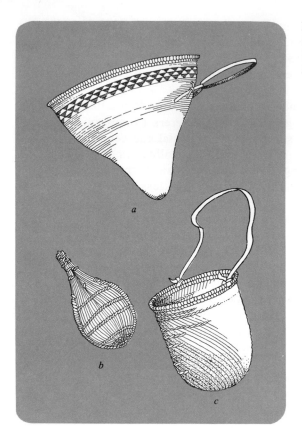

Figure 7–23 Coiled and twined basketry. (a) Coiled carrying basket; (b) twined seed beater; (c) twined carrying basket. (After Mason.)

peared later and in time became the dominant basketry technique as it is in the historic cultures of the region. In coiling, rods or rodlike bundles of grass are sewn together. This technique is especially well adapted to making tight trays and baskets capable of containing water and serving for hot stone boiling. (See Chapter 17 for a number of further examples of basketry.) Without basketry and nets the seed collectors could not have functioned.

The collectors, so deeply involved with plant life, seem most likely to have begun the domestication of plants and the shift from food gathering to food production. Considerable evidence that this was the case is now known for the domestication of maize and associated plants in Mexico. For other centers of domestication the matter is less clear. The postglacial Natufian cultures known archaeologically from the eastern end of the Mediterranean may represent collectors in transition to farming with stone sickles and querns for harvesting and processing grass seeds similar to the domesticated grains. The evidence of early basketry in Shanidar Cave further east, the only such evidence comparable in age to that of the North American desert cultures, is suggestive. If collectors once were common in the arid and semiarid lands of the Near East, none persisted into historic times. The same is true of the tropical forest

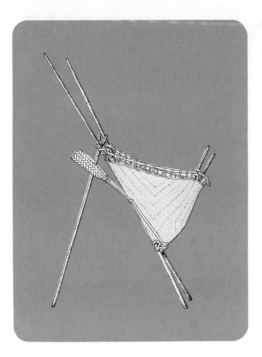

Figure 7-24 Papago Indian carrying net and frame. The basketry band goes over the forehead while the stick at the left allows the frame to be set upright. (After Mason.)

areas of South America and Southeast Asia, the likely centers for the domestication of numerous root, tuber, and fruit crops. These regions have a sufficient variety of plant foods to have supported cultures based heavily, if not predominantly, on collecting.

6. Summary

Previous to the industrial revolution, human societies fell into three major technological categories. These included hunting and gathering, leading to specialized hunting and collecting; plant and animal husbandry; and urbanization. Depending upon the productivity of the environment and upon a variety of historical circumstances, each of these technological adaptations led to the emergence of a variety of cultural types. Although hunter-gatherer societies were as variable as any other kind, they tend generally to be characterized by the existence of low population density, scarce and widely dispersed food resources, and organization into family bands. The Australian aborigines and the Bushmen exemplify some of the shared characteristics of desert-dwelling hunter-gatherers. Although both groups lacked any elaborate development of material culture, both possessed an extensive technology consisting of the knowledge required for survival in a harsh environment. Both groups, the Australians in particular, possessed complex systems of social relationship governing behavior and permitting the exchange of membership between nearby lands.

Specialized hunters and fishermen and collectors are characterized by the development of comparatively elaborate technology required to exploit one or a few major resources within the environment. Although changes in climate and the introduction of agriculture led to the disappearance of many specialized hunting peoples, the Crow with their rather recently developed buffalo hunting technology, exemplify the pattern of complex technological development characteristic of such specialized peoples. Both the Crow and the somewhat less specialized Eskimo possessed elaborate technologies and, compared to hunter-gatherers and many agricultural peoples, an abundance of material culture.

Fishing peoples, especially where fish are abundant, are capable of developing permanent settlements and high densities of population. Thus, the peoples of the Northwest Coast of North America could develop a way of life that in its broad outlines was hardly distinguishable from that of prosperous agricultural peoples. The archaeological record shows little evidence of the early emergence of fishing peoples or adequate seagoing vessels. Although the early record of the existence of fishing peoples may have been hidden by postglacial rises in the sea level, specialized fishing as a way of life seems to be no older than the emergence of agriculture itself. In favorable environments dense populations could also develop without benefit of agriculture as the result of the development of specialized methods for the collection of vegetable produce. The desert cultures of western North America, although they possessed highly specialized techniques for the collection and processing of acorns, pine nuts, and seed grasses, were prevented by harsh environmental circumstances from developing a population much more dense than that of the Australians or the Bushmen. In California, where the desert gave way to lush oak-covered grasslands, a population more dense than that of many agricultural peoples could develop. With this went the development of permanent village sites — perhaps not occupied throughout the year — and an elaborate artistic, religious, and ceremonial life. Because such adaptations as the specialized fishing of the Northwest Coast or the specialized acorn collecting of California were more successful than any simple form of agriculture would have been, the origins of agriculture, as we shall see in the next chapter, are more commonly attributed to specialized seed collectors living in semiarid environments in the Near East and in Central America.

Collateral Reading

Bicchieri, M. G. (ed.) *Hunters and Gatherers Today*. New York: Holt, Rinehart and Winston, Inc., 1972. Recent studies of several peoples.

Borgoraz, Vladimir. *Chuckchee* (Landmarks in Anthropology). Reprint of 1909 ed. New York: Johnson Reprint Corp., 1969. Fishermen and pastoralists.

Chance, Norman A. *The Eskimo of North Alaska*. New York: Holt, Rinehart and Winston, Inc., 1966. A good brief account.

Clark, Graham. *The Stone Age Hunters*. New York and Toronto: McGraw-Hill Book Company, 1967. Deals with prehistoric hunters with some modern parallels.

Damas, David (ed.). *Contributions to Anthropology; Band Societies.* National Museum of Canada Bulletin 228, Anthropological Series 84, 1969. Fresh view of hunter-gatherers.

Furer-Haimendorf, Christoph von. *The Aboriginal Tribes of Hyderabad.* Vol. I.: *The Chenchus, Jungle Folk of the Deccan.* London: Macmillan & Co., Ltd., 1943. Hunters and gatherers in India.

Goodale, J. C. *Tiwi Wives: A Study of the Women of Melville Island, N. Australia.* Seattle: University of Washington Press, 1971.

Hodges, Henry. *Artifacts, An Introduction to Early Materials and Technology.* London: John Baker, 1964. Perhaps best study of the tools and technologies relevant to hunters and gatherers.

Honigman, John J. *The Kaska Indians: An Ethnographic Reconstruction.* (Yale University Publications in Anthro.) New Haven: Yale University Press, 1954. Canadian hunters.

Lee, Richard B., and Irven DeVore (eds.) *Man the Hunter.* Chicago: Aldine Publishing Company, 1968. An excellent discussion of contemporary hunter-gatherers.

Oakley, Kenneth. *Man the Toolmaker,* Corrected Edition. Chicago: University of Chicago Press, 1963. Contains good material on the technology of hunters.

Rohner, Ronald, and Evelyn C. Rohner. *The Kwakiutl: Indians of British Columbia.* New York: Holt, Rinehart and Winston, Inc., 1970. Contemporary versus "Potlatch Period" Kwakiutl culture.

Service, Elman R. *The Hunters.* Englewood Cliff, N.J.: Prentice-Hall, Inc., 1966. A perhaps overgeneralized view of uniformities among hunter-gatherer cultures.

Spencer, Sir Baldwin, and F. J. Gillen. *The Arunta: A Study of a Stone-Age People.* Oosterhout N.B., Netherlands, Anthrop. Pub., 1966. A republication of a classic study.

Turnbull, Colin M. *The Forest People.* New York: Simon & Schuster, Inc., 1961. A romantic ethnography of the Congo Pygmies.

Warner, W. Lloyd. *A Black Civilization: A Social Study of an Australian Tribe,* rev. ed. Harper & Row, Inc., 1958. One of the most detailed accounts of an Australian people.

Ethnographic References

Australian Aborigine: Berndt, 1970; Hart and Pilling, 1960; Tindale, 1972.
Bushmen of South Africa: Lee, 1968, 1972; Thomas, 1959.
Chumash: Anderson, 1968; Kroeber, 1953, 1925; Landberg, 1965.
Crow: Lowie, 1935.
Eskimo: Oswalt, 1969; Spencer, 1959.
Haida: Swanton, 1909.
Nisenan: Beals, 1933.
Nomlaki: Goldschmidt, 1951.
Shoshoni: Kelly, 1964; Stewart, 1938.

8/Food Producers

1. The Transition to Food Production

The first several million years of human existence led to the development of a rich variety of cultures whose economic base was the systematic harvesting of wild plants and animals. Resources available to such hunter-gatherer cultures varied greatly with environmental circumstances. Large and geographically concentrated resources of the kind that were available in California and on the Northwest Coast of North America often permitted large concentrations of population and the development of permanently settled communities. The scarce and scattered resources of desert and tropical forest regions permitted only small populations lacking extensive material equipment and moving constantly from place to place.

If studies of recent and currently existing hunter-gatherers are a reliable index of past circumstances, hunter-gatherers as a whole enjoyed stable relationships with their environments. Populations were generally well below the maximum number of people the environment could support, and human beings were rarely in a position to exterminate the animals they relied upon for food. They could and did use fire to make substantial changes in the plant cover, and they may have modified the animal population of many regions they occupied, but even here, once fire-adapted vegetation and hunter-adapted animal populations were established, stable relationships to the environment were maintained. Even in harsh, desert environments the average hunter-gatherers may, like their primate relatives, have spent only a few hours a day in the quest for food. Environmental stability and low population density restricted the incidence of disease, so that hunter-gatherers may have been far more healthy than their lack of access to modern medicine might suggest.

Ten thousand years ago, as the last ice age drew to a close, the environments occupied by human beings began to undergo radical change. A rise in the sea level flooded rich coastal plains. Dryer and warmer times led to the development of vast grasslands where forests had flourished in earlier times. At the same time the retreat of the glaciers opened new lands for human settlement. Improved hunting techniques, in particular the widespread use of the bow and arrow, and improved fishing techniques involving the use of boats, increased the human capacity to exploit the environment. Many animal species that were hunted for food became extinct. Specialized technologies for the harvesting and processing of grass seed became widespread and in some places may have led to the establishment of permanently settled communities of collectors largely dependent upon abundant stands of wild grass.

Exactly how all of these various elements came together during the uncertain centuries following the retreat of the ice is not known in detail. One possibility is that agriculture began as a kind of desperate attempt to survive and adapt within environments that were overpopulated and rapidly deteriorating. Another possibility is that the increased density of human beings resulting from improved hunting and gathering technology caused certain plants and animals to adapt to the special circumstances created by human habitation sites or by human hunting and collecting activities. Ultimately these plants and animals, having started their career as weeds and pests, might have become sufficiently useful as food to have justified human effort in caring for them.

At first this incipient agriculture probably had little influence upon established patterns of hunting and collecting. The plants used would have been

Figure 8–1 Both gatherers and farmers process seeds and grains by pulverizing or grinding them. (a) stone mortar and pestle from Santa Cruz Island, California, a nonfarming culture; (b) Mohegan Indian, New York, mortar and pestle of wood used to pound maize; (c) Pueblo metate and mano for grinding grain and seeds. (Not to scale.)

only semidomesticated, and the technology required to produce significant crops would have been nonexistent. Assuming that in many parts of the world the yields from hunting and gathering had become borderline for survival, even a small agricultural crop would have been sufficient to tide people over in a bad year. Many recent and modern peoples use agriculture in much the same way as a means of supplementing hunting, gathering, or pastoral means of subsistence.

As crops became increasingly adapted to the unique environments provided by the practice of agriculture, and as human beings developed improved agricultural technology, yields from early agriculture must have increased markedly, especially in favored locations. Such increased agricultural production almost certainly went hand in hand with increased population. The need to care for crops required people to remain for long periods in a single place, and this, combined with increased population, would have resulted in the excessive harvesting of such wild crops as plants, animals, and fish. Once hooked on agriculture, there was an almost inevitable slide in the direction of increasing dependence upon cultivated plants. Casual farming, probably carried out almost exclusively by women, was gradually replaced in favorable environments by much more intensive agriculture carried out by both men and women.

Although some specialized hunter-gathers lived in permanently settled communities and some agricultural peoples did not, the development of agriculture meant that most human beings came to live in permanently established settlements. Tallensi household compound. Tongo, Ghana. (Kindness of David Kronenfeld.)

The attribution of the invention and early practice of agriculture to women stems from the fact that virtually all known hunting and gathering societies practice a division of labor in which men deal with animals and women deal with food plants. In many existing agricultural societies, women tend to play a predominant role in agriculture, while the men engage in hunting, warfare, animal herding, or elaborate ceremonial activities. Men tend to play a predominant role in agriculture when the plow, which involves animals, is used, or when special ecological conditions give them nothing else to do.

Early agriculture appears to have been of two general kinds: root or tuber cultivation and seed crop cultivation. Tuber cultivation seems to have been generally characteristic of tropical forest regions, although it also developed in the Andean highlands in South America, where the domestic potato originated. Seed crop cultivation appears to have developed primarily in highland grassland regions, generally in the subtropics. Early agriculture, because the

In much of highland Bolivia and Peru, the potato remains the staple food. Potatoes are preserved by allowing them to freeze at night and then mashing them with the feet and drying them. Long-term storage of food is usually essential to the establishment of permanent settlements. (Courtesy of the United Nations.)

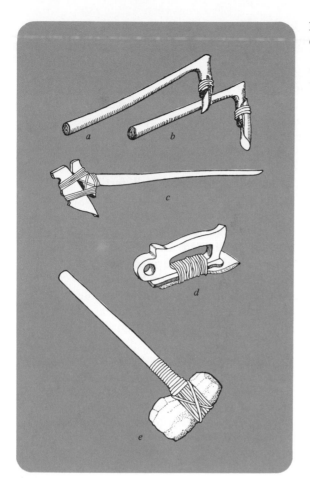

Figure 8–2 Farmers tend to use more complex tools. (a,b,c) adzes for woodworking (after Willoughby); (d) adze (after Goddard); (e) ax (after Moorehead). (Not to scale.)

distinction between weeds or self-domesticated plants and cultivated or artifically domesticated plants was trivial or nonexistent, almost certainly involved the growing of a wide variety of edible and nonedible crops on a single field. When agriculture had developed sufficiently to make weeding worthwhile, the nonedible crops would have been removed from the field, leaving a mixture of leafy vegetables, tubers, fruit-bearing vines, and grasses.

In this form of agriculture, usually called interculture, three or four kinds of seed are deliberately planted and several other types of seed are merely encouraged. In recent history, especially following the development of the plow, many of the seed crops have come to be grown by monoculture, in which only one species is planted and allowed to survive within a given field. Interculture—*polyculture* would be more appropriate—remains common in the raising of maize, beans, and squash in classical American Indian fashion, and in the less well-known African and South Asian pattern of raising millet, legumes, and gourds or melons within a single field. In modern times many of the tuber crops characteristic of the moist tropics have been raised through monoculture, but the prevailing pattern for all tropical agriculture has been the development of a profusion of domesticated plants within each patch of cultivated ground.

Interculture, especially when it involves leguminous or nitrogen-producing plants, tends to preserve the fertility of the soil. It also preserves a mixture of plants more typical of tropical environments and more resistant to weather conditions or diseases that might wipe out a single species. Except in a few, quite exceptional environments, all forms of early agriculture appear to have had a tendency to exhaust the soil when a single patch of land was farmed over a period of several years. Thus nearly all early forms of agriculture appear to have relied upon natural regeneration as a means of restoring soil fertility. This meant the periodic abandonment of fields and the continuous clearing and development of new fields. The classic pattern for such swidden agriculture involves a gradual movement of the farm village from place to place within a larger territory as fields in one place are exhausted. Because, at any one time, only a small part of the existing arable land can be farmed, population density, except in favored regions such as Western Africa or Yucatan, is relatively low and communities tend to be scattered. Lacking a plow capable of uprooting tropical grasslands or an iron ax capable of clearing large areas of forest, the proportion of arable lands is likely to be very small. Until the

Figure 8–3 Head coverings are standard equipment among many peoples. Almost all farmers have them; many hunter-gatherers do not. (a) decorated wooden hat; (b) coiled basketry cap worn by Pomo acorn collectors of California; (c) Indian maize farmer of northeastern United States; (d) Albanian mountain man's head covering; (e) hat worn by reindeer-herding Lapps of Scandivavia.

In swidden agriculture, trees are girdled or chopped down. After drying, trees and underbrush are then burned. Seeds or tubers are planted in the soft ash with a digging stick. The effort required to remove large unburned tree trunks is unrewarding; planting takes place around them. Semai of Malasia. (Kindness of Clay Robarchek.)

development of systematic manuring practices and irrigation, neither grain agriculture nor tuber agriculture, except as in Egypt and Mesopotamia where fields were renewed by annual floods, could support very large or very dense populations.

With the development of agriculture the pattern of ecological limitations upon human behavior was markedly changed. Human activities now had to be planned with regard to the characteristics of the particular plants and animals upon which human life depended. Increased population density led to increased problems in the relationships among human beings. It also led to increased disease. Where yields were high in relation to labor costs, agriculture could support large numbers of specialists who contributed little to food production. Where yields were large and harvesting had to be completed within a short space of time, solutions had to be found to the problem of mobilizing large numbers of workers at harvest time. Depending upon the nature of the environment, the most efficient use of the land might involve many different and complicated balances among a variety of plant and animal species. Decisions on which plants to grow or which animals to raise have important effects upon the structure of human life, especially on family size and community organization. In many parts of the world, long-term planning and complex decision making are required in order to develop productive fields, large herds, or systems of irrigation.

Women preparing packets of rice seedlings from seedbed at lower right. Seeds will be planted in rice plots in immediate foreground. On lower left is stubble from freshly harvested rice (to be eaten by water buffalo). Rice plots in background are in four stages: (a) dry plots on left are fallow, (b) plots in center are flooded and ready for planting, (c) nearby plots have just been planted, (d) distant fields are ready for harvest. Wet rice agriculture may involve dramatic changes in the environment. Gurun-Batusangkar, West Sumatra, Indonesia. (Kindness of Lynn Thomas.)

Overall, the effects of agriculture included a longer workday, increased disease, the development of an exploitative or manipulative approach to the environment, and, in many places, a regular regime of overpopulation and famine. Even under the best of conditions, one might even say particularly under the best of conditions, agriculture may result in the extermination of wild animals and a decline in the proportion of domesticated animals. The resulting diet, consisting largely of yams, potatoes, maize, bread, or rice, is almost certain to cause widespread malnutrition and protein deficiency. One happy solution to this problem is the wholesale consumption of crude beers and wines containing large quantities of yeast (rich in protein and B vitamins).

2. Incipient and Marginal Farmers

Archaeological work both in southwestern Asia in such sites as Jarmo and Jericho and in the valleys of Tehuacán and Oaxaca in Mexico demonstrate that with the domestication of the first plants people did not immediately

Hillside cultivation of wheat by planting in shallow pits. Agricultural operations may involve large-scale environmental changes. Pits and cleared spaces made by agriculturalists in the tropics often provide ideal breeding places for malaria-spreading mosquitoes. Tanzania. (Courtesy of the United Nations.)

become farmers. (See Chapter 6.) The transition from the first cultivation to the establishment of permanent or semipermanent farming villages may have taken 1,000 or 2,000 years. Some recent collecting peoples did approach the first stages of farming. Australian women sometimes cut the tops from wild yams and buried them again. The Owens Valley Paiutes gathered seeds from certain areas only in alternate years. Moreover, they dug ditches and diverted the waters of mountain streams to spread out over wider areas and so promote the growth of a good crop of wild grasses. In some cases the Indians even scattered seeds over the irrigated areas. Both the Australians and the Paiutes, then, were but a step removed from farming in that they employed with wild plants techniques of irrigation, casual sowing, and crop conservation.

Many Apachean peoples of the American Southwest, including the Navajos, were marginal farmers before European contact. The western Apache of Arizona probably learned farming from the Pueblo peoples after migrating into the Southwest.[1] Farming was sufficiently important to the western Apache that their farms were the basis of the local settlement group, but they provided only part of the diet. Located in the arid West, the western Apache could farm only in a few places where the lands retained moisture or, more commonly,

[1] Grenville Goodwin, *The Social Organization of the Western Apache* (Chicago: University of Chicago Press, 1942).

Plowing rice field. Gurun-Batusangkar, West Sumatra, Indonesia. (Kindness of Lynn Thomas.)

could be irrigated by short canal systems from flowing springs or streams. Farmlands belonged to clans and sometimes to individuals; outsiders might be permitted to farm such lands by agreement but trespass otherwise was resisted. Around the farmlands was an area with a radius of eight to ten miles that was regarded as the range primarily of the local group and a still larger area considered to be the range of the band to which the local group belonged. Trespass on these lands, however, was not resented; people ordinarily hunted or gathered in the places most convenient to their local settlement. If they went

Winnowing rice by hand. Burma. (Courtesy of the United Nations.)

Winnowing sorghum to separate particles of straw or chaff from grain. Gopalpur, South India. (Photo by Alan R. Beals.)

farther it was because of necessity or because some special resource was not available nearby.

The first significant wild plant harvest came in April when mescal (*Agave* sp.) sprouted. Parties traveled to areas where the plant was abundant and brought back the roasted buds to the local settlement. In May maize planting took place and most of the population was present at the farms, preparing soil, planting, and repairing irrigation ditches. Ditch bosses supervised this work and apportioned the water. Farmowning families stayed in the home settlement until July, when the maize was 6 to 8 inches high; after that only old people and dependents remained in the settlement. Others began to collect wild foods. In July some went to the lowlands to collect saguaro (a cactus) fruits. Many more, however, went to higher country to collect acorns. Only sweet acorns were used; the western Apache lacked knowledge to leach the bitter acorns. In late August a few families went again to low country to gather mesquite beans; some perhaps visited the farms to see if any green corn was ready to eat. September saw most families in the home farms for the harvest; they remained there until the harvest was complete and stored safely away. In November piñon nuts and juniper berries were the major wild crop. Although some sporadic hunting took place the year round, November to April was the principal hunting time. During this season most people lived in the home settlement or in family clusters nearby.

Public ceremonies occurred throughout the year but especially in June, July, and August. These attracted many people from other localities and bands. Some of the ceremonies were spectacular and feasting, dancing, and social intercourse were among the attractions. Families and clusters of related families were basic to western Apache social organization. Matrilineal clans

Cleaning plow and harrow (rake) before storage. Burma. (Courtesy of the United Nations.)

tied these families together and in a few instances the local settlements might all be members of a single clan. If more than one clan was represented in a given locality, the most numerous clan dominated local affairs. The clans extended kinship ties far beyond the family and, although individuals belonged to their mother's clan, both maternal and paternal clan members were important. Clan chiefs, subchiefs, locality chiefs, and war chiefs advised and led people in many activities. If a chief was not involved, usually one mature and able individual was regarded as the leader for a particular purpose.

The western Apaches were more mobile than many of the California acorn collectors or the fishing peoples of the North Pacific Coast. They were marginal farmers because they had not completely accepted the farmer's way of life in a precarious environment. Some, of course, lacked sufficient lands; on the other hand, some families did not cultivate all the land available to them. Except for irrigation, the Apache technology differed little from that of the arid lands collectors. Their social organization and ceremonial life was, however, more complex and resembled that of established farming peoples.

When studied by Fejos in 1943,[2] the Yagua, who lived in tropical forests north of the upper Amazon river in South America, practiced extensive farming, but obtained their main food supply from hunting. Plants cultivated include sweet manioc (a starchy tuber), maize, yams, sweet potatoes, pumpkins, papayas and pineapples, bananas, and sugar cane. (The last two were introduced by Europeans.) Fields were created by clearing the forest, girdling large trees with stone axes, and burning. Although fields might be cultivated more than one year, some new fields were cleared each year and old fields abandoned. Men cleared the fields but other farming work was done by women using only a digging stick. There was no weeding or later cultivation.

Despite the variety of cultivated plants providing a year-round source of food, hunting not only provided the majority of the diet but was the activity of consuming interest. Game animals included deer, tapir, peccary, five kinds of monkeys, agouti, sloth, anteater, armadillo, river turtle, and freshwater dolphin. Dogs and poisoned spears were used for hunting some large animals; for others and for smaller animals and birds poisoned blowgun darts were employed. Large animals were hunted in groups under the direction of the chief; other activities were individual, sometimes from hunting blinds. Important were a great variety of traps, snares, pitfalls, and deadfalls. Fish were poisoned but no other fishing techniques were used.

Some food was pulverized in a wooden trough with a wooden rocker. Meat was preserved by smoking. Most food was boiled in pottery vessels and flavored with salt and capsicum (chili peppers).

The Yagua community consisted of an extended patrilineal and patrilocal family occupying a single large house with a frame of poles set in the ground and bent over and tied together to form an arch, and then covered with thatch or palm leaves. These large houses may have been a late innovation replacing small huts. Usually they were six or seven miles away from the next settlement and locations shifted from time to time as fields were exhausted nearby.

[2] Paul Fejos, *Ethnography of the Yagua* (New York: Viking Fund Publications in Anthropology, No. 1, 1943).

The Yagua lacked either the bow and arrow or the spear thrower, although both were used by nearby tribes. At times they used dugout canoes obtained from other tribes, but their water travel was ordinarily on the balsa raft, which might be large enough to accomodate an entire family. They also manufactured bark cloth, woven fabrics, and pottery. Except for the stone ax, stone implements were almost lacking, as raw material had to be traded from elsewhere. Hardwood points were used as weapons, and split bamboo provided knives.

The Yagua, hence, were marginal farmers, as were the western Apache, apparently by choice. Many of their neighbors in similar environments gained most of their food from farming. The technology was limited but highly specialized and included such things as some weaving and pottery making, arts more commonly found among more settled farmers. Architecture was more ambitious than that of the western Apache, but this was perhaps necessary in a region of very heavy rainfall.

3. Pastoralists

Pastoralists are people who live primarily by herding domesticated animals. Before the industrial revolution, pastoralism occurred mainly in the arid and semiarid lands stretching from North Africa to Central Asia. Specialized rein-

Flock of karakul sheep grazing in northern Afghanistan. Astrakhan, the skin of karakul lambs, has long been an important export. (Courtesy of the United Nations.)

Bedouin from southern Algeria grazing sheep and camels. (Courtesy of the United Nations.)

deer pastoralists also existed in the Arctic regions of the Old World from Norway to Siberia. Sheepherders, characteristic of parts of southern Europe and India, and other kinds of specialized herdsman often existed in a kind of subordinate or symbiotic relationship to farming peoples. Many farming peoples, especially those practicing plow agriculture, but also those raising tuber crops attractive to pigs, are also partly pastoralists. In general, pastoralists are either directly involved in agriculture or depend for agricultural supplies upon neighboring agricultural peoples. In the New World, despite the domestication of the llama, pastoral peoples did not exist as separate social or political entities.

Although pastoralism was at one time regarded as a stage in evolutionary development, it is now apparent that pastoralism developed in connection with agriculture and that pastoralism represents an adaptation to specific environments in which lands are suitable for herding but not for agricultural production. Peoples, specialized in the herding of animals, tend to be more mobile than agricultural peoples because they must habitually move their animals from place to place in order to take advantage of good grazing conditions. Because animals are highly portable, pastoral peoples are often involved in patterns of raiding and warfare in order to augment their own herds or to avenge losses suffered when others have attacked them. Herding tends to become an occupation largely restricted to males, and thus, in pastoral societies, the inheritance of property and patterns of marriage generally stress the solidarity of the male descendants of the same ancestor. In technical terms pastoral societies tend to be patriarchal, patrilineal, and patrilocal.

The Nuer, as described by Evans-Pritchard in 1940,[3] represent a people entirely dedicated to the raising of cattle, but reluctantly engaged in fishing and in agriculture. Located in the Sudan in Africa, the Nuer occupy a plateau region consisting of extensive marshes and grasslands. During the summer rainy season much of Nuerland is a grass-covered swamp. During the winter the grass is burned off, and the countryside becomes an arid, dusty plain. During the summer the floods drive the Nuer and their cattle to a few precious patches of heavily overgrazed high ground. During the winter the Nuer must move closer to the rivers in search of water and grass.

Although Nuer local groups moved and pastured their herds as a single unit, ownership of cattle was vested in the male membership of joint families often including grandfathers, married sons, and male children. Cattle were used to provide milk, meat, and blood (obtained by piercing a neck vein). Because there are few stones and trees in Nuerland, cattle also provided hooves, bone, and horns for making tools. Hides were used to make containers, beds, cords, and drumheads. Dung was used for fuel, plaster, and bandaging. Cattle were given away before a man could obtain a wife, and cattle served as currency in many other sorts of transactions. A murderer could escape vengeance only by making a suitable payment in cattle to his victim's relatives. In traditional times wealth in cattle was augmented by stealing them from neighboring peoples.

As soon as Nuer children were old enough to crawl, they played in the kraal (corral) with calves, sheep, and goats, often drinking milk directly from the udders of the animals. Small children collected urine in gourds and washed themselves with it; they helped with the milking and herded the smaller animals. Children were named after oxen; poems were written about oxen; and descent was calculated in terms of oxen. Because the cattle were passed down from father to son, the local group tended to be patrilineal. Although the Nuer preferred to live entirely upon the cow, the possibility of severe drought and of cattle raids and cattle disease made necessary a reluctant reliance upon agriculture.

During the summer rainy season, when the Nuer retreated to more or less permanent villages on high ground, each family began to cultivate a patch of land behind their homestead. The cultivation was done with hoes by all members of the family. Should the crop survive subsequent floods or dry spells, it had to be weeded repeatedly until harvest time and defended from elephants, birds, locusts, ostriches, antelopes, and other interlopers. Millet and beans—and in more recent times, maize—formed the principal crops. Millet was planted in late spring and again in early fall and harvested in September and January. Crops were never rotated and manure was never used. Thus the Nuer practiced a kind of swidden agriculture (see §4 of this chapter) and moved their homesteads after a few years of cultivation in a single place. Much of the ordinary agricultural work was carried out by older people, while younger people herded the cattle at camps separated from the village. The

---

[3] E. E. Evans-Pritchard, *The Nuer: A Description of the Modes of Livelihood and Political Institutions of a Nilotic People* (New York: Oxford University Press, 1968) (c1940).

Encampment of nomadic pastoralists near Bojinoord, Iran. (Courtesy of the United Nations.)

young people returned periodically to help harvest the fields and to carry away supplies of millet for porridge and beer. During the winter the village site became uninhabitable because of the absence of water. Cattle and people then moved to the banks of streams and the people subsisted largely upon a diet of fish and game. Throughout the year the principal diet consisted of milk, mush, and beer supplemented by beef from an occasional sacrifice, by fish, or by game.

The Nuer pattern of subsistence, like that of hunter-gatherers living in difficult environments, involved the use of all available technology to exploit every conceivable environmental niche available to them. The practice of agriculture and pastoralism together provided for a much denser population than could be supported by hunter-gatherers occupying the same environment.

4. Swidden Farmers

Where special circumstances or the specialized use of animal or chemical manures makes it possible to maintain the fertility of agricultural lands, the same fields can be used year after year. Marginal agriculturalists, like the Yagua, and even some pastoralists, like the Nuer, must perforce practice a form of shifting or swidden agriculture, moving their fields when existing fields give out. Practices resembling swidden are still maintained in parts of Europe and North America where fields are left idle or fallow when their yield begins to decline. The surviving forms of swidden agriculture tend to occur in the tropical forest regions of the New World, Melanesia, Indonesia, South and Southeast Asia, and Africa. Although swidden agriculture is sometimes regarded as a single ecological or evolutionary type, it is often found in association with other types of agriculture and might best be regarded as one of several available alternative forms of agriculture and pastoralism that are used in the process of adapting to different sorts of environments.

Swidden tends to be characteristic of tropical forest environments because large animals capable of providing manure are usually not viable in such regions and because the various forms of plow agriculture are impractical. Because swidden involves clearing relatively small patches of forest at any one time, it creates less disruption of the forest ecology than would massive plow agriculture. In many environments swidden agriculture is extremely productive because it involves a variety of different crops and thus reproduces to some extent the tropical forest environment. Swidden crops are often managed by women, although men clear away the forest and help with heavy work. Consequently women often own the fields and may exert considerable economic and political power. A comparatively large proportion of swidden agriculturalists are matrilocal and matrilineal.

When described, the Tapirapé of central Brazil lived in densely forested areas interspersed with extensive semiarid savannahs with scrub growth and groups of palms.[4] Flooded in the rainy season and arid during the dry season, the savannahs were visited only occasionally for hunting. Note the similarities

[4] Julian H. Steward (ed.), *Handbook of South American Indians* Washington, D.C.: Bureau of American Ethnology, Bulletin 143 (six volumes), 1946–1959); Vol. II, 1946, pp. 167–178.

A Kurdish tribe of northern Iraq moving to a new location. Both donkeys and cattle bear packs. Women look after the water supply and raise chickens, geese, and turkeys which accompany the tribe on its travels. (Courtesy of the United Nations.)

Unirrigated rice growing in a swidden field in the Amazon basin. Brazil. (Courtesy of the United Nations.)

to the Nuer environment. Within forest areas on high ground above flood levels, the Tapirapé cleared extensive garden sites and planted them with both sweet and bitter manioc, four kinds of maize, yams, beans, pumpkins, squash, peanuts, peppers, bananas, papaya, and cotton. Food was abundant, but manioc was the basic staple. Gardens were cleared either individually or cooperatively but in the latter case were divided for individual cultivation. Clearing and most garden work were done by men, but women also took part. Each gardener ordinarily had two plots, a newly cleared area and the area cultivated the previous year, in which only manioc was planted. After two years plots were abandoned.

Meat was regarded as a luxury, although game was abundant in many seasons. The men hunted throughout the year but the major hunting season was on the dry savannahs from June through October. In September and October, after fields had been cleared but before planting, most families moved into temporary camps where the men hunted deer, peccary, and wildfowl with the bow and arrow, using a club to finish off the wounded game. Fish were shot with the bow and arrow or stupified with vegetable poisons. Turtle eggs and wild fruits were collected.

Residential houses were quadrangular structures of poles tied to a roof beam and covered with palm or banana thatch. They averaged about 13 by 33 feet and sheltered four to eight related simple or nuclear families. The residential houses were set in an oval about a large (approximately 20 by 65 feet) men's ceremonial house which women were forbidden to enter. Each family in a residential structure had its own sleeping and cooking area. Settlement populations numbered originally about 2000 persons. Exhaustion of available farm sites as well as fear of the ghosts of the dead led to abandonment of the settlement every four to five years. The household equipment, owned by the women, included sleeping hammocks, cooking pottery gourds, and basketry. Many of these, as well as the weapons used by men, were decorated. No clothing was used, but the body was tattooed and many ornaments worn. Canoes were not used, and all goods were transported on the human back.

The house groups were matrilocal, that is, they normally consisted of related women, husbands, and children. Kinship was bilateral, reckoned through both parents, and was extended so that a large number of people in the settlement could be addressed by kinship terms. Kinship ties were the most important force for solidarity. In addition, both men and women inherited membership from their fathers in a feasting group which met periodically for ceremonial meals; they were means of distributing food surpluses. Finally, all men belonged to one of two patrilineal groups or moieties with primarily ceremonial functions. Each of these in turn was divided into three

Swidden agriculture may persist after more intensive forms of agriculture have been developed. Note swiddens on hills at left foreground and background. Gurun-Batusangkar, West Sumatra, Indonesia. (Kindness of Lynn Thomas.)

Woman carries baby in net bag suspended from her head while another woman performs ritual to ensure that baby will sleep well. House in background is testimonial to permanent settlement. Gururumba Tribe, Eastern Highlands of New Guinea, Upper Asaro Valley. (Courtesy of the American Museum of Natural History.)

age grades: youths under fifteen, warriors from fifteen to forty, and elders. Very old men might drop out of the group activities. The functions included group hunting, group work activities, competitive dancing in ceremonials, and reciprocal feasting. Neither the settlement nor any of the organized groups were exogamous. For various activities special leaders were recognized; because of their prestige, shamans often occupied these positions and headed residential groups. Ceremonials were especially frequent during the rainy season, when hunting or garden work was impossible.

5. Village Farmers: The Kapauku

When practiced in association with intensive gardening and pig raising, swidden agriculture can give rise to relatively permanent settlements and to the development of complex political and economic structures. The Kapauku of western New Guinea followed in 1963 the same basic agricultural patterns as did the peoples previously discussed before they were affected by modern influences.[5] But a favorable environment, combined with the advantages of pig raising and the systematic use of green manure, created a quite different pattern.

The Kapauku lived in a rainy and mountainous country where they subsisted primarily by the raising of sweet potatoes both in swiddens chopped out of the surrounding forests or in perennial gardens on valley bottoms. Virgin forests were almost never cleared for fields; they were too difficult to clear and too valuable as a source of timber and rattan. Preferred lands for hillside cultivation were secondary forest previously cultivated but abandoned for a period of about ten years. In the marshy valley bottomlands, both swidden fields and gardens required the construction of drainage ditches to keep water from standing on the crop and ruining it. The gardens were fertilized with composted vegetable material, and the crops planted on raised beds. In addition to the sweet potato, sugar cane, taro, greens, bananas, and many minor crops

[5] Leonard Pospisil, *Kapauku Papauan Economy*, Publications in Anthropology, No. 62 (New Haven: Yale University Press, 1963).

Steps in the making of a pottery vessel. Use of pottery and other hard-to-transport articles is a characteristic of permanently settled peoples. Bili, near Madang, New Guinea. (Courtesy of the United Nations.)

could be grown in the gardens. Many of these plants, including perhaps the sweet potato itself, may have been introduced over the past three hundred years by Europeans.

A special complication of Kapauku farming was the necessity for a sturdy and pigproof fence around all cultivated plots. The Kapauku fed their pigs at night and in the morning, but during the day the pigs roamed about, foraging. Domestic pigs, along with wild pigs and rats, could devastate a garden very quickly. Because a pigproof fence is practically impossible to construct, there was an advantage in developing contiguous fields so as to make it easier to keep watch and to construct fences.

The heaviest work of the Kapauku male was clearing forest land. Before steel tools reached the area, he used a polished-stone blade set in a handle for cutting or girdling trees and a stone "machete," a polished-stone blade about 20 centimeters long, held in the hand for girdling or cutting smaller plants. Wooden digging sticks were used for planting and harvesting. A more elaborately worked stick with a bladelike end was used for weeding, and a similar tool with a broader blade was used for digging drainage ditches. Net bags were used to carry produce.

Pig breeding and trading was the usual avenue for acquiring wealth and status. A significant part of the sweet potato crop was fed to pigs. The animals provided a major part of the protein in the diet and were also slaughtered on almost any special occasion. In some districtwide events several hundred pigs might be slaughtered. Although men paid a great deal of attention to their pigs, much of the care and feeding was in the charge of women. Young pigs often were carried around by women in their carrying bags or in the arms.

In addition to farming and pig-raising activities, many wild plants were gathered, mainly leafy vegetables and fruits. In addition, a large number of wild plants were used for the manufacture of artifacts and houses. Numerous varieties of bark provided bast for thread or string. Hardwoods were used for arrow points; other woods were employed for bows, handles, and frames for netted containers; and yet other woods were used for canoes, house building, and thatching. Reed, bamboo, and rattan were used for arrows, containers, and bowstrings and for construction of houses. Some plants were used for magical or decorative purposes. Many plants were gathered whenever accidentally encountered; others were searched for when the need arose. About 150 named plants were considered useful. Numerous insects, reptiles, amphibians, eggs, and larvae were collected whenever encountered, and were considered delicacies.

Fish were virtually absent in Kapauku territory, but small lakes had an abundance of several varieties of crayfish. These were collected mainly by women and children from the shores or with dugout canoes, using a variety of nets. Water insects, eggs, and larvae were also collected. Men, if they fished, preferred diving and spearing crayfish, but none did this systematically, and some adult males had never fished.

Because of the scarcity of game, hunting for many of the Kapauku was primarily a men's sport. A number of specialized types of arrow for different kinds of game were used with the bow; fire drives were practiced; and a variety

Bolivian Indian woman spinning thread. The right hand twirls the spindle. Actually the woman is spinning the thread a second time to tighten it and eliminate irregularities in the yarn. (Courtesy of the United Nations.)

of traps were used. Wild boar and rats appeared to be the most common animals hunted; the first was dangerous, and both damaged crops. Quantititatively, hunting and fishing seem to have provided a relatively small return for the time and energy involved.

Kapauku settlements consisted of scattered houses which, because they had to be replaced from time to time, resulted in a certain amount of movement over time. Except when a territory was abandoned because of pressure of neighbors or land shortages, these movements were for only short distances. Houses represented substantial labor. They varied in size according to the wealth of the owner and the size of the household. Basic floor plans were similar: a central men's room, where all males over about seven years of age slept, and a series of rooms, each with a separate outside entrance, for each married woman and her small children. Walls were made of two or more layers of planks separated by insulating material. Roofs were of thatch. Floors were raised platforms with an opening in which a stone and clay fireplace was built.

The Kapauku made a number of basic stone tools, some of which have been mentioned, using both polished and chipped-stone techniques. More striking was the use of animal teeth and bone for many purposes; split bamboos provided most knives. Containers were almost all made of netting, or occasionally of wood or bamboo. Basketry and pottery were unknown. Food

Member of Shepherd caste, near Gopalpur, South India, weaving a woolen blanket. (Photo by Alan Beals.)

was either roasted on hot ashes or steamed by wrapping thickly in leaves and placing on hot ashes. Clothing was minimal but there were elaborate ornaments. Examined in detail, the technology was quite complex and many individuals could make only part of the objects they used regularly; this was more true of men than of women. In one survey more than half the men had never chipped a flint and over one-third had never made a bow.

Specialization, in the sense that not all the culture is equally known to everyone, occurs in many societies; this is particularly true of village-farming communities. The Kapauku were perhaps unusual in the degree of internal specialization in the technological aspects of culture. This may possibly have been encouraged by the possession of a true all-purpose monetary system facilitating exchange and a great preoccupation with wealth, both its accumulation and its use for social purposes. A contributing factor may be the uneven food supply from farming. Sweet potato fields take about eight months to mature; some families thus might sell surpluses part of the year, yet purchase part of their food in other times of the year. Moreover, there were a number of families that concentrated on other activities and made no serious attempt to produce all of their food.

Kapauku villages were spatially separated from other villages but they all formed part of a confederacy, divided into lineages, sublineages, and villages. The headmen at upper levels were headmen of lower-level groups. Several criteria determined headship: the size of the lower-level groups a man headed,

Kpandu, Togo (Africa) man weaving on introduced European loom having foot treadles to shift the heddles. (Courtesy of the United Nations.)

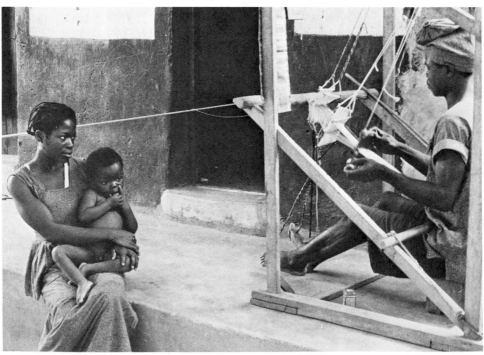

age and health, and wealth and generosity. At times more than one headman was recognized but the one with greatest wealth and who was head of a large household would normally take precedence. Political factions often formed about competing headmen.

Each Kapauku was a member of one or another patrilineal descent group. These were not localized and sometimes included people belonging to other confederacies. Other unilineal groupings included clusters of sibs called phratries, and lineages and sublineages. The latter are localized groupings, but might be larger than a village. The nuclear family might be a production and consumption unit, but the household frequently included a number of nuclear families forming extended or augmented families. The extended family consisted of related kin; the augmented family included distant kin. Young men from poor families might elect to join, as apprentices, a household headed by a man who was a good manager and leader. In normal patrilocal residence, wives in the household were not related. Nevertheless, for many purposes the extended bilateral family was as important as the unilineal descent group.

6. Village Farmers: The Hopi

Traditionally, the Hopi Indians lived in several independent farming villages located on top of spurs of Black Mesa in Arizona. Although Hopi culture has changed in many ways since the Coronado expedition first exposed them to European influences, the Hopi have been more sucessful than most American Indians in preserving their way of life, while selectively borrowing that which seemed useful from European culture.

To some extent even today, the Hopi represent an example of a self-sufficient and independent farming community exploiting the same lands year after year. The gardening tradition followed by the Hopi has been practiced in the southwestern deserts of the United States for more than 1,000 years. Although rainfall is deficient and the growing season short, the Hopi and their ancestors have developed special techniques for raising maize, beans, squash, and cotton. Although in a few locations the water table is sufficiently high to permit raising crops dependent upon rainfall, the principal Hopi techniques involve small-scale irrigation near flowing springs or flood plain farming following heavy rains. The Hopi have developed special varieties of plants accommodated to drought and to a growing season that can be as short as ninety days. Although Hopi farming involves a number of ingenious specializations, it was traditionally carried out with simple digging sticks, wooden spadelike instruments, and the baskets required to transport the harvest.

Until recent increases in population, Hopi farmlands were sufficient, but often located at considerable distances from the village. Traditionally farmers often ran long distances to their fields. Although the Hopi farmlands were never considered desirable by European standards, the Hopi traditionally produced more than enough for their needs and kept a year's reserve in storage as protection from drought. Agricultural production was supplemented by wild plants and by hunting. Deer and antelope, the only large game, were scarce, but organized rabbit drives provided some additional meat. Large animal skins were used for footwear, belts, shields, pouches, drumheads, and bowstrings. House beams and firewood were obtained with some difficulty by trips into the interior of Black Mesa. Markets held in the Hopi villages were often visited by otherwise hostile Navajos who traded bear skins and other items for agricultural produce.

Hopi architecture was mainly of stone with mud mortar and plaster, and earthen roofs supported by rafters. Such roofs, if made of carefully selected clays, can be remarkably watertight. Both sexes collaborated in house building, but women owned and maintained the house. Structures were built contiguously and were often two or more stories high. A single dwelling would usually include workrooms, sleeping rooms, and storage rooms. Large ceremonial chambers called *kivas* were used as lounging and workrooms by the

Andean Indian woman, Cauca Valley, Colombia, weaving on vertical loom. The loom differs from that of the Hopi in having a continuous warp looping around the beams at either end of the loom. (Courtesy of the United Nations.)

men, who wove textiles, and as meeting places for religious associations devoted to the carrying out of elaborate ceremonies. Properly maintained Hopi dwellings and kivas will last for a long time. The Hopi village of Oraibi, although its population has dwindled, is the oldest continuously occupied settlement in North America.

Kinship ties are important even today, and the Hopi are organized in matrilineal clans. Crosscutting these were a number of corporate groups revolving about a variety of ceremonial functions. Some were oriented toward curing, others toward weather control and various supernaturals. Most social and political functions were distributed through the kinship and other groupings, although clan chiefs and town chiefs exercised considerable influence. No formal political or other institutions existed between villages, although some visiting and intermarriage has always occurred.

In addition to their complex social and ceremonial life, the Hopi also had highly developed many technologies found frequently among food-producing peoples but rare or nonexistent among gathering peoples. The Hopi were able to make good chipped-stone implements, but like most food-producing peoples, they made a number of polished-stone artifacts. They depended heavily upon the slab grinding stone, as did the gathering peoples of the desert or arid-lands cultures, but they shaped it carefully and usually set it in a stone-lined box to contain the meal produced. Ground axes, mauls, and a number of ornaments were also made. (See Figures 8–1 and 8–2.) Except for the grinding stones, none of these articles is essentially superior to chipped- or flaked-stone

Figure 8–4 Elaborate Pueblo Indian woman's dress achieved without tailoring or fitting cloth.

tools; they require more time and patience to make, but perhaps less skill, and suitable stone for grinding is easier to find than that for chipping.

Clothing was worn normally in cold weather, including kilts, dresses, and belts; men wore sandals and women often wore elaborate buckskin moccasins and leggings. Clothing was not tailored. (See Figure 8–4.) A good deal of attention was paid to hairdressing and ornaments, and the masks, carved figures, and other ceremonial gear were often very elaborate. (See Figures 8–5 and 8–6.)

As is the case with many village farmers, weaving was important. Cloth was woven on the true loom. The Hopi were unusual, although not unique, in using a broad loom, which produced wide fabrics, rather than the backstrap loom, which produced only narrow fabrics. (See Figures 8–7 and 8–8.)

Most cottons used for weaving were cultivated; the Hopi were unique, in that a special variety of cotton had been developed to mature in the short growing season available. Cotton fibers must first be separated from the seeds and then combed to make the fibers lie parallel. Although thread may then be rolled out by hand on the thigh, a spindle is much more efficient. This is a stick weighted by a spindle whorl of clay or wood to maintain rotational

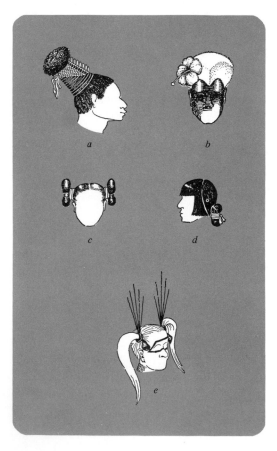

Figure 8–5 Most people rearrange their hair—out of vanity, to indicate status, or for ceremonial purposes. (a) New Guinea (Papuan) hairdress; (b) Melanesian (Solomon Islands) hairdress; (c) Hopi Indian hairdress worn only by unmarried girls; (d) Hopi man's clubbed hairdress; (e) hairdress of a priest (Rio Grande Pueblos, southwestern United States).

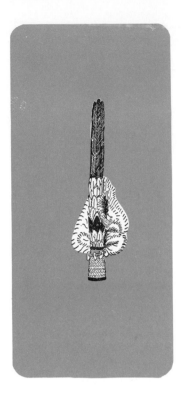

Figure 8–6 Pueblo Indian (Zuñi) head ornaments. At top right is a ceremonial mask. (After Stevenson.)

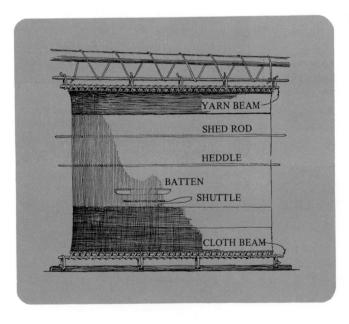

YARN BEAM

SHED ROD

HEDDLE

BATTEN

SHUTTLE

CLOTH BEAM

Figure 8–7 A complex Hopi Indian loom showing main parts. The Hopi loom has no foot pedals to move the heddles.

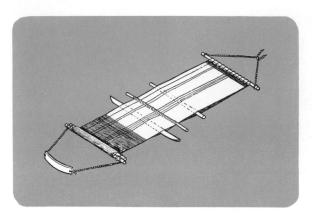

Figure 8-8 Belt or backstrap loom most commonly used in Middle America. The fabrics are usually narrow but may be many feet in length.

momentum when spun with the fingers. A starting thread from a mass of prepared fiber is worked out with the fingers and attached to the spindle. The latter is then spun or twirled and a thread is drawn out from the fiber bundle. (Figure 8-9.)

Most weaving was done on a loom. In its simplest form a loom consists of two poles connected by evenly spaced threads called the warp. Cross threads, called the weft, may be introduced by the fingers alternating over and under each warp thread or combination of warp threads. The traditional Hopi loom is considerably more complex. A shed rod separates alternate warps to make two sheds. A weft may thus be passed through in one operation, using a supply of weft thread wound on a stick called a shuttle. A heddle, another stick with thread looping around it and catching up every other warp, can be lifted to reverse the position of the sheds and the shuttle passed back between them. A batten, a flat piece of wood, is used to pound down each weft. Additional heddles may pick up various combinations of warp threads, thus permitting designs to be woven into the cloth. By using several shuttles, different colored

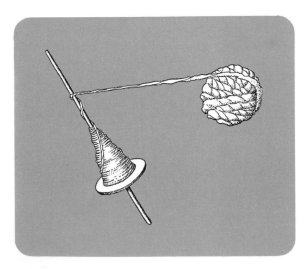

Figure 8-9 Spindle with wooden disk serving as fly wheel to maintain momentum when the spindle is twirled with the fingers. A loosely twisted yarn in the ball on the right is here being respun.

threads may be introduced. The Hopi further use a yarn beam, on which reserve warps are wound, and a cloth beam, on which the woven cloth is wound up. This permits making a cloth much longer than the distance between the two beams. A further refinement, not known originally to the Hopi or other New World weavers, is an added mechanism operated by foot pedals which mechanically raises the heddles without using the hands and which speeds up the weaving process. The foot-pedal loom is basically the loom used in industrailized weaving, although many mechanical refinements have been introduced.

Even simple weaving involves a complex technology requiring training and the development of skills for its successful use. The equipment takes time to make and is too bulky to be transported by people frequently on the move. Weaving hence is primarily found among relatively stable food producers, although it is not practiced by all.

The Hopi differed from the other farmers we have described in the making of elaborate pottery containers. The Hopi did make some basketry containers, although basketry trays and large storage containers were their principal product. There was some village specialization in the kinds of baskets made. Pottery making centered on the first Mesa. Pottery is rarely found among people who must move frequently, for it is too fragile and too heavy for people who transport all their household belongings. Pottery making is not necessarily confined to farming peoples, but it is quite rare among all but a few semisedentary peoples. The Hopi, along with other Pueblo peoples, were perhaps the most skilled potters in North America. Clay suitable for pottery making consists mainly of silica and aluminum oxide. Because the proportions of these substances vary in natural clays, it usually is necessary to mix in other materials to make the clay either more plastic or less sticky and less apt to crack in drying. Such materials, called tempers, include sand, mica, pulverized fragments of broken pottery (sherd temper), quartz, lime, or feldspar. Organic materials such as straw are also added at times, although such tempers are usually less satisfactory. The process of modeling the clay also sets up stresses in the finished vessel that may cause breakage during firing or make the completed pottery very fragile. Many of these stresses may be avoided by the use of special techniques for shaping. Among most nonliterate peoples the coiling method is used: the vessel is built up by pinching on successive rolls of clay. A smooth surface is then produced by scraping or rubbing, although sometimes the coils are left as an ornament on the exterior. Pottery vessels also may be modeled from a lump of clay, or clay may be shaped with a mold. (See Figure 8–10.)

The most efficient method of shaping pottery is by rotating a lump of clay on a turntable or potter's wheel. With the hand or an implement, the rotating clay is quickly shaped into the desired form. (See Figure 8–11.) Usually a pedal arrangement is added so that the wheel may be rotated by the foot, leaving both hands free for manipulation of the clay. Generally the potter's wheel is limited to complex cultures in which the wheel is also used in transportation and in other devices. The earliest wheel-made pottery appears to be in the Tigris-Euphrates region of the Near East, where it is found in sites

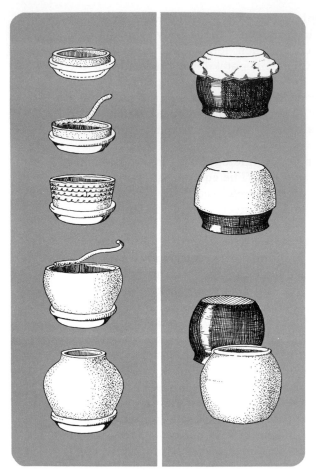

Figure 8–10   Two techniques of shaping pottery. Left: the coiling technique, in which the vessel is built up by pinching on successive rolls or coils of clay and may later be smoothed by scraping and rubbing. Right: the molding technique, in which soft clay is pressed over a mold or another vessel and the shoulder and rim added by coiling.

slightly earlier than the first use of bronze. By 3000 B.C. the wheel was widely used in the Near East, although not employed by everyone, and it seems to have spread with the use of bronze. The wheel was unknown to the Hopi or any other New World potters before European contacts.

After shaping, clay vessels must be thoroughly dried, for an excess of moisture in the clay will cause breakage in firing. Firing must also be carefully done; temperatures of 400 degrees centigrade or higher are best to ensure the transformation of the material into pottery. If subjected to lesser heat, the material will revert to clay when wet. On the other hand, firing at excessive heats will fuse the materials and the vessel will be too fragile for use if it does not simply melt out of shape. Many peoples, like the Hopi, bake their clay vessels in open fires, but others use enclosed heating chambers, such as kilns or ovens.

Pottery may be decorated in various ways. Very frequently the vessels are decorated before firing by incising or engraving designs on the surface in various ways, or by adding special rims, legs, bases, or other details made

Figure 8–11 The potter's wheel. The platform is turned rapidly by hand or by the feet with a lower kick wheel. The lump of soft clay is shaped while spinning by using the hand or an implement. The potter's wheel was not used until relatively late and first appeared in Southwestern Asia.

separately and fastened to the finished pots. Among the Peruvian Indians, pots were not infrequently shaped to represent animals and other creatures, and in some regions of Peru there are found great numbers of so-called portrait pots, shaped, it has been suggested, to represent the heads of particular individuals.

Painting is the most common form of pottery decoration, and there are literally thousands of painted designs, geometric, representational, and abstract, found among the nonliterate peoples of the world. (For illustration, see Chapter 17, "The Arts.") Painted designs are usually added before the pottery

Kpandu woman, Togo, shaping a pottery vessel by paddle and anvil method. The vessel is first shaped out roughly from a lump of clay and then paddled into shape holding a curved "anvil" inside the vessel. (Courtesy of the United Nations.)

Figure 8–12 Left: Tungus saddle (after McCreery); right: Mexican Charo saddle (after Toor).

is fired, and the pigments used not infrequently change their color as firing progresses. Some pottery may also be slipped; that is, given an added smoothness or a particular color by coating the dried but unfired vessel with a very thin clay. Painted pottery designs tend to vary both regionally and in time, and thus form, where written records are lacking, one of the best indicators of cultural contracts between diverse people and of cultural change within the history of a single society.

Most untreated pottery is more or less porous and so permits liquids to escape slowly. Many peoples make no effort to remedy this condition, though we do find some instances of resin-coated pottery. In the Near East, however, the discovery of glass led to the technique called glazing, in which materials simi-

Shaping clay on crude wheel. Colombia. (Kindness of Sylvia Broadbent.)

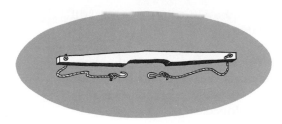

Figure 8-13 A carrying yoke held on the shoulder with loads of equal weight dangling from each rope.

lar to glass were applied to pottery to make it waterproof and to give it a smooth and highly polished finish. Some American Indians apparently developed a similar glazing technique independently of the Old World. The ultimate discovery in the use of glaze was made by the Chinese, who, after several centuries of experimentation, learned to mix glaze materials with the clay to produce porcelain, or "china." The technique of making porcelain spread to Europe several centuries later and is today a very important industrial process in our culture, with many applications in chemistry, medicine, and sanitation. In medical biology, for example, the filterable virus is an organism sufficiently small to pass through a porcelain filter.

Pottery does more than merely make the storage and transportation of liquids easier. It can be used for the storage of small grains, seeds, and other materials. Foods can be boiled directly over the fire rather than by the stone-boiling technique. Pottery is also used for pipes, ornaments, ladles, lamps, and other objects, and some peoples use large pottery vessels for burial of the dead. Except where the use of metal has become cheap and common, pottery still provides one of the most important sources of containers for most of mankind. Even in many areas of Western civilization pottery is extensively used for

Potter's kiln and pots. Colombia. (Kindness of Sylvia Broadbent.)

cooking and the transportation of liquids, and in the United States we still employ pottery or china dishes for eating and baking.

The Hopi, then, exemplify three important technological developments whose first appearance is closely associated with the early stages in the development of food producing: permanent architecture, weaving and handmade (rather than wheel-made) pottery. Not all of these are present among all simple food producers, nor are they always as highly developed.

7. Summary

Dramatic environmental changes at the close of the last ice age appear to have set the stage for human experimentation with plant and animal husbandry. Early agriculture appears to have involved the cultivation of either roots and tubers or of seed crops, and probably involved a number of different crops raised on the same field. This pattern of interculture, probably carried out without systematic fertilization of the fields, led to swidden agriculture in which new fields were planted each year and exhausted fields restored through a process of natural regeneration. The necessity for coadaptation among human beings and domesticated plant and animal species led to many changes in the pattern of human life. These often included permanent residence in a single spot, complex and long-term planning, a longer workday, increased population density and increased disease, declining protein consumption, and cyclical overpopulation and famine.

At the beginning, the practice of agriculture was probably undertaken as a means of supplementing more traditional hunting and collecting activities. The incipient or marginal practice of agriculture, for this reason, probably did not have any very radical impact upon the hunting and collecting way of life.

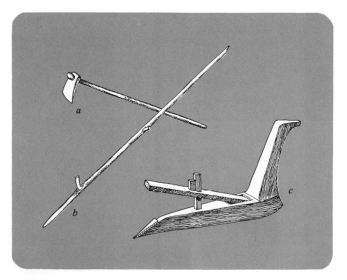

Figure 8–14 The basic farming tools. (a) hoe; (b) digging stick; (c) the wooden plow.

The technology and social life of the Western Apache and the Yagua, while in many ways more complicated than that of such peoples as the Australian aborigines or the Bushmen, seems little more complicated than that of the Indians of the Northwest Coast or even the Eskimo.

Although pastoralism was at one time regarded as an adaptation quite distinct from the cultivation of plants, most pastoralists appear to be dependent in one way or another upon plant cultivation. Pastoral peoples, such as the Nuer, are often warlike, mobile, and patriarchal. Because herds represent portable wealth that must be protected from human thieves and animal predators, the dominant economic role in most pastoral societies appears to be played by men. In swidden agriculture, the dominant economic role is often played by women, who have the primary responsibility for the production of food crops. The Tapirapé, although living in an environment somewhat like that of the Nuer, were dependent upon extensive cultivation of gardens by women. Gardens were inherited in the female line, and house groups were formed primarily through matrilocal residence. Men, however, had important roles in hunting, warfare, and the conduct of ceremonial activities, and this is probably reflected in the presence of patrilineal organizations.

Swidden agriculture also figures prominently in the economy of the Kapauku but in association with pig raising and intensive gardening. The heavy economic contribution of the Kapauku man seems to lead to a heavy male emphasis in the inheritance of property and the organization of society in terms of patrilineal descent groups. The permanent occupation of farmlands and the productive agricultural economy made permanent settlements possible, and the density of population encouraged economic specialization. In all of these cases the relationship between such types as pastoralism, hunting, swidden agriculture, and intensive gardening is a complicated one. Such features of social organization as matrilineality or patrilineality cannot be explained in terms of one-to-one correspondence with types of economic activity, but must be explained in terms of the overall pattern of economic activity.

The Hopi, like the Eskimo, represent a fairly complicated technology applied to a fairly harsh environment. Thus Hopi agriculture was in some ways more sophisticated than Kapauku agriculture, but it remained considerably less productive. The Hopi lacked the elaborate patterns of internecine warfare characteristic of the Kapauku. Both the Kapauku and the Hopi possessed an elaborate ceremonial and artistic life. Hopi religion and philosophy and production of textiles and pottery have received much praise, but perhaps only because they are better known and more familiar than the ideas and productions of the Kapauku.

Peoples like the Hopi and the Kapauku who are largely dependent upon agriculture and who have developed permanently settled communities best illustrate the problems and advantages of the agricultural way of life. The chronic warfare afflicting the Kapauku, to say nothing of the Nuer or the Tapirapé, is matched among hunting and collecting peoples perhaps only by the Indians of the Northwest Coast, who are exceptional in any case. The problems of carrying out agriculture in an arid environment are demonstrated by the ruined monuments of Hopi-like peoples scattered throughout the southwestern United States. On the other hand, the village farming way of life has produced rich localized traditions of art and religion, many of which were lost as village farmers became peasants or joined the faceless masses in the city.

Collateral Reading

Chagnon, Napoleon A. *Yanomamo: The Fierce People*. New York: Holt, Rinehart and Winston, Inc., 1968. Shifting agriculture in Venezuela.

Conklin, Harold C. "An Ethnoecological Approach to Shifting Agriculture," in Andrew P. Vayda (ed.), *Environment and Culture Behavior: Ecological Studies in Cultural Anthropology*. Garden City, N.Y.: The Natural History Press, 1969. A defense of swidden agriculture as an ecological type.

Dentan, Robert Knox. *The Semai: A Nonviolent People of Malaya*. New York: Holt, Rinehart and Winston, Inc., 1968. Marginal agriculture, compare with Yanomamo.

Dozier, Edward P. *Hano: A Tewa Indian Community in Arizona*. New York: Holt, Rinehart and Winston, Inc., 1965. Sojourners among the Hopi.

Ekvall, Robert B. *Fields on the Hoof: Nexus of Tibetan Nomadic Pastoralism*. New York: Holt, Rinehart and Winston, Inc., 1968. High altitude ecology, care of livestock, use of products.

Flannery, Kent V. "The Origins of Agriculture," *Annual Review of Anthropology*, 2:271–310. Palo Alto, Calif.: Annual Reviews, Inc., 1973. Discussion and bibliography of recent work.

Hammond, Blodwen, and Mary Shepardson. *The Navajo Mountain Community: Social Organization and Kinship Terminology*. Berkeley: University of California Press, 1970. A recent study of the Navajo.

Hudson, Alfred B. *Padju Epat: The Ma'anyan of Indonesian Borneo*. New York: Holt, Rinehart and Winston, Inc., 1972. Swidden technology and its effects, adjudication process, religious groupings.

Leeds, Anthony, and Andrew P. Vayda (eds.). *Man, Culture and Animals: The Role of Animals In Human Ecological Adjustment*, Publication No. 68. Washington, D.C.: American Association for the Advancement of Science, 1965. A symposium on the subject.

Leonard, Jonathon N. *The First Farmers*. Boston: Little, Brown and Company, 1973. A summary.

Mason, Otis T. *Types of Basketry Weaves, Source Book in Anthropology*, ed. A. L. Kroeber and T. T. Waterman. New York: Harcourt Brace Jovanovich, 1931. Chapter 26. The standard work on the technology of basket making.

Pelto, Pertii J. *The Snowmobile Revolution: Technology and Social Change in the Arctic*. Menlo Park, Calif.: Cummings Publishing Co., Inc., 1973. Industrialized pastoralists.

Redfield, Robert. *The Primitive World and Its Transformations*. New York: Cornell University Press, 1953. (Reissued 1957 as a Great Seal Book.)

Semenov, S. A. *Prehistoric Technology*. London: Cary, Adams and Mackay, 1964. A handbook of prehistoric technology.

Streuver, Stuart (ed.). *Prehistoric Agriculture*. Garden City, N.Y.: The Natural History Press, 1971. An overview.

Ucko, Peter J., and Dimbleby, G. W. *The Domestication and Exploitation of Plants and Animals*. Chicago: Aldine Publishing Company, 1969.

Von Furer Haimendorf, Christoph *The Konyak Nagas: An Indian Frontier Tribe*. New
    York: Holt, Rinehart and Winston, Inc., 1969. Complex agricultural society
    without an urban center.

Ethnographic References

Apache: Basso, 1971.
Hopi: Dozier, 1970; Eggan, 1950; Titiev, 1944, 1972.

9/Food Production and Urban Life

1. The Origins and Basis of Urbanism

Both the gathering and food-producing peoples discussed in the preceding two chapters live in essentially autonomous societies variously identified as tribes, communities, or villages. The autonomy of these societies is not only political; it extends to all aspects of culture. Economically, virtually all the food, needed implements, shelter, and clothing are both produced and consumed within the community, and some form of the family or household is the principal production and consumption unit. Specialization occurs but it functions primarily within the social unit or within a group of linked units. External trade may include foodstuffs but tends to be limited to raw materials unavailable in the territory accessible to members of the society, to luxury items, or to items of symbolic value. Although villages or even tribes may be linked into confederacies, as is the case with the Indians of the eastern United States or the Kapauku (Chapter 8), most political decision making and the resolution of legal problems take place within the small community. Religious ideas may be shared with others but are not controlled by them. Such ceremonies as the famous Hopi rain dance may benefit all Hopi; performance, however, is largely by the inhabitants of a single village. In effect, so long as members of such societies do not come in conflict with their neighbors, they are subject to no external controls and are free to make their own decisions.

Early anthropology dealt very largely with such autonomous societies. Two kinds of problems showed this approach to be insufficient. One was the growing interest in the origins of urbanism. The early food-producing villages in the Middle East clearly were followed by large towns and cities. Similar developmental patterns came to be recognized in other parts of Asia and Africa as well as in Middle America and the Andean regions of the New World. These urban centers represent a radically different way of life, and the relation between them and the village-farming community became a focus for research. About the same time many anthropologists began to realize that most of the farming villages they studied were in fact peasant societies or were becoming so.

The earliest urban centers appeared in the lowland alluvial drainages of the Tigris and Euphrates rivers in Mesopotamia of the Old World around 3000 B.C., followed shortly by urban centers in the lower Nile Valley of Egypt, the Indus Valley in Pakistan, and the Yellow River basin of northern China. In the New World urban centers developed on the Peruvian coast and in Mexico before the beginning of the Christian era. All of these regions have substantial areas of cultivable land, capable under favorable circumstances of supporting dense populations. In each there is evidence of the practice of irrigation appearing at about the same time as the cities, together with massive public religious architecture, and of some social stratification indicated by differences in domestic architecture and associated material goods. The appearance of cities is usually accompanied by an efflorescence of material and artistic culture and, in the Old World, metallurgy, new means of transportation, and writing.

In the Mesopotamian region, where the earliest cities developed, only precarious farming is possible along lowland river banks and swamps unless irrigation is practiced. Irrigation, on the other hand, permits the cultivation of large contiguous areas and produces a high return in relation to the labor involved. Large-scale irrigation works give much the best returns, but they involve the organization of a sizable labor force and controlled distribution of the water. It is possible, therefore, that cities developed out of the need for centralized control of the large irrigation works necessary to support dense populations. These centers of organization and control attracted various full-time specialists and traders. They and the richly productive areas they controlled also were obvious targets of raiders from the less fertile highlands nearby. As centers grew they also came into competition for lands and water. Both factors presumably contributed to the building of defensive works and establishment of a military system.

Similar sequences of development seem to have occurred in the Indus Valley and in China. The evidence for Egypt is less convincing, for the annual flooding of the Nile made large irrigation works unnecessary. However, the effectiveness of the floods is improved by diking to retain waters and channeling waters into areas not normally flooded. An analogous situation seems to have existed in Peru, especially along the coast, where most cultivation depends upon spreading the waters of the rivers descending from the Andes into the

Yadgir, a small city in South India. Photographed from ruins of ancient fortress overlooking city. Intensive agriculture, practiced on irrigated rice lands in background, permitted the development of an urban concentration of population in ancient times. (Photo by Alan Beals.)

desert. This can best be done if each valley is treated as a unit. In Middle America again the case is less clear. Irrigation appeared quite early in the development of farming in parts of Mexico. However, the areas suitable for irrigation are broken up into many relatively small basins and valleys, so that large irrigation works were not needed and often impossible.

Whether irrigation is the sole or the primary factor leading to the appearance of early cities or is but one of a cluster of causes, in each area secondary or derived urbanism in other regions soon followed, in some measure a response to or a copying of the early cities. Many of the derived urban centers seem related to the rapid growth in trade and commerce; others perhaps arose out of the need for defensive positions against expansionist tendencies of the military forces of the new states or protection against pastoral raiders who became increasingly troublesome about the same time. It also is clear that a

301

necessary precondition of urbanism was the refinement of food-producing techniques to permit the support of dense populations and a nonfarming class or classes within a society. Where our information is adequate this precondition was provided by village-farming communities.

2. Peasants and Cities

Although peasants are defined differently by many writers, the basic definition still seems that of A. L. Kroeber, who considered them part cultures or part societies.[1] By this he meant communities, usually villages, that are no longer completely autonomous and are located within a territory claimed or in some way administered by a larger society. Among the characteristics generally associated with peasant communities are the following:

(1) Most of the population is engaged in food production and the community produces most of the food it consumes.

(2) The community is dependent on outside sources for some of the tools and other goods believed to be essential.

(3) It no longer has complete control over its relations with other communities and in many cases has lost control of many of its internal legal and political affairs.

(4) Many of its institutions are local manifestations of national institutions. Examples are the presence of a national church or national educational system or the use of a national currency in economic exchange.

In most cases peasants produce some exchangeable surplus food which goes to support towns or cities which in turn provide certain types of manufactured or processed goods and services. These exchanges frequently are organized and carried on through a system of marketplaces, usually in the towns or cities.

The definition of an urban center is sometimes given in terms of size. The official definition of an urban settlement or place by the United States Bureau of the Census is a community of 2,500 persons or more. Such a definition in the United States is meaningful because of the absence in this country of any extensive peasantry or village farming pattern. A community of 2,500 in the United States usually is a service center attending to the needs of a significant farming population living outside the settlement on separated individual farmsteads, a pattern much less common in most of the world. In this discussion an urban community is defined as one in which less than half of the population is engaged in food production.

The first major attempt to define the relation of peasants to urban centers was the folk-urban hypothesis of Robert Redfield.[2] Anthropologists working in Latin America and Africa had begun to find themselves involved with urban-type communities. Both they and the urban sociologists had begun to be aware

[1] A. L. Kroeber, *Anthropology* (New York: Harcourt, Brace, 1948 (c1923)).

[2] Robert Redfield, *The Folk Culture of Yucatan* (Chicago: University of Chicago Press, 1941).

that substantial differences existed between the way of life of urban and that of rural populations. Louis Wirth, an urban sociologist of the University of Chicago, in a famous article published in 1938, attempted to define the characteristics of urbanism as a way of life.[3] Accepting this, Redfield suggested that the way of life of the people he called the "folk" was in the antithesis of the urban lifeway. (See also Chapter 19, §4.) Most activities in the cities are secular and religion is institutionalized; among the folk all life is permeated by religion. The folk produced their own food, material goods, and shelter; family and kinship are important; relations between people are personal and face to face; most knowledge is transmitted through oral traditions; and the world view looks inward, toward the local community. In contrast, the city dweller is a specialist engaged in making and exchanging things or providing services and dependent upon others for most necessities; family and kinship are replaced by other institutions; most relations between people are impersonal and often at a distance; knowledge is transmitted by formal institutions, the written word, and similar devices; and the world view is outward. The city is the center not only of power but of innovations which spread outward ultimately to the folk. Between the folk and the city are intermediate communities, the towns, in which the influence of the city is stronger. Communities can thus be arranged in a hierarchy, the folk representing an archaic way of life, the city the modern way of life.

[3] Louis Wirth, "Urbanism as a Way of Life," *American Journal of Sociology,* **44**:1–24 (1938).

Urban clustering in a village community. Houses in northern Afghanistan. (Courtesy of the United Nations.)

Redfield initially was not clear whether the folk were peasants, village farmers, or tribal societies, but the specific communities he discussed are of peasants. His cities and his folk were essentially ideal polar types, and as more research was done it became evident not only that cities never conform wholly to Redfield's ideal type, but that there are substantial differences between cities at different times and places. The same became evident with folk cultures. Among the Yucatán Mayas, the peasants Redfield knew best, various religious practices and beliefs are essential parts of farming practices. Among the Tarascan peasants of Michoacán, Mexico, this is not the case; farming is strictly secular and practices are empirically evaluated. Peasants involved in marketing systems often have numerous impersonal social relationships and a broad world view.

Redfield's folk–urban hypothesis is now recognized as inadequate, but it stimulated a great deal of research and rethinking of the problems of both peasants and cities. It now seems clear that neither peasants nor cities may be studied in isolation from one another. Although for various purposes peasant communities may be studied as special systems, they are an aspect of a larger culture which includes cities. In some cases peasants may be studied as traditional communities with unique cultures that have been modified or penetrated by external influences from the city. In other cases they may be studied most profitably as integrated local modifications of national institutions and idea systems to some degree with independent and even competing characteristics. Studies of national institutions tend to emphasize their formal characteristics; the ethnographic study of a peasant or other type of community relates these institutions to the people who live or are affected by them.

Urban sociologists have by and large fallen into the same error of studying cities in isolation rather than recognizing them as parts of larger cultural systems. Cities cannot exist without organized methods of food production, and in many urbanized cultures food production is organized primarily through the peasant village. But this is not the only possible arrangement. Food production may be organized through manor or hacienda or plantation systems, or even, as was the case with the northern United States in the last century, through individual or family farmsteads. Moreover, as Sjöberg and others have recently made clear, a distinction must be drawn between the preindustrial and the industrial city.[4] The differences between cities and between peasants revealed by comparative studies stem in part from their participation in different cultures and cultural systems.

3. Peasants

Most of the Indians of Oaxaca, Mexico, probably have lived as peasants since before the beginning of the Christian era. In this state the Mexican census recognizes more than 3,000 localities, so identified either by law or custom,

---

[4] Gideon Sjöberg, *The Preindustrial City: Past and Present* (New York: Free Press, 1960).

classified as cities, towns, villages, and hamlets (*rancherias*). In the valley of Oaxaca, the largest upland valley in the state (over 4,000 feet elevation), a complete sequence is known archaeologically from incipient farming through the formation of permanent villages to the establishment of urban centers. The basic modern political unit is the *municipio*, a unit similar to the county in the United States. If we except those *municipios* containing towns or cities, the *municipio* contains either a single village or, very frequently, a large village, the *cabecera*, and a number of dependent smaller settlements. The archaeological evidence suggests this pattern probably existed as early as the formative period some centuries before the birth of Christ.

Although at first sight the valley may appear to be homogeneous, in fact it contains several different soil types requiring different methods of cultivation and suitable for different kinds of crops. These include alluvial bottomlands, with moisture-retentive soils, flood plains, and various sandy or loamy soils of differing fertility. Rainfall is likewise variable. Not only does rainfall differ locally from year to year, but the western end of the valley receives on the average about twice as much rainfall as does the eastern end. The moisture-retentive alluvial bottomlands and most of the sandy or loamy piedmont soils depend upon rainfall to produce crops. Where water tables are high, wells are dug for irrigation by dipping water out with pots and pouring it about the plants. Permanent and semipermanent streams from the mountains are used to irrigate both piedmont and alluvial soils through local systems of permanent ditches. Sometimes villages share these ditches and in some cases may charge villages lower down the system for "transit" rights for the water. Finally, somewhat different ditch systems with replaceable weirs divert the seasonal floodwaters of some streams over farmlands. In all villages maize, the basic staple of the diet, and varying amounts of beans and squash are cultivated. Villages with favorable soils also plant other crops; some specialize in certain vegetables, flowers (in demand for ceremonial purposes), agave, or oil plants. Many families also raise pigs, sheep, goats, chickens, turkeys, or milk cows.

A number of conclusions emerge from detailed study of these villages: (1) In most villages some families do not produce enough maize to provide their basic requirements; many villages do not produce enough maize to meet the villagewide requirements. In all villages goods considered essential must be imported. Probably a majority of villages import tomatoes, onions, garlic, herbs, and chili peppers. All villages must import chocolate, an essential drink in most ceremonies and a favored breakfast drink by those who can afford it, for it is not grown in Oaxaca. (2) Most of the artifacts for farming and household use, clothing or the materials for it, and very often the beams, poles, and rafters for houses are not produced in the village. (3) In order to survive, most men have at least one other source of income—barber, musician, mason, carpenter, trading, or some handicraft, or as a last resort they sell their labor to more fortunate fellow villagers, to haciendas (now mostly gone and the remnants converted into commercial farms), or to farmers in other villages; or they go temporarily outside the valley. Moreover, most handicraft specialization is by village. Only four villages make pottery, perhaps five weave broadloom fabrics or belts, two small districts provide most of the basic vegetables con-

Peasant house in Oaxaca, Mexico. Tile and corrugated iron roofs show influence of industrialized urban centers. Cane-pole walls and large water jar filled by hand are traditional. (Photo by Ralph Beals.)

Zapotec Indian woman with goats. Oaxaca, Mexico. (Photo by Alan Beals.)

Procession in Oaxaca, Mexico. The organization of such village fiestas involves a complicated hierarchy of civil and religious officials. Large balloonlike object is carried by one man who dances while balancing it with his hands. (Photo by Alan Beals.)

sumed. Household inventories or material objects show that usually most of them come from a large number of other village sources or from the urban industrializing world. In this case the self-sufficient peasant image cannot be maintained, and the village specialization requires a large market network for interchange between villages as well as between village and city.

Although the Oaxaca peasant village is not autonomous economically, traditional villages have a remarkable degree of political and religious autonomy. Farmlands are individually owned and cultivated, but the village controls a definite territory; outsiders may live or buy land in the village only with the permission of village authorities. All authorities are elected locally, and most disputes and minor crimes are adjudicated internally. Only violent internal factionalism or conflict between villages brings the intervention of outside authorities. Nevertheless the pattern of public offices to some extent conforms to state-established norms. Religion nominally is Catholic and certain principles are widely accepted. Not all villages have resident priests and each village has a complex and to some extent uniquely local ceremonial pattern centering around the cult of the saints and not controlled by the priests. Both ceremonial and civil offices are organized in a complexly interrelated prestige ladder, and people reach the ultimate goal of elders, or *principales,* only by progressing through the hierarchy of offices. Since the early 1920s the villages have been increasingly involved with outside institutions. The introduction of schools, health services, and more recently, potable water systems, road building, and electricity have involved intrusion of new state or national agencies. Both state officials and church officials try to modify the traditional ceremonial system. Population growth has resulted in more and more people leaving the village, sometimes permanently, but usually sending back cash remittances.

The basic unit of production and consumption is the nuclear family or some modification of it. Kinship ties nevertheless are important and are greatly extended by a system of ritual kinship, the *compadrazgo*. Marriage is mostly within the village, although compulsory rules of endogamy are lacking. Power is determined partly by wealth, which in turn may be affected by inheritance and the cooperation of the kinship group, but hoarding of wealth does not give much power or status. Wealth must be expended in support of public works and the ceremonial systems. These leveling mechanisms and a system of equal inheritance among all children prevent wide differences in wealth. Poor individuals may, and frequently do, improve their economic position through their own efforts; hard work and intelligent management are

Village plaza in Oaxaca, Mexico. Competition between villages is now expressed through basketball matches held during fiestas. An earlier form of basketball may have filled the same function in ancient times. (Photo by Alan Beals.)

highly respected, but must be coupled with involvement in village affairs and village welfare. Despite intense loyalty to the village, the Oaxaca peasants are strongly individualistic and deeply concerned with such matters as prices and the operation of the market.

Gopalpur, in southern India, is one of the half million villages of that country in which live perhaps one out of every six or seven people in the world. There is no such thing as a typical Indian village, but there are a number of widespread similarities among them. Located in a densely settled region, Gopalpur is classed as a small village (300 to 700 people). Nearby are to be found other small villages, hamlets (under 300 people), medium villages (700 to 1,200 people), and large villages, usually with a marketplace. These various communities differ in part because of ecological variables; the smaller types tend to be adapted to a special limiting environmental situation; the larger communities have more varied productive possibilities.

The main crop of Gopalpur is sorghum; foods from this grain form the basis of almost every meal. Legumes are also important. Much of the farming depends on rainfall, but in some places shallow wells provide water to irrigate patches of onions, eggplant, and chili. Small areas are planted to rice watered from a reservoir made by damming a small stream. Peanuts, tobacco, or cotton are grown primarily for sale; surpluses of other crops may be sold also. Large mango trees scattered through the fields provide the only fresh food in the dry season. In one area seepages of salty water are processed into salt; sheep and cattle are grazed in nearby areas. Each farming family tries to have a female water buffalo for milk, two draft bullocks, and a few goats, sheep, and chickens. An important function of the animals is to provide manure for the fields.

Major cultivation involves an archaic bullock-drawn plow, harrow, and various rakes, seed drills, and planks. A hoelike short-handled spade, baskets, and a two-wheeled cart are needed for manuring; the cart is used for other transport as well. Sickles are used for the grain harvest; grain must be threshed, usually by driving animals over it, and winnowed, using special trays. Unlike the Oaxaca peasant, except for baskets most of these things are made by the farmer and his family, working when necessary with the local carpenter or blacksmith.

Kinship is important in Gopalpur, but participation in the system is limited until marriage occurs. This activates a whole set of responsibilities toward as well as claims upon kinsfolk. Paternal and maternal descent lines are distinguished; marriage with any person related through the paternal line is incest, even though the relationship may be essentially mythological. Only the male seed is believed to be transmitted to offspring, for the woman is regarded as the passive vessel in which the seed is implanted. Hence, not only is marriage to relatives in the female line possible, but marriage with the mother's brother's daughter or own sister's daughter is preferred. As women live with their husband or husband's family, wives often must be sought outside the village. Marriage, hence, involves alliances not only between families, but between villages. Both a man's family and the other members of the village must approve of a marriage. As a man extends and properly maintains his ex-

Traditional peasant farm implements are often simple in construction. This plank used to level rice fields contains no metal parts. Gopalpur, South India. (Photo by Alan Beals.)

Improved transportation permits application of manure to distant fields. Technology required for manufacture of wheels with spokes has not yet reached this part of India. Gopalpur, South India. (Photo by Alan Beals.)

panding chain of relationships within and without the village, his power and influence increase.

An entirely different set of relationships involve the jatis or castes. The jatis are endogamous groupings; far more important, they also have a variety of reciprocal social, economic, and ceremonial functions regarded as essential by the people of Gopalpur. The jatis are ranked partly in terms of occupation. Highest ranked are the Brahmins, who are vegetarians, who are usually educated, and who alone can perform certain ceremonial roles considered essential to village welfare. The landlords often are Brahmins and the village headman, or Gauda, comes from a Brahmin family. The people of Gopalpur know of about fifty jatis, but members of only fifteen live in the village. The singer for the village, essential to any marriage, entertainment, or the curing of illness, lives in another village. Members of other jatis pass through Gopalpur periodically, bringing special goods or performing special services, and then disappear; their residence is not even known to the people of Gopalpur. Some of the jatis are linked together, then, by exclusive rights to perform certain services and traditional forms of payment for these. In other cases arrangements are more or less contractual. For example, a farmer agrees to give a carpenter a specified quantity of grain a year; in return the carpenter takes care of the farmer's needs. Failure to meet an obligation may result in withdrawal of services or refusal to provide goods; usually other members of the jati of the aggrieved person will also refuse to deal with the offending person.

Economic class divisions also exist in Gopalpur which are not directly determined by jati membership. The landlord here is a Brahmin; this is not true in all villages. The middle class includes those members of the farmer jatis who own land they farm themselves; members of other jatis may own land and farm it but also have other occupations. The lower class consists of the landless farmers as well as landless members of other jatis, who must rent land or work as hired laborers. The lower class also includes all the members of some of the lower-ranking jatis. The ranking of the various jatis represented in Gopalpur is not necessarily the same as would be found in other villages.

Operation of the kinship network and the reciprocal obligations between jatis serve to resolve or suppress many conflicts, but not all. Factions and cliques form or re-form about many issues. A number of traditional officials carry on some ceremonial functions, especially the headman, but also mediate disputes and seek to maintain order. These offices, most of them filled from particular jati or lineages within a jati, include a police headman and a crier. Others who can lend money, rent lands, advance credits, or grant other favors also are influential.

Gopalpur manages to feed itself using traditional methods of cultivation that are essentially centuries, perhaps millennia, old. Clearly, at present and perhaps also in the past, this self-sufficiency depends on an out-migration of surplus population. The village also is largely autonomous with respect to its internal order and its relations with neighboring villages. It is not, however, a closed system, for it is dependent upon other villages for most of its wives and many of its services. Three major religious traditions are represented in

Gopalpur—Brahmins, Lingayats, and Muslims. People are aware that each of these is part of a more extensive system. Particularly in their major deities, ceremonials, and oral traditions, people of Gopalpur are aware that they participate in a widespread culture. But no external religious pressures are felt and the pattern of ritual and ceremonial is essentially village centered. Gopalpur and villages like it contribute to the support of the towns and cities of the plain, but the mechanisms appear indirect. Since Indian independence, outside agencies of government have begun to impinge upon the larger communities, but in Gopalpur outsiders are rare and only mildly disturbing temporary visitors. In the past the people of Gopalpur not only thought their way of life adequate, but that they were skillful in meeting the demands of their environment. They felt proud that they were participants in a great civilization. The outside world has changed and the people of Gopalpur now feel inadequate and poor, but reluctant to change their ways.

Gopalpur appears to be more self-sufficient in food than do most villages in the valley of Oaxaca. In both cases, however, villages are interdependent for a wide variety of goods and services; in Oaxaca these are distributed through the active impersonal market system; in Gopalpur they depend much more on the exogamous marriage and jati systems, including a regional network of villages. The political and ceremonial organization of the Oaxaca village seems

Threshing grain with bullocks and water buffaloes. Production of grain crops beyond the needs of the individual household usually require large labor force at harvest time. Friends and debtors assist and are rewarded with food and liquor. Threshing parties usually last until dawn. Gopalpur, South India. (Photo by Alan Beals.)

Stacking hay. The size of a family's haystack and manure heap is a measure of wealth and suitability for marriage. Hay is the major food source for milk cows and bullocks essential for milk and traction. Gopalpur, South India. (Photo by Alan Beals.)

more structured and more autonomous. Kinship ties are important in both cases but they are structured very differently. In Oaxaca the household seems smaller and more independent. Both are involved in different ways in a regional village network as well as with the more distant city.

The examples given far from exhaust the varieties of peasantry in the world. Everywhere, however, peasants share the predominance of food producing as the basic activity, however much they vary in ecological conditions; technological adaptations; dependence upon some economic exchange between village, town, and city; and degree of autonomy in different aspects of culture. Village communities engaged primarily in other forms of production such as mining, crafts, or the raising of nonfood crops by traditional means may sufficiently resemble neighboring food-producing communities as to justify their inclusion under the heading of peasant.[5]

[5] Edward B. Harper, "Two Systems of Economic Exchange in Village India," *American Antropologist,* **61**:760–778, No. 5 (October, 1959).

Large labor force is needed to harvest grain before it is eaten by rats, birds, or insects, or destroyed by bad weather. A substantial portion of the crop will ultimately feed people in city. Gopalpur, South India. (Photo by Alan Beals.)

Some groups are but recently entered into peasantry or quite unconsciously are on the verge of becoming peasants. The Papuan Kapauku, discussed in Chapter 8, already are perhaps irrevocably involved in the transition to peasantry. On the technological side they find steel tools increasingly indispensable. As these and other products of industrial society begin to seem equally indispensable, they will have to increase their production of salable crops. Such economic involvement may still be relatively slight and develop slowly. Other changes, however, impend. Sooner or later the colonial power — formerly the Netherlands, now Indonesia — will begin to interfere in political processes and modify laws; health services, clinics, and schools will be established, altering population structures and changing values and world views. Soon or late, and perhaps sooner than might be expected, the Kapauku will no longer be village farmers but village peasants.

The area of Africa south of the Sahara offers some problems to the definition of the peasant type. In both east and west Africa there are many densely populated areas, such as the Yoruba-speaking region, occupied by village-dwelling farmers. In nearby regions urban centers are known to be fairly old. Kano, in northern Nigeria, is mentioned in documents more than 1,000 years ago. Timbuktu is nearly as old and at one time supported a Moslem university rivaling those of Spain, Sicily, and the Near East. Both cities were near the terminus of important trans-Saharan trade routes. Pre-European cities also existed on the east coast, although their history is in some dispute. In other cases, particularly in West Africa, cities seem either to have been related to the penetration of Moslems into the Sudan or grew out of European trading activities. Certainly some small kingdoms developed in several areas, but whether such more developed large kingdoms as Dahomey antedated European contacts is still debatable. In East Africa great emphasis is placed on cattle breeding. Although cattle are highly valued, often they contribute little to the food supply. In a number of cases, such as Baganda, fairly complex states existed. These seem to have arisen through the domination of prior farming peoples by conquering cattle breeders who established themselves as a dominant ruling caste. Whether the farmers in many of these regions were peasants at the time of European contacts seems still in debate. There is little difference of opinion, however, that most of the African farmers, if not originally peasants, are in the process of becoming so.

Some peasants are very persistent. Through much of the Mediterranean area as well as in more industrialized western Europe many villages of peasants still exist. Large numbers of people also follow many peasant ways of life, although they no longer are organized in communities. These people still produce much of their own food, using agricultural and animal husbandry techniques characteristic of European peasants. Many own their own land, preferably by inheritance, or are tenant farmers with long-standing arrangements with the landlord. Their houses (in Germany, for example) are large, with animals and farm equipment on the ground floor, living quarters above. But although they still produce much of their own food, they produce much more for the market. They use tractors and mowing machines, drive automobiles, and have modern inside plumbing, electricity, and a variety of electrical appliances in houses often two or more centuries old. The community in which they live, if near an urban center, may also include many commuters and nonfarming personnel. The village may contain modern apartment houses, restaurants, automobile and appliance distributors, and a variety of other commercial and service enterprises. The nonfarmers participate in such political and religious activities as still center in the community quite as much as do the cultivators. The term *peasant*, hence, is no longer appropriate for the cultivators. Although they may perpetuate many peasant technologies and ways of life, essentially they are commercial farmers. As a type, they may perhaps more properly be compared with the family farm operator once predominant in much of the United States.

The peasant community provides one way in which the relations between food producers and urban centers have traditionally been organized. As a type of arrangement, however, it may be primarily suited for the preindustrial age. Even then it was not the only way in which food production could be organized in an urbanized society.

4. Manor, Hacienda, and Plantation

In medieval Europe much agricultural production was organized in a manorial system. Land was owned in large tracts and worked by tenants or serfs. The manor was largely self-sufficient and there usually were reciprocal relationships and responsibilities between owner and worker. The worker owed not only labor or produce to the owner, but often military or other services. The owner, reciprocally, owed protection from violence, the maintenance of various services, and aid in crises and emergencies. Where tenants gave labor or serfs worked the land, they served as laborers under the supervision of foremen. To call these workers on the manor peasants is a confusing error. The serf especially made no decisions even about farming activities. However traditional the life style might be, it was a way of life controlled by others. There was little autonomy legally, politically, or religiously.

In Latin America the hacienda, although perhaps influenced by memories of the manorial system already in decay or abolished in much of Europe, seems to have developed relatively independently. Actually several types occurred. In one, sometimes viewed as the classical type, the hacienda is a family-owned, large-scale agricultural enterprise. The heart of the establishment is the residence of the owning family, although much of the year the

Tanzania produces two-fifths of the world's commercial sisal fiber. Such commercial farming provides cash required for modernization. It may also deplete the soil and convert farmers to plantation laborers dependent upon world markets for food and clothing. (Courtesy of the United Nations.)

family might be absent. Like a medieval chateau in France, this might be a fortress. About this or within the walls are the quarters of the hacienda manager, the foremen, and a number of permanently employed specialists, such as blacksmiths, leatherworkers, and carpenters. Surrounding these or in more distant quarters live the permanent labor force, theoretically paid wages, although usually these are mainly in food and goods. Ideally the first goal of the hacienda is to be as self-sufficient as possible. Secondly, it must produce some salable products to support the owners in some luxury and obtain the necessary goods or materials that the hacienda cannot supply. Landowning by itself gives prestige in Latin America society; the amount that the land produces is of secondary importance once the desires of the owners are satisfied. Once this point is reached there is little concern with increasing production or improving technology, especially if capital investment is necessary.

This ideal model was rarely achieved, either in past or contemporary haciendas. Most haciendas require more labor than can be attracted to or held on the hacienda, even when laborers are held as virtual slaves working to pay off debts, for adequate wages cannot be paid. Solutions for this differ. If peasant-type villages exist nearby, wage labor at peak periods might suffice. The need for such labor provides an incentive for the hacienda to encroach on village lands so that the villagers support themselves only through part-time wage labor. In some cases, especially in Peru, some villages are so short of land that they are completely dependent upon the hacienda. Either the village as a whole makes some arrangement with the hacienda, or individuals enter into tenancy relations. A very common form of tenancy is for the village or the individual tenants to be given enough land to cultivate to provide for basic subsistence. In some cases they also receive pasturage rights for animals. In return the tenants are required to give a minimum number of days of labor to the hacienda, either without pay or at a very small fixed wage. Sometimes household services are required as well. In Ecuador such tenants were often called *huasipungeros*, an adaptation from Quechua, meaning "keepers of the gate."

Even without land reform, where the hacienda system still survives in parts of Latin America it seems to be dying. The hacienda depends upon a large stable and cheap labor supply. Even so, its production costs are so high that it cannot compete with more efficient food production systems. The modern agricultural industry draws away the essential labor supply. Only those haciendas which have modernized farming methods and which have shifted toward a competitive wage labor system seem to be prospering.

The plantation system involves growing specialized crops for a large market. Like the hacienda system, it requires a large supply of cheap labor, and it was responsible for the expansion of slavery in the sixteenth to nineteenth centuries. Although the great development of plantation production began mainly in the New World with the introduction of sugar production and an expanded world demand for this product, it has earlier counterparts. In pre-Columbian Mexico, cacao (chocolate) plantations using slave labor existed in what is now the state of Tabasco. The Caribbean area and coastal Brazil were the great areas of plantation-type production in the sixteenth to eighteenth centuries, followed by cotton plantations in the southern United States after the invention of the cotton gin in 1765. At its best the plantation retained some of the paternalistic features of the hacienda and manorial systems. The plantation provided housing and sometimes other services to its workers, helped them in emergencies, and maintained some personal relationships between patron and workers. This pattern is still seen in Ceara, in northeastern Brazil. Here labor may still move from one plantation to another. If the patron, or *patrão,* is too demanding or fails to look after his workers, or *moradores,* properly, they may seek another patron. A patron with a bad reputation may thus find it difficult to get workers. In this case the plantation often retains some features of the hacienda in that workers may have plots of land for subsistence farming.

The plantation in its early form often is associated with colonialism. The United States development shows that was not necessarily the case, although precursors of the cotton plantation existed in the colonial tobacco plantations of Virginia in the eighteenth century. These depended upon indentured labor, that is, labor under contract arrangements for a specified number of years, although slaves also were used. This pattern spread through many parts of the world, notably in Oceania and Africa, following the termination of slavery in much of the world in the last century. Finally, many plantations continue today with the use of wage labor in regions where labor is cheap.

The greatest spread of the plantation system of production is associated with the rise of industrialism and the industrialized city. With mechanization and the application of scientific methods and its technological derivatives, the plantation either converted into or was replaced by the industrial farm, the "factory in the field." In Brazil, for example, with the invention of the steam-powered sugar mill, it became difficult for family-owned sugar plantations using the old animal-powered mills to compete. Not only did they lack capital to build mills, but the mill, in order to succeed, had to control the production from large cane-producing areas. Thus plantations increasingly became corporate-owned enterprises run by a hired manager. The personal relations between management or owner and workers ceased and wage labor became the rule. Most such enterprises can be operated with a small permanent wage labor force, with additional labor hired for peak periods. The management assumes no responsibility for workers in the rest of the year and migratory labor forces become common. In parts of the United States these labor forces once were drawn in part from the city, or where variation in crops permitted, were moved from region to region. At times labor is drawn from Mexico or Puerto Rico. In Peru the commercialized sugar and cotton plantations of the coast draw part of their seasonal labor from the land-poor peasant villages of the mountains, which thus free themselves from dependence upon the hacienda.

The commercial or industrialized farm has the virtues of high productivity, adequate capital, ability to use the latest in machinery and scientific technology, and relatively low production costs. From the standpoint of the welfare of the national economic system it has many advantages in feeding the industrial areas. Most farm workers, however, lose virtually all participation in any social or political system. It is difficult to identify a specific cultural or social system of the commercial farm; the workers are a specialized manifestation of working-class people in the total society and lack membership in either a community or any other institutions of the society. The industrialized farm eliminates tenant farmers and needs less labor. In the United States, as elsewhere, the displaced population moves to the urban ghetto.[6]

The corporate farm or the large industrialized "family" farm is not, of course, the only possible solution to modern production problems. The collective farms of most communist countries are equivalent solutions; in many cases the main difference is that managers and technicians are named by the state rather than by the corporation. Profits, if any, also go to the state, whose bureaucrats may also set production goals, decide what crops are to be grown, and what capital investments are to be made. Cooperatives are another possible solution. If they are to be more than subsistence enterprises they must also depend upon a managerial and technical staff, in this case chosen by the members of the cooperative, to make most of the crucial decisions. The problems of seasonal labor still remain; either the cooperative or collective farm members must be seasonally idle, if they are numerous enough to meet peak labor demands, or a migratory labor force must be sought. The main difference between the collective or cooperative and the commercial farm seems to be that the members of the former participate in a local social and cultural system. The relatively harmful social consequences, low yield, and high energy consumption of factory farms have cast some doubt on their inevitability. Japanese agriculture, although somewhat industrialized, is more productive.[7]

5. The Urban, Industrial, and Scientific Revolutions

Earlier we spoke of the Neolithic or food-producing revolution as radically modifying human ways of life. It is common also to speak of the urban revolution as similarly changing culture and lifeways. The urban revolution grew out of the change to food production, but it was accompanied by a number of important technological changes. The industrial revolution also refers to a major change in technology and lifeways. The single most important development perhaps was the utilization of fossil fuels for energy sources, which permitted a tremendous rise in productive capacities and transportation efficiency.

The food-producing technology that characterized the Neolithic revolution spread over most of the world in which farming was possible; Australia and some subarctic regions and arid regions were almost the only exceptions. The spread of the later urban industrial revolution was less complete. Few cities existed in the heavily forested tropics or in Oceania before the last century; in these regions cities often represent less the development of urbanism than

---

[6] Walter Goldschmidt, *As You Sow* (New York: Harcourt Brace Jovanovich, 1947).

[7] Richard K. Beardsley, John W. Hall, and Robert E. Ward, *Village Japan* (Chicago and London: University of Chicago Press, 1959).

Peasants in El Salvador making rope of sisal fiber. Such simple machines lie at the origins of industrialization. (Courtesy of the United Nations.)

they do the spread of the effects of the industrial revolution in Europe and the United States. They arose as centers of administration and commerce.

The industrial revolution had two effects not always noted. The more widely recognized are the needs of the growing industrial economies of western Europe and the United States for expanding markets for their products and increasing supplies of raw materials. Consequently, industrialism was accompanied by expanding commercial activity and colonialism. Less often recognized is that the new industrial technology permitted the establishment and growth of cities even though an adequate local food-producing base did not exist. Thus in the less industrialized parts of the world—Latin America, Asia, and Africa—we find cities which must be fed in part by foodstuffs from abroad. The industrial technology also allowed a great increase in size and functions for the older preindustrial cities.

The industrial revolution not only accelerated urbanism and changed its character, it also increasingly drew the village world into its orbit. The Kapauku villager who treasures his steel ax has already taken the first step toward involvement in the industrial revolution. Today the industrial revolution has been overtaken by a scientific revolution which has enormously increased potential control over nature and given a new dimension to technology.

The early industrial revolution developed within a few countries; the rest of the world, so far as it was involved, was in a dependent situation. Now, stimulated by the newer scientific revolution, the world is rapidly becoming industrialized. The industrialized city and the megalopolis are recent developments. Today the village world is rapidly becoming involved as well. The urban-industrial-scientific culture type probably will spread as inevitably as did the Neolithic revolution, regardless of political ideologies. Many problems that face most of the world are not problems of ideology, but of industrialism. A major difference from the Neolithic revolution is an increasing consciousness of what is happening. The modern social sciences offer some hope of ultimately controlling and directing the course of industrialization, or at least mitigating some of the effects of the transformation it is bringing.[8]

6. Technology and Urbanism

Just as such technological developments as stone polishing, weaving, and pottery making are closely associated with the beginnings of food production in the Neolithic, so in the Old World metallurgy and new techniques of transportation are associated with the rise of urbanism. In neither case were these technological innovations causal factors; urbanism in the New World developed without either metallurgy or significant improvements in transportation. Moreover, in the Old World some of the innovations became important to people in nonurban societies. They were, however, essential to the development of industrialized urbanism.

Discovery and Spread of Metalworking

The first metals to be used were copper and gold, which often occur in relatively pure form. One of the earliest peoples to make tools and ornaments of copper were the American Indians around Lake Superior, who cold-hammered or annealed (heat-treated and hammered) copper into chisels, spear and harpoon points, knives, and ornaments. They did not, however, discover smelting or other advanced metallurgical techniques.

In the Old World, the earliest evidence of the use of native copper appears at Cayonii Tepesi in eastern Anatolia at about 7000 B.C. Copper artifacts ap-

---

[8] Ralph L. Beals, "The Village in an Industrial World," *The Scientific Monthly*, 77:65–75 (1953).

pear at many other sites in Turkey, Syria, Iraq, and Iran before 5000 B.C. Many of these artifacts were annealed or heat treated. Ultimately the practice of annealing led to the smelting and casting of copper under higher temperatures, and ultimately to the reduction of copper from ore. Other metals may have been discovered in the slag resulting from the smelting of copper. Although copper may have been obtained by the reduction of ore by 4000 B.C. or even earlier, the use of copper tools had little economic impact. Copper tools are relatively soft, do not take or maintain a sharp cutting edge, and for many purposes are inferior to more easily made stone tools.

Much more important was the discovery of bronze, a very hard alloy of arsenic and copper or tin and copper. Arsenic and tin bronzes have been found at the Royal Cemetery at Ur and in other sites as early as 2600 B.C. and, judging by their wide distribution at that time, may have been in use for a considerable period. A limiting factor in the development of bronze from a rare metal to a useful source of tools was the difficulty in obtaining tin. After 2000 B.C. bronze was being traded by the hundreds of kilograms from the East through Mesopotamia and as far as Crete. Crete was also importing tin from

Sawing planks by hand in Ghana. Three men are required to pull the saw downward on the cutting stroke. The development of metallurgy brought about this improvement over splitting logs with wedges and smoothing them with the adze. (Courtesy of the United Nations.)

Cornwall. Where bronze is rare, it may be associated with the development of aristocratic and warrior classes because it conferred a definite military benefit upon those wealthy enough to afford it.

Copper and silver smelting were independently developed in the Andean region of the New World, and the production of fine ornaments and other objects through hammering, welding, and sophisticated casting techniques was characteristic of most of the major New World urban civilizations. Bronze was developed shortly before the coming of the Europeans, probably in Bolivia. An alloy of copper, silver, and gold, equal in hardness to bronze, was used in Colombia and Panama.

Iron, known from Anatolia as early as 2500 B.C., appears originally to have been a virtual monopoly of the Hittites, who used it to good military advantage. Afterwards it spread rapidly, although in many places the art of ironwork remains a secret carefully guarded by trained specialists. Iron reached China, Southeast Asia, Romania, England, and Nubia during the thousand years before the birth of Christ. Nearly all of the peoples of Africa use iron and have apparently used it for some time. In India, ironworking techniques arrived comparatively early and led to the discovery of steel.

Techniques of Metalworking

Metalworking requires a far greater knowledge of the environment and its resources than stoneworking. In a stone-using society, almost any adult individual can recognize and find the raw materials used for tools, for stones may be taken as they occur in nature and chipped or ground to the required shape. The same is true, of course, of free copper and meteoric iron, which are probably regarded by many peoples as particular varieties of stone.

But making tools of metals imbedded in ores is not so easy. Neither copper nor tin ores nor iron-bearing sands or ores look at all like the metals that may be extracted from them; they are, rather, raw materials that must first be altered radically in form and appearance to be made into tools. Metalworking, then, requires the development of numerous techniques, each of which is of equal or greater complexity than the finding and shaping of stone. Among the more important of these are (1) mining, the discovery and collection of suitable ores or metal-bearing sands; (2) smelting, the extraction of pure metals from ores or sands; (3) alloying, the mixing of different metals to produce others that are harder or otherwise more useful; and (4) forging and casting, the techniques whereby metals are finally shaped into tools and artifacts. To practice these techniques, a people must also be able to build adequate furnaces and other devices to produce the heat necessary both to the smelting of ores and the forging or casting of metals. Finally, anvils, hammers, tongs, molds, and other tools are needed to complete the process of shaping metal artifacts.

Smelting was first applied to copper, gold, silver, and lead ores, and the metals so obtained were cast into various tools and implements. The finest casting technique is the *cire perdu*, or "lost-wax" method. The object to be cast is first modeled in wax; this model is then covered with a coating of clay, or more commonly, with a mixture of clay and other materials. One or more openings are left in the clay envelope, which is then hardened by baking, and the wax, melted by the heat, is "lost" and runs out of the openings. Molten metal is finally poured into the clay mold so prepared, thus producing in metal the artifact originally modeled in wax. Objects of great complexity and intricacy of design may be made by this method, but each is unique, for the model is destroyed in the process.

The next metalworking technique to be discovered was alloying, which was first applied to the making of bronzes. Several types of bronze are found in prehistory, each of which consists mainly of copper hardened by a small admixture of tin, phosphorus, arsenic, or, more rarely, gold or silver. Copper-tin mixtures are, however, the most widespread, and the alloy so formed — of 90 percent copper plus 10 percent tin as the optimum mixture — makes far more serviceable cutting tools than copper alone; it is, in addition, an ideal metal for casting. We do not know how bronze was first discovered, but it may have been accidental and derived from the smelting of copper ores mixed in nature with other ores.

There is a similar mystery in the discovery of iron and its smelting, for iron ores and iron-bearing sands give little or no clue to the metal that may be obtained from them. Here again we may lay it to accident or, possibly, to a deliberate search, following discovery of the technique of smelting, for other metal-bearing ores.

Smelting, forging, and casting require the use of furnaces and devices to increase the heat of fires by supplying them with plenty of air. Most primitive furnaces are made of clay, and the most commonly used fuel is charcoal. Many techniques are employed to supply a forced draft: the Aztecs of Mexico had a number of men blow on the fire through hollow reeds, the Incas of Peru set their furnaces on mountain ridges swept by strong winds, and many Old World peoples devised bellows of one sort or another.

In Africa two principal types of bellows are employed. One is a large leather bag, which is opened as it is lifted. The upper opening is closed and the bag is then compressed, with the air escaping through a nozzle or tube directed at the fire. Because two bags are used, each alternately raised and compressed, the draft is made continuous. The second type is a solid chamber of wood or pottery fitted on top with a loose diaphragm of leather and at the bottom with a nozzle (often of clay) leading into the fire. Alternately raising and lowering the diaphragms of two such drum bellows forces a continuous draft through a common nozzle at the fire.

The Europeans, until the recent introduction of the rotary blower, used an accordionlike bellows, now familiar for its use in many households with a fireplace. There is also an African accordion bellows — possibly a compromise, recently developed, between the native drum bellows and the European accordion bellows.

In Indonesia, we find a quite different bellows, the so-called piston type. It consists of two hollow cylinders, made of bamboo, each of which is fitted with a close-fitting piston or plunger. Tubes from the two cylinders are joined

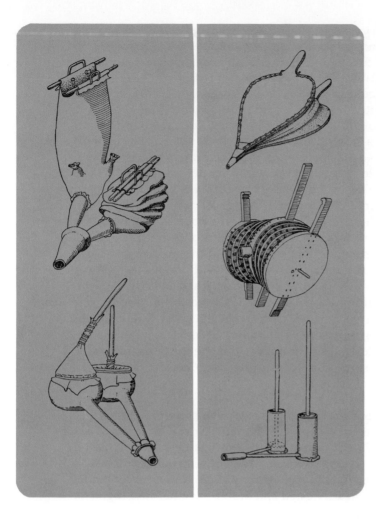

Figure 9–1 Left: Two types of leather and pottery bellows used in metallurgy.

Figure 9–2 Right: Top: two accordion-type bellows; bottom: piston bellows

into a nozzle that leads into the fire. The operator pumps the pistons alternately, thus directing a continuous stream of air into the fire.

To make the process of simple metalworking more vivid, let us turn to the Akikuyus, a Bantu-speaking people of East Africa, well known for their skill in the smelting and forging of iron. We should note, however, that Akikuyu ironworking is primitive only in contrast to our highly mechanized techniques; the Akikuyus, though lacking the machines and extensive knowledge of our culture, possess all the major techniques of ironworking and produce by hand extremely well-made and efficient tools and artifacts.

The Akikuyus obtain their ores in open quarries from decomposed iron-bearing rocks. These quarries are in gorges where streams have broken down the rocks and washed out iron-bearing sands. Sometimes the Akikuyus hasten this process by directing a stream against the rocky sides of a gorge and so increasing the supply of sands. The ferriferous sand is gathered in bags and carried to the lower portion of the stream, where women and children pan and wash it in much the same way as gold miners pan out gold dust from river sands. Large quantities of sand are heaped in the pans, and water is poured on it to remove, by continuous washing, the lighter particles and leave behind the heavier iron-bearing sand. After repeated washings of this sort, the last of which takes place in small gourds, the residue is made up largely of quartz grains, magnetite, and ilmenite ores, with a high iron content. The process is laborious, and the yield is about one pint of well-cleaned ore per hour of labor.

The ore is then taken to a furnace for smelting. The furnace is a hole in the ground lined with clay and so constructed that the clay lining is brought well over the edge of the hole in a convex, everted border around the entire oval mouth of the furnace. The bellows is a cone of sewn goatskins, 4 feet long, and 6 inches in diameter at the large end. A wooden tube, 6 inches long, is set into the small end of the cone. When in use, the cone is pegged to the ground, and the nozzle is set toward the fire. Over the mouth of the nozzle is fitted a pipe of pottery, which runs over the everted lip of the furnace and down into it just above the fire. Two straight slabs of wood, with thongs at their top ends, are attached to the two sides of the cone. Two such bellows are employed so as to produce a continuous stream of air. To work the bellows, one thong is caught by the thumb, the other by the fingers and palm. The operator then closes his hand, so bringing the slabs of wood together to compress the goatskin cone. As his hand closes, he also pushes the cone over against itself and so increases the air pressure directed into the fire. One operator works both bellows, squeezing each alternately.

The furnace is filled with alternating layers of charcoal and ore and allowed to burn, under draft from the bellows, all day long. As the charcoal is consumed and the furnace contents sink to the bottom, more charcoal and ore are added, a little at a time. Finally, when all the ore has been added and all the charcoal burned, the slag is left overnight to cool. In the morning it is removed and knocked to pieces, and the pure iron is removed in small lumps from the slag. These are again heated and beaten together into ingots or blooms weighing about 2 pounds each.

The iron blooms are then taken by the smiths, the most skilled of the ironworkers, who forge the iron into a variety of tools. The smith uses a smooth river boulder as an anvil, and a hammer, tongs, chisel, and other tools, which he makes himself of iron. Other tools and artifacts made include spearheads, arrowheads, swords, axes, adzes, knives, razors, tweezers, branding irons, bells, rattles, earrings, and rings. Akikuyu smiths make wire by beating iron into a long, thin rod and drawing this through a hole in another piece of iron. They also make chains, among the most difficult of the smithing arts. There is, in fact, no forging technique possible by hand that is unknown to the Akikuyu smiths. They do not, however, cast iron; all their artifacts are made by forging.

Metalworking: Its Effect upon Society

It is quite often erroneously assumed that the acquisition of metalworking techniques by itself raises a society to a new stage of culture, superior in every respect to that of earlier and contemporaneous stone users. That this is not necessarily the case is demonstrated by the fact that some metal-using societies are not very different in their total technologies and cultures from some stone users.

The Ifugao of the Philippines, for example, make excellent iron axes and other tools, but from the standpoint of technology their culture as a whole is not greatly different from that of the Neolithic lake dwellers of Europe. Nor is it very different, even in technology from the cultures of such contemporaneous peoples as the aboriginal Hawaiians and Maoris of Polynesia, who lack iron. Similarly, though the Negroes of the Congo have highly developed ironworking techniques, their lack of massive architecture, the wheel, and urban communities is in contrast to the Bronze Age Egyptians. In brief, one cannot adequately compare cultures solely in terms of the presence or absence of toolmaking techniques, for these do not necessarily accompany other cultural features of equal and even greater importance.

Nevertheless the introduction of metalworking does often affect materially the rest of culture. Stone-using peoples nearly always are food gatherers or live

Flow of water causes this waterwheel to turn and raise water to trough at top. In many places efficient irrigation was fundamental to the development of intensive agriculture and urbanization. (Courtesy of the United Nations.)

in small, isolated villages as farmers. Most such communities tend to be isolated, to engage in relatively little trade or other forms of contact with others, and to practice few or no specialized crafts.

With metalworking, this picture often changes. Metals, unlike stones, have a limited distribution, and the use of them stimulates trade, in both raw materials and finished artifacts, over considerable areas. Trade leads of course to wider contacts between disparate peoples and as well to the wider diffusion of cultural innovations. Metalworking, too, because it requires the development of many complex techniques, tends to develop specialized crafts, a feature of economic organization often lacking among stone users. Thus the Akikuyus have at least two specializations related to metalworking: some people spend all their labor in collecting and smelting ores; others are smiths whose task it is to forge iron into tools and artifacts. This leads to internal trade: the smelters sell their iron to the smiths, and the smiths sell the completed tools to others.

It follows, then, that the onset of metalworking is frequently associated with increased specialization of labor and internal trade. It also is associated with expanded external trade, for the raw materials for metallurgy are unevenly distributed. The regions of dense population and high demand for metal products rarely are near the locations of metallic ores. In the Old World metalworking was also associated with a number of other technological innovations, such as improved transportation, the beginnings of written records, and the growth of cities and more complex social and political organization. The history of the urban cultures of the New World proves that none of these things are causal or even necessary for urbanism to appear. They are, however, essential to the later developments leading to industrialization and the industrialized city.

Types of Transportation

All human groups have some technology associated with transporting goods by land, even if human beings provide the only motive power. The contemporary nonhuman primates, such as the gorilla, lacking technical aids, can only transport articles in their hands. Gorillas, because of the dispersed nature of their food supply, spend most of their lives moving from place to place securing food, which they eat on the spot. Though they may return to the same spot repeatedly to spend the night, they do not accumulate any possessions (assuming, for which there is no evidence, that they want possessions). Only small infants are transported, usually clinging to their mothers by their own efforts.

In contrast to the gorilla and other apes, human groups of even the simplest culture establish camps or locations that they may occupy for several days or weeks. The economically productive members of the group leave the camp in search of food, and though they may eat part of the food on the spot, some is transported back to the camp to be eaten over a period of time or to feed the aged or young who may have been left in camp or to be stored for a

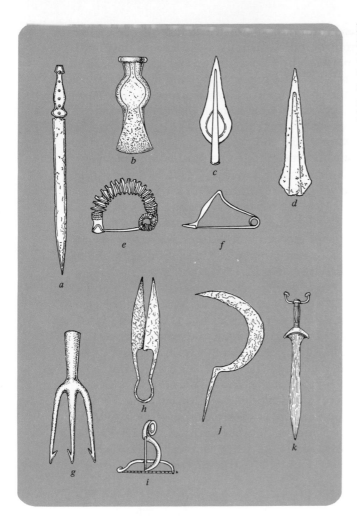

Figure 9–3 Tools and weapons from the bronze and iron ages of Europe: (a and k) swords; (b) adze; (c and d) spear heads; (e,f, and i) fibulae or safety pins; (g) fish spearhead; (h) scissors; (j) sickle. Not to scale. (After McCurdy.)

period of scarcity. When the nearby food supply is exhausted, the camp may be moved to a more convenient location, but some possessions are also transported from one camp to another. Thus a skin shelter or tent cover may be preserved for many years, being moved from one camp to another. Extra clothing and ornament, tools, weapons, containers, and ceremonial objects are similarly transported.

If techniques of transportation are very simple, the number of objects preserved is small. Moreover, the size of the group is also limited unless food supplies are very abundant. As a rule a large group will exhaust food supplies in the vicinity of a camp so rapidly that the group will have to move too frequently. Thus the size of the group tends to conform to the amount of food available and the efficiency of transportation techniques.

Obviously, good transportation also makes a much wider variety of raw materials available to a given people. It further encourages specialization of occupation with a resulting increase in interdependence of groups occupying larger areas. Yet, though good transportation usually is related to advanced techniques and improved motive power, much evidently can be done by proper organization of simple kinds of transport. The great Negro kingdoms of Africa and the complex and extended cultures of Mexico, Central America, and Peru depended mainly on the efficient organization of human power for transportation and communication.

No direct evidence of transportation exists for the Paleolithic. Though it is probable that Late Paleolithic people had means of crossing smaller streams by swimming or using floats or rafts, there is no certainty that they did so. The sole exception known is from the Maglemose culture of Scandinavia in the Mesolithic. The Maglemose people may have lived on floating rafts on lakes and apparently possessed simple dugout canoes hewn or burned from a single log. On the other hand, by analogy with modern nonliterates, we may be fairly confident that most Paleolithic people had simple transportation techniques involving human motive power and the use of crude containers. Such a conclusion is suggested by the fact that even Lower Paleolithic people evidently occupied the same camps for some time and so may have transported food to these camps. Upper Paleolithic people sought or traded desirable stone materials over considerable distances, and inland dwellers used shells and fish from the sea, such facts again arguing some simple means of transport.

The use of domesticated animals for motive power effects a great improvement in land transportation, however crude the methods. Larger groupings of people are possible because food can be transported over longer distances. At the same time face-to-face interaction becomes possible among more widely separated peoples. Trade can be over longer distances and in bulkier goods. Migratory people may own more possessions. All these factors apparently contribute to the formation of larger social units and the development of politically organized groups.

The least efficient use of animal power is by packing or riding. The Peruvian Indians of South America utilize the llama for packing. The llama is a relatively poor beast of burden; it can carry only about 40 pounds, and it travels slowly, grazing along the trail, and so covers only about ten miles a day. Nevertheless, one man can pack and drive a considerable number of llamas and so transport far more goods than he can by himself.

Some of the Plains Indians of North America use the dog as a pack animal. It is even less satisfactory than the llama, but it is still an improvement over human transportation. The Eskimos likewise use their dogs in this fashion in summer.

In the Old World a variety of animals are used for packing. Cattle, horses, donkeys, and camels are so employed over fairly wide areas, whereas the yak, elephant, and reindeer have a more limited distribution. Cattle may carry as much as 500 pounds, but can travel only about ten miles a day with this load. Camels, on the other hand, can carry 1,500 pounds as far as twenty miles a day. Both animals are thus more efficient than the horse, and peoples who possess all three, such as the Kazaks of central Asia, customarily use the horse mainly for riding. In the Mediterranean area the donkey seems to have been the principal beast of burden for a very long time, whereas the camel is the main animal employed in the deserts of North Africa and southwestern Asia. In central Europe, however, the principal pack animal is the horse.

In the extreme North many European and Asiatic peoples use reindeer as pack animals. The Lapps of northern Scandinavia and many people in Siberia pack reindeer during the summer season. Each animal can carry about 80 pounds, divided between two bags or pouches slung on each side, and a herd so loaded is capable of covering long distances.

The riding of animals apparently developed first among the herding people of central Asia, who used both the horse and the camel. Horse riding, rare or absent in the early Mesopotamian cultures, became far more common after contact with migrants from central Asia. Saddles are generally used with both animals, but the horse requires as well a special bridle.

Some reindeer breeders, such as the Tungus, applied the techniques of horse riding to reindeer. Elsewhere such animals as cattle, yaks, elephants, and water buffalo are ridden, but the practice is not extensive, and often it is confined to women and children or to herdsmen caring for animals at pasture. It is perhaps notable that the American Indians, some of whom became excellent horsemen after European contact, had no riding animals at all in the aboriginal period. Animals can transport more goods when used as draft animals than as pack animals.

The simplest type of land vehicle, the sledge, was in use by the Mesolithic of Finland. This earliest known vehicle was for use on ice or snow, but it was usable also on the alluvial plains of the Near East, where it probably existed before 4000 B.C. Again we may guess that Neolithic people harnessed oxen to the sledge as well as to the plow.

The Copper Age provides the earliest definite use of draft animals from Nearer Asia where two- and four-wheeled carts were in general use before 3000 B.C. (see Figure 9–4). By 1000 B.C. wheeled vehicles were used from western Europe to China. In many regions, though, their use was limited until

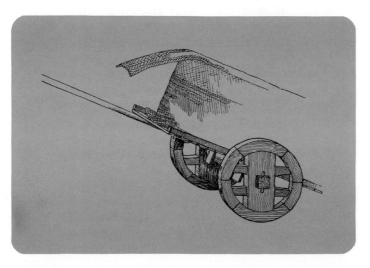

Figure 9–4 A Chinese two-wheeled cart with basket-woven top.

the invention of ironshod wheels and the development of roads and bridges. Pack animals, consequently, continue to be used in parts of Europe up to the present time and in most sections were superseded only with the advent of railroads and automobiles.

Early water transportation probably was confined to canoes and rafts or floats. The first evidence of larger boats comes with the Copper Age cultures of Egypt, where evidently some sort of seagoing craft was in use perhaps as early as 3500 or 4000 B.C. Human motive power was in the main employed, though sails are represented on Egyptian vases dated shortly before 3000 B.C. Navigation techniques were poor and long-distance ocean voyages, except along coasts or in such enclosed seas as the Mediterranean, were rare and hazardous. Not until after the discovery of America were there any real improvements in ocean navigation.

Sails are only rarely used with canoes. Although sails were used by the Peruvian Indians on rafts, and in the Caribbean area and on the North Pacific Coast on canoes, the New World made little use of sails. Canoes are too unstable to use wind power safely. In any case the craft must generally sail straight before the wind or it is in danger of capsizing. In this respect the Oceanians had a great advantage; with the outrigger not only was danger of capsizing reduced to nil except in high winds, but the craft could tack—that is, sail into the wind at an angle, an art unknown to Europeans at the time of Columbus.

By all odds the greatest navigators until after the voyage of Columbus were the Polynesians. Not only had they mastered the art of sailing into the wind, but they had developed crude navigation devices for determining latitude. Planned voyages of over 2,000 miles are known to have occurred, and the Polynesians discovered and occupied most of the habitable islands in the vast expanse of the central Pacific at a time when European sailors dreaded leaving sight of land.

Although there is evidence that Egyptian and Phoenician sailors may have circumnavigated Africa before the beginning of the Christian era, such voyages were in short stages within sight of land. Sails were employed early, but because the knowledge of sailing into the wind was lacking, oars remained important, particularly in the relatively calm waters of the Mediterranean. In Roman times and after, vessels designed for speedy travel or for warfare, where continuous mobility was essential, relied on large numbers of rowers to take the place of unreliable or opposing winds. Navigation in the open sea was precarious and uncertain.

The Arabs probably were responsible for the first real advance in European navigation in several thousand years when they adapted the compass, an invention of the Chinese, to purposes of navigation. The compass was particularly useful in waters near Europe, where long-continued cloudiness often made it impossible to observe the stars. Nevertheless, though aided by the compass, Columbus could only order the sails furled when his ships encountered an adverse wind and wait for a breeze in the right direction, for the sailing abilities of his ships were little superior to those of the Egyptians and Phoenicians.

Fanti men working on fishing boat. Block of wood is base for mast. Like many agricultural peoples, the Fanti of Ghana rely upon fishing as a source of protein. (Kindness of David Kronenfeld.)

The development of ocean travel had important effects on the history of culture. During the Paleolithic, cultural inventions could only spread by the slow process of diffusion from one tribe to the next. Even with the invention of boats, communication was limited except in inland seas and along coasts and waterways. Nevertheless, for the first time it became possible for people separated from one another by intervening groups to come in contact. Only with the development of efficient long-distance travel by Europeans, however, did a revolution take place in the spread of culture. The earlier voyagers, except for the Polynesians, generally either were very limited in their range or made long voyages so infrequently that these had little or no effect on the transmission of culture. Even the Polynesians seem to have had little or no effect on the cultures of the Americas, although it seems very likely that they reached the American coast more than once.

The social conditions existing in Europe after the discovery of America, coupled with rapid improvement in navigation and boat design, resulted in radical changes of culture in widely separated areas of the world. Trade introduced European ideas throughout the world, and in turn brought Europeans in contact with myriad new ideas, concepts, and culture elements. Europeans also settled many portions of the globe. The result was not only the enormous flowering and enrichment of European cultures as old habits and mental barriers were broken, but also the wide diffusion of European culture patterns to many parts of the globe and to peoples who had long lived in almost complete isolation.

Transportation and Urbanism

The New World examples remind us that urbanism is not dependent on great technological developments in transportation and that much could be done with the efficient organization of human labor for transport. Nevertheless, in the Old World more efficient transportation using animal power expanded the area of potential urban food supplies and the possibilities of trade over longer distances. Equally obviously, peasants cannot exist if there is no way of exchanging surplus foods for other goods. More efficient transportation by both sea and land significantly expanded the potentialities for long-distance trade in more bulky items and in securing supplies of raw materials. Thus the Phoenicians appear to have stimulated exploitation of the tin mines of Spain and Cornwall long before the beginning of the Christian era.

Transportation and trade also stimulated the development of secondary urbanism. Sometimes this took the form of trading settlements, sometimes of ports for shipping or of assembly and distribution points for goods. Primary urbanism did not depend upon advances in transportation. But both improved transportation and metallurgy enhanced the importance of urban centers and greatly stimulated the spread of secondary or derived urban centers.

7. Summary

Peasants, today the most widespread type of food producers, represent one facet of urbanism. Both the peasant way of life and the urban one are parts of complex cultures. Although the peasant way of life is very different from the urban way of life, both types of settlement share aspects of some common institutions and are dependent upon one another. The city, once established, tends to be the center of specialization, administration, and innovation. The causes of urbanism are still obscure, but it is clear that cities arose first in areas with sedentary village food producers. In a number of places where cities first appeared, the need to construct and maintain large irrigation works may well have provided the impetus for the concentrations of power and authority characteristic of cities. The evidence is not equally clear in all centers of primary urbanism, and other factors, such as the importance of exchange between areas of differing products, may well have played a part.

In the Old World primary cities are also associated in time with the appearance of metallurgy, advanced animal transportation using the wheel, improved water transportation, and such things as record keeping and public architecture. None of these is essential to urbanism, whereas metallurgy and some of the improvements in transportation are important in nonurban societies. Iron-working is, for example, important in nonurban Africa and Indonesia, and pack animals and sometimes wheeled vehicles were employed by the non-urban nomads of Asia and eastern Europe.

Although peasantry is a widespread way of organizing food production in urbanized societies, it is not the only possible form. Large estates owned by large landowners, such as lords or religious institutions, could be worked by slaves, serfs, or dependents, as they were in early Mesopotamia and Egypt. The manor in medieval Europe and the hacienda in colonial America are examples of similar organizations. Yet another way of food production is the plantation, worked by slaves, indentured servants, or a combination of tenants and wage labor and usually devoted to the large-scale production of a single crop for the world market. The industrial revolution, particularly with the increasing application of scientifically derived technologies, led to the industrial farm, with high capitalization and large-scale production, and dependent upon constantly diminishing amounts of wage labor, which today increasingly dominate modern economies. Alternatives to the corporate farm common in many parts of the world are the collective farms and cooperatives. In each type, however, control of the operations is characteristically in the hands of specialized managers and technicians, and most of the workers have little control over the use of its labor. Whatever the managerial system, the workers are essentially a rural proletariat.

Metallurgy and improved transportation are not essential to the beginnings of urbanism, but they contribute greatly to specialization and the growth of trade and to the spread of secondary or derived urbanism. They have made possible the rise of industrialism and the industrial city or megalopolis of today, phenomena today penetrating all parts of the world. They illustrate clearly that the interplay between technology, culture, and society is far more complex than a simple cause-and-effect relationship.

Collateral Reading

Adams, Robert M. *The Evolution of Urban Society*. Chicago: Aldine Publishing Company, 1966. New perspectives on the archaeological record.

Beals, Alan R. *Village Life in South India: Cultural Design and Environmental Variation*. Chicago: Aldine Publishing Company, 1974. Ecology and rural communities.

Beardsley, Richard K., John W. Hall, and Robert E. Ward. *Village Japan*. Chicago: University of Chicago Press, 1959. Excellent for Japanese agriculture.

Firth, Raymond William. *Malay Fishermen: Their Peasant Economy*, 2d. rev. ed. Hamden, Conn.; Archon Books, 1966. Fishermen in urban society.

French, Robert Mills (ed.). *Community: A Comparative Perspective*. Itasca, Ill.: F. E. Peacock Publishers, Inc., 1969.

Homans, George C. *English Villagers of the Thirteenth Century*. New York: Russell & Russell Publishers, 1960. A famous reconstruction.

Lewis, Oscar. *Life in a Mexican Village: Tepoztlán Restudied.* Urbana: University of Illinois Press, 1951. A detailed ethnography.

Pitt-Rivers, Julian Alfred. *The People of the Sierra.* New York: Criterion, 1945. Chicago: University of Chicago Press, 1961, 1966. Life in a Spanish village.

Potter, Jack., May N. Diaz, and George M. Foster (eds.). *Peasant Society, A Reader.* Boston: Little, Brown and Company, 1967. A variety of well-selected articles.

Redfield, Robert. *Peasant Society and Culture: An Anthropological Approach to Civilization.* Chicago: University of Chicago Press, 1956.

Spindler, George. *Burgbach: Urbanization and Identity in a German Village.* New York: Holt, Rinehart and Winston, Inc., 1973. Persistence of tradition despite industrialization.

Wertime, Theodore A. "Pyrotechnology: Man's First Industrial Uses of Fire," *American Scientist,* **61**:670–682, No. 6 (November–December, 1973), A recent review.

Wolf, Eric R. *Peasants.* Englewood Cliffs, N.J.: Prentice-Hall, Inc. 1966. A brief survey.

Ethnographic References

Africa: Hill, 1963, 1970a, 1970b.
Brazil: Castro, 1966; Johnson, 1971.
India: Beals, 1962.
Mexico: Beals, 1946, 1966, 1975.

10/Economic Anthropology

1. Economics and Economic Anthropology

Because the formal science of economics has developed largely out of the study of the economic systems of modern industrialized nations, more fundamental scientific questions concerning the nature of all human economic systems are shared between economics proper and anthropology. *Economic anthropology* is the comparative, cross-cultural study of economic systems. Economics is sometimes defined as the study of economizing. Economizing, in turn, is defined as the allocation of scarce resources among alternative ends. Some definitions of economizing are restricted to material goods, but others include services and other nonmaterial phenomena in the definition. Resources may also be broadly defined to include such nonmaterial "things" as skill and knowledge. Ends may be regarded as material goal objects or more broadly defined as anything that human beings desire or need.

In the very broad sense of goal satisfaction, economics and economizing behavior can be seen as applying to any human act. Any behavior can be interpreted as a conscious or unconscious decision to engage in that behavior instead of some other behavior and it is easy to conclude that in making such a choice the individual has, however inaccurately, made some calculation of the profits and losses involved. Even the act of doing nothing can be construed as a choice among alternative ends. Broadly interpreted in this fashion, the concept of economizing or maximizing holds a useful place in all the sciences of human behavior.

Although it may seem extravagent to assert that all human decisions are economic decisions, the narrow definition of economics as concerned solely with the production, consumption, and distribution of material goods also presents difficulties. Under the narrow, materialistic definition economics would be unable to calculate the value of the "goodwill" attached to a business or an economic institution and it would be hard pressed to explain gift giving, charity, public relations, or other activities involving a mixture of material and nonmaterial goods. The reason for the difficulty involved in the definition of economics is that the economic system, however it is defined, is an integral part of the larger cultural system. The economic system is separated from the cultural system for analytic purposes; it does not have any independent existence as a system. In other words, it is easy to focus upon the production, exchange, and consumption of material goods—they are comparatively easy to weigh, measure, and compare—but that does not mean that the nonmaterial world can be or should be ignored. Economic anthropology generally deals with material goods, but it is also concerned with the relationship of these economic things to the other aspects of the sociocultural whole.

The relationships between economics, especially economic theory, and anthropology have been the subject of a long and continuing debate. At the heart of this debate lies the fact that economics developed as an essentially practical discipline dedicated to an understanding of modern industrial economies. Among the basic assumptions that have contributed to formal economic theory are:

1. *Maximization.* When engaging in production and exchange activities, people will seek to get the maximum possible returns or benefits.
2. *Rationalization.* People will seek by consciously rational means to improve their productive or exchange capacities.
3. *Supply and demand.* The value of goods and services will increase when they become scarce or when demand increases.

The operation of supply and demand will be affected by the possibility of substituting other goods or services or by the existence of competing demands. In cash economies, characteristic of industrial society, the operation of supply and demand can be measured by examining relationships among supply, demand, and price. The economist recognizes that these basic assumptions may be affected by culturally determined preferences, by monopolies, and by government policies such as wage and price controls.

Economic theory derived from these assumptions often deals with large-scale or macroscopic phenomena that can be studied by statistical methods. In such studies individual decisions that might constitute exceptions to the theory being tested tend to be submerged by larger numbers of individual decisions that are made in accordance with the theory. The existence of exceptional circumstances in which large numbers of people make decisions that are not in accord with macroeconomic theory has led to the study of micro-economic — individual and small group — phenomena such as motivations to produce, the operations of individual firms and businesses, the processes of economic decision making, the significance of information flows, and the formation of consumer preferences.

Although many of the fields of microeconomics are directly applicable cross-culturally, there are serious problems involved in applying the findings of macroeconomics to small-scale societies. Economic anthropology, then, raises a number of questions: (1) How universal are the basic assumptions the economist makes about human behavior? (2) Are data concerning nonindustrial societies significant for the development of economic theory? (3) To what extent is formal economic theory useful in the understanding of the economics of nonindustrial societies? (4) What are the different ways in which economic systems, however conceived, are related to other aspects of sociocultural systems? (5) Are the economic systems of nonindustrial societies fundamentally different from those of industrial societies or do they differ mainly in scale, complexity, or emphasis?

When a large animal is killed, it yields a supply of meat that cannot readily be consumed by the hunter and his immediate family. Among hunter-gatherers and other small societies, distribution is generally handled by traditional rules obligating the hunter to distribute his kill among particular sets of relatives or associates. Among agricultural peoples, where there is a larger population, meat is likely to be sold in a market. Here a Fanti hunter sells his venison after the price has been fixed by community leaders. Ghana, Africa. (Kindness of Ed Plummer.)

Some forty years ago Bronislaw Malinowski, although very interested in the economic problems of nonindustrial peoples, suggested that formal economic theory had little to offer the anthropologist. About the same time, in a famous exchange, Frank Knight, a prominent economist, suggested that the study of small societies had little or no relevance to economics, and Melville Herskovits, an anthropologist, argued that although formal economic theory was of little use to the anthropologist, anthropological studies cast considerable doubt on its universality. Herskovits was later to change his position somewhat, admitting that most anthropologists were insufficiently familiar with economic theory to make proper use of it. In part this change of position was influenced by the work of Raymond Firth, who took the position that the fundamental principles of economics have universal application but that many of its assumptions must be tested. Not only did he make effective use of economic theory, but he devised methods of fieldwork which provided more precise and quantified data about economic activities.[1]

With the rise of interest in the problems of less industrialized countries, these considerations have acquired great practical importance. Many economic aid programs as well as the economic policies of developing countries have been formulated on the assumption that the expansion of economic institutions on the Western model will bring about the desired goals of economic development. Enough failures in such programs have occurred to raise the question again of whether the fault is in the economic theories or models used or in lack of attention to the different ways in which economic activities are embedded in differing social structures or systems.

Some economists have challenged the role of classical economic theory outside Western societies. This group, led by the late Karl Polanyi, represents the "substantive" approach in economics. In anthropology Paul Bohannon and George Dalton have been the leading exponents of this approach. In very simplified terms, the substantivists argue that existing economic theory was developed in relation to the market economies characteristic of Western industrial nations involving, at least theoretically, the free play of supply and demand in determining value and exerting a powerful influence on production and consumption. Initially it was argued that "primitive" economies were oriented primarily toward meeting subsistence needs and hence were different in kind from market economies. The principles controlling the exchange of goods in subsistence economies were reciprocity and redistribution with a virtual or complete absence of the operation of market principles, maximization, or rationalization. Reciprocity involved the exchange of goods and services in kind or, if unlike goods were involved, in accordance with traditional values. Redistribution involved mechanisms to maintain substantial equality in goods, that is, moving goods from the "haves" to the "have nots," and preventing the accumulation of goods. Basically, the substantivists maintain that "primitive" subsistence economies differ in kind from industrial market economies in opposition to those who maintain the differences are not in kind but

---

[1] Raymond Firth, *Malay Fishermen: Their Peasant Economy*, 2d rev. ed. (Hamden, Conn.: The Shoestring Press, 1966; 1st ed., 1946).

Any reasonably rare and portable material, sea shells for example, can serve as a medium of exchange. Topoi, paramount *luluai* (chief) of a village near Rabaul, Melanesia, in his treasure-house, holding a short length of shell money. The circular objects are coils of shell money covered in cord or basketry. Topoi's shell money is estimated to be worth more than 12,000 Australian pounds. (Courtesy of the United Nations, Australian Official Photograph.)

in degree. Economic activities in subsistence societies are seen to be embedded in the social system, to involve a system of mutual give-and-take according to set equivalencies, and are guided by generosity. These involve cooperative relationships which diminish hostilities and foster solidarity. Market economies, in contrast, involve bargaining (Polanyi uses the term *higgling-haggling*), to arrive at a mutually satisfactory price motivated by desires for personal gain or profit. This leads to antagonism, hostility, and anxiety.

The substantive approach has been sharply criticized by Scott Cook,[2] who points out that the substantivists have romantically idealized the subsistence

[2] Scott Cook, "The Obsolete Anti-Market Mentality: A Critique of the Substantive Approach to Economic Anthropology," *American Anthropologist*, **68**:323–345 (1966).

Mothers and children offering produce for sale. Fanti, Ghana. Open-air markets like this are a common means of distribution among agricultural and urban peoples. (Kindness of David Kronenfeld.)

economies while attributing various social disadvantages to the market-oriented economies. He suggests that so far the substantivists and the formal economic theorists have essentially ignored each others' points of view; rather than engaging in a discussion, they have "talked past" each other. He points out that the substantivists were forced to modify their views because of the existence of simple peasant societies in which market principles clearly operate. This problem generally was dealt with by the substantivists by formulating an intermediate class of peasant societies which in varying degree had been "contaminated" by the influence of market economies. This does not solve all dilemmas, for there are well-studied subsistence economies with little outside influence in which market principles clearly are operative to some extent. Cook also suggests that the majority of the world's people outside the industrial market economies are peasants functioning to some degree according to market principles. For Cook, the major function of economic anthropology today is in relation to the problems of development.

In another critique of the substantivist position, LeClair[3] suggests that (1) general economic theory is possible; (2) current economic theory may be inadequate because it is based too exclusively on the special case of Western

[3] Edward E. LeClair, Jr., "Economic Theory and Economic Anthropology," *American Anthropologist*, **64**:1179–1303 (1962).

industrial economies; (3) it should be possible either to demonstrate that non-Western economies are special cases to be subsumed under existing theories or to use them to develop new or expanded general theories. The function of economic anthropology in such a view is to provide descriptions of these special cases and to attempt to relate them to economic theory. This third view dominates the following discussion. A second important job of the economic anthropologist is to investigate the different ways in which the functions of the economic system may be distributed among institutions that are widely different from those performing the same functions in Western society. This is a task for which few economists are prepared.

Three fundamental economic questions may be identified:

(1) How are the goods and services wanted or needed by human societies produced? Technology is involved here only in that it determines the potential means for the conversion of raw materials into usable foods and artifacts. More important are the patterns by which an economic system functions to govern the human activities and interactions involved in the production of goods and services. Economic anthropology seeks to discover how the work of production is divided among members of human societies and whether or not individuals or groups within a society specialize in particular occupations. In our society, for example, there are a large number of specialized trades, crafts, and professions, many of which require years of apprenticeship or learning. In contrast, smaller and more homogeneous societies, such as those of the Australian aborigines, have few or no specialized occupations; every individual of the same age and sex group performs or is capable of performing the same tasks, most of which are learned in youth as part of the process of growing up.

(2) How are the goods and services that are produced distributed or allocated among the members of human societies? Here again the emphasis lies on the patterns of human interaction that govern the processes of distribution, not on the techniques employed to achieve this end. Is distribution, as in many of the simpler societies, primarily a family concern, in the sense that members of the family produce virtually all that is necessary to meet their needs? Or is the family part of a larger unit, within which goods and services are distributed by some system of barter or trade? In modern societies, the organization for distribution is exceedingly complex; nearly all the needs for daily living must be obtained by trade, and many of them come from distant places and go through many hands before reaching the ultimate consumer.

(3) How are the goods and services that are produced and distributed in human societies eventually put to use and consumed, and what patterns of behavior govern this process? In many societies, in which the techniques of production and distribution are extremely simple, production, distribution, and consumption take place within one small group, whose members live in daily face-to-face contact with each other. In such societies the distributive mechanisms may be relatively simple; but they are not nonexistent. Surpluses may be small, but they exist whenever an individual or a family produces more of anything than it consumes. The problems of economic power and political control found in complex societies where individuals produce large surpluses

are, of course, much more complex. It does not necessarily follow, however, that they are wholly different in kind.

In the sections that follow we shall examine each of these questions in some detail in an attempt to learn how a comparative study of human societies may result in a better understanding of the economic aspects of human culture.

2. Problems of Production

Broadly defined, *production* has to do with the process of obtaining goods from the natural environment. This involves consideration of the abundance and distribution of resources; the technology used in obtaining and processing resources; the energy available for the tasks of production; the kinds of things that particular humans seek to produce; and the various elements of risk, effort, investment, and yield involved in the production of particular goods. At the outset, in considering the resources available for production, a distinction must always be made between the resources that might be discovered by an all-wise and all-knowing outsider and the resources that are perceived to exist by the members of any particular group. In many cases, probably in all cases, human beings ignore or fail to utilize resources that an outsider perceives to be present. For example, the Indians of California relied heavily upon the natural acorn crop for subsistence, but with a few exceptions neglected the possibilities of agricultural production. Modern Californians, for their part, make almost no use of the natural acorn crop, despite the fact that it is one of the largest food crops in the state.

Utilization of the environment, then, is not an automatic process, but rather the result of an interaction between the ultimate resources available and the capacity of the members of a particular cultural system to perceive such resources and to develop the technology required for their utilization. In almost every environment there are nutritious food plants that are not used because the technology required to process them is not available. Even where technology and knowledge are available, costs of energy and labor may cause a resource to be neglected. Such abundant metals as aluminum and titanium were unused until large amounts of energy and relatively economical ways of processing the ores became available. In our own culture many items common in the diet of other peoples—such as grasshoppers, horses, dogs, cats, and acorns—are rarely utilized. Many of our decisions concerning the utilization of the environment are based, not upon rational choice, but upon the fact that people seek to perpetuate existing or traditional agreements. The same is true elsewhere. The Eskimo, although often faced with hunger, maintained a large number of rules forbidding the consumption of certain foods. Although such rules, often called food *tabus,* may sometimes have positive value in preventing overuse of natural resources, it is difficult to explain all such rules in economic terms.

Although human needs and wants are always the product of interaction between various biologically and culturally decreed minima and it is therefore extremely difficult to estimate the absolute requirements of human survival, any society must produce the necessities of life in sufficient quantity to permit the survival and reproduction of its membership. As a minimum, any culture must provide the food necessary to sustain life and the equipment necessary to obtain food. It is more difficult to establish universal needs for clothing, shelter, ornaments, toys, art objects, medication, or household furniture. It might almost be said that human beings have a need to regard certain unnecessary things as necessary. Although production may often represent a response to some biological need, it may also be carried out in response to needs that are socially derived or to needs whose origins are puzzling or inexplicable. Those who join Thorstein Veblen in saying "Invention is the mother of necessity" are probably as correct as those who claim the opposite.

There have been, of course, many cultures which failed to meet the basic needs of their memberships and so disappeared. Many existing and recent cultures seem to fall close to that dark region where basic human needs are barely met. According to Allan Holmberg,[4] the Sirionó of the forests and savannahs of eastern Bolivia are one such people. Holmberg found the Sirionó to be constantly hungry or in fear of hunger. Hunger dominated their activities, even their dreams. Wives constantly scolded husbands for failing to bring in sufficient meat; husbands accused wives of hiding food and not giving them a fair share. Although the Sirionó, in fact, consumed quite considerable quantities of meat—which might lead us to suspect that they were somewhat better off than they seemed to think—there can be no doubt that they lived in a difficult environment and faced severe problems of survival.

Nevertheless their life was not without its luxurious aspects. Although the Sirionó moved camp with some frequency and transported all of their belongings on their backs, their inventory of "necessary" material objects was surprisingly large. They required shelter from rain; continuous fires to protect them from insects; hammocks for sleeping; tools and weapons including digging sticks and bows and arrows; and containers for storing, transporting, and cooking food (almost no food was eaten raw). Further, despite the tremendous limitation on economic choice characteristic of any harsh environment, the individual Sirionó was constantly involved in the making of decisions. Each day the male decided whether to gather vegetable food or hunt. In either case he faced a host of decisions about where to go, what kind of plant or animal to seek, and so on. When food was available he faced the options of making and repairing tools, improving the family shelter, or resting. Although these decisions may be regarded as basically practical or survival-oriented, there was also the possibility of engaging in drinking, singing, or dancing. Similar patterns of economic decision making apply to Sirionó women as well. So despite

---

[4] Allan Holmberg, *Nomads of the Long Bow: The Sirionó of Eastern Bolivia* (Garden City, N.Y.: The Natural History Press, 1969; first published 1950).

the Sirionó view of themselves as under constant survival pressure, they nonetheless found themselves involved in economizing, that is, allocating their means among various ends.

3. Division of Labor by Age and Sex

Although the technology and skills of the Sirionó were relatively simple and might well be learned by anyone, not all Sirionó engaged in all kinds of Sirionó activities. Instead, as seems to be universal among human beings, tasks and activities were allotted to different individuals on the basis of age and sex. The very young and the very old were not expected to produce. The young were valued and given affection; the aged might be neglected or abandoned, as sometimes happens in Euro-American cultures. Men hunted, fished, built shelters, and made weapons, tools, and some utensils. Women cooked, cared for children, carried water and firewood, and made hammocks, mats, woven or twined containers, pottery objects, and ornaments. Both sexes performed tasks associated with producing vegetable foods, dressing game, or carrying burdens. Sirionó work often involved the interdependency of the sexes. Women made the strings for the bows men used in hunting; men made the spindles used by women in making thread.

Because the very young in all human societies often lack the knowledge or the physical strength required to perform certain tasks, and the very old often lack the required strength, the division of labor in terms of age is often a direct reflection of ability. It may also be based upon more arbitrary criteria such as the attainment of puberty or upon social criteria such as marriage or the completion of initiation ceremonies having little connection with the tasks at hand. Similarly, in the division of labor by sex, true physiological differences between men and women seem to be involved in some cases but not in others. Thus it seems logical that women involved in the nursing of babies be assigned tasks close to home while their husbands are involved in hunting and other tasks involving prolonged absence. Similarly the fact that men tend to be on the average somewhat larger and stronger than women might have contributed to the assignment of certain tasks requiring great strength to men. Obviously there is an element of arbitrariness involved in a division of labor that assumes that all women are either pregnant or lactating or that all men are more muscular than all women. In South India, where, as is customary in many other places, the women are expected to collect firewood, a nursing mother may be away for as much as eight hours while her husband performs relatively easy work in a nearby field.

In general, especially in nonindustrialized cultures, the tasks that are to be performed are simple and can be performed by almost anyone. The division of labor by age and sex, although not carried out independently of biological criteria, is probably directed, not so much by problems of production as by problems of social organization and convenience. The assigning of different tasks to old and young and to male and female probably creates an economic

The division of labor by sex is sometimes explained in terms of the fact that men are stronger than women on the average and that women have child-care responsibilities. Heavy work, such as the transportation of firewood, is nevertheless assigned to women in many places. Ruanda-Urundi, Africa. (Courtesy of the United Nations.)

Although construction work is frequently assigned to men, this rule does not always apply when things are constructed for women's use. Fanti women (Ghana) constructing an earth oven for smoking fish. (Kindness of David Kronefeld.)

interdependence that serves to strengthen family organization. An economizing decision is also involved in an arrangement that ensures that all persons need not learn to perform all tasks.

Among the Mixe Indians of Mexico the processing of maize, which forms the mainstay of the diet, lay entirely in the hands of women. Men received no training in the processing of maize and were incapable of surviving unless a woman was available to process the maize that the man produced. Although man's work involving the planting and raising of maize constituted a complicated technological process, it only represented one-half of the food-producing revolution. The other half, the processing of the crop, was equally complicated and time consuming. The processing involved removing the maize from the cob; boiling it with the proper amount of lime for a sufficient time to remove the hard outer shell and soften the kernel; grinding it on a flat stone slab until it reached the proper texture; working water into the dough; and shaping it between the palms until a flat cake of uniform thickness was formed. The cake was then cooked at the correct heat on a flat griddle, properly treated to prevent sticking. A Mixe woman with a family of five would spend about six hours a day manufacturing tortillas. Under such circumstances it would be impossible for her to engage in the raising of maize, just as

Water, one of the heaviest substances normally transported, is usually carried by women. Denokil tribeswomen filling animal skins with water. Awash Valley, Ethiopia. (Courtesy of the United Nations.)

it would be impossible for her husband to engage in the processing of maize. Here it was the division of labor that permitted the use of maize as a staple food, and the maintenance of the division of labor depended to some extent upon the incapacity of men to make tortillas and of women to farm. Because both men's and women's skills were taught from early childhood without consideration of the individual's abilities or inclinations, the end result was adult ignorance of the skills mastered by the opposite sex and, very often, a *trained incapacity* such that the adult found it virtually impossible to acquire a skill normally belonging to the opposite sex. Small wonder that most people accept the myth that the sexual division of labor is biologically ordained. A division of labor by sex and age occurs in all known human societies. It is firmly anticipated in primate societies and was almost certainly a factor in the biological evolution of humanity, especially as it affected the development of male responsibility for the care of mothers and infants.

4. Specialization in Production

Specialization, sometimes referred to as true division of labor, occurs when full- or part-time specialists exist. Where population densities are low and technology relatively uncomplicated as in most hunting and gathering groups, specialization, if it exists, is usually confined to a few part-time specialists who may play leadership roles, undertake special medical or religious tasks, or, more rarely, produce arrows or other items requiring special skill or talent. When population is dense and complicated technologies must be employed, specialization becomes much more likely. Here again, as in the case of the division of labor by age and sex, specialization of labor need not be carried out primarily as a means of rationalizing production, but may be developed as a means of creating economic interdependence between different families, villages, or even tribes.

In the American Southwest the village-dwelling Pueblo Indians possessed a far more complicated division of labor than was characteristic of the less-settled Navajo and Apache. Among the Pueblo Indians, pueblos that were isolated and that had small populations generally possessed a less complex division of labor than did larger and more closely spaced pueblos. According to Edward Dozier, the Western Pueblos, including the Hopi (see Chapter 8, pp. 283–294), were primarily organized in terms of age and sex.[5] Each village was structured in terms of matrilineal clans and, while the members of these clans carried on the same kinds of day-to-day production labor, the task of carrying out ceremonial functions believed to be essential to survival was assigned to individual clans. Each clan had the responsibility for organizing an association, which could have members from other clans or even other villages and which performed a particular ceremonial activity.

[5] Edward P. Dozier, *The Pueblo Indians of North America* (New York: Holt, Rinehart and Winston, 1970).

Carpenter working with chisel. He is a full-time specialist who has inherited his status as village carpenter from his father. If a member of the Carpenter caste is available, no other person may serve as village carpenter. Clients pay the village carpenter annually and must furnish wood and unskilled labor. (Photo by Alan Beals.)

Although the Western distinction between economic and religious activity is difficult to apply to the Pueblo Indians, some of the "ceremonial" associations supervised activities that we would consider economic. Thus there were associations for hunt, war, social control, and rainmaking.

Although Western Pueblo specialization of labor might well bear such labels as incipient or part-time and be considered primarily a socially integrating rather than an economic device, two of the pueblos, notably Zuñi and Acoma, had developed an increased degree of specialization. At Zuñi, there was a hierarchy of priesthoods which had ultimate control of the village, and at Acoma, the Antelope clan had virtually absolute control over many aspects of community life.

Where farming communities are close together and numerous and, especially, where individual communities occupy quite different ecological niches, the extent of specialization increases markedly. In the Pacific, especially in Melanesia where islands are large and close together, trade between coastal and inland communities or between different islands often leads to considerable specialization in production by the populations of different tribes or communities. Community productive specializations are also common among peasant agriculturalists, especially in Mexico. In areas of rich agricultural production, most individuals are farmers, but the farming is very often combined with other specializations that may become full-time specializations if the market warrants it. The Baganda of Africa depended upon specialized groups of ironworkers, carpenters, canoe builders, leather workers, drum makers, potters, house thatchers, and floor makers. Suye Mura, a village in Japan, contained a carpenter, a stonecutter, a cake maker, two midwives, a barber, two priests, and a variety of minor or part-time specialists such as roof makers. There were also many specialists who offered their services in nearby villages, and a variety of specialists not regarded as traditional. In all, there were some 34 different kinds of specializations involving about 80 people, but most of them were engaged mainly or part-time in farming.

In India the concept of specialization and complementarity of function provides one rationale for a system of specialized castes which theoretically exchange economic services within each village. Even though only a few families in each caste may pursue such traditional professions as blacksmith, carpenter, or washerman, all members of the caste will consider themselves to be specialists, perhaps only temporarily employed in agriculture. In India the concept of specialization goes beyond what might be considered necessary for efficient or rational production alone and is used to provide a rationale for the interdependence of different groups of people. To the extent that specialization actually reduces conflict between castes, it can be regarded as an efficient and rational device for maintaining society. Arrangements that seem inefficient or irrational from the point of view of production alone may seem efficient and rational, even ingenious, when viewed in broader perspective.

Specialization in production becomes possible only when an individual or group possesses a technological adaptation that permits them to produce more than they require for their own consumption. Although this is often called a surplus, it should be remembered that an individual is likely to produce more than he consumes only if he can exchange the resulting product for something else that he consumes. In many cases farmers in highly specialized societies, despite the fact that they may produce twenty times more food than they consume, are less well fed than hunter-gatherers because such a large fraction of their production is traded away or taken away. On the other side of the coin, specialization permits increased production because the specialist is likely to be a more efficient producer than the jack-of-all trades.

Four brothers plowing rice field in Gopalpur, South India. Membership in a large family permits economies of scale which substantially increase per acre production. (Photo by Alan Beals.)

5. The Organization of Production

The concepts of specialization and division of labor cover the situation in which different individuals or groups produce different things and then exchange whatever they do not consume themselves. In many hunter-gatherer societies, many of the tasks of production are carried out by individuals. The Eskimo hunter must often creep up on his prey as quietly as possible in order to get close enough to use his bow and arrow, spear, or harpoon without frightening the animal. This is a task performed more efficiently alone because the presence of others could only produce noise and confusion. Similarly, although groups of individuals may travel together in search of wild plants for food, the actual task of locating and harvesting the plants is usually performed by the individual.

Other sorts of tasks may require the carefully coordinated effort of large numbers of individuals. The Plains Indian buffalo hunt often involved the total available man and woman power of the tribe. Once a large herd was located, the men constructed a stout corral and, extending from its entrance, a pair of diverging fences. Near the corral the fences were strongly built, but as they moved outward the construction became lighter. When the corral and the fences had been completed, a group of men stampeded the buffalo in the direction of the corral. As the herd moved between the converging lines of fence, the remaining men, women, and children would take up positions along the fence lines where they could urge the herd along and keep it from breaking through the weaker portions of the fence. Once in the corral, the buffalo were killed by the men standing safely outside. Once the buffalo were killed, the women would skin and butcher them, preparing choice bits of meat for immediate consumption, and drying the rest for storage and later eating. The profits of the hunt were divided among the participating families.

Techniques such as the buffalo hunt require careful organization and precise timing. Each individual's efforts must coordinate with those of others, or the project will fail. Among the Plains Indians, coordination was achieved by a buffalo chief, assisted by a men's club which served as messengers and police force. For the duration of the hunt, the word of the buffalo chief was law. Anyone who hunted individualistically or disobeyed the chief or his messengers would be promptly punished, often by being stripped of his possessions and publicly whipped.

The Plains Indian buffalo hunt took place during the summer when vast herds of buffalo gathered. Had individuals carried out their own hunting independently, it would have scattered the herds, making hunting more difficult. The communal hunt, then, represents a technological means of increasing the size of the buffalo harvest. It also required the coming together of an entire tribe during the summer months and thus necessitated a variety of social as well as economic adjustments. During the winter, when the buffalo herds scattered, the tribe broke down into component families and bands, and hunting became uncoordinated and individualistic.

Although the Plains buffalo hunt required complex coordination and timing in order to produce results, it involved relatively little specialization of individual labor. By contrast, a modern factory might have a work force composed of large numbers of subgroups each of which performs a single specialized task. In such a setting the individual may lose sight of the common enterprise to the point where he regards his own performance as unimportant and therefore not worth doing well. In some cases, then, the planned economic efficiency of an assembly line may be disrupted by the existence of unforeseen personal and social needs on the part of individuals who have become mere cogs in the machine.

In South India, weaving was traditionally carried out as a family enterprise in which each child and adult carried out specialized functions. The need for child labor within the household made it difficult, in many cases, for children in weaving households to attend school or even to become familiar with other sorts of tasks or occupations. As handloom textiles have gradually been replaced by manufactured textiles, handloom weavers, in sharp contrast to specialists in other occupations such as blacksmithing where child labor is not used, have found it almost impossible to find other forms of employment for which they were suited. Here, as in the case of the buffalo hunt or the modern factory, the organization of work in such a way as to maximize production produces important consequences for the organization of society and the fate of the individual.

6. Distribution in Subsistence Economies

When each individual or family unit is engaged in the same type of production as all others, the vast bulk of all production is distributed and consumed by the individual or within the family. In such systems, should an individual or a family have insufficient supplies of food, there would be relatively few resources available that might be traded for additional food. Under such circumstances the common pattern is one of sharing or reciprocity. The person or family that has run short of supplies accepts a gift from someone else or may simply move in with relatives who are better off until economic conditions improve. Among peoples who depend for meat supplies upon the hunting of large animals, the successful hunter cannot begin to consume his production. Consequently there are almost invariably arrangements — sometimes quite elaborate — for distributing the meat resulting from a successful hunt. On a future hunt, when the hunter is unsuccessful, he is likely to receive meat from someone else's kill. Such reciprocative distribution arrangements probably occur in all societies.

Among the Hopi the nuclear family consisting of husband, wife, and children was traditionally the basic unit of production and consumption. The family lived in a house its members had built, ate the food its members produced, made its own clothing, and made all the tools and equipment it required. The lands used for hunting and gathering were owned by no one.

Farming land was owned by matrilineal clans (groups of families tracing descent from a common ancestor through the female line) and assigned equitably to each family.

When, by reason of crop failure or lack of success in hunting and gathering, a family was unable to sustain itself, food and other necessities were provided by related families as gifts, thus imposing on the recipients the obligation to give similar aid when required. Families did not hoard foods or other necessities when others were in want, for such actions would have violated every canon of Hopi behavior. Generosity and a "good heart" were among the highest Hopi ideals; stinginess was tantamont to a confession of witchcraft. As a result the families and clans making up a Hopi village achieved an internal distribution of most goods without having any formal marketing or trading system. Because some clans possessed fewer or less productive lands than others, and because the distribution of ages and sexes within each family created differences in productivity, not all families were equally productive. Although the more productive families were expected to be generous, their generosity rarely extended to the point of share and share alike.

The Zapotec Indians of Oaxaca, Mexico, also made use of reciprocative arrangements, despite their participation in a complex system of trading and marketing. For important events, such as weddings, or to meet ceremonial obligations a man might solicit help from relatives, friends, and neighbors. Such aid might take the form of money or, more commonly, foodstuffs, liquor, and, more recently, soft drinks. Generally the donor expected to be repaid on some future occasion when he had a costly special obligation to meet. Careful records were kept by both recipient and donor and the latter expected to receive exactly the same goods in return. Thus, if a man had donated a 15-pound turkey, he expected to receive a turkey of the same weight in return. If there was any discrepancy in weight the difference might be made up in other goods or, more commonly, in money.

Such exchanges can be considered as examples of reciprocity. However, other members of the community with few social contacts with the host might make unsolicited donations. This most commonly occured when a man embarked on a program of "planting" as many obligations as possible in anticipation of a wedding or ceremonial expenditure of his own. In this case he definitely considered this a form of noninterest-bearing savings and the transaction may be analyzed in formal economic terms. It is further illuminating to find that the Zapotecs had other forms of credit or loans. Individuals facing a shortage of food or with some emergency to meet could borrow food or money from friends or neighbors without paying interest. Such loans usually were paid back in a week or so. In addition, the Zapotecs clearly distinguished gifts from the formal reciprocity just described. Even in the formal context, donors of a carton of beer or soft drinks could specify that they were making a gift and did not expect a formal return. Gifts were also given on other occasions. No formal repayment of gifts was expected, although, as in much of the giving in our own society, some eventual return was expected. However, this return was not normally in kind, nor was an exact equivalent expected. Returns might include friendship, casual assistance, useful information, or support in some social-conflict situation. In many instances the formal reciprocal exchanges involved no continuing social relationships. When a relative stranger entered into a formal reciprocal arrangement, once it was repaid, the relationship could come to an end. Gifts, by contrast, were for the purpose of maintaining a continuing social relationship. Reciprocal exchange, then, is amenable to a strict economic analysis concerned only with the value of the goods exchanged. Gifts, although of significance in strict economic terms, require a far greater consideration of such imponderables as the value of friendship and thus lead us away from consideration of the exchange of material goods into complex political and social concerns.

Simple subsistence economies in which distribution is primarily reciprocative were once considered examples of "primitive communism" because it seemed that all goods in such societies were the property of the group or community. Although it is often true that the hunter's kill or even the farmer's food crop is automatically distributed to a variety of individuals other than the producer and that such distribution is based not so much upon the producer's desires as upon traditional patterns of sharing, it is false to suppose that the producer is denied any profit from such transactions. Indeed, the hunter or

Wheat field was rented by group of partners from wealthy landholder. Harvest must now be divided equally and measurement of grain carefully observed. Gopalpur, South India. (Photo by Alan Beals.)

farmer in a reciprocative system is very much in the position of a producer in a market economy who must pay taxes, social security, interest on loans, and support for his parents or children. The successful hunter, when he "gives away" or shares his kill, is equally paying off outstanding debts and obtaining social security against the time when his hunting is unsuccessful.

In almost all societies the individual has rights of private ownership to the tools and clothing that he himself uses and wears. The practice of sharing hunting territory and holding it in common reflects the fact that access to hunting territories, like access to air, is essential to individual survival in a society that lives by hunting. Where agricultural lands are involved, ownership is often determined by complicated means, and different individuals may have different sorts of rights to the lands or to the produce of the lands. Among the Hopi, lands pertain to the clan, but the individual clan member owns the right to farm an equitable share of the land. In the final analysis this is not too different from a situation in which the bank owns the land, while the farmer owns certain rights, usually not mineral rights, in the use or sale of the land.

Related to such mechanisms as reciprocity, gift giving, and sharing ownership rights is the question of redistribution. In almost any society it is possible for a few individuals to acquire goods or property in excess of their ordinary needs. Such acquisition is likely to lead to the collapse of systems of exchange, unless mechanisms exist for the periodic redistribution of goods and property. In the United States the requirement that the rich pay a higher percentage of their income in taxes than do the poor represents such a redistributive mechanism. In some communities in Latin America, individuals who become wealthier than their fellows are asked to assume special burdens in connection with the carrying out of fiestas or folk religious festivals. These special burdens, known as *cargos,* or *mayordomias,* usually involve expenses connected with the provision of food and drink or entertainment to the community.[6] In many cases the expenses connected with serving a cargo are large enough to wipe out the individual's accumulated wealth and cause him to incur substantial indebtedness. The individual who serves a cargo accumulates such intangible business assets as goodwill and prestige; he also moves closer to a position of power as a community leader. In the United States a politically ambitious individual may buy votes through lavish entertainments or the performance of costly public services. Thus redistributive mechanisms often work in terms of the trading off of wealth for such intangibles as power or prestige. In the case of redistribution, as in the case of gift giving, an analysis based simply in terms of buying and selling objects in a market has limitations because it is difficult to evaluate intangible items that are not bought and sold in a market. There is some controversy concerning the amounts of wealth actually distributed by such redistribution mechanisms. The safest guess is that the rich generally remain rich even after a fraction of their wealth has been distributed to the poor.

[6] For a good recent study see Frank Cancian, *Economics and Prestige in a Maya Community: The Religious Cargo System in Zinacantán* (Stanford: Stanford University Press, 1965).

7. Trading

Most anthropologists use the term *trade* to identify transactions in which goods are directly exchanged for each other or for money. Outside of certain kinds of special circumstances, we may anticipate that individuals normally engage in trade primarily for the purpose of profit. When people exchange apples for oranges, we may presume that they do so because they value the oranges more than they value the apples. Even if this were not literally the case, so long as they are willing to make the exchange it seems reasonable to assume that they perceive some benefit or advantage, some profit, from the transactions. If two individuals are willing to exchange apples and oranges, it must mean that both see themselves as profiting in some way from the exchange. Such a situation, in which there is a demand for a transaction of a cer-

Environmental differences and specialization of labor make it advantageous to develop patterns of trade. Here inland dwelling agriculturalists exchange yams directly for fish caught by coastal fishermen. New Guinea. (Courtesy of the United Nations.)

talm type, constitutes a market A market must exist before goods can be exchanged. Although we may speak of going to the "market" to buy oranges, what we are really doing is going to a marketplace. A market will exist at the marketplace only if oranges are available and only if their price is low enough to create and maintain demand.

Where societies lack any substantial internal division of labor and produce primarily for internal consumption, various forms of reciprocation, sharing, and gift giving are likely to be of greater economic importance than trade. Nevertheless trade, especially among neighboring societies, almost always exists. The Hopi, for example, traditionally engaged in trade with neighboring tribes exchanging farm products and cotton textiles for *piñon* nuts, *mescal*, red ochre, shell beads, and tanned deerskins. The Aruntas of Australia, although dependent upon hunting and gathering, obtained a number of goods by trade, including *pituri*, a narcotic, which was traded from Queensland some 200 miles away.

Trade between societies tends to be stimulated by the fact that certain materials are not equally available throughout a region. Such goods as salt or seashells, which are portable but not widely distributed in nature, may in fact become the object of long-distance trade. Intersocietal trade is also stimulated where the several societies occupying different environments within the same region have markedly different technologies. As a result, even though such societies may have no internal division of labor, each separate society may specialize in some particular form of hunting, gathering, horticulture, or animal husbandry. The Plains Indians, who devoted nearly all of their primary productive efforts to hunting the buffalo, exchanged, where possible, a portion of the meat and hides so obtained with neighboring tribes. Trade between the Pueblo Indians bordering the Plains and the Plains Indians traditionally involved the exchange of meat for farm products and textiles.

A similar trading relationship has been noted between the inland Chukchee of Siberia and the maritime Chukchee, the inland people exchanging reindeer meat and hides for sea mammal meat and hides, differences in taste and in the quality of the hides evidently being sufficient to maintain demand.[7] At the simplest level of analysis, trade between societies is dependent upon environmental and technological differences between them and upon their capacity to produce goods that can be used for exchange. Other needs, for marital and military alliances, or simply for human contact, may also stimulate trade. If there is little to be exchanged and if the items exchanged have no regular demand, trade between societies may be casual and irregular. Even where two societies each produce barely enough for their own consumption, extensive and highly elaborate patterns of trade may develop surrounding the exchange of such staple foods as shellfish and acorns or yams and fish.

---

[7] Vladmir G. Bogoraz, *The Chukchee* (Landmarks in Anthropology). (New York: Johnson Reprint Corp., 1969; reprint of 1909 ed.).

8. The Kula Ring

Where intersocietal trade is complicated and formalized, it generally takes one of three forms: trading partnerships, a system of traveling merchants or peddlers, and organized marketplaces. The *kula* ring involving several different island and coastal populations to the east of New Guinea is an excellent example of the first of these forms. Although the following description is based upon Malinowski's account of the *kula* ring as it existed before 1920, many aspects of the system still persist.[8] Harding has described a similar Melanesian trading system as it existed in the early 1960s.[9]

The Trobriand Islands, occupied by one of the member groups of the *kula*, lie directly north of the eastern tip of New Guinea. The people of these islands were and are productive horticulturalists and fishermen, as well as boat builders and navigators. Trobriand gardeners regularly produced large quantities of food, sufficient to support boat builders, religious practitioners, and other specialists. Many specialized occupations, whether they applied to food production or to manufacturing, were localized on particular islands or in particular communities. The Amphletts, to the south of the Trobriand Islands, are situated between flat and extremely fertile coral islands that lack a variety of important resources and rich, jungle-covered volcanic islands that possess large timber and mineral resources. The principal export of the Amphletts was pottery. Food imports, such as sago, pigs, coconut, taro, and yams, were exchanged for pottery. In addition, from the islands to the north, the Amphletts obtained stone for implements, wooden dishes, lime pots, baskets,

[8] Bronislaw Malinowski, *Argonauts of the Western Pacific* (New York: Dutton, 1961; first published 1922).

[9] Thomas G. Harding, *Voyagers of the Vitiaz Strait, A Study of a New Guiana Trade System* (Seattle: University of Washington Press, 1967).

Long-horned African cattle grazing near the cattle market of Kitega, Ruandi-Urundi. (Courtesy of the United Nations.)

ebony lime pots, and mussel shells. These items were exchanged for pots and other articles obtained locally such as turtle-shell earrings, special nose sticks, red ochre, pummice stone, and obsidian and also for articles imported from the south such as wild banana seeds for necklaces, strips of rattan, bird feathers, belts, bamboo, and barbed spears. Clay for Amphlett pottery was obtained from nearby larger islands as a result of special arrangements between pottery-making communities and those that were sources of clay.

Systems of exchanges similar to those characterizing the Amphletts extended over many miles of open sea and involved many different islands or groups of islands, each inhabited by peoples who spoke different languages and followed different ways of life. Warfare was endemic on many of the islands, and fear of sorcery created a constant and dangerous suspicion of any stranger. Nevertheless constant trade took place. Granted the differences in the resources available to the different islands and groups of islands, such trade may be regarded as having been essential to the maintenance of traditional ways of life characteristic of the region.

The Trobriand and Amphlett Islanders and their many neighbors had a solution to the problem of maintaining trade among hostile peoples. On each group of islands there existed trading communities that were to some extent specialized in the exchange of items produced locally. In each of these trading communities there existed individuals, generally wealthy individuals, who made periodic voyages to visit trading partners located on other island groups. The exchange of visits among trading partners involved elaborate rituals and ceremonies connected with the exchange of symbolic objects. At each meeting between the trading partners, the first partner provided the second with a red shell necklace, which the second partner exchanged for a white shell bracelet. Red shell necklaces moved in a clockwise direction from trading partner to trading partner, while white shell bracelets moved in a counterclockwise direction. Because both bracelets and necklaces had to be passed continuously from partner to partner, within a few years both would pass through the district of their origin as they circulated endlessly within what has been called the *kula ring*. The value of each bracelet and necklace was calculated in terms of the length of time it had been circulating in the ring.

Elaborate ceremony was involved in the building of trading canoes and in the making of visits to trading partners, and it was the ceremonial itself, combined with the awesome perpetuation of the kula ring as bracelets and necklaces mysteriously reappeared after legendary travels, that was considered the most important aspect of the relationships among trading partners. The exchange of boatloads of goods between the two trading partners was considered almost incidental to the objective of exchanging ceremonial objects in a ritually correct manner.

It is possible to interpret the extensive ceremonial attached to the *kula* as comparable to the luxurious expenditure of wealth that has been labeled "conspicuous consumption" in industrialized societies. Granted an abundance of goods and free time, and a comparative freedom from strong selective pressures, we can certainly anticipate the development of elaborate and impractical or uneconomic games, rituals, and displays. An alternative expla-

Livestock market. Villa Bruzzi, Somaliland. (Courtesy of the United Nations.)

nation of the ceremonial attached to the *kula* is that it had the effect of enveloping the *kula* ring with such awesome and mystical importance that the interruption of the trading cycle by warfare or other means became virtually unthinkable. In terms of this interpretation the ceremonial was, in fact, the most important aspect of the *kula* because the survival of ordinary economic trade depended upon it.

The all-important relationship between trading partners also has a practical explanation because a long-term business relationship has a value of its own beyond the immediate profits to be gained by trading one cargo for another. A trader who sailed from the Trobriands to the Amphletts with a particularly rich cargo might experience temporary difficulty in obtaining a similarly rich cargo from the Amphletts. The existence of a permanent and ritually important relationship between trading partners would permit the ironing out of such inequalities during future voyages. When an individual must take great risks to convey goods to a market in which both supply and demand are unstable and unregulated, the existence of a trading partnership tends to lessen the risks by permitting them to be extended over several trips or voyages. A trading partnership is also most useful when the seller is a foreigner who is unfamiliar with local language, culture, and business practice. The Amphlett resident who received a trading partner from the Trobriands had a religious obligation to ensure the success of the partner's journey in every detail. The religious obligation supported the thoroughly rational objective of continuing a business relationship that could not fail to be profitable to both parties so long as the Trobrianders required pots in which to cook their yams and the Amphlettese required yams to cook in their pots.

9. Aztec Marketplaces and Traveling Merchants

Although the *kula* ring is a complex trading device, it is primarily a system of barter involving the exchange of specialized production among different communities and regions. It involved no specialized medium of exchange, and its continuation depended upon firmly established traditional practices rather than upon bargaining or systematic regulation.

The Aztecs of the Valley of Mexico, by contrast, developed a system of trade that involved an established system of pricing and an elaborate mechanism for bargaining and for regulating trade. The Aztecs used mainly stone tools and had no beasts of burden or machines, yet they managed to support an extremely dense and fully urban population in which only a portion of the working force was directly engaged in food production. Others engaged in a number of such specialized crafts and professions as priests, merchants, gov-

Pots and cooking stands for sale in Gopalpur, South India. Payment is made directly in cash or grain. If there were a resident member of the Potter caste, payment for all potting services would be made annually at harvest time. (Photo by Alan Beals)

ernment and court officials, carpenters, fishermen, wood carvers, masons, stone cutters, goldsmiths, silversmiths, jewelers, weavers, tanners, and many others. In brief, the machinery of production was complex rather than simple, characterized by a high degree of specialization of labor and large exchangeable surpluses. Further stimulus to trade was provided by marked differences in natural resources through the close proximity of environments ranging from the tropical lowland to the temperate and even arctic highland.

The Aztec Empire was a loose organization of city-states held in subjection by force of arms by a confederacy of three city-states in the valley. The confederacy in time came to be dominated by one of the members, Tenochtitlán, situated where Mexico City stands today. Each subject city and locality—and these extended at the time of the Conquest in 1521 through most of central Mexico—paid tribute to Tenochtitlán and acknowledged its sovereignty. Throughout the empire there existed, in each city, large marketplaces for the local distribution of goods. These were connected to each other and Tenochtitlán by a system of traveling merchants who had their headquarters in the capital.

At Tenochtitlán local markets were held daily in various portions of the city for the sale of provisions. In addition a great market, located in an outlying suburb, took place every fifth day. To this came artisans, producers, and purchasers from miles around. Each kind of merchandise had its special place in the great market square, an arrangement very similar to that which exists in many Mexican markets today. Great varieties of goods were offered. Bernal Diaz, the historian of the Cortes expedition in the 1520s, notes, among many other things, gold, silver, jewels, feathers, clothing, chocolate, tobacco, tanned hides and rawhides, footwear, slaves, meats of many varieties, vegetables and fruits, salt, bread, honey, tools, pottery, and household furnishings. The market was under the direction of special officers who maintained order, supervised weights and measures, and adjudicated disputes.

Although many of the market transactions were simple exchanges of one kind of goods for another, certain articles, such as cacao beans, squares of cotton cloth, copper ax blades, and quills of gold dust, served as media of exchange. Details about the standards of exchange values are lacking, but there is no doubt that such standards existed, at least in rudimentary form. There was also a system of credit whereby loans were made on good security but without interest. The penalty for failure to pay a debt was severe—the debtor was enslaved until his obligation was discharged.

Linking the market of Tenochtitlán with others within and outside the empire was the function of the traveling merchants. These formed a special, closed guild centered in the capital, with hereditary membership and its own insignia, officials, gods, ceremonies, and system of justice. Merchants traveled together in strongly armed bands, their goods carried by retinues of porters. They moved from one market area to another, distributing local specialties throughout the empire and beyond, and bringing back to the capital goods from outlying regions. The merchant bands functioned as spies, informing the home government of important military and political matters. They were protected by the Aztec government; any injury to a merchant was a cause for war.

In Aztec society, then, we find a developed system of commerce and trade, based on a complex specialization of labor and an efficient system of production. Each Aztec community depended in part upon trade for the fulfillment of its wants; unlike the societies with subsistence economies, local production was not organized to meet all these needs. In short, as increased production made possible the development of specialization, and as specialization provided goods for exchange, there arose a system of distributing goods and services through trade to a widespread group of interlinked communities.

10. The Consumption of Wealth in Unspecialized Societies

In unspecialized societies where virtually all goods are produced through a simple division of labor by age and sex and where distribution involves largely the exchange of goods within the household, patterns for the consumption of goods are as uncomplicated as the patterns of production and distribution. Although some households inevitably produce and consume more than others, there is little incentive for the individual to increase production beyond immediate requirements because such surplus production can ordinarily be exchanged only for the same things produced. Because most articles of production represent immediate requirements for food, clothing, and housing, there is little opportunity for the development of luxury goods or of elaborate patterns of consumption.

Eskimo culture illustrates this situation. As described in Chapter 7, §3, the Eskimo level of production was low and the population was thinly scattered. Each nuclear family had to be largely self-sufficient, for it often traveled alone, rejoining other related families only during seasons of abundance. The man hunted and fished and made the tools and weapons required for those pursuits. The woman cared for the house and children, made and repaired clothing, and gathered plants when they were available. The husband and wife team could support itself and a small number of children. If children came too close together or if people became too old to contribute to the household, children might be left to die and old people might simply wander off to commit voluntary suicide.

To ensure survival of the local group, it was essential that any surplus beyond the immediate needs of the household be shared with other households. Large animals and other foodstuffs to be shared were distributed according to complex rules. Food stored in caches was available to anyone who needed it. Adults made their own tools and maintained ownership as long as they used them. Housing, even if the family constructed their own, was regarded as private property only while in use. Although an individual household might have more or less heating oil or better or worse clothing than another household, survival of the local community upon which all depended required that items of basic necessity be shared whenever possible. A hypothetical renegade who refused to share or to receive gifts and who accumulated property would perish the first time he was unsuccessful at hunting.

Even where existence is not quite so marginal, as among the Bushmen, the convenience of an accumulation of food or other property is counterbalanced by difficulties of preserving it from the elements and by the need to carry it from place to place as the household moves. Where, as among such Australian groups as the Tiwi, the environment permitted production in excess of individual household needs, an older man, who had successfully accumulated a number of hardworking wives, would enjoy considerably enhanced power and prestige. Such big men often played a socially integrative role, organizing religious ceremonies, settling disputes, and carving wooden grave markers required for the sumptuous funerals of other big men. Although the carving of wooden grave markers can be counted as an example of specialized production, Tiwi production was, on the whole, unspecialized. The assets of the Big Man consisted primarily of personal relationships, the most fundamental of these involving the possession of many wives.

11. Wealth and Status Among the Tlingit

With abundant resources, productive technology, dense population, specialization of labor, and most important of all, the development of long-lasting and portable assets, complex patterns of distribution and consumption are likely to develop. In particular, continuing the pattern already noted for the Tiwi and in connection with the Latin American *cargo*, systems of ranking and hierarchy are likely to develop in which individuals may exchange wealth for power and prestige. One of the most notable examples of such a pattern occurred among the traditional American Indian cultures of the Northwest Coast of North America.

The Tlingit, the northernmost of the Northwest Coast groups, occupied a coastal and island region in southeastern Alaska. Traditional Tlingit adaptations to the environment were primarily based upon fishing, especially salmon fishing. The mainland Tlingit also hunted a variety of animals. In season, the Tlingit also collected berries, greens, and tubers. The Tlingit made use of a wide variety of tools and highly specialized fishing and hunting equipment. Canoes and houses were made of planks. Many Tlingit goods were made by specialists or imported from distant places. Large canoes were obtained from the Haida; copper plates were obtained from inland tribes. The Tlingit also produced a variety of artistic and luxury goods.

All, or nearly all, Tlingit belonged to one of two halves or moieties of the tribe and were accordingly described as Wolves or Ravens. All marriages took place between Wolves and Ravens. Each moiety was divided into a number of smaller groupings, matrilineal clans whose membership ideally consisted of persons descended in the female line from the same female ancestor. A Tlingit village traditionally consisted of several different lineages corresponding to different local clans and drawn from both moieties. Each local clan was divided into households, each consisting of a number of different, but related, nuclear families. Clan property traditionally consisted of salmon streams,

Village market, Damodar Valley, India. (Courtesy of the United Nations.)

hunting grounds, berry patches, sealing rocks, house sites, and trading routes into the interior. The house-group owned the house, slaves, large canoes, important tools and food boxes, important weapons, ceremonial gear, and the food produced by community effort. These objects were held in trust by the *yitsati*, or "keeper of the house," usually the senior male resident, for use by household members. Individual property consisted of tools, weapons, small canoes, clothing, decorations, and ceremonial objects.

Within the household, staple foods and necessities were usually produced by cooperative effort under the direction of the yitsati. Individuals might also hunt or fish and cook their private feasts over the communal fire. Economic relationships between households involved elaborate systems of reciprocal exchange in which goods or the services of various specialists were obtained in exchange for gifts. Beyond the goods needed for daily life and either produced in the household or obtained through reciprocal exchange were rights to ceremonial objects, songs, spirits, and ritual privileges. These things, some belonging to the clan and some to the individual household or to the individual, were important factors in establishing the rank of the clan among other clans and of the household within the clan.

Although ownership of symbols of status was inherited, status itself had to be constantly validated through the giving of elaborate feasts and ceremonials. Such feasts and ceremonials reaffirmed property rights in both ordinary and

367

ceremonial objects and served to develop and maintain the status of the household or clan that served as host. At the simplest level, household heads, whenever they possessed surplus food, would invite neighbors and friends to feasts. Such feasts, very much like North American dinner parties, are intended to repay those who had served as hosts at previous feasts. Naturally there was every effort to ensure that the feast was somewhat more sumptuous than previous feasts.

More elaborate rituals in which the household entertained guests were called *potlatches*. Potlatches celebrated within the village, usually in connection with house building, funerals, or life-cycle events, were generally a part of the system of reciprocal gift giving and were carried out in a relatively cooperative and harmonious fashion. Potlatches involving visitors from other communities tended to be much more elaborate and to emphasize competition and self-aggrandizement. Such a between-village potlatch could be given only with the consent of the village and of other houses in the clan, for it involved elaborate planning and assistance from the home village. The potlatch itself was usually a four-day ceremonial involving elaborate feasting, with special foods, ritual, theatrical performances, eating contests, conjuring acts, speeches, and jokes. On the last day the host presided over a huge pile of gifts which he distributed to the visitors in order of their rank. The guests were expected to return these gifts with gifts of equal or greater value at a future potlatch. If such a potlatch was not held within a reasonable amount of time, the visitor's clan suffered a loss of status and might even lose possession of one of its totemic crests (symbols of status) until the debt was paid.

Especially as it concerned relationships between villages, the potlatch served as an index of the personal resources available to the host both in terms of his ability to amass wealth and of his ability to obtain the help of kinsmen and neighbors in performing the potlatch. Where the total humiliation of an enemy was desired, wealth might be literally destroyed by breaking or burning objects of value. The host, of course, was not impoverished even when he engaged in massive destruction of his own wealth, for his enemies had either to admit their inferiority through the transfer of status and privilege to their host or to return the potlatch with interest.

The economic impact of the potlatch upon Northwest Coast society is not entirely understood. The potlatch provided an incentive toward hard work and the accumulation of property that was undoubtedly useful during years of poor harvest. It also ensured that at least some of the wealth accumulated by persons of high status was redistributed to their followers, but we possess no quantitative measures of the amount of wealth redistributed. In terms of the social system, the potlatch provided a means of demonstrating power short of actual warfare. Thus it may have inhibited conflict within the tribe and among neighboring villages. On the other hand, the potlatch between villages was scarcely friendly and did at times serve as a cause of conflict or at least ill will. Although the potlatch is sometimes viewed as an unusual or even perverted social practice, it is little more than a dramatic intensification of patterns of reciprocity, competitive hospitality, and gift giving that occur in almost all known societies.

12. The Consumption of Wealth Among the Aztecs of Mexico

In §9 of this chapter we outlined the system of trade and markets that prevailed among the Aztecs of Mexico in pre-Conquest times. As a result of this system the Aztecs of Tenochtitlán, the dominant city-state, became enormously wealthy, for it was the concentration point of most of the surplus production garnered throughout the empire by the far-flung Aztec network of trade and conquest. We may now complete the picture and learn how the wealth was consumed by the population at Tenochtitlán.

At the time of the Conquest (1521), Aztec society was divided into three major classes: a large middle class composed of members of the *calpulli* landowning units, which may have been clans, a smaller but increasingly important upper class (*tecutin,* or honorary lords), and a small but growing lower class composed of those who had lost *calpulli* membership for various reasons. There was as well a class of slaves who, except for the fact that they had no choice of employers, may for our purposes be included in the lower class.

The *calpulli* were twenty in number. Each owned large tracts of land, which were distributed among its members for as long as they or their descendants put the land to use. *Calpulli* lands could not be alienated, and if abandoned by the grantees, reverted to the *calpulli*. One member of each *calpulli* represented the group in the minor council, a governing unit that declared war, made peace, decided disputes between *calpulli,* and carried on ordinary administrative duties. The *calpulli* were also represented in the great council, which met every eighty days to decide matters of larger importance to the empire and which also elected a new emperor at the death of the incumbent.

It is evident, then, that *calpulli* members were on the whole well off. They had direct access to land, the major source of wealth, which could not be taken from them. They also had a part in government, and some of them at least had opportunity to gain fame and fortune as war leaders, merchants, minor political figures, and craftsmen.

Calpulli members whose services to the state in trade, warfare, politics, or religion were exceptionally meritorious were elevated by the emperor to the status of *tecutin,* or honorary lords. By such elevation they not only retained their rights in the *calpulli,* but they received in addition freedom from all but nominal taxes, a share as individuals in the rich tribute that flowed into Tenochtitlán from conquered city-states, and individual grants of land made from conquered territories at the disposal of the emperor. They were also members of the great council along with *calpulli* representatives and other officials, and so had a share, as appointees of the emperor, in the government of the nation. Though *tecutin* were in theory appointed only for life and so could not pass either their titles or their privately owned lands to their sons, it had become increasingly common, at the time of the Conquest, to appoint sons of *tecutin* to the offices and statuses of their fathers. Thus in actual fact, if not in legal theory, the *tecutin* were on the way to becoming hereditary lords and a small but powerful class of wealthy landowners.

Members of the lower class included, as we have noted, individuals expelled from the *calpulli*, aliens who had never had *calpulli* membership, serfs attached to the lands of the *tecutin*, and slaves — war captives, debtors who failed to meet their obligations, and those who sold themselves into slavery or were so sold by their parents by reason of poverty. These underprivileged folk had of course no access to land, tribute, or public office; they made their living as farm laborers for wealthy *calpulli* members and *tecutin*, or as porters for merchants. There was little hope for them to rise in status, for *calpulli* expulsion was seldom if ever reversed and there was usually no way in which they could acquire land, nor was there the free time to learn and practice a craft or profession.

Among the Aztecs, then, the consumption of goods and services was not uniform throughout the society. The *tecutin* class, together with the emperor and his family, wealthy merchants, and *calpulli* members who held high governmental positions, were marked by conspicuous consumption; they lived in large houses, wore fine clothing, ate the best foods, and provided the best in education and training for their children. Members of the middle class, though secure in economic position by virtue of *calpulli* membership, had less than the upper class. Most numerous, they formed the solid backbone of the empire, furnishing its farmers, craftsmen, merchants, soldiers, minor military leaders, and the bulk of its political officers. Finally, the lower class, lacking property and direct access to the land, consumed least. For their services as unskilled laborers, the freemen among them earned only a bare living and, when this was lost through disability or misfortune, had only themselves or their children to sell in return for subsistence.

13. Some Problems of Consumption

The preceding discussion and the examples given suggest that (1) in all societies, even those that seem to produce primarily for the purpose of subsistence, consumption involves a wider variety of goods than might be thought to be required for mere survival, and (2) there are complex relationships among production, distribution, and consumption. For any group of human beings, from a household to an entire society, it is theoretically possible to divide consumption processes into a number of separate budgets, each fulfilling a different sort of need. Unless, as is rarely the case, the members of a group recognize the same sorts of needs that an outsider might recognize and divide them analytically into the same sort of categories, the division of consumption activities into separate budgets is a fairly arbitrary procedure. Nevertheless, even crude estimates of the consumption budgets of different groups make possible interesting comparisons between them.

The following budgets can usually be recognized:

(1) *The subsistence budget:* the expenses, calculated in terms of goods, labor, and cash, required to provide food and otherwise to meet the ordinary necessities of life.

(2) *The capital budget:* the outlays made in order to acquire the buildings, equipment, human beings, livestock, and other permanent or semipermanent items required for production, distribution, and consumption.

(3) *The maintenance budget:* outlays involved in maintaining or replacing the various items in the capital budget.

(4) *The rental budget:* outlays required in order to maintain the group's rights to property, members, and other assets vis-à-vis other groups. This would include the costs of defense, taxes, rents, and other activities designed to ensure a secure position within society or in relationship to other groups.

(5) *The expansion budget:* outlays required in order to enlarge the group or its activities or in order to improve the position of the group relative to that of other groups.

To this, some would add a sixth budget to cover expenses and outlays which seem to have no practical purpose whatsoever or which, if they have a practical purpose, do not achieve it. In strict terms, such outlays would be considered nonproductive and maladaptive, and it would be assumed that a group having such a budget would encounter difficulties in surviving. While some groups live in relatively unforgiving natural and social environments and so can ill afford error or extravagance, any group must have a margin of survival sufficient to cover some level of inevitable miscalculation and extravagance. At the same time the possibility of classifying some kinds of outlays as maladaptive often leads to the conclusion that outlays for religion, art, recreation, prestige, or even education are unnecessary or impractical. Without entering into the possibility that these things could be placed, at least partly, in the subsistence budget as reflecting various kinds of psychological necessity, we can consider them to fall, under ordinary circumstances, into either the rental budget or the expansion budget.

The rental budget, in particular, covers the requirements that must be met if the group is to survive in its social as well as in its natural environment. For example, the *potlatch*, which might be seen as an extravagant waste of resources, is essential to the maintenance of a Tlingit household's position vis-à-vis other households. Because a *potlatch* validates the right of the household to make use of certain resources, it can be regarded in at least some of its aspects as exactly equivalent to the paying of rent or taxes. Just as taxes support a government which maintains cooperation and cohesion on a tribal or national scale, so the *potlatch* could be interpreted as supporting a more informal system of relationships which maintained cooperation and cohesion among the Tlingit.

The expansion budget includes outlays required to increase political power, prestige, or social standing. The *potlatch* or the financing of *cargos* in Latin America may also be interpreted as contributing to the expansion of social influence. In village communities and small towns, fairs, festivals, athletic contests, and the like may also be interpreted as contributing to the rental and prestige budgets of such communities.

In comparing patterns of production, distribution, and consumption that occur in modern industrialized nations with those of less industrialized societies, it is easy, as Polyani and other substantivists have done, to emphasize the differences between them. In particular, societies with large and highly specialized populations are more likely to possess specialized economic institutions than are small and less specialized societies. The presence of formal market institutions where goods are exchanged for cash may sometimes lead to a belief that the study of economics can be subsumed under and limited to transactions in which goods are exchanged for cash. In the same way, study of other specialized institutions such as churches or schools can lead to the belief that the study of religion or education is merely the study of what happens in church or at school.

When consideration of consumption budgets is undertaken, it is difficult to see any fundamental difference among societies. Subsistence, capital, and maintenance budgets seem logically inevitable in all societies, and there is good reason to believe that the social needs which call forth rental and expansion budgets are also universal. Particular groups, households, communities, and societies will allocate different proportions of their resources to the different budgets. A hunter-gatherer household might be expected to devote a large proportion of its outlays to its subsistence and rental budgets, the last especially where it is economically dependent upon its neighbors in sharing the spoils of the hunt. A peasant farmer household practicing a highly productive form of agriculture could be expected to have a high proportion of its outlays in the rental and expansion budgets because a large part of its production would go to support cities and states. An urban household might well follow a pattern similar to that of a peasant farmer household, except that the outlays would be in cash rather than in grain or produce.

Another sort of difference between societies, then, would have to do with the kinds of outlays involved in the various budgets. If the rental budget is conceived, as it might be by an economist familiar with an industrialized economy, strictly in terms of cash rent paid to a landlord and cash taxes, it might seem that the *potlatch* or the taking of a *cargo* in Latin-American culture belonged in a separate category of useless ritual expenses. As we have attempted to suggest, the problem of applying the principles of economics to nonindustrialized economies is primarily a matter of identifying areas where bargaining and marketlike exchanges take place and of interpreting price and value in areas where cash values are not assigned. Once economic theory has been transformed to meet the new set of circumstances, it will be seen that maximization, rationalization, and supply and demand operate in all human societies.

14. Summary

Economic anthropology is the comparative, cross-cultural study of economic systems. Although economics and economic anthropology place emphasis on the problems involved in the production, distribution, and consumption of material goods, both fields must often deal with nonmaterial goods, and their findings may often be applied to a wide range of economizing behaviors. Among the basic assumptions of economic theory are maximization, rationalization, and supply and demand. Many of the current applications of economic theory in our society are based upon the study of macroeconomic phenomena which can be studied by statistical and quantitative methods. The principles and methods of small-scale or microeconomics are often easier to apply in the small-group or small-community settings often studied by anthropologists. Economic anthropology raises a number of questions concerning the universal validity of economic theory and concerning its applications outside of those sectors of modern industrial economies dominated by cash transactions.

Although some economic anthropologists, labeled "substantivists," have emphasized qualitative differences between modern industrial economies and all others, whereas formal economic theorists have stressed the broad similarities among all societies, the modern view is that such basic principles as maximization, rationalization, and supply and demand operate in all societies, though not necessarily in the same aspects of the economy. Therefore economic theories based upon industrial society need to be modified in order to be made universally applicable, but such modifications will generally increase their value even in the interpretation of the industrial economies from which they were originally derived. Economic anthropology calls attention to phenomena such as gift giving and sharing, whose importance in industrial societies has not always been recognized by economists.

Production is the process of obtaining goods from the natural environment. Such utilization of the environment is a result of interaction between the character of the resources available and the capacity of each group to perceive their existence and develop technologies for utilizing them. Although production may be interpreted in terms of the satisfaction of needs, the line between needs that are necessary to survival and needs that are socially created is difficult to draw. Even groups such as the Sirionó, who believed themselves to be living at the margin of survival, seem to make a variety of economic decisions in which needs for food, shelter, and rest are weighed against such less obviously practical needs as drinking, singing, and dancing.

Almost all societies possess a more or less natural division of labor in terms of age and sex. Although such division of labor is not strictly rational because criteria of age and sex do not always reflect actual abilities to perform tasks, it may have the function of creating interdependence between individuals which serves to strengthen family ties. Any division of labor is economically valuable to the extent that all individuals need not learn to perform all tasks. True division of labor, or specialization, occurs when individuals perform different economic tasks, usually on a full-time basis. It is usually found where populations are relatively dense, technologies relatively complex, and the individual specialist can produce more than he consumes. Because some tasks can be best performed by a single individual, whereas other tasks may require the coordinated efforts of a number of individuals, significant differences between societies obtain in terms of the organization of productive activities. Buffalo hunting requires a more complicated organization of production than does the stalking of game, as practiced by the Eskimo. The organization of production may have important consequences for the organization of society and the fate of the individual.

Where everybody produces the same things, there is little incentive toward the development of complex economic institutions. Where such circumstances exist, the common tendency is the development of patterns of sharing or reciprocity. Although such patterns are the dominant form of distribution in many hunting and gathering societies, they also exist among the Zapotec Indians, who participate in a complex market economy, and in our own society. Almost all societies also possess redistributive mechanisms by means of which accumulations of wealth are redistributed, often in exchange for such intangibles as power or prestige. The progressive income tax in the United States or the taking of a *cargo* in Latin-American village communities function, at least in part, as such redistributive mechanisms.

Trade occurs when goods are directly exchanged or exchanged for money for the purpose of profit. Where there is a demand for such a transaction or exchange, a market is said to exist. Although trade is characteristic of most societies, it may be less important than various reciprocative arrangements in societies that lack substantial internal division of labor or the capacity to produce in excess of immediate consumption needs. Trade between societies is often stimulated by environmental circumstances in which materials available to one group are unavailable to another. The *kula* ring exemplifies a complex pattern of trade between societies that is strengthened and maintained by ceremonial features and the institution of trading partnerships. The development of marketplaces and media of exchange is characteristic of urban societies having a dense population and a complex specialization of labor, as illustrated by the case of the Aztecs.

In the absence of dense populations or specialization of labor, the production of goods in excess of household needs is often neither practical nor rewarding because everyone enjoys virtually equal access to goods required for basic consumption. Where resources are abundant and technology productive, complex patterns of distribution and consumption are likely to emerge. Such specialized fishermen as the Tlingit were able to develop an elaborate system of distribution and consumption typified by the *potlatch*. Among the Aztecs of Mexico, patterns of consumption were governed, in part, by the development of a system of social class. One way of understanding patterns of consumption and making comparisons between them is in terms of the allocation of consumption among budgets for subsistence, capital, maintenance, rental, and expansion. Although this implies that all consumption is in pursuit of practical ends, some allowance must be made for maladaptive or impractical consumption caused by extravagance or miscalculation. Many phenomena, like the *potlatch* or the taking of a *cargo*, which seem maladaptive at first glance, may turn out to be far less extravagant then they appear. The line between practical and impractical economic expenses is often hard to draw. Extravagance, miscalculation, and impracticality occur wherever there are human beings, but maximization, rationalization, and supply and demand can be seen to operate most of the time in all human societies.

Collateral Reading

Beals, Ralph L. *The Peasant Marketing System of Oaxaca, Mexico.* Berkeley: University of California Press, 1975. One of few existing studies of a regional marketing system.

Belshaw, Michael. *A Village Economy: Land and People of Anecorio.* New York and London: Columbia University Press, 1967. A good study of a Tarascan Indian village by an economist.

Bernard, H. Russell, and Pertti J. Pelto. *Technology and Social Change.* New York: Macmillan Publishing Co., Inc., 1972. Well-described recent examples of the influence of new technology.

Boserup, Esther. *Woman's Role in Economic Development.* London: Athlone, 1970. The importance of women is often neglected in economic studies.

Dalton, George (ed.). *Tribal and Peasant Economies, Readings in Economic Anthropology.* American Museum source books in anthropology. Garden City, N.Y.: The Natural History Press, 1967. A collection of important articles.

Dalton, George (ed.). *Studies in Economic Anthropology,* Anthropological Studies, 7. Washington, D.C.: American Anthropological Association, 1972. Some more good articles.

Firth, Raymond. *Malay Fisherman: Their Peasant Economy.* London: Routledge & Kegan Paul Ltd, 1939. A classic study.

Firth, Raymond. *Themes in Economic Anthropology.* London: Tavistock Publications, 1967. British points of view.

Harding, Thomas G. *Voyagers of the Vitiaz Strait.* Seattle: University of Washington Press, 1967. Another view of Melanesian trading patterns.

Herskovits, Melville J. *Economic Anthropology.* New York: Alfred A. Knopf, Inc., 1952. The pioneering textbook in the field.

LeClair, Edward E., Jr., and Harold K. Schneider. *Economic Anthropology.* New York: Holt, Rinehart and Winston, Inc., 1968. A good recent textbook.

Plattner, Stuart (ed.). *Formal Methods in Economic Anthropology.* Washington, D.C.: American Anthropological Association, 1975. New ways of studying economic phenomena.

Polanyi, Karl. *Primitive, Archaic and Modern Economies.* (Essays edited by George Dalton.) Garden City, N.Y.: Doubleday & Company, Inc., 1963. Presents the substantivist point of view.

Polanyi, Karl, D. M. Arensberg, and H. W. Pearson (eds.). *Trade and Market in Early Empires.* New York: The Free Press, 1957. Essays on the transition to market-dominated economies.

Pospisil, Leonard. *Kapauku Paupan Economy.* New Haven: Yale University, Department of Anthropology. (Yale University Publications in Anthropology No. 67, 1963). Excellent field study controverting the substantivist approach.

Rappaport, Roy A. *Pigs for the Ancestors.* New Haven: Yale University Press, 1968. Attempted ecological explanation of complex economic and social relationships.

Salisbury, R. F. *From Stone to Steel: Economic Consequences of a Technological Change in New Guinea.* New York: Cambridge University Press for Melbourne University Press, 1963. A sophisticated study of economic change.

Vayda, Andrew P. (ed.). *Environment and Cultural Behavior.* Garden City, N.Y.: The Natural History Press, 1969. Essays concerning ecological relationships.

Ethnographic References

Aztec: Coon, 1948, Chapter 15; Murdock, 1935, Chapter XIII; Thompson, 1933; Vaillant, 1941.

Baganda: Murdock, 1936, Chapter XVIII; Roscoe, 1911.

Eskimo: Birket-Smith, 1936; Coon, 1948, Chapter 4; Murdock, 1935, Chapter XII; Rasmussen, 1908, 1931.

Hopi: Eggan, 1950, Chapters II, III; Murdock, 1935, Chapter XII; Titiev, 1944.

Mixe: Beals, 1945.

Oaxaca: Beals, 1975.

Plains Indian (Crow): Lowie, 1935.

South India: Beals, 1962.

Suye Mura, Japan: Embree, 1939.

Tiwi: Hart and Pilling, 1960.

Tlingit: Oberg, 1973.

11/Marriage

1. Household Formation

The last four chapters dealt with the various means by which human beings adapt to their environments and engage in the production, distribution, and consumption of material goods. All of these worldly activities involve the organization of human beings into various kinds of groups. Even where, as in the case of the Eskimo seal hunter, people carry on activities in solitude, they rely upon other human beings for knowledge about how the activity is to be carried out, for the supply of items of equipment that they cannot obtain or manufacture by themselves, and for the provision of food and other necessities when they cannot obtain them by themselves. Because no human being can ordinarily survive without the help of other human beings, the study of human adaptation involves an understanding of the complex relationships among human beings as well as an understanding of ecological and economic relationships interpreted in materialistic terms. Relationships among human beings and the means by which they are organized and regulated constitute the field of *social organization*.

As we have seen in the previous chapters, the most widespread form of social organization among human beings involves the existence of households related to each other in various ways to form bands, neighborhoods, or communities. Because the form of the household varies

377

greatly from place to place and may differ greatly from the kind of familial organization that we generally think of when we think of households, it may be an overgeneralization to consider the family household biologically necessary or otherwise fundamental to all human society. Nevertheless the household is the most common form of human organization. Today it exists in every part of the world, and there is reason to believe that it existed as soon as or even before human beings became fully human.

The most common form of human household is the nuclear family household. Ideally such a household consists of a married couple and their children. Simpler forms of the household—single-person households, single-parent and child households, or childless households—also exist in most societies, but only the mother–child household is likely to be preferred or frequent. The formation of a nuclear family household involves two kinds of relationship: descent and marriage. Descent is the relationship between parent and child; mar-

Carrying the bride across an obstacle. Part of a Philippine Negrito wedding ceremony. (Courtesy of the American Museum of Natural History.)

riage is the relationship between husband and wife. Although some primates appear to recognize descent at least from the female parent and some birds and other animals engage in practices resembling marriage, the combination of the principles of descent and marriage in the formation of a long-lasting cooperative organization appears to be unique to human beings. The existence of, and apparent necessity for, cooperation between households also seems to be a uniquely human trait. As noted in previous chapters, the prolonged helplessness of the human infant must very early have necessitated the development of something like a household organization, and so it can be argued that the household, together with the band or troop organization characteristic of the primates, must have existed very early in human evolution.

Although descent may be fictitious, as in the case of adopted children, the parent–child relationship among human beings is generally sufficiently close to the biological relationship of descent as to require little discussion. In the case of marriage the situation is quite different, for human marriage, although it generally involves sexual relationships between the spouses, is primarily a social and cultural relationship. If marriage is to be understood at all, it must be sharply distinguished from sexual intercourse. Sexual unions are likely to be transitory or casual, and they ordinarily impose no familial obligations or responsibilities upon the participants. Nearly all societies provide for various kinds of sexual encounters, and in many societies it is considered either inevitable or desirable that young adults engage in a variety of casual and transitory affairs before undertaking the serious business of marriage.

Marriage, which usually involves some kind of formal ritual or ceremony before it is considered to exist, represents a union that is recognized and publicly approved by the other members of society. Married persons are expected to cooperate with each other and sometimes with other relatives in the maintenance of a household. The couple is also expected to produce children, the production of children often being necessary to the validation of a marriage. When children do come, the married couple usually acknowledge them as their own and provide for their care and rearing. Although most cultures provide means for the dissolution of marriage, it is ordinarily expected that those who marry intend the union to be lifelong and not just a transitory affair to be broken off at the whim of one or the other partner. Marriage is ordinarily a set of cultural patterns that sanction parenthood and provide a stable background for the care and rearing of children. It is the major cultural mechanism involved in the formation of the household, the continuation of the family, and the maintenance of relationships based upon kinship.

The distinction between marriage and sexual encounters is strongly marked among the Samoans of Polynesia.[1] In this society young men and women were traditionally expected to engage in a number of sexual encounters before marriage, none of which need necessarily result in marriage. These affairs took place clandestinely; couples did not live together openly but

---

[1] Lowell D. Holmes, *Samoan Village* (New York: Holt, Rinehart and Winston, 1974); George P. Murdock, *Our Primitive Contemporaries* (New York: Macmillan, Inc., 1935); G. Turner, *Samoa* (London: Macmillan and Co., Ltd., 1884).

met at night on the beach or in palm groves. If a girl was afraid to venture out at night, her sweetheart might even slip into her house. Both boys and girls ordinarily participated in many such affairs, and it was not unusual for an individual to carry on several at one time. The Samoans did not share our romantic ideal that love is lifelong or is necessarily centered upon one particular person.

Eventually, however, the Samoan youth was expected to marry and settle down to the serious business of establishing a family. When a young man made this decision, he initiated formal and public courtship of the girl of his choice. With his *soa,* or go-between, he called upon her, bringing with him a ceremonial gift of food for her family. If they approved the marriage, the gift was accepted and the young man and his *soa* were invited to dine and spend the evening. While the young man sat watching, his *soa* paid elaborate court to the young girl, urging her to accept the suitor as her husband. Several such calls might be necessary, for Samoan girls were reluctant to give up the pleasant and easy life of an unmarried girl for the serious responsibilities and hard work of marriage. Once the suitor was accepted, he went to live with his bride-to-be, although the marriage ceremony might not take place until all the necessary arrangements were made some months later.

An even more explicit approval of premarital intercourse occurred among the Masai, a people of Kenya, in East Africa.[2] Masai young men, after a series of ceremonies marking the end of boyhood, traditionally left their native village and went to live in a nearby warriors' encampment, or kraal. Here they learned the arts of war from older men and took part in occasional raids for cattle and other booty. Ordinarily a Masai male spent from ten to fifteen years as a warrior, during which he accumulated property in cattle, turned over to his father for safekeeping.

Masai warriors were not permitted to marry, but this did not mean that they remained celibate during their years in the warriors' kraal. Young unmarried girls also lived in the kraal, to serve as the warriors' sweethearts and sexual partners, a relationship openly maintained and approved in Masai society. As with the Samoans, these arrangements were explicitly transitory and solely for purposes of sexual gratification; the men and girls involved were not considered married. Living with the warriors placed no stigma on the girl, for every normal Masai girl had this experience in her youth. Should a girl become pregnant, she returned to the village to be married. Having a child out of wedlock stigmatized neither the girl nor the child. Indeed, it aided a girl in securing a husband, for the Masai welcomed children and regarded barrenness as a principal cause for divorce.

When a man completed his service as a warrior, he returned to the village, took charge of the property he had accumulated, and married. He had now acquired the status of a houschold head and assumed the burdens and responsibilities of establishing a family.

---

[2] C. Daryll Forde, *Habitat, Society and Economy* (New York: Dutton, 1950); A. C. Hollis, *The Masai* (Oxford: The Clarendon Press, 1905).

It is evident from these examples, which may be multiplied endlessly, that the human need for sexual gratification, though served by marriage, is in no sense wholly responsible for it. Marriage in every human society that we know is a complex cultural phenomenon, in which the purely biological function of sex plays but a small role in comparison to such sociological functions as the care of children, the maintenance of the household, and other culturally imposed needs of the family.

2. Selecting a Spouse: Marriage Regulations

Because marriage is a lasting relationship, usually considered to be of great social importance, human societies provide guidelines and rules concerning the persons with whom marriage, and very often sexual intercourse as well, can be consummated. Although these guidelines and regulations take quite different forms in different places, almost all such rules, directly or indirectly, require that children marry outside the nuclear family. Marriage between mother and son, father and daughter, or brother and sister is universally forbidden with the exception of a few societies, such as those of Ancient Egypt and the traditional Marquesas, where brother-sister marriages were permitted among the royalty and perhaps among others as well. Very often marriage and sexual intercourse are also forbidden, often by the same rules, with a variety of other relatives both close and distant.

Although regulations prohibiting marriage within the nuclear family household are universal, they are not always of the same form. In our own society father-daughter marriage is usually forbidden by a law specifically mentioning the father-daughter relationship. In other societies it may be forbidden by a rule stating that no woman can marry within a descent group consisting of those descended in the male line from the same male ancestor. It has been argued that such a rule is merely an extension of nuclear family exogamy (out-marriage) to a set of analogous relatives. Certainly, if the rule forbidding marriage between father and daughter, for example, is merely an accidental consequence of a broader rule, it is an accident that has been repeated in every known society.

The universality of nuclear family exogamy has led to considerable speculation about possible biological origins. An early theory held that a rule prohibiting both sex and marriage with close relatives, although it is rare among other species, was necessary in order to prevent the expression of such lethal recessive genes as those for sickle-cell anemia or hemophilia. Because a father and daughter or a brother and sister would have identical genes on 50 percent of their chromosomes, the chances of an encounter between two recessive genes would be greatly increased if they produced offspring. Early human beings, taking note of the increased mortality of the offspring of incestuous marriages, must have, it was argued, discovered that such marriages were biologically dangerous. Plausible as this argument seems, an equally plausible argument can be made in the opposite direction. Frequent marriage between close relatives would expose lethal recessive genes to the forces of natural selection causing them to be quickly eliminated from the population. In short, if human beings once practiced incest on a regular basis, there would have been few lethal or crippling recessive genes in the gene pool, and it would have been impossible to make the observation that incestuous marriages or sexual relationships led to a higher mortality.

There is, of course, an important distinction between rules governing sexual relationships, technically called incest rules, and rules governing marital relationships, technically called rules of exogamy and endogamy (out-marriage and in-marriage). If marriage rules are regarded as a consequence of rules governing sexual relationships, then the argument that both incest rules and marriage rules have some sort of biological importance is strengthened. If, however, incest rules are regarded as a reflex of marriage rules and sex is forbidden because marriage is forbidden, then it is more difficult to make a biological argument. Because both sex and marriage are almost always forbidden within the nuclear family, it is difficult to imagine which sort of rule came first. Outside the nuclear family, rules governing marriage and sex are identical in some cases, quite different in others. The commonest case is probably the one in which the individual is permitted to establish sexual relationships with many more kinds of persons than can be married. Rules compelling marriage outside the nuclear family are, of course, much easier to enforce and much more consistently enforced than are rules against incest. If a decision must be made, then, marriage rules would seem to be both more important and more enforceable than rules governing sexual encounters. If such rules were based primarily upon a biologically based aversion or upon a recognition of biological peril, then it would be expected that rules governing sexual relationships would receive much more emphasis than rules governing marriage.

Another problem involved in relating nuclear family exogamy to recognition of some sort of biological peril lies in the fact that while all societies forbid marriage and usually sex between individuals who share 50 percent of their genes, quite the reverse often occurs in connection with individuals who share 25 percent of their genes. Among the Kariera of western Australia, each male has four sets of kinsmen within his own generation. These sets are (1) his brothers, his father's brother's sons, and his mother's sister's sons, (2) his sisters, his father's brother's daughters, and his mother's sister's daughters, (3) his father's sister's sons and his mother's brother's sons, and (4) his father's sister's daughters and his mother's brother's daughters. Each of these classes is extended to include a wide range of other individuals, so that all human beings of the same generation can be divided into four distinct groups.

The rules of Kariera marriage are now obvious. A man cannot marry his brother, his sister, or his father's sister's son or anyone belonging to the same marriage class that they belong to. The ideal marriage, then, is between a man and his father's sister's daughter or his mother's brother's daughter. This form of marriage, usually called cross-cousin marriage, tends to involve a stated preference for marriage between first cousins whose parents are cross-siblings (brother and sister) rather than parallel siblings (sisters or brothers). It is im-

Bride being escorted to groom's house for wedding ceremony. The main wedding ceremony will be held later at the bride's house. Parcels contain gifts of food. Gurun-Batusangkar, West Sumatra, Indonesia. (Kindness of Lynn Thomas.)

possible to explain Kariera marriage rules in terms of biological closeness because cross-cousins and parallel cousins (whose parents are parallel siblings) are both first cousins. The marriage rules, in fact, because they render half of all females of marriageable age unmarriageable, force the marriage of close relatives even when distant relatives are available but in the wrong category.

It is not just that human beings are indecisive about whether marriage to close relatives or distant relatives, or both, should be forbidden or encouraged. The principles upon which such rules rest vary greatly from society to society. Australian aborigines, South Indians, and many other peoples divide the world into classes of people you can marry and classes of people you can't marry. The Navajo are one of many peoples who trace descent in the male line in such a way as to form a small number of clans, each of which is exogamous (the individual must marry outside the clan). In North India the individual must usually marry endogamously within his caste, but exogamously outside his village, outside a rather wide circle of people considered close relatives of his father or his mother, and outside his clan. Very often, he must also receive his bride from the west and send his daughter in marriage to the east.

The existence of this kind of variation in marriage regulations in general suggests that although biological or universal psychological factors may lurk somewhere in the background as one of several possible sources of such regulations, biological factors alone are not adequate to explain them. Incest and marriage rules pertaining to the nuclear family, despite their differences in form, seem more likely to have some sort of universal biological or psychological basis because they too are virtually universal. Several authors have suggested that the incest rule finds its basis in a kind of automatic aversion to marriage and sex with persons who are psychologically close for other reasons. As an example, individuals raised together on Israeli collective farms seem to prefer to marry strangers.[3] Arthur Wolf has noted a similar tendency among the Chinese of Formosa.[4] On the other hand, marriage to the girl next door is an ideal in the United States, and individuals in South India have been observed to go to great lengths in order to marry a first cousin or sister's daughter raised in the same village. Furthermore, although there are difficulties in collecting accurate statistics on the frequency of sexual relationships within the nuclear family household, such incest occurs frequently enough to rule out the existence of any universal aversion to close relatives.

Although the literature contains almost endless discussion of incest rules and of their possible relationships to rules governing marriage, there is still very little agreement on their origins. This may well be because incest rules forbidding sexual relationships within the nuclear family are far less universal

[3] Yonina Talmon, "Mate Selection in Collective Settlements," *American Sociological Review*, **29**:491–508 (1964).

[4] Arthur P. Wolf, "Childhood Association, Sexual Attraction, and the Incest Taboo: A Chinese Case," *American Anthropologist*, **68**:883–897 (1966).

than they are supposed to be. Rules governing marriage, on the other hand, are clearly universal and there are several good reasons why they should almost universally insist upon marriage outside the nuclear family and household.

3. Functions and Effects of Marriage Rules

In addition to whatever universal biological or psychological factors may contribute to the development of marriage rules, there are a number of social and cultural factors that seem important. These factors are of two kinds: those that apply to relationships within the family and those that apply to relationships outside the family. Within the family and especially within the household, such roles as parent, child, husband, wife, brother, sister tend to be sharply defined and long enduring. Some authors have wondered, then, if a sudden change in role from son to husband, from daughter to wife, or from brother and sister to husband and wife might not have unpleasant side effects. It seems likely that a son-husband or daughter-wife would have great difficulty in attaining emotional maturity and would certainly have problems in dealing with other members of the household. In addition to a whole host of possibly unpleasant psychological consequences, there would also be problems concerning the inheritance of property or centered about the early death of a father-husband or a mother-wife. Many of these problems do occur in societies where there are sharp age discrepancies between husband and wife or where male or female offspring are expected to continue living in the parental household after their marriage. Presumably mother-in-law problems would be intensified if one's mother-in-law were also one's wife or mother.

Although it appears evident that the emotional and social problems involved in marriage within the household would unbearably intensify the problems that can be observed to exist in almost any nuclear family household, the general thrust of anthropological opinion has been to emphasize the functions and effects of marriage outside the household. One good reason for this is that we are unlikely ever to find answers to questions concerning what might happen if marriage within the household were permitted. The necessity of marrying outside the household requires the existence of other households sufficiently friendly to cooperate to the extent of participating in a marital relationship. Granted the existence of the household and of rules forbidding marriage within it at an early stage of human evolution, then there must have existed some kind of community of households engaged in the exchange of offspring. Other rules requiring marriage outside the local group of cooperating households, which may also have existed quite early in human evolution, would imply the cooperative exchange of marital partners among a number of local groups. Although exchanges, whether of trade goods, marital partners, or ideas, do not always generate affection and may sometimes generate discord and hostility between the two parties to the exchange, the necessity for an exchange of marital partners requires that some sort of relationship must be maintained between any one household and several others.

Wedding in Gopalpur, South India. Groom wears elaborate headdress and carries knife. Eight-year-old bride is accompanied by her mother. Another ceremony and consummation of the marriage will take place after bride reaches puberty. (Photo by Alan Beals.)

In brief, the primary effect of marriage regulations is the formation of households and cooperating groups of households. The differing forms of marriage regulations in different societies can be explained in terms of the differing kinds of groupings that the members of each particular society attempt to achieve either as a means of adapting to external circumstances or as a means of maintaining an organization that is simply traditional. The Chiricahua Apaches, who forbid sexual intercourse and marriage with any consanguineous, or "blood," relatives, can be used to illustrate these points.

Among the Chiricahua as described in 1937 and 1941,[5] the individual traditionally began his life in the wickiup of a nuclear family, tended as an in-

---

[5] Morris E. Opler, "An Outline of Chiricahua Apache Social Organization," in *Social Anthropology of North American Tribes,* ed. Fred Eggan. (Chicago: University of Chicago Press, 1937), pp. 173–242.

faนt by his parents and older siblings, and sometimes by his maternal grand-parents and mother's sisters as well. As soon as he was able to move about for himself, his social world enlarged to include other children in the encampment of the joint family. These were the children of his mother's sisters and their husbands. The encampment might also have included older relatives of his mother such as his mother's mother and her husband or her unmarried and visiting brothers. Less often, he would have contact with the joint family of his father where he might most often encounter his father's sisters and their children.

Within the encampment, boys and girls were taught to play and amuse themselves separately. This separation became more rigid as they grew older. Gradually they learned to behave with restraint and formality toward siblings and cousins of the opposite sex, whether they lived in the same encampment or elsewhere. This attitude was encouraged by differences in training and occupation. Boys were trained to hunt and make weapons, while girls worked with their mothers and other female relatives.

At or soon after their first menstruation, girls underwent a complex four-day ceremony designed to prepare them ritually for womanhood and to symbolize their readiness for marriage. These ceremonies were attended by all the joint families of the local group and sometimes involved visitors from other local groups within the band. Social dances took place at the same time and offered many opportunities for unmarried youths to meet, even though under the watchful eyes of the girls' elderly female chaperons.

Boys marked their advance to manhood by participating as novices in four successive raiding parties. Under the supervision and protection of older and experienced warriors, they learned the techniques of raiding and warfare. During these trips the novices carefully observed certain ritual procedures, spoke only when addressed and even then answered only in a special war-path language, and performed all the petty and menial tasks incident to camping and traveling away from home. When the four raids were done, the boys, if they had proved their ability, were welcomed as men, free to marry and assume all the responsibilities of adult status.

As a result of their training in the joint family, capped by the puberty rites, youths of both sexes were directed to seek their wives and husbands outside the bonds of consanguine kinship. They had learned, under threat of severe penalties, to avoid all siblings and cousins of the opposite sex, or to treat them, when contact was inevitable, with extreme formality and respect. But the joint family and the local group also provided, on numerous social occasions, opportunities to meet nonrelatives of the opposite sex, and older members of the joint family not infrequently arranged appropriate marriages for their offspring.

Such marriages linked joint families, as well as the bride and groom, in affinal ties not easily dissolved. The importance of these is evident when we remember that the Chiricahua local group was not a highly organized body held together by a tight political apparatus. It was, rather, a more or less unstable confederation of joint families, united by mutual compatibility and a common respect for an outstandingly able and experienced leader. When the joint families of such a group were also united by intermarriage, the unity and permanence of the local group were further ensured. And because the local group was a principal agency of offense and defense in a society that spent much of its time in raiding and warfare, its preservation was important to the security of all its constituent families.

To summarize this section, it seems clear that incest regulations function in at least two important ways: (1) to maintain a stable and cooperative family unit for the care and training of children, and often for economic purposes as well, and (2) to ensure that the sexual impulses of men and women are directed to the end of establishing essential relations between families. Although these social functions of incest regulations may not throw much light on their origins, they do illuminate their relation, as patterns, to the rest of the culture.

4. Preferential Marriage

The data presented in the preceding section suggest that marriage involves not only a contract between individuals but also one between families. Marriages are frequently so arranged, by means of marriage rules, as to cement alliances between families and larger exogamic units and so provide a wider base for intrasocietal cooperation than would otherwise be possible.

Even in our own society marriage may still involve the family as much as the individual. Many a man or woman has discovered, before or after marriage, that he or she has acquired not only a spouse but also a number of new relatives whose claims are difficult, it not impossible to ignore. Moreover, families often contrive to have their offspring marry individuals similar to themselves in religious faith, racial or ethnic group membership, and socioeconomic status. In a broad sense, all such limitations on the choice of a spouse may be defined as preferential marriage—the preference or even requirement that a spouse be found among individuals of a certain defined subgroup within the society.

In other societies, and especially in those very largely governed by kinship usages, preferential marriage may be more precisely defined and more rigidly enforced. As noted in §2 of this chapter, the Australian Karieras required that an individual marry his cross-cousin, near or remote; the spouse may come from no other group. This practice may sometimes result in two patrilocal joint families more or less regularly exchanging marriageable women, with the daughters of one family marrying the sons of another, and vice versa.

An arrangement of this sort has certain obvious advantages, both to the stability of the family itself and to the maintenance of interfamilial cooperation. The women coming into the family at marriage are known to it as relatives of the women already there; their coming has been anticipated and they have already begun to adjust to their future in-laws. Accordingly, when these women actually take up residence with their spouses, there is little disturbance of intrafamilial harmony and cooperation. Similarly, two large families, united by many affinal ties and the promise of more to come, have increasingly more in common and every incentive to cooperative effort.

Another but rarer form of preferential marriage is found in parallel-cousin marriage, illustrated by the camel nomads (the Bedouins) of northern Arabia as described in 1948 and 1950. The Bedouins lived in a desert environment, moving from place to place in search of water and pasturage for their camels, their most important means of livelihood. To care for their camels and to protect them against the raids of enemy groups, the Bedouin bands required a strong force of men, united in close bonds of kinship, for kinship usages were the principal means of social control. It was therefore desirable that a young male not leave the band at marriage but remain in it and either bring his bride to his paternal band or find one within the band. Marriage outside the band would, however, divide the male's loyalties between the band of his birth and that of his bride, a contingency hardly in keeping with the extreme hostility between bands as a result of an intense competition for the little water and pasturage available. Bedouin bands tended, therefore, to be endogamous — that is, marriages took place within the band — and the preferred marriage was with the father's brother's daughter, a parallel cousin, born and reared in the same band. By this means young males not only were kept in the band but also had their relation to the father's brothers, already a strong one, further reinforced by the affinal tie.

Preferential marriage, then, may be viewed as a further technique of reinforcing social solidarity and broadening the cooperative base within a society. It takes on particular importance in societies governed largely by kinship usages, in societies in which cooperation between distinct familial groupings is essential to survival. In the history of our own society, as it has moved from an earlier preindustrial stage with emphasis on familial ties and kinship usages to the modern industrial civilization in which the family is small and kinship usages play but a small role in social control, preferential marriage — and indeed the whole role of the family in respect to marriage — has decreased in importance. In the earlier period the family played a large role in selecting the spouses of its offspring, even to the point of arranging preferred marriages for their children without consulting them or taking their feelings into account. Today, though the family undoubtedly plays some role in the marriages of its young, arranged marriages are rare.

5. Levirate and Sororate

In most societies it is probable that ideal patterns of culture hold marriage to be a more or less permanent tie, one not to be dissolved easily at the whim of either partner. More than this, marriages, once begun, establish enduring ties between families in many societies — ties that outlive even the principals to the marriage. The expression of this fact in cultural terms is found in the *levirate* and *sororate,* two widespread patterns of culture. According to the levirate a man is required to marry the wife or (in a polygynous society) the wives of his deceased brother. The sororate, in turn, requires that a widower ordinarily accept an unmarried sister as successor to his deceased wife. The precise manner in which these customs operate to maintain once-established marital relations between families is illustrated by the Chiricahua Apaches, who practice both the levirate and the sororate.

Among the Chiricahuas, as we have noted, the functioning social and economic unit was the large family with matrilocal residence. Young men became members of their wives' families, taking the place, in an economic sense, of the sons who left the family upon marriage. Should these sons-in-law turn out to be economic assets to the family, it is obvious that they must be encouraged to stay and, indeed, their contract to marry assumes that they will stay.

Marriage ceremony in village of Teteman, British Togoland. (Courtesy of the United Nations.)

To effect this permanence of residence was the function of the levirate and the sororate. If a man's wife died while he was still of an age to marry again, he could not do so until his deceased wife's sisters (or those of her cousins resident in the family) had had the opportunity to claim him as husband. Should one of them make such a claim, he was required to marry her, and such marriage would take place very soon after his wife's death. Only if no eligible women existed, or if those eligible did not press their claim, could the widower seek a spouse outside his deceased wife's family. Even then, he could not properly marry until the deceased wife's family had given him permission to do so, and such permission could not be given until the appropriate period of mourning — a year or more — had passed. It should be noted too that a widower who was not claimed by members of his deceased wife's family eligible to do so might find it quite difficult to find another spouse outside. It was more or less assumed, in such cases, that the widower remained unclaimed because he was more a liability than an asset to his deceased wife's family. Accordingly, few if any other families could be found who were willing to take him in.

When a woman's husband died while she was still marriageable, she was under the same obligation to her deceased husband's brothers and male cousins, provided, of course, these were unmarried. Should one of these ask to marry her, and so take the place of her deceased husband in the economic life of her family, she had no recourse but to accept. Of course, if none of those eligible to claim her did so for a period of a year or more, she was permitted to take another husband, if one offered himself.

The import of these patterns of conduct is clear. Marriage, in the view of the Chiricahuas, established a bond between families that was not dissolved by the death of either man or wife. The wife's family, even after her death, retained an indissoluble claim on her husband that, should they choose to exercise it, could not be declined by him or by his family. The family of a deceased married man held a similar claim over his wife, in the sense that they could, at their discretion, provide her with a husband she was bound to accept. In these instances, it will be noted that the family interest in a marriage of one of their number took considerable precedence over that of the individual concerned.

6. Monogamy and Polygamy

Anthropologists commonly distinguish three forms of marriage: monogamy, the marriage of one man to one woman; polygyny, the marriage of one man to two or more women; and polyandry, the marriage of one women to two or more men. Polygyny and polyandry are often linked under the single term *polygamy*, a marriage of one individual to two or more spouses. Very rarely, a fourth marriage form is found, a combination of polygyny and polyandry in which sets of men and women enjoy more or less equal conjugal rights over each other. This form, often called "group marriage," will be discussed in §7 of this chapter.

Although there are many societies that permit or even encourage polygamous marriages, it does not follow in such socieites that every married individual, or even that a majority of them, has more than one spouse. Quite the contrary is true, for in most so-called polygamous societies monogamy is statistically the prevailing form. The reason for this is clear: the proportion of male to female births in any human society is roughly the same, and if this proportion is maintained among the sexually mature, a preponderance of plural marriages means that a considerable number of either men or women must remain unmarried. In societies, such as those of Australia or East Africa, when the age of marriage for men is delayed, while women are married at puberty, older men are likely to have several wives. Adultery and discord result between older married men and young unmarried men. Otherwise, monogamy not only prevails in most of the world's societies, either as the only approved form of marriage or as the only feasible form, but it may also prevail within a polygamous society, in which, very often, only a minority of the population can actually secure more than one spouse.

To illustrate polygynous marriage, let us turn to the Baganda, a society numbering about 1 million members living in Uganda, East Africa. The Baganda were a cattle-raising and horticultural people living in a region extremely favorable to both these pursuits. Their political system was an autocratic monarchy, and the king, aided in governing by a large number of chiefs and subchiefs appointed by himself, had almost absolute political powers. As the supreme ruler and the wealthiest man in the kingdom, the monarch had hundreds of wives. Chiefs and petty chiefs could have ten or more wives, depending upon their wealth and political status. Farmers, petty officials, and artisans, the lower strata in the population, worked very hard to secure at least two wives (as a symbol of their status and wealth), and some of the more fortunate might have three or even four. But the poorer peasants often had but one wife, largely because they were unable to raise the high price necessary to the acquisition of a second. Although accurate figures are unavailable, it appears that the Baganda were among the few peoples of the world among whom plural marriages formed a large percentage, perhaps even a majority, of the whole.

In a polygynous household the husband supplied a house and garden for each of his wives. The wives lived with him in turn, cooking and serving for him during the period of their visit. Although they came only at his invitation, and though the husband might actually have preferred one to the rest, he had to be careful not to arouse jealousies and resentments that might destroy the peace and harmony of the household. The first wife took precedence over the others and had charge of the household fetishes, objects in which ghosts or spirits were believed to reside and that were important in Baganda religious rites. The second wife too had important duties: she shaved her husband's head and trimmed his nails, occupations that gain their significance from the fact that hair and nail clippings had to be carefully protected against the machinations of enemies, who might use them to injure or even kill the husband.

The wide dispersal of polygyny among the Baganda was made possible by the high mortality rate among Baganda males. In chiefly families, male children were often killed at birth; the princes of the royal house, once the successor to the throne had been chosen, were put to death; the king arbitrarily killed off male retainers and servants who displeased him; males, never females, had to be sacrified in great numbers to the gods at appropriate ceremonies; and great numbers of men were killed in the annual wars the Baganda conducted with their neighbors. As a result of these factors, plus the fact that large numbers of women were taken as booty in war expeditions, the women outnumbered the men by three to one. It was this disparity in the relative numbers of men and women that made polygyny on so wide a scale possible.

Polyandry is much rarer than polygyny; a typical example is found among the Todas, a people of southern India who traditionally lived largely on the dairy produce of their herds of water buffalo. The ideal pattern of marriage in Toda culture was fraternal polyandry, which dictates that when a woman marries a man she becomes in theory at least, the wife of all his brothers, both the living and those as yet unborn. Frequently such marriages occurred in fact as well as in theory, and a set of brothers (or clan brothers) with but one wife lived together in a single hut. There was little jealousy or friction. When one of the brothers was with the wife, he placed his mantle and staff outside the hut as a warning to the rest not to come in. During the wife's first pregnancy, one of the brothers performed over her a ceremony known as "giving the bow" and so became the recognized (or legal) father to her children. The remaining brothers were fathers only in a secondary sense.

Occasionally polyandry was nonfraternal (the men belonging to different clans). When these lived in different villages, the wife customarily spent about one month with each in turn. The men performed the ceremony of "giving the bow" in turn, so that the first was father to the first two or three children and the others, in sequence, fathers to the rest. Because these arrangements frequently led to much dispute and bickering, fraternal polyandry tended to be a preferred form.

As with the Baganda, Toda polyandry was undoubtedly the result of a disproportion in the ratio of men to women; in a population of 800 there were about 100 more men than women. This disproportion arose through the pattern of female infanticide. Single girl babies were frequently killed at birth, and when twins of different sexes were born, the female twin was always killed. Because twins were believed "unnatural," one was killed even if both were boys, and if the twins were girls, both were killed.

It is of interest to note, however, that polyandry remained a preferred form of marriage, even after infanticide had greatly decreased and the proportion of males to females was approaching normal equality. The practice of polyandry then took a somewhat different form. Thus, a set of brothers would take two or even more wives instead of just one. But the persistence of the older cultural form was indicated even where each brother had a wife, for these wives were clearly considered to be held in common by all the brothers.

Our ideal and compulsory pattern of marriage, which holds that monogamy is the only appropriate form, is not shared by all peoples, not even by some of those who regularly practice monogamy. In a great many societies, monogamy is only one possible form of marriage, with polygyny or polyandry as perfectly possible, though less frequent, alternatives. And in some societies, as among the Baganda, monogamy may be regarded as a poor substitute for polygyny, symbolic of a low status both economically and socially.

7. "Group" Marriage

Some of the earlier theories about the origins and ancient history of human cultures have postulated that man, in his primeval state, had no marriage forms at all but lived in a state of promiscuity. Later there developed, according to these theories, a kind of "group" marriage, whereby sets of males and females shared more or less equal conjugal rights over each other. Still later, it was supposed, came polygyny and polyandry, with monogamy representing the latest and highest form of marriage.

Evidence for this hypothesis was sought in "primitive" cultures, on the assumption that these preserved ancient forms relatively unchanged. But, as we have noted, polygamy is by no means general among so-called primitives. Rather, monogamy occurs far more often, if only for the reason that polygamy is difficult except under rare and special circumstances. Moreover, polygamy, or at least polygyny, occurs often among peoples who are by no means primitive in culture—for example, among such peoples as the modern Muslims, the Chinese, and the ancient Incas of Peru. Polygamy, as we have seen, is conditioned not by a supposed primitivity in culture, but by particular social and environmental circumstances.

No evidence of a state of promiscuity has ever been recorded, whether among hunter-gatherers or others. Every human society known has rigid rules of marriage, similar in kind and complexity to those we have illustrated. And group marriage, although it occurs, is so rare as to be notable, and, like polygamy, is not confined to hunter-gatherers. We have already mentioned one instance among the Todas, in which a set of brothers may possess a number of wives in common, and here it may be a recent development from an earlier polyandry, caused by a decrease in female infanticide. Another instance of group marriage is reported by Linton for the Marquesans of Polynesia. We shall examine this in some detail for the light it throws on this unusual form of marriage.

The Marquesans were traditionally a fishing and agricultural people, by no means "primitive," who lived in isolated villages along the coasts of the larger islands of the Marquesas group. Each village was made up of large extended families, and each family had a headman and a small cluster of buildings set on a platform. The platform, by its size and elaborateness, symbolized the family's wealth and prestige; the larger and finer it was, the higher was the socioeconomic status of the family. To gain such status and to retain it, the family required, above all, a large supply of manpower. It took much human labor to build a family center and to cultivate and collect the food and other resources necessary to maintain it. The chief of the village had the largest and wealthiest household, and from there the households in the village graded down to the small families of little status who occupied the lowest stratum of the class structure.

The headship of a household was inherited by the firstborn child, who acquired this title as soon as he was born. Active control was not achieved until maturity and marriage; in the meantime, the former head acted as regent for the child. Younger children had no position at all in their family of birth, but at marriage attached themselves to the households of their spouses.

Girls among the Marquesans were encouraged to take many lovers, for by this means their chances of a good marriage were improved. This was because a young household head sought by marriage, not only to gain a wife suitable to his station in life, but also to add to his house as many young men as possible in the capacity of secondary husbands. Secondary husbands of course were younger sons, not eligible to the headship of their households of birth, who sought their fortune by attaching themselves to a wealthy and powerful house.

When a young household head married, he attempted to set up a polyandrous family. But he might, if he was wealthy enough, marry more than one woman and so add even more secondary husbands to his house. In this situation, the result was a kind of group marriage, with the head and the secondary husbands having equal conjugal rights over the wives. The head and the first wife ruled the household, which also included the older relatives of the head and the children born of these marriages.

It should not be assumed that the secondary husbands lacked any means of enforcing their rights. To keep them there, and so to retain the manpower necessary to maintain the family status, the household head had to treat the secondary husbands fairly. Should he fail to do so, they were under no compulsion to stay, but might well seek to attach themselves to another household in which they had the promise of better treatment.

Linton indicates that only the wealthier Marquesan households had more than one wife, whereas most of the rest tended to be polyandrous to a greater or lesser degree. In only the poorest households was there but one husband and one wife; in these cases, apparently, the head was unable to attract secondary husbands to his group. Frequently such a household head might even fail to find a wife and therefore be obliged to abandon his heritage and join another household as secondary husband.

The prevalence of polyandry among the Marquesans, as among the Todas, arose through a scarcity of women due to the practice of female infanticide. Group marriage, where it existed in the Marquesas, was obviously an extension of the polyandrous family by adding to it one or more wives. It derived, not from any excessive primitivity of Marquesan culture, but from socioeconomic circumstances peculiar to it.

8. Bride Price and Dowry

The customs of bride price and dowry so frequently associated with marriage are much misunderstood, especially in societies, such as our own, in which these patterns of culture are lacking. Bride price is often conceived as reducing women to the status of chattels to be bought and sold, and dowry as a means of securing husbands by purchase. Neither conception is accurate; there is no necessary implication in either bride price or dowry that spouses may be bartered as insensate pieces of property.

Bride price may roughly be defined as a marriage payment made by a prospective husband, or more often by his family, to the family of the bride. This payment serves many functions, among which are symbolizing the socioeconomic statuses of the families to be united affinally, establishing an economic tie between the families of the bride and groom to ensure further the stability of the marriage, and providing the family of the bride with a means of replacing her with daughters-in-law. To illustrate these points, let us turn to the Baganda of East Africa, where, as in so many African societies, bride price was a highly developed pattern of culture.

Among the Baganda of East Africa, men could marry as early as sixteen, and girls at fourteen. A young man wishing to marry must ordinarily have accumulated enough property to pay the bride price and to supply the numerous other gifts necessary to a somewhat complex marriage ritual. He could secure wives by other means; by inheritance from a deceased older brother (the levirate), as a reward for meritorious serivce from a superior, as a gift from a subordinate who desired to curry favor, or as part of his share of loot from a raiding expedition. But the most frequent and preferred way of securing a bride, especially in the case of a first marriage, was through negotiation and the payment of a bride price.

Because the task of accumulating a bride price was likely to be long continued, and to require as well the assistance of his family, a Baganda young man learned to choose his wife with care. Good health, the ability to bear children, skill in gardening and household arts, and a reputation for industry and obedience were qualities to be desired in a bride; relative to these, other considerations, such as good looks, were minor. Having found a girl to his liking, and one who could meet the critical scrutiny of his family, the young man initiated negotiations with her older brother and paternal uncle, whose duty it was to arrange the marriages of the girls in their family. If the young man gained their consent, he brought several gourds of native beer and swore before witnesses (the usual form of contract among the nonliterate Baganda) to be a good husband. At this point the girl also signified her assent by serving the beer to those present; if she refused to do this, negotiations were broken off and the young man had to go elsewhere for a bride.

If the girl consented, however, the couple were considered betrothed, and the clansmen of the girl proceeded to set the bride price. The customary base price was 2,500 cowry shells (roughly the equivalent of a single head of cattle), to which could be added an amount in domestic animals, beer, bark cloth, and other materials in keeping with the status of the girl's family and with the ability of the young man to pay. To set too small a bride price might lower the family status, but too high a bride price might discourage the prospective husband. The girl's family had to steer a middle course, both to preserve their social position and to make the best marriage possible for their offspring.

The marriage did not take place until the bride price had been paid. For a poor man this might require some time; for one better endowed with worldly goods the interval between betrothal and marriage might be shorter. During this interval the girl was carefully fed and groomed by her family so that she might become plump and attractive to her husband. The sisters of the young man visited the prospective bride frequently, to bathe her and to examine her critically for physical defects.

The whole tenor of these arrangements reflects the concern of both families that the marriage be successful. The bride price ensured that the girl, once married, became mistress of her husband's household, engaged in gardening and other gainful occupations for him; her labor power could no longer be claimed by her family of birth. Similarly her children belonged to her husband's clan, though here it is interesting to note that every third child belonged to the wife's clan unless redeemed by further payment by the father or his clansmen. If the wife ran away from her husband, her clansmen had to send her back or return the bride price. But when a marriage was successful, the bride price was ordinarily used by a family to secure wives for their young sons and so replace the daughters who married out with daughters-in-law, whose labor power and children would add to the resources of the clan.

Although the pattern of providing brides with a dowry had often degenerated into one of permitting noble but impoverished families to recoup their fortunes by marrying wealthy commoners, dowry, it is evident, had originally a function not dissimilar to that of bride price. As the custom existed in Europe (and to some extent is still practiced) the dowry represented a gift in money, goods, or both made by the bride's family toward the establishment of her household. Because the husband was head of the family, and because it was considered unfitting that a woman handle business affairs, the dowry usually became the property of the husband, with the understanding that it be used to the best advantage of both himself and his wife. It did not represent a payment for an agreement to marry, but simply a means of assisting a young man (who was often similarly assisted as well by his own family) to begin the expensive business of establishing a home for his wife and the children to come. Like bride price, dowry united the families of the bride and groom in an endeavor to provide the best possible economic base for marriage, and so to ensure its permanence and success.

Dowry appears to be a rarer cultural form than bride price. It was apparently very common in Europe, at least among the upper economic strata, but is scarcely represented at all elsewhere. The custom has now largely disappeared even in Europe, though the modern custom of providing a bride with household equipment and a stock of new clothing possibly represents a survival of the older cultural pattern.

Many peoples lack both bride price and dowry, though among some of these, gift giving is considered a necessary prerequisite to marriage. A typical example is found among the Chiricahua Apaches, where, according to one of Opler's informants, "A man must give a present to his wife's relatives or be disgraced; the woman is disgraced too if this is not done."[6] But there is no limit to the number of such gifts, nor does the size of the gift affect the status of the principals. The gifts are not a bride price; they "do not entitle the husband or his family to any extraordinary control over the wife or her property. . . . Moreover, these gifts or their equivalents are never returned, not even in cases of unfaithfulness on the part of the woman or of dissolution of the marriage tie."[7]

But it is of interest to note that the marriage gift "functions as initial evidence of the economic support, cooperation, and generosity which a man owes to his wife's close relatives. The promise of future assistance can even take the place of a gift on occasion. . . ."[8] This correlates with what we already know of the Chiricahua family — the young man joins his wife's joint family at marriage and becomes one of its economic supports. It is obvious that his gifts cannot be interpreted as a compensation to the girl's family for the loss of her services and children. The marriage gifts, divided among the wife's kin, serve only to cement ties between the families of husbands and wives and to symbolize their economic parity.

9. Divorce

Although we have emphasized the fact that marriage is universally conceived as a permanent tie and have illustrated many cultural patterns designed to secure this end, there are few if any societies that do not provide some means, easy or difficult, of terminating unsuccessful marriages. No society known approves of divorce in principle — to do so would of course be tantamount to denying the permanence of the marriage tie — and no society encourages divorce. But nearly all societies, in practice, recognize that certain conditions, diversely defined, make it better to terminate a marriage than have it continue as a failure, and perhaps as a deterrent to others approaching marriage.

Recognized causes for divorce vary widely from one society to the next and even from one period to another in the history of a single society. In a study of divorce in forty non-European societies, Murdock gives a table listing the more commonly recognized grounds for divorce and indicating opposite each the number of societies that permit or forbid for this reason (Table 11–1).

It will be noted that this table also emphasizes the fact that, in most of the societies studied, divorce was as easy for women to secure as it was for men. According to Murdock, in thirty of the forty cultures surveyed no difference

[6] Morris E. Opler, *An Apache Life-Way* (Chicago: University of Chicago Press, 1941), pp. 161–162.

[7] Ibid.

[8] Ibid.

Table 11-1 Reasons for Divorce (Forty Sample Societies)*

| | Permitted | | | | Forbidden | | | |
| | Definitely | | Inferentially | | Definitely | | Inferentially | |
Reasons	To Man	To Wife	To Man	To Wife	To Man	To Wife	To Man	To Wife
Any grounds, however trivial	9	6	5	6	14	13	12	15
Incompatibility without more specific grounds	17	17	10	10	6	7	7	6
Common adultery or infidelity	19	11	8	12	8	10	5	7
Repeated or exaggerated infidelity	27	23	8	10	5	5	0	2
Childlessness or sterility	12	4	15	18	7	7	6	11
Sexual impotence or unwillingness	9	12	24	21	3	4	4	3
Laziness, nonsupport, economic incapacity	23	22	11	9	4	5	2	4
Quarrelsomeness or nagging	20	7	7	12	6	11	7	15
Mistreatment or cruelty	7	25	19	9	3	4	11	2

* G. P. Murdock, "Family Stability in Non-European Societies," copyright November, 1950, by *Annals of the American Academy of Political and Social Science, 272*, 195–201, p. 200. Reprinted by permission.

could be detected in the rights of men and women to terminate unsatisfactory marriage.[9] The rights of men were superior in six societies—the Moslem Kurds of Iraq, the Siwans of Egypt, the Japanese, the Baganda, the Siriono of Bolivia, and the Guaycuru of the Gran Chaco of South America. Women held superior rights in four of the forty societies—the Kwomas of New Guinea, the Dahomeans of West Africa (in the case of "stable" marriages with patrilocal residence and payment of bride price), the Yurok Indians of California, and the Witotos of Brazil. Some questions may be raised about the representativeness of the forty tribes surveyed, but the findings suggest that in comparison with them divorce practices in the United States, far from being unusual, are very nearly average.

From time to time the suggestion has been made that sexual rights in initiating divorce are related, roughly at least, to the relative status of men and

[9] George P. Murdock, "Family Stability in Non-European Societies," *Annals of the American Academy of Political and Social Science, 272*:195–201 (1950).

women in the society concerned. Among the Aruntas of Australia, for example, divorce was made very easy for the man, who could send his wife away on the slightest pretext, whereas the woman had no right to a divorce at all. If she was badly treated or her marriage was otherwise made intolerable, her only recourse was to run away, and even then she was subject to recapture and might be made to return to her husband.

A similar differentiation between the rights of men and women in divorce was found among the Baganda of East Africa. Here a man might also divorce his wife at will, sending her back to her family and demanding the return of the bride price. He was almost sure to do this if she was barren, for barrenness was not only a great misfortune but a positive danger to the fruitfulness of his gardens. However, because a barren woman had practically no chance of remarriage, her husband might simply neglect her, reducing her to the status of a household drudge and near slave.

The Baganda woman could not divorce her husband, though if she was badly treated, she might run away and claim the aid of her clansmen. These individuals would seek a meeting with the husband and attempt to mend matters; but if, for good reasons, the woman persisted in running away, she would be given sanctuary by her kinfolk, and all or part of the bride price would be returned to the husband.

Among both the Aruntas and the Baganda the ease of divorce for men and the corresponding difficulty of divorce for women appear to be correlated with the relatively low status of womanhood. An Arunta woman, though she was hardworking and contributed considerably to the economic resources of the household, lived in the joint family of her husband and was subject to the rule of men. She had no political rights and held no position of importance in the band, nor was she permitted to participate in sacred ceremonies. Especially among the Arunta and other Australian groups the low status of women is sometimes exaggerated by male informants. Studies based on female informants have provided a somewhat different picture.[10] Similarly the Baganda woman lived among her husband's clansmen and was often only one of several wives. Her work was gardening, an occupation important to Baganda well-being but despised by the upper ruling class, who were cattle keepers. Women did not participate in politics, held no important positions, were often forbidden to partake in religious rites, and were forbidden even to approach the cattle. Among both the Aruntas and Baganda, then, it is not surprising to find that the woman's right to dissolve a marriage was nearly nonexistent, whereas a man might divorce his wife whenever he saw fit, with or without cause.

Quite a different situation existed among the Chiricahua Apaches. Here, men and women had almost equal rights to a separation and on similar grounds. Unfaithfulness, barrenness or impotence, brutality, nagging, laziness, or even incompatibility could result in divorce, and a woman could initiate such proceedings just as easily as a man. When a divorce took place, the couple simply separated, each retaining his or her own property, the man leaving his wife's joint family to return to his own family or to remarry. Unless

[10] Phyllis M. Kaberry, *Aboriginal Woman, Sacred and Profane*. (Farnborough, Eng.: Gregg International Publishers, 1970; first published 1939).

she was the guilty party—being divorced, for example, for ill temper, barrenness, or laziness—a divorced woman had no difficulty in remarrying, and the same applied to men. This equality of opportunity for divorce is again probably related to the status of women, which in Apache society was quite high. Woman's work was not despised, and though women did not hold important positions of leadership in Apache society, they did play a considerable role in influencing their husbands. Moreover, the woman lived in her family of orientation after marriage, the joint family was matrilocal, and it was the husband who had to prove his worth to critical in-laws.

An even better situation for women was found among the Iroquois of Upper New York. Here also the joint family was matrilocal. The newly married couple lived in a room of the longhouse, owned by the wife's clan and ruled very largely by her older female relatives. The men had neither political nor economic rights in their wives' longhouse; these they exercised only in their houses of birth. Consequently a wife could put her husband out whenever she decided it was necessary, with no more formality than putting his belongings outside the house. But the man had equal access to an easy divorce; he needed only to stay away.

Although the relative status of males and females is an important factor in divorce rules, Murdock's data suggest that equality in initiating divorce is widespread and occurs even where men are markedly dominant.

> It is . . . surprising to encounter an equal facility in divorce among patrilocal and even patriarchal peoples like the Mongols, who see no reason for moral censure in divorce and say in a perfectly matter-of-fact manner that two individuals who cannot get along harmoniously together had better live apart.[11]

On the relative frequency of divorce as between different societies, Murdock finds only sixteen societies in which

> the stability of marital unions is noticeably greater than in our society. . . . In the remaining twenty-four societies, constituting sixty per cent of the total, the divorce rate manifestly exceeds that among ourselves. Despite the widespread alarm about increasing "family disorganization" in our own society, the comparative evidence makes it clear that we still remain well within the limits which human experience has shown that societies can tolerate with safety.[12]

Neither Murdock's data, nor any other, are evidence that most societies regard the marriage relationship as casual. On the contrary, as even our brief survey of marriage forms has shown, there is, in nearly all societies, a constant effort toward the end of encouraging and rewarding permanent unions, not toward dissolving them. The general attitude toward divorce, as Murdock says,

> is clearly that it is regrettable, but often necessary. It represents more of a practical concession to the frailty of mankind, caught in a web of social relationships and cultural expectations that often impose intolerable pressure on the individual per-

---

[11] Murdock, "Family Stability in Non-European Societies," op. cit., p. 191.
[12] Ibid., p. 197.

sonality. That most social systems work as well as they do, despite concessions to the individual that appear excessive to us, is a tribute to human ingenuity and resiliency.[13]

10. Summary

Relationships among human beings and the means by which they are organized and regulated constitute the field of social organization. The most common form of organization is the family household which takes its form through operation of the principles of descent and marriage. Although marriage differs from society to society, it generally involves a union between a male and a female which is socially sanctioned and provides a stable background for rearing children. There is a sharp distinction, illustrated by the examples of Samoan and Masai cultures, between the institution of marriage and various formal and informal means of securing sexual gratification. Most societies provide extensive guidelines and rules concerning the persons with whom marriage is expected to take place. Marriage and sexual relationships within the nuclear family are almost universally forbidden. Although the origins of the incest taboo forbidding sex within the nuclear family and rules of exogamy forbidding marriage within the nuclear family remain controversial, there is considerable agreement that the practice of out-marriage plays an important role in contributing to the development of cooperation between households and the formation of larger groups and communities. Different sorts of marriage rules and different patterns of preferential marriage play an important role in determining patterns of organization permitting the adaptation of different sorts of bands, neighborhoods, or communities to particular environmental problems. Very often social relationships established by marriage are considered more important than any particular marriage. This accounts for patterns of arranged marriage as well as for such institutions as the levirate and sororate, which guarantee the perpetuation of the relationship between families even after the death of one of the spouses.

Three major forms of marriage — monogamy, polygyny, and polyandry — are generally recognized by anthropologists. Of these, monogamy occurs most frequently even in societies that encourage polygyny or polyandry. In a few societies, like that of the Baganda, polygyny is actually more frequent than monogamy. Polyandry is by far the rarest form of marriage, and occurs with relatively low frequency even in societies where it is considered desirable. With the possible exception of traditional Toda polyandry, polyandry is usually a step in a progression in which a group of brothers marry first one and then several wives, sometimes reaching a state of polygyny. Such an arrangement, noted by Linton in the Marquesas, may approach what has been referred to as group marriage.

[13] Ibid., p. 201.

Marriage payments such as bride price and dowry help to establish the sincerity and commitment of the families involved. By ensuring that marriage cannot take place unless resources are available to support the new household, marriage payments often play an important role in controlling the growth of population. Although impressive and expensive marriage ceremonies and the making of large marriage payments seem designed to reinforce the marriage tie, most societies recognize the inevitability of divorce. Grounds for divorce and the assignment of responsibility for initiating divorce proceedings differ from society to society.

Collateral Reading

Bohannan, Paul, and John Middleton (eds.). *Marriage, Family and Residence*. Garden City, N.Y.: The Natural History Press, 1968. Useful articles.

Goody, Jack (ed.). *The Developmental Cycle in Domestic Groups*. Cambridge: University Press, 1971. Cyclical changes in household organization.

Evans-Pritchard, E. E. *Kinship and Marriage Among the Nuer*. (First Published in 1951.) London: Oxford University Press, 1960. Marriage patterns of pastoralists in Africa.

Fortes, Meyer. *The Web of Kinship Among the Tallensi*. (First Published in 1949.) London: Oxford University Press, 1967. An agricultural people in Africa.

Fox, Robin. *Kinship and Marriage*. Baltimore: Penguin Books, Inc., 1967. A fairly recent survey.

Friedl, Ernestine. *Women and Men: An Anthropologist's View*. New York: Holt, Rinehart and Winston, Inc., 1975. Sex roles in hunting and gathering and horticultural societies.

Goody, Jack, and S. J. Tambiah. *Bridewealth and Dowry*. Cambridge Eng.: Cambridge University Press, 1973. An examination of payments connected with marriage.

Murdock, George P. *Social Structure*. New York: Macmillan Publishing Co., Inc., 1949. A theory of kinship terminologies tested cross-culturally.

Schneider, David M. *American Kinship: A Cultural Account*. Chicago: University of Chicago Press, 1968. A brief survey of patterns in the United States.

Schneider, David M., and Kathleen Gough (eds.). *Matrilineal Kinship*. Berkeley and Los Angeles: University of California Press, 1961. A comparative study of matrilineal societies.

Ethnographic References

Apache: Basso, 1971; Opler, 1937, 1941.

Baganda: Kagwa, 1934; Murdock, 1935, Chapter XVIII; Roscoe, 1911.

Bedouin: Coon, 1948, Chapter XIII; Forde, 1950, Chapter XV.

Marquesan: Linton, 1939; Suggs, 1966.

Masai: Forde, 1950, Chapter XIV; Hanley, 1971; Hollis, 1905.

Samoan: Holmes, 1958; Mead, 1928; Murdock, 1935, Chapter III; Turner, 1884.

Toda: Murdock, 1935, Chapter V; Rivers, 1906.

12/Kinship and Kinship Groupings

1. The Nature of Kinship

Relatives, or kin, are people who are related to each other through some combination of the principles of descent and marriage. Although descent and marriage are genealogical principles and therefore reflect biological realities to some extent, it must never be forgotten that descent and marriage are primarily social and legal principles. It is never easy to be certain about one's biological ancestors, but sociological ancestors are easily identified as the people who socially and legally play the role of mother and father. A similar distinction was made earlier between sexual relationships and marriage.

Despite the importance of the distinction between biological and social relationships, all human societies appear to possess sets of terms that are primarily applied to persons who are, or are thought to be, genealogically related. Any such set of terms is referred to as a kinship terminology. In our own kinship terminology, the male ("Ego") refers to his male parent as "father" and his female parent as "mother." His parent's siblings and their spouses are "uncle" and "aunt." Thus the mother's sister (MoSi) and the father's brother's wife (FaBrWi) are described by the same term, even though their biological relationship to Ego is quite different. Like most kinship terms, the term "aunt" covers several different types of genealogical relationships.

405

Proboscis monkey, *Nasalis larvatus*. Human beings are unique in their ability to maintain lifelong recognition of a variety of kinship ties. Various forms of family life are, however, characteristic of a variety of other species. (San Diego Zoo photo by Ron Garrison.)

In his own generation, Ego refers to other children of his parents as "brother" and "sister." The children of his uncles and aunts are referred to as "first cousins." Ego refers to his children as "son" and "daughter" and to the children of his brothers and sisters as "nephew" and "niece." He refers to his parent's parents as "grandfather" and "grandmother" and to his children's children as "grandson" and "granddaughter." He refers to distant relatives as "cousin." Relatives by marriage, except in the case of "husband," "wife," "uncle" and "aunt," are referred to by use of the suffix "-in-law."

To individuals who are familiar only with the English kin terms outlined above, the English kin terms are likely to seem biologically right and natural. In fact the English system of kin terms, like all other systems of kin terms, represents a conventional selection that lumps different kinds of relatives such as mother's sister and father's brother's wife together under a single term. The use of a term such as "aunt" is conventional because there is no real necessity for considering MoSi, FaBrWi, MoBrWi, and FaSi to be the same. It would be equally reasonable, for example, to have separate terms for all four relatives or, as some English speakers do, to refer to MoBrWi and FaBrWi as "aunt-in-law." Because MoSi and FaBrWi are like mother, it would be perfectly reasonable to do as many people do in other cultures and call all three of them "mother," reserving some other term for MoBrWi and FaSi.

The units of a kinship terminology, like the individual trees in a forest, are such *kin types* or types of kin as MoBrWi, FaSiHu, or FaBrDa. Just as the trees in a forest can be divided into useful and useless trees, evergreen and deciduous trees, or tall and short trees, so can the hundreds of possible kin-types within a genealogy be divided and classified in a variety of ways. With a few possible exceptions, classifications of kin types make use of principles derived from various combinations of descent, marriage, and sex.

In the English terminology given above, all of the terms except "cousin" involve a generation principle. "Father," "mother," "uncle," and "aunt" are all one generation above Ego, while "son," "daughter," "nephew," and "niece" are all one generation below Ego. Because application of the generation principle simply involves counting the lines on a genealogical diagram, Ego's generation is usually referred to as the zero generation; his parents fall in the "plus one" generation, and his offspring fall in the "minus one" generation.

Figure 12–1 Kin types and kin terms. Each person shown on the genealogical diagram represents a single kin type. The kin terms—"uncle," "aunt," and "cousin," each summarizes a number of kin types. In the English terminology, the terms "father" and "mother" are usually applied to the single kin types "Fa" and "Mo."

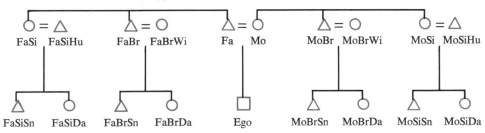

Uncle = FaSiHu, FaBr, MoBr, MoSiHu
Aunt = FaSi, FaBrWi, MoBrWi, MoSi
Cousin = FaSiSn, FaSiDa, FaBrSn, FaBrDa,
        MoBrSn, MoBrDa, MoSiSn, MoSiDa

A second principle involved in the English terminology is that of sex. All terms except "cousin" imply the sex of the individual. A third, and rather confusing, principle is the principle of collaterality ("sidewaysness"). On the genealogy (Figure 12–1), Ego's father, Ego, and Ego's son form a single vertical line or lineage. Looked at in this way, FaBr, MoSi, FaSi, MoBr, BrSn, BrDa, SiSn, and SiDa — all seem to stray sideways from the direct line even though they are connected to it. Hence the principle of collaterality. Figure 12–2 uses lines to represent the principles of classification used in English. The distinction between relatives by marriage (affinal) and relatives by descent (consanguine) represented by use of the term "in'law" is not represented, but it is the fourth major principle of classification used in the English kinship terminology.

As the above discussion suggests, a kinship terminology is a set of terms or labels applied to the various kin types or positions in a genealogy in accordance with various principles of classification such as generation, sex, lineality-collaterality, and consanguinity-affinity. Although the English kin terms can be understood in terms of these four principles, five additional principles are of common occurrence in other kinship terminologies. In English usage a distinction is commonly made between "big brother" and "little brother" or "big sister" and "little sister"; such a *distinction in terms of relative age* is quite common and frequently involves the use of quite different words for older and younger siblings. In English the sex of Ego is of comparatively slight importance except in the use of the terms "husband" and "wife." Obviously only a female can have a husband and only a male can have a wife, but both males and females can have fathers, mothers, brothers, sisters, cousins, and so forth. In other kinship terminologies male and female Egos may use quite different terms in a large number of different contexts. This principle is usually referred to as *sex of speaker*.

A number of closely related principles have to do with the *nature of connecting relatives*. In many South Indian kinship systems, for example, different terms are used for older sister's husband and younger sister's husband. Here, the acting principle is the age of the connecting relative compared to that of Ego. In systems that distinguish between cross-cousins and parallel cousins, cross-cousins are cousins whose parents, the two connecting relatives, are real or classificatory siblings of opposite sex. Parallel cousins are cousins whose parents are real or classificatory siblings of the same sex. A classificatory

Figure 12–2 English kin terms excluding affinal and grandperson terms.

	Lineal		Collateral		Distant
	m	*f*	*m*	*f*	
+1	Father	Mother	Uncle	Aunt	
0	Brother	Sister	Cousin		
−1	Son	Daughter	Nephew	Niece	

sibling is a person who is commonly referred to by the same term used in referring to a sibling.

The *principle of reciprocity* refers to the situation in which two relatives refer to each other using the same term. In English, if a grandchild referred to his grandparent as grandkinsperson, reciprocity would be observed if the grandparent also addressed the grandchild as grandkinsperson. Using reciprocal terminology, if Ego said, "Good morning, sibling," the proper reply would be, "Good morning, sibling." The term "cousin" is the only truly reciprocal term in English.

A final principle has to do with the *condition of the relative* to whom a term is to be applied. If a relative is dead, married, or otherwise different from what he was before, it may make a difference in the terms to be applied. If "maiden aunt," "rich uncle," "bachelor uncle," "widow," or "widower" were used as kinship terms in English, it would reflect the operation of such a principle.

In summary, the common principles used in the classification of kinsmen are as follows:

1. Generation
2. Sex
3. Lineality–collaterality
4. Affinity–consanguinity
5. Age (usually relative age within a generation or within a set of siblings)
6. Sex of speaker
7. Nature of connecting relative
8. Reciprocity (two kinsmen use the same term in referring to each other)
9. Condition of relative referred to

2. Two Kinship Terminologies

The English kinship terminology adopts the overall strategy of separating relatives in terms of progressive distance. The primary lineal relatives — mother, father, son, daughter, brother, and sister — are surrounded by a thin layer of collateral relatives — uncle, aunt, nephew, niece, first cousin. All other relatives are lumped together regardless of sex and often regardless of distance or generation under the utility term "cousin." Among the Chiricahua Apache, there is also a core of central relatives, but it consists only of terms for father, mother, son, daughter. All other known relatives are divided into a series of classes based primarily upon generation and sex of the connecting relative.

All relatives of Ego's generation, including Ego's siblings, first cousins, and distant relatives if the connection is remembered, are divided into two classes: "Cikis," meaning relatives of the same sex; and "Cilah," meaning relatives of the opposite sex.[1] Persons who are "Cikis" to each other are expected

[1] Morris E. Opler, "An Outline of Chiricahua Apache Social Organization," in *Social Anthropology of North American Tribes,* ed. Fred Eggan (Chicago: University of Chicago Press; 2d ed., 1955), pp. 173–239.

	Lineal		Connected To Male Relative	Connected To Female Relative
	m	*f*		
+1	"Father"	"Mother"	Cided	Cidai
0 Same Sex	Cikis			
Opposite Sex	Cilah			
−1	"Son"	"Daughter"	Cided	Cidai

Figure 12–3 Chiricahua Apache kin terms excluding grandperson terms.

to cooperate closely, much in the manner expected of ideal brothers or sisters in Euro-American societies. Persons who are "Cilah" to each other must never marry regardless of how remote their relationship might be. "Cikis" and "Cilah," like most other terms in Chiricahua kinship, are reciprocal. A person addressed as "Cikis" by Ego will address Ego as "Cikis."

All relatives separated from Ego by one generation are also divided into two classes on the basis of the sex of the connecting relative. Thus all relatives of a male Ego's father, both his father's "Cikis" and his "Cilah," are referred to as "Cided." All same-generation relatives of Ego's mother are referred to as "Cidai." In reverse, Ego refers to all descendants of his same generation male relatives as "Cidede," and to all descendants of his female relatives as "Cidai." They of course use the same term in referring to him because he is related either on their father's side or on their mother's side. There are four separate terms covering grandparent–grandchild relationships. Four terms are needed because the sex of two connecting relatives has to be taken into account. For example, father's father and his people form a different grouping from father's mother and her people.

One of the problems in the analysis of kinship terminologies centers on the question of the extent to which the terminologies reflect the existence of actual groupings or other social realities. In some cases kinship terminologies may simply be a set of labels applied to kinsmen which are applied, like the names of vegetables, without any particular regard to existing social groupings or relationships. In other cases a kinship terminology may create distinctions between marriageable and unmarriageable persons or may serve to define membership in particular groupings. Chiricahua Apache kinship terms can be said to reflect social relationships in the sense that they make a clear distinction between relatives, with whom marriage is unthinkable, and nonrelatives. Beyond that, if we remember that the Chiricahua Apache were hunters and gatherers who lived in widely scattered family encampments, the kinship terms can be seen as defining particular family encampments and the people in them. Thus a sizable proportion of Ego's same-sex peers and opposite-sex peers are likely to be found in his mother's encampment, where he is brought up, or in his father's encampment, which he may visit frequently. In the same

Apache hunters with bows and arrows. Existing American Indian photographs were often posed by early photographers who provided suitable ethnic clothing, often removing the subjects' boots and trousers. (Courtesy Smithsonian Institution, National Anthropological Archives.)

way many of Ego's "Cidede" will be found in his father's encampment, and many of his "Cidai" in his mother's encampment. Because relatives who live far away or with whom Ego has little contact are likely to be forgotten, the effect of the kinship terms is to define the particular family encampments that contain relatives and that must be avoided in searching for a spouse, even though they may be depended upon for assistance in other matters. The complete ban on marriage to known relatives has the effect of forcing young people to search for spouses in distant or unrelated encampments. Such wide-ranging bride search serves to integrate a larger tribal society in which many different encampments share the same language and are interconnected by ties of marriage.

Chiricahua Apache marriage rules forbid marriages between individuals who have a remembered blood relationship. This distinction is clearly marked in the kinship terminology. Other Apache kinship terminologies, as well as a wide variety of terminologies used on every continent, solve the problem of arranging marriages by dividing large numbers of individuals — very often all individuals — into two groups between which individuals are exchanged in marriage. In the Urabunna tribe of Central Australia, described by Spencer and Gillen,[2] all individuals on earth are considered to belong to one of two groups, the Matthurie or the Kirarawa. The Matthurie and the Kirarawa, then, form exogamous marriage classes or moieties. No Matthurie can marry a Matthurie; no Kirarawa can marry a Kirarawa.

At the outset, then, all Urabunna kinship terms make a distinction between membership in Ego's moiety or membership in the complementary moiety. In order to keep track of who belongs to which moiety, it is necessary to introduce a lineage principle. In the case of the Urabunna, descent is calculated matrilineally. Thus all members of each moiety are treated as if they were in some sense related by matrilineal descent. In each generation there is one set of brothers and sisters belonging to one moiety and one set of brothers and sisters belonging to the complementary moiety. Because grandparents and grandchildren rarely figure in marriage negotiations, such systems generally simplify kinship terms referring to individuals two generations removed from Ego. For the Urabunna, all such grandpersons belonging to the complementary moiety are referred to as "Kadnini." All grandpersons, both grandchildren and grandparents, who belong to Ego's moiety are called "Thunthi." Ego's daughter's children, because they belong to Ego's moiety, are called "Thunthi." Ego's son's children, who belong to their mother's moiety, are called "Kadnini."

Finer discriminations, taking note of the individual's sex and marriage-ability, are required for individuals in Ego's generation and in the generations of Ego's parents and offspring. (Figure 12–4.) Within Ego's moiety, all women in the first ascending generation arc divided into two classes: those mother's age and older and those younger than mother. Mother, mother's older sister, and all analoguous women are referred to as "Luka." Younger women in

[2] Baldwin Spencer and F. G. Gillen, *The Native Tribes of Central Australia* (London: Macmillan and Co., Ltd., 1938; first published 1899).

	Ego's Moiety		Complementary Moiety	
Generation	*Female*	*Male*	*Female*	*Male*
+1	Luka Senior - - - - - - Junior Namuma	Kawkuka	Nowillie	Nia
0	Nuthie Kupuka	Kakua Senior - - - - - - Junior	Nupa Apillia	Witewa
−1	Thidnurra		Biaka	

Figure 12–4   Urabunna terms excluding grandperson terms.

mother's generation and moiety are referred to as "Namuma." Mother's brothers and Ego's wife's father or husband's father, in other words all male members of the same moiety one generation above Ego, are referred to as "Kawkuka." Ego's sister's children and other children in Ego's moiety and one generation below Ego are referred to as "Thidnurra."

Ego's older brother and the sons of all men in his father's generation who are older than his father are referred to as "Nuthie," while older sisters, etc., are referred to as "Kakua." Younger brothers, younger sisters, and the offspring of men in the parental generation who are younger than father are all classed together as "Kupuka."

The complementary moiety is divided into the various classes representing the spouses of the people in Ego's moiety. The husband's of parental women in Ego's moiety are "Nia," while the wives of parental men are "Nowillie." A male Ego's mother-in-law is a "Nowillie" and his brother is a "Nia," just like Ego's father.

In Ego's generation, all men in the complementary moiety are "Witewa." This includes father's sister's sons, sister's husbands, and wife's brothers. Because Ego can marry only the daughters of women older than his father, a distinction is made between "Nupa" or marriageable women and "Apillia," including father's younger sister's daughters. All persons in Ego's children's generation in the complementary moiety, including Ego's sons and daughters, are "Biaka."

Although the Urabunna kinship terminology is bound to seem complicated and difficult at first glance, it actually possesses, as do many other such systems of terminology, an elegant simplicity. In fact the Urabunna seem positively reluctant to bestow kinship terms on people that don't matter. Thus grandparents, grandchildren, Ego's sister's children, and even Ego's own children are simply lumped into broad categories that might be translated as "grandperson," "kids in my group," and "kids in the complementary group." Where terms really matter in connection with Ego's status, careful note is taken not only of sex but also of relative age. Because Ego's position in his lineage presumably depends upon his mother's seniority, women junior to his mother are carefully identified. The same thing holds in Ego's generation, where unimportant younger siblings are simply lumped together regardless of sex. The terminology functions as a part of a complex set of marital restrictions, and it serves to define the class of women (or men) Ego can marry.

3. Kinship Groupings

Especially in small, relatively stable communities where just about everyone is related to everyone else, the division of society into groups often takes place in terms of kinship. Kinship groupings are often—perhaps about half the time—foreshadowed by distinctions made within the kinship terminology. In almost all societies a household, composed largely of kinsmen, forms a fundamental social grouping.

The most common form of family household consists of a husband and wife and any children they might have. Such a unit, technically described as a nuclear family household, is sometimes regarded as universal. Certainly it is convenient in many kinds of analysis to treat the nuclear family household as a basic unit and then to discuss various exceptional forms. Even where the nuclear family household is the ideal form, there are inevitably a great many exceptional sorts of family households. Households may be formed by single men or women, by married couples who do not produce children, or by single men or women who happen to have children but lack spouses. Very often, out of convenience or necessity, a nuclear family household may be supplemented by the addition of a grandparent, a married child, or other relatives or even nonrelatives. It is convenient to regard all of these different sorts of family households as variations on a basic nuclear family household, but this should not blind us to the fact of widespread and inevitable variation. One of the characteristics of the nuclear family is that it tends to break up when the children marry, when the parents die or divorce, or at other established points in the human life cycle. The male raised in a nuclear family will usually begin his life in a household headed by his parents and conclude his life in a family that he himself heads.

Families headed by single parents, especially single female parents, are frequently regarded as a variety of nuclear family. Some authorities consider such a mother–child family household to represent a more basic form than the nuclear family. Such families occur with some frequency among other primate species and may well have been the common form of family among species ancestral to humanity. On the other hand, a mother–child family is not well

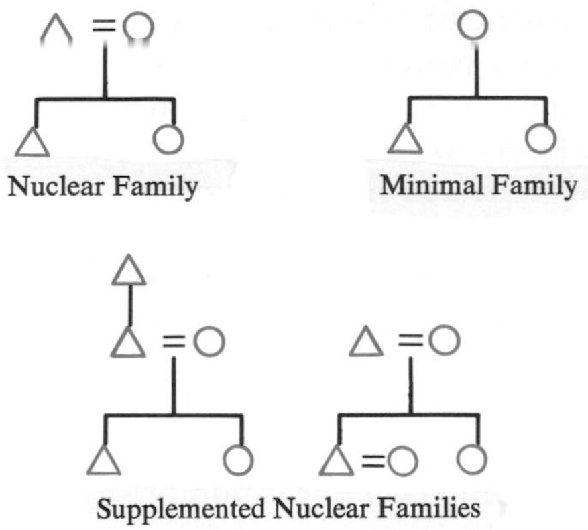

Figure 12–5 Basic types of families and family households. In real life, other relatives may often join the household as suggested by the diagrams of enlarged nuclear families.

adapted to survival in most human environments, especially where a hunting and gathering technology is employed. It seems to occur most frequently in urban settings, where women can find employment or draw welfare checks but men can not.

Larger "extended family households" consist of groupings of the various kinds of nuclear families described above. Thus a polygamous household involves several wives (polygynous extended family) or several husbands (polyandrous extended family) who share a single spouse. A polygamous family may also involve separate households that are visited in turn by a single spouse. The polygynous family, where one man has several wives living either separately or in the same household, usually occurs as an exceptional form of the family within societies having predominantly nuclear family households. The multiplication of wives is usually an expression of wealth and status. The polygynous family is also a possible adaptation to shortages of males created by endemic warfare or even, as in traditional Tibet, by customary monasticism. The polyandrous family is comparatively rare and seems to exist mainly where female infanticide produces a shortage of women, and extreme poverty makes it impossible for brothers to acquire more than one wife. Among the Nayar of South India in traditional times, a woman might contract formal marriages with a number of different men. Such men were not, however, members of the household even though they might be reasonably frequent visitors. The household itself consisted of mothers and grandmothers and their brothers and children.

The Marquesans of Polynesia, especially if they were wealthy, sought to marry women who had many lovers in the hope that the lovers would join the household as secondary husbands. The resulting household consisted of a household chief and his principal wife, together with a number of secondary wives and husbands, all of whom, in theory, enjoyed conjugal rights with each other.

Another type of extended family household, the extended nuclear family, consists of several nuclear families usually united by parent-child and/or sibling relationships. Because many societies follow patrilocal residence, the most common form of extended nuclear family is organized around a set of brothers and their wives and children; very often such a family is headed by the older brother or by their father. A matrilocal extended family household consists of sisters and their husbands and would be likely to be headed either by the mother's brother or by the father. An eclectic extended nuclear family household is possible and occurs with considerable frequency usually when relatives connected by a variety of ties join together under one roof. Such eclectic families are rarely the ideal form and are often reported as being either matrilocal or patrilocal.

There are a number of situations in which unrelated families or individuals form households. In such cases it is often difficult to determine whether these should be regarded as a local group or band consisting of nuclear family households or as an extended family household. In some cases members of extended family households, both nuclear and polygamous, eat together but sleep separately. In other cases they may eat and sleep separately but hold property in common.

4. Larger Kinship Groupings

As suggested above, the extended family household may merge somewhat imperceptibly into a local group or neighborhood consisting of nuclear families practicing various forms of cooperation and related to each other in a variety of ways. Because a local group, particularly where population density is low, generally controls a specific environment or territory which it exploits through cooperative effort, local group composition tends to be affected by the necessity of maintaining a ratio of territory to people such that the environment is neither over- nor underutilized. The prototypical form of the local group, like the patrilocal extended family, consists of brothers and their wives and children. Such a group may attain a size of perhaps twenty or thirty households by including within it, usually as brothers, the male children of father's brothers.

In real life, especially in hunting and gathering societies and agricultural societies having low population density, a purely patrilocal grouping is difficult to maintain. Men may go off to live matrilocally with their wives' local groups. If there is need for manpower, unrelated or distantly related persons may be invited to move in. Thus, even though the model for the local group may be patrilocal or matrilocal, it is much more likely to be eclectic in actual composition than a household. The terms *patrilocal* and *matrilocal* applied to territorial groups such as the household or the local group are intended to describe the situation in which the married couple lives in the father's group or in the mother's group. For greater precision, some anthropologists prefer to use "virilocal" in reference to residence in the husband's group and "uxorilocal" in reference to residence in the wife's group. Where a newly married couple may reside any place they choose, residence is "neolocal." If the choice is either in the husband's group or in the wife's group, residence is "bilocal"; where they shift back and forth between the husband's and the wife's group, residence is "ambilocal." Although these terms are useful in describing ideal cultural patterns, a proper description of the actual process involved in forming a local group involves a quantitative description of the decision-making process actually involved in the determination of postmarital residence.

A local group formed primarily by patrilocal or by matrilocal residence will tend to coincide with a patrilineal or matrilineal descent group or lineage. If all the men in a group obtain their wives from other groups and take up residence in the households or local groups of their fathers, the result is an exogamous patrilineal and patrilocal group. If an exchange of marital partners takes place between two local groups, the pattern of actual marriage is likely to consist predominantly of cross-cousin marriage if patrilocal or matrilocal residence rules are strictly followed. Thus father's sister will marry a man residing in Group B, while father marries a wife from Group B. Father's wife's brother (Ego's cross-cousin) will be available to marry Ego. For demographic reasons an exchange of daughters between two small local groups is usually impossible because one group or the other is likely to run short of daughters before all the men in the other group are married. The Chiricahua Apache marriage system makes it virtually impossible to exchange brides repeatedly between just two local groups by defining Ego's father's and mother's relatives as consanguines, who cannot be married. Under systems of cross-cousin marriage, such as that of the Urabunna, exchange takes place between two sharply delimited groupings, but they have to be much larger than a local group.

In Australia and in other places where population density is low, most marriages take place within a *dialect tribe* composed of individuals speaking the same dialect of the same language. Although such a *dialect tribe* has no tribal leadership or governmental structure, it attains its unity through the fact that everyone in it is related by marriage or descent. Because a *dialect tribe* will consist on the average, of about 500 individuals,[3] with a maximum size of a few thousand individuals, it will rarely contain more than ten or twenty local groups ranging in size from 5 to 100 families. Marriage rules generally require that most of the local groups regularly exchange marital partners with each other.

Cooperation between the local groups composing a dialect tribe and the sharing of a common language and culture is generally ensured by the fact of close family relationship and intermarriage. When environmental circumstances and technology permit the formation of larger groupings, a number of special devices are called into play in order to ensure communication and cohesion. Such devices may involve complex governmental structure or the development of groups of nonrelatives such as age-mates or friends. Very often larger groupings are formed by the extension of kinship ties far beyond the possible limits of remembered relationships. Although such extended kinship groups may be territorial — for example, when a tribe is divided into two intermarrying segments, each occupying a distinct territory — they are more often

[3] Joseph B. Birdsell, "Local Group Composition Among the Australian Aborigines," *Current Anthropology*, 11:115–142, No. 2 (1970).

Groom under umbrella at left being escorted to bride's house by members of his matriclan and phratry. The mat and mattress indicate that the groom will be changing his residence to his wife's house. The umbrella is symbolic of a clan chief (the groom). Gurun-Batusangkar, West Sumatra, Indonesia. (Kindness of Lynn Thomas.)

organized into segments which crosscut existing territorial boundaries. Although an extended kinship group can sometimes be based upon kinship relations calculated bilaterally through both the mother and the father, the common method of forming such groups involves tracing descent either patrilineally or matrilineally. Typically, then, an extended kinship group consists of a number of lineages which usually form local groups or segments of local groups and are considered to be descended from the same male or female ancestor. The local lineage is usually in some sense a corporate or organized group in that its members interact and cooperate in the performance of certain tasks. The larger group, composed of several local lineages, may or may not constitute a corporate group. Although the term "clan" is generally applied

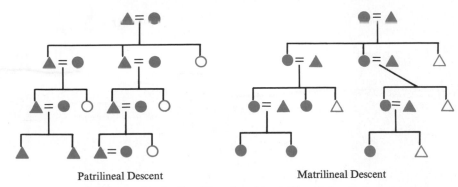

Patrilineal Descent   Matrilineal Descent

Figure 12-6 Patrilineal and matrilineal descent.

indiscriminately to both corporate and noncorporate extended kinship groups, there is some justification for using the term "clan" where some corporate organization exists and the term "sib" where it does not. Thus a matriclan or a patriclan is a large organization of kinsmen, often living in separated localities, but usually possessing a name and engaging in some sort of corporate activity. A matrisib or patrisib is a more vaguely defined grouping which may possess a name, but which has no internal organization and does not engage in any corporate activities. There is, however, wide disagreement among anthropologists on how such terms should be defined. Terms like "clan" and "sib" may, in fact, lump together organizations that are quite different in different places. Hence, many anthropologists prefer to use the terminology used by the people themselves or else to adopt the terminology commonly used by anthropologists working in the region.

The important thing to remember is that extended unilineal kinship groupings such as clans and sibs are exogamous units. The members of a clan are regarded as brothers and sisters from whom familial affection and cooperation can be expected, whereas members of other clans are likely to be relatives by marriage who are treated in the manner appropriate to "in-laws." In effect, societies organized in terms of clans or sibs are families writ large, and they derive their solidarity from the affection accorded to unrelated individuals who are regarded as, and to a degree treated as, close kin because they belong to the same clans as Ego's close relatives.

In societies with elaborate status systems, individuals within clans are often ranked in terms of seniority, and the same ranking may also be applied to clans. Clans may also be organized into phratries or moieties consisting of groups of clans which are regarded as sharing the same descent lines and are therefore exogamous. Clans or sibs may be divided into a variety of smaller regional units and organizations, or they may be truly international in scope transcending tribal and national boundaries. In modern society international religious, fraternal, and labor union organizations are modeled on patrilineal clans, and members refer to each other as brother and sister. Such brotherhoods and sisterhoods make use of what may be a universal dream of glory—to be supported in life's crises by a large, steadfast, and loyal group of sisters and brothers.

Minangkabau *rumah gadang* or large house. Rice shed on left, kitchen just visible at rear of house. House is maintained for matrilineage or sublineage, but such houses are now giving way to smaller, simpler houses. Gurun-Batusangkar, West Sumatra, Indonesia. (Kindness of Lynn Thomas.)

In many societies marriage with outsiders is restricted or forbidden. Within societies marriage between classes, occupational groups, or ethnic groups may also be forbidden. Such groups, to which the term "caste" is sometimes applied, exist in most modern nations and existed traditionally among a wide range of densely populated agricultural and urban societies. In Mesoamerica, village communities are often endogamous, and it has been suggested that the Aztec *calpulli*, rather than being clans, were actually endogamous groups at least in some cases. In many parts of Africa, blacksmiths and other specialized groups form endogamous castes within larger tribes and states. In India, *jatis* are usually endogamous groups composed of exogamous clans. Indian *jatis* are usually ranked and are expected to maintain distinctive occupational and religious practices. Because such endogamous ethnic groups or castes are often believed, like clans, to be composed of kinsmen, the distinction between caste and clan often turns on the single issue of exogamy versus endogamy.

Functionally a system of ranked clans, each possessing distinctive occupational and other attributes, differs little from a system of ranked castes. Francis Hsu,[4] who has compared the castes of India with the clans of China and the clubs of Euro-American nations, finds essential parallels among them even though they seem to lead to rather different ways of thinking and acting.

5. Summary

Relatives, or kin, are people who are related to each other through some combination of the principles of descent and marriage as applied to socially recognized familial ties. Such genealogically related individuals are addressed and referred to through the use of a set of kin terms collectively constituting a kinship terminology. Each kinterm is generally applied to a series of similar kin types such as MoSi, FaBrWi, MoBrWi, and FaSi, all of which call for the use of the term "aunt." The several hundred kin types that can be located upon a genealogical diagram can be classified in a variety of ways, depending upon the particular principles used in forming the classification. In the English kinship system the principles used in classifying relatives are generation, sex, lineality–collaterality, and consanguinity–affinity. The principles of age, sex of speaker, nature of connecting relative, reciprocity, and condition of relative referred to have been identified in other kinship terminologies. A comparison of the English, Chiricahua Apache, and Urabunna kinship terminologies illustrates the range of results that can be obtained by varying the principles of classification and the order in which they are applied. Although kinship terminologies need not necessarily be connected to social realities, most play a role in defining groups of people who are to be treated in more or less the same way.

The principles of kinship may also be used to define various kinds of nuclear and extended family households or to establish larger kinship groupings. Of particular importance in this matter is the question of residence after marriage, which may be patrilocal, matrilocal, neolocal, ambilocal, or some combination of these logical alternatives. Patrilocal or matrilocal residence, if practiced consistently, will tend to generate a patrilineal or matrilineal descent group or lineage. Patterns of marriage play a role in defining larger groups such as tribes, generally by ensuring consistent patterns of bride exchange among the various local groups of which they are composed as illustrated by the marriage rules characteristic of the Chiricahua Apache and of Australian tribes. Where large numbers of people must be integrated into a single social organization, exogamous clans or sibs may serve as a means of encouraging wide-ranging marital exchanges. By contrast, endogamous groupings, usually referred to as ethnic groups or castes, may restrict marital exchange to particular subgroups within the larger society.

[4] Francis L. K. Hsu, *Clan, Caste, and Club* (New York: Van Nostrand, 1963).

Collateral Reading

Barnes, John A. *Three Styles in the Study of Kinship*. Berkeley: University of California Press, 1971. An impressive treatment of different approaches.

Bohannon, Paul J., and John Middleton (eds.). *Kinship and Social Organization*. Garden City, N.Y.: The Natural History Press, 1968.

Buchler, Ira R., and Henry A. Selby. *Kinship and Social Organization: An Introduction to Theory and Method*. New York: Macmillan Publishing Co., Inc., 1968. Describes some of the newer approaches.

Graburn, Nelson H. (ed.). *Readings in Kinship and Social Structure*. New York: Harper & Row, Inc., 1971. A good selection.

Keesing, Roger M. *Kin Groups and Social Structure*. New York: Holt, Rinehart and Winston, Inc., 1975. An up-to-date survey.

Schusky, Ernest L. *Variation in Kinship*. New York: Holt, Rinehart and Winston, Inc., 1974. A survey.

Schusky, Ernest L. *Manual for Kinship Analysis*. New York: Holt, Rinehart and Winston, Inc., 1965. A much improved version of an earlier edition.

Tyler, Stephen A. (ed.). *Cognitive Anthropology*. New York: Holt, Rinehart and Winston, Inc., 1969. Sections contain examples of formal and mathematical methods for the study of kinship.

Ethnographic References

Chiricahua Apache: Opler, 1937, 1941.
Marquesan: Linton, 1939.
South India: Beals, 1962.
Tibet: Ekvall, 1968.
Urabunna, Australia: Spencer and Gillen, 1899.

13/Social Organization

1. General Principles

A social organization is a set of members related to each other in ways that facilitate the carrying out of activities characteristic of a particular group or society. An organization can be viewed structurally, in terms of the relationships or principles by means of which its members are organized, or processually, in terms of the various activities by means of which it is maintained. Thus a kin group such as a patrilineal clan can be viewed structurally, in terms of the relationships of descent which define each member's position within the clan, or it can be viewed processually, in terms of the behaviors expected from and/or exhibited by its membership.

Although there are several useful ways of viewing social structure, the most common is in terms of a set of positions or statuses that are occupied by the members or groups of members. The arrangement of the statuses in terms of various principles of relationship constitutes the social structure. Thus the nuclear family can be characterized by such statuses as parent, child, husband, wife, father, mother, son, daughter, brother, and sister. These statuses are given positions within a genealogical diagram representing the social structure of the family by the relationships of descent and affinity. In terms of process, each status carries with it a role that the individual occupying that status is expected to play and the various behaviors that the individual actually exhibits. The statuses of mother and child, for example, carry with them certain roles that every mother and child is expected to play. In many societies the role of mother involves feeding, protecting, and emotionally supporting the child, while the role of child involves displaying obedience and affection toward the mother. A "good" mother is one whose actual behavior closely conforms to role expectations. In real life the mother and child may attempt to avoid performing certain aspects of their roles or may engage in bargaining about the manner in which their respective roles are to be played. In the nuclear family, as the child's status moves from that of child to adult, the roles of mother and child are placed under increasing strain and there are likely to be increasing divergences from the ideal expectations provided in the definition of the role. In the course of time the child will occupy the new status of grown-up child and role, and status will again be consistent.

Within an organization individuals may move from one status to another and, over the course of time, new statuses may develop or old statuses disappear. The roles attached to each status may also change, and particular individuals may differ in the extent to which they exhibit conformity or nonconformity to the roles attached to their statuses. An individual may occupy several statuses at once and the roles attached to such statuses may sometimes conflict.

Distinctions must also be made between social classifications, which involve sets of labels or terms applied to statuses and the statuses themselves. In parts of South India the name for the status of "mother" is "tayi," and in the United States it is "mother." The status is the same, but the label is different. Needless to say, the status of mother continues to exist, even if there is no name for the status. Further, although names like "tayi" and "mother" refer to a particular status within a family group, it is important to note that mothers do not form a group. Labels or names used in social classification do not necessarily refer to organized groups or even to interrelated individuals. Barbers, workers, the younger generation, and right-thinking persons, all constitute social classifications. We expect certain things of the members of these classes because we have seen fit to lump them together under a single label, but the label need not tell us very much about their position in society or the kinds of activities in which they engage. Most important of all, individuals who are classified together under the same label are not necessarily related or connected to each other in any way. A mere label can tell us nothing about social structure because it tells us nothing about any interconnectedness that might exist among barbers, workers, or other persons who happen to be classified together.

In our own society the label "family" can be used either to describe the occupants of a nuclear family household or the entire set of individuals to whom kinship terms apply. Both types of family consist of interconnected persons, but only the nuclear family household forms a "true" or corporate group possessing an organization and exhibiting characteristic behaviors. The nuclear family household is, in fact, a subcultural system with its own environment, cultural tradition, and social organization. The family consisting of all known kinsmen may contain persons that Ego has never seen. It is also likely to lack any clearly defined boundary or membership and there may be no circumstances in which its members interact as a group. Concepts of social organization, social structure, status, and role apply primarily within true or corporate groups. It is important, then, to consider some of the various ways of classifying groups and their members.

A group where all, or nearly all, of the members interact directly with each other is generally called a *face-to-face*, or *primary*, group. A group composed of interacting groups is generally called a *secondary* group. A primary group can consist of two people. As it acquires additional members, it is bound to reach a point, which may vary from culture to culture or situation to situation, at which subgroups will form within it. Under most circumstances a true primary group will probably contain fewer than ten persons, but under special circumstances the upper limit in size may reach as high as twenty.

In previous discussions of marriage and kinship, continual reference was made to households and local groups. If individuals are to interact and so to form groups, it is essential that they possess some place in which to do so. Thus coresidence, or at least the temporary sharing of a territory, is essential to the formation of any kind of group. Occupation of a common territory is more fundamental than kinship as a means of organizing human groups. Households, local groups, bands, tribes, states, nations, and many things in between are all primarily territorial groups, even though their members may visualize them also in other terms.

Beyond kinship and territorial principles, almost anything that can be regarded as a common bond between individuals can serve as a basis for social structure. At the primary group level, people who work in the same place may form teams, work groups, or crews. They may also form secondary groups such as factories, unions, or social and recreational clubs. People who work at the same jobs or professions may also form guilds, unions, and other sorts of groups based on common occupation. In fact any kind of common interest, from chess to revolution, may serve as the basis for the organization of some kind of group.

Groups need not be classified solely in terms of the basis of membership. Like individuals they can be arranged in terms of the roles they play in society and the contributions they make or are thought to make to it. Groups can have recreational, economic, religious, educational, political, artistic, and other purposes or functions singly or in combination. Specialized groups devoted to the carrying out of a single specialized set of purposes and/or tasks are, of course, characteristic of societies possessing specialization of labor.

Acquisition of membership status in a particular group, or for that matter of any status, may fall anywhere along a continuum of achieved to ascribed status. An achieved status is one that must be earned through the demonstration of ability; an ascribed status is one that is acquired by virtue of descent or some other arbitrary criterion. Even in the family, where descent is supreme, such statuses as "mother" represent achievement, from which it may be concluded that there is no society that does not possess both achieved and ascribed statuses as well as a variety of statuses that combine both principles. Graduation from college is generally regarded as an achieved status, but it certainly helps if the student is born into a family that can afford to pay tuition. Another sort of continuum used in classifying groups has to do with the extent to which membership is voluntary or involuntary. Birth into any group is involuntary as is conscription into a labor gang or military force. Membership in social or recreational clubs is usually regarded as voluntary, even though various subtle and not so subtle pressures may be exerted upon the individual to make him or her join.

Groups may also be classified in terms of such things as the manner in which goods, both material and nonmaterial, are distributed within them and the extent to which such things as membership requirements and duties and responsibilities are spelled out. In ideal egalitarian groups the members are peers or equals, decisions are made collectively, and the material and nonmaterial costs and profits of membership are divided equally. At the other extreme is the ranked or hierarchical group in which the members are considered unequal, decisions are made by the higher-ranking members, and many of the costs of membership are assigned to lower-ranking members, while many of the profits are assigned to higher-ranking members. Most groups fall somewhere on a continuum between such extremes. Further, groups that are egalitarian in some senses may be ranked in others. An authoritarian group is one in which a few high-ranking individuals make the decisions. Such a group need not be, although it usually is, hierarchical in other respects. As an example, a University department with a rotating chairmanship is egalitarian in providing access to positions of authority, but authoritarian in the sense that one person holds decision-making power at any moment. Authority itself is not a single characteristic. Hence it is possible for a group to possess several authorities, each of whom "takes charge" under different circumstances. The division of power in medieval Europe between the church and the state is a case in point.

Where requirements for membership and other aspects of group functioning are spelled out in formal detail, a group is said to be a formal group. An informal group, by contrast, is one in which the members are vague about who belongs, what they are supposed to be doing, who is the leader, and so on. The classical form of the informal group is the neighborhood play group consisting of children of about the same age. Although a few children may form the nucleus of such a group, other children may come and go. Careful observation will enable an outside observer to discover who the members are, who the leaders are, and so on, but such information usually cannot be gained through interview techniques. In contrast, a formally organized children's club may well have a constitution, a list of members, formally elected leaders, and so on.

When social organizations are considered as structures, our attention is directed to the number and arrangement of the individuals and groups out of which they are composed and to the various principles, such as kinship, friendship, common interest, territoriality, exchange, and hierarchy, which establish relationships between the individuals and groups and determine their position in relationship to each other. Other ways of classifying groups and organizations have to do with such things as the manner in which membership and status are acquired, the kinds of activity that take place within the group, the degree to which the group is formally organized, the kind of cultural tradition the group possesses, or the kinds of functions or impacts the group has upon other aspects of society. Because ways of classifying groups and individuals can be multiplied endlessly, it is possible to be skeptical about any classification that is not justified in terms of some particular research question or theory. For example, a distinction between primary and secondary groups or between formal and informal groups is useful only if we have some substantial reason for believing that the differences are important.

2. Types of Social Structure

Although virtually all anthropologists would agree that human societies have evolved structurally in the sense that new ways of organizing and developing relationships between individuals and groups have developed over the years, there is a great deal of disagreement on the details. Hunter-gatherer societies, especially those that have low population density, are generally considered to be primarily organized in terms of kinship and territory or propinquity and to contain at most three levels of organization: nuclear families or nuclear family households, local groups, and bands. Each level of organization is composed, very roughly speaking, of perhaps 10 or 20 units from the next lower level of organization. Thus a local group contains 10 or 20 nuclear families, and a band contains 10 or 20 local groups. As noted earlier, the average size of the band or "dialect tribe" is believed by some to be approximately 500. Even among hunter-gatherers with low population density, there are many exceptions to this pattern. Both the Tiwi of Australia and the Chiricahua Apache traditionally included several bands within a dialect tribe which must have been considerably larger than 500.

Bands and tribes of hunter-gatherers, on the whole, often lack specialization of labor beyond that based on age and sex. Consequently access to positions of power and leadership, which are usually informal anyway, is usually egalitarian in the sense that an individual's power and prestige increase gradually with age. Although men are generally of higher status than women, strict distinctions between the spheres of action of the two sexes often make the question academic. Among the Tiwi and many other Australian groups, men were strongly ranked in terms of the power and influence they acquired in both economic and social spheres as they accumulated wives. Older men, who failed to accumulate wives, held relatively low status. In a sense, wives were the capital of the Australian male, and as he acquired wives and relatives by marriage, he became a more and more powerful and authoritarian leader.

Among Eskimo hunters, as among most hunter-gatherers, the accumulation of more than one or two wives was presumably ruled out by ecological circumstances. The Eskimo shaman, who possessed special training that permitted him to encounter and hopefully control the spirits responsible for misfortune and illness, might, so long as he carried out his spiritual duties successfully, rise to a position of considerable power and influence. He was, however, a part-time specialist who supported himself and his family as everyone else did by hunting and fishing.

The increased resources and population densities characteristic of some specialized hunters or collectors and of several of the less productive forms of gardening or animal herding seem to lead to the development of more complex social structures often based upon factors other than kinship. The Hopi and other Western Pueblo peoples, although primarily organized in terms of kinship (see pp. 283–294), also possessed more or less voluntary kiva organizations composed of individuals interested in the performance of particular ceremonial activities. Western Pueblo clans were also, to some extent, ranked, with important leadership positions often belonging exclusively to certain clans. Village councils, usually composed of the leaders of the various clans, provided a formal governmental organization of a sort that usually exists only informally among hunter-gatherers.

Among the Nuer, all boys initiated into manhood within the same period of years formed a single age group, or *ric*. After an age group had been formed, "the knife was hung up" and traditionally there were no more initiations for a period of approximately four years. At any one time there were usually about six age groups in existence. Members of the same age group were regarded as being on terms of equality. They joked together, played together, ate together and were associated in work and war. Members of the same age group also fought each other, and it was considered improper to fight with a man of a senior age group. Members of an age group were expected to show respect to members of senior age groups, and any relationship that was not already fixed by kinship was fixed in terms of the relative seniority of the individual's age group. The members of an age group were considered brothers and could not marry each other's daughters. Similarly a man could not marry a woman drawn from his father's age group unless her father or his father had died. Thus, among the Nuer, the age group system operated very much like a system of cross-cousin kinship terminology to divide the group into broad classes with formally specified relationships between the classes.

Age groups are one of many forms of social organization characteristic of the Igbo of Nigeria. The Igbo, even before modern times, were one of the most densely populated and highly urbanized groups in the world. Ottenberg, writing in 1968, gave the total population of the Igbo at between 5 and 7 million with a density reaching up to 1,000 persons per square mile. (The population density of Russia and the United States is closer to 50 persons per square mile.) Despite the density of population, the Igbo did not until recently possess or participate in a national government in any organized or formal sense. The major formal social unit was a village group consisting of a set of neighboring villages and ranging in size from several thousand to over 75,000. Although Igbo social organization was expressed mainly through patrilineal and matrilineal clans and a variety of voluntary organizations, groupings of men and women in terms of age were also of vital importance.

Starting at about the age of twenty-eight, men joined age sets covering a

Masai youth (Tanzania) during a respite in the coming-of-age ceremonies performed every six or seven years to induct youths into the warrior age grade. (Courtesy of the United Nations.)

span of about three years. Each village contained between fifteen and twenty age sets, each having its own organization and leadership. Membership was compulsory for all men in the village and so included men from different clans. The sets were grouped into grades consisting of two or three different age sets. An executive grade consisting of younger men was responsible for the direction of communal work, the safeguarding of community funds, police work, and assistance in the performance of rituals and sacrifices. The elder's grade, which included elders from other villages as well, administered the entire village group. Within the village the elders were responsible for village properties, for the settling of disputes, for legislation, and for the conduct of village feasts and ceremonies.

Organizations similar to age groups may also be formed on the basis of achievement, and achievement may sometimes form the basis for admission to age-graded organizations. In the United States the transition from junior high school to high school is based partly upon age and partly upon the ability to perform certain tasks which may be specified in great detail. Among the Hopi, children without political ambition might attain to manhood through participation in the relatively mild rituals of the Powamu society. Children whose parents and mother's brothers had greater ambitions for them were encouraged to undergo the much more difficult and painful initiation into the Kachina society as well.

Although membership in an age grade or age group is often involuntary, age groups may also come to be a specialized form of voluntary association. In Bamako, the capital of the African state of Mali, traditional age groups of the Bamana tribe have become one of a large variety of voluntary associations by means of which the city is organized. The traditional age groups, which existed in rural areas in 1968, consisted of boys and girls of about the same age who were initiated at the same time. The oldest boy and the oldest girl in the age group of "hand" was chosen as leader, and each organized the boys and girls respectively into an association. Boys and girls in the different hands might pair off, but the boy was likely to be whipped if the girl was not a virgin when she reached marriageable age. The girls and boys associations performed odd jobs about the village, using the income for private celebrations or for other purposes. The boys association also organized dances and performed plays for public entertainment. In addition to the young people's associations, there were associations for the old men. Age grading was less of a factor in such societies as the *komo* and the *nama*, which consisted of individuals graded in terms of their success in acquiring esoteric knowledge which was used to frighten nonmembers, and sometimes to punish or poison them. The *kore*, another association, was composed of young adults who practiced buffoonery and joking. Finally, there was an association of hunters that had its own exclusive cults, secret knowledge, and magic.

As the city of Bamako became progressively urbanized and came to include different tribes and peoples, the traditional rural voluntary associations as described above appear to have proliferated and become a wide variety of mutual aid, sports, political, cultural, youth, regional, religious, veterans, and caste organizations. During the 1950s, even though Bamako was a relatively small city, there were about 149 associations that were actually registered with the government. There were, of course, many more that were informal or social and not registered.

The proliferation of voluntary associations in most modern cities is generally attributed to the fact that kinship, and even ethnic ties, tend to lose their effectiveness because immigrants to the cities often have difficulty in locating or living near kinsmen or members of their own ethnic group. Initially, and as a means of locating kinsmen and tribesmen, voluntary associations tend to develop along ethnic or locality lines and to have highly generalized economic, political, and religious functions. They help their members to find jobs, marital partners, and housing; they provide entertainments and religious services; and they develop political influence in the name of some region, language, or religion with which they identify. Later, as their members become increasingly urbanized and successful, membership in ethnic associations tends to be replaced or supplemented by membership in increasingly specialized associations reflecting some particular common interest ranging from athletics to local history. Because associations differ in such things as the size of their membership fees and the economic and social demands made upon their members, associations tend to be ranked, with the highest ranking sometimes exerting great political and economic influence.

In Bamako the Ambiance Association was started about 1956 by people of relatively humble status as a mutual aid society. By 1963 it had over 300 members including many of the most influential people in the city. Its primary efforts were directed toward the performance of elegant marriage ceremonies and other folk art performances generally attended by the highest-ranking government officials. In addition to such large organizations as the Ambiance, there were a ranked series of small clubs dedicated to the pursuit of modernity. The oldest and highest ranking of these clubs was the Bourbon, founded in 1953 by students returned from France. The Bourbon Club introduced bebop and associated modern ways of dressing and behaving. Wealthy young men who had not been to France also formed a club and by 1968 a whole series of ranked clubs developed largely for the purpose of organizing modern dance parties.

Although complicated arrangements of different kinds of voluntary associations occur only within complex and highly specialized cultural systems, voluntary associations, especially such highly informal ones as work groups or play groups, together with kinship organizations and organizations based on age or sex, can be regarded as the most widespread and presumably earliest and most basic ways of forming human groups. Bureaucracies, those complex and specialized structures dedicated to government, religion, education, adjudication, medical care, and so on, appear to develop and to acquire increasing complexity as population growth and other factors permit the development of specialization of labor to the point where hierarchies of specialists develop within particular fields.

3. Examples of Social Structure

In Chapters 11 and 12, examples have been given of social structures in which the arrangements of individuals and groups with regard to each other were almost entirely governed by principles of kinship. At a level of slightly increased complexity, the organization of the Hopi into clans and kiva associations has been mentioned. In the following examples, although kinship organizations, age grades, and voluntary associations of various kinds continue to be of considerable importance, additional forms of organization acquire an equal or greater importance.

Crow Indian social structure resembled that of the Hopi in that the "tribe" was divided into autonomous subdivisions, pueblos in the case of the Hopi, bands or tribelets in the case of the Crow. Both Hopi and Crow were also organized primarily in terms of matrilineal clans. Among the Hopi, political power derived primarily from position within the clan as determined by seniority and participation in ceremonial activity. Among the Crow, wealth and military achievement as determined by the individual's success in acquiring power through the vision quest were the prime determinants of political influence. To be a leader among the Crow, it was essential that the individual perform a creditable military exploit (counting *coup*). Such "good and valiant" men were the leaders and decision makers of the band. One of the good and valiant men, usually an older man with many honors, was chosen to be head of the camp. The camp head made decisions about the movement of the band. He also appointed one of the several military clubs to serve as police. The police regulated the communal buffalo hunt, punishing anyone who killed game illegally. The camp head was also assisted by a herald, or crier, who made announcements throughout the camp and transmitted the decisions of the camp chief.

In addition to membership in the mother's clan, most men belonged to a social and military association. Membership in particular associations was generally voluntary, although parents might pledge an infant to replace a brother who had died while a member. As seems to be the rule with voluntary associations, the Crow were constantly forming new associations and allowing older ones to die out. In 1833 there were eight clubs. In the 1870s there were four clubs: the Foxes, Lumpwoods, Big Dogs, and Muddy Hands. Members of a particular club generally met each evening or so in a member's tipi for friendly socializing. Fellow club members, even those from different bands, treated each other like brothers, helping each other through economic crises and aiding with burial expenses. Although the clubs were run by older and prestigious members, younger officials who were supposed to undertake the most dangerous military duties were chosen each year. Each club was, of course, ready to undertake police duties if chosen to do so by the camp head. During the 1860s and 1870s, when the Lumpwoods and the Foxes were the two most important clubs, the two clubs competed for the honor of striking the first coup of the season. After the spring elections, the two clubs challenged each other to participate in the mutual abduction of wives. A man had the right to kidnap any woman whose lover he had previously been. If the husband attempted to visit his wife after she had been kidnapped, he would be tied up and smeared with dog dung, and his fellow club members would be forced to flee lest their blankets be chopped to pieces by members of the opposing club.

With the ever-present possibility of feuds between clans and of an outbreak of hostilities between fiercely competing clubs, Crow social structure seems almost frighteningly centripetal. What held things together was probably the existence of crosscutting loyalties: a conflict between clans is the same thing

European introduction of the horse and gun vastly increased the productivity of buffalo hunting and resulted in the intensification of patterns of raiding and warfare. A Cheyenne Indian in special war dress with pistol and cartridge belt. (Courtesy of W. H. Over Museum.)

as an opposition between husband and wife or even father and children, while conflict between clubs could involve opposition between brothers and between members of the same clan. A small group may be held together by virtue of the fact that its members are totally interdependent in both economic and social activities; a larger group, such as the Crow band, may be held together by the fact that any attempt at division involves the rupture of such important ties as those connecting fellow club members or fellow household members.

The Samoans of the South Pacific were traditionally village dwellers who supported themselves by fishing and agriculture. The basic unit of their social structure was a family household consisting of a family head (*matai*) chosen at the death of the previous family head by all adult household members and officially appointed by the village council. With the family head lived his immediate family and other close relatives. The average household in recent times contained nine or ten people. Related households formed an *aiga*, or extended family. Such a family had an elected head and, although it was usually associated with a particular village, its members might live in a number of different villages. Membership in a particular *aiga* could be claimed on the basis of any relationship to its present or previous heads. Thus an individual could claim membership in a number of different extended families, and each extended family tended to be quite large. The extended family participated in gift exchanges at the time of weddings and funerals and carried out religious and ceremonial activities. Member households contributed goods to the extended family head to permit him to carry out these functions.

The different household and family heads inherited the titles of Chief or Talking Chief. These titles were strictly ranked in terms of traditional achievements. The highest-ranking chiefs were the High Chiefs of the village. The High Chiefs occupied a special place within the Council House with progressively lower-ranking chiefs seated at increasing distances from them. The lowest-ranking chiefs lacked assigned positions and usually sat on the floor near the highest-ranking chiefs of their extended families. High-ranking Talking Chiefs were spokesmen for the High Chiefs and served as village orators and executive officers. High-ranking chiefs, because their persons were sacred, were usually represented by Talking Chiefs. Lower-ranking chiefs and Talking Chiefs were not necessarily paired. The High Chiefs presided over Village Council meetings, settled disputes brought before the Council, and served as advisors to the Talking Chiefs. The High Talking Chief, who carried an enormous fly whisk as his badge of office, was the principal village orator, settled disputes between villages, welcomed important persons to the village, and oversaw distributions of food and other property.

Although succession to office involved inherited position, selection from among those eligible depended upon their achievements in war, their knowledge of ceremonial lore, and their oratorical ability. The rigidly hierarchical seating in the Village Council, combined with the use of a special chief's language and a vast importance attributed to oratorical skills, probably meant that high-ranking chiefs and Talking Chiefs possessed much greater influence upon decisions than did their inferiors. Alliances of villages possessed similar councils, High Chiefs, and Talking Chiefs, but such alliances were often temporary and rarely survived the lifetime of their elected High Chief.

Untitled men within the village formed a voluntary association responsible for cooperative labor and for assisting the chiefs in the carrying out of ceremonial activities. The organization was usually led by the son of the High Chief or by some other close relative. In organization, the untitled people's association closely paralleled that of the village, having its own council and its own hierarchy of chiefs. The untitled people's association also had social and recreational functions involving courtship, the organization of soccer matches, and the holding of dances and beer parties. Unmarried women formed a parallel group which also contributed to the general welfare by carrying out economic, social, and ceremonial activities.

South Indian village organization traditionally involved, as does that of Samoa, a combination of households and extended families. Each household had a head, and the senior head of a group of patrilineally related households occupied a seat on the village council. He also, however, occupied a seat on a clan council which administered the affairs of local village lineages within a region. If there were two lineages, belonging to the same caste within the

The throne is a widespread symbol of authority. Yoruba, Nigeria. (Courtesy of the UCLA Museum of Cultural History.)

village, membership in the village council went to the head of the senior lineage. Thus the village council was formed by representatives from each important caste in the village. Because the castes were ranked, it follows that the members of the village council were also ranked. Nevertheless all decisions of village, lineage, and caste councils had to be unanimous.

In addition to council membership on the part of household heads, there were hereditary village officers and servants. The most important of these were the Headman and the Accountant. The Headman settled disputes and administered punishments to those who behaved improperly. The Accountant, usually a member of the literate and high-ranking Brahman caste, kept village land and tax records. The Headman and the Accountant, together, were responsible for meeting with government officials and arranging for the payment of taxes or for other services they demanded.

Ceremonies, necessary for the welfare of the community, were generally carried out by hereditary officers drawn from all or nearly all of the castes of the village. The different castes often had highly specialized economic responsibilities as well, such as conducting worship, blacksmithing, barbering, and carpentry. Village unity, then, had to do with the perception that the cooperation of representatives of many different castes was necessary for the wellbeing of the community. Because marriage had to take place outside the clan, but within the caste, many marriages took place between villages, with the result that kinship ties served as links between villages, while economic and ceremonial ties served as links between the castes composing a village. Here, a pattern of crosscutting loyalties provided each individual with horizontal loyalties to caste and clan which stretched across villages, and with vertical loyalties and economic interdependencies to friends, neighbors, and functionaries within the village.

Although most voluntary associations within the village were informal peer groups, work groups, loafing groups, and political alliances, formal associations were often organized in connection with intervillage competitive sports such as wrestling and, more recently, volleyball, and religious activities, especially the performance of religious dramas and the organization of hymn-singing groups. Although even in recent times state bureaucratic organizations have not penetrated very deeply into most villages, the traditional village often had a school organized by groups of parents who made gifts and payments to a schoolteacher. State organization, although it was highly complicated even several thousand years ago, was quite simple from the village point of view. At the time of harvest, the local chieftain or his representative, sometimes supported by mercenary soldiers, appeared and demanded their traditional share of the crop. Problems that could not be resolved in the village could also be taken to the local chieftain or to an important religious shrine. The most important social responsibility of chieftains and of higher-ranking rulers as well was to regulate disputes between castes concerning their rank, privileges, and duties. Chieftains and rulers were also responsible for dealing with bandits and for the defense of the state.

4. Summary

A social organization is a set of members related to each other in ways that facilitate the carrying out of activities characteristic of a particular group or society. Such an organization can be viewed structurally, in terms of the principles by means of which its members are organized, or processually, in terms of the various activities which account for its maintenance. Social structure is

commonly viewed as a set of positions or statuses arranged in terms of principles of relationship such as kinship or rank. Within social structure, distinctions are often made among statuses or positions, roles, and labels. A social
structure is a property of a group or society defined as interconnected people
who engage in decision-making behavior with sufficient frequency to establish
patterns of characteristic behavior. An important distinction can be made
between primary, or face-to-face, groups and secondary groups. Groups have
been classified in a number of other ways: in terms of how membership is
achieved, what the members do, how decisions are reached, how formal they
are, or how hierarchical they are. The value of such classifications is dependent upon their relevance to some particular research question or theory.

There is general agreement that human societies have evolved structurally,
but vast disagreement on the precise order in which new structural arrangements came into being. Hunter-gatherer societies with low population density
seem almost always to be organized primarily in terms of kinship and territory
or propinquity. Somewhat larger hunter-gatherer societies often had systems
of rank in which some individuals were more important and more powerful
than most others. Voluntary organizations and formal age grades, such as the
Hopi kiva group or the Nuer *ric,* though not absent among hunter-gatherers,
seem to occur with more frequency in agricultural or herding societies and
other relatively complex societies such as the Igbo and the United States. Like
age grades, voluntary associations are associated with a wide range of societies. Voluntary associations tend to proliferate, however, in certain kinds of
urban settings, as illustrated by recent developments in Bamako. Bureaucratic
organizations and institutions tend to be limited in distribution to complex
and highly organized societies. The complex possibilities inherent in the
arrangement of individuals and subgroups in terms of a variety of principles of
organization are illustrated by reference to the social structures of the Crow
Indians, the Samoans, and the South Indians.

Collateral Reading

Banton, Michael. *Roles, an Introduction to the Study of Social Relations.* London:
     Tavistock Publications, 1965.
Bradfield, Richard M. *A Natural History of Associations: A Study in the Meaning of
     Community,* 2 vols. New York: International Universities Press, 1973. Voluntary
     associations in kin-based societies.
Kuper, Hilda. *The Swazi: a South African Kingdom.* New York: Holt, Rinehart and
     Winston, Inc., 1963.
Lowie, Robert H. *Social Organization.* New York: Rinehart and Co., 1948. A broader
     coverage than most recent works.
Mayer, Adrian C. *Caste and Kinship in Central India.* Berkeley and Los Angeles: Uni-
     versity of California Press, 1970.
Meillassoux, Claude. *Urbanization of an African Community, Voluntary Associations in
     Bamako.* Seattle and London: University of Washington Press, 1968. A society
     dominated by clubs.

Mitchell, John C. (ed.). *Social Network in Urban Situations*. Manchester, England: University of Manchester Press, 1971. Networks are now seen as fundamental to the structure of many urban communities.

Newman, Philip L. *Knowing the Gururumba*. New York: Holt, Rinehart and Winston, Inc., 1965.

Rubin, Morton. *The Walls of Acre: Intergroup Relations and Urban Development in Israel*. New York: Holt, Rinehart and Winston, Inc., 1974.

Sugarman, Barry. *Daytop Village: A Therapeutic Community*. New York: Holt, Rinehart and Winston, Inc., 1974.

Warner, W. Lloyd. *Structure of American Life*. Edinburgh: University Press, 1952.

Ethnographic References

Bamana; Mali: Meillassoux, 1969.

Crow: Lowie, 1935.

Eskimo: Birket-Smith, 1936; Coon, 1948, Chapt. 4; Rasmussen, 1908.

Hopi: Dozier, 1970; Eggan, 1950; Titiev, 1944, 1972.

Igbo, Nigeria: Ottenberg, 1968.

Nuer: Evans-Pritchard, 1940.

Samoan: Holmes, 1958; Mead, 1928:

South India: Beals, 1962.

14/Social Organization: Process

1. Maintaining A Social Structure

In the previous chapter a distinction was made between social structures and social processes, processes being the culturally significant patterns of behavior by means of which a cultural system is maintained. In forming a social structure, individuals occupy statuses and develop relationships between those statuses through behavior; that is, they do the things they need to do in order to be regarded as occupants of particular statuses and to maintain the social structure. Individuals, then, create social structure by means of behavior, and a social structure can be regarded as an artifact of behavior. It differs from a physical artifact, such as an item of material culture, in that the parts are human beings and the relationships between them are such immaterial things as kinship and friendship.

The coordination of individual activities in the construction and maintenance of social structure is assured by virtue of the presence of behavioral standards, including various sorts of rules, laws, and regulations, by means of which people assess the correctness of each other's behaviors. When individuals violate the behavioral standards that define their roles in particular situations, they are likely to encounter results that are aversive or unrewarding. Political processes in general deal with those aspects of

439

social behavior that have to do with the establishment and enforcement of behavioral standards (legislation and social control) and with the circulation of individuals from status to status. Because our own society includes specialized institutions for the carrying out of political processes, we tend to think of these processes in terms of such things as getting elected, making laws, administering justice, and so on. Even in our own society, the realm of such formal political action is a highly restricted one. Most behavior is governed by informal or traditional behavioral standards which do not have the force of law and which need not be enforced by such formal institutions as law courts or police forces. For example, most family households in the United States settle their affairs informally, appealing to formal institutions only when ordinary informal mechanisms fail. Such questions as the expenditure of funds by different household members, the division of labor within the household, or the hours at which meals are to be served fall normally within the realm of informal process.

2. Establishing Behavioral Standards

Legislation or the establishment of behavioral standards is often regarded as a highly formal process involving the "passing" of laws or the systematic preparation of regulations. Laws are enforced, at least in theory, through the use of police forces and other police powers of the state, while the normal sort of bureaucratic regulation is usually enforced by denying certain services or privileges to violators. Laws and regulations differ from behavioral standards, however, to the extent that some laws and regulations are unknown to the public or are not enforced. Active laws and regulations, those that people know about and are expected to conform to, are behavioral standards, but they differ from ordinary behavioral standards to the extent that they are formally stated or written. Although there is probably no way of classifying behavioral standards that will permit us at once to specify in any society the distinctions among laws, regulations, rules, and informal behavioral standards, standards that are called laws generally have several of the following characteristics: (1) They are enacted through a formal process of legislation; (2) they are formally written down or otherwise codified; (3) they involve some specific and formal method of adjudication and enforcement. In addition they have to be behavioral standards in the sense that they are generally known and expected to be obeyed.

In informal groups and unspecialized societies, legislation is generally an informal process, and there are relatively few behavioral standards that can be confidently identified as laws. In many situations, even in complex societies, the legislation of behavioral standards is a difficult process to observe. For example, in modern world culture standards of dress and hairstyle seem to come into being without benefit of formal processes of legislation. During the 1960s a rapid, and to some people frightening, lengthening of men's hair occurred almost simultaneously in such regional centers of fashion as Bombay, Moscow,

Council members listening to a visiting administrator. In complex societies legislative processes are complex and are carried out at many levels. Lower Juba, Somaliland, Africa. (Courtesy of the United Nations.)

Tokyo, London, San Francisco, and New York. Although several governments immediately announced that the new hairstyle had been legislated as a part of a Communist or capitalist plot, the originators of this new behavioral standard have not as yet been identified, nor has the legislative process involved been investigated. Further, although the new behavioral standard involved no mechanisms of enforcement, many men adhered to it despite expulsion from school, loss of employment, and imprisonment.

Although the example of hairstyle may seem trivial or exceptional, the fact remains that in all known cultures most of the standards that govern behavior are of unknown origin. The processes of legislation that created them are either buried in antiquity or hidden by the casual and informal processes by which they are developed and changed. In most cases the legislation of new behavioral standards is probably a largely unconscious process in which individuals respond to changing circumstances by relaxing their allegiance to behavioral standards that become boring, inconvenient, or unworkable. The relaxation of allegiance, identified by A. L. Kroeber as pattern exhaustion, permits experimentation with new forms of behavior. Because nobody really cares very much about the old standard, the new forms of behavior meet relatively slight opposition. In the end, one of the new forms of behavior, through a process akin to natural selection, is accepted as more convenient or more workable than the traditional standard, and becomes itself a standard of behavior.

In many societies where individuals are permitted direct access to supernatural forces, legislation may be accomplished by visionaries who receive new laws or behavioral standards directly from deities or spirits. In our own tradition, Moses, who introduced the Ten Commandments, Joseph Smith, the founder of the Church of Jesus Christ of Latter Day Saints, and many leaders of Protestant sects are reputed to have had such direct access to supernatural figures. In the same way, the Koran was written directly in the words of God by Mohammad. Among the Plains Indians and other American Indian groups, almost all individuals sought supernatural knowledge and power through the vision quest. Once a vision was demonstrated to be genuine either through exhibitions of power or through careful analysis by elders and other men of power, it could form the basis of legislation. The Ghost Dance, a religious movement which spread among the Indian groups of western North America during the latter part of the nineteenth century, was based upon a series of visions given to the Paiute Indian Wovoka and secondarily to a number of Plains Indian leaders. These visions, which foresaw the disappearance of the white man and the return of the buffalo, were accepted as genuine by many groups of Indians and resulted in the development of substantial changes in behavioral standards.

In most cases visions and other sorts of inspiration come under the heading of proposed legislation which is then carefully considered by appropriate decision-making groups. In small or informally organized groups, decisions on new behavioral standards may be made by the group acting as a whole or by an informal council of elders or high-status individuals. In complex societies with specialization of labor, the task of conceiving and approving new legislation falls into the hands of formally appointed chiefs and councils, bureaucratic organizations, authoritarian rulers, and other sorts of political organizations.

In the small group, which is, after all, the place where most legislation occurs even in complex societies, the close contact or even identity between the legislator and the member tends to generate a close fit between behavioral standards, the things that people are expected to do, and the things that they actually do. Another way of saying this is that there is sufficient feedback of information to guarantee the rejection of proposed legislation that is unpopular, unenforceable, or unrealistic. In complex societies the development of formal systems of law, together with the development of agencies for enforcement, easily leads to situations in which laws fail to reflect actual practices or in which laws place unrealistic or impossible burdens upon large segments of the population. Bogoraz describes a situation in which the Russian Czar ordered all of his administrative officers to introduce beekeeping into

The need to coordinate tribal activities in hunting and warfare contributed to the development of political organization on the Plains. The ability to have visions and acquire powers was an important attribute of leadership. Cheyenne Indians dressed for a council meeting. (From the Morrow Collection. Courtesy of W. H. Over Museum.)

the territories under their control. The Chukchee, and other groups living north of the Arctic Circle, were compelled to break the law because domesticated bees cannot survive in the polar environment. Such a state of affairs can develop only in complex societies that have failed to develop patterns for the appropriate feedback of information from the ruled to the rulers.

The efficient functioning of a complex society also requires that feedback operate from the rulers to the ruled, and it is often the case that legislative bodies generate vast quantities of legislation of which the ruled are totally unaware. In the University of California system, for example, legislation governing the behavior of faculty members can be developed by the Board of Regents, by the University Administration, by the statewide Academic Senate, by the campus Academic Senate, and by a host of other bodies and committees. The bulk of this legislation is contained in four or five fat volumes which few faculty members have ever seen. Similarly most states in India have had on the books since the 1930s laws permitting women to inherit property. Only a few urban sophisticates are even aware that the laws exist. The massive proliferation of laws and regulations with which the average citizen is totally unfamiliar is, of course, characteristic of most societies that possess written documents. In this case it is perhaps just as well that adequate feedback mechanisms do not exist. In any modern state the systematic enforcement of all the laws on the books would result in inconceivable chaos.

<h3>3. Social Control</h3>

Social control is the means by which the members of society are encouraged to conform to behavioral standards. In small societies and groups, where legislation and behavior coincide fairly closely, nonconforming behavior is not likely to be very frequent. People acquire behavioral standards quite early and rarely see any good reasons for violating them. In many cases rules concerning proper behavior are self-enforcing. Consider such rules as, "Don't make noise when you're stalking antelope," or "Don't put your hand in the fire."

On the other hand, although most people feel that their cultural traditions provide them with rules governing "what to do upon any occasion," no cultural tradition can encompass all the decisions that might be forced upon the individual. Behavioral standards tend to cover ordinary people in ordinary circumstances. If they attempted more than that, they would become too numerous to remember. The individual who seeks to behave as a proper member of his group or society is nevertheless often placed in situations requiring the generation of behaviors on the basis of little more than the hope of doing the right thing. Especially among children, but quite commonly among adults as well, the individual may inadvertently exhibit behavior that is considered improper or illegal.

The overall thrust of mechanisms of social control is to ensure that the balance of gains and losses associated with proper behavior is more rewarding than the balance of gains and losses associated with improper behavior. In cases where the individual is asked to make important sacrifices for the welfare of the group, conformity to behavioral standards is correspondingly difficult to arrange. In most societies and groups responses to exhibitions of improper behavior tend to vary along a spectrum ranging from mild disapproval to severe or life-threatening punishment.

Although it is easy to think of all behavior in terms of the extent to which it conforms to or violates standards, the situation is not always that simple. Some individuals such as clowns, scapegoats, children, and strangers are expected to violate certain standards. The routine violation of standards may be characteristic and necessary for some patterns of social control. Among the Eskimo, for example, there are a whole set of standards forbidding the eating of particular substances at particular times and covering various other aspects of everyday behavior. Very often the Eskimo lack the time or inclination to observe all such rules. The constant violation of the rules eventually irritates the spirit world and the Eskimo are afflicted with bad weather or bad hunting. When this happens, the members of the band gather together and confess their sins while a religious practitioner, a shaman (Chapter 15, §9), intercedes with the spirits and begs forgiveness. The spirits are expected to restore good weather and good hunting once all of the guilty and unclean Eskimo have confessed their sins and purified their minds. Here the violation of standards provides a mechanism for explaining misfortune and also for coping with it. Rule-breaking itself, then, is very frequently a part of normally expected behavior — a form of conformity to a more general standard.

Because Eskimo communities are generally quite small, violation of standards of interpersonal behavior is a very serious threat to the integrity of the group. Jean Briggs, in her account of a group of eight Eskimo households living to the northwest of Hudson's Bay, has described in detail the subtle techniques used to control her own behavior and that of others. One family in the group was particularly despised for unhelpfulness, greed, and bad temper. When the husband was overheard in the distance scolding his wife, people narrowed their eyes and murmured disapprovingly to each other. Such faults as this were, however, never mentioned in front of the nonconforming family. Social disapproval was expressed primarily by a refusal to initiate social contacts or to follow up when contacts were initiated by the nonconformists. If the wife smiled, other women smiled back, but when she asked questions, other women simply replied, "Yes," or "Who knows?" thus shutting off the attempt to initiate conversation. The effect was of a quiet shunning in which there was no overt act that could be described as anything but friendly. Nonconforming behavior that cannot be handled in this way triggers increasing tension within the group which may ultimately result in murder.

The Eskimo fear of violence or of the slightest display of hostility is in sharp contrast to the open display of hostility and violence characteristic of the Nuer of Africa. From earliest childhood the Nuer male was traditionally expected to respond to real and fancied slights or insults through fighting, and skill in fighting was highly valued. Although such a system of pervasive violence does not appear to represent a system of social control, a man's success in fighting, especially in fighting with those who were not members of the same age group or kin group, was dependent upon the kind of support he received from others. If a man justified stealing another man's cattle in terms of an unpaid debt, his chances of receiving assistance were increased. In effect the Nuer preferred to fight just wars, at least within closely related local groups or lineages. Each man's need for supporters placed a limit upon the violence and deadliness of fighting within his circle of intimate friends and kinsmen and created a need to conform to group standards lest he be alienated from his normal allies.

Within small groups generally, especially when the members are linked by kinship ties, conformity to most behavioral standards is assured by the fact that individuals are unaware of any alternatives. Where alternatives exist, the situation is usually structured in such a way both by the natural environment and by other people that the alternatives don't appear to be worth trying. Where the alternatives do appear to be worth trying — for example, when an Eskimo family wishes to enjoy the luxuries of stinginess and bad temper or when a Nuer wishes to steal more cows from a man who has injured him than is justified by the injury — the most common means of social control is simply to shun or to turn away from the malefactor. In the Eskimo case ridicule or some other direct challenge to the malefactor was considered dangerous and was not attempted unless repeated offenses made murder a psychological necessity. In the Nuer case the offender could be ridiculed or challenged, but the result was invariably a fight.

Among the Hopi, the Arunta of Australia, and many other peoples, repeated violations of behavioral standards are considered symptomatic of deadly and malevolent intent. The Hopi traditionally recognized a class of "two-hearts" who survived only by virtue of the fact that they supernaturally killed at least one close relative each year. The two-heart was considered to be unaware of his or her own evil nature. Direct accusation could only strengthen a two-heart, but a two-heart could be gravely injured by kindly and courteous treatment. A two-heart could of course be recognized by the exhibition of stinginess, bad temper, and other violations of behavioral standards. The Arunta believed that most deaths were caused by witches living in other groups. When a death occurred, they might, after identifying the local group responsible, visit the other group, identify individuals who persistently violated behavioral standards, and kill them. In most cases of death by witchcraft, it is not essential that anyone be actually involved in the practice of the black art, but only that someone, a scapegoat, can be identified and dealt with. Scapegoating is the process whereby persons who violate behavioral standards are accused of being responsible for a wide range of misfortunes affecting the group and are punished by ostracism or execution. The existence of scapegoats serves as an object lesson to others as well as providing a rationale for disposing of a particular offender. All Hopi and Arunta had to avoid scrupulously any behaviors that might conceivably be considered symptomatic of witchcraft. Among the Plains Indians, where power could be obtained through visions and used against other people, leaders were in a position to enforce behavioral standards through the threat of actually using witchcraft against an offender. In South India a thin sheet of copper inscribed with appropriate Sanskrit words could be tied around the neck of a suspected thief. If he was guilty, he was afflicted with severe stomach pains. Hardly an unlikely possibility, so long as the thief believed in the effectiveness of the charm.

Except among groups resembling the Hopi and Eskimo, where gossip and criticism were carefully kept away from the malefactor, accusations of witchcraft or of other serious violations of behavioral standards always pose the danger of counterattack. Very often — for example, when a person is accused of witchcraft because of a tendency to scream at small children — the malefactor has no way of knowing which behavioral standards he is accused of violating. This appears also in the Eskimo case given above where the family accused of stinginess and bad temper was never told why it was being shunned and, as is so often true in these cases, was unable to reform.

To a degree, all forms of social control involve some kind of punishment or reward. People who are shunned or avoided because they are ill-tempered or because they are thought to be witches are certainly punished in a sense. So are those who are accused by gossip of sexual irregularities, dishonesty, or other violations of standards. Similarly those who are treated with respect and admiration because they exemplify the highest possible standards of conduct

Positive appeals of friendship and conviviality are major factors in social control. Fanti men enjoying themselves. Ghana. (Kindness of David Kronenfeld.)

can be considered to be rewarded. All this is quite different from systematic reward and punishment distributed intentionally and in a formal manner. In ancient Egypt and in modern South India each person's good and bad deeds were weighed in the balance by the gods after his death and appropriate rewards or punishments assigned. Hopi deities, the kachinas, were frightened by the presence of the two-hearts or by the existence of mean thoughts. If there was disharmony in the pueblo, the kachinas remained at home and so did the life-giving rain clouds. Eskimo children who played roughly and noisily while their parents were away were likely to attract the attention of the many-armed spanking monster. An obvious advantage of supernatural punishment is that those who get punished have no one to blame but themselves.

In complex societies, where large populations are involved, such informal means of social control as ridicule or shunning become increasingly difficult to apply. In many cases rule-breakers are associated with subgroups or subcultures (countercultures) within which they receive moral and psychological support for rule-breaking activities. It is generally under these circumstances that informal behavioral standards become laws and that informal methods of social control are supplemented by systems of formal punishment. In the traditional South Indian village, violators were formally tried by village or caste councils and punished by fines, or in severe cases by banishment from the village or expulsion from the caste. Execution and imprisonment were virtually unknown. Such a system of punishment involving immediate trial is effective, even though the punishment may seem mild to those of us raised in a more punitive civilization, because the punishment follows directly upon the violation.

In our own society and in parts of Europe where punishments are severe, trials long delayed, and the culprit often marked for life as a criminal, it has often been argued that the system of punishment is ineffective as a means of social control. At best, the relegation of a large segment of the population to permanent membership in a criminal class may serve as a deterrent to those who fear the severity of the punishment. Physical violence directed against the person or psychological violence directed against a person's identity always creates the risk of resentment and counterattack. The need for violent punishments seems to characterize groups and societies that have conflicting moral standards and a lack of any strong consensus concerning behavioral standards. In the end, the use of punishment, especially of violent punishment, is a confession that milder forms of education and social control designed to encourage conformity to behavioral standards have failed.

In the vast majority of human societies, mechanisms of social control are a means of ensuring that the things that people want to do are in close conformity to the things that they are supposed to do. Some years ago, Edward Sapir made a distinction between genuine cultures in which the promised rewards for conformity to behavioral standards were given and spurious cultures in which people were given expectations that could not be met.[1] Along these

[1] Edward Sapir, "Culture, Genuine and Spurious," in *Selected Writings of Edward Sapir in Language, Culture, and Personality,* (ed.) David G. Mandelbaum (Berkeley: University of California Press, 1949).

Kachina spirits "visiting" the Hopi in order to participate in the Powamu or "bean-planting" ceremony. After initiation into the kachina cult, young men are told that the kachinas no longer visit in person, but must be impersonated by initiated men. Photograph by James Mooney of the Bureau of American Ethnology, Walpi Pueblo, Arizona, 1893. (Courtesy of Smithsonian Institution, National Anthropological Archives.)

lines, a genuine culture can be regarded as one in which the opposition between freedom and conformity is minimized because existing behavioral standards provide an efficient means by which a free individual can achieve his goals without causing harm to others. In a spurious culture the individual is brainwashed and made to conform regardless of the personal and psychological sacrifices involved in doing so. Cultures and their associated mechanisms for social control always represent restrictions on human freedom, but there is a difference between cultures in which individuals willingly give up short-term gains in order to secure the benefits of membership, and those in which conformity to behavioral standards is secured by violence or the threat of violence.

4. Conflict

Most people, most of the time, are addicted to propriety. People conform to behavioral standards and in the process of doing so they engage in behaviors that symbolize membership and participation to those around them. Because behavioral standards tend to be loosely phrased and because they do not always cover all possible situations, it is impossible for any individual to behave with uniform and consistent propriety. Everybody breaks rules; everybody sometimes engages in behavior that to at least some other members symbolizes a rejection of membership and participation, in a word, opposition. In the normal course of events, the individual who has expressed opposition encounters opposition in return. Those who have observed his behavior express their own opposition through laughter, reproof, frowns, or violent action.

When an expression of opposition is countered with opposition, the individual who initiated the dialogue has the choice of expressing further opposition or of indicating submission by expressing symbols of participation. Thus, not counting behavior that is meaningless or irrelevant, or the possibility that behaviors will be ignored or disregarded, there are three basic modes of human dialogue: (1) cooperation or the exchange of symbols of participation, (2) submission or the reply to symbols of opposition with symbols of participation, and (3) conflict or the exchange of symbols of opposition. Most of our actions mean something to somebody else—they are symbolic. Taking off one's shoes at the beach symbolizes participation; taking off one's shoes at the college president's tea symbolizes opposition, unless the president is exceptionally progressive.

In most situations, as among the Eskimo, direct exchanges of behaviors symbolizing opposition are avoided whenever possible. In all human societies conflict behavior is much less common than cooperation, submission, or the avoidance of interaction. By the same token, conflict that is considered appropriate or desirable is far more frequent than conflict that is considered inappropriate or disruptive. Among the Eskimo, the Hopi, and many other small and closely knit societies, most kinds of conflict, even playful exchanges of opposition, were traditionally considered frightening or disruptive. Although the Hopi were fond of foot races, it was considered bad form to outdistance the other runners. The goal was not to win but to finish together. The Hopi did, however, maintain "joking relationships" between boys and their father's sister's husbands in which the uncle might threaten to castrate the boy, and the boy, when asked to carry a bundle, might well carry it several miles to the bottom of the mesa instead of to its intended destination. Such playful conflict evidently symbolizes a relationship so close as not to be threatened by even the most disagreeable sorts of practical joking. It may also serve as a means of informing individuals that aspects of their behavior are considered inappropriate or improper.

The virtual absence of conflict and competition in some human societies can be explained in various ways. In some cases, perhaps among the Semai of Malaysia, a comparative absence of conflict may simply have reflected a genuine culture in which an affectionate regard for others rendered self-assertiveness unnecessary. However, because the Semai represent a victimized and isolated population with a history of long contact with more numerous and more warlike peoples, the reported absence of conflict among the Semai may simply reflect an adaptation in which flight or withdrawal was a successful stratagem, whereas fighting invariably ended in defeat.

Neither explanation would fit the case of the Eskimo and the Hopi, for both peoples were traditionally capable of exceptional violence. The Greenland Eskimo are known to have exterminated at least one Viking settlement, and in other Eskimo groups there seem to be no intermediate steps between the passive shunning of offending individuals and their deliberate murder. Evidently it is easier to kill someone than to tell him to his face to mend his manners. The Hopi responded to Navajo raids, which might result in the death of one or two Hopi, with literal wars of extermination in which a Navajo camp would be surrounded and all persons in it murdered. When the pueblo of Awatovi displayed hospitality to the Coronado expedition, the neighboring pueblos exterminated its entire population. American Army officers who dealt with the Hopi describe the rage with which Hopi leaders met opposition.

Because both the Eskimo and the Hopi lived under extreme environmental conditions where total cooperation was considered a requirement for survival, it may be that any failures of cooperation simply could not be tolerated or that the frustrations of daily life were so great that even playful opposition was likely to trigger rage. Another explanation is that the individual was simply not trained to deal with opposition and therefore tended to ignore it until it became unbearable and could only be resolved through unlimited violence.

In other societies conflicts tend to be highly ritualized and controlled, and there is often a hierarchy of conflicts ranging from children's play to warfare. In the United States, for example, in addition to constant exposure to every kind of conflict on the television screen, children compete for grades in school, engage in competitive sports, play cowboys and Indians, play competitive board games, practice wrestling and boxing, and engage in quarreling and fighting. Of these forms of conflict only quarreling and fighting are considered undesirable, but even here, it is assumed that fighting among children is inevitable and must be tolerated so long as the degree of violence involved is kept within carefully defined limits—no biting, no throwing rocks, no use of weapons, no kicking, no scratching, and so on.

Among adults and children large enough to hurt each other, fighting, except in play, tends to be ruled out except as it takes place in highly ritualized form between urban street gangs or among individuals frequenting lower-class bars or dance halls. Adults, however, are free to quarrel, to engage in debates, to participate in elections, and to compete freely at the workplace, or for positions of high status. Even in the United States, as among the Eskimo and the Hopi, it is not unusual for those involved in potentially competitive or conflictful situations to combine to prevent competition. Students in a northern California high school routinely removed the pants of any student who received an "A" grade and hung them from the flagpole. Workers on piece rates have been observed to combine against "rate busters," making life difficult for any worker who produced above a certain amount. Business people, of course, are notorious for their ingenious schemes for avoiding competition with other business people.

The tendency in the United States to ritualize and to make a game out of conflict extends even to murders. It is all right to murder a suspected burglar or an escaping felon, and it is also legitimate to murder in self-defense. Cold-blooded murder is a serious crime, but it is much better if it is done with a legitimate weapon such as a gun rather than with a knife (lower class) or with poison. The use of unorthodox weapons is considered bizarre and may draw a relatively stiff punishment. Traditionally the same restrictions upon the appropriateness of particular weapons, to say nothing of rules forbidding the killing of women, children, and noncombatants, also applied to wars.

The above listing of just a few of the kinds of conflict that occur in the United States points to the fact that there are many kinds of conflict, just as there are many kinds of cooperative activities. War, which can be defined as external conflict or conflict between independent political groups, also exists in a variety of different forms. The understanding of conflict in general depends to a considerable extent upon our ability to develop ways of sorting out the different kinds of conflict and to consider the various causes and effects of each of the kinds.

The most widely accepted distinction among kinds of conflict is that given above between internal conflict and war. Another series of distinctions have to do with the extent to which conflict is desired and expected and the extent to which it is considered undesirable and unexpected. On this scale, competitive sports, no matter how many people get killed or injured, are generally considered desirable and may be rationalized as alternatives to war, as practice for war, or as character-building activities. Competitive sports also have the character of games; that is, they have a "let's pretend" quality, and the fighters are expected to shake hands after the match if they are both conscious. Competition for grades or for business profits is certainly not a sport or game, but it is generally considered desirable by the people involved. *Competition* is a somewhat elastic word and may sometimes be applied to any socially approved conflict involving status or position. Thus elections, duels, and even some kinds of feuds may be regarded as forms of competition. A less elastic definition would make a distinction between violent and nonviolent competition similar to the distinction made between sports involving body contact and all others. Quarrels (verbal conflicts) and fights (physical conflicts) are rarely socially approved, and third parties generally try to stop them if they can.

The distinction made above between nonviolent and violent forms of conflict can be extended to form a scale for the severity of any kind of conflict ranging from the expression of verbal opposition to deadly attack. Other ways of classifying conflict have to do with the kinds and numbers of people involved and the extent to which conflicts are regulated or ritualized. Thus husband-wife conflict is quite different from conflict between political parties in the number of people involved, in their identities, and in the extent to which it is regulated.

Most students of conflict agree that a distinction can be made between conflicts that are functional or adaptive in the sense that they contribute to the efficient working of society and the long-term survival of its membership and conflicts that are dysfunctional or maladaptive. Games and competitions are generally regarded as functional. Factionalism or conflict within a society is generally considered dysfunctional to the extent that it disrupts normal productive activities, but functional to the extent that it leads to adaptive changes in the organization of the society. Some kinds of warfare are considered functional and adaptive to the extent that they contribute to the internal solidarity of the societies involved or to the adjustment of populations to environmental resources. Wars of extermination are functional and adaptive only for the victor, and must be considered dysfunctional and maladaptive if the net result is mutual extermination. Although this general view seems to be held by all students of conflict, there is sharp disagreement on the possibility of actually measuring or describing the extent to which conflict is functional or adaptive. For example, a demonstration of the functional value of the two-party system would seem to require a series of controlled experiments in which the functional value of the two-party system was compared with that of various other arrangements. The argument that the two-party system is functional because both it and the United States survive is plausible but hard to distinguish from the argument that "all that is, is good."

Because conflict is universal among human beings, the beginnings of an explanation of conflict are to be sought in general characteristics of human beings or of the societies they create. Although the universal tendency toward conflict has been given a variety of labels such as "territoriality" and "aggression" — human beings have even been given the label of "killer ape" — such labels convey very little information. It would be as useful to explain culture by saying that human beings have a culture-building instinct. Conflict is also sometimes explained as the result of physiological conditions arising from poverty, malnutrition, fatigue, or overcrowding. In parts of northern California, wife beating reaches its peak on Sunday night. In India and in the United States, many kinds of conflict seem to occur with greatest frequency during the hottest months. For all societies, there are times of the year or of the day or week when conflict becomes more probable than at other times. A fatigue-irritability explanation of conflict helps to shed light on the timing of certain kinds of conflict, but it says very little about the form or severity of the resulting conflict or about the kinds of people likely to be involved.

Another approach to an explanation of conflict inquires about the circumstances under which an individual might choose to signal opposition rather than participation. The expression of opposition might reflect misjudgment or a lack of understanding of behavioral standards; it might reflect the existence of inconsistent or confusing behavioral standards; or it might reflect a situation in which the individual is led to believe that net gains and losses from involvement in conflict are less than net gains and losses involved in conforming to behavioral standards. These various situations in which individuals or groups are likely to display behaviors that are interpreted as symbols of opposition are collectively labeled "strains."

Each society, then, has its own characteristic pattern of strains involving areas where behavioral standards are confusing, contradictory, or unrealistic. In South India, for example, where property was traditionally supposed to be owned jointly by the male members of the household, there is generally relatively little conflict when the property is divided. Imagine, however, a household composed of two brothers and their male children in which one brother dies before the property is distributed. Should the male children of each

Marital relationships are frequently a source of strain. People use rituals, feasts, and exchanges of wealth in an often vain attempt to cement relationships once and for all. Wedding feast in Indonesia. (Kindness of Lynn Thomas.)

454

brother receive half the family property, since each brother owned half, or should all of the children receive equal shares even if one brother has more children than the other? Because this situation is somewhat rare, rules governing appropriate behavior have never been formulated, and violent conflict between the two groups of brothers becomes almost inevitable.

In the United States the traditional pattern, in which the husband dominates family affairs, has always run counter to the frontier egalitarian pattern, in which both husband and wife participated in family decision making. As a result, marriages in the United States have always been characterized by a relatively high level of conflict and divorce. In recent years the success of the women's liberation movement has accentuated the existing inconsistencies between behavioral standards favoring male dominance and those favoring equality or even female dominance. The result has been a sharp increase in marital conflict. Because a male-dominated or a female-dominated family contains a single unimpeachable authority, it is probable that such families will always have less conflict than egalitarian families, in which decision making involves the agreement of both husband and wife. Conflict within a family dominated by a single spouse is likely to have more serious effects because it is unprecedented and therefore less subject to regulation.

Although the concept of strain helps to explain why particular situations or particular social relationships are especially afflicted by conflict, an understanding of the course likely to be followed by particular conflicts requires a detailed understanding of the behavioral standards involved in the conduct of a particular type of conflict. Although we may think, for example, of wife beating as an improper activity having the character of an unplanned outburst and triggered by a combination of hunger, beer, a bad day at the office, and wifely misbehavior, the expression "wife beating" gives the game away. At a given point in what may be a prolonged exchange of oppositions between husband and wife, it is expected, but not always approved, that the husband engage in wife beating. He is expected to do it properly, without causing extensive physical damage and, in our society, without using a stick or other weapon. Thus wife beating is a specific, highly symbolic, and very precisely defined or ritualized way of expressing opposition. Whether the act of wife beating leads to further escalation of the conflict and to divorce or to termination of the conflict and reconciliation depends upon the interpretation put upon it by the married couple. The meaning of a wife-beating episode depends very much upon the social class or ethnic subcultures to which the wife and husband belong.

In South India, where wife beating, sometimes with a stick, is also an accepted aspect of marital conflict, wife beating may symbolize a very real desire on the part of the husband to preserve the marital relationship. If the husband, after hearing that his wife has been making advances to another man, fails to beat her, divorce is the likely outcome.

The words and actions that express opposition also convey information about the seriousness of the conflict and the anticipated outcome. In well-organized groups, active and perceptive leaders can often identify conflicts in their early stages and intervene in such a way as to prevent their development.

In South Indian villages, where the suspicion of adultery is the most common cause of marital conflict, active village leaders can reduce marital conflict almost to the vanishing point simply by preventing flirtation. Traditionally a wife who looked boldly at other men was seized by the village leader, dragged to the temple, and beaten with a sandal.

When conflict or potential conflict is not interrupted in some such manner, it has a tendency to escalate, that is, to become increasingly loud and violent. It may also increase in scale involving larger and larger numbers of people. Although the individual may escalate a conflict or involve other persons in it with the purpose of winning or causing the opponent to submit, he may also do so with the idea of securing third-party intervention in the dispute. Thus conflict can sometimes be a means of directing the attention of outsiders to a problem that the disputants are unable to resolve.

In South India where all forms of public conflict except for a limited number of athletic and status competitions are considered improper, participants in a conflict obtain third-party intervention simply by making their dispute public. Thus the wife runs out of the house with her husband chasing her, or aggrieved individuals initiate conflict during festivals when visiting dignitaries from other villages are present. In any case of public conflict all observers immediately bring the conflict to a halt. They then proceed to hear the complaints of the two parties and to propose a mutually acceptable solution. If such informal arbitration fails, the case goes to more formal village councils or to outside political or religious authorities who enforce their decisions through the use of fines or, as in the case of police, the collecting of bribes. Attempts to assign guilt are quite rare, and probably were absent in traditional culture. The basic goal of conflict resolution techniques is that of explaining proper conduct and applying pressure to ensure that both parties adhere to it in the future.

In the United States public conflict, other than competition and some forms of verbal conflict, also tends to be considered improper, but third-party intervention is generally secured through a formal complaint to the authorities. The authorities tend to make distinctions between victims and aggressors and to resolve the conflict by punishing the aggressor. In the United States the question of who started the conflict becomes vitally important, whereas in South India the key question is what started it and how the bone of contention is to be removed.

Among the Nuer, if a homicide appears likely to lead to a blood feud between two segments of the tribe, the murderer can appeal to a leopard-skin chief to persuade the victim's relatives to accept compensation in lieu of revenge. The leopard-skin chief, unlike third parties who intervene in disputes in South India or the United States, possesses no particular authority, but because of his important role as a mediator, he can generally obtain a respectful hearing. His task is not that of establishing facts or proprieties but simply that of getting the two parties to agree to the amount of compensation to be paid. His success as a negotiator depends upon the fact that a blood feud, damaging to both parties, is certain to erupt if his efforts fail.

The prime requisite for the resolution of undesired conflict, whether it is accomplished by discussion, negotiation, or the intervention of authorities, is the existence of moral authority within the group either in the form of general agreement on moral issues or in the existence of individuals within whom moral authority resides. The exercise of moral authority consists in interpreting behavioral standards in such a way as to minimize inconsistencies between them or to identify particular behavioral standards that apply to a given situation. Once the parties to a conflict have accepted a consistent set of behavioral standards governing their future relationships, the basis for conflict is removed. Conflict between nations or societies having different behavioral standards and lacking shared acceptance of any body of moral authority tends to be irresolvable, except in the case where it becomes evident that further conflict will be damaging to both parties. Wars, then, tend to end in the conquest, flight, or extermination of the weaker party. If the two parties to a war are evenly matched, so that the conflict is indefinitely prolonged, the conflict is likely to become highly ritualized with the opponents tending to accept common standards for the conduct of war. In such cases, war sometimes appears to acquire functional value for both participants and is therefore continued intermittently over long periods of time. Very often a balance of power is maintained by neighboring states or societies through complex and shifting alliances. Although patterns of endemic warfare can be halted through the mediation of neighboring states or the evolution of a transnational moral authority, patterns of endemic warfare seem almost universal among agricultural and industrial societies, and by no means absent among hunter-gatherers.

Although conflict, especially when it is not socially valued, is often regarded as being opposed to such socially valued behaviors as cooperation and submission, a good case can be made that conflict is essential to the formation of human groups because some degree of competition or hostility toward other groups is required for the maintenance of group boundaries. Similarly the possibility of warfare between societies leads inevitably to cooperation or alliance among societies possessing a common enemy. If cooperation is based upon the existence of similar people possessing similar goals, the recognition of such similarity is dependent upon the existence of dissimilar and therefore hostile people possessing dissimilar goals.

Because conflict seems to occur in all known human groups, it seems reasonable to conclude that conflict is an inevitable and adaptive aspect of the human condition. The argument that some conflict seems to be necessary or adaptive is not the same as the argument that all conflict is necessary or adaptive. Even in situations where violent or deadly conflict seems to have adaptive consequences, it may be wondered if such costly interchanges truly represent the most adaptive or most efficient solution possible to the problems that the pattern of conflict appears to solve. The fact that many groups and societies manage to survive indefinitely or for long periods without engaging in violent or deadly conflicts suggests that there are, indeed, alternative solutions. Although there is no reason to expect that there will ever be a world without conflict, there is every reason to believe that there can be a world without deadly or injurious conflict.

5. Law and Lawlike Phenomena

In the comparison of cultures it is always possible to make a sharp distinction between large societies with a complex division of labor and small societies lacking a complex division of labor. If law is characterized in terms of such formal properties as the existence of written codes, governing bodies, legislatures, law courts, and prisons, together with the presence of such full-time specialists as chiefs, judges, policemen, and professional criminals, then it follows, automatically, that law is an exclusive property of complex societies. In another view, the existence of laws and legal systems can be seen as a property of small societies and of small groups within larger societies. In such a case, laws are viewed as special sorts of behavioral standards for which there exist special measures designed to ensure conformity to them, and legal systems are viewed as those relatively formal arrangements by which reported violations of laws are investigated, miscreants identified, disputes resolved, and corrective measures taken.

Whether one thinks of small groups and small societies as possessing law or merely lawlike phenomena, the heart of the matter lies in the fact that different sorts of behavioral standards have very different sorts of implications in terms of the extent to which they are violated or the consequences of their violation. Thus, although bad grammar or bad manners may have serious consequences for the individual, such consequences rarely involve any kind of

In many societies decisions are reached and conflicts resolved through more or less democratic discussion. Because all are free to speak, the result is often boredom, which may in itself have a cooling effect. Banso Council, Cameroons, discussing school fees and land taxes. (Courtesy of the United Nations.)

formal investigation, adjudication, punishment, or arbitration. In most societies the behavioral standards governing good grammar or good manners cannot be elicited by means of direct questions. In most cases the relevant behavioral standards are not legislated in any obvious way, and people do not have any ready access to a formal list of do's and don't's. Although bad grammar or bad manners may elicit laughter or ridicule, there is on the whole no standard list of punishments or other appropriate actions that should be administered or taken when a participle is dangled or an infinitive split. When behavioral standards are violated with some frequency and the violations are considered of important consequence to the entire group, then it is safe to expect that efforts will be made to define them clearly and formally and to enunciate as well the various appropriate actions that will be taken when they are violated.

In previous examples drawn from Eskimo culture, it was seen that an individual or a household might acquire a considerable reputation for meanness or selfishness and might therefore be the object of considerable gossip and criticism. Nevertheless, granted the Eskimo reluctance to make waves, the individual displaying such bad manners might never throughout an entire lifetime be made aware of the nature of the behavioral standards that were being violated. Similarly Eskimo rules of life traditionally forbade sleeping on the sea ice at night, but this formally stated rule was enforced only by the fact that supernatural harm would come to the individual who did so. A person who violated such a rule would be thought to be strange or crazy, but on the whole nothing would be done about it. Other rules of life specifying how and when certain foods were to be eaten were taken much more seriously, for violations of food tabus could anger important spirits and so seriously affect the food supply of the entire village. When there was a shortage of food, then, the Eskimo traditionally gathered together and attempted to cleanse themselves of such violations through a ritual of public confession and forgiveness. Thus the violation of a food tabu was likely to be followed by a public procedure in which those responsible for violations were publicly embarrassed. Here the clear statement of the law and the presence of formal procedures that could be invoked when the law was violated serve to give the food tabu a status quite different from that of more ordinary behavioral standards.

Among the Nuer the leopard-skin chief, who traditionally served as a kind of arbitrator in the case of disputes between closely related groups, clearly lacked the sanction of force that would be available to a judge in a modern courtroom. His lack of formal political power was undoubtedly in most cases more than compensated for by the many strands of informal power and influence that must be associated with any person of importance in a small-scale society. Because everyone was aware of the details of the cases he handled and of the manifold and universally bad consequences of a failure of arbitration, the powers of a leopard-skin chief, even though not displayed, must have been formidable indeed. Here law and legal action in small societies and groups differs from that characteristic of larger organizations in that both the facts of the case and the powers of the persons involved are totally familiar to all. Elaborate symbolism and legal ritual, tedious investigations of the facts, and the living presence of armed enforcers are essential to legal situations in societies in which the parties to the case are unfamiliar with each other or with the power relationships involved; hardly necessary in a small group.

Among the Tiwi, where old men had many young wives and young men often had none, the seduction of wives by young men was a common cause of trouble. Generally old men complained about such goings-on at large gatherings, and a trial ensued. In the trial the old man harangued the young man, lecturing him concerning his social responsibilities, and then began to throw hunting spears at him. The young man could generally dodge the spears quite easily, but if he was well behaved and well brought up, he would eventually allow a spear to inflict a minor but sensational wound. If the young man was ill-behaved and did not know his place, he might continue to dodge the old man's spears indefinitely or even throw a few spears back. In such cases some elders would line up to assist the accuser, while other elders would restrain the young man's potential supporters. If the young man did not now give in gracefully, there was a likelihood that he would be seriously injured or killed. In the Tiwi case, the trial proceeds without presentation of evidence and without determination of guilt. The reason for this is that the facts are not in question. The law, however, is a formal one—everyone knows that it is wrong to seduce another person's wife, and the nature of the punishment and the setting in which it is to be administered are clearly and formally established. Tiwi culture is hardly unique in setting up a situation in which law is certain to be violated. Perhaps the purpose was not to eliminate seduction but to preserve the honor of the elders when seductions were carried out too obviously or too frequently.

In his study of Congo Pygmies, Colin Turnbull relates the case of the Pygmy named Cephu. Cephu and the small group of families associated with him tended to camp somewhat separately from the other families in the local group and was somewhat reluctant to participate in communal rituals. So there was tension in the camp between Cephu and the others. This tension reached a climax when during a hunting party Cephu deliberately set his nets in front of those belonging to others and thus "stole" the game that was rightfully theirs. When the hunting party arrived, everyone gathered in the clearing, and Cephu was sent for. When Cephu arrived no one paid the slightest attention to him and, although several younger men were seated in chairs, no one rose to offer him a place of honor. Once this had been settled, one of the more influential members stood up and began listing the various misdeeds that Cephu had committed. Others responded to Cephu's protestations of innocence by shouting at him and listing further misdeeds. Cephu burst into tears, but continued to defend himself. Finally it was suggested that Cephu was a big chief (the Pygmies have no chiefs) and that he therefore could take his group and go off and do his hunting and chiefing elsewhere. At this point Cephu apologized profusely and agreed to turn over all of his meat to the others. After the meat was taken, Cephu remained in his hut crying and making noises indicative of extreme hunger until a relative brought him a potful of meat and mushroom sauce. Later in the evening he joined the group in singing, and the incident was over.

Although Turnbull suggests that formal legal processes were not involved in this case, its lawlike nature is evident. The behavioral standard that Cephu violated was known to all and applied to all. The violation was followed by a trial that was certainly formal by Pygmy standards, and the subsequent sentence proved acceptable to all. Here, the difference between Pygmy law and Euro-American law lay not so much in what happened—a violation, a trial, a suspended sentence conditional on return of the stolen property—as in the lack of specialized legal functionaries and elaborate ritual proceedings. Although Cephu's habitual bad manners and generally uncooperative spirit figured in the trial, it was clear throughout that these breaches were not breaches of the law in the same sense that stealing game was a breach of the law. Cephu's other offenses had, after all, been a tolerated cause of unhappiness long before he dared go so far as to break the law. Thus, even in a highly informal and small-scale society, it is possible to make clear distinctions between laws and ordinary behavior standards. The violation of the law called forth a definite and established procedure used for no other purpose.

Although studies of the law in complex societies tend to emphasize law courts and other formal institutions which apply to an entire tribe, state, or nation, there is good reason to believe that the study of less formal law characteristic of subgroups within the larger society will lead to much better understandings of the larger formal structure of law. In India, and in many other countries where European systems of law have been imposed by colonial power, the contrast between local or folk law and national law is especially marked. Especially in rural villages, almost all legal violations and disputes are settled within the village or within groups of related villages. Because recourse to regular law courts, government officials, or other state and national legal institutions tends to be expensive and to lead to unpredictable results, law cases and trouble cases generally tend to move outside the local area only in the case of certain kinds of murders and disputes that cannot be resolved at the local level. Even at the local level there is a strong tendency to settle things informally at the small-group level. In the case of family disputes, for example, every attempt is made to settle the argument within the family. Where this cannot be done—for example, if a husband persists in beating his wife for no reason—the wife may appeal for help by fleeing from the house. In such a case, where a private dispute becomes public, it is almost always settled by an informal committee of neighbors. This may be the case even in the city, where a dispute between two individuals draws a crowd and individuals within the crowd attempt to settle the dispute. Many kinds of legal violations and disputes, including justifiable homicide, theft, borrower–lender arguments, and parent–child conflicts, may then be settled by informal committees which constitute themselves as courts, hear both parties to the dispute or complaint, and attempt to arrive at a settlement.

When the trouble cannot be confined to household, neighborhood, peer group, or other small group, it is likely to be brought to the attention of somewhat formal bodies, called *pancayats*, which are most often composed of male household heads representing such larger groupings as lineages, castes, or villages. When a pancayat sits as a court of law, its proceedings are hardly

Elected village headmen meet to discuss regional problems. Faridabad, India. Government officials seated at table make the actual decisions. (Courtesy of the United Nations.)

more formal than those of the Pygmy. On the other hand, precedents are discussed and knowledgeable persons formally enumerate the various behavioral standards that may have been violated. Normally the pancayat seeks a far-reaching agreement through a process of unanimous decision that will lead to mutual satisfaction and a removal of the sources of illegal behavior or disagreement. There is a marked lack of concern with justice in the abstract or with punishment. Justice is done and punishment administered only when justice or punishment seem appropriate ways of ending the trouble once and for all. If the pancayat fails to reach agreement or if individuals fail to abide by its decision, the final recourse is to appeal to a higher-level pancayat or to an official municipal, state, or national court. Here the formally constituted legal system is seen as dealing only with a residue of cases that cannot be settled informally at lower levels. If we are to understand what laws exist, how often they are violated, what sorts of persons violate them, or what sorts of legal decisions are made, we must trace the origins of trouble cases from their small beginnings through a complex chain of increasingly formal legal institutions. Following such a route, we may wish to define a progression from informal law through customary law toward official law and we may wish to speak about the unique properties of each kind of law, but, in all of this, we cannot really speak of what is happening to people or how the law affects people unless we consider numerous cases from beginning to end.

The desire to find out what really happens, as distinct from what gets recorded by the court clerk, has led many students of anthropology and law to view law as a property of all human groups including very small and informal groups within larger societies. This view in turn leads to the conclusion that lawlike behavioral standards formulated at different levels within society may be quite different. Thus the law as understood and used by lawyers can be seen as only a fraction of the law that exists, and the way is opened up to more general understandings of lawlike behavioral standards and the variety of mechanisms by which they are applied or enforced.

6. Changing Status

If an organization is to be maintained by means of the activities of individuals, there must be a means by which the activities of individuals are coordinated. In any social situation it is vital that the individual be able to identify the other actors and the roles they are supposed to play. Thus a good part of social life consists of the exchange of symbols or symbolic behaviors which serve to indicate the statuses which individuals occupy or intend to occupy and consequently the roles they intend to play. Many of the works of Erving Goffman, such as *The Presentation of the Self in Everyday Life*,[2] deal with the ordinary day-to-day means that people employ in identifying themselves to others. Especially in complex societies, the daily life of the individual involves a constant movement from one status to another, and this movement is signified by constant changes in the dress or manner of the individual.

The necessity for constant communication about status and role arises from the fact that each individual member of a society, in addition to the wide variety of formal labeled statuses occupied more or less permanently, has accessible a number of informal, often unlabeled statuses that may be occupied as the situation warrants. Even with a formal status, such as mother, there are

[2] Erving Goffman, *The Presentation of Self in Everyday Life* (Garden City, N.Y.: Doubleday, 1959).

Host displays his generosity before party begins. In many cultures prestige and increasing status can be obtained through hospitality. Fanti, Ghana. (Photo kindness of David Kronenfeld.)

likely to be a wide variety of substatuses, each carrying a slightly different role, such as angry mother, tired mother, overworked mother, playful mother, or loving mother. A mother, of course, is not free to occupy these statuses voluntarily or without restriction. For example, it would be inappropriate to display angry mother or overworked mother at a family picnic, for this would "ruin" the picnic. In daily life mother signals her intention to occupy a particular maternal substatus through the use of tiny gestures, intonations, bodily postures, or costumes. For the most part she can play out the roles associated with each of her many substatuses only with the acquiescence of her children and only in their presence. The role of mother can be practiced only in the presence of persons willing to play the role of child. When a mother–child situation exists, both mother and child must acknowledge acceptance of the situation and indicate the roles they hope to play in it. In a sense they must begin the encounter by entering a bargaining situation concerning the roles that are to be played in it. At the outset a combination such as angry mother and loving child creates an impossible situation, and it is therefore necessary for one of the parties to the dialogue to offer some sort of compromise. The situation might then become loving mother and loving child, angry mother and angry child, or, in response to different signals from the child, the mother might cycle down from angry to forgiving to loving. Much of the friction that occurs in everyday life is a result of the confusions that arise as different participants in particular social situations attempt to occupy unacceptable statuses or insist on maintaining some particular status or substatus, even when it is inappropriate.

In addition to the movement from substatus to substatus within a single status, there is a constant shifting of status as the individual moves from social setting to social setting. During the day an individual may wear many hats — mother, shopper, employee, neighbor, friend, daughter, sister, and so on. Each of these statuses has its own collection of substatuses and roles and each situation has its own relevant behavioral standards. Although the pioneering work of Erving Goffman and of Roger Barker[3] has laid bare many features of the almost incredible complexities of daily life, research on the ordinary and continuous shifting of statuses and roles is still in its infancy. Almost no cross-cultural research along such lines has been completed. Evidently the learning and practice of the arts of self-presentation are largely informal and unconscious. Because it seems probable that people are incapable of actually learning how to behave in every status and situation that they occupy, it seems safe to conclude that individual behavior in particular situations stems from the application of broad general principles akin to grammatical rules. For example, the role of angry person is probably a generalized role that can be applied with appropriate changes to any situation in which the display of anger seems appropriate. The individual need not know in detail how to be an angry mother, an angry pedestrian, or an angry something else, but only in a general way to be capable of adapting the symbols of anger to the requirements of particular statuses and situations. An angry mother can legitimately hit her children, but an angry pedestrian usually cannot hit other people. Otherwise the display of anger involves very much the same facial expressions, gestures, and vocabulary. A good part of the phenomenon of cultural shock or being upset in strange places results from the fact that the symbolic exchange used in establishing status is likely to be misread or misunderstood. In many parts of South India or Mexico, an angry citizen of the United States may be a figure of fun, often because people do not recognize the early symptoms of the onset of anger. Resort to the more universal symbolism of a two-year-old temper tantrum, besides being embarrassing, may get the message across but may also provoke even more hilarity.

[3] Roger G. Barker, *Ecological Psychology, Concepts and Methods for Studying the Environment of Human Behavior* (Stanford: Stanford University Press, 1968).

Seated Oba or king wearing beaded crown and carrying a fly whisk accepts homage of woman seated before him. Carved wooden door from the Yoruba of Nigeria. (Courtesy of the UCLA Museum of Cultural History.)

The difficulties involved in studying and understanding the complex and largely unconscious behaviors involved in everyday changes of status and role, especially in cross-cultural contexts, have led to a tendency to emphasize the processes involved in the manipulation of the grander and more formal expressions of status and role. Very often, and perhaps with some reason, the concepts of status and role have been reserved for important labeled positions that could be conveniently placed upon a diagram. Kinship statuses that can easily be placed upon genealogical diagrams, class and occupational statuses that can be conveniently arranged in hierarchical order, and such stages of life as birth, marriage, and death have received much more attention than the shifting everyday statuses that form the basis of daily interaction. Similarly such processes as becoming a chief, getting married, or obtaining a promotion and the often complex rituals that accompany them have received considerable attention.

The questions involved in these grander sorts of studies have to do, not with how people get by on a day-to-day basis, but with how major and important lifetime statuses are conferred. Because a social organization cannot operate unless the more important statuses within it are filled by appropriate role-playing individuals, it follows that one of the most important forms of political activity within an organization is creating and filling vacancies. Where vacancies are created only by the death of the incumbent, there is the advantage that there can be no dispute over the question of removing the incumbent, but, then, of course, there is no way of removing an incompetent incumbent. If the incompetent can be removed through some sort of legal procedure, then there is always danger of disagreement on the propriety of such a removal. In the same way, if there is some sort of principle of age, heredity, or seniority that can be used to select the one and only one individual entitled to occupy a given vacancy, there is no way of passing over an incompetent incumbent. If there is no such agreed-upon principle of succession, then disputes over entitlement to a vacant position are a probability. Theoretically all of these problems could be avoided in situations where ability to perform the role was the only criterion and the currently most capable individual

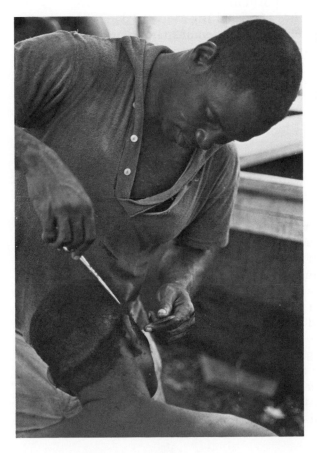

Hereditary and elected officials in formal political systems can rely upon power. In informal systems, the position of Big Man often depends upon merit and performance. Fanti leader performing unpaid barbering services for a friend. Ghana. (Kindness of David Kronenfeld.)

was entitled to occupy the position. The advantages of such a merit system are likely, however, to prove illusory in those many and frequent situations where merit cannot be unequivocally established.

Succession to office on the basis of merit is a common, perhaps universal, way of filling informal statuses. In South Indian villages, in New Guinea, in many American Indian tribes, and in many informal situations within complex cultures, important positions of power and leadership are filled by "Big Men." The Big Man's merit is generally measured by the quantity of wealth he possesses and by the number of followers he is able to control, and he is likely to retain his position as long as he continues to provide benefits to his followers greater than those offered by other aspirants to Big Man status. Among the Plains Indians of North America, a man who acquired spiritual powers as a result of the vision quest would, of course, confer upon himself and his followers success in hunting and in warfare. He could occupy a Big Man status only so long as his spiritual powers were strong, a matter that had to be continuously demonstrated by success in hunting and warfare. Thus a Big Man system tends to involve a continuous turnover in leadership as individuals shift their allegiances rapidly to whichever individual appears to possess the most merit at any particular time. Although an occasional Big Man might become so big as to absorb all opposition, the most common characteristic of a Big Man system is the presence of several Big Men and potential Big Men involved in more or less constant efforts to demonstrate their comparative merit. In the modern United States such star systems occur in competitive sports or in various fields of art and drama. They also occur less obviously in determining the occupation of such informal positions as political boss or "power behind the throne."

A variant on the Big Man system, probably equally common, involves selection on the basis of merit followed by long-term or permanent occupancy of the position. Such a system of selection is the basis of marriage, of civil service appointments, and of specialized occupations generally. When there is a permanent Big Man, there is little point to continuous attempts at replacement, but obvious problems will develop if he fails to remain the most meritorious person available. In general a merit system poses problems of deciding what constitutes merit and who has the most of it. Serious and disruptive conflicts can arise over any of these issues.

An alternative to the various sorts of merit systems is to transmit jobs like property through some form of inheritance. In South Indian patrilineages, for example, the headship of the lineage is generally transmitted to the previous headman's oldest surviving brother and ultimately to his son. In effect every person in the lineage has a numbered rank and succession is determined, unless the individual candidate can be shown to be incompetent, simply by promoting individuals in order. The right to perform particular jobs ranging from ruler of a principality to barber for a particular village was transmitted in similar fashion. Such a system of inherited status has the advantage that an individual can receive lifelong training for a particular position, but there are obvious problems of maintaining such a system when incompetent persons succeed to positions of importance.

With regard to succession to high political office, Robbins Burling has defined four major patterns in addition to hereditary succession: seizing control by force, appointing one's successor, replacement of a single ruler by a committee, and contested elections.[4] Although Burling finds weaknesses in all of these modes of succession, he argues that contested elections come closest to providing a means of choosing a meritorious leader without resort to violent conflict. On the whole the movement of individuals from one status to another within society, and especially the movement of individuals into high political office, appears to be one of the central unsolved problems of all human cultures. It depends upon widespread agreement on who is to occupy a vacant office and a continuing agreement on the conditions under which a present occupant may retain his position. As Burling has pointed out, patterns of succession to office are quite different in different cultures and in all cultures are likely to undergo cyclical change as new mechanisms are tried and found wanting.

7. Summary

A social structure can be regarded as an artifact of behavior. It comes into being and maintains its existence only when individuals play roles and occupy statuses within it. Behavior relevant to the perpetuation of a social structure can be broadly defined as political. Political processes, then, have to do with the establishment and enforcement of behavioral standards and with the circulation of individuals from status to status. Although laws and regulations are behavioral standards, most of the rules by means of which individuals govern their behavior are much more informal. One of the problems involved in identifying behavioral standards lies in the fact that the processes of legislation by means of which they came into being are buried in antiquity or hidden by the casual and informal processes by means of which they are developed and changed. In most cases the legislation of behavioral standards is probably a largely unconscious process. In many societies new behavioral standards may be promulgated by visionaries who receive their inspiration directly from deities or spirits. In such cases supernatural inspiration is often treated as proposed legislation which is then examined to determine if it is genuine and acceptable. In small groups, which is probably where most legislation occurs even in complex societies, there is likely to be a fairly close fit between behavioral standards and behavior. In larger societies, where it becomes increasingly difficult to arrange for communication and feedback among different parts of the society, laws and behavioral standards may develop which fail to reflect actual behavior or which place impossible burdens upon large segments of the population. In many cases people may be totally unaware of the vast majority of the laws and behavioral standards supposed to govern their behavior.

Conformity to behavioral standards is encouraged by means of mechanisms

---

[4] Robbins Burling, *The Passage of Power: Studies in Political Succession* (New York: Academic Press, 1974), p. 260.

of social control. The requirement of conformity must be broadly interpreted, for there are rules that are intended to be broken, situations in which rules must be broken, and kinds of rules for which many kinds of behavior may be regarded as conforming. Mechanisms of social control may range from a kind of quiet shunning, as among the Eskimo, to the patterns of violence characteristic of the Nuer. Among many peoples fear of being accused of witchcraft may serve as a mechanism of social control. Although most means of social control involve elements of reward and punishment, formal patterns of reward and punishment are more commonly associated with complex societies such as that of South India. Although the term *social control* may have an ominous ring, the presence and frequent use of the more oppressive means of social control is generally a mark of what Edward Sapir called "spurious" cultures.

Even in the most smoothly running societies, behavioral standards cannot provide information about what to do on every occasion, and it is impossible for individuals to behave with consistent propriety. Under such circumstances disagreements may arise; individuals may engage in conflict through the exchange of behaviors symbolizing opposition. Although conflict behavior is probably less common than cooperation, submission, or the avoidance of interaction, it is likely to have serious repercussions. Among the Eskimo, the Hopi, and many other small and closely knit societies, the open expression of conflict in any form was avoided whenever possible. In many other societies conflict tends to become highly ritualized and controlled, and there are many kinds of conflict that are considered desirable or acceptable. In the United States, for example, many kinds of conflict are considered acceptable and appropriate forms of behavior, and even those that are not considered acceptable are likely to be governed by behavioral standards.

Conflicts may be classified in many different ways, the most important being the distinctions among internal and external conflict, violent and nonviolent conflict, small-scale and large-scale conflict, regulated and unregulated conflict, and functional and dysfunctional conflicts. Although conflict may be interpreted as having roots in general human characteristics or in conditions causing irritability, it may also be regarded as resulting from circumstances that cause individuals to violate behavioral standards or to otherwise signal opposition. Such circumstances, having to do with situations where behavioral standards are misunderstood, inconsistent, or unenforceable, can collectively be labeled "strains." Where patterns of strain lead to the recurrence of particular kinds of conflict, such as husband-wife conflict in the United States or India, behavioral standards are likely to develop governing the ways in which such conflicts are to be carried out. Thus there may be proprieties governing even the conduct of such improprieties as wife beating. When the parties to a conflict cannot themselves bring a conflict to an end, there are usually mechanisms available for resolving or settling the conflict. The prime requisite for any kind of conflict resolution or mediation is the existence of moral authority. Worldwide variation in the frequency and variety of conflict and in the mechanisms required to control and resolve it suggests that the abolition of deadly and injurious conflict falls well within the range of human abilities.

If law and lawlike phenomena are considered primarily in terms of formal characteristics such as the existence of written codes, policemen, or judges, it follows that the study of law must be restricted to complex societies. When laws are regarded as special sorts of behavioral standards and legal systems as relatively formal mechanisms for dealing with violations of laws and the settlement of disputes, it becomes possible to identify laws and lawlike phenomena in all existing human societies. Thus, although Eskimo life is largely governed by behavioral standards that lack the force of law, there are a number of cases where violation of a particular standard, such as a food tabu, will involve the individual in a relatively formal and public procedure involving considerable personal embarrassment. Again, although the leopard-skin chief of the Nuer appears to lack the formidable police powers available to a judge in a Western court, there is every reason for believing that he had access to substantial public support for his decisions. Thus the differences between a judge and a leopard-skin chief may be more apparent than real. Other examples taken from the Tiwi and the Congo Pygmies suggest a range of variation in legal affairs, but illustrate the general proposition that law and the lawlike phenomena can be identified under a variety of circumstances. The importance of a combined consideration of law in the narrow and official sense and law in a broad sense is suggested by the example of South India in which individual trouble cases can be shown to pass through a variety of informal and traditional procedures before they reach the formally constituted, Western-style, law courts. Although it is legitimate to view law in either a broad or a narrow sense, the tendency in anthropological studies of law is to consider law a property of even the smallest of human groups. This opens up the possibility of reaching general understandings of lawlike phenomena and of understanding possible conflicts and inconsistencies arising out of the existence of different levels and varieties of law.

In addition to legislation, social control, conflict, and law, political processes involve the means by which individuals indicate status and move from one status to another. Looked at in one way, the life of the individual involves a constant daily and yearly progression among a wide variety of accessible statuses and substatuses. Although, following the work of Erving Goffman and Roger Barker, considerable interest in the microscopic study of status changes has developed, most published work in anthropology continues to emphasize the processes of movement into major and important lifetime statuses. Although mechanisms for determining succession to office range over a variety of alternatives, including strict inheritance and selection on the basis of merit, it would appear that few if any societies have solved the problem of transferring important statuses without conflict or uncertainty.

Collateral Reading

Bailey, F. G. *Strategems and Spoils: A Social Anthropology of Politics.* Oxford: Basil Blackwell, 1969. The role of decisions and self-interest in politics.

Bailey, Fred G. (ed.). *Gifts and Poison: The Politics of Reputation.* Oxford: Basil Blackwell, 1971.

Balandier, Georges. *Political Anthropology.* New York: Pantheon Books, Inc., 1970. A viewpoint from French anthropology.

Banton, Michael (ed.). *Political Systems and the Distribution of Power.* New York: Frederick A. Praeger, Inc., 1965. Collected articles.

Bohannan, Paul (ed.). *Law and Warfare: Studies in the Anthropology of Conflict.* Garden City, N.Y.: The Natural History Press, 1967.

Boissevain, Jeremy. *Friends of Friends: Networks, Manipulators, and Coalitions.* New York: St. Martin's Press, Inc., 1974.

Cohen, Ronald, and John Middleton (eds.). *Comparative Political Systems: Studies in the Politics of Pre-industrial Societies.* Garden City, N.Y.: The Natural History Press, 1967. Good articles.

Diamond, A. S. *Primitive Law, Past and Present.* London: Methuen and Co., Ltd., 1971. A survey.

Douglas, Mary (ed.). *Rules and Meaning: The Anthropology of Everyday Knowledge.* Baltimore: Penguin Books, Inc., 1973.

Gluckman, Max. *Politics, Law and Ritual in Tribal Society.* Chicago: Aldine Publishing Company, 1965. Based on studies in Africa.

Goffman, Erving. *Interaction Ritual, Essays on Face-to-Face Behavior.* Chicago: Aldine Publishing Company, 1967. Symbolizing status through words and gestures.

Greul, Peter J. *The Leopard-Skin Chief: An Examination of Political Power Among the Nuer. American Anthropologist,* **73:**1115–1120.

Hoebel, E. Adamson. *The Law of Primitive Man: A Study in Comparative Legal Dynamics.* Cambridge, Mass.: Harvard University Press, 1964.

Nader, Laura (ed.). *Law in Culture and Society.* Chicago: Aldine Publishing Company, 1969.

Pospisil, Leopold J. *Anthropology of Law: A Comparative Theory.* New York: Harper & Row, Inc., 1971.

Selby, Henry A. *Zapotec Deviance: The Convergence of Folk and Modern Sociology.* Austin: University of Texas Press, 1974. Misbehaviors in a Mexican community.

Swartz, Marc J. (ed.). *Local-Level Politics: Social and Cultural Perspectives.* Chicago: Aldine Publishing Company, 1968. Collected articles.

Ethnographic References

Arunta, Australia: Spencer and Gillen, 1927.
Congo pygmy: Turnbull, 1961.
Eskimo: Birket-Smith, 1936; Briggs, 1970; Coon, 1948, Chapter 4; Rasmussen, 1908.
Hopi: Dozier, 1970; Eggan, 1950; Titiev, 1944, 1972.
New Guinea: Pospisil, 1963.
Nuer: Evans-Pritchard, 1940.
Semai: Dentan, 1968.
South India: Beals, 1962.
Tiwi: Hart and Pilling, 1960.

15/Religion

1. The Nature of Religion

Religious beliefs and practices are those that have to do with relationships between humans and supernatural forces or beings. Although the definition sounds simple enough, its use depends upon the anthropologist's capacity to distinguish clearly between things that are natural or social and things that are supernatural. In many cases the attempt to distinguish between natural and supernatural leads to a kind of ethnocentrism in which the beliefs of scientists, including anthropologists, are considered to define the realm of the natural, whereas all other beliefs are held to deal with the supernatural. As an example, the belief that garlic will prevent plague is likely to be placed in the area of the supernatural until such time as some scientist demonstrates that garlic really does prevent plague.

Another way of distinguishing between the practical or the scientific sphere and the religious sphere is in terms of the particular attitudes that people hold in regard to different sorts of things. Where people hold a secular and pragmatic attitude and are willing to investigate, examine, test, explore alternatives, and ask questions, it often seems reasonable to conclude that religion is not involved. When people display attitudes of awe and reverence, where they accept things on faith, and where they are reluctant to make changes or explore alternatives, a sense of sacredness and religiosity seems to be involved.

473

In the end, a great many beliefs and practices are neither completely secular nor completely sacred and have to do with phenomena that are not clearly natural or supernatural. People who believe that flying saucers are optical illusions or actual visitors from outer space would consider them natural phenomena, while others might consider them sacred and religious phenomena. Marxists who believe that a socialist utopia will emerge automatically as a result of the workings of inexorable historical processes regard themselves as dealing with a thoroughly documented scientific finding. Some of their opponents, on the other hand, see elements of supernaturalism in Marxist beliefs and therefore interpret Marxism as a modern form of religion. Marxism, capitalism, and many other political doctrines tend to be idealistic and utopian. Because none are derived in any direct way from scientific knowledge about human behavior, the least that can be said about them is that they are strongly tinged with a religious mystique. Many physicists and biologists have a strongly religious attitude toward their disciplines. For that matter, Alfred Kroeber, one of the leading anthropologists of his time, once wrote, "Anthropology is my religion."

Granted that religious ideas and practices cannot always be strongly separated from other sorts of ideas and practices, every culture nonetheless seems to possess a core of beliefs and activities that are unmistakably religious in quality. All cultures possess a more or less systematic set of understandings about the nature of things and the purposes of life which serve to place not only the supernatural world, but the natural world as well, within a religious framework. Such a set of fundamental and important ideas is generally described by the term *world view*. Stemming from the world view are a variety of religious practices and associated practitioners which can be subsumed under the general heading of *religious ritual*. Religious ritual refers generally to the various techniques used in dealing with those areas of life defined within the world view as being especially awesome, sacred, or concerned with the supernatural.

Religious ideas and behaviors seem to arise out of situations in which human beings find themselves unable to provide simple explanations or solutions to events they consider important. Most religion has to do with natural phenomena lacking explanation or with important and recurrent events that cannot easily be predicted. Sudden death, drought, mysterious prickling sensations, and other things that arise without warning and without apparent cause are likely to produce anxiety and a search for explanations. Although in any culture a few things may be dismissed as unknowable or inexplicable, the common tendency is to invent an explanation if a natural explanation is not readily available. Although there seems to be no particular reason for anxiety about such things as the rising or the setting of the sun, people tend to feel uncomfortable unless they feel they have some means of controlling the process or of ensuring that it is not brought to a halt.

Social arrangements that produce discomfort or arouse feelings of guilt or anxiety are also explained in religious terms. In South India poor people were traditionally considered to have committed sins in previous lifetimes for which they were being punished. Closer to home is the idea that the meek will

The Siva dance, the "national" dance of Western Samoa. Such dances in Polynesia were originally enactments of important myths or legends. (Courtesy of the United Nations.)

inherit the earth, or that it is easier for a camel to pass through the eye of a needle than for a rich man to enter heaven. Religious explanations of things seem to cluster around situations characterized by strain and uncertainty and to serve the function of resolving doubts and anxieties, very often by providing activities in which people can engage. A curing ceremony or an elaborate course of hospital treatment may have little effect upon a terminal illness, but both the religious ritual and the supposedly pragmatic course of hospital treatments are probably psychologically helpful to patients and their associates.

Although one anthropologist has cynically defined religion as "a strong belief in what you know ain't so," the truth is that there are many areas of life where, even with the aid of hopefully omnipotent science, it is impossible to find a rational and all-encompassing explanation or an infallible way of obtaining results. Did the curing ceremony fail because the payment to the ancestral spirit that caused the illness was inadequate? Did the hospital treatment fail because the patient was not brought to the hospital soon enough?

Can it be scientifically demonstrated that ancestral spirits do not exist or that the disease was inherently incurable? Of course not, and yet some of us must explain the patient's death. For the Azande of Africa, Evans-Pritchard records their willing acceptance of the fact that an illness might be caused by a disease organism.[1] But the Azande asked the perfectly reasonable question, Why did this man get sick and not some other man if witchcraft was not involved? Is the scientific answer that the sick man's resistance to infection was lower because his family situation was stressful? If so, isn't that witchcraft? The Azande explanation of illness and means of treating it is not the same as ours, but it may not be entirely false either and it is certainly not illogical. For those who believe, it provides an answer to a question that has received very little scientific attention.

2. World View

A world view consists of understandings that people have about why things are the way they are. If technology is that part of a cultural tradition that tells people what to do on every occasion, then world view is that more essential and basic part of the cultural tradition that tells people what is worth doing and why. In the United States the following statements represent the kinds of data associated with world view: (1) Ours not to reason why; (2) If you work hard, you'll get ahead; (3) If at first you don't succeed, try try again. But world view also has to do with our general understandings of the nature of the universe and of the forces at work within it. It has to do with the five medieval elements—earth, air, fire, water, and ether. It has to do with the number of directions that exist, with a concept of time that can be killed or wasted, and with such mysterious forces as gravity or electromagnetism. World view contains the answers to the questions: (1) What is going on? (2) What is the meaning of it all? (3) What is the purpose of life? (4) How can I find my way?

In essence, world view consists of inferences that people make about the world around them. Such inferences are not, on the whole, illogical, but they are very often based upon inadequate information and premature generalization. When students of the English language say, "I swinged from a tree," they are making a logical inference concerning the proper way of forming the past tense. Such an inference is based upon experience with large numbers of verbs that form their past tense by adding *-ed*. The existence of classes of verbs that have a different sort of past tense is ignored until a behavioral standard is violated and the individual who said "swinged" is treated to the punishments of laughter or reproof. Different cultures have different world views primarily because they use different sorts of reasonable inferences to explain the same things. The Azande world view is concerned with explaining why particular individuals get sick. To explain injury and sickness in general, they use the

[1] E. E. Evans-Pritchard, *Witchcraft, Oracles and Magic Among the Azande* (London: Oxford University Press, 1937), p. 479.

Mask used at conclusion of circumcision ceremonies. Face of wood, collar of grass. Yake, Congo, Africa. (Courtesy of the UCLA Museum of Cultural History.)

reasonable inference that an angry or jealous person will physically injure his opponent. The inference that hostility can lead to physical assault is entirely reasonable and would not normally be regarded as a religious idea. The extension of the inference to the idea that a hostile person can cause illness through the manipulation of an unseen force or power seems to involve the supernatural and would therefore be classified as a religious belief in witchcraft.

To gain success, power, or courage, Crow Indians traditionally relied upon supernatural assistance. They gained such assistance by fasting and mortification of the flesh designed to arouse the pity of supernatural beings. Half-dead from hunger, pain, and loss of blood, the seeker would often fall into an unconscious state. While the seeker was unconscious, animal spirits or other supernatural figures would take the seeker to their *tipis* and make gifts of powerful songs or other charms useful in attaining goals. One of the key ideas here, perfectly reasonable, is that suffering arouses pity. Equally reasonable is the idea that, as the band is controlled by human beings, so the world is controlled by essentially similar supernatural beings. Both generalizations were supported by the fact that individuals could visit with the supernatural figures and, later, achieve success in life on the basis of the powers that were given them.

We do not really know why human beings seek explanations for imposing or impossible events. Indeed, we are not even sure that they do, for some peo-

Male effigy used in initiation ceremonies in one of the grades of a men's secret organization, probably symbolic of a mythological personage. Made of fiber-wrapped reeds, modeled over with painted vegetal paste. New Hebrides Islands, Melanesia. (Courtesy of the UCLA Museum of Cultural History.)

ples are remarkably unconcerned about events that are of overwhelming concern to others. The extent to which such explanations are realistic or unrealistic has a great deal to do with the development of technological aids to perception, such as the telescope and microscope, and with the development of systematic devices for exploration, such as the controlled experiment or the random sample. Even granted the existence of an imposing basis for realism, there is no likelihood, in a world that the scientific world view perceives to be affected by indeterminacy, that all explanations will be reasonable or all events predictable. In fact the failures of the scientific world view may serve as a greater source of annoyance and anxiety than the failures of less rigorous world views that make a smaller pretense of perfection. In the modern United States, soldiers still carry lucky charms, basketball players still pray for supernatural assistance, sufferers from arthritis still wear copper bracelets, and teenage lovers still seek astrological assistance.

In all of these cases the religious belief and its associated practices are usually understandable as a simple extension of general principles that may well be realistic and practical under other circumstances. Two of these general principles, impersonal power and animism, are considered in the following sections.

3. The Concept of Impersonal Power

A growing individual acquires increasing strength and power. A leader often has the power to force or persuade others to do his bidding. In the United States these elementary concepts of power are extended to gravity, electricity, magnetism, and luck. Very often in many different cultures, similar concepts of power are generalized to refer to an inherent ability to influence the course of events. The Algonkin Indian term for impersonal power, *manitou*, refers to a property that can be possessed by gods or spirits, religious practitioners, and others as well. It can also be possessed by things or events that are extraordinary or inexplicable.

The term *mana* used in Micronesia, in Polynesia, and in parts of Melanesia refers similarly to concentrations of force analogous to our concept of impersonal power. Success, especially exceptional success, in any enterprise is attributed to the possession of *mana*. In Polynesia, where there were traditionally elaborate systems of rank, *mana* was often used as a direct measure of social position. High-ranking individuals might, in fact, possess so much *mana* that it was dangerous for ordinary people to approach them. Although a chief's *mana* served to protect the village from disaster, the first indication that his *mana* had drained away was often defeat in war or other misfortune. The Polynesian attitude toward divinities and chiefs was often pragmatic; they wasted little time on gods or humans who appeared to have lost their *mana*.

On some islands, *mana* was obtained by inheritance, and individuals traced their descent bilaterally, as is the custom in the United States, through those relatives that had the greatest achievements and therefore the most *mana*. Very often, when a child inherited *mana* from both parents, it possessed more *mana* than either of them and therefore had to be treated with the greatest respect. A similar "spoiled child" syndrome appears in the United States when the child is expected to become superior to either parent.

Artifacts, especially tools, weapons, and canoes, were given *mana* by careful construction and the rigorous performance of rituals pertinent to their building. Building a canoe required close cooperation between craftsman and priest to ensure that it would possess *mana*. Should the canoe prove slow and unwieldy or the ax dull, it would be evidence that the careful rituals required for its construction had failed to imbue it with *mana*.

An individual possessing *mana* was in a position to place a *tabu* or prohibition upon his property and so to forbid persons with lesser *mana* to touch it or use it without penalty of supernatural punishment. In the Marquesas, Linton[2] observed a situation in which the eight- or nine-year-old son of a chief had quarreled with his father and tabued the house by naming it after his head. The boy, looking glum but triumphant, sat in the house, while his father and the rest of the family camped in the front yard until such time as the son was willing to remove the tabu.

[2] Ralph Linton, "Marquesan Culture," *The Individual and His Society,* ed. Abram Kardiner (New York: Columbia University Press, 1939), pp. 158–159.

Tabu also resided in gods, humans, and artifacts possessing great *mana*. Often a high chief was considered physically dangerous to others and was forced to live in virtual isolation. The notion of mystical power inherent in the body of high-ranking individuals or in artifacts associated with them is extremely widespread. Consider the western European belief that kings could cure by the laying on of hands, or the more modern cult worship of popular actors and singers in which sycophants attempt to obtain bits of their hair or small pieces of their clothing and other associated artifacts. The Western concept of luck as something that can be enhanced by the performance of rituals, such as moving to a different chair or wearing a good luck piece, is a similar concept of impersonal power.

As an explanatory principle, impersonal power is complete and self-sufficient. It accounts for all events in the past and for all future events. Exceptional success, outstanding leadership, unusual performance, and all that is divine, supernatural, and wonderful are so because they are associated with the possession of power. Such power is amoral—neither good nor evil, accounting equally for god and demon, priest and sorcerer, good person and scoundrel. Because a single accident or slipup can cause the loss of power, the concept of power rationalizes both success and failure. Success is the sure indicator of the possession of power; failure, the sure indicator of its loss or absence.

4. Supernatural Beings

Although impersonal power can function independently of any belief in special sorts of creatures that possess it, most religious systems also involve various sorts of beliefs about supernatural beings. Animism, or the belief in supernatural beings, was first defined by E. B. Tylor.[3] He saw animism as involving a belief in souls capable of existing after the death or destruction of the body and as also involving immaterial spirits and deities capable of influencing events in the material world. Anthropologists have traditionally made a distinction between animism and animatism, the belief that certain natural objects are capable of sentient action, and movement. Although animated objects, such as a TV set that refuses to function, may be kicked or slapped, animatism is not a major part of most religions. The forest-dwelling California Indian believed that a tree might kill, if it so desired, by dropping one of its branches upon its victim. Like the modern logger, who also recognizes the existence of such "widow makers," the Indian does not therefore venerate the tree or believe that the tree contains a spirit to be worshipped. The Indian merely exercises great care when passing under it. The same person would have avoided a certain pool because it was believed to contain a malevolent spirit that might have been propitiated by means of offerings. Animism, illustrated in the second example, is a belief in the existence of

[3] E. B. Tylor, *Primitive Culture* (Boston: Estes and Lauriat, 1874), Vol. 1, pp. 426–427.

Figure 15–1 Left: impersonation of the Shalako, a supernatural being, Zuñi pueblo, New Mexico; right: priest of a ceremonial society, Zuñi pueblo, New Mexico.

supernatural beings, whether they originate in the souls of once-living creatures or have existed from the beginning of time as supernaturals.

The following discussions of Chiricahua Apache, Baganda, and Aztec supernaturals illustrate the complexities that can develop from the comparatively simple idea that events in nature are controlled by spiritual beings. Because there is generally a close relationship between the numbers and characteristics of supernatural beings and the kinds of interpersonal relationships existing within any particular culture, beliefs in supernatural beings are generally attributed to the generalization of interpersonal experiences within the family and community. If human relationships are complicated and hierarchical, as they were among the Aztecs, then relationships to supernatural beings are likely to become complex and hierarchical. If father is stern and all-powerful, there may well be a stern and all-powerful deity supervising the human family with the same unforgiving attention that a real father gives to his children. It is not unreasonable to suppose that the same techniques used in obtaining favors from father will be effective in obtaining favors from similar supernatural beings.

Although beliefs in supernatural beings and religion itself can be regarded as originating in the extension of various kinds of concrete and predictable experience into other realms, such beliefs can also be interpreted as psychological projections—fantasies, dreams, or stories—by means of which human beings strive to comprehend and to render predictable those things that they do not comprehend and that are not predictable.

5. Apache Supernaturals

Like many peoples living in small and scattered camps or settlements, the Chiricahua Apache lacked a tightly structured or hierarchical social order. As might be expected, their relationships to the environment were highly personal. Accordingly the deserts and mountains within which the Apache lived were populated by beings whose relationships to the Apache closely resembled those characteristic of relatives, friends, and enemies within the social world. There were three major classes of supernatural beings—gods, spirits, and ghosts. The most important gods included Life Giver, White Painted Woman, Child of the Water, and Killer of Enemies. These deities figured in myths and ceremonies, but their major importance lay in the past. For example, Child of the Water, aided by Killer of Enemies, made earth habitable by killing the Giant, the Great Eagles, the Bull Buffalo, and the Antelope.

Spirits were more numerous and more intimately concerned with day-to-day events. The Mountain Spirits, representatives of a "people" said to live in the Holy Mountains, frequently visited the Apaches, particularly during ceremonies, and they played important roles in mythology and in the performance of masked dances. The Mountain Spirits were believed to live in particular localities and to be custodians of the animals found in the vicinity of their homes. Visitors to places believed to be inhabited by the Mountain People would sprinkle pollen in the direction of their "Holy Homes" and pray for protection from enemies or other harm. Individuals faced with trouble or danger would pray to the Mountain People in the hope that they would emerge and offer their protection.

Other spirits included the benevolent Controller of Water, the malevolent Water Monster, and a host of others connected with places, natural phenomena, and animals. A whole series of stories deal with the sly and mischievious Coyote, who violates almost all standards of proper behavior and whose attempts at mischief almost always backfire. During his rare successes, he brought the Chiricahua some of their most valued cultural possessions. Although techniques used in attracting the support of spirits were less dramatic than those used by the Crow, the Apache also sought familiar spirits from whom they received powers that enabled them to cure illness and sometimes to cause it. Owl, snake, bear, and the various economically important game animals were the most frequent sources of such familiar spirits. Power obtained from the Mountain Spirits permitted the individual to present the Masked Dancer rite, an important ceremony for curing and for community welfare. Spirits were the means by which the Chiricahua obtained access to supernatural power and so the ability to cure illnesses, to stave off death and misfortune, and otherwise to ameliorate the problems of existence.

The third category of supernaturals, the spirits of the dead, were greatly feared, and the Chiricahua made every effort to obliterate the memory of the dead as quickly as possible. Occasionally the ghosts of the dead did not remain in the underground afterworld to which they were consigned, but returned to visit, often in dreams, their living friends and relatives. Such visits were

Spirits carrying bows and arrows and swords appear at Apache encampment. Called "Devil Dancers" by their early photographer, the costumed individuals portrayed here probably represent mountain spirits who, like the Hopi kachinas, were expected to provide supernatural assistance to the group. (Courtesy of Smithsonian Institution, National Anthropological Archives.)

dreaded as indications that the one visited might soon die himself. Careful precautions were taken to avoid any direct or indirect reference to the dead in the hope of discouraging ghostly visitations.

6. Baganda Supernaturals: The Ghosts of the Dead

The Baganda (Chapter 11, §6) were traditionally horticulturalists and cattle herders who lived in the hilly and well-watered grasslands of Uganda. The relatively complex social relationships characteristic of the Baganda kingdom were reflected in their hierarchy of supernaturals. Their gods fell into three major classes: clan gods, the deified spirits of former kings, and tribal or "national" gods. Clan gods (one for each of the thirty-six clans) and deified kings were essentially ancestral spirits who had been elevated to godly rank. Clan gods represented the ancestor of the clan and were worshipped only by their descendants, the living members of the clan they represented. Kingly gods were honored by all—as they were during their lives as kings—but were especially worshipped and consulted by members of the royal clan.

Each of the national or tribal gods had a temple and a cult of priests supported by contributions from the royal treasury. The national gods were arranged in a hierarchy, not unlike a governmental organization, with each deity having a particular area of greatest influence and particular functions for which he was responsible. Katonda, the "father of gods," created the universe and all that was in it, but, like a distant monarch, left the universe to be run by his descendants. Accordingly his cult was relatively small and unimportant.

Mukasa, the god of Lake Victoria, was the dominant Baganda deity, responsible for providing fish and controlling storms. More important, he was the god of fertility, who sent twins, received with great rejoicing, and provided children to childless women. He was responsible for good crops and increases in the cattle herd. He served to stimulate and provide good living for all. The king frequently consulted Mukasa at times of crisis, gave generously to his temples, and provided him with rich sacrifices.

Other gods included Walumbe, the god of death; Kaumpuli, the god of plague—kept hidden in a hole in the earth by his priests; Kibuka and Nende, the gods of war; Dungu, the god of hunters; Musuka, the rainbow god and patron of fishermen; Gulu, the sky god; Kitaka, the earth god; Musisi, controller of earthquakes; Nagawonyi, the goddess who sends rain, protects the crop, and receives the first fruits of harvest; and Nabuzana, the goddess in charge of childbearing women, whose priestesses function as midwives.

Spirits were particularly associated with streams, lakes, wells, trees, hills, and other identifiable natural places and things. Shrines were built to serve as spirit dwellings and as repositories for offerings. When a Baganda crossed a stream, took water or fish from a lake or stream, chopped down a tree, or

Sioux and other Plains Indian groups traditionally disposed of the dead in trees or on platforms. (From the Morrow Collection. Courtesy of W. H. Over Museum.)

Mask with headdress worn in rituals of the Ekpo society, Cross River tribes (probably Ekoi), Nigeria. Made of skin-covered wood; originally human heads were used, which may account for realism of mask. (Courtesy of the UCLA Museum of Culture History.)

otherwise altered the landscape, he was careful to propitiate the resident spirits by leaving an offering. Hills were especially sacred because of the many spirits who lived there, and could be used as places of sanctuary by those who had incurred the wrath of the authorities.

When a person died, the soul left the body and was immediately transformed into a ghost, invisible but subject to the same appetites, passions, and feelings as the living. The ghost felt cold, pain, and heat; it might be kindly and affectionate, or angry and vindictive; it might suffer a second death by fire or by drowning. Still a member of the society, clan, and family to which it belonged while alive, the ghost remained an important figure in the life of relatives and friends.

A newly made ghost went first to the god of death to give an accounting of his life. The ghost then returned to its place of burial and took up residence in a shrine built at the head of the grave. In the case of a male ghost the wives who had borne him children and who survived him lived also at the grave, tending his gardens, his domestic animals, and his shrine. If these proprieties were well observed and if suitable offerings were provided, the ghost did not disturb his living relatives and friends but functioned, invisibly, in much the same way he did during life.

Annoyed by the neglect of shrine or grave, or by any improper action on the part of surviving relatives, a ghost might bring illness, misfortune, or death upon relatives or friends. When this happened, a specialist was called upon for advice. The specialist might seek to propitiate the ghost by offerings and by repairing whatever omissions there might have been in regard to care of the ghost's shrine or grave. If these measures failed, the specialist might try to catch the ghost and kill it by fire and drowning. Father's sisters were said to be particularly malevolent and so often had to be disposed of in this manner. Angry ghosts sometimes took possession of the bodies of the living, causing delirium and attacks of frenzy. Such ghosts were exorcised by requiring the patient to inhale the smoke of burning herbs.

Two years after death the ghost was reincarnated in the body of a newly born child of the same clan and family. The identity of each child was determined at a naming ceremony when the father recited the names of his deceased clan relatives to the baby. If the child laughed when the name was spoken, it was a sign that the proper name had been found. Once a ghost had been so reincarnated, the grave and shrine could be abandoned and offerings need no longer be made.

Through their beliefs in ghosts and reincarnation, the Baganda achieved a cyclic social continuity that linked the society of the living to the dead and to the unborn. The Chiricahua Apache rejected death and journeyed to the underworld with the greatest reluctance. The Baganda interpreted death as a temporary condition soon to be cured by rebirth. Because both sets of beliefs established certainties about the problem of death, both probably served to allay anxiety. The Baganda and the Chiricahua understood death, they had no cause to worry about it.

7. The Gods of the Aztecs

Among the Baganda we have noted the beginnings of a godly hierarchy, with a number of tribal or national divinities, each more or less specialized in function, and each honored by a temple and cult. Nonetheless, the Baganda gods were in general less important than the ghosts of the dead; the national gods represented, as it were, a form of religious specialization, the province of a limited number of priests or other religious practitioners.

The tendency toward specialization in religious belief was even further developed among the Aztecs of Mexico. The Aztecs, as we have said before, were a powerful and warlike people who at the time of the Spanish Conquest in 1520 dominated most of present-day Mexico. Although their basic economic dependence was on horticulture, we noted also the presence of extensive trade, external and internal, an almost continuous aggressive warfare for conquest, and the development of numerous specialized arts and crafts. (See Chapter 13, §8.)

Like the other peoples whose supernaturals we have described, the Aztecs probably also peopled their universe with gods, spirits, and ghosts. We know little of their concepts of ghosts; however, the souls of most of the dead went to a place called Mictlan, an underworld home of the dead, and, though this was not a place of punishment, it was pictured nevertheless as a dreary and uninviting spot. Other ghosts were more fortunate. Those who died of drowning, lightning, or diseases such as dropsy and leprosy went to a paradise called Tlalocan, the residence of the rain gods, or Tlalocs, where they enjoyed perpetual summer and all they wanted to eat and drink. Warriors killed in battle, women who died in childbirth, and victims sacrificed as offerings to the gods went to the home of the sun, an even more attractive place than the country of the Tlalocs. Warriors' souls were believed to appear during the day, after having accompanied the sun to the zenith, as hummingbirds, whereas the souls of women who died in childbirth escorted the descending sun to the horizon and then spent their nights on earth in the guise of moths. But, though offerings were made to the dead at ceremonies taking place at stated times after their demise, there is no evidence that the Aztecs had any such elaborate cult of the ghosts as we have described for the Baganda.

Spirits also played some role in Aztec religion, though our knowledge is again fragmentary. Hosts of spirits are reported for springs, fields, mountaintops, households, and individuals (guardian spirits). There were also, apparently, many minor deities, similar to the clan gods of the Baganda, that served as tutelary divinities of families, *calpulli*, occupational and trade groups, and many similar social segments. It is notable that the latter appear to be closer to spirits than to ghosts, as among the Baganda.

But the Aztec gods far outshone these lesser supernaturals. There were literally hundreds of gods, specialized in a great variety of functions. They were apparently not too well organized into a hierarchy, or pantheon; single gods often appear with a variety of names and are even differently represented in paintings and carvings. The attributes of gods are also frequently confusing, with considerable overlapping between one god and another. Part of this confusion undoubtedly springs from inadequate reporting; our only firsthand accounts of Aztec religion are from Spanish priests and soldiers. In part, also, it is likely that the Aztecs, as a result of years of conquest and the gradual absorption of alien peoples, added many foreign gods to their own earlier, and probably much more limited, stock.

No one of the Aztec gods stood out as a supreme deity. Indeed, the idea of an organized assemblage of gods with one as the supreme ruler is relatively rare. It was apparently approached by the Inca of Peru, who regarded the sun as at least a dominant divinity, but the idea is much more common in the older religions of the Near East and in the offshoots of those found in ancient

Greece and Rome. The concept of a single, all-powerful deity is even rarer and is apparently lacking among all nonliterate peoples. As we know it in Old World history, it seems to have appeared first in Egypt, about 1400 B.C., and after many centuries, diffused into Asia Minor. Here, about 800 B.C., the concept emerges in Judaism and Zoroastrianism, and later in Christianity and Mohammedanism. Even in these religions, however, we find constantly cropping up the concept of other, opposed divinities, such as the evil principle symbolized by Satan, and numerous lesser supernaturals, as represented by angels, cherubim, and saints. These are, to be sure, regarded more as derived divinities than divinities in their own right; they possess divine power solely by virtue of their attachment to the supreme being.

To return to the Aztecs, it seems clear that four of their deities stood out as more powerful and important than the rest. One of these was called Tezcatlipoca, who was said to be omniscient, all-seeing, and possessed of eternal youth. In one of his dual characters, he personified the breath of life and had the functions of judging and punishing sinners, humbling the haughty and overbearing, presiding over feasts and banquets, and serving as the patron of military schools. In his second character, symbolized by his representation with a black face, limbs, and body, Tezcatlipoca was the god of darkness, even the malevolent enemy of mankind, and served as the patron of those who practiced black magic, sorcery, and witchcraft. Here, then, is a god that combines into one character both a beneficent and an evil — or at least antisocial — principle.

Quetzalcoatl, the "plumed serpent," had a much wider range in Mexico and Central America, and was found, under various names, among many peoples. To the Aztecs, Quetzalcoatl was the divinity of wind and air, the special patron of the priesthood. According to myth and legend, he brought to the Aztecs the calendar and all their priestly arts and sciences. Once he headed a rich and peaceful empire in Mexico but, yielding to temptation under the machinations of enemies, he fell from his high position, traveled eastward, and disappeared into the ocean. The Aztecs, however, confidently expected Quetzalcoatl to return as a Messiah to restore the golden age, and, when Cortes, the Spanish conqueror, first appeared, the Aztecs thought for a while that he was Quetzalcoatl. This of course gave Cortes a great advantage, even though the Aztecs soon discovered their mistake.

The third of the four great Aztec divinities was Huitzilopochtli, the god of war and more remotely of the sun and of horticulture. He was especially important to the Aztecs, and perhaps original with them rather than borrowed from alien peoples. His great importance lay in his connection with war, which, as we have seen, was a major activity of the Aztecs, and in his patronage of agrarian arts, also basic to Aztec economy.

Finally we find the Tlalocs, apparently a group of divinities in control of rain, water, thunder, and the mountains. As we noted earlier, the land of the Tlalocs was one of the special "heavens" of the Aztecs, reserved for people who died in certain specified ways. As gods of rain and water, the Tlalocs were of obvious importance to a nation of cultivators.

In addition to these, there were many separate gods: for each phase of growing maize plants and all other cultivated plants; for fire, lightning, the planets, the sun, and the moon; for the many regional divisions of the empire. There were the god of death and the underworld; the god of hunters and the morning star; the goddess who had charge of sexual sins, confession, and purification; and, finally, the many gods for warriors, weavers, traders, and other similar groups. All these and more had their special cults, priests, and ceremonies. The Aztec calendar of rites and ceremonies was long and complicated, and, we may be sure, was under the charge of a trained priesthood, men and women who devoted their lives to this calling.

It is perhaps worth noting here that as gods assume greater importance in a religion, there is apt to appear as well a greater organization of religious ceremonies and a specialized body of priests to conduct them. An elaboration of supernaturalism is apt to occur in societies that produce sufficient goods to support the priests, temples, and cults involved. We shall return to this point in later sections.

8. Other Aspects of World View

By themselves, the concepts of power and animism do not necessarily imply the existence of supernatural forces. The concept of electricity, for example, involves a concept of impersonal power without involving any supernatural agencies or forces. In the same way the concept of personality involves ideas of planning and purpose that have supernatural implications only when it is believed that natural objects or intangible beings are animated by or associated with personalities. Happenings that are motivated by power and happenings that are motivated by beings must, however, be dealt with in quite different ways. If a crop fails because a field has lost supernatural or natural power, the logical response is to take practical and mechanical measures required to restore the field. Attention is directed to the accumulation, storage, and transmission of power by whatever means seem practical and effective. In Hindu mythology any being, whether human or supernatural, is capable through knowledge of magical formulas or through fasting and abstention of acquiring vast quantities of supernatural power. Such powers can be used beneficently to increase the fertility of fields and perform other useful functions, but they can also be used malevolently because power is inherently neutral in any conflict between good and evil. Such powers can be used in precisely the way that fertilizer is used to increase crop production. They can be labeled "supernatural powers" only by those who believe that they are not actually effective.

If the crop fails because a supernatural being is angry with the farmer, the kinds of measures that can be taken to restore the productivity of the field are quite different. What is needed now is prayer, bribery, blackmail, or other highly personal techniques designed to influence a being who is motivated essentially in the same ways that a human being is motivated.

Although any event, such as crop failure, can be explained in an infinite number of ways, not all possible explanations are equally satisfying. One would certainly hope that any explanation would provide a program of action designed to prevent a recurrence of the problem. If some being has caused crop failure, then a way can be found of coping with that being. It would be a rare human being who believed that nothing could be done about crop failure, illness, death, or the awesome possibility that the sun might not rise tomorrow. Where such cases of real or potential misfortune are attributed solely to impersonal power, the individual has little choice but to blame himself. He should have applied more fertilizer, abstained from sex, gone to bed early, or performed other actions that would have prevented the loss of power. Of course, the idea of loss of power can be combined with ideas of personality, in which case misfortune can be attributed to the activities of malevolent or temporarily disaffected human beings, spirits, or deities. Where misfortune is generally attributed to natural and supernatural beings, the obvious tendency is to blame others for whatever has gone wrong. If the affected individual has failed in his obligations to neighbors or to supernatural beings and so has provided them with justification for their vengeful actions, he again has no one to blame but himself. Here the concept of automatic punishment is almost as mechanical as the idea of loss of power. Both ideas set up the proposition that good fortune follows from doing the right thing, while bad fortune follows from doing the wrong thing.

The idea that bad fortune is the result of malice and not the result of one's own mistakes or shortcomings is the fundamental idea underlying the concept

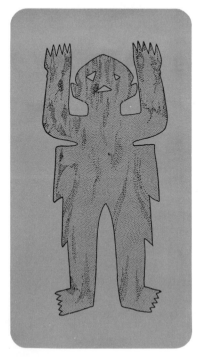

Figure 15–2 Doll of handmade paper used by some Mexican Indians in witchcraft. (After von Hagen.)

of witchcraft. Such a concept greatly reduces the burden of guilt that must be carried when the individual has no one to blame but himself, but his release from guilt must often by purchased at the price of aggression and conflict. The Arunta of Australia, for example, traditionally attributed all death to covert enemies living in neighboring groups. Such a view has the merit of reducing internal conflict and suspicion, but obviously does little to contribute to friendly relationships between neighboring groups. In the American Southwest the Navajo tended to attribute death and misfortune to fellow members of the group with the result that hostilities among neighbors often led to murder. Against this backdrop the Baganda tendency to attribute misfortune to the often inadvertent neglect of deceased relatives seems positively inspired because it steers a middle course between excessive guilt and the need to blame others. Similarly the Hopi belief that witches were best dealt with by being civil to them offers a hopeful strategy for avoiding direct confrontation and violence.

In many cultures different sorts of misfortune are attributed to different sorts of causes. In South India a person who became ill could attribute his misfortune to witchcraft ("poisoning"), to divine punishment, or to improper diet, depending upon the kind of illness involved. The same sort of thing is true in the United States, where psychological illnesses tend to be attributed to others, while physical illnesses are attributed to diet, loss of sleep, cigarette smoking, or other factors controlled by the individual.

Although the concepts of impersonal power and animism are probably the most important general explanations of the things that happen in the world, they are inevitably found in association with a wide variety of other concepts which, taken all together, contribute to the uniqueness and fascination of the world views characteristic of different peoples. For example, the principle of limited good as developed by George Foster consists essentially of the idea that the goods of this world are limited and that the more goods someone else has, the less will be available for oneself.[4] Such a view is quite realistic in particular contexts—for example, where grades are based on a rigid statistical formula or where a pie is to be divided—but it is not realistic when applied to situations in which goods are unlimited or, as in the case of affection, where the act of sharing, itself, may well multiply the available good. The opposed view, that goods are unlimited, leads—as Garrett Hardin has pointed out—to the "tragedy of the commons" when individuals are given unlimited access to a particular good and use it up.[5] Air and water pollution and overgrazing are examples of this. The view of unlimited good has been characteristic of the early stages of the development of industrial societies and is probably characteristic of all sorts of societies in the early stages of technological revolution or in the most productive stages of pioneering a rich environment. The extent to which particular goods are considered limited or unlimited in any society is bound to have important effects upon the quality of human relationships as

---

[4] George M. Foster, "Peasant Society and the Image of Limited Good," *American Anthropologist*, **67**:293–315 (1965).

[5] Garrett Hardin, "The Tragedy of the Commons," *Science*, **162**:1243–1248 (1968).

well as upon the interpretation of human relationships with natural and super-natural forces.

The idea of natural order, a basic assumption of the scientific method, is probably essential to most religious interpretations of the nature of things, but it is certainly weakened by the hypothesized existence of malicious spirits or deities capable of souring milk, ruining crops, or sending pestilence for no particular reason whatsoever. Individuals who believe that they may at any time be the objects of unprovoked and unavoidable misfortune almost certainly lack the confidence and security afforded to those who live in a safe world guarded by benevolent and predictable deities.

The above examples represent a tiny fraction of the many ideas, concepts, and principles that have been identified as fundamental to human interpretations of the nature of things. Although there are probably fundamental rules of logic and ideas of causation that exist among all peoples, the precise weighting and importance given to particular ideas about the nature of things tend to be quite variable. Such variation seems to be deeply influenced by differences in the life experience of different peoples and by the special nature of the problems they encounter in organizing their societies and in coping with their particular environments.

9. Religious Practitioners

Wherever supernatural forces are considered to be at work, there are likely to be individuals whose control of the technology required for dealing with such forces provides them with a part-time or full-time occupation. Regardless of what may be said concerning the world's oldest profession, there will always be a solid argument that the first specialist was a religious practitioner. In many societies lacking specialization of labor, the closest thing to a specialist is a *shaman* or a spirit medium. Although the term *shaman* refers specifically to part-time religious practitioners found among tribes of the Siberian Arctic, it is often used in the literature to refer to a variety of practitioners who deal in one way or another with spirits. Because the Arctic shaman plays an active role in dealing with spirits, whereas a spirit medium is simply a passive vessel through whom spirits communicate, it may be sensible to maintain a distinction between them.

Among the Polar Eskimo, shamans, or *angakok*, were numerous at the time the group was first studied. Almost every family had one and there would be several in a winter village. Both men and women became shamans and, although they were often compensated for their services, none devoted full time to shamanism. Shamans were usually older and highly respected individuals, successful in other pursuits as well as in the religious sphere. In becoming a shaman, the individual was usually visited by spirits when walking alone. One or several of these would later become "familiar" spirits, who could be depended upon for assistance. Following this, the individual would seek advice from an older and more established shaman. Once trained, shamans possessed the ability to call forth or suppress storms and to banish or summon game animals. Their most important function was to cure disease, interpreted as the loss of the soul. Soul loss, a condition not unlike the identity crisis that periodically afflicts individuals in industrialized nations, is regarded as serious, and if the soul is not recovered, the individual will eventually die.

Curing rites were held by the shaman at the request of the patient. The shaman initiated the rites by addressing a familiar spirit in a special language. The shaman gradually entered a trance state by singing spirit songs, beating on a drum, and dancing in a wild and uncontrolled manner. When the trance state was achieved, the shaman trembled and groaned, sometimes foaming at the mouth, and ultimately becoming rigid and insensible to pain. In this state the shaman's own soul might leave the body and rescue the patient's soul, sometimes after a bloody fight. Once the soul had been recovered, the patient was expected to improve. Because the shaman obtained his power from contacts with familiar spirits, the shaman was also capable of stealing and hiding the souls of enemies. Powerful shamans were, thus, regarded with fear and respect, but their lives were in jeopardy if too many of their patients died.

By contrast, Chiricahua Apache curers, although they obtained their powers by visions obtained ordinarily while in a state of trance, rarely made use of the trance state in the actual process of curing. The spirit gave powers, usually expressed as special songs or rituals, to the curer, who then made use of them. A Chiricahua curer generally commenced a healing ritual by rolling a cigarette and blowing smoke to the four directions, saying each time, "May it be well," and perhaps intoning a brief prayer for peace and security. A prayer was then addressed to a familiar spirit for assistance, perhaps describing how supernatural powers were obtained and expanding upon their virtues.

Once the preliminaries were completed, the curer began to sing the songs obtained from the familiar spirit, interspersing them with prayers. Once the spirit's attention was obtained, the spirit might indicate privately to the curer the nature of the disease and the techniques to be used in curing it. Typical cures involved the administration of medicinal herbs, the sucking of foreign objects from the patient's body, or the continued performance of ritual songs or dances. At the end of the ceremony the curer often imposed a special diet upon the patient and provided an amulet for further protection. Like Eskimo shamans, the Apache curers might turn their powers to evil purposes. Successful Apache curers were ultimately required to repay their familiar spirits for their many kindnesses by providing them with their own lives or the life of a younger relative. Consequently successful curers, especially if they were old and enjoyed excellent health, were regarded with extreme respect and with fear amounting to terror.

In South India religious specialists and other individuals as well could be possessed by spirits at any time and were almost always possessed by dieties or spirits on ceremonial occasions. The behavior of the individual at such times depended entirely upon the nature of the spirit doing the possessing. Thus a daughter-in-law possessed by an evil spirit might direct a stream of obscenities at her mother-in-law and generally behave in an undignified fashion. By con-

Religious specialist blowing smoke on a tree struck by lightning to "cool" it. Otherwise, it is believed, the lightning that struck tree a few days earlier might kill somebody. Gururumba tribe of eastern highlands, New Guinea. (Courtesy of the American Museum of Natural History.)

trast, an individual possessed by a deity might be contented with dignified but enigmatic statements or perhaps a formal set of demands that needed to be met before the deity's favor could be obtained. In all of these cases the individual functions solely as a spirit medium — a passive receptacle.

Shamans and spirit mediums obtain their powers through a direct experience with supernatural beings. The term *priest* is generally used to describe an individual whose powers are derived primarily from traditional lore passed down as the tradition of a particular organized religious group, sometimes referred to as a cult. Among the Zuñi, traditionally a horticultural, pueblo-dwelling people of New Mexico, individuals became priests by means of prolonged and specialized training involving the rise through a succession of offices to the position of head priest of a religious society. In Zuñi curing societies the priests conducted elaborate ritual performances that involved the careful memorization of long sequences of ritual activity. Among the Zuñi, priests were part-time specialists. In more complex specialized societies, priests are likely to be organized in complex hierarchies and to have a variety of specialized functions. Although shamans and other sorts of free-lance and part-time religious practitioners continue to operate in most complex societies, the tendency is toward the organization of priesthoods based upon traditional knowledge handed down through religious cults. Evidently a priesthood offers the organizational advantage that only a small number of individuals have direct access to information about the supernatural, and the possibilities for dramatic changes in religious belief and practice are correspondingly reduced.

10. Religious Rituals

Religious rituals represent the various techniques that are applied as a means of controlling or influencing the supernatural world. Like other forms of technology, religious rituals can be classified in terms of the social units by which they are enacted. Idiosyncratic rituals are those performed by the individual in response to private and personal religious beliefs. Individual rituals are culturally sanctioned rituals enacted by the individual in response to specific, culturally defined events. Such actions as drinking a love potion or other sovereign remedy, sending one's spirit helper to do harm to another, or crossing one's fingers to ensure good luck and safety, all constitute rituals carried out privately by individuals. Group rituals — performed by a family, village, nation, or other collectivity — are generally classified as ceremonies and tend to be much more elaborate than rituals performed by individuals.

Rituals that have a compelling effect upon the supernatural are generally classified as magical. In magic, if the ritual is performed properly, the result follows automatically. Magic involves the assumption that such impersonal forces as power or natural law can be manipulated in such a way as to force the supernatural world and any beings that might be in it to obey the wishes of the magician. In other forms of religion, particularly those involving supernat-

Figure 15–3 Animal impersonations are often part of ceremonial dances. Left: deer dancer, important personage in ceremonies of the Yaqui Indians, Sonora, Mexico; right: deer impersonator, Taos pueblo, New Mexico.

ural beings, rituals derive their impact through their success in persuading supernatural beings to provide help and to withhold harm.

In Crow Indian religion, persuasion and magic are combined. The individual obtains his powers by arousing the sympathy of a supernatural being, but once he has his powers they are magical in effect unless, of course, they are contravened by some greater power. For example, Lone-tree, while still a young boy, went on a war party. The war party was disastrously defeated and Lone-tree found himself lost and alone in a terrible thunderstorm. At this point he was visited by a large white eagle who said that he would adopt Lone-tree and gave him the power to make rain or hail or to stop a storm. Later, Lone-tree told his enemy, Short-bull, "You will nearly die this summer." Short-bull was struck by lightning, but survived.[6]

In traditional South India, people had available to them a wide range of effective medical treatments. They lacked, however, any effective means of dealing with the great epidemic diseases such as cholera or smallpox. These diseases were believed to be caused by disease goddesses. When "sin was up," the disease goddesses would go to one of the high-ranking male gods, Shiva, and ask permission to punish the people for their sinful behavior. Accordingly, when an epidemic struck, people would clean up their villages, sweeping the streets, whitewashing houses, and doing everything they could think of to compensate for their past sins and to appease the goddess. Nevertheless the epidemic would cease only when the goddess decided that sinful behavior had been brought to an end and the people adequately punished for their misdeeds. In other contexts, traditional South Indians made frequent use of magic, and in many cases made no distinction between magical and natural processes. A bad wife, for example, might poison her husband by putting "dirty stuff" in his food. Whether the "dirty stuff" was cyanide or menstrual blood made no difference; both were poisonous and both were described by the same word.

All religious rituals are, of course, triggered by some sort of tension or transition in the life of the individual or group. Simple rituals tend to go with minor events, while complex and elaborate ceremonies composed of many different rituals in combination tend to go with major crises and important events. The daily use of a deodorant designed to compel the attention of the opposite sex reflects a specific tension or anxiety concerning the personal attractiveness of the individual. Such use of a deodorant is magical to the extent that the individual imagines that the substance used will do anything more than create a change in body odor. Obviously the line between a social ritual or technique and a religious ritual can become extremely thin.

In all cultures there are a host of minor social and religious rituals that provide a time frame for events, especially by marking beginnings and endings, or that serve to indicate the current status of the individuals or the group. A religious ritual such as the saying of grace or the opening prayer is often interchangeable with such secular rituals as the saying of "let's eat" or "let's play ball." Nevertheless the more religious ritual is likely to be laid on in connection with special occasions or times when there is a desire to

[6] Robert H. Lowie, *The Crow Indians* (New York: Holt, Rinehart and Winston, 1956), p. 242.

On eve of circumcision ceremony boy rides a horse accompanied by musicians and dancers. Legog village, Indonesia. (Courtesy of the United Nations.)

emphasize particular events. Religious ceremonies, in the form of calendrical rituals, are especially likely to mark particular times of the year such as the completion of harvest or the coming of winter when marked shifts in the activities of the group and its members are likely to occur. Rites of passage, similarly, mark the transitions in the life of the individual such as birth, puberty, marriage, childbirth, and death.

Rituals of succession, ranging from the "taking around" of a new office worker to the coronation of a monarch, play a similar role in dramatizing, explaining, and sanctifying changes in the composition or status of the group. Other rituals and ceremonies deal with specific crises such as illness, drought, floods, war, or other disasters. Without exhausting all of the kinds of rituals and ceremonies there might be, we can sum up by saying that the most common kinds of rituals are (1) calendrical rituals, marking the times of the day, month, and year; (2) rites of passage, marking the phases of an individual life; and (3) status or crisis rituals, marking threats to or abrupt shifts in the status of the individual or the group. Rituals of greeting and parting, as well as rituals of succession, can be regarded as forms of status ritual.

The scientist, who assumes that all events are governed by natural law, and the dedicated religionist, who assumes that all other religions are false, are among the first to inform us that curing rituals do not cure people, that planting rituals do not ensure a good harvest, and that a coronation ceremony does not ensure divine support for the king or queen so coronated. From this point of view, it is evident that the practice of religion is a waste of time and resources. If there is no supernatural or if most people worship false gods, then the ritual technology used for coping with the supernatural can only be ineffective. But there is a problem here, especially for the scientist. The problem is that most known peoples do, in fact, expend very considerable efforts and resources upon the practice of religion. Even in the United States, which lacks a state religion, and in countries dominated by Marxist philosophies, which consider religion unnecessary, the place of religious ceremonies has been filled by an elaborate series of secular ceremonies that are fully as wasteful and time consuming as anyone else's religious ceremonies. If elaborate ceremonial activities are unnecessary, then they are probably maladaptive. In short, by Darwinian standards societies that practiced religion should long since have been displaced by societies that did not. In another view, societies that worshipped false and ineffective gods should long since have been displaced by societies that practiced the one and only one true religion.

At the beginning of this century Emile Durkheim considered this problem and emerged with the dictum, "There are no false religions." [7] Durkheim argued that although it might be pointless to argue about the reality or lack of reality of any particular supernatural force, there could be no disputing the fact that religions contributed to the adaptation and survival of the societies in

[7] Émile Durkheim, *The Elementary Forms of the Religious Life*, trans. Joseph Ward Swain (New York: Collier Books, 1961), p. 15.

Funeral of an Indian. Guambia township, Colombia. (Courtesy of the United Nations.)

Corpus Christi festival. Chocontá, Colombia. (Kindness of Sylvia Broadbent.)

which they were found. His basic argument was that religious rituals provided a means of organizing the sentiments of the group, thereby making possible the maintenance of social solidarity. Let us consider, then, some specific ceremonial activities and their possible effects upon the survival of the group.

11. South Indian Ceremonials and Their Effects

Years ago, not far from the city of Bangalore in South India, a local chieftain constructed an irrigation dam. Shortly after the construction of the dam, a man of one of the very lowest-ranking castes, a man doomed by the sins of his previous lives to be an eater of beef and a landless laborer or serf, was walking along the top of the dam. Looking toward the water he noticed that the surface of the water was disturbed and he heard the voice of Gangamma, the goddess of the waters, saying, "I want out." The landless laborer answered Gangamma, saying, "Don't leave now, just wait awhile until I come back." Gangamma promised to wait until the man returned. The man rushed into the presence of the local chieftain and told him what had taken place. The chieftain immediately drew his sword and killed the landless laborer. Consequently Gangamma was still, as of 1966, pent up behind the dam awaiting his return.

To reward the landless laborer for his supreme sacrifice, the chieftain ordered his descendants to be given lands in each of the villages served by the

irrigation dam. In return they were to serve as ditch riders and water regulators in all the villages and to maintain the irrigation dam. Each year after
that, until the government banned the ceremony because tourists complained
about blood on the road, all of the descendants of the landless laborer held a
great ceremony at the temple to Gangamma on top of the dam. During the ceremony hundreds of water buffalo were slaughtered and thousands of people
fed. In supernatural terms the purpose of the ceremony was to ensure that
Gangamma remained happy and peaceful inside the dam. Because Gangamma
is one of the disease goddesses, inordinately fond of such impure substances
as meat and alcohol, a diet of water buffalo blood is second only to human
blood as a means of appeasing her.

For people like the government officials who banned the ceremony, the
usefulness of the ceremony was not readily apparent. Nevertheless a number
of important effects can be attributed to the ceremony. First, the ceremony
served as a means by which the largely illiterate population could be reminded

Religious procession Gopalpur, South India. An important aspect of all weddings and
annual ceremonies is a procession to all important shrines in the village. (Photo by
Alan Beals.)

of the myth of Gangamma and the social arrangements resulting from it. These social arrangments, because they resulted in the maintenance of the dam and in the efficient distribution of the irrigation water flowing from it, were of considerable importance. However, some fifty years before, the government had largely disrupted the traditional system of maintenance by deciding that the lands given to the descendants of the landless laborer were the property of the government and charging rent for them. When this happened, the dam, like many other dams in the region, ceased to be repaired, and British officials complained angrily about the "stupid" farmers' unwillingness to repair their irrigation dams. The descendants of the landless laborer continued to serve as ditch riders and water regulators, however, and to share some of the fruits of their position with their poor relations by holding the annual ceremony.

In addition to maintaining and organizing the vast set of social relationships required for the maintenance of the dam and the distribution of the irrigation water, the ritual had the thoroughly concrete impact of providing meat protein to low-caste people most likely to suffer from protein malnutrition. Considering that the undernourished poor might also be fed, especially during the season when agricultural work was unavailable, at a wide variety of similar ceremonies including weddings and village fairs, the importance of animal sacrifice as a means of augmenting the diet was probably substantial. From a cynical point of view, religious ritual provided a means of keeping the poor alive during times of the year when their labor was not required in the fields and made it possible to keep their wages low. During hard times resulting from overpopulation or drought, ceremonies were not held as frequently and did not feed as many people. Thus rituals like the Gangamma ceremony could be regarded as playing a role in ecological relationships by regulating the population of landless laborers.

Speaking of ecology, one of the interesting features of the Gangamma ritual is the slaughtering of water buffaloes. Water buffalo cows are extremely useful animals which, in India, give milk in greater quantity and of better quality than ordinary cows. Male buffaloes, although sometimes used for plowing, are generally regarded as useless in the region surrounding Bangalore. It is the male buffaloes that are eaten. Male buffaloes yield enormous quantities of meat, yet only members of the lowest-ranking castes are permitted to eat such meat. The Gangamma ceremony provided a rationale for the slaughter of male buffaloes which would otherwise have been competing with human beings and more useful animals for available food. It also provided a gathering of thousands of persons ready and willing to consume water buffalo meat. In this regard the ceremony may have outlived its usefulness by the time the government banned it, because water buffalo meat could easily have been sold to Muslims and Europeans living in Bangalore.

In South India, as in other urban civilizations, pilgrimages and tourism are an important aspect of life. The Gangamma ceremony, because it provided an opportunity to observe the slaughter of large numbers of water buffalo and to participate in parades and other ceremonial activities, must have attracted many visitors to the nearby town and swelled the coffers of its merchants.

Religion aside, taken as spectacle, the Gangamma festival must have had as many practical side effects as such California ceremonies as the Salinas rodeo or Mule Days in Bishop.

As a matter of fact almost all large villages and towns in South India and many small ones as well hold annual fairs or festivals which center about religious rituals but which have as their main purpose the attraction of visitors from neighboring and sometimes distant communities.[8] Such interlocal festivals are quite common across the world and in fact seem to be characteristic of urban civilizations. Although festivals vary in content from place to place, even within South India, their main features, besides the criterial feature of the host-guest relationship between the performers of the festival and the audience, include (1) the performance of ritual, (2) commercial activities, (3) athletic competitions, (4) dramatic and musical events, (5) an impressive mythol-

[8] Alan R. Beals, "Conflict and Interlocal Festivals in a South Indian Region," *Religion in South Asia,* ed. Edward B. Harper (Seattle: University of Washington Press, 1964), pp. 99–114.

Pots contain offerings to be placed before the village deity. Gods are likely to possess the men carrying the pots and make oracular statements or criticize the conduct of the ceremony. Gopalpur, South India. (Photo by Alan Beals.)

ogy, (6) general participation of members of the host village in the ritual, and (7) joyous feasting and celebration.

In Northern Mysore State, mythologies concerning individual festivals inevitably stress the importance of the festival as a means of securing divine favor and promoting the general good. In addition to this official excuse, it is apparent that the festival provides opportunities to display the athletic or dramatic talents of its marriageable young men. It also provides lucrative opportunities for village religious functionaries and businessmen. Some villages have also become "famous places" as a result of their annual festivals and may be visited by several hundred thousand people who may travel up to a hundred miles in order to attend. The majority of villages celebrating interlocal festivals do not thereby become famous; very often both the gods and the guests publicly express their dissatisfaction with the conduct of particular festivals. We may then entertain the possibility that the United States is not the only place in the world where expensive and ineffective promotional schemes are developed by community leaders at the expense of ordinary community residents.

With very few exceptions, however, the villages that celebrate interlocal festivals are confronted with serious internal divisions, often leading to armed conflict between different factions in the village. Villages that do not hold festivals rarely exhibit such conflict. One speculation about the reason for this curious state of affairs is that interlocal festivals are held in an attempt to compensate for the bad reputation that a village gains when it has extensive conflict within it. The holding of the festival may serve as a means of arresting internal conflicts because a cooperative spirit must be maintained if the festival is to be held. Just as the threat of war may create solidarity in the face of an outside threat, so the necessity of preparing for a festival may create solidarity.

Another feature of interlocal festivals is the frequency with which violent conflicts occur during the course of wrestling matches involving competition between different guest villages. In recent history seven people were killed during a riot that erupted during the wrestling matches at one festival. Although the evident hostility displayed at the wrestling matches would suggest a general pattern of conflict between villages, such conflict occurs in few other contexts. For the most part, people from rival villages may visit each other's villages freely, and unarmed travelers may move freely from place to place without fear of violence. It is possible that the interlocal festival, especially the interlocal athletic competition, like the Olympic games at Munich, creates tensions and hostilities between communities and is therefore violently disruptive of the social fabric. On the other hand, some theorists view the interlocal festival as an alternative to war. In terms of actual effects, the interlocal festival ensures that conflict between villages is almost totally restricted to riots that take place at wrestling contests and between unarmed individuals.

Across the world, interlocal festivals generally involve villages, universities, and other social divisions within a state or nation. Where they involve tribes or nations with which open warfare is a possibility, the invited guests generally consist of allies or potential allies. Among the Tsembaga of New Guinea, interlocal festivals were a means of sealing alliances preparatory to the waging of war.

Within the South Indian villages observed in 1960 and 1966, the most important and most frequent ceremonials were calendrical ceremonies, which occurred throughout the year, usually at the time of full moon, and marriage ceremonies, which tended to be concentrated during periods when agricultural work was limited. Both types of ceremonies required the participation of representatives of all the major castes in the village. In South Indian world view, the various castes were believed to possess different functions similar to the functions possessed by the different organs of the body. Although this suggests that every village possessed an elaborate and complicated specialization of labor, the fact is that most of the people in any particular village were employed most of the time in agriculture. Here it seems probable that the required participation of a range of different castes in the conduct of vital calendrical and marriage ceremonies served to encourage the belief that a variety of different castes was necessary to the proper working of the village organization. This, then, is yet another example of the manner in which religious ceremonies can contribute to social harmony and integration.

Calendrical and marriage ceremonies in South India were frequently interrupted by conflict, especially when representatives of one caste or another

Carved South Indian door frame with "god photos," garland, and mango leaves. "God photos" are the basis of daily family rituals carried out before each meal. Photo on right shows Hanumantha carrying mountain to drop on enemy. Near Gopalpur, South India. (Photo by Alan Beals.)

refused to attend or to do their part. It was no accident that distinguished visitors were invariably asked to attend such ceremonies or that they played an active part in settling disputes that arose while they were taking place. The common pattern was that ceremonies were halted following the outbreak of a dispute or a refusal to participate. Village elders and distinguished guests then held hearings to determine the cause of the conflict and attempt to arrive at a suitable settlement. If they failed to do so, they risked the vengeance of angry gods, and, equally perturbing, they missed the joyous feasting that should accompany the completion of the ceremonial.

Marriage ceremonies involved considerable expense, and the proposed marriage required the approval of a wide range of people as signified by their participation in the various stages of the ceremonial. A father who had been unscrupulous in his dealings with other people in the village might have great difficulty in arranging the marriage of his son or daughter. The ceremony itself, then, can be interpreted as a major device for social control. Further, because marriage ceremonies were expensive, such ceremonies could be held only when harvests were good and only when families could accumulate the required resources. The ceremony then had important ecological effects because it served to control the frequency of marriage and, hence, the growth of population. Because marriage was considered essential to the happy life, young men who lacked the resources required for the conduct of the ceremony were forced to leave the village, perhaps seeking wealth in the stinking slums of Bombay. Some found jobs and returned to be married. Others disappeared or returned to spread tuberculosis among their already impoverished relatives.

In South Indian villages elaborate rituals and ceremonials designed to appease and appeal to the gods seemed to have a variety of impacts upon the organization of the village, the regulation of conflict, the stimulation of trade, the feeding of the poor, and the control of both animal and human populations. Although many of these effects are difficult to demonstrate in any detail — we don't really know what would happen if the ceremonies were not held — it seems reasonable to conclude that religious ceremonials play a vital role in regulating the relationships among human beings as well as the relationships between human beings and the environment.

12. Summary

Religion has to do with those areas of life where supernatural forces are believed to operate and where the appropriate attitudes are those of faith and reverence. Because religious ideas and practices are pervasive, it is not always easy to separate them from other aspects of culture. Even in terms of the definition given above, supernatural forces are not always regarded with awe or reverence, nor are attitudes of faith and reverence restricted solely to supernatural things. Within the sphere of religion a distinction can be made between world view, or fundamental and important ideas about the nature of things, and religious ritual. Although the connection is not inevitable, religious ideas and practices seem to arise in connection with natural a[nd social?] phenomena that are important but difficult to predict or control. The [?] relationship between religion and the inexplicable suggests that reli[gion?] remain characteristic of human cultures so long as there continu[e?] puzzling and inexplicable events in the universe.

A world view is that part of a cultural tradition that contains the an[swers to?] fundamental questions about what is worth doing and why. In broad[er terms a?] world view is a set of inferences that people make about the world [around?] them. In general, world view acquires its religious character from the [all-too-?] human tendency to overgeneralize and to extend inferences that are [logical?] and reasonable in one context into another context where their appli[cation?] cannot be so easily demonstrated. Thus Crow Indian supernaturals [are be-?] lieved to be subject to the same appeals for pity that are likely to mov[e ordi-?] nary human beings. Although in theory the scientific method offers a m[eans of?] examining the objective value of many of the inferences contained in any world view, there is little likelihood that it can justify all of them. Thus all world views including our own continue to be dominated by essentially religious attitudes.

The concepts of impersonal power and animism are characteristic of many world views. The concept of power, as applied to individual growth or to electricity or magnetism, it not by itself a religious concept. It becomes a religious concept when it is applied broadly, as in the example of *mana*, to a wide range of situations, objects, and individuals for which its applicability is doubtful. Similarly the principle of animism is a belief in the existence of beings, such as human beings, that act with feeling and purpose. When these beings become nonhuman, invisible, unpredictable, or all-powerful, the ordinary idea of beings doing things becomes a supernatural idea. For most cultures supernatural beings appear to represent, in their relationships and behavior, generalizations based upon experiences with human beings. Thus Apache spirits, like the Apaches, were often simply proprietors of particular aspects of the landscape. The more complicated social relationships of the Baganda and the Aztecs are reflected in a much more complicated hierarchy of supernatural figures. The belief that events are caused by supernatural beings calls for strategies of action characteristic of interpersonal relationship, whereas the belief that events are caused by impersonal power calls for the application of more impersonal sorts of strategies. Very often ideas of impersonal power and supernatural beings are blended. Thus automatic punishment caused by supernatural beings acting impersonally may also be dealt with by essentially impersonal strategies.

In different cultures, concepts of impersonal power and animism are found in association with a wide variety of other concepts such as the principle of limited good, the idea of natural order, and the fundamental rules of logic or ideas of causation. In essence a world view tends to involve the creation of general and sweeping explanations of the nature of things out of the familiar principles and concepts that work so well in the conduct of practical affairs.

Almost all peoples possess full-time or part-time religious practitioners who are responsible for the technology considered necessary in dealing with supernatural forces. Even where specialization of labor is virtually absent, most peoples possess shamans or spirit mediums who are capable of communicating with the spirit world and sometimes of taking action within it. Equally common are individuals, like the Apache curer, who have acquired or have been given special powers. In more specialized societies spirit mediums and curers are likely to be more specialized, and their efforts are often supplemented by priests and other authorities who derive their powers, not from direct contact with the supernatural, but from participation in a religious cult within which specialized religious knowledge is handed down.

Religious rituals represent the technology that is used in dealing with the supernatural world. Some rituals are individual and private; others are characteristic of such groups as family, village, or nation. Rituals that have a compelling effect upon the supernatural are usually classified as magical, although very often magic and persuasion are combined. The dividing line between religious and magical rituals and secular rituals is often very thin, and may turn upon such small things as the actual effectiveness of a particular poison or a brand of deodorant. Religious rituals are often classified in terms of the kind of event involved in their scheduling. Thus a distinction can be made among calendrical rituals, rites of passage, and rituals of succession.

To the skeptical outsider, whether scientist or true believer, the conduct of religious rituals which seem, almost by definition, to be incapable of influencing events often seems pointless or maladaptive. An opposed view is that religious rituals play an important role in mobilizing sentiments crucial for the maintenance of social solidarity and that they may have important economic and ecological effects as well. This latter view, of the functional value of religious ritual, is illustrated by reference to several South Indian rituals.

Collateral Reading

De Waal Malefijt, Annemarie. *Religion and Culture: An Introduction to Anthropology of Religion*. New York: Macmillan Publishing Co., Inc., 1970. A textbook.

Durkheim, Émile. *The Elementary Forms of the Religious Life*, trans. J. W. Swain. New York: Macmillan Publishing Co., Inc., 1915. The first systematic attempt to relate religion to society.

Evans-Pritchard, E. E. *Theories of Primitive Religion*. New York: Oxford University Press, 1965 (paper). Good expression of functionalist influenced views.

Frazer, Sir James G. *The Golden Bough*, One-volume-abridged edition. New York: Macmillan Publishing Co., Inc., 1928, Chapters III, IV. One of the great classic works; primarily of historical interest.

Geertz, Clifford. *The Religion of Java*. New York: The Free Press, 1964. One of the outstanding studies of the religion of a major emerging nation.

Kluckhohn, Clyde. *Navajo Witchcraft*. Boston: Beacon Press, 1962. Methodologically and theoretically a landmark study of witchcraft.

Lessa, William A., and Evon Z. Vogt, Jr. *Reader in Comparative Religion: An Anthropological Approach*, 3d ed. Evanston, Ill.: Row, Peterson & Company, 1972. Good selection from published materials.

Lowie, Robert. *Primitive Religion*. New York: Liveright Publishing Corp., 1948. Old but still useful survey.

Malinowski, Bronislaw. "Magic, Science, and Religion," *Science, Religion, and Reality*, ed. J. Needham. New York: Macmillan Publishing Co., Inc., 1925. Concise statement of views of a famous functionalist.

Middleton, John (ed.). *Gods and Rituals*. Garden City, N.Y.: The Natural History Press, 1967a. Collected articles.

Middleton, John (ed.). *Magic, Witchcraft and Curing*. Garden City, N.Y.: The Natural History Press, 1967b. Collected articles.

Middleton, John (ed.). *Myth and Cosmos*. Garden City, N.Y.: The Natural History Press, 1967c. Collected articles.

Norbeck, Edward. *Religion in Primitive Society*. New York: Harper & Row, Inc., 1961. Essentially an advanced textbook.

Radin, Paul. *Primitive Religion, Its Nature and Origin*. New York: The Viking Press, Inc., 1937. Stimulating presentation by an original mind.

Rappaport, Roy A. *Pigs for the Ancestors: Ritual in the Ecology of a New Guinea People*. New Haven: Yale University Press, 1968. Sweeping hypotheses about the role of religion in ecosystem regulation.

Wallace, Anthony F. C. *Religion: An Anthropological View*. New York: Random House, Inc., 1966. Some new approaches.

Ethnographic References

Azande: Evans-Pritchard, 1937, 1971; Gero, 1968.

Aztec: Caso, 1937; Coon, 1948, Chap. 15; Murdock, 1935, Chap. XIII; Soustelle, 1968; Thompson, 1933; Vaillant, 1941.

Baganda: Murdock, 1935, Chap. XVII; Roscoe, 1911.

Chiricahua Apache: Opler, 1941.

Crow: Lowie, 1935.

Eskimo: Birket-Smith, 1936; Murdock, 1935, Chap. VIII; Rasmussen, 1908, 1931.

India: Beals, 1962.

Marquesan: Handy, 1923; Linton, 1939; Suggs, 1966.

Zuñi: Cushing, 1921; Eggan, 1950, Chap. IV; Stevenson, 1904.

16/Language

1. The Uniqueness of Language

Perhaps the most important defining characteristic of human beings is the ability to develop and use language and other similar symbolic codes. Other animal species communicate in a variety of ways. Some species, like the chimpanzee, may have a limited capacity to learn symbolic codes resembling language, but chimpanzees have not as yet been observed to create languages of their own. The essential feature of all known human languages is the use of a small number of basic elements arranged in various ways to form complex messages. Language shares this property with the genetic code in which complex messages are formed by the combination and recombination of four basic chemicals.

The principle of combining basic elements can be illustrated by rearranging the letters in *dog*. The same three letters can be used to form *dog*, *do*, *go*, *god*, and *good*. Although it is easy to think of the basic sounds of the English language as equivalent to such letters of the alphabet as "d," "o," and "g," there is an important difference between basic sounds (phonemes) and alphabetical letters (graphemes). This is evident in the fact that the letter "o" in the above examples represents five different basic sounds.

509

A language involves the use of a small number of phonemes to form complex messages. The basic sounds of a language cannot be arranged haphazardly and still make sense: there has to be a set of behavioral standards, a phonology, that defines the kinds of sound combinations that will be meaningful. In English, standards governing the arrangement of graphemes forbid such things as *doog, gdo,* or *odg.* Similar combinations of phonemes are also forbidden.

Language can be considered to consist of arrangements of phonemes in accordance with phonological and grammatical rules. Even that is not enough. It is necessary that some sort of meaning be conveyed by the different arrangements of phonemes. In other words, what does "dog" mean and why? The answer is that the connection between "dog" and the various meanings of "dog" is entirely arbitrary. The word "dog" does not look like a dog; it does not sound like a "dog"; it has absolutely no physical connection with any kind of naturally existing dog. It is as if someone had once said, "Let the sound "dog" stand for that animal that barks, for an unpopular person, for a foot, and so on. "Dog" means dog for the same reason that "dit, dit, dit" stands for "s" in Morse code or that "AC" stands for the hypotenuse of a right triangle. Somehow it was *arbitrarily* decided that it should be so. The difference between language and Morse code or algebra is that Morse code and algebra are artificially constructed codes, while languages are natural codes in which meanings tend to be assigned by relatively unconscious processes.

Language consists, then, of arbitrary symbols with meanings that must be learned. For human beings, the tendency to attach symbolic meanings not only to words but to a variety of other things as well is an important aspect of the development of culture. For human beings, unlike other animals, things are not what they seem. A snow-capped mountain is not just a mountain. It may symbolize the home of the gods, freedom, achievement — whatever the members of a particular cultural system have come to feel that it should symbolize. Anthropologists have only recently begun to turn their attention to the role of symbolism in human life, but it is evident that nonlinguistic symbols such as body movements, artifacts, and natural objects form an important aspect of communication among human beings. Although the use of arbitrary symbols is often considered a property of language different from the basic property of combining and recombining phonemes, there is no way that words and utterances formed by combining a few basic elements could acquire anything but an arbitrary meaning.

Once sentences can be formed by combining words having arbitrary meanings, it follows that new or unusual combinations of words will arise. The same idea that underlies the use of phonemes can give us the power (*productivity*) to create green dogs, four-legged men, flying horses, and the spirits of our ancestors. Through similar mechanisms all human languages also give the power (*displacement*) to talk about things that are elsewhere (in the other room) or elsewhen (in the next week). Another important feature of language is its capacity for abstraction. Symbols can stand for symbols. Thus "animal" stands for or symbolizes all of the symbols that stand for particular kinds of animals.

Because the existence of language depends upon the arbitrary assignment of meanings to sets of sounds in accordance with a set of behavioral standards (grammatical rules), it follows that language, like other aspects of culture, must be identified with particular groups and societies. Just as different societies may share virtually identical cultures, so different societies may share virtually identical languages. In such cases distinctions between languages are generally based upon the criterion of *mutual intelligibility*. If people can understand each other, they speak the same language; if they can't, they don't. Except in cases of total incomprehension, the criterion of mutual intelligibility involves degrees of understanding that are difficult to measure. There is some merit, then, in the proposal that both languages and cultures be considered the property of specific decision-making groups with known memberships. It is such groups, and only such groups, that can establish and maintain behavioral standards concerning the appropriateness of either linguistic or cultural behavior.

In the United States, although Spanish sometimes acquires at least a semiofficial status in some of the southwestern states, English is the official language, and other languages are officially discouraged. The English spoken in the United States is not, however, a single uniform language. It is, rather, a collection of very similar languages having a considerable degree of mutual intelligibility. Official English has been called *standard* English and is considered to consist of at least two dialects: one is literary or *formal* English, which is used in formal discourse or in writing, and the other is *colloquial* standard English used in informal speech. Southern, New England, or Middlewestern dialects of English are usually described as *provincial* standards. Most citizens of the United States also speak various local dialects or home dialects which are usually referred to as *nonstandard*. Such nonstandard dialects are sometimes associated with isolated communities such as those in Appalachia or New England, but they may also be associated with ethnic groups or age groups. Dialects may also be associated with work groups and professions, physics and sociology having mutually unintelligible jargons.

Just as each individual and each primary group is likely to have a unique interpretation of behavioral standards, so it follows that each individual has an idiolect and each group a dialect which may differ microscopically or dramatically from that used by other individuals or groups. Although languages, like animals, can be assigned to families, genera (languages), or species (dialects), there is nothing to prevent the exchange of materials even between quite unrelated languages. Just as in animal classifications where the distinctions between two different species in the same genus can range between slight and large, so the distinctions between two dialects or idiolects of the same language can range between trivial and just short of unintelligibility.

In describing a language, just as in describing a culture, the first step is to identify a community whose members are more or less uniform in speech. The next step is to collect examples of linguistic behavior (utterances) from which rules governing such things as pronunciation, meaning, and grammar can be derived. Here it is important to remember that linguists, like other cultural anthropologists, do not simply wish to learn the language and culture of the people they study. They wish to understand the rules and principles that are involved in its operation. Just as an anthropologist's construct of a culture is a theory about the rules that influence behavior, so a linguist's grammar or construct of a language is a theory concerning the rules and principles used in the generation of speech or linguistic behavior.

To illustrate the difference between rules of language and speech, consider the utterances *Sing!, March!, Go!,* and *Come!* Each of these is made up of a single word and each has the same intonation pattern or pitch. The same words, spoken with a slight rise in tone, yield quite different utterances: *Sing?, March?, Go?,* and *Come?* From this comparison (and many others like it) we may note two characteristic patterns of the English language: (1) the commands (for example, *Sing!, March!, Go!,* and *Come!*) have a high-level intonation which contrasts markedly with (2) the rising intonation of interrogatives like *Sing?, March?, Go?,* and *Come?* These patterns — the command (or imperative) and interrogative intonations — it should be emphasized, are not in themselves utterances, but are rather modes of speaking peculiar to certain classes of utterance.

If we now compare utterances like *Sing!* with others illustrated by *Bill!* or *John!,* we may note another pattern characteristic of commands in English. For *Bill!* and *John!,* though they are spoken with the same intonation as *Sing!,* are not commands but exclamations, utterances occurring under a strong stimulus, such as surprise at seeing the individuals so named. They differ from commands in that they include words such as *Bill* and *John,* which are nouns rather than verbs. Thus we derive another pattern of English: that a command not only has a characteristic high-level intonation but is made up of a verb, with or without modifiers. In contrast, nouns spoken with a high-level intonation are classed, not as commands, but as a kind of exclamation. (There are also other varieties.) A full description of a language includes many statements such as these, which describe as accurately as possible the particular ways of speaking that characterize the speech of a given community. Needless to say, the examples given are very simple ones; most of the patterns descriptive of a language are far more complicated.

2. "Primitive" Languages

In discussing the several aspects of culture in preceding chapters, we have had frequent occasion to contrast the cultures of small hunting and collecting or agricultural peoples with those of large urbanized societies, such as our own. We have noted, in such contrasts, that these peoples frequently possess cruder or less-developed technologies, or that their systems of social organization or religious belief are relatively simple and uncomplicated. When we come to the study of language, however, this does not appear to be true, for the languages of other peoples, even those with the crudest technologies, are apparently not less well developed or more primitive than the languages of so-called civilized folk.

This statement may come as a surprise to most readers, for popular opinion tends toward a contrary view. We are sometimes told that "primitive" peoples have "primitive" languages; that "primitive" languages have only a few hundred words as compared to the many thousands of, let us say, English; that "primitives" are not infrequently obliged, because of the poverty of their languages, to eke out their utterances with manual and facial gestures; or that "primitives" have neither the vocabulary nor the grammar to express the finer and subtler nuances of meaning.

None of these statements is true. All languages, whether spoken by Navajos, Australian aborigines, or cultivated Englishmen or Frenchmen, have highly perfected systems of significant sounds and equally well-developed grammars. As to vocabulary, every language known to us possesses all the vocabulary that is required by the culture of the people who speak it. What is more significant, all languages have equal potentialities. If some languages, such as English, French, or German, have greater resources of expression by reason of a richer and more fully developed cultural background, any other language placed in a similarly developed culture will develop equal vocabulary resources.

To illustrate these points, let us consider briefly the Navajo language, today spoken by over 100,000 Indians living in Arizona and New Mexico. The Navajo system of distinctive sounds includes thirty-six consonants and eight vowels, a total of forty-four. English has twenty-five consonants and nine vowels, ten fewer than are found in Navajo.[1] Languages vary greatly in the number of distinctive sounds: some have as few as fifteen, others sixty or more. But these numerical variations are not indicative of superiority or inferiority in the structures of languages. There are many differences between the English and the Navajo sound systems, but these, when examined, are nonsignificant for the relative efficiency of the two languages. All we can demonstrate by comparing the two systems is that they differ.

Navajo grammar, like its system of sounds, is very different from that of English. Thus, the Navajo noun has the same form in both the singular and the plural — there are no plural noun endings (such as the *-s* of *book-s* or the *-en* of *ox-en*) in Navajo. Similarly, the third-person pronoun of Navajo is singular or plural and nondistinctive in gender: it can be translated *he, she, it*, or *they*, depending on context. Finally, we find no adjectives in Navajo. The function performed by the English adjective is in Navajo performed by a verb.

We can also show, however, that Navajo possesses grammatical distinctions lacking in English. Navajo has two third-person pronouns; one is used to refer to persons with whom the speaker has rigidly formal relations, the other to refer to those with whom his relations are informal and familiar. Navajo also distinguishes between two kinds of possession, inalienable, when speaking of something such as a body part that is inseparable from its owner, and alienable, when speaking of a possession — for example, a horse — of which he can divest himself. In the Navajo verb it is possible to distinguish gram-

---

[1] Some simplifications of the two systems are made here, to avoid technicalities irrelevant to the discussion.

matically between actions that are endlessly repetitive (*he sings again and again. . .*), actions that are customary or habitual (*he generally sings*), and actions that have been completed (*he has finished singing*). As our translations show, these notions can also be conveyed in English, but they are conveyed, not by a grammatical device (similar to the English grammatical distinction between present and past tense), but by the employment of adverbs such as *again and again, generally,* and the auxiliary *has* plus *finished.* To conclude: in grammar, as in sound features, Navajo and English are widely divergent. Despite this divergence, there is no evidence that either the Navajo speaker or the English speaker has the slightest difficulty in expressing himself, or that either language provides in its grammar for greater wealth of expression than the other. Speakers of all languages have at their command rich symbolic systems (of distinctive sounds and grammatical devices) all of which are very much at the same level as far as efficiency of communication is concerned.

A comparison of the vocabularies of languages such as English and Navajo at first sight reveals differences that appear to be significant. There is no questioning the fact that the Navajo vocabulary is smaller and has fewer resources of expression than that of English. It is easy to exaggerate this difference and to make it appear that a vocabulary like that of Navajo is so poor as to forbid any but the simplest statements. The matter is not so simple: Navajo has a wealth of vocabulary in areas (for example, the art of making ritual sand paintings) that are peculiar to their culture; here English often appears to be deficient. Conversely, English has, in areas of culture unknown to the Navajo (for example, machine technology) a vocabulary not found in Navajo. The fact is that in Navajo, English, or any other language, the size and resources of a vocabulary are not determined by the structure of the language but rather by the cultural matrix in which the language exists. A language has as large and as comprehensive a vocabulary as is required by the culture of which it is a part. When a culture increases in complexity, the language will almost at once respond by the development of richer vocabulary resources. This point is demonstrated in the known history of the Navajo and other American Indian tribes, in which, by reason of several centuries of contact with peoples of European origins, the cultures and the vocabularies of the Indians have increased considerably in scope and volume.

3. The Diversity of Language

No less striking than the universality of language is its extraordinary diversity. There are probably thousands of distinct languages spoken in the world of today, not to mention numerous ancient idioms of which we have only scanty written records, and probably many others that have been lost without a trace. Linguists customarily divide the languages of the world into stocks or families. (We shall later, in §7, see how this is done.) In this section, our purpose is simply to provide a brief summary of the languages of the world and their classification, so far as it is now known.

Most important to us is the far-flung Indo-European family of languages, which includes most of those best known to us. It is usually divided into nine subgroups: Germanic (including, among others, German, English, the Scandinavian languages, and Dutch), Celtic (mainly Gaelic and Welsh), Baltic (Lithuanian, Lettish, and others), Slavic (principally Russian, Polish, Czech, Bulgarian, and Serbo-Croatian), Romance (the languages derived from Latin, such as French, Spanish, Italian, Roumanian, and Portuguese), Greek, Indo-Iranian (including Persian, Kurdish, and many modern languages of northern India), Armenian, and Albanian. These languages, some of which, like English, have spread to many areas of the world, are now spoken by about one-third of the present world population. Though many are obscure and little-known tongues, others (for example, English, French, German, Spanish, and Russian) are exceedingly important for an understanding of the complex cultures of the Western world.

Although most of the languages of Europe belong to the Indo-European family, there are a number of tongues that do not. Basque is one of these, spoken by fewer than 1 million people in the Pyrenees and unrelated to any other known tongue. Traces, in scattered inscriptions, are also found of older non-Indo-European languages, once spoken in the European area but now extinct.

The other non-Indo-European languages of Europe (Finnish, Lappish, Hungarian, and Estonian) belong to the large Finno-Ugric family. This family includes also Karelian, Olonetsian, Ludian, Vepsian, and others (spoken in the portions of Russia adjacent to Finland) and several (among them Mari, Permian, Mordvin, and Ob-Ugrian) that are scattered farther east in northern Russia. Hungarian, with 13 million speakers; Finnish, with 5 million speakers; and Estonian and Mordvin, with 1 million speakers each, are the largest of the Finno-Ugric group.[2] The remaining languages have fewer than a half million speakers each, and some of them are near extinction. Samoyedic, a language spoken by about 18,000 people living along the Yenisei River in Siberia, is remotely related to Finno-Ugric.

The Turkic or Altaic group is sometimes linked with Finno-Ugric and Samoyedic into a larger Ural-Altaic family. Altaic includes, among others, Turkish, with 38 million speakers, Azerbaijan (in Iran and the U.S.S.R.), with 8 million, and Uzbek (U.S.S.R.), with 9 million. Yakut, the language of a small, isolated community in northeastern Siberia, also belongs to the Altaic group.

A small group of languages, the Mongol, are spoken by about 3 million people who live in Mongolia and in scattered communities in various parts of Asia and even European Russia. Another small group is made up of Tungusic, spoken by some 70,000 people of Siberia, and Manchu, spoken north of the Mongols, which today has well under a million speakers. Mongol was the language of Genghis Khan and his followers, and its oldest record is an inscrip-

---

[2] The population figures are only estimates as of 1975 and probably vary a good deal in accuracy. They do serve, however, to give some notion of the relative sizes of the major language populations of the world.

tion dating to the thirteenth century. Manchu printed records go back to the seventeenth century and the language is found in manuscripts of an even earlier date.

Still farther north and east are a cluster of languages, usually called the Hyperborean group, though this is a geographical rather than a linguistic classification. The communities speaking these languages (for example, the Chukchi, Koryak, and Kamchadal) are small and nonliterate, and too little is known of their languages to state their relationships with accuracy.

In eastern and southern Asia we find the large Sino-Tibetan family, of which Chinese (with its several distinctive dialects) is the most important subgroup. In addition to Chinese, the family includes Tibetan, Thai (of Siam), Burmese, and a number of lesser-known tongues. The Sino-Tibetan family, like the Indo-European, has a large number of speakers, estimated to include nearly one-fourth of the world's population. Most of the Sino-Tibetan languages are written, and some records in Chinese go back as far as 2000 B.C.

On the southern fringes of Asia we find, beginning in the west, the languages of the Caucasus Mountains, a still little-known group of considerable diversity. The best-known of these is Georgian in the southern Caucasus, with 3 million speakers and written records dating back to the tenth century. The Dravidian languages (including, among others, Tamil, Malayalam, Kanarese, and Telugu) are spoken in central and southern India by more than 156 million people. Munda is a group of languages spoken on the southern slopes of the Himalayas and in central India by perhaps 3 million or more people. Mon-Khmer includes Vietnamese, with about 36 million speakers, and a number of smaller idioms scattered over southeastern Asia, the Nicobar Islands and portions of the Malay Peninsula.

Japanese, with about 109 million speakers, is apparently unrelated to any other group. The same is true of Korean, spoken by 51 million people. In northern Sakhalin and the adjacent coast around the mouth of the Amur River is Giliak, a far smaller but also isolated tongue. Ainu is another such language, spoken by a small nonliterate group who today live in the northern portions of the Japanese Archipelago.

Except for the languages of the Australian aborigines and a small cluster of Papuan languages spoken in New Guinea, all the languages of Oceania belong to a single stock, Malayo-Polynesian. This language group includes Malay-Indonesian (93 million speakers), Javanese (45 million speakers), Tagalog (in the Philippines; 20 million speakers), and numerous others in Madagascar, Indonesia, Melanesia, and Micronesia. Included in the Malay-Indonesian category are eleven languages (mainly in Indonesia and the Philippines) with 1 million or more speakers. Tagalog, it should be noted, is now the national language of the Philippines. Indonesians, as a result of their establishment of a new nation, have developed a national language, called Indonesian, based largely on Malay.

Africa presents a complex variety of languages: it is estimated that approximately 1,000 mutually unintelligible tongues are today spoken by about 200 million Africans. In addition to the languages native to Africa, there exist also a number of imported European tongues, among them English, French, Portuguese, and Afrikaans, the last-named being a variety of Dutch. The native African languages are divided by Greenberg[3] into four major stocks: Africo-Asiatic, Nilo-Saharan, Khoisan, and Niger-Kordofanian.

The Afro-Asiatic group, as the name implies, includes not only African languages but related tongues spoken in the adjacent regions of Asia. One of the most important subgroups is Semitic: the modern Hebrew of Israel (3 million speakers), Arabic in North Africa and Asia (121 million speakers), the several languages of Ethiopia (among them Amharic, with 9 million speakers), and Cushitic, which includes, among others, Galla, with 7 million speakers and Somali, with about 4 million people. There are also a number of Semitic languages known to us only from written records: among these are ancient Hebrew, Aramaic, Phoenician, and Akkadian (Babylonian and Assyrian). The remaining branches of the Afro-Asiatic group are Berber (Morocco, Algeria), with about 6 million speakers, and Chadic, a small group of languages in northern Nigeria that includes Hausa, today spoken by more than 18 million people. Ancient Egyptian, known only from records dating from 4000 B.C., is also put into the Afro-Asiatic family.

The Nilo-Saharan languages are found in several detached areas in or just south of the Sahara. Most of these languages are spoken by small populations; the largest is Kanuri, which is spoken by well over 2 million people and is a major language of northern Nigeria.

The Khoisan languages, which together have fewer than 100,000 speakers, are the smallest of the four language families. Most of the Khoisan speakers now live in southwestern Africa; these are the Hottentot and the Bushmen. The Khoisan group also includes two languages, Hatsa and Sandawe, of Tanganyika in East Africa, which was probably the original homeland of all Khoisan speakers.

The remaining languages of Africa are placed by Greenberg in the large and widespread Niger-Kordofanian group. This family of languages extends from Dakar in West Africa eastward to the coast of Kenya and south to the tip of Africa. It includes an enormous number of languages, among them the well-known Bantu group. About forty of the Niger-Kordofanian languages are spoken by populations of more than a half million speakers each.

North and South America, in the period just before European contact, had a population conservatively estimated at about 15.5 million. This population spoke about 2,000 mutually unintelligible languages. One-third of these were spoken north of Mexico; the remaining two-thirds were spoken in Mexico, Central America, the islands of the Caribbean, and South America.

Today, except perhaps in Latin America, the number of languages is greatly reduced, and those that remain have few speakers as compared with those speaking the languages of the Old World. Quechua and Aymara, spoken in adjacent areas of Peru and Bolivia, Guarani in Paraguay and Brazil, and

---

[3] Joseph H. Greenberg, "The Languages of Africa," *International Journal of American Linguistics,* **29,** No. 1 (1963), Part II (Publication 25 of the Indiana University Research Center in Anthropology, Folklore, and Linguistics). We are also indebted to Dr. William E. Welmers, who gave us access to a preliminary draft of Chapters 1 and 2 of a proposed textbook on African language structures.

Nahuatl (or Aztec) in Mexico and Guatemala are the only ones with a million or more speakers. Two language groups—the Otomian of central Mexico and the Mayan of Yucatan and Guatemala—have between 300,000 and 500,000 speakers each. Mayan, Otomian, and Nahuatl were languages of Indian empires before 1500 A.D., and both the Mayans and the Aztecs had systems of writing that have now disappeared.

Only a few Indian languages of America north of Mexico are still flourishing: among them are Navajo, with over 100,000 speakers; Ojibwa (northern United States and southern Canada), with 30,000 speakers; Cherokee (Oklahoma and North Carolina), with 50,000 speakers; and Dakota-Assiniboine, with 42,000 speakers. The remaining languages of this area are slowly dying out. Nearly half of the aboriginal tongues have become extinct, and half of the surviving languages have fewer than 1,000 speakers.

Because relatively little work has been done on American Indian languages, it is difficult to determine their classification. Earlier scholars estimated about 40 language families for North and Central America and between 80 and 100 for South America and the Caribbean area. There is no doubt that these figures are too high; more recent investigation has drastically reduced this number, especially in North and Central America. We cannot review these studies here; it is enough perhaps to mention some of the more widespread and better-established families.[4]

American Indian languages, it should be noted, are not demonstrably related to any in Europe or Asia. Several such relationships have been proposed, but there is not as yet sufficient evidence for any of them.

Some American Indian language families are spread over considerable territories: Eskimo-Aleut, on the coasts of the Arctic from Alaska to Greenland; Athapaskan, in northwestern Canada, Alaska, and in smaller enclaves on the Pacific coast and in New Mexico, Arizona, and Texas; Algonkin, over much of northeastern and midwestern United States, Canada south and east of the Athapaskans, and in two or three places in the northern plains; Siouan, the languages of many of the Plains Indian tribes; Uto-Aztecan, from Utah south through much of Mexico; Carib and Arawak, which extend from the West Indies through much of eastern South America; Tupi-Guarani, on the coast of Brazil; Araucanian in Chile; and the Kechuan family, spread by Inca conquests from Colombia to southern Peru.

Other language stocks are much smaller, and we often find regions of remarkable linguistic diversity. In California, according to Kroeber, an aboriginal population of about 150,000 spoke 135 languages that are conservatively grouped into twenty-one families. Edward Sapir noted for this region that it illustrates "greater and more numerous linguistic extremes that can be

---

[4] A summary of American Indian language families is given in the *Encyclopaedia Britannica* (1961) under the headings "Central and North American Languages" and "South American Languages." See also Harry Hoijer et al., *Linguistic Structures of Native America* (New York: Viking Fund Publications in Anthropology, 1946), Vol. 6, especially the introduction. This portion of the book is also available in the Bobbs-Merrill Reprint Series in the Social Sciences, number A-118.

illustrated in all the length and breadth of Europe."[5] Similar areas of great linguistic complexity are found along the northern Pacific coast from Oregon to Alaska, on the Gulf coast from Texas to Florida, in southern Mexico, and in several places in the tropical lowlands of South America.

As our brief review of world languages demonstrates, there are few if any areas of culture that are so diverse as language. The range in modes of speaking is almost beyond description and yields one of our most valuable storehouses of data for the comparative study of human behavior.

4. The Structure of Language: Phonology

All languages have two aspects: a phonological aspect, or phonology, and a grammatical aspect, or grammar. Phonology is the study of the basic units, or phonemes, of the language and of the rules governing sequences of phonemes. The study of grammar involves the identification of morphemes, recurring sequences of phonemes that carry a meaning, and the rules governing the sequences in which they occur. In all languages phonemes are finite in number generally ranging between thirty and forty-five. Morphemes, the meaningful units composed of phonemes, are much more numerous, and there seems to be no necessary limit to the number a given language might contain.

Although phonemes are somewhat like letters of the alphabet and it may be that the letters of the alphabet were originally intended to represent the basic speech sounds of the English language, it is vital to remember that graphemes (alphabet letters) sometimes are used to describe several different phonemes and that two different graphemes may sometimes describe the same phoneme. It is necessary to discover the phonemes of a language by listening to the actual sounds that people make rather than by examining any system of writing they might have. The linguist begins work by attempting to transcribe utterances by means of a phonetic description. A phonetic description is an attempt to indicate all of the sound qualities of a given utterance that might conceivably turn out to be important in defining it. Traditionally phonetic description has been based upon the analysis of the means by which sounds are produced.[6] Thus a phonetic transcription of an utterance involves consideration of such things as the position of the speaker's lips, tongue, and glottis, the vibration or lack of vibration of his vocal cords, the extent of nasalization, loudness or emphasis, and so on. The question is, which of these many features that a sound may naturally have are considered significant by speakers of the language?

---

[5] Edward Sapir and M. Swadesh, "American Indian Grammatical Categories," *Word,* 2:103–112 (1946), p. 103.

[6] There are a number of systems of phonetic transcription, but the one most often used is the International Phonetic Alphabet (I.P.A.). For a brief description of the I.P.A. and the principles of phonetic analysis, see H. A. Gleason, Jr., *An Introduction to Descriptive Linguistics,* rev. ed. (New York: Holt, Rinehart and Winston, 1961), Chapter 15.

Consider some of the occurrences of the phoneme /k/[7] in one English dialect.[8] It occurs, among other places: (1) at the beginning of a syllable or word (as in *kind*), (2) preceded in a syllable by *s* (as in *sky*), (3) at the end of a syllable and followed by another consonant (as in *tract;* the phoneme /k/ is often represented by the grapheme *c*), and (4) in the middle of a word and preceded by a strongly stressed syllable (as in *picket;* where it is represented by the graphemes *ck*).[9] The sounds actually found in these four classes of utterance include the phone [kʰ] in which the [k] sound is followed by a puff of air or aspiration and the phone [k⁼] in which the aspiration is not present. Because two distinct sounds are represented, should we consider that /k/ is really two phonemes? In this case, no; because the distribution of [kʰ] and [k⁼] is complementary. [kʰ] never occurs under conditions (2), (3), or (4) and [k⁼] never occurs under condition (1). Further study of the English language would reveal rules governing the use of aspiration for other phonemes as well, and it would be seen that in English, aspiration alone is not sufficient to distinguish between one phoneme and another.

In many of the languages spoken in India, the situation is quite different because both [kʰ] and [k⁼] can be used at the beginning of words as well as under other conditions, and the result is a substantial difference in meaning. In other words, the distribution of the two phones is contrastive rather than complementary. The same thing can be said about /k/ and /g/ in English. Phonetically, the difference between the two phonemes is slight; a /g/ is simply a /k/ pronounced with the vocal cords vibrating. Nevertheless the substitution of /g/ for /k/ can make a substantial difference in meaning as in *beck* and *beg, could* and *good,* or *candor* and *gander.*

Although in practice the identification of phonemes may be a partly intuitive process in which the linguist makes shrewd guesses about the relative importance of particular sounds, the linguist's hypotheses about which sounds are phonemes is usually subject to rigorous test by examining patterns of complementary and contrastive distribution. Examination of the distribution of phonemes also leads to the development of rules governing the arrangement of phonemes in sequence. For example, why do *sky, spy,* and *sty* exist in English, but not *sgy, sby,* or *sdy?* The answer is probably that in the environment provided by *s* and *y*, it is impossible for English speakers to distinguish between [k], [p], and [t] and the closely similar [g], [b], and [d]. Once the various phonemes and the rules governing their use have been identified, it becomes possible to move on to a consideration of morphemes and the rules governing their arrangement.

---

[7] A symbol put between slant lines always denotes a phoneme; one between brackets denotes a speech sound or phone.

[8] That is, the variety of English spoken in Chicago. Although the rules given here apply to many varieties of English, it should be remembered that phonemic systems may differ widely from one dialect to another as well as from one language to another.

[9] We have given only a partial statement of the variations of /k/ because we seek only to illustrate the method, not to provide a full description of /k/.

5. The Structure of Language: Grammar

Although there is a tendency to think of language in terms of letters that are combined into words, the situation is not quite that simple. Phonemes are combined to form *morphemes,* which may in some cases be considerably smaller than words. The morpheme is a meaningful unit recurring with essentially the same meaning in the utterances of a language; it is not itself divisible into two or more meaningful units. In effect the morpheme is the smallest meaningful unit that can be constructed by the combination of phonemes. Morphemes are identified in much the same way as phonemes.

To illustrate this process let us examine the utterance *a dog barks at the moon.* What elements in this phrase can occur in other phrases and retain the same meaning they have here? Each of the words in the above phrase occurs in one of the following: *a* rose is red, my *dog* is lost, he *barks,* we looked *at* it, *the* man is dead, the *moon* shines. Thus each of the words in the original phrase has its own distinct meaning and can be used with that meaning in other utterances.

We may now ask if any of the six words or segments of the phrase can be divided into additional meaningful units. Five of the words—*a, dog, at, the, moon*—cannot be divided into meaningful expressions. The sixth word, *barks,* contains the segment *bark,* which recurs in such phrases as *the dogs bark* and the segment *s,* which recurs in such forms as *he sinks, he talks, he walks,* and *he speaks.* Our phrase, then, contains six words but seven meaningful units or morphemes.

Morphemes, it is evident, are not necessarily words; one of the words in our phrase (that is, *bark-s*) contains two morphemes. Many words in English are equally or more complex, as evidenced by the following examples (hyphens separate morphemes): *work-er, sing-er, nice-ly, slow-ly, un-tie-s, un-like-ly, in-act-ive-ly.* These examples also make clear that some morphemes may occur independently (for example, *dog, cow, walk, run, at, in*), whereas others (for example, the *-s* of *dog-s,* the *-er* of *walk-er,* the *un-* of *un-tie*) appear only in combination with other morphemes. The former are called free morphemes, the latter bound morphemes.

All languages employ large numbers of morphemes (free and bound), and as we said in §2, the number found in a language is determined in large part by nonlinguistic factors. But just as we do not learn a language simply by memorizing its words, so we do not completely describe the grammar of a language by listing its morphemes. A grammar includes more: the finite number of arrangements whereby morphemes, which rarely occur alone, are combined into words, phrases, and sentences. In no language do we find that its morphemes occur in all possible arrangements. The number of possible arrangements is always limited by rules peculiar to the language under study. A knowledge of the possible arrangements of English, for example, tells us little or nothing of the possible arrangements of another language.

To illustrate what is meant by the general term *arrangement,* let us analyze a simple English sentence: *The waitress brought the soup.* Our first step is to divide the sentence into its largest segments — segments called immediate constituents. In this case we compare the given sentence with another that is very like it: *The waitress brought the soup?* The first sentence, it is clear, is declarative; the second is interrogative. Furthermore, the first differs from the second in intonation: roughly, the first sentence terminates with a falling intonation, whereas the second terminates with a rising intonation.[10] It is apparent, then, that the sentence under analysis has two immediate constituents: a feature of intonation that marks it as declarative plus the meaningful sequence of words *the waitress brought the soup*. The intonation feature is a morpheme; the sequence of words obviously requires further analysis.

By a similar process of comparison, we next show that the sequence *the waitress brought the soup* also has two immediate constituents: *the waitress* and *brought the soup*. The evidence for this division lies in the fact that we can substitute other forms for either of these divisions without altering the other. Thus we find phrases such as (*she, he, the girl,* or *the man*) *brought the soup,* or *the waitress* (*served the meal, dropped a spoon,* or *set the table*). It will further be noted that in phrases of this type, one immediate constituent (that is, *the waitress, she, he, the girl,* or *the man*) precedes the other (that is, *brought the soup, served the meal, dropped a spoon,* or *set the table*). The phrase *the waitress* and those that may be substituted for it, all function as grammatical subjects, and the phrase *brought the soup* and its substitutes as predicates.

Next, the phrases *the waitress* and *brought the soup* are each divided into immediate constituents: *the waitress* (by comparison with such phrases as *a waitress, this waitress, the man, the girl*) divides into *the* and *waitress,* and *brought the soup* (by comparison with *brought the bread* and *dropped the soup*) divides into *brought* and *the soup.* In each case one immediate constituent precedes the other; any other sequence (for example, *waitress the* or *soup the dropped*) is not in accord with rules of English grammar. Finally, it should now be clear, the phrase *the soup,* like the phrase *the waitress,* has two immediate constituents: *the* and *soup,* arranged in this order. In *the waitress* and *the soup,* the article *the* gives definiteness of reference to the following noun, and in *brought the soup,* the second immediate constituent is the grammatical object of the preceding verb.

Up to this point we have been concerned with the rules governing the construction of sentences and phrases; this aspect of grammar is called *syntax.* We are left with a series of words (morphological constructions) and the problem of dividing these, where necessary, into their constituent morphemes. *Morphology* is the term usually applied to this aspect of grammar.

With regard to the words we now must analyze, the task is a simple one. All the words but two (*waitress* and *brought*) contain but a single morpheme. *Waitress* is clearly related to *waiter;* it is a combination of *waitr-* (a variant form of *waiter*) and the bound morpheme *-ess* (as further illustrated in forms such as *princ-ess* from *prince* and *deacon-ess* from *deacon*). One of the immedi-

---

[10] The phoneme difference is here much simplified to avoid technicalities irrelevant to the present discussion.

ate constituents of *waitress* (that is, *waitr-* or *waiter*) may also be divided into two immediate constituents: *wait* (in the sense *to wait upon*) and the bound morpheme *-er* "one who. . . ." Note that the three morphemes *wait*, *-r* from *-er* and *-ess* are combined in two steps: *wait* plus *-er* gives us *waiter*, and *waiter* plus *-ess* yields *waitress*, in which the morpheme *waiter* assumes a special combinatory variant, written *waitr-*, the hyphen indicating that this variant does not occur independently. English has quite a few instances of such variants: *duch-* (from *duke*) in *duch-ess* and *duch-y; dep-* (from *deep*) in *dep-th; leng-* (from *long*) in *leng-th*, and many others.

Brought, it is clear, contains only two morphemes, *brough-* and *-t*, the preterit ending. Note, however, that *brough-* is a variant of *bring*, found only in the preterit (*he brought it*) and the participle (*he has brought it*). Many English verbs show this kind of variation: *sought* from *seek, thought* from *think, caught* from *catch*. The study of alternations like these in morphemes is called *morphophonemics;* that is, alternations in the phonemic shapes of morphemes that are a consequence of their combining with other morphemes.

Although the features of arrangement we have illustrated in the sentence *The waitress brought the soup* seem obvious to speakers of English, it does not follow that all languages exhibit the same arrangements. Take, for example, the rule governing in English the order of subject (for example, *the waitress*) and predicate (for example, *brought the soup*). In Navajo this rule does not exist; in a Navajo sentence of roughly the same type the subject comes first, the object second, and the verb last. Thus, the Navajo will say *hastiin šaš yiyiiłxé* (*the man kills the bear*) where *hastiin* (*man*) is the subject, *šaš* (*bear*) the object, and *yiyiiłxé* (*he kills it*) the verb. Here we find not two but three immediate constituents arranged in the sequence noted. Moreover the verb can function alone as a sentence: *yiyiiłxé* (*he kills it*) belongs to the same sentence type as the longer sentence — a feature of arrangement that does not apply to declarative sentences in English.

A more detailed study of Navajo would reveal many other contrasts. To give only one more example, we know that Navajo has borrowed the Spanish word *loco* (*crazy*), which in Navajo assumes the shape *lóogo*. In Spanish, *loco* is an adjective and as such follows the noun it modifies: *un hombre loco* is roughly the equivalent of English *a crazy man* (note the contrast in arrangement between Spanish and English). But in Navajo the word *lóogo* is taken as a verb: *hastiin lóogo* is only in meaning the equivalent of *a crazy man* (or the Spanish equivalent). Grammatically, *hastiin lóogo* is a sentence, literally translated (*the*) *man is crazy*.

To summarize this and the preceding section, we may say that every language possesses the following:

(1) A set of phonemes, finite in number, and a set of rules governing the ways in which phonemes are combined.

(2) A large number of morphemes, free and bound, which make up its lexicon.

(3) A finite number or arrangements that govern the ways in which morphemes are combined to produce intelligible utterances.

Taken together, these three items make up the structure of a language, in terms of which any utterance current in a given speech community may be fully described.

Although the general procedures outlined above are sufficient for a rudimentary understanding of phonology and grammar, modern linguists have gone considerably beyond them in attempts to achieve increasingly detailed and precise descriptions of languages. The student who wishes to continue the study of language structure, perhaps by reading some of the works suggested at the end of the chapter, will encounter a world of controversy in which such basic aspects of linguistics as the definition of the phoneme and the morpheme become the subject of heated dispute.

6. Linguistic Change

Though linguistic structures, at any given point in their history, may appear to be rigid and unchanging, this appearance is illusory. In actual fact, all living languages (that is, all languages still being spoken) undergo continual change, manifest in both their phonological and their grammatical structures. Such changes become most evident when we contrast languages at different points in their history or when we observe that two or more mutually unintelligible tongues are nevertheless derived from a common source, as the modern Romance languages are from Latin.

English affords a good example of linguistic change. Its first written records appear about 900 A.D., and from that time on we have a more or less unbroken line of documents connecting the oldest recorded English with that of the present. Linguists customarily divide the history of the English language into three main periods: Old English (or Anglo-Saxon), from 900 A.D. to about 1100 A.D.; Middle English, from 1100 to about 1550; and Modern English, from 1550 to the present. During this relatively brief span (little more than 1,000 years), English has altered so radically in both phonology and grammar as to make it quite impossible for a native speaker of Modern English to read either Middle or Old English without a good deal of special study.

We can illustrate some of the changes in English phonology from 900 A.D. to the present by comparing the following words as they occur in Old English, Middle English, and Modern English.

Note that the differences of sound are greater than is indicated by the orthography. Old English and Middle English *a* is pronounced roughly as in *pot* (the macron—for example, *ā*—indicates length; Old English *ae* as in *man;* Old and Middle English *i* as in *see;* Old English *ē* and the vowel of Middle English *dēp* roughly like the *é* of French *été* (but longer); Middle English *ē* in *dēl* and *drēm* as in *bed;* Old and Middle English *ū* as in *boot;* Old English *ō* and the vowel of Middle English *mōd* as in German *Sohn;* Middle English *ō* in *stōn* roughly like the British English *law;* Old English *ȳ* as the *u* of French *une*. In Old English vowel combinations, as in *drēam* and *dēop*, both vowels are pronounced.

Old English	Middle English	Modern English
mann	man	man
stān	ston	stone
dāel	del	deal
wīn	wīn	wine
drēam	drēm	dream
dēop	dēp	deep
sunu	sune	sun
hūs	hūs	house
mōd	mōd	mood
fȳr	fīr	fire

We may note further that the differences in pronunciation between Modern English and its earlier forms are consistent and systematic, not random. The vowels *ā*, *ū*, and *ȳ* of Old English, for example, nearly always become *o* (as in *stone*), *ou* (as in *house*), and *i* (as in *mice*) in Modern English, provided of course we compare these in words that have been retained in the language since Old English times. Examples of these regular phonetic correspondences are found in the following pairs: *stān, stone; hāl, whole; bāt, boat; gāt, goat; gān, go; hūs, house; mūs, mouse; cū, cow; lūs, louse; hū, how; fȳr, fire; mȳs, mice; lȳs, lice; brȳd, bride; hwȳ, why.* By means of similar phonetic correspondences we may eventually link up all the phonemes of Old, Middle, and Modern English, thus summarizing in systematic form all the changes in habits of pronunciation that have taken place in English-speaking communities during the past 1,000 years, insofar as these are reflected in written documents.

But differences in phonology are not the only ones that separate Old, Middle and Modern English forms, for these may also differ in grammar. Old English *stān*, for example, had a total of six case forms: *stān*, nominative singular; *stāne*, dative singular; *stānes*, genitive singular; *stānas*, nominative plural; *stānum*, dative plural; and *stāna*, genitive plural. In the Middle English period, these reduced to four: *stōn*, nominative singular; *stōnene*, genitive plural; and *stōnes* in the remaining three cases (genitive singular, nominative plural, and dative plural). Today English has but two forms: the general singular *stone* and the form *stones*, which functions indifferently as a genitive singular (written *stone's*), a genitive plural (written *stones'*), and a general plural.

Verbs, too, were conjugated differently in Old and Middle English as compared with the present. The Old English verb *bindan* (*to bind*), for example, had the following forms in the present indicative singular: first person *binde*, second person *bindest* or *bintst*, and third person *bindeth* or *bint*. These were retained essentially unchanged through most of the Middle English period, but today there remains only *bind* for the first and second persons (*I bind, you bind*) and *binds* for the third (*he binds*).

It is clear from these examples, few as they are, that Old, Middle, and Modern English, though obviously distinct languages (or better, sets of languages), are nevertheless linked in a continuous historical tradition. Old English is a set of languages spoken in England until 1100 A.D., when, by slow changes, it merged into a new set of languages which we have called, collectively, Middle English. In the same fashion, linguistic change being continuous, the Middle English languages gave way to the many modern forms of English now spoken, by reason of migration and colonization, both in England and in numerous other areas of the world. Both Old English and Middle English, once the languages of many thousands of people, no longer exist, save in the scanty remnants preserved in ancient documents.

7. The Comparative Method

Although written records afford us the best and most direct evidence of linguistic change, for a great many languages such records are unavailable. Writing is a relatively recent invention, no more than 5,000 years old. Linguistic change, like language itself, is evidently much older. There is no reason to believe that unrecorded languages are less subject to change than those for which we have ancient documents.

The evidence that all languages change is found in the fact that groups of modern tongues reveal, on careful examination, the same sorts of resemblances in phonology and grammar that we have just noted between Old, Middle, and Modern English. Ways of speaking in modern English are similar to those of modern German, Dutch, Swedish, Norwegian, and Danish, even though these idioms, like the older forms of English, are languages very different from modern English. To illustrate this point, let us compare English, German, and Swedish in respect to the following words.

English	*German*	*Swedish*
brother	bruder	broder
daughter	tochter	dotter
door	tür	dörr
father	vater	fader
foot	fuss	fot
hair	haar	hår
heart	herz	hjärta
knee	knie	knä
man	mann	man
mother	mutter	moder
son	sohn	son

As a result of resemblances like these, which in the languages concerned are so numerous as to affect almost every aspect of the vocabulary, it is inferred that English, German, and Swedish are modern divergent varieties of an earlier protolanguage common to all three. English ways of speaking, in modern times, represent one set of divergences from those of the earlier speech community, whereas German and Swedish ways of speaking represent two other sets of divergences, different both from each other and from English. The resemblances between English, German, and Swedish, too many to result from coincidence, are evidence of their common origin in the remote past, and hence of the fact that all three languages have changed, though in different ways, from their common ancestor.

This means of describing linguistic change is called the comparative method. It involves, as our example above illustrates, a sorting of the vocabularies of the languages compared to ferret out the forms that are cognate to each other; that is, the forms that, in each of the languages compared, represent modern divergences from a single prototype form and hence are historically connected. Where investigation reveals many such cognates between two or more different tongues, these languages are presumed to be members of a single stock or family, or to be connected historically to a single protolanguage. If thorough comparison of two or more languages discloses no cognates, there can be no relationship between them.

Further examination of the cognate forms of related languages reveals, as in the case of Old, Middle, and Modern English, that their divergences in pronunciation may be reduced to orderly statements of phonetic correspondence. A sound correspondence evidenced in one set of cognates is ordinarily paralleled by scores of others containing the same sounds. Note, for example, that the correspondence of English and Swedish *d* (in *daughter-dotter* or *door—dörr*) to German *t* (in *tochter* and *tür*, respectively) is found also in the following sets: *dew, dagg, tau; death, död, tod; deep, djup, tief; day, dag, tag; deaf, döv, taub; dear* (expensive), *dyr, teuer; dance, dansa, tanzen; dive, dyka, tauchen;* and *dream, drömma, träumen.* Similar correspondences may be set up between nearly every English phoneme and its Swedish and German counterparts.

It is this systematic correspondence between the sounds of different contemporaneous languages that, like the same order of correspondence between different historical periods of the same language, truly evidences their common origin. Random similarities between languages, on the other hand, do not mean that they have a common antecedent, but only that such similarities are due to chance. Thus, it is mere coincidence that the English *ma* (*mother*) resembles Navajo *-má* (*mother*). Borrowing may also account for some similarities, as in the case of Navajo *lóogo* (*crazy*) from Spanish *loco*.

It is by the use of the comparative method that linguists divide the languages of the world into separate stocks or families. As we noted in §3, there are many such families of languages—a reflection both of the diversity of modern tongues and the antiquity of language as a human faculty. As more and more languages are studied and compared intensively with each other, we may expect that the number of linguistic stocks will decrease. Families now apparently unrelated will eventually be shown to be related, though remotely. But it is not likely, by the comparative method alone, that we shall ever be able to demonstrate the common origin of all modern tongues. The rate of divergence of languages is too rapid, in relation to the great time span of human history, to make it probable that enough remains of a possible primeval uniformity of speech to link all present-day languages into a single great family.

8. Language in Culture

To the anthropologist the study of language is important not only for practical purposes, but also for the fact that linguistic researches may often prove essential to an understanding of the deeper problems of ethnology and social anthropology. As Boas pointed out many years ago,

> . . . the study of language must be considered as one of the most important branches of ethnological study, because, on the one hand, a thorough insight into ethnology cannot be gained without a practical knowledge of the language, and, on the other hand, the fundamental concepts illustrated by human languages are not distinct in kind from ethnological phenomena; and because, furthermore, the peculiar characteristics of languages are clearly reflected in the views and customs of the peoples of the world.[11]

The importance of language lies obviously in the fact that all linguistic forms have meaning and, as we have seen, these meanings represent not single items of experience, but one or more categories of experience. As Boas puts it,

> Since the total range of experience which language serves to express is infinitely varied, and its whole scope must be expressed by a limited number . . . [of linguistic forms], it is obvious that an extended classification of experience must underlie all articulate speech.[12]

All such classifications or categories of experience represent the end result of a long historical tradition and are indissolubly tied to a particular cultural milieu. It is not surprising, therefore, to discover that societies that differ in culture differ as well in the categories that attach to their linguistic forms. A careful and precise determination of the categories of meaning found in language will then reflect, to a greater or lesser degree, the views and customs of the people who speak that language.

To illustrate this point, let us consider the two English words *house* and *home*. The former, in its nuclear meaning, is defined as a dwelling; a person may own several houses and live in none of them. A home, on the other hand, is the fixed residence of a person or family; one has only one home at a time.

If we now attempt to translate these two forms into Navajo, we discover

---

[11] Franz Boas, "Introduction," *Handbook of American Indian Languages*, Part I, Bulletin 40 (Washington D.C.: Bureau of American Ethnology, 1911), p. 73.

[12] Ibid., p. 24.

that Navajo also has two words: -*yan*, a form that never occurs independently but only when preceded by a possessive prefix as, for example, in the form *biyan* (*his home* or *house*). Forms of this category are said to be inalienably possessed. The second Navajo word is *kin*, which may occur independently or with a possessive prefix, as in *bikin* (*his home* or *house*).

A careful examination of the nuclear meanings of these two forms reveals that *biyan* refers only to a Navajo's native dwelling, the six-sided house of logs in which many Navajos still live. *Biyan* is never used for houses or homes belonging to non-Navajos, whether these be other Indians, Americans, or Mexicans. The houses or homes of non-Navajos are always designated by the word *kin*.

Similar difficulties arise when we examine grammatical categories rather than the lexical categories just illustrated. In English, the expression *that house*, by virtue of its place in the series *this house, that house, these houses, those houses*, defines, roughly, a singular house at some distance from the speaker. But among the Kwakiutl Indians of British Columbia, according to Boas, a similar expression belongs to a more complex series, to wit:

1. the house (singular or plural) visible near me.
2. the house (singular or plural) invisible near me.
3. the house (singular or plural) visible near thee.
4. the house (singular or plural) invisible near thee.
5. the house (singular or plural) visible near him.
6. the house (singular or plural) invisible near him.[13]

Kwakiutl, it is evident, has six demonstratives, whereas English has but four (that is, *this, that, these, those*). In Kwakiutl, one must specify visibility or invisibility as well as location in reference to the speaker, the person addressed, or some third person. Note, however, that the English distinction between singular and plural is not required in Kwakiutl, for all six of the Kwakiutl demonstratives refer indifferently to one or more than one.

In Eskimo, Boas continues, demonstratives are even more specific. An English expression such as *that man* must appear in one of the following forms: *that man near me, that man near thee, that man near him; that man behind me, that man in front of me, that man to the right of me, that man to the left of me, that man above me, that man below me*, and so on for person addressed (*thee*) and the third person (*him*).

To take a more complex and revealing example, suppose we attempt to translate the English sentence *I give it to him* into Navajo, assuming just the literal sense of presenting another with a gift. At first, we can find no Navajo equivalent, for there is no Navajo verb that has the meaning *give*. But if we persist, we find not one but twelve Navajo forms that are at least the rough equivalents of our English sentence. All these are simple verb expressions, for in Navajo the verb is quite often as expressive as a whole phrase or sentence in English.

[13] Boas, op. cit., pp. 40–41.

The first part of all twelve verbs (called the prefix complex) is the same. It may be written *bàaniš-*, where *b* and *n* are pronounced much as English *p* and *n*, respectively, *š* is like *sh* in *ship*, *a* is about the same as the vowel of *palm*, and *i* is like the vowel of *sit*. The vowel *a* is doubled to indicate that it is long; it has about twice the duration of *i*. *Bàaniš-* is made up of four morphemes: *b-*, from *bi-* (*him*), *àa-* (*to, toward*), *ni-* (*completively*), and *š-* (*I*). Arranged in this way, these morphemes together have the meaning *I cause it completively to him*, obviously only a partial meaning, as *bàaniš-* is only part of a larger form.

To complete the Navajo form we must add one further morpheme, a verb stem. Twelve of these may be used, the choice depending on what sort of object is referred to by the *it* of the prefix complex. If it is a living object, the stem *-tèeh* (*a living object moves*) is added to form *bàaništèeh* (*I cause it* [a living being] *to move completively to him* or, roughly, *I give a living being to him*). Similarly, we can form *bàaniškàah* (*I cause a container with contents to move completively to him*), *bàanišłé* (*I cause a ropelike object to move completively to him*), and so on through a total of twelve categories of objects to be given. If the speaker is in doubt as to the nature of the object given, he uses *bàanisʔàah* (*I cause a round solid object to move completively to him* or *I cause it* [unknown] *to move completively to him*).

It is clear, then, that the notion expressed by English *give*, as a separate category of action, does not exist in Navajo. Rather, the Navajos speak of giving as a special instance of "objects moving," where an agent causes an object of a particular type to move completively from himself to another. The act of giving, in other words, is differently conceived in the two speech communities, and this difference is codified in their styles of speech.

To conclude this section it would appear that language functions far more importantly in a culture than simply as a neutral device to represent or symbolize the flow of experience. A language does more; it furnishes the categories and divisions of experience in terms of which its speakers cope with the universe about them. Sapir, in an article called "The Status of Linguistics as a Science," made this fact amply clear when he said:

> Language is a guide to "social reality." Though language is not ordinarily thought of as of essential interest to the students of social science, it powerfully conditions all our thinking about social problems and processes. Human beings do not live in the objective world alone, nor alone in the world of social activity as ordinarily understood, but are very much at the mercy of the particular language which has become the medium of expression for their society. It is quite an illusion to imagine that one adjusts to reality essentially without the use of language and that language is merely an incidental means of solving specific problems of communication or reflection. The fact of the matter is that the "real world" is to a large extent unconsciously built up on the language habits of the group. No two languages are ever sufficiently similar to be considered as representing the same social reality. The worlds in which different societies live are distinct worlds, not merely the same world with different labels attached.[14]

[14] Edward Sapir, "The Status of Linguistics as a Science," *Language* (Charlottesville, Va.: Linguistic Society of America), 5:207–214 (1929), p. 209.

9. Writing

In our own society, where nearly everyone learns to read and write early, we often confuse language with writing and frequently speak of writing as though it were a special kind of language. The "written language" is contrasted to the "spoken language," with the former being regarded as somehow more accurate and precise than the latter. In some circumstances, indeed, we speak as though nonliterate peoples (that is, peoples who lack a writing) also lack a language and so can communicate with each other, if at all, only with the greatest difficulty.

The error implicit in these beliefs is obvious: language and writing, though clearly related, are not the same. They are, in fact, two very different aspects of culture. Writing, roughly defined, is a set of techniques for the

Pupils in this New Guinea school speak five different languages. They were formerly hostile to each other and first came to school with bows and arrows. Pupils are taught to read and write in their own language, then in a trade language called "Police Motu," and finally in English. (Australian Official Photograph, Courtesy of the United Nations.)

graphic representation of speech, whereas language, as we have seen, is a complex of patterns that governs or controls speaking. All of us learn to speak early in life; with minor and unimportant exceptions, we have acquired all our habits of speaking before we are six years old. But we do not ordinarily learn to read and write until much later, if at all, and this learning has, on the whole, very little effect upon our speaking habits. Literate peoples, then, possess two cultural techniques related to language: the art of speaking, which they share with all humans, literate or not, and that of writing or representing their spoken forms graphically, a cultural possession that distinguishes them from nonliterate societies.

Writing probably originated from drawing, a technique as widespread among human beings as language itself. But we must emphasize that drawings, even in the form of conventionalized pictographs, are not the equivalents of writing. A drawing may well serve to recall an event, or even, as among the Plains Indians, to tell a story. However, narrative drawings — often miscalled picture writing — differ from true writing in that the pictographs are not tied specifically to spoken words, syllables, or sounds, but may be interpreted by any of a number of equivalent utterances. The pictograph ∧, as used by the Plains Indians, stands simply for a dwelling, whatever word might be used to name it, whereas our graphic symbol *house* is linked specifically to one spoken word and no other. The Plains Indian ∧ can be read *house, dwelling, tipi, tent*, or any similar equivalent, but *house* can stand only for this word and no other.

True writing began, then, when conventionalized graphic symbols (derived, it would seem, from earlier pictographs) became associated with the sounds of a language. In all the earliest writings known, many or most of the symbols are logographic; that is, they stand for words, particular combinations of speech sounds. Some early systems are also syllabaries, in which the symbols stand for syllables rather than whole words. Although logographic systems of writing exist (as in Chinese) and many peoples (for example, the Japanese) employ syllabaries, most modern systems are alphabetic; that is, the graphic symbols represent, more or less accurately, the distinctive sounds or phonemes of the languages written. The history of the development from the earliest known logograms to modern alphabetic writing is very complicated and still imperfectly known. We shall summarize only the major developments in the following paragraphs.

Writing was certainly invented twice in human history, and possibly oftener. The earliest invention occurred in the Near East, probably among the Bronze Age Egyptians. It is possible that this invention spread, with many changes, throughout Europe and Asia, so giving rise to all modern systems of Old World origin, but many scholars believe that Chinese writing (and possibly other systems) was invented independently. Later, and quite independently of the Near East, writing was invented by the American Indian Mayas of Yucatan and Guatemala (or by near neighbors). But Maya writings gave rise to no modern forms, and today even the few surviving Maya records are only partly decipherable. The Aztecs of Mexico also possessed a writing, very like that of the Mayas and probably derived from it.

The earliest Egyptian writing was a mixed system, combining logograms and even pictographs with symbols that stood for syllables. Later it became standardized to some twenty-four characters, each of which stood for a consonant plus a vowel. In this form the Egyptian writing was taken over by a neighboring people who spoke a Semitic language.

These people reworked the Egyptian system to suit the needs of their language. Each symbol came to represent a consonant alone; vowels were not represented at all. Semitic writing thus became alphabetic, in that each symbol stood for a single sound. It was, of course, incompletely alphabetic in that the vowels were not represented. This was no great handicap in a Semitic language, in which the vowels may easily be supplied from the arrangement of consonants in a word and the context in which the word appears.

The alphabet so formed spread quickly to all the Semitic-speaking peoples of the Near East, including the Phoenicians, traders living at the eastern end of the Mediterranean and the founders of the city of Carthage in North Africa. As a result of trading contacts with the Phoenicians, and probably under the stimulus of trade, which requires written records, the Greeks soon took over the Phoenician alphabet, adapting it to their uses as the Semites had adapted the Egyptian syllabary.

The Greeks made many changes in the Phoenician alphabet, but the most important of these was the invention of vowel symbols. Greek, like English, cannot be written intelligibly in consonants alone; vowels must also be represented. The Greeks, however, did not create many new symbols; rather they simply reinterpreted some of the Phoenician characters, especially those that were not necessary to the writing of Greek consonants. Thus the Phoenician aleph (a consonant pronounced deep in the throat) became the Greek vowel alpha, and two Phoenician symbols for *h*-like or breath sounds (absent in Greek) became Greek epsilon and eta, both vowels. Greek *o* was made from another Phoenician consonant, and *i* and *u* from two more.

From the Greeks, in a long series of borrowings extending over centuries, the alphabet spread to the Romans, the Germanic-speaking peoples, and so to all of Europe. At the same time, there was also a spread from the Near East eastward, for it is probable that the Indian systems of writing are from the same source as the Semitic and European. In all these borrowings, modifications were made: in the values of the signs used, in the form of the writing, and in numerous other details. Many problems in the complex history of writing remain unsolved. Whole systems of writing are still undecipherable in large part; until recently this was true of the ancient inscriptions of Crete. And most of the later systems, though well known in general, still offer many problems of interpretation. Scholars are even today in doubt, for example, as to the proper reading of many Greek and Latin characters, and even of a number of particulars in the writing of Old English.

Nevertheless, it is clear that writing has a history definitely apart from that of language. Our central point—that language exists independently of a system of writing—should never be lost sight of. Writing adds a valuable set of techniques to a culture, but it adds nothing to the language.

Though writing marks an important step in the development of human cultures, it does not in itself provide all the features of long-distance communication, the keeping of accurate records, and the spread of learning so frequently attributed to it. In many societies writing remained a technique restricted to a small elite and even prohibited to the bulk of the population. Among the Mayas and early Egyptians, writing apparently functioned mainly as a magico-religious device; it was an art difficult to learn and laborious to perform. And even though the development of extensive trade in the Near East caused the spread of writing to secular uses, it still remained in the province of a few highly skilled specialists.

True literacy and the spread of learning and education came only when writing was supplemented by means, such as printing, for the rapid duplication of written records.

10. The Antiquity of Language

There is general agreement that the adaptive advantages of improved communication were a major factor in the evolution of humanity and that human biological evolution proceeded by gradual stages as a result of the interaction of improved communication, toolmaking, and other factors noted in Chapter 6. There is general disagreement concerning the steps by which human language evolved. The diversity of modern languages and the fact that all known languages are fully developed structurally suggest that the development of language was completed some time before the dispersion of *Homo sapiens* to his present locations. If we assume that those Neanderthals, who some 75,000 years ago were practicing systematic burials, possessed something like religion that required an ability to conceptualize the supernatural, then it would appear that they must also have possessed a productive language, that is, a language in which morphemes could be combined in new ways to produce such expressions as "life after death." Perhaps all of the elements required for the development of a modern language were present some 100,000 years ago and these elements contributed heavily to the rapid evolution of *Homo sapiens sapiens*. At any rate, there is agreement that fully modern human beings speaking fully modern languages came into being about fifty thousand years ago.

The fact that chimpanzees seem to possess at least rudimentary language skills suggests that our early ancestors possessed comparable abilities. It is difficult to imagine how early humans could have managed a complex tool kit and a comparatively elaborate social life without some reasonably efficient means of communication. Presumably the earliest human beings possessed some sort of protolanguage. Such a protolanguage must have involved coding in which basic elements of sound or gesture were combined and recombined in order to transmit and perhaps generate new information. Without this, protolanguage would have been no different from other animal communication systems and could not have been a factor in human evolution.

Lieberman suggests that the evolution of human language, from whatever its early forms might have been, involved three kinds of change: (1) improvements in cognitive ability, especially the ability to encode, (2) improvements in speaking abilities making it possible to speak rapidly and clearly, and (3) increases in cultural complexity which provided more things to talk about.[15] Of these, only the increase in cultural complexity is easily documented. Here, it is tempting to suppose that the introduction of new and especially complicated means of tool construction or hunting technique go along with improvements in cognitive or communicative abilities. We did this earlier in suggesting a relationship between the development of language and the development of religion and art. On the other hand, the rate of development of cultural complexity may depend very much upon the interaction between environmental challenges and the amount of existing complexity. The accumulation of culture may, like other forms of learning, be one of those processes that starts slowly and then accelerates.

Although research on the problem is in its earliest stages, there is a possibility that changes in language can be documented through the study of the vocal tracts of fossil skulls. Lieberman, Crelin, and Klatt have made casts of the vocal tracts of modern and fossil humans which seem to demonstrate differences in their ability to enunciate particular sounds.[16] Their studies suggest that the ability to articulate the sounds used in modern human languages developed comparatively recently, and was in fact absent among most specimens classified as Neanderthal. Despite an evident ability to develop complex technology, *neandertalensis* may have lacked a fully modern language. This possibility is quite puzzling to most scholars and it is unlikely that there will be general agreement concerning Neanderthal language until our guesses concerning possible protolanguages can be given better support.

Progress in our understanding of the nature of language has, especially in the last few years, led to the development of increasingly ingenious ways of detecting its possible presence in the past. Ultimately the fossil record and the associated archaeological remains may yield considerably more information about the evolution of language than is currently available. As is always true in the study of the past, we will never know precisely what happened. It seems probable that our developing knowledge of animal communication, language, physiology, cognition, and human biological and cultural evolution will soon provide a much more exact picture of the evolution of language than is available at present.

11. Summary

The use of language may be the most important defining characteristic of human beings. Language involves the use of a small number of phonemes combined and arranged in accordance with phonological and grammatical rules. The meanings assigned to words and other units of language are arbi-

[15] Philip Lieberman, *On the Origins of Language* (New York: Macmillan, Inc., 1975).

[16] Philip Lieberman, E. S. Crelin, and D. H. Klatt, "Phonetic Ability and Related Anatomy of the Newborn, Adult Human, Neanderthal Man, and the Chimpanzee," *American Anthropologist*, **74**:287–307 (1972).

trary. The human capacity to assign arbitrary meanings applies to many things other than language, and the study of symbols has come to be of major importance for the understanding of human beings. When words with arbitrary meanings are combined in new or unusual ways, the resulting productivity leads to the emergence of new concepts. Language also provides the ability to communicate about things that are elsewhere or elsewhen and to develop abstractions in which symbols are used to symbolize symbols.

Distinctions between languages are generally based upon the criterion of mutual intelligibility. Within any single language, mutually intelligible dialects and idiolects are likely to be characteristics of particular regions or groups. Languages that are mutually unintelligible, but nevertheless similar in certain respects, can be classified together as members of a single language family. In describing a language, a community of speakers must first be identified and, then, examples of utterances collected. Analysis of such utterances leads to the formulation of rules of language such as those governing the use of commands in English.

Cultures can generally be compared and even ranked in terms of their technology or patterns of social organization, but it has not proved possible to rank cultures in terms of language. Although some languages possess more complex vocabularies than others, all possess equally well-developed grammars and the capacity to increase their vocabularies as circumstances warrant. For example, although Navajo and English are very different languages, both seem equally efficient as means of communication. Although all languages have the same basic properties, language itself is one of the most variable aspects of culture, and the number of distinct human languages must be counted in the thousands.

In the analysis of language a distinction is generally made between phonology, which deals with phonemes, and grammar, which deals with morphemes. Phonemes are the minimum sounds that are considered significant by the speakers of a language. The presence of particular phonemes can be rigorously established through the examination of patterns of complementary and contrastive distribution. Such an examination also permits the formulation of rules governing the arrangement of phonemes in sequence. The morpheme is the smallest meaningful unit that can be constructed by the combination of phonemes. Morphemes are not necessarily words, and a distinction must be made between free morphemes and bound morphemes. Arrangements of morphemes are limited by grammatical rules that specify appropriate ways of combining morphemes to form words, phrases, and sentences. Rules governing the construction of sentences and phrases represent an aspect of grammar called syntax. Morphology is the study of the rules governing the arrangement of morphemes in the formation of words.

In the process of being spoken, all languages undergo change as illustrated by a comparison of Old English, Middle English, and Modern English. The evidence that all languages change can also be based upon a detailed comparison of similar languages. Thus it can be inferred that English, German, and Swedish are all modern varieties of an earlier protolanguage. The comparative method, which involves the comparison of similar languages, permits the reconstruction of earlier languages and the classification of languages into families.

Because language is the means by which people communicate with each other and label the various elements in the world around them, it follows that the study of language is a valuable means of understanding the views and customs of those who speak them. A language furnishes the categories and divisions of experience in terms of which its speakers cope with the world.

Writing is a set of techniques for the graphic representation of speech. Writing probably originated from pictographic drawings. Although systems of writing can be logographic, with each symbol representing a word, or syllabic, with each symbol representing a syllable, most modern systems of writing are alphabetic, with each symbol representing a speech sound. Writing, by itself, does not provide all the features of long-distance communication, accurate record keeping, and the spread of learning so often attributed to it. In much of the world, widespread literacy did not occur until after the invention of the printing press.

The history of the evolution of language must be inferred from the indirect evidence provided by human fossil and archaeological remains. There is general agreement that *Homo sapiens sapiens* possessed an essentially modern language some fifty thousand years ago. There is debate concerning the possession of fully developed language by the Neanderthals. The possession of at least rudimentary language skills by the chimpanzee suggests that some form of rudimentary language may have been used by the earliest human beings. As yet there is no plausible explanation of the form such a rudimentary language might have taken or how it might have evolved into modern language.

Collateral Reading

Bloomfield, Leonard. *Language*. New York: Holt, Rinehart and Winston, Inc., 1933. A classic still useful despite its age.

Blount, Ben (ed.). *Language, Culture and Society: A Book of Readings*. Cambridge, Mass.: Winthrop, 1974. Collection including both classic statements and current research.

Burling, Robbins. *Man's Many Voices: Language in Its Cultural Context*. New York: Holt, Rinehart and Winston, Inc., 1970. Recent introduction to sociolinguistics.

Gelb, I. J. *A Study of Writing*. Chicago: University of Chicago Press, 1952. The best available study of writing and its development.

Giglioli, Pier Paola (ed.). *Language and Social Context: Selected Readings*. Penguin Modern Sociology Readings. Baltimore and Hammondsworth, Middlesex, England: Penguin Books, 1972. Collection of recent articles on sociolinguistics.

Gleason, H. A. *An Introduction to Descriptive Linguistics*, rev. ed. New York: Holt, Rinehart and Winston, Inc., 1961. A sound and useful text.

Greenberg, Joseph H. *Anthropological Linguistics: An Introduction*. New York: Random House, Inc., 1968. Useful introduction.

Gudschinsky, Sarah Caroline. *How to Learn an Unwritten Language*. New York: Holt, Rinehart and Winston, Inc., 1967. Basic techniques.

Gumperz, John J., and Dell Hymes (eds.). *Directions in Sociolinguistics: The Ethnography of Communication.* New York and London: Holt, Rinehart and Winston, Inc., 1972. Series of articles that provide important insights into sociolinguistics.

Hymes, Dell. *Foundations in Sociolinguistics: An Ethnographic Approach.* Philadelphia: University of Pennsylvania Press, 1974.

———— *Language in Culture and Society: A Reader in Linguistics and Anthropology.* New York: Harper & Row, Inc., 1964. An exceptional collection of articles, together with a detailed bibliography on anthropological linguistics.

Langacker, Ronald W. *Language and Its Structure: Some Fundamental Linguistic Concepts.* New York: Harcourt Brace Jovanovich, 1967, 1968. An excellent and well-written text, especially useful for its clear exposition of Chomskian Theory.

Lehmann, Winfred Philipp. *Historical Linguistics: An Introduction,* 2d ed. New York: Holt, Rinehart and Winston, Inc., 1973. A recent textbook.

Sapir, Edward. *Language.* New York: Harcourt Brace Jovanovich, 1921. Although the book is now outdated, it still presents a stimulating treatment of general and historical linguistics.

17/The Arts

1. Nature and Origin of the Arts

In our own culture we tend to think of the arts as a fairly well-defined group of activities, usually carried on by specialists. Painting, sculpture, music, dancing, drama, opera, and the writing of fiction and poetry are all generally recognized as "art" if they are done under certain circumstances and possess certain qualities. Fabric design, furniture design, ceramics, household decoration, and many other activities may also be classified as art, but they are generally distinguished from "fine arts" by such labels as "practical" or "applied" art. Art that is not produced by specialists or that is enjoyed by large numbers of people is also likely to carry a derogatory label such as "folk art" or "popular art."

In other cultures, especially those that lack a high degree of specialization of labor, it is often difficult to make the same kinds of distinctions. In many cases it is difficult to make any very clear distinction between artistic and everyday activities. The anthropological definition of art, then, centers about the extent to which any given activity seems to involve, over and above any practical or utilitarian value, elements that have an impact on the senses of a performer or an audience. Artistic activities are not just carried out properly; they are carried out with grace, style, and beauty as these concepts are understood by the members of any particular culture. Although artistic productions are sometimes defined by the sentiments they arouse in an anthropologist or other outside observer, the ultimate authorities on what is art and what is not art are the artist and the audience for whom the activity was performed.

Although a sunset, a bird's nest, or some other natural effect may be classified as beautiful, ugly, or otherwise important in terms of its impact upon the senses, the productions of nature are not generally regarded as art. In the same way, accidental productions of human beings are not art in a technical sense. Natural and accidental productions have an artistic component to the degree that they have a special impact upon the senses, but they are not technically art because they do not involve a relationship between performers and audience. Art, like other cultural productions, is an activity carried out with reference to a real or imagined audience. Like other cultural productions, artistic activities involve cultural standards which in this case are usually referred to as style or artistic tradition. In other words, art possesses the attribute of grammaticality; there are rules concerning the proper performance of artistic activities. The artist may work within the framework of rules or he may deliberately use "bad grammar" in order to secure particular effects. In the same way, an audience possesses critical standards that permit it to assess artistic performances and to react accordingly with rage, delight, boredom, or excitement.

From some perspectives it seems apparent that the artistic impulse is much older than the human species. Many of the nest-building and vocal activities of birds clearly transcend mere utility. Köhler's chimpanzees[1] hung strings and rags about themselves, smeared themselves with paint, and engaged in single-file circuits of a post in which they stamped one foot harder than the other, although not in unison. In the archaeological record it is evident that some of the earliest human beings gathered attractive and nonutilitarian stones and very often did more work than they had to in order to produce utilitarian tools. It is not, however, until the emergence of the Neanderthals that the evidence for the existence of art becomes convincing. The Neanderthals collected mineral pigments, such as ochre, and engaged in the apparent decoration of burials. With the emergence of *Homo sapiens sapiens,* the archaeological record exhibits elaborately chipped stone tools, carved figurines, engravings, and cave paintings. Evidently, the forms of artistic expression were fully developed some fifty thousand years ago and have been characteristic of all modern or historically reported peoples.

Although, in terms of the standards of our culture, some peoples seem less artistic than do others and some peoples are interested in some kinds of art and not in others, it has not been possible to trace any clear pattern of the evolution of art forms. The cave paintings of the Upper Paleolithic, which are among the earliest art forms known, possess a degree of skill and sophistication that appeal strongly to twentieth-century art critics. In much of rural South India, houses, tools, pottery, and most textiles were traditionally undecorated and were not regarded as artistic creations. In these fields many of the earliest agriculturalists of six or seven thousand years ago engaged in far

[1] Wolfgang Kohler, *The Mentality of Apes,* trans. Ella Winter (London: Pelican, 1957).

In some cultures almost every object must be beautified. Lime spatula from the Massim area, Trobriand Islands, near New Guinea. The blade, moistened with saliva, was dipped into a container with powdered lime, which was then licked off to chew with a mixture of areca nut and betel leaves. (Courtesy of the UCLA Museum of Cultural History.)

greater artistic exertions than the modern South Indian farmers. On the other hand, almost every South Indian village stages elaborate plays, dances, and religious ceremonials involving extensive literary and musical training. Some peoples seem reluctant to leave a piece of wood uncarved or a piece of pottery unpainted, whereas other peoples, for no obvious reason, prefer their wood and their pottery plain and unadorned.

In sharp contrast to South Indian potters, Tarascan potters in Mexico, at least during the 1940s, preferred to decorate all aspects of the pottery they produced, both inside and outside. Many potters refused to make any two pieces with identical designs. On the evidence of differences of this sort, it can be concluded that different peoples disagree on the importance of particular kinds of art. Peoples also disagree on the manner in which a story should be organized, the kinds of sounds that are considered musical, and the relative merits of representational and geometric drawings. On the Northwest Coast of North America, representational art involved highly stylized drawings and carvings often depicting both sides of the animal on the same flat surface. Side by side with this highly stylized, almost geometrical art, some Northwest Coast tribes produced three-dimensional portrait carvings that were both representational and startlingly realistic.

Although many students of art are prepared to examine the enormous variety of human art and pass judgments on the relative merits of different artistic traditions, it has proved difficult to find any objective basis for judgments of artistic quality. Some artistic traditions involve more training and greater skill than do others, some allow greater freedom of expression than do others, and so on. All human artistic creations are the products of age-long dialogues between the artist and his audience. They reflect traditions of art and art criticism in which any particular audience has learned to appreciate artistic nuances that might pass unnoticed by the uninitiated. The critical standards applied by the audience represent cultural standards that have been learned along with other cultural standards. A New Yorker may find artistic enjoyment in a piece of Pueblo pottery, a Northwest Coast mask, or a pre-Colombian necklace, but he cannot evaluate such art unless he is familiar with the cultural tradition out of which it emerged. He may like it, but he doesn't understand it. He doesn't know what the artist was trying to accomplish; he doesn't know the principles of proportion or symmetry under which the artist was working.

Chilkat blanket, northwest coast, North America. An example of fine finger weaving done on suspended warp without a loom. Designs are the same as those used in wood carving; such curved lines are difficult to weave. (Courtesy of the UCLA Museum of Cultural History.)

In the end, there is very little that can be said about why a given production or performance should be more beautiful or more appealing than another. If one statue is beautiful because of its simplicity, the next is beautiful because of its complexity. If one piece of music is beautiful because of its harmony, the next is beautiful because of its disharmony. Many Muslim artistic traditions are regarded as superb because they are purely geometric and nonrepresentational; other artistic traditions are superb because they are nongeometric and representational. The fact that art is universal among human beings suggests that there is somewhere a common basis for the human appreciation of art. Certainly there are sounds no human ear can hear and colors no human eye can discern. Art, like all other aspects of culture, exists within biological limits that we shall someday discover, but art too, like other aspects of culture, is profoundly influenced by cultural standards.

2. Art and the Individual

The processes involved in the production of a work of art have rarely been studied in detail. Many factors operate in artistic production, each of which is necessary to the completed procedure. Among these factors two stand out as paramount: the culture and period in its history in which the artist participates, and the people with whom the artist lives and works, whether these are critics, collaborators, or simply friends and relatives. Although in this section we shall concentrate on the individual and his relationship to art, we cannot neglect either the social or the cultural setting in which the artist works.

In one sense, all of art is produced by individuals. Even when many people collaborate, as in a dramatic production, a ballet, a symphonic concert, or the writing and production of a motion picture, the many forms, actions, and patterns that make up the completed production do not arise spontaneously. All may be traced ultimately to the contributions of this individual or that. Groups as such create nothing; the act of creating is always an individual's action.

Nevertheless, it is a mistake to conclude that a work of art, even a painting or a novel, is exclusively the production of one person, or that a group product, such as a motion picture, can be reduced to a mere sum of individual contributions. Actually, the processes of artistic production are more complicated; the artist, in effect, gives expression to sentiments, emotions, and ideas that arise through and by interactions with others. It is in this sense that all art owes its inception to its social and cultural setting rather than to the artist alone. The unique genius of the artist lies in sensitivity to the social and cultural milieu, and in ability to respond in an esthetically satisfying medium.

To exemplify this point is difficult, for few have studied the artist at work. But we can sometimes infer something of the process of artistic creation from an analysis of the work produced. Numerous studies of literature illustrate such analysis, and demonstrate that no artist truly works in isolation but is continually subject, in one way or another, to many influences originating in the culture, the historical period, and the audience. Similar illustration may be found in nonliterate societies, particularly in the telling of myths and legends. The storyteller truly interacts with an audience and may frequently add to the tale and embellish it in response to their reactions to the performance. The storyteller will also adapt the tale to particular cultural circumstances by illustrating and developing the plot in terms of current events and happenings known to the audience. In this way, the tale gradually changes in both form and content as it is told over and over again by different narrators, to different audiences, and at different times in the history of a people.

In our society, individual artists—that is, painters who paint pictures or novelists who write books—are customarily given great prominence; their dependence on other people and on their culture is frequently overlooked. In other societies, and particularly among nonliterate peoples, works of art—such as the stories told, the songs sung, and decorations on pottery, basketry, and other media—are often anonymous, or at least the individual artist is given only a subordinate role in their production. It is this difference that we recognize when we speak of folk art, in which, as in the art of nonliterates, the role of the individual as creator is much reduced, if not lost altogether.

The anonymous nature of folk art and the art of nonliterate peoples has frequently led to the observation that everyone in a folk or nonliterate society is an artist, whereas in our society the artist is usually a professional. In one sense this is true, for folk arts and those of nonliterates are often practiced, to some degree, by nearly everyone. Most Navajo adults are at one time or another storytellers; many Navajo men sing at ceremonies or social dances; and nearly all Navajo women weave decorated blankets. But it may be worthwhile to examine this observation in more detail, and so learn more of the role of the individual in the arts. Are all members of a nonliterate society artists? Are they all equally able? Are no differences recognized between artists?

Unfortunately there are few concrete studies that enable us to answer these questions directly. One of the best researches in this field is a study by the late Lila O'Neale of the basket weavers of the Karok and Yurok Indians of northwest California.[2] These two groups, almost identical in culture, are widely known as technically skillful basket makers. The baskets display a variety of shapes and have a geometric ornamentation that is generally admired in our culture. In her investigation of these people, O'Neale found that many women made baskets; in aboriginal times, probably every woman did so, for baskets were an important part of the household equipment. Yet considerable differences in skill, both in weaving and in the use of design, are evident. These differences are clearly apparent to the Indians themselves; they recognize that one woman is a better artist than another. The superior weaver appears to get some satisfaction from this recognition, but also to get satisfaction from her own feeling of ability and skill.

The designs placed on baskets vary considerably, but there was a clear distinction between old design elements and new. There were also traditional ways of placing designs on baskets of different shapes. Approved originality in

---

[2] Lila O'Neale, "Yurok-Karok Basket Weavers," *University of California Publications in American Archaeology and Ethnology*, **32:**1–182 (1932).

Figure 17–1 Variations in design elements and their placement on California Indian baskets. (After O'Neale.)

design consisted of making slight variations in the traditional design elements or motifs and in their placement on the basket. Variations or completely original innovations were more apt to be accepted and perhaps copied, however, if the weaver was a recognized leader in the field. Innovations by a poor weaver were certain to be criticized and were not copied. According to O'Neale, "Far from being deadened by a craft in which so much is reduced to conformity, the women of the two tribes have developed an appreciation of quality, design-to-space relationships, and effective color dispositions which are discriminating and genuine." [3]

In the preceding case, we are dealing with a craft that imposed technical limitations on the artist to begin with, one that took years of instruction and practice before great skill could be developed. In addition there were conventions as to what was acceptable and what was not. Yet within this framework there were recognized differences of ability. There was also limited but real originality. Artists appear to have developed conscious esthetic standards and apparently derived satisfaction both from achieving these standards and from the recognition accorded them by others.

Such evidence as we have indicates that other arts among nonliterates are similarly regarded, at least to some degree. There are recognized standards in all artistic activities, whether it be painting designs on pottery, weaving cloth, carving wood, dancing, or telling stories, and there are, as well, recognized differences in ability. The maker or performer gets satisfaction from his skill or virtuosity, in his creativeness within the limits imposed by the culture, and from the recognition of his fellows.

Similar points are also made by Paul Bohannon writing about the Tiv of central Nigeria. Some Tiv wood carving was a communal project; for example, several people might work casually on the decoration of a wooden staff.

[3] Ibid., p. 165.

Figure 17–2 Carved wooden plate, Haida Indians, Northwest Coast, illustrating a formalized shark design adapted to a round flat surface.

Carving design on bark waist band. Mount Hagen area, New Guinea. (Courtesy of the United Nations.)

Mask from the Kaigani-Haida, Kasaan, Prince of Wales Island, British Columbia. It may represent a mythological sea monster "which had a head like a house" or symbolize the hero who, after having killed it, was able to perform deeds of valor in its guise. The most prized possession of Chief Skowl who died in the winter of 1882–1883. (Courtesy of the UCLA Museum of Cultural History.)

Nevertheless there were differences in ability between wood carvers, and the best did not wish to be observed at work. Similarly most Tiv were critics who did not hesitate to say whether a piece of carving was good or bad. Moreover, they usually could give reasons for their preferences. At the same time, the critical abilities of some Tiv seemed more highly developed than others. Bohannon suggests, indeed, that more can be learned about Tiv art by the study of criticism than by the study of artistic creation.[4]

In our own society there is considerable evidence that the same factors operate, although with varying force among different individuals. Some artists, writers, and others have seemed indifferent to the recognition of their fellows, but some have derived their principal satisfaction from such recognition. In a society that supplements recognition with monetary rewards, the latter have usually fared better economically.

It is not assumed, of course, that artists work only to gain personal gratification, whether by their own creativeness or by recognition from others. Art-

[4] Paul Bohannon, "Artist and Critic in an African Society," in Marian W. Smith, *The Artist in Tribal Society* (London: Routledge & Kegan Paul, 1961), pp. 85–94.

ists frequently have something to say, some emotion or idea that they hope to communicate to others who may view their productions. This is particularly true in our own society, and probably occurs as well in others. Indeed, there are some who believe that all of art everywhere communicates, whether or not the artist is conscious of such communication, and whether or not a society recognizes the art medium as a means of communication.

The "socialist realism" of some Marxist ideologists is the most explicit formulation of the arts as communication; it not only recognizes this function but argues that this is its major purpose. Lenin believed that art belonged to the people and should be understood and loved by them. The major goal of art, thus, should be realistic reflection of the class struggle and proletarian achievement. Idealistic, and even more, abstract modern art, was criticized as concealing these realities or as lacking in social significance and hence to be rejected. This view emphasizes the artists' search for approbation by their fellows and denies the validity of individual self-satisfaction. At the other extreme, apparent among some modern artists, artistic creation is seen as primarily or even solely for the gratification of artists who use whatever medium they choose to express their own ideas and emotions without reference to conventional symbols or meanings.

Whatever view is accepted, it appears that emotions and ideas are more explicitly expressed in such fields as painting, literature, music, and the dramatic arts than in others. We shall discuss the communication function of the arts further in the section that follows.

3. Art as Communication: Conventions and Formal Symbols

In the preceding section it was suggested that artists often seek to convey ideas and emotions. Insofar as they succeed, they are communicating to their fellows. In the discussion of Yurok and Karok basketry, it was pointed out that artists operate within a closely limited set of conventions. Such conventions are always present where communication is achieved.

This statement may be challenged by many artists in our society. In part, this is because the conventions within which the artist operates, whether in our own society or in a nonliterate society, are very largely unconscious, just as is most of cultural behavior. Literary artists, for example, operate within the framework of a system of symbols known as language, and language is taken for granted by most artists. Linguistic conventions, though in many ways rigid and unyielding, do of course allow for a certain degree of individuality and originality in the arrangement and handling of their elements. But these variations are severely limited; even an e. e. cummings, whose innovations are after all mainly in writing rather than in language, will not write in nonsense syllables. A Joyce or a Stein achieves certain effects by violating some superficial writing and linguistic conventions, but in so doing, limits the audience, at least until these innovations become more widely understood and appreciated.

And it should not be forgotten that unknown artists, or those of lesser stature, cannot so easily persuade their readers to tolerate radical innovations of writing and linguistic expression; their variations on the commonly accepted conventions may cause artists to lose touch with their readers altogether. In short, literary artists are bound rather closely by both a system of language and a system of writing that language, a bondage they cannot escape if they seek to communicate to any but a chosen few.

Similarly, in the field of painting, we accept in the first place the convention of two-dimensional representation of three-dimensional space. That this is a convention, and that the interpretation is learned, is indicated by reports that some peoples in Oceania, who have no two-dimensional art, are at first incapable of recognizing and interpreting photographs. In our own culture everyone is familiar with two-dimensional representation from a very early age. With a few exceptions, most modern painters still operate within the convention of two-dimensional representation, however much they may ignore other conventions.

In the theater, likewise, a room is commonly represented with only three sides; the fourth is, of course, removed so that the audience may view the action. Audiences accept this convention without question, despite its arbitrary and artificial character. Indeed, in recent years, audiences have even become accustomed to central staging, in which all walls are dispensed with and actors are surrounded by an audience on all four sides.

More elaborate and rigid conventions may depend upon formal symbols, which differ very little from the symbols used in language. In our own religious art, for example, a golden ring or halo above the head of a figure is used to denote a divine being and is so understood by most people in our society. It would have no such meaning to an ancient Mayan, who, on the other hand, would find no incongruity in a human figure with one arm ending in a serpent symbol to identify him as a particular deity. Symbolism, then, can be of two kinds: the acceptance of certain basic conventions upon which a whole art form is based, such as representing three-dimensional space on a two-dimensional canvas, and the use of particular symbolic items, such as a halo. In our own culture the use of specific symbols in art is relatively rare and is mainly associated with religious art. In other cultures, such as that of the ancient Mayas, the number of specific symbols was very great.

One of the truly great art expressions of the world was that of the Maya Indians of Central America, an art that maintained itself with varying but high quality over nearly 2,000 years. The Mayas were extremely skillful painters and sculptors and were able to represent the human body accurately in its most difficult positions; that is, as reclining, full face, three-quarter face, and so on. Their artists had also made a rather able development of perspective a number of centuries before it began to develop in European painting. Despite its technical excellence, however, much of Maya art is incomprehensible at first sight to people of our culture. Two major reasons exist for this. One is the Maya convention that deemed large vacant spaces in a composition to be undesirable. Accordingly, they filled these spaces with elaborate and ornate designs, and even used wholly meaningless elements merely to fill space. The

Cambodian woman making baskets. Mekong Valley. (Courtesy of the United Nations.)

second, and in some ways more important, reason was the high degree of religious symbolism involved. Maya art was primarily a religious art and incorporated a large number of formal symbols. These all conveyed significant meaning to a Maya; to the modern observer unversed in Maya art they are apparently meaningless insertions and even distortions of the main figures.

Not all art traditions utilizing formal symbolism are related directly to religion. The Indians of the Northwest Coast developed a great art tradition that is even more difficult for a person of our culture to understand than is that of the Maya. Again the element of formal symbolism is large. The Northwest Coast Indians represented a great many animal forms as well as mythical beings. The latter, of course, would not be understandable without a knowledge of the religious beliefs, but even representations of animals often may not be recognized by the untrained observer.

The Northwest Coast Indians sought, first, to adapt the form of the animal represented to the object to be decorated, and second, to represent, as far as possible, the whole animal. They did not, however, attempt a realistic view; as Boas has said, "with the exception of a few profiles, we do not find a single instance which can be interpreted as an endeavor to give a perspective and therefore realistic view of an animal." [5] Animal representations were, then,

[5] Franz Boas, "The Decorative Art of the Indians of the North Pacific Coast," *Bulletin of the American Museum of Natural History*, **9**:123–176 (1897), p. 176.

550

Argillite dish from Haida
Indians of Queen Charlotte
Islands, British Columbia.
(From the Sir Henry Wellcome
Collection. Courtesy of the
UCLA Museum of Cultural
History.)

Carving in granite of killer whale and human
figure. Tshimshan, northwest coast, North
America. (From the Sir Henry Wellcome Collection. Courtesy of the UCLA Museum of
Cultural History.)

"combinations of symbols of the various parts of the body of the animal," so arranged "that the natural relation of the parts is preserved, being changed only by means of sections and distortions, but so that the natural contiguity of the parts is observed." [6]

As an example, let us describe briefly a wooden box decorated with a carving or painting of the beaver. The front of the beaver was represented on the front of the box, the sides of its body on each side of the box, and the tail on the back of the box. On the bottom of the box was a view of the beaver's underside, and on the top, a similarly disconnected view of the beaver's back. In brief, the animal was, as it were, sectioned by the artist, and each section represented separately, but in its proper relation to other sections, on the object to be decorated.

Excellent designs were thus achieved, but of course the animal represented was completely unrecognizable to anyone ignorant of north Pacific coast culture. To the native, however, the representation was clear and unmistakable, for included in every design were formal symbols identifying the animal. Thus the beaver representation in the example given above would show two large incisor teeth, a scaly tail indicated by an ovaloid area hatched in a particular way, and a stick held between the forepaws. However differently a beaver might be pictured on objects of differing size and shape, these symbols would always be included, and so would identify the picture to the initiated viewer.

It is obvious from the preceding examples that visual art operates through symbolism to some degree and that it will convey certain meanings to persons familiar with the symbols. Similar circumstances could be demonstrated for the other arts also. As a vehicle for communication, however, the arts operate on a much broader and more subtle scale than through symbolism. Their effectiveness seems to stem from the fact that in general the arts entertain, they produce a certain "suspension of disbelief," and generally have some emotional quality to them. These other aspects of communication should be examined briefly.

4. Art as Communication: Uses

One of the uses of the arts as communication is to reinforce belief, custom, and values. In some art traditions this may be extended to instruction or propaganda. Thus religious art, whether expressed in the architecture of churches, in the presentation of religious scenes, or in the images of saints, serves first of all to create the emotional and intellectual atmosphere considered proper for religious exercises. It also serves as a constant reminder of aspects of belief, and in the form of drama it may take on a direct instructional purpose.

For example, throughout the Middle Ages, the Church, confronted with the problem of a large illiterate population in Europe, developed dramatic representations of important religious events or dogmas (the so-called mystery

[6] Ibid.

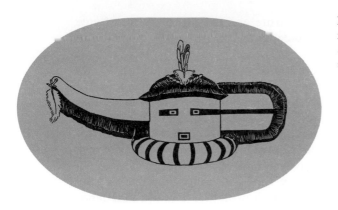

Figure 17-3   Dance mask used in religious ceremonies, Pueblo Indians, Southwestern United States, showing sophisticated use of asymmetry.

plays), both to educate and to reinforce knowledge of fundamental Christian doctrine. This device was transferred to Latin America for use in educating the Indian, where it met with considerable success and still persists in many places. Often such religious dramas are coupled with the dance, as in the Mexican *Pastores,* one of the better-known, but far from the only, survival, of the mystery plays in Latin America. Plays and pageants for children are common in many of the churches in the United States as well, particularly around Christmas, and are commonly used in many primary schools to teach young children. Adult schools for illiterates also use dramatic performances as teaching devices, especially in modern China.

Such use of the arts is common among many nonliterate peoples as well. The Pawnees, for example, had a ceremony before planting time in which the whole routine of the proper planting and care of corn was reviewed. Similar ceremonies occurred among a number of northwest Amazon tribes, among whom many religious ceremonials and dances occurred before planting time, interspersed with long recitatives regarding the proper planting and care of the plants appropriate to the season. In this way conservation of knowledge on a practical level was interwoven with religious belief; artistic performance involving drama, music, dance, and poetry; and a social occasion of considerable importance.

The study of nonliterate myth and folk tale also provides many similar examples in which beliefs and the value systems are reinforced and transmitted to the young. Such functions are not always obvious from the mere reading of tales, but they often become clear when the setting of the storytelling is examined. Many Indians of western North America, for example, told elaborate tales centering around the mythical figure of Coyote. Coyote was usually represented as a trickster who indulged in more or less malicious pranks as well as activities of the grossest and most immoral character, judged by native standards as well as our own. Such tales were frequently told in the presence of the young. Almost invariably, however, Coyote met with misfortune as a result of his behavior. The adults treated the stories as extremely funny, making clear that their laughter was at the improper behavior of Coyote and pointing the moral at the end that no good can come of such behavior. The parallel between the inevitable triumph of virtue and the discomfiture of vice in our own popular literature, from the so-called comic strip to many motion pictures, seems obvious.

The function of the arts in reinforcing knowledge, beliefs, attitudes, and values is fairly easily recognized in a simple homogeneous society. In a complex and heterogeneous society such as ours, the problem becomes more difficult, for not all groups within our society have the same beliefs, attitudes, and values. We may agree that virtue should always triumph, but definitions of virtue differ from group to group. The successful labor leader who wins better wages, hours, and working conditions may be a proper hero to members of his union, but he must be portrayed as a villain to satisfy many members of the employing group in our society. Making a motion picture about a real labor problem—certainly a significant aspect of our culture—is fraught with great difficulties, for a motion picture is very costly to make and hence must draw sizable audiences. The common assertion that commercialization of the arts is at the root of this problem seems an inadequate explanation. A ceremonial among nonliterates, which may give rise to expressions of design, dance, music, drama, and poetry, may involve many weeks of labor by virtually the entire group—the weaving of special baskets, the making of ceremonial regalia, the extensive rehearsals, the accumulation of large quantities of food—and hence economically requires much greater outlay proportionately than the making of a motion picture. The real point may be that in the homogeneous society everyone is agreed on the nature and purposes of the performance. The motion picture, on the other hand, can at best satisfy only a portion of the members of the society, and the temptation is strong to make it appeal to the widest possible audience. In the attempt to offend the fewest people, the motion picture product, then, is often trivial and inane.

On the other hand, the motion picture offers many possibilities for presenting, under the guise of entertainment, the viewpoints of special groups. Controlled primarily as they are by large financial interests, motion pictures are criticized by some as presenting a view of American life and aspirations conforming to that of bankers and employers. On the other hand, because motion pictures are made by individuals who are essentially employees, some people suspect the movies of being colored by contrary views. Pictures dealing with religion, race relations, labor relations, politics, and other similarly controversial topics almost always draw strong criticism from one group or another, to say nothing of Congressional investigations.

Although the element of communication is most obvious in such things as motion pictures and television, it is present frequently in most forms of art. Moods and emotions, rather than ideas, may be communicated, especially in music, the dance, poetry, and many forms of painting. And it must not be forgotten that an important function of the arts is the evoking of pleasure. The dance, for example, in our own society is very largely devoted to the pleasure of the participants, if we except the relatively small amount of professional dancing. Most young people in our society participate in dancing, and it has come to be closely associated with many other aspects of our culture, such as those that govern social occasions, courting procedures, and mate selection. It

Bark cloth mask, Papuan Gulf, New Guinea. (From the Sir Henry Wellcome Collection. Courtesy of the UCLA Museum of Cultural History.)

remains one of the few arts in our culture in which great numbers participate rather than being the observers of professional activities.

The whole problem of the arts as a means of communication is a very large one and, despite the very considerable literature, much research remains to be done. In the last two sections we have tried merely to indicate a few of the problems and to discuss some of the more obvious general conclusions. It is clear, however, that the problem is not confined to our own culture, where most of the research has been done by psychologists and sociologists, but that it presents universal aspects common to all cultures.

5. Art as Cultural Tradition

In the preceding sections we have noted that art invariably involves the use of conventions and symbols. The use of symbols, in art as in language, implies a body of common understandings among the members of a society, and carries as well the implication that these understandings are transmitted from generation to generation. Although the conventions and symbols of art are, at any particular time, more or less rigid and conservative, they do undergo change through time, just as any other aspect of culture.

Symbols and conventions afford perhaps the best indication that the arts belong to culture and partake in cultural processes and change. It is obvious, however, that all other aspects of art are likewise culturally determined. Techniques, the choice of subject matter, the preference or emphasis on this or that art, the functions of the arts, attitudes toward art and the artist—all these are cultural in character. To illustrate these points, we shall present a concrete example, drawn from a study of the potter's art among the Pueblo Indians.

The region around Kayenta in northeastern Arizona was occupied by a Pueblo people with a special local pottery-making tradition that lasted from about 700 A.D. to about 1300 A.D. In the course of those 600 years, the tradition underwent numerous changes in techniques, forms, and most particularly, in the character of the painted designs utilized. It is the painted designs that we shall discuss in subsequent paragraphs.[7]

During a period known as Pueblo I (±750–900 A.D.), the dominant pottery was decorated with poorly painted black designs on a white background. These were built upon a foundation of horizontal lines encircling the vessel. From these lines, in some cases, depended enrichments, such as ticks, dots, hooked triangles, and other geometric forms; in other cases, the spaces between lines were filled by various elements set in panels. (See Figure 17–4a.)

The second period, Pueblo II (900–1100), had two phases. The earlier was marked by a development of Pueblo I design but with thicker lines (Figure 17–4b). Some new fillers appeared, but the fussier decorations of Pueblo I disappeared. On the inside of bowls, the layout became radial in appearance (Figure 17–4c), although this was actually accomplished by widening the band with filled panels until it nearly covered the interior of the bowl. The changes were gradual and represent the development of a unified tradition.

In the later phase of Pueblo II, two new styles appeared. One shows many characters of the earlier style but with much more careful painting and design layout. Treatment of design elements changed, and many new elements, such as interlocking scrolls and frets, appeared (Figure 17-4d). Bowl interiors were treated quite differently: they were usually divided into three sections, the two outside being occupied by characteristic fillers, modified to fit the shape (Figure 17-4e). The second late Pueblo II design was simpler, with banding lines from which depended outlined figures, or with outlined fillers between lines, the figures then being filled with hatching (Figure 17-4f and g).

Although these three Pueblo II designs can be clearly distinguished from one another, there are many individual pieces of pottery that show elements

---

[7] Ralph Beals, George Brainerd, and Watson Smith, "Archaeological Studies in Northeastern Arizona," *University of California Publications in American Archaeology and Ethnology*, **44**:1–236 (1945).

Figure 17-4 Pottery designs from the Kayenta region, northeast Arizona, showing historical sequence over several hundred years. (a) Pueblo I black on white design elements; (b, c) early Peublo II black on white designs and arrangement on a shallow bowl divided in thirds; (d, e, and f) late Pueblo II black on white design elements and arrangement in bands or on shallow bowl with bilateral symmetry; (g, h) designs on Peublo II black on orange ware; (i) late Peublo III black on white design containing elaborations of elements in Pueblo I; (j) a late Pueblo III black on white element; (k) the same element on Peublo III black on orange ware. See text for fuller discussion. (After Beals, Brainerd, and Smith.)

from two or more. Or perhaps this can be better put by saying that many elements were common to the three traditions. The two late Pueblo II traditions, although using decorative elements in common with the earlier, seem to represent the effects of influences from outside the area under study. We also find in Pueblo II an orange pottery, usually covered with a red slip or coating on which were sometimes painted black designs similar, on the whole, to those on the black-on-white pottery of the same period. (See Figure 17-4g and h.)

Pueblo III (1100–1300) saw a tremendous variety of black-on-white pottery decoration. On certain large jars the layout of the design involved the elaboration of the hooked triangle used as a line enrichment in Pueblo I. (Compare the solid black lines of Figure 17–4i with the middle element of the second line in Figure 17–4a.) Elaborations of design on this basis also involved development of interlocking scroll designs. (Trace the white lines in Figure 17–4i.) The interlocking scroll design and many other elements as well as other types of design layout in Pueblo III black-on-white of the Kayenta area can be shown to appear earlier in the nearby Flagstaff area. Kayenta Pueblo III black-on-white pottery designs thus show some continuity from earlier designs in the region, but the influx of new elements and layouts creates a considerable discontinuity between Pueblo II and Pueblo III pottery designs in the region.

The case is quite different when we turn to the orange-ware pottery of Pueblo III. Shortly before the beginning of Pueblo III black-on-white types, there appeared a great flowering of the orange-ware types with polychrome decoration of red, black, and white paints in various combinations. To a very

Pottery stirrup-shaped bottle with painted bird-warrior figure. Mochica, Peru. (From the Sir Henry Wellcome Collection. Courtesy of the UCLA Museum of Cultural History.)

Portrait stirrup jar. Chimu, Peru. (From the Sir Henry Wellcome Collection. Courtesy of the UCLA Museum of Cultural History.)

Owl stirrup bottle. Truxillo (?), Peru. (From the Sir Henry Wellcome Collection. Courtesy of the UCLA Museum of Cultural History.)

Polychrome painted bowl in several colors. Nazca, Peru. (Courtesy of the UCLA Museum of Cultural History.)

considerable degree, the design layouts and the motifs used are those from the late Pueblo II black-on-white pottery (cf. Figure 17–4j and k). For perhaps 100 years, both black-on-white and orange-ware polychrome were at their climax in richness of design and abundance. In some instances they were certainly made by the same potters (evidenced by complete outfits for both types together with partially completed vessels found in the same graves), yet almost at no point are they identical in either design layout or design elements. In the case of polychrome pottery, we have a continuous tradition going back to the Pueblo I black-on-white, modified and elaborated, it is true, and enriched by some infiltration of outside influences. In the case of the black-on-whites, we have a discontinuity, with the Pueblo III black-on-whites derived mainly from outside, although utilizing a modification of the old spurred triangle in layouts of design, and developing quickly a great local richness and variation. Indeed, in the latter part of Pueblo III, the period of great cliff dwellings and open, large, multiple houses, there seems even marked differentiation in pottery decoration from town to town.

The great pottery tradition of the Kayenta area came to an end with the abandonment of the area about 1300. We could trace its influences among the ancestors of the modern Hopis, and perhaps even into modern Hopi pottery, but this seems unnecessary for our point.

The function of the decorated pottery of the Kayenta area is not certain. Cooking vessels were made in a different unpainted ware not described in this section. It is possible that the painted pottery was used for storage and perhaps for water carrying. It also seems likely that some, at least, of the pottery was used for ceremonial purposes. The decoration can only have been made for esthetic purposes. The variety and character of the decoration preclude the possibility that it had symbolic values to any extent. It seems reasonably certain that the decoration represented an esthetic design tradition that gave satisfaction to the maker through exercise of skill and taste, within the limits of the conventions of the group, and gave pleasure to the observer or user.

To recapitulate, then, Kayenta pottery design developed in black-on-white designs in Pueblo I, either through a wholly local development, or more probably, through the local adaptation of a design tradition borrowed from elsewhere. Through a long period of time it flourished through gradual enrichment and growth of skill, influenced from time to time by stimuli from other regions, but always keeping its distinctive local character.

At the beginning of Pueblo III times, attention focused on the previously little-decorated orange ware, and there was a great efflorescence of design and the addition of new colors, still basically in the same design tradition. Because of the general appearance of polychrome pottery in the Southwest about this time, we can guess that the stimulus for the new development came from outside, but again it was, in detail, primarily a local development. Shortly after the beginning of this efflorescence in orange ware, strong outside influences resulted in a considerable modification of black-on-white design. Although some influence in layouts of design persisted, in the main the elaborate Pueblo III decorative development in black-on-white came from borrowed designs and motifs. Yet this borrowed design tradition had come from a related tradition so that there is no absolute break.

As an art movement, then, we have a tradition continuing over some six hundred years with fairly narrow limits to the conventions employed. Within the limits of this tradition, however, there were opportunities for originality and change, which took place through both internal developments and external influences. At no time was there a complete break with the past, nor, if one viewed the whole area of painted pottery-making in the Southwest, would there be any doubt of the distinctiveness and continuity of the tradition. In the detailed study of this art form, we can see illustrated the general principles of cultural continuity and culture change.

With such a relatively limited area and concrete geometric designs it is possible to follow the movement as a cultural tradition fairly easily. But wherever we have a long documented tradition, we may see similar processes at work in other cultures. Painting in our own culture, in a general way, seems to indicate the same sort of history, although it is harder to document exactly. We shall summarize this history briefly in the section that follows.

6. Art as Cultural Tradition: European Art

The great tradition of painting in Euro-American culture began with the Renaissance. The development of perspective, perhaps the influence of the rediscovery of Greek civilization, the patronage of the Church, and the great intellectual ferments associated with the beginnings of the age of exploration, all apparently contributed to a great efflorescence of an art that had been relatively dormant, although not absent, in earlier periods.

A major characteristic of painting in the Renaissance was its realistic character. Great attention was paid to painting human and animal figures with correct anatomy. Landscapes show plausible if not exact trees, streams, hills, or buildings. Exact conformance to the conventions of perspective was required. Certain general, although not usually expressed, rules of composition were developed. Symbolism was present but confined mainly to religious art. Because much of early Renaissance art was religious, however, the amount of symbolism was considerable. Individual variation was in technical skill and virtuosity and in the individualization of landscapes and figures, particularly the human figure.

This tradition flourished through succeeding centuries, and seems not to have been seriously challenged until virtually the early part of the present century and the development of *abstract* schools of painting. (This term, *abstract*, as used here covers a variety of developments, but space does not permit additional elaboration.) Abstract artists in part turned inward, devoting themselves primarily to the expression of inner and personalized emotions and observations. Public reaction, on the whole, was adverse, because the new type of interest, for its failure to conform to the older conventions, did not communicate. Artists condemned the public for its inability to appreciate the new art, yet this lack of appreciation was the inevitable result of abandoning one set of conventions for another. The small but appreciative audience for modern art forms must be viewed as a group that has begun to understand the new conventions. It is difficult to see how artists who wish to paint for anyone but themselves can avoid either conforming to existing conventions or the establishment of new conventions that are understood by their audience. Many modern artists continue to conform to the convention of two-dimensional representation of three-dimensional objects. Others have entered upon a high degree of symbolism as well, employing, however, the less well-established symbols of psychoanalysis.

On the whole, the public has so far failed to absorb or understand the new conventions. The tradition of Renaissance art has continued to flourish where communication is demanded, for example, in the "socialist realism" of Russian painting. In western Europe and the United States, popular art (but not Pop art) and advertising are a direct continuation of the Renaissance tradition.[8] It is true that in both instances there has been some change of detail and, to some extent, a change of function. It perhaps is not irreverent, however, to suggest that the religious painting of the Renaissance was in effect a form of advertising.

The present period, then, is one in which most of the public and some of the artists are continuing in a long-established art tradition, in a fashion not dissimilar to the development of the pottery-painting tradition of the Kayenta region. For some decades, however, we have had a group of artists interested in a different type of art and endeavoring, unconsciously at least, to establish a new set of conventions. It would be interesting in this connection to know how the artists were regarded who first introduced the new Pueblo black-on-white tradition into the Kayenta region. Very likely they evoked the kind of responses so common in our society when new, radical, or modern art forms, whether in painting, sculpture, or music, are first presented to the public. Modern art is frequently condemned (both in Russia and the United States) as meaningless, crude, and fuzzy in conception and execution, childlike, or even disgusting or obscene. Those who make such criticisms, like most Americans, are steeped in Renaissance art conventions and deeply resent efforts to alter this tradition or to establish a different set of conventions. It is indeed entirely impossible to say at this time whether the innovations of modern art will succeed or not, but we may expect, at the least, that the Renaissance tradition will undergo slow but continuous change, and that there will be further changes of function, similar to that which has occurred with the movement of the tradition into the field of commercial and popular art.

7. Music

Our discussion has so far been couched in very general terms, with illustrations drawn mainly from various kinds of pictorial and decorative art. In this and the following section we shall offer a brief discussion of other art forms: music, poetry, and prose narratives.

[8] We are indebted for this idea to a suggestion by the late S. MacDonald Wright, although he is not responsible in any sense for the interpretation and development we have given here.

Of all the arts, music perhaps best illustrates the effect of cultural tradition in determining both social and individual standards of what is desirable and approved. The influence of the cultural tradition on standards of musical appreciation results often in a kind of physiological conditioning, to the extent that music that is pleasing and satisfying to members of one society may be no more than a physically painful cacophony to those of another. An excellent example is found in our own reaction to some types of Chinese music.

As is the case with most music outside the western European musical tradition, classical Chinese music uses a different scale from our own. In both scales each note represents a physically determinable sound wave. This, reaching the human ear, causes vibrations, which generate nerve impulses that are transmitted to the brain of the listener. Any musical scale can thus be described, in physical terms, as a set of wavelengths of varying size with fixed intervals between them. The major difference between the Chinese scale and our own rests in the use of a different system of intervals between the fixed points of the scale. It is these intervals rather than the absolute pitch of each note that the ear "perceives," and that cause acceptance or rejection of a particular type of music.

To the Western ear, classical Chinese music seems meaningless, inharmonious, and often downright unpleasant. To the Chinese, our music sounds much the same. Inasmuch as the physiological apparatus for the perception of sound is identical among the two peoples, we must conclude that the difference in appreciation is due to cultural conditioning. (Some simple kinds of Chinese folk songs, in contrast to the classical forms, may be quite appealing to the Western-trained ear.)

Dancing for pleasure is an important means of artistic expression in many cultures. Gopalpur, South India. (Photo by Alan Beals.)

This fact becomes clearer if we examine the history of Western music itself. Over a period of several centuries we find that various kinds of intervals within our own scale have varied in popularity. Sound combinations that one century considered dissonances have become commonplaces in another. Thus, little more than a half a century ago, Debussy was considered a radical in music. Most people considered his work ugly and full of dissonance. Today his works are generally regarded rather highly, for people have, through repetition, become accustomed to the intervals he employs. The history of the development of jazz likewise shows the influence of conditioning. Intervals once condemned as "barbaric" in early jazz music have in many cases crept into so-called classical music and are accepted today.

Such innovations are continuing. Arnold Schoenberg, for example, experimented with an entirely new arrangement of intervals, using in effect a twelve-note musical scale. For years his work was condemned by many, and public performances of his music were almost unknown. Only a small group of people gave them any appreciation. It is too early to say whether the work of Schoenberg will have a lasting influence on contemporary music, but it is interesting to observe that in recent years many of his works have been performed by major symphony orchestras in concerts for the general public. Perhaps most people are still puzzled, or even repelled, by Schoenberg's music, but many people who formerly would have rejected it entirely now find it at least interesting for an occasional performance. In the light of the past history of musical changes, it is entirely possible that in another half century Schoenberg's music will be entirely accepted and that the work of earlier composers will be considered insipid, meaningless, or even ugly.

In a somewhat similar fashion, the music of nonliterate peoples seems to most of those reared in European traditions to be a formless and meaningless jumble of sounds. On analysis, this proves not to be the case. It is true that the music of many nonliterate peoples emphasizes rhythm rather than melody, and that it is performed mainly by singing and simple percussion instruments rather than by a number of instruments producing different tones. Similarly the melodic intervals usually differ from our own, and harmony or tonal accompaniments to the melody are rare. Nevertheless the studies of musicologists have clearly shown that the music of all nonliterate peoples shows very definite patterns, and is not in the least random or chaotic. Usually, in any particular nonliterate society, there exist only a few acceptable patterns for the opening and closing phrases of songs; the series of melodic phrases making up the song are of standard length and utilize a limited number of combinations of intervals, with other possible combinations rarely if ever appearing. Moreover certain patterns can be shown to extend beyond a single tribe, and it is often possible to map out areas of common or similar musical tradition, just as it is possible often to establish culture areas for other phases of culture.

Recent studies by Alan Lomax suggest strongly that some aspects of musical style are associated with particular cultural types or levels. The implication is that the formation and spread of a particular musical style follow the same general processes as may be found in the origin and spread of a particular type of harpoon or other similarly tangible artifact class.

The occasions for music, among many nonliterate peoples, are extraordinarily varied and numerous. In Robert Lowie's account of the Crow Indians, to which we have frequently referred, songs are mentioned in connection with almost every activity. Mothers sing, and even compose, lullabies to their children. In many cases the children learn these as they grow older and sing them while playing, and sometimes all the children in the camp will learn a particular song. Young men wander through the camp at night, playing flutes to amuse and entertain their sweethearts, and not infrequently a young man may compose a love song to be sung outside the tipi of the girl he loves. Many men have their own sacred songs, which are learned in the course of their contact with supernatural powers in vision experiences and which are sung at times of grave personal crisis or in ceremonies and rituals. Ceremonial occasions are replete with singing, a principal technique of appealing to the supernatural powers.

Songs are also used to build up a martial and aggressive spirit for war parties. When a war party returns successfully and its members distribute their booty, the recipients of gifts will compose and sing songs of praise, recounting the brave deeds and extolling the generosity of the warriors. There are also mourning songs to honor the dead. But perhaps most frequent are songs of mockery, sung to ridicule a member of the society who has in some fashion failed to conform to accepted standards of Crow behavior. Clearly, music plays a most important role in Crow life, and the same appears to be true of many, if not all, nonliterate societies.

An interesting musical event, reminiscent of our own musical competitions, occurs among the Eskimos. During the spring, when many Eskimo families come together for feasts and ceremonies, there are frequent song contests. A man who has been injured by another, whether by theft, the destruction or misuse of his property, or another means, will compose a song ridiculing his opponent and challenge him to a contest. If the challenge is accepted, the injured man, to the accompaniment of furious drumming, will mock his opponent in song, accuse him of a long series of misdeeds, refer disrespectfully to his relatives, and otherwise expose him to ridicule. The opponent appears not to listen but in his turn sings a similar song, returning the charges in kind. No other hostilities take place; there is simply a long exchange of satirical and derogatory songs, which may go on for many evenings, and may even continue, at intervals, over several years. The spectators attend these contests with great interest, urging the contestants to their best efforts, and judging the skill with which each contestant composes and sings his songs.

8. Poetry and Prose

In many cases it is difficult to separate poetry from song. As among the Crows, most poetry is sung. Discussion of poetry likewise is hampered by its figurative and allusive language, often coupled with elaborate symbolism—qualities difficult to render in translation. Nevertheless the poetry of nonliterates clearly follows culturally determined traditions and often is of considerable charm even in translation.

Frequently poetic expressions are very brief, emphasizing in vivid form some cultural ideal. Lowie gives the following two songs or chants, revealed in visions to Crow warriors:

> *Whenever there is any trouble, I shall come through it. Though arrows be many, I shall arrive. My heart is manly.*
> *Eternal are the heavens and earth; old people are poorly off; do not be afraid [that is, do not be afraid of dying on the warpath]*[9]

Densmore quotes one of a Papago woman's curing songs as follows:

> *Brown owls come here in the blue evening,*
> *They are hooting about,*
> *They are shaking their wings and hooting.*[10]

[9] Robert H. Lowie, *The Crow Indians* (New York: Rinehart, 1935), p. 104.
[10] Frances Densmore, "American Indian Poetry," *American Anthropologist,* **28**:448–449 (1926), p. 448.

A visiting band entertains in Gopalpur, South India. Modern bands playing songs from motion pictures are gradually replacing traditional musical forms. (Photo by Alan Beals.)

Similarly, a Chippewa song is translated by Densmore:

> *I hear the birds before the day,*
> *I see the flowers beside the way.*
> *How can you sing, happy and free,*
> *How can you sing so close to me*
> *When I have lost my sweetheart?*[11]

The Polynesians are especially noted for their chants, which are applicable to many occasions, and often include long historical genealogies. The following example, without a genealogy, is given by Peter Buck; it is sung on the death of a chief.

> *Alas, the bitter pain that gnaws within*
> *For the wrecked canoe, for a friend who is lost.*
> *My precious heron plume is cast on Ocean's strand,*
> *And the lightning, flashing in the heavens,*
> *Salutes the dead.*
>
> *Where is authority in this world, since thou hast passed*
> *By the slippery path, the sliding path to death?*
> *Lone stands Whakaahu mountain in the distance,*
> *For thou art gone, the shelter of thy people.*
> *Flown has my singing bird that sang of ancient learning,*
> *The keel of Tainui, the plug of Aotea,*
> *Now bewailed by women's flowing tears.*
> *Beautiful lies thy body in thy dogskin tasseled cloak,*
> *But thy spirit has passed like a drifting cloud in the heavens.*
> *All is well with thee who liest in state on chieftain's bier.*
> *Ah, my precious green jade jewel, emblem of departed warriors!*
> *The dragon emerged from his rocky fastness*
> *And sleeps in the house of death.*[12]

The following chant expresses a major preoccupation of the Polynesians, famous for their long sea voyages:

> *The handle of my steering paddle thrills to action,*
> *My paddle named Kautu-ki-te-rangi.*
> *It guides to the horizon but dimly discerned.*
> *To the horizon that lifts before us,*
> *To the horizon that ever recedes,*
> *To the horizon that ever draws near,*
> *To the horizon that causes doubt,*
> *To the horizon that instills dread,*
> *The horizon with unknown power,*
> *The horizon not hitherto pierced.*

[11] Ibid., p. 449.

[12] Peter H. Buck, *Vikings of the Sunrise* (New York and Philadelphia: Stokes and Lippincott, 1938), pp. 282–283.

The lowering skies above,
The raging seas below,
Oppose the untraced path
Our ship must go.[13]

The poems given above illustrate a preoccupation with cultural ideals, with nature and supernatural forces, and the sheer expression of emotions so common in the poetry of all peoples. Similar examples are legion in non-literate societies; the items quoted are by no means unusual.

Little has been done so far in the purely literary analysis of the poetry of nonliterate peoples. Although extensive collections exist for some groups, most of these have been translated, more or less adequately, into English or some other European tongue; but precise analysis can be made only by studying poetry in the original language. Such features as prosody, rhyme, alliteration, and other similar poetic devices are necessarily lost in translation. Yet even in translation, certain literary characteristics may be seen, such as the parallel structure evidenced in the Polynesian sea chant given above. The few comparative studies so far made emphasize the fact that the poetry of all societies, like their music, adheres to well-defined standards of form and employs a common stock of poetic images and other literary devices that is often as standardized and as complex as our own.

Literary forms in prose, written or merely told, are found among all peoples. Major types include narratives (such as myths, legends, and other tales), proverbs, riddles, and puns. Whereas prose narratives, like songs, appear to be universal, proverbs and riddles appear to be most frequent in the Old World and are relatively very rare among the aboriginal peoples of the Americas. Puns are probably universal, but are so dependent upon an intimate knowledge of the languages in which they occur as to be extremely difficult to collect.

Among most nonliterate peoples, prose narratives are often of great functional importance. In many instances two major types may be discerned: myths and legends. Myths are usually stories laid in another world, quite different from that of the present, and stories in which the principal actors are gods, spirits, and other supernaturals. Legends, on the other hand, recount events that took place in the world as it is today, though often at some earlier time. Men are actors in legends, though supernaturals too not infrequently play important roles. The distinction between myths and legends, though a convenient one, is none too sharp; there are many tales that cannot easily be ascribed to one or the other category.

Myths frequently are concerned with origins—the creation of the universe and its various aspects, the origin of important cultural aids such as fire, the origins of significant food animals and plants, the beginnings of death or illness, the origins of the society itself and of its clans or other social segments, and the origins of ceremonies and rituals. We find many such tales among the Navajos; for example, a recent collection lists such titles as the origin of the Night Chant (an important curing ceremony), the people of the

---

[13] Ibid., p. 40.

lower world (an episode in the creation story), the origin of the Salt Clan, the origin of horses, the building of the first hogan (or Navajo house), and the first louse.

Other myths center about the actions of a culture hero or spirit, often individualized under the name of some animal. These tales are not infrequently arranged in a cycle or connected series of episodes. An example is found among the Mescalero Apaches, who tell a long cycle of stories dealing with Coyote, a trickster who is pictured sometimes as a human, sometimes as an animal. Coyote undergoes a host of experiences, now with this animal, now with that, which illustrate almost infinitely his dominant characteristics of greed, cupidity, cunning, and gluttony. Coyote is also impious and often stupid, and the stories of his adventures frequently evoke roars of laughter from the audience. But, at the end of this long cycle of tales, and after Coyote has run the gamut of his adventures, he is possessed by the culture hero, a divinity, and made the instrument of creation. Through him, the present universe and all living things of the earth, excepting only human beings, are brought into being. Once this has been accomplished, Coyote is himself reduced to the status of an animal, and the culture hero, together with other divinities, completes the creation and makes the world habitable for humans.

Legends are more mundane in content, though these tales too include their share of the wonderful, the awesome, and the supernatural. The Mescaleros relate numerous tales of the Mountain Spirits and of man's contacts with them. These are, in a sense, vision experiences, that tell how a person, often caught up by some crisis or dangerous situation, is assisted by the Mountain Spirits, taken to their holy home, instructed in a ceremony, and returned to his people.

Proverbs and riddles are exceedingly common in Africa, where they function as a kind of repository for the wisdom of the group. In some parts of Africa, indeed, proverbs are used much as legal precedents are used in our courts; both the complainant and the defendant, in West African court procedure, quote proverb after proverb to support their claims.

As with the other forms of art, the prose literature of a group shows a definite style and reflects aspects of the culture. In a study of Hawaiian literary style, it is pointed out that the choice of subject and the treatment of character reflect the aristocratic society of aboriginal Hawaii. The tales characteristically use hyperbole or exaggeration, especially with respect to the hero of a tale, colorful metaphors and similes, symbolism, great emphasis on details such as long name lists, antithesis, and repetition. Humor is abundant but is mainly based either on punning or on scatological reference; sarcasm is rare. Certain Polynesian linguistic features that make alliteration and repetition or parallel structure easy are extensively developed.

In general, tales show their derivation from the cultural and social setting in which they occur more clearly than other art forms. The function of tales is likewise usually more obvious than with other arts; in most cases they clearly either afford explanatory statements about the universe and its origins or emphasize group values and ideals, often with a definitely didactic purpose. Very often a single tale will combine several such functions. With all the reasonably obvious functional significance of the tale, however, it should not be overlooked that the tale also entertains. Tales are not told simply to impress the young or one's fellows with proper and improper ways of behavior, or to explain the gods; they are also told because the teller and his hearers enjoy the process.

9. Summary

Although not all of the arts are equally developed, or even represented, in every culture, there are no societies that lack artistic activities altogether. Moreover, it seems clear that art was a part of culture from its earliest beginnings, though its traces are few even in Paleolithic cultures and are restricted to art forms such as painting and sculpture. It is the universality of art and its probably great antiquity that suggest that artistic activities apparently satisfy some deeply rooted psychological need, common to all mankind.

Art forms are numerous and include such major activities as pictorial or representational arts (for example, painting and sculpture), literary arts (including the songs and stories of nonliterate peoples), the dramatic arts, and decorative arts. Art is defined as an activity that, over and above its practical or utilitarian values, brings satisfaction both to the artist and to those who participate in his work as beholders, audience, or collaborators. It is this esthetic component that distinguishes art from other aspects of culture.

Works of art, like tools, weapons, and other artifacts, are of course made by individuals, working alone or in collaboration with others. Groups or societies, as such, produce nothing. Yet it should also be understood that artists do not live in isolation; they are always members of a particular society and they always participate in a particular culture. As such, their work is profoundly influenced by the cultural patterns of their times, and becomes not an entirely individual product, but a product of the culture as well.

In addition to the fact that artistic activities result in esthetic satisfactions to artists, performers, audiences, or participants, they also have other functions. One such function is communication; to a greater or lesser degree, all arts serve as media for the communication of emotions, ideas, attitudes, and values. The efficiency with which artists communicate depends on the degree to which the conventions and symbols they use are understood and appreciated by their fellows. In small and homogeneous societies, there is often only a single system of conventions and symbols, common to all members of the society. In large heterogeneous societies, on the other hand, conventions and symbols may differ from one group to another within the society, and so often restrict the artist's audience. Systems of conventions and symbols, though they vary in their rigidity from one society to another, always allow for some degree of individuality and innovation, even in nonliterate societies. Changes in systems of conventions and symbols are slow and come about through innovations by individual artists or by the adoption of new ideas from other cultures.

Because art serves often as a medium of communication, it functions also to conserve and reinforce beliefs, customs, attitudes, and values. Nearly all arts have this function, though it is perhaps most evident in the literary and pictorial arts. In some instances the arts may be used for instructional purposes or to propagandize; an instance is found in the so-called mystery plays of the medieval European church.

Art may be identified as activities involving an esthetic component, but artists and their products function within a larger cultural context. It is possible to isolate the subsystem of art for special study, but it cannot be understood fully except as part of the total sociocultural system in which it occurs. The social context of art—that is, the portion of the sociocultural system within which art is made and used—not only reveals the relationship between art and society, but "is a main junction point of the process by which the art forms are transmitted through time and space."[14]

Collateral Reading

Beals, Ralph L., George W. Brainerd, and Watson Smith. "Archaeological Studies in Northeast Arizona," *University of California Publications in American Archaeology and Ethnology*, **44**:1–236 (1945). Includes effort to trace the changes of a unified design style over time.

Boas, Franz. *Primitive Art*, New Edition. New York: Dover Publications, Inc., 1955. An anthropological classic still worth reading.

Boas, Franz. *Race, Language and Culture*. New York: Macmillan Publishing Co., Inc., 1940. See "The Development of Folk-tales and Myths," pp. 397–406; "Mythology and Folk-tales of North American Indians," pp. 451–490; "Stylistic Aspects of Primitive Literature," pp. 491–502; "Representative Art of Primitive People," pp. 535–540; "The Decorative Art of the North American Indians," pp. 546–563. A series of essays on special problems still of basic importance.

Day, A. Grove. *The Sky Clears, Poetry of the American Indians*. New York: Macmillan Publishing Co., Inc., 1951. A convenient collection.

Dundes, Alan. *The Study of Folklore*. Englewood Cliffs, N.J.: Prentice-Hall, Inc., 1965. Outlines new methods in the study of folklore beyond tracing distributions and motifs.

Fontenrose, Joseph. *The Ritual Theory of Myths*. Berkeley and Los Angeles: University of California Press, 1966. Examines the relation of ritual and myth.

Jacobs, Melville. *The Content and Style of an Oral Literature: Clackamas Chinook Myths and Tales* (Viking Fund Publications in Anthropology, No. 26). Chicago: University of Chicago Press, 1959. An unusual and important approach to the study of oral literature.

Kirk, G. S. *Myth: Its Meaning and Functions in Ancient & Other Cultures*. Berkeley and Los Angeles: University of California Press, 1973. Evaluation of diverse approaches to the study of myth.

[14] Phillip H. Lewis, "The Social Context of Art in Northern New Ireland," *Fieldiana*, **58** (1969), 9 (Chicago: Field Museum of Natural History.)

Lewis, Phillip H. "The Social Context of Art in Northern New Ireland," *Fieldiana*, Vol. 58, 1959. Chicago: Field Museum of Natural History. An art historian decides his subject must be put in social context and goes to the field to try out his ideas.

Lomax, Alan. *Folk Song Style and Culture*, Publication No. 88. Washington, D.C.: American Association for the Advancement of Science, 1968. A major new approach to the study of music in relation to culture.

Malinowski, Bronislaw. *Myth in Primitive Psychology*. New York: W. W. Norton & Company, 1926. A functionalist approach to the explanation of myths.

Marschack, Alexander. *The Roots of Civilization: The Cognitive Beginnings of Man's First Art, Symbol and Notation*. New York and Toronto: McGraw-Hill Book Company, 1972. Argues for presence of complex notational systems associated with day, lunar, seasonal, and ceremonial sequences.

McAllester, David P. (ed.). *Readings in Ethnomusicology*. New York: Johnson Reprint Corp., 1971.

Nettl, Bruno. *Music in Primitive Culture*. Cambridge, Mass.: Harvard University Press, 1956. Presents views of a leading student of non-Western music.

O'Neale, Lila M. "Karok-Yurok Basket Weavers," *University of California Publications in American Archeology and Ethnology*, **32**:1–182 (1932). One of rare studies focusing on the makers rather than the objects produced.

Rothenberg, Jerome (ed.). *Shaking the Pumpkin: Traditional Poetry of the Indian North Americas*. Garden City, N.Y.: Doubleday & Company, Inc., 1972.

Smith, Marian W. (ed.). *The Artist in Tribal Society, Proceedings of a symposium at the Royal Anthropology Institute*. New York: The Free Press, 1961. These papers are unusual in emphasis on the artist rather than his products.

Spradley, James P., and George E. McDonough (eds.). *Anthropology Through Literature*. Boston: Little, Brown and Company, 1973.

Turner, Victor. *Dramas, Fields and Metaphors: Symbolic Action in Human Society*. Ithaca, N.Y.: Cornell University Press, 1974.

18/Culture and the Individual

1. Replication of Uniformity: Organization of Diversity

It is sometimes convenient to regard a cultural tradition as something that is learned by successive generations of individuals who then obediently execute the various kinds of behavior encouraged by tradition. In this view, human beings are passive receptacles of cultural materials. They are indoctrinated, brainwashed, enculturated, socialized, trained, or educated to become conforming members of their society. Here the effect of a cultural tradition is to encourage what Anthony F. C. Wallace has called "the replication of uniformity."[1] Deviance and mental illness, to say nothing of creativity, can be considered to result when the individual is improperly enculturated and hence is unable to perform conformingly as a member of his culture. From this point of view, some cultural traditions make greater demands upon the biologically given capabilities of human beings than do others, and the individual members of such cultural systems accordingly have much greater difficulty in maintaining their mental health than do members of more "natural" cultural systems.

The view of cultural traditions and their transmission as involving the replication of uniformity is essentially a

[1] Anthony F. C. Wallace, *Culture and Personality* (New York: Random House, 1961), pp. 26–27.

distant and outside view of the processes of personality formation. It is a way of examining questions about the ways in which the members of a particular cultural tradition are like each other and different from the members of other cultural traditions. In other words, there are some ways in which all Crow Indians respond to the world around them differently than do Japanese or Englishmen. Although this general approach may sometimes lead to a glib labeling in which whole peoples are characterized as "neat," "aggressive," "fearful," or even "paranoid," there is little doubt that members of particular cultural systems tend to share particular personality traits that may contrast sharply with some personality traits shared by members of another cultural system.

By the same token, and on the basis of closer examination, the personalities of different members of the same cultural tradition may be quite different. On many dimensions the range of variation in personality within a particular culture may be much greater than the range of personality variation between cultural systems. In this view, to use Wallace's words again, the range of personalities within a cultural system reflects "an organization of diversity" even more than it reflects a "replication of uniformity." Individuals within a cultural system are bound to differ in many ways because (1) they are biologically different, (2) they have different life experiences, and (3) different things are expected of them depending upon such things as their age, sex, birth order, bodily appearance, stature, and social position.

Another tendency of the early research concerning child training or enculturation was the assumption that all children in the same culture were raised in much the same way and that all learned much the same things. While it is true that all children must learn enough about their culture to be able to function successfully within it (there are certain things that everyone must learn), it is not true that all must function in the same ways within their culture or that all must have access to identical information about their culture. In the common situation, where the infant interacts primarily with its mother and the mother is therefore the primary agent of enculturation, the child who lacks a mother or an effective substitute mother may still learn to function adequately. A firstborn child, who has exclusive access to the mother, receives quite different treatment from later-born children, who must share their mother with others. Although there are ideal patterns of child rearing in every culture, it is folly to expect that very many children will be reared under conditions approaching the ideal. The fact that children in any culture are reared in a variety of different ways places further difficulties in the way of establishing precise relationships between child-rearing practices and adult characteristics of behavior and personality.

In the end, we may be certain that there are great differences in the ways in which children are reared in different cultures, and that these differences both result from and account for observable differences between cultures in adult behavior. In addition to the fact that it is impossible to produce a set of individuals with identical personalities, there is the question about why anyone should want to do so. Cultural systems operate because their memberships share particular attributes that enable them to work together, but they also

Fanti father and child. Ghana. In most cultures fathers play an important role in child care. (Kindness of David Kronenfeld.)

operate because their members are sufficiently different from each other to permit them to carry out different kinds of tasks effectively and to express different viewpoints. Within the limits set by the need to find some common ground, cultural systems not only permit but positively encourage the development of a wide range of personality types.

Although the concept of personality is a familiar one, many of the problems involved in explaining the relationships between culture and the individual lie in the considerable difficulties involved in conceptualizing personality. When we collect verbal statements and behavioral observations about a cultural tradition, we suppose that we are collecting something resembling the rules of a game or the script of a play. When we do the same thing, using personality as a guiding concept, we suppose that our observations of some particular individual will lead us to some sort of understanding of why he behaves the way he does, how he understands the rules of the game, and the manner in which he proposes to play it. Presumably, if an individual plays Ping-Pong in an aggressive way, he will also play tennis, golf, and double solitaire in an aggressive way, and we might be justified in saying that he or she has an aggressive personality. Of course, we know from common experience that an aggressive Ping-Pong player is not necessarily aggressive in other activities. We could ask if the individual's aggressive way of playing Ping-Pong is some sort of personality trait or if it is some sort of cultural trait, perhaps reflecting the sports tradition in which the player was educated. In the United States it is strictly forbidden to tell the hostess at a dinner party that the vegetables were underdone and the meat tough. It is a strongly reinforced cultural imperative that the dinner be praised and the hostess thanked. If we interpreted this cultural standard as an example of personality, we would have to say that people in the United States have deceitful personalities or perhaps a weak grasp of reality.

Perhaps the most useful way of distinguishing between the concept of culture and the concept of personality is to view personality as a theory concerning the consistencies in the behavior of the individual and the manner in which they are generated. Culture, by contrast, has to do with the consistencies evident in the functioning or operation of a cultural system. The usefulness of the concept of personality depends upon the extent to which the individual maintains his special way of acting as he moves from situation to situation; the usefulness of the concept of culture depends upon the extent to which individual behaviors can be seen as taking place with reference to a particular set of cultural standards. All of these problems — the replication of uniformity, the organization of diversity, the development and maintenance of the personality, and knowledge of cultural standards — involve processes of teaching and learning, which are discussed in the following sections.

2. Learning to be Human

Enculturation is the process whereby all normal human individuals learn how to talk, to act, and presumably to think in the ways characteristic of their cultures. Terms like *socialization* and *cultural transmission* are generally used as synonyms for *enculturation,* but all three terms are sometimes given specialized meanings. The primary meanings of all three terms have to do with the manner in which the infant and child is transformed into an adult, but all three may also be used to refer to more specialized training and learning that take place in later life.

At the time of birth the human infant has already spent some nine months in the mother's womb. During that time development of the infant has been affected in a largely undetermined degree by the various cultural forces that have affected the mother. In particular, the mother's state of health and nutrition and the kinds of activities she has engaged in may have an impact upon the unborn child. Before birth, environmental forces have commenced the process of interaction with the infant's genetic potentials which will determine their expression. The newborn infant is already a biocultural, rather than a purely biological, being.

The fact that cultural and other environmental forces begin to exert an influence upon the development of the child while it is still in an embryonic stage should not be taken to mean that the child's genetic potentials will automatically be warped or frustrated. Very often a cultural setting provides precisely the circumstances which, as far as we know, lead to the optimum develop-

Sioux Indian child asleep on cradle board. Child spends early months of its life completely immobilized except when removed for morning and evening clean-up. Once removed from the board, child rapidly acquires normal physical skills. (From the Morrow Collection. Courtesy of W. H. Over Museum.)

ment of the individual's genetic potentials. Because the biological and cultural factors in human development are inextricably tangled from the very beginning, it has proved impractical to identify the purely biological aspects of human development in any detail. From a biological point of view, certain abilities and receptivities appear to develop in fairly regular order. The child must stand before it can walk, babble before it can talk, and so on. The onset of such stages of life as puberty and menopause seems to relate to biological programming, and there is considerable evidence of the progressive development of intellectual or cognitive abilities. Although it is possible to chart these and many other evidently biological developments in terms of the order in which they develop and the age of the growing organism, cultural and environmental influences may slow or speed the process of growth and may even change the order in which particular characteristics appear. South Indian rural infants, who are constantly carried by parents or older siblings, tend to develop verbal abilities comparatively rapidly but are rather slow in learning to walk. The reverse is true of infants in the United States, who are encouraged to walk but are isolated from the flow of conversation.

Psychologists in recent years have shown that in many animals the capacity to respond to various stimuli appears at different stages in the development process. In some cases, if appropriate stimuli are not presented at the right period of development, the organism loses its capacity to respond. Newborn chicks kept in total darkness and fed by hand past a certain age may never learn to peck at objects or to feed themselves. Although there is little evidence that human beings ever lose their ability to learn new tricks, there is evidence that many abilities are best learned at particular stages in development. Many educational psychologists now believe that abilities to read and count, as well as to develop many social skills, should be developed long before the child enters the first grade.

The growth of the child represents in part the unfolding of a largely predetermined set of biological capacities; it also represents the very often conscious efforts of parents, siblings, peers, and other interested parties to create a particular kind of person. Each culture establishes certain conventional ways of rearing an infant—how often the baby is to be held, how frequently it should be allowed to nurse, when it should be toilet trained, whether it should be breast-fed or bottle-fed, whether it should be confined or allowed to wander, when it should be punished or rewarded, when it should be spoken to or listened to, and infinitely more questions and possibilities form the kinds of materials that make up the conventional standards of child rearing in particular cultures.

Early students of the relationship between culture and the individual, often influenced by Freudian emphases upon the importance of traumatic experiences, attempted to interpret personality formation in terms of the influence of particular child-training practices upon development. Swaddling (wrapping a child tightly in blankets), early weaning, or harsh toilet training were all thought to mark the child for life and to play a major role in the establishment of adult patterns of neurosis which were thought to be characteristic in each culture. A more current view is that although some particular practices in almost any system of child rearing are unpleasant for the child and may have important consequences in particular cases, personality formation depends more upon the context in which particular practices are carried out and the degree to which particular sorts of messages are reinforced or repeated. The simple fact of early weaning is unlikely to have a major impact upon the child, unless it is reinforced by a whole series of related practices that involve punishment, withdrawal of affection, or pressure to achieve in similar ways.

The Manus, a Pacific Island people studied by Margaret Mead in the 1920s, were a water-dwelling people who lived on pile houses set in the midst of a lagoon.[2] For the Manus child one of the challenges of life involved an ability to survive in the water. By the time the child was a year old, it had been trained to grasp its mother firmly about the neck while it was carried from place to place. It could now ride with its mother in a canoe, clinging fast to its mother even when the canoe overturned and plunged both into the cold and salty water. Parents continually watched their children and were always there to pull them out of the water should they fall through the floor boards of the house or off the canoe. Once the baby could toddle, it was put down in shallow water to play. Watching older children, the child learned to swim by the age of three. As soon as swimming was mastered, the child was given a 5- or 6-foot canoe, and soon, before his fourth birthday, was able to punt a large canoe while the father sat at ease amidships.

During this process of learning, each improvement was noted and lavishly praised. Once a child learned to perform, it was never permitted to refuse to perform. The child was never nagged or afflicted with don't's; it was constantly watched. When it failed, the failure was overlooked or the child might be scolded. Invariably the child was rescued and encouraged to continue the activity. The child who attempted to walk and suffered a painful fall received no sympathy; favorable attention was reserved for the child who tried and succeeded. Although the child might suffer the pain and upset of falling in the water or falling down, the parent was always there to prevent serious injury.

What were the effects of this pattern of training? First, children had no fear of serious injury as a result of drowning or falling. Second, no child failed to learn basic water skills. Third, all children, and of course adults as well, developed what Mead describes as "perfect" motor coordination. Clumsiness was unknown, and there was no word for clumsiness in the language.

Although people in Manus considered property sacred and might even mourn lost property as one might mourn a dead relative, no attempt was made to place property out of the reach of children. Rather, the mother constantly watched the baby, rebuking it and chastising it if it touched anything not its own. In dealing with Mead, Manus children would not expropriate so much as a piece of wastepaper without asking permission first. Theft of the tail of a fish, the expropriation of bits of food found floating in the water, or the taking of an extra bit of food were considered crimes as severe as any other kind of theft. The breaking of an old cracked pot was no more permitted than the breaking of a new one. Whether encouraging physical proficiency by means of

[2] Margaret Mead, *Growing up in New Guinea* (New York: Dell, 1968).

praise or discouraging theft by means of punishment, the Manus parent was inexorably consistent and eternally vigilant, with the result that desired behaviors emerged rapidly and solidly while undesired behaviors were extinguished. By the age of three, the child had developed basic physical skills, an abhorrence of theft, an ability to talk, and an extreme fastidiousness about undressing in the presence of others. Following this, there was virtually no attempt to teach obedience, respect, or deference to parental wishes. A two-year-old might refuse to go home with its mother; children were not expected to be home at mealtime; and no work was expected of them.

Language skills and many of the skills learned later in life tend to be learned through a process of repetition and imitation. The Manus seem to develop early what Mead has called "an affection for repetitiousness"[3] and a love of imitation. When the baby uttered a word, a nearby adult was almost certain to repeat it, and baby and adult might then repeat the same word up to sixty times. Adults also imitated children's gestures. Children freely imitated adult behavior, copying every gesture and expression. Dancing, drumming, fighting, and fishing were also learned primarily by direct imitation of adults or older children.

In the traditional South Indian village of Gopalpur during the 1960s, observed child-rearing practices were strikingly different from those employed at Manus. South Indian parents believed that children were incapable of learning anything else until they learned to talk. Thus virtually all attempts to teach the small child involved teaching it to talk. In doing this parents or, more likely, grandparents would hold the child in their arms and point things out to them: "There goes your sister; there goes your mother; look, there's a bird." Children's verbalizations were usually not imitated. The child learned language quickly as a result of being constantly addressed by adults and older children.

People in Manus placed a heavy emphasis on physical competence, people in Gopalpur made no effort to develop muscular skills in children. The baby was in fact prevented from crawling or attempting to walk during the first two or three years of life. It was kept either in a hanging cradle or, if restless, carried about by a parent or older sibling. Older siblings who put the child down while they went off to play were severely thrashed. As soon as the child began to talk, parents began to give it orders and instructions. Although parents scolded children vigorously when such instructions were ignored, serious attempts at discipline by slapping or beating did not begin until the child was six or seven years old. Children old enough to walk were generally kept outside the house, coming inside only to demand food, at which time they might well be assigned some small task or sent off on an errand. By the age of four, certainly by the age of six, the child was gradually inducted into adult work, and children soon learned to eat and run out of the house while ignoring the mother's complaints about their laziness and unproductivity. Between four and six, the child spent most of its time in a play group composed of other children. For girls, children's play consisted of grinding grain

South Indian father with children. Except when asleep, children are held and carried constantly by whoever is available. Gopalpur, South India. (Photo by Alan Beals.)

and preparing food and, for boys, of planting and plowing. Older children played more elaborately but still very often in imitation of adult activities. Although imitation was an important means of learning in both Manus and South India, imitation in South India was mostly indirect. In South India, the child observed adult activities and later tried to imitate them, whereas in Manus, the child directly imitated whatever the adult was doing at the time. In both societies the children's play group was the prime means of enculturation following early childhood. In both societies the few toys were scaled-down versions of adult equipment. In South India children's play tools and equipment were rarely manufactured by adults, and sticks and branches often served as poor substitutes for plows, drama costumes, or cooking utensils.

Although South Indian girls were sometimes able to avoid all forms of work and training on the grounds that they would soon enough, perhaps at the age of eight or nine, be victimized by their future mothers-in-law, boys were often pushed to work as early as six when they might be asked to herd sheep or cattle. Fathers generally turned such heavy agricultural chores as plowing over to their sons by the time they were nine or ten. Otherwise, attempts to push or encourage the development of the child were negligible, and men pro-

Grinding with toy handmill. Many of children's play activities mimic adult work. Gopalpur, South India. (Photo by Alan Beals.)

tected by fathers or older brothers might live their whole lives without acquiring any knowledge of such essential techniques of life as political maneuver or economic exchange. In contrast, Manus children were expected to perform early and excellently at a variety of tasks.

Child-rearing techniques in both Manus and India are strikingly different from our own, although there are many parallels. Neither in Manus nor in South India is there the fear of failure that characterizes the relationship of parents and children in the United States. In Manus much is expected of children, but the child that fails is simply considered to be "not ready," and training efforts are redoubled until the child succeeds. In the United States the child that walks or talks a little later than its peers is likely to be labeled "slow" or "dumb" by its parents, and affection may be withdrawn from a "spoiled" or "rotten" child that has thus disgraced its parents. The Manus parent reacts with total dismay to the destruction of the least bit of property; the U.S. parent discriminates between valuable property, which should not be destroyed, and valueless property, which the child is permitted to destroy virtually at will. The U.S. child is surrounded with objects and property, in-

Boys pretending to be actors in drama. Gopalpur, South India. (Photo by Alan Beals.)

cluding toys, to a degree that would be astounding to Manus or South Indian children.

It would be possible to go on at almost infinite length concerning variation in child-rearing techniques between cultures. What is to be learned varies from culture to culture, and so does how it is learned. There is important variation in the manner in which children in different cultures learn such standard things as how to walk and to talk. Without question, differences in child-rearing techniques lead to characteristic differences in the ways people in different cultures behave. These differences may involve deep-seated personality characteristics as well as relatively shallow ones. There are, however, difficult problems involved in determining just what sorts of personality differences exist or just how important they are in determining differences in behavior.

Due to differences in individual experience and genetic inheritance, there is a wide range of personality types in any culture. Further, individuals in all cultures must react in a variety of different ways to a variety of different situations. A young man who is a husband or father, or a young woman who is a wife or mother, surely behaves differently from a young man or woman who has acquired neither role. Does this mean that a deep-seated personality change has taken place, or does it mean that the personality is simply obscured by the assumption of some particular social role or by the adjustment to some particular situation?

For example, in the case of Manus, Margaret Mead discovered that following her initial visit during the late 1920s, the people of Manus had engaged in a rapid modernization of their culture. Mead attributes the rapid change in Manus culture to "the form of their educational experience [which] gave them potentialities for change which would be lacking in people differently educated."[4] Certainly we can see in the physical ability of the Manus children, and in their self-confidence and willingness to learn, a potential for change and adjustment. This could be taken to mean that there was a happy and fortuitous correspondence between the traditional Manus personality and the personality required for modernization.

In South India the village of Gopalpur remained relatively traditional and unmodern in the 1960s. Perhaps the lack of modernity in Gopalpur could be attributed to particular aspects of child-rearing techniques. Certainly people in Gopalpur lacked mechanical skills, and their training or lack of training may

[4] Mead, ibid., p. 6.

School radio receiving set at Kavieng, New Guinea. The rapid introduction of new and sometimes conflicting ideas is a characteristic of modernization. (From the Australian Government, Courtesy of the United Nations.)

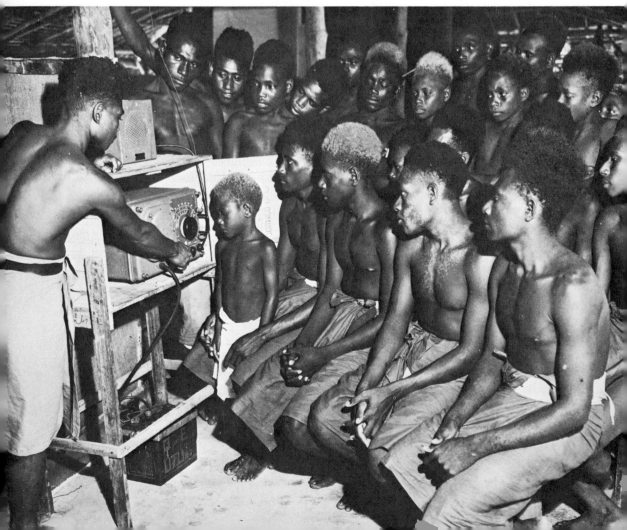

have made them notably incurious about the world around them. Equally important perhaps, and in contrast to both the United States and Manus, was the
lack of any strong pressure to learn things quickly. Perhaps if the children of
Gopalpur were taught in the way that the children of Manus or Middletown,
U.S.A., were taught, rapid modernization would occur.

On the other hand, many villages in India have in fact modernized as
quickly as Manus and presumably on the basis of a child-rearing pattern and a
personality development little different from that characteristic of Gopalpur.
In fact, at the present moment almost all peoples of the world are modernizing
in different ways and in different degrees, and it can be argued that the wash of
modernization across the world proceeds at its own pace and in blithe
disregard of differences in child-rearing techniques or personality characteristics. This could mean that the range of personality types in any society is
sufficient to permit the development of individuals capable of implementing
modernization, or it could mean that any ordinary human being, regardless of
his or her training or personality, is capable of adjusting to a wide range of
new circumstances including modernization.

Modernization often has to do with the interaction of small traditional
societies or communities with massive economic and political forces over
which they have little control. It is surely helpful if people have child-training
practices and personalities that are adapted to modernization combined with
a strong desire for modernization. Besides this, people must have a source of
cash income, for modernization costs money. They must also exist in a political and economic setting in which it is possible for them to act cohesively and
to avoid being robbed, enslaved, or exterminated. A host of conditions must be
met before modernization or any other kind of change can take place. Having
the right kind of child-rearing technique or the right kind of personality is
probably one of those conditions, but its importance is likely to vary from situation to situation.

The same kind of logic applies to the question of personality change and
stability. Modernization probably does require deep-seated personality change
in some peoples or in some individuals, and the habits of a lifetime are difficult to change. Nevertheless abrupt change in personality is a feature of the
careers of many individuals in all cultures. In cultures like Manus such a
change, sometimes called a discontinuity in child rearing, was actually institutionalized. The Manus child's complete freedom from adult control and
responsibility ended abruptly at marriage, when the man assumed the burden
of repaying those who paid for his wedding, and the girl became the slave of
her in-laws and the victim of her husband's wrath. It is hard to believe that
such grim, hardworking parents evolved from such merry and irresponsible
young people.

The process of becoming human, of learning one's culture and acquiring a
personality, is extraordinarily complicated and therefore hard to study in any
complete and detailed way. The events of childhood almost certainly have a
considerable effect upon the development of adult character, but so do many
other things. Personality change and development continue throughout life,
some people changing more than others. Child-rearing practices and personal-

ity types characteristic of particular societies undoubtedly have an impact upon the manner in which each society adapts to changing circumstances, but it is unlikely that very many societies or individuals possess rigidities so great as to make adaptation impossible. Thus all peoples modernize, but perhaps some have child-training practices and a range of personality types that make it easier for them than for others. Existing differences among human societies and among human individuals create the possibility that particular kinds of child-rearing practices and personality types may be more suited for some kinds of situations than for others. Cultures that are "conservative," whose members refuse to do what some outsider thinks they should do, are sometimes held to be dominated by those of ineffective or deficient personality. Opposed to this idea is the thought that cultural "conservatism" often results from the wisdom of people who are unwilling to buy a pig in a poke or who are unable for economic and political reasons to make the changes that someone else recommends. The society that won't change is analogous to the child that won't learn. Is it because the child is deficient or because the conditions for learning are absent? These questions will be taken up again in discussions of cultural change. For the moment it is sufficient to note that important problems in ethics and public policy hinge upon the answers that may be found for them.

3. Education and Anthropology

The study of ways of rearing children characteristic of different cultures leads naturally to questions concerning the effectiveness and impact of different ways of teaching and learning. The field of educational anthropology, broadly construed, has to do with the ways in which people teach and learn. More narrowly defined, educational anthropology often involves the study of formal and institutional settings, especially the role of the school and the schoolteacher in the process of teaching and learning. An important problem in educational anthropology has to do with the comparative effectiveness of different patterns and techniques of education. Although this problem can be defined narrowly in terms of the speed with which people learn under particular sets of circumstances, a broader approach involves detailed consideration of the impact of particular ways of teaching upon the individual's personality.

Among the Chaga, an African group described by Raum in 1938 and 1940, techniques used by parents in educating their children emphasized the use of fear and punishment.[5] If a child refused to stop crying, the mother called a spirit, presumably to carry it off. An older brother might even be asked to hide behind a hedge and imitate the noises made by a threatening spirit. Children were told that low-sailing clouds might carry them off. If the child ate improper foods, its mother might die. If the child broke certain rules, the

[5] Otto Raum, "Some Aspects of Indigenous Education Among the Chaga," *From Child to Adult,* ed. John Middleton (Garden City, N.Y.: The Natural History Press, 1970), pp. 91–108.

mother might call the spirits to kill it. Grandparents, being close to death, were especially powerful, and children who lived with their grandparents were given special warnings about the consequences that might follow if the grandparents were angered.

When the child approached the fire, ate earth or manure, or refused to eat solid food when it was being weaned, the mother gave it a quick slap and then later fondled and licked it. As the child grew older, the frequent slap was replaced by more drastic punishments. A disobedient child might be locked in an empty hut without food. A lazy child might be tied to the house post for a night. Children were often deprived of food, sometimes for a day or two. A boy who was careless in herding animals might have manure smeared on his face in the presence of his male relatives, or his father might give him fifteen strokes with a stick.

The necessity for constant punishment is evidence that punishment is not a particularly effective way of compelling children to eat, or herdboys to be diligent. The Chaga were, however, a warlike people, and it may be that the constant emphasis on violence in child training contributed to effectiveness in war. The Chaga also lived in considerable fear of witchcraft, and it might well be, although these things are difficult to measure, that they were considerably less trusting and affectionate toward each other than other peoples who rely less on punishment might have been. In short, the combination of fear and punishment might have been an extremely effective way of producing fearful and violent individuals.

Writing in 1971 about the Menomini Indians of Wisconsin, George and Louise Spindler describe a pattern of education radically different from that of the Chaga.[6] Traditional Menomini never whipped their children, and such punishments as were administered were mild. Menomini parents scolded their children reluctantly, and under great provocation might throw cold water in their faces. It is believed that young children especially might sicken and die if scolded or punished. Children were, however, frightened by stories about spirits or ghosts, and reminded of the threat of death posed by the owl. The principal techniques of instruction, however, were storytelling and "preaching." The child was gently but constantly given verbal instructions concerning the right way to behave and the consequences of bad behavior. Like the Chaga, the Menomini lived in fear of witchcraft, especially that practiced by grandparents. In evaluating Menomini reared under the traditional pattern, the Spindlers found them, among other things, to be lacking in rigidity, and without evidence of high anxiety, tension, or internal conflict. They also suggested that the traditional Menomini were "unsuited for competitive struggle in a society that is structured around social and economic manipulation and requires focused interpersonal aggression for achievement within its framework."[7]

Chaga punishment and Menomini "preaching" are plainly different from Manus praise and indulgence or from South Indian "benign neglect." Cer-

[6] George Spindler and Louise Spindler, *Dreamers Without Power, the Menomini Indians* (New York: Holt, Rinehart and Winston, 1971).

[7] Ibid., p. 29.

tainly we should expect such differences in childhood education to result in differences in attitude and behavior. Nevertheless we are not yet on firm ground when it comes to specifying the precise results of specific educational techniques. Parents like the Menomini parents, who behave respectfully toward their children and treat them with affection, are likely to receive much more respect and affection from their children than do such stern disciplinarians as the Chaga father. Manus children, subjected to constant praise, almost certainly have more self-confidence than do Chaga children, subjected to humiliation and criticism. The significance of such differences in terms of abilities to perform is hard to interpret. All four different styles of childhood education appear to have resulted in the development of comparable abilities to perform culturally assigned tasks. It would be hard to demonstrate, except as matters of style, any sharp differences in the comparative efficiency of South Indian herdboys and warriors and Chaga herdboys and warriors. All four peoples have faced the challenge of modernization. Although modernization has affected them in different ways and probably at different rates of speed, none of the four groups have proved incapable of modernization, and where they have failed to modernize, it has been for economic and political reasons that are generally obvious. Although some educational techniques don't work at all and some educational techniques don't work on people who have been raised in particular ways, most traditional techniques of education are quite effective. People learn to act like human beings and more specifically like members of their cultures. They also learn, quite generally, how to adapt to new circumstances of life. Some peoples seem to be more friendly, more trustworthy, more hardworking, or more fun loving than others—there are literally hundreds of psychological dimensions upon which they can be compared—but there is as yet no certainty that such variations among peoples are sufficiently great to justify either praise or condemnation of their systems of childhood education.

Traditional school in South India. Village priest teaches elite children to read, write, and recite verses from scriptures. School runs from dawn to dark, and master uses stick. Gopalpur, South India. (Photo by Alan Beals.)

The situation is considerably different when studies are made of methods of education used in schools. Over most of the world, childhood education carried out in schools is a means of education largely imposed from without. Parents rarely have direct control of their children's schools. The schoolteacher is often an outsider interested in applying educational methods, learned at outside institutions, to children who may have been raised up to that point by means of quite different methods. For example, Menomini children and parents, when first exposed to "Whiteman" schools, reacted with shock and horror. The children were unaccustomed to strict discipline, to abrupt interference with their activities, to the use of criticism instead of praise, or to the use of corporal punishment. Small wonder that Menomini children performed badly in the Whiteman school, or that their parents reacted angrily to what they perceived as cruel and unnecessary punishment.

In recent times the educational level of the Cherokee Indians of eastern Oklahoma has been one of the lowest in the United States. Thomas and Wahrhaftig reported in 1971 that 40 percent of adult rural Cherokee were functionally illiterate in English; many did not speak English at all.[8] Most Cherokees dropped out of school the moment they could do so. But this was not always true of the Cherokee. In the later part of the past century, the Cherokee ran their own schools, using bilingual teachers and textbooks written in Cherokee. The Cherokee school system was considered the finest west of the Mississippi.

By the 1890s the Cherokee nation was divided into two factions representing a division between those who wished to maintain a Cherokee identity and those who wished to become completely "American." As the school system became dominated by those who insisted upon teaching in English a standardized curriculum suitable to middle-class Americans, the desire of conservative Cherokee for education correspondingly diminished. In studying traditional rural Cherokee children in the classroom, Dumont and Wax found that where teachers insisted upon a curriculum designed to "teach out" Cherokee culture the students responded by the development of subtle devices which gave the students control over what was to be taught and learned.[9] In class, having learned at home to conduct themselves with unfailing courtesy and social skill, the Cherokee children displayed all the behaviors of the model student. They sat quietly with perfect posture, rarely talked, and never fidgeted. They devoted long periods of time to their assignments, instructed younger brothers and sisters in arithmetic, and were eager to return to the classroom after recess. In fact the teacher was allowed to teach the students how to behave in a classroom, but the students made plain from the beginning that they had no intention of learning English or other foreign subject matters useless to their future lives as tribal Cherokee.

[8] Robert K. Thomas and Albert L. Wahrhaftig, "Indians, Hillbillies, and the 'Education Problem,'" *Anthropological Perspectives on Education,* ed. Murray L. Wax, Stanley Diamond, and Fred O. Gearing (New York: Basic Books, 1971), pp. 230–251.

[9] Robert V. Dumont and Murray L. Wax, "Cherokee School Society and the Intercultural Classroom," *Human Organization,* **28**:217–226 (1969).

As the children advanced to the seventh and eighth grades, the tension between what the children wished to learn and what the teacher chose to teach gradually increased. When the teacher chose to display an interest in Cherokee ways and to teach materials that the children perceived as useful in the matter of becoming Cherokee, then and only then would the children display an interest in the teacher or in the teacher's interests. The Cherokee demanded an exchange in which topics of instruction were chosen democratically and in which the individual most qualified to teach taught. Because few teachers could endure reduction to the status of first among equals, especially when the equals were impoverished and "un-Americanized" Indians, most teachers encountered a conspiracy of silence by means of which the children protected themselves from the "alien intrusiveness of the teacher and the discourtesy and barbarity of the school."

Because they are often students of the deprived, depressed, or disadvantaged, anthropologists often tend to encounter the school as an alien institution imposed from without upon the people studied. Often they see incompetent teachers who have been assigned to the worst possible teaching position possibly as a punishment for previous displays of incompetence. Sentenced to a one-room schoolhouse in a rural area and asked to teach children who are poor, culturally different, or ethnically segregated, the teacher, even though from the same background as the children in class, may focus his or her bitterness and racial and ethnic prejudices upon the students. Convinced that the students can't or won't learn, the teacher acts out a self-fulfilling prophecy. Other, more zealous teachers must yet teach the students, in an unfamiliar language, materials that are totally irrelevant to the student's interests or life expectations. It is, for example, extremely difficult to explain the computation of compound interest to students who have no money and have never seen a bank. Added to the teacher's other problems is the fact that the teaching methods used in the school and the traditional patterns of discipline adopted by the school are often in conflict with the methods used by the student's parents. Thus Menomini children are prepared to hear lectures, but they are unaccustomed to the patterns of competition, criticism, and failure involved in the system of grading students.

Although the school may offer to some students the promise of social mobility into a cultural setting where such things as a knowledge of the method of calculating compound interest may actually be of value, the vast majority of students find themselves expected to learn materials that are irrelevant to their daily lives taught in a language they barely understand by means of methods that are repugnant to them. At the heart of the problem lies the fact that most modern nations seek to establish systems of universal education in which the same basic "national" way of life is conveyed to all students. Individual communities, on the other hand, seek to establish systems of local education which preserve the unique values and special attributes of their own cultures or subcultures. Middle-class and upper-class parents and communities representing the cultural "mainstream" in most modern nations are capable of exercising political and economic power in order to maintain productive compromises between the school system and the needs of the local community. Parents and communities who are culturally different by reason of poverty, foreign origin, or ethnic group membership tend to lack political and economic power and therefore to lack the means of influencing the school system so as to reach a compromise between local and national needs and expectations. The school system then becomes an alien intrusion, the teacher an enemy, and the building itself an object of vandalism.

Although the discrepancy or discontinuity between life and learning in the school and life and learning outside the school is perhaps most marked in the case of those parents and children who are labeled "culturally different" from some sort of idealized national norm or goal, rapid cultural change in all modern cultures and the development of an increasingly specialized educational bureaucracy have led, in many modern nations, to the development of an increasing discontinuity between school learning and home learning. In the United States, even middle-class parents and children often find themselves powerless to effect substantial change in what have become large and impersonal school bureaucracies. Thus dramatic and sometimes paralyzing conflicts have developed in some communities over policies of racial integration, the busing of young children out of their local neighborhoods, sex education, the new math, and the new social science.

Although individual parents and communities have many highly specific reasons for objecting to various changes in the schools or in the subject matters taught, it is a safe guess that two fundamental issues are involved. One is the degree to which parents and local communities should be permitted to control and influence the schools attended by the children. The other, which is related to the first, has to do with the flow of information in complex bureaucratic systems. Curriculum changes, in particular, tend to be developed by specialists outside the school system in response to appropriate scientific findings dealing with new discoveries about what and how children should learn. The new curriculum is then introduced into classrooms across the nation, with little attempt at explanation or discussion. Classroom teachers, children, and parents have little input into the planning stages of such programs and are often powerless to modify them. The result may be an emotional rejection of the new program, and even of the school itself.

The new math, for example, was developed by mathematicians and educational psychologists on the basis of findings that children could learn mathematical operations more readily if they were first given a grasp of number theory, especially the theory of sets. Parents, who had never learned number theory, were, predictably, dismayed when they discovered that their children were learning things that they themselves could not understand. They also felt that such traditional operations as learning the multiplication tables, or adding long columns of figures had practical and character-building significance which the new math lacked.

In the same way, one aspect of the new social science curriculum has revolved around an attempt to introduce accurate descriptions of other peoples into the grammar school curriculum. Traditional curricula dealing with the California Indians, the Eskimo, or Mexico presented romanticized and inaccurate information that conveyed a general message concerning the superiority of middle-class white American culture in every department of life. The replacement of the traditional stereotypes and prejudices that constituted the old "social slop" with more accurate and detailed information that could be properly labeled "social science" has been viewed in some quarters as posing a threat to the American way of life and even to the psychological well-being of the child. Although the existence of a generation gap reflecting a discrepancy between the education of parents and children and the existence of an institutional gap representing a discontinuity between school education and home education can be looked upon as an inevitable consequence of rapid cultural change, it seems probable that these gaps would not seem so wide if reasonable efforts had been made to keep them from developing in the first place.

One example of a case where the accidents of history prevented the development of such gaps can be drawn from the recent history of the village of Namhalli in South India. Located near the rapidly developing city of Bangalore, Namhalli received a grammar school as early as 1903. The grammar school, which formed a part of an educational bureaucracy designed to bring English education to a relatively small number of South Indians, was attended by a relatively small proportion of the village children. Those children who successfully completed grammar school and, later, middle school were able to obtain jobs as teachers. Further, although the principles of the educational bureaucracy involved transferring teachers frequently so that they would not become attached to or influenced by local communities, the desirability of a teaching post so near the city led Namhalli's teachers to a policy of systematically evading transfer. Thus, in contrast to the situation that obtained in more rural villages, Namhalli soon came to possess teachers who were permanent residents of the village and in many cases were born in the village. Almost from the beginning, by a policy of what amounted to subversion of the educational bureaucracy, children in Namhalli were taught by teachers who spoke their own dialect and who could be readily influenced by their parents.

Although Namhalli parents could not exert influence upon school curricula, they could exert great influence upon the methods and manner of teaching. Because traditional education in Namhalli had involved the largely irrelevant and impractical memorization of the great Indian epic poems, parents in Namhalli were accustomed to the idea of education for the sake of education. There was no traditional precedent for any concern with the content of education. All that mattered was that the children were successful in school, receiving appropriate diplomas, and so on. Up until the 1940s the school was seen as an avenue whereby a few children from the village could become low-paid schoolteachers. During the 1950s and 1960s, however, the school became an avenue whereby large numbers of people from the village could obtain relatively high-paying factory jobs.

Once the firm connection was made between schooling and good jobs, virtually all of Namhalli's children over the age of three began to attend school regularly. Parents, who saw their children's school achievement as a means of achieving economic security, displayed an overwhelming interest in every detail of the child's school day. In addition they spent long hours teaching and learning from their children's schoolbooks. To the extent that Namhalli

Namhalli school. School meets half day. Master believes in progressive education and rejects parents' demands that he use stick. Curriculum prepares all children in village for modern middle school and high school. Girls attend because educated young men seek educated wives. Namhalli, South India. (Photo by Alan Beals.)

developed a generation gap, it was with the total knowledge and consent of Namhalli's parents. In one case a mother born in a village that used a different language from that used in school, reared her first child in her native language, and her second child in the school language, Kannada. Her youngest child, seven years old in 1975, refused to address her in any language but English. Thus parents have been swept up in the learning process generated by an overwhelming desire to make sure that their children obtain high school diplomas and factory jobs. In this case the enormous value attached to a high school diploma (most students during the fifties majored in English history) has obscured the enormous gap between school education and home education. For the rural Cherokee or the ghetto dweller in the United States, the school offers neither practical reward nor information useful in the conduct of daily life. The South Indian example suggests that where parents feel they can exert some influence upon the school, even if they can't influence the curriculum, and where the school is seen as offering a practical advantage, a curriculum unfamiliar to the parents and, in fact, culturally foreign may nevertheless be accepted with enthusiasm.

Although the anthropology of education is in its infancy, it has demonstrated a capacity to ask a variety of questions concerning the manner in which education can be carried out. Anthropological techniques of close observation of relatively small numbers of people offer a means of discovering what actually happens between parents and children or teachers and students in particular contexts. Depending upon the situation, some kinds of education work and some kinds of education don't work; educational anthropology is a means of discovering why.

4. Cognitive Anthropology

Somewhat apart from questions about how people become enculturated or educated are questions that have to do with the nature of what they learn and the kinds of things that happen when information is introduced into the human brain. These larger questions about ways of thinking are the domain of Cognitive Anthropology. Looked at in strictly mechanical terms, a human being is a device that absorbs information through various senses, stores some of it, analyzes and evaluates some of it, and then, finally, generates some kind of behavior. These information-processing activities are carried out primarily in the brain and the nervous system. Although there are differences among individual human beings in the precise details of brain and nervous system, the basic design is similar in all normally functioning human beings. Although human beings don't all think the same way, there is little evidence to support the possibility that any very substantial differences exist in the machinery with which we think. To be sure, some individuals appear to use their built-in biological computers a bit more effectively than others. Perhaps some individuals have a slightly greater information storage capacity than others, and so on, but basically all of our biological computers bear the same model number.

In general, then, such differences as exist between human beings in ways of thinking or cognition are to be attributed to the kinds of information received through the senses, to the selection of information for storage in the memory, and to learned ways of processing information. Perception or the selection of information to be remembered or processed depends upon the importance attributed to particular sorts of information and upon the availability of such information within the environment. What people think and how they think about it presumably is related to the kinds of experiences they have had as members of a particular culture and as speakers of a particular language. The anthropological study of cognition has to do with the exploration of differences in ways of thinking and perceiving that are characteristic of the members of different cultures.

The idea that people in different cultures use their brains in different ways places a formidable obstacle in the way of attempts to find out how they do use their brains. If we attempt to present the same stimulus—perhaps a simple problem—to individuals raised in two different cultures, we immediately encounter the difficulty that representatives of two different cultures may perceive the problem in totally different ways and may therefore, in fact, be working on different problems. For example, in seeking to understand how the

Different people may interpret the same experience in different ways. Fanti children. (Kindness of Ed Plummer.)

members of an African group, the Kpelle, handled geometric concepts, Cole, Gay, and Glick discovered that the Kpelle language possessed relatively few terms for naming geometric shapes.[10] For example, the Kpelle used the same word to describe both a circle and an ellipse. Presumably the reason that they did not have two different words for these two concepts had to do with the fact that they were raised in an environment in which survival rarely depended on the making of fine discriminations between circle shapes and elliptical shapes. In any event, when presented with a problem involving an ability to tell the difference between a circle and an ellipse, the Kpelle required considerably more practice before they could solve the problem than did kindergarten or first grade students in the United States.

Although it seems sensible to conclude that the difficulties encountered by the Kpelle in making a distinction between circles and ellipses was related to

[10] M. Cole, J. Gay, and J. Glick, "Some Experimental Studies of Kpelle Quantitative Behavior," *Culture and Cognition*, (ed.) J. W. Berry and P. R. Dasen (London: Methuen, 1974), pp. 159–196.

their language and probably to their experience and was thus a mere matter of perception, it is very difficult to identify the precise stage of information processing at which the Kpelle encountered difficulty. On a whole series of geometric tests, despite any language problems they might have had, Kpelle schoolchildren who had been exposed to geometric concepts performed better than other Kpelle and slightly better than schoolchildren from the United States. Kpelle schoolchildren live in a world slightly different from that of other Kpelle. The experiences they have had and their ways of thinking about those experiences are therefore different.

The situation is much more complicated than simply asking people in various ways about the difference between a circle and an ellipse or between a straight line and a curved line. Do people reared in different cultures have the same desire to perform, are the questions that are asked given the same interpretation in different cultures, are the relationships between the investigator and the people being studied the same in both cultures, is unconscious communication between the investigator and the people being studied likely to bias the results? The answer to all these questions is likely to be, no, if the assumption that people in different cultures think differently is correct. This does not mean that cognitive differences are impossible to study—only that they are very difficult to study.

Granted that reasonable techniques can be found for comparing the reactions of people in different cultures to more or less the same sets of stimuli, a serious problem still remains. We can describe some of the stimuli that confront the black box represented by the human brain and body, and we can describe some of what comes out of the black box in terms of behavior, but we don't know what has happened between the time the problem or set of stimuli was presented to the individual and the individual responded with an attempted solution. One of the major problems in cognitive anthropology has to do with the creation of theoretical models that would explain exactly how it is that human beings in general or human beings in different cultures actually process information. Although the problem is analogous to that of reconstructing a computer program from an analysis of input data and computer printout, it is a bit more complicated than that because we cannot know what sorts of data, already stored in the human memory, may be used, or, in detail, what sorts of data are being absorbed at any particular moment.

Attempts to solve this sort of problem generally involve attempts to construct models that can be used to generate some particular aspects of behavior that closely approximate some limited form of behavior characteristic of real people. Although such a task appears to be difficult or impossible, it turns out in practice to be fairly simple. Thus a grammar of a language is in some sense a model that tells us how people might go about arranging words in their heads when they are talking. If a person can read a grammar of French and then form correct French sentences, it is a fair guess that the cognitive operations that he is performing are somewhat like those performed by at least some speakers of French. In normal scientific practice, granted two equally useful analyses of French grammar, the simplest analysis would be identified as the correct one. Should we therefore conclude that the normal speaker of French uses precisely the same approach to the speaking of French as that used in the most elegant possible grammar of French? If we did so, it would come close to a conclusion that acting like a Frenchman is the same as thinking like a Frenchman.

It is possible to write several grammars of French using different approaches, and it is possible that all of these grammars will be equally effective as a means of generating linguistically correct statements in the French language. We now have several models (grammars) that will correctly predict an aspect of French behavior, and we might choose to rest there with the argument that it is sufficient to predict behavior without bothering to worry about whether or not the cognitive model that works for us is the same one that works for other French speakers.

A cognitive anthropologist, however, would seek to determine which of the models most closely approximates the actual thought processes taking place within the speaker's head. One approach to this sort of problem would be to examine the kinds of mistakes that French speakers make when they use their language. Very often one sort of model would tend to produce one kind of error, whereas an alternative model would produce a different kind of error. The model that produced patterns of hesitation or error most closely resembling the patterns displayed by actual French speakers might then be considered to be the model most closely resembling that concealed in the speaker's head.

In attempting to choose between two models both designed to explain how speakers of American English assigned kinship terms to particular individuals, Romney and D'Andrade used a test in which individuals identified the degree of closeness or similarity between particular kinship terms.[11] When the terms were placed on a diagram in terms of their relative closeness, the result was found to approximate one model much more closely than the other. Further study of American English kinship terminologies has led to the development of five or six alternative ways of explaining and predicting the individual's actual use of kinship terms. Because these models are useful in different ways, cognitive anthropologists now suspect that each individual makes use of several different models in the process of deciding where and when to use any particular kinship term. The different models or different ways of deciding what to do seem to be applied in different situations.

All human behavior is a product of a decision-making process that begins with the individual's choice of some particular model or procedure that past experience has shown to be useful in the solution of a problem of that type. Perhaps the easiest way to see how this works is to consider the problem of adding two numbers together in order to obtain a total. Simple sums like 3 plus 2 have often been memorized in the first grade. Thus $3 + 2 = 5$ is stored in a readily accessible portion of the individual's memory, and the response is made automatically with a minimum of calculation. Confronted with $25 + 2$, the individual would not be likely to have the answer immediately available,

[11] A. Kimball Romney and Roy D'Andrade, "Cognitive Aspects of English Kin Terms," *American Anthropologist,* **66**:146–170 (1964).

but would be aware that a rapid solution could be obtained by counting on the fingers or by breaking the problem down into such elements as $20 + 5 + 2$ which are immediately available in his memory. Confronted with the problem of adding 3,742 and 9,835, the individual would recognize the impossibility of using any of the techniques available for simple problems and would therefore apply some other learned technique of problem solution. The choice of a particular technique would depend upon such things as the availability of a pencil and paper or the degree of speed and accuracy that seems to be required. An answer phrased "a little less than 14,000" is obviously calculated in quite a different way from an answer accurate to the last digit.

Because we are used to thinking about arithmetic in terms of problems and solutions, it is comparatively easy for us to think about the specific problem-solving procedures that might be stored in the individual's head. The basic approaches of cognitive anthropology depend upon the realization that every word spoken and every action taken by the individual involves some degree of problem solving and decision making. Even automatic or memorized responses such as $2 + 2 = 4$ involve unconscious decisions to respond automatically; the automatic process can be interrupted at any time as in the joke, $2 + 2 = 5$. When we look at individuals as computers — as problem-solving machines — it is apparent that the production of anything beyond such simple, memorized phrases as "Good morning. How are you?" requires an enormous amount of calculation. The situation must be appraised, the appropriate words must be chosen, the words must be arranged in grammatical order, and the various muscles must be instructed to produce appropriate noises. All this must be done within the limitations of memory and reliability of the human brain.

Although the study of the human brain and associated organs is in its infancy and must be approached through the collaboration of many different disciplines, anthropologists are now making substantial contributions largely through the study of individual informant's abilities to generate sets of related words. An example of research of this type is Berlin, Breedlove, and Raven's attempt to discover general principles involved in folk classifications of plants and animals.[12] Here it seems that the individual's ability to remember sets of more than ten to twenty plant and animal names conveniently depends upon the existence of a hierarchial classification.[13] This tells us simply that the human memory cannot easily handle long lists of undifferentiated words. Without special effort, the individual cannot name 100 animals without first classifying the animals into types, such as fish and birds. A simple test of this proposition is to attempt to produce a disordered list in which the names of plants, animals, kitchen utensils, or some other category of things occur without any clustering or arrangement in terms of type. Human beings arrange the names of things in taxonomies in which specific things are included

[12] Brent Berlin, Dennis E. Breedlove, and Peter H. Raven, "General Principles of Classification and Nomenclature in Folk Biology," *American Anthropologist*, **75**:214–242 (1973).

[13] Michael Cole and John Gay, "Culture and Memory," *American Anthropologist*, **74**:1066–1084 (1972).

under particular headings or types. In classifying plants and animals, human beings rarely use in ordinary discourse taxonomies involving more than five or six levels. Thus the English classification of animals begins with the term "animal" (Level 1). Included under animal are a series of life forms such as fish, birds, reptiles, and mammals (Level 2). Then come the names of kinds of genuses of animals (Level 3), followed by specific names such as "horse" and "cow" (Level 4), and by varietal names such as Arabian or Mustang (Level 5). Typically, folk taxonomies contain between five and ten life forms in which are included approximately 500 genera. Normally there are fewer names for species and varieties than there are for genera; that is, many genera have few or no species listed under them.

Although it is not yet possible to assert confidently that *all* folk biological classifications share certain common features, the work done so far seems to suggest that universal regularities can be found through the analysis of systems of classification and that these universal regularities will provide useful information about the nature of human cognitive processes. Ultimately these and other explorations in cognitive anthropology have to be related to the work of psychologists and neurologists who are engaged in complementary approaches to the study of human ways of thinking.

5. Anthropology and Mental Illness

"Cracked" Narsappa lived in a small village, not far from the city of Bangalore in South India. Before he acquired the label "cracked," Narsappa had a good job with a government agency in the city. In the village he had adequate lands and property, and a large and apparently supportive network of relatives and friends. Nevertheless the day came when Narsappa concluded that he was destitute. Instead of going to work he roamed the village streets weeping and begging for handouts. Narsappa's relatives and friends cared for him and supported him until one day, several years later, he decided he was no longer destitute. Plainly, because they gave Narsappa the English label "cracked," Narsappa's fellow villagers considered him to be insane. Equally plainly, they did not consider his insanity to require treatment or confinement. Indeed, because he recovered in time, it may be that treatment was not required.

Although Narsappa's particular exhibition of mental illness took a form similar to certain forms of mental illness in the United States, his particular symptoms, such as his method of begging, were related to South Indian culture. The expression of his mental illness was to a large extent a cultural matter. The particular form his mental illness took—the illusion of poverty—could be sustained only in a culture like that of South India or of the United States in which major distinctions were maintained between wealth and poverty. In a culture like that of the Eskimo or the Bushmen, where the accumulation of wealth is but weakly emphasized, it is hard to imagine that mental illness could ever take the form of delusions of destitution.

The anthropological study of mental illness begins with the fact that the forms of mental illness tend to vary from one society to another. Even where, as in the case above, forms of mental illness are pretty much the same in two different societies, the frequencies of the various forms and the kinds of people affected are likely to be quite different. Although some early students of anthropology and mental illness saw whole societies as suffering from such diseases as megalomania, blanket categorizations of entire populations are now seen as the result of a confusion between culturally approved forms of behavior and culturally disapproved forms of behavior such as are characteristic of mental illness. An emperor of Japan in former days who believed himself to be a direct descendant of the sun god would simply be expressing an aspect of traditional Japanese religion. A citizen of New York who believed the same thing would almost certainly be considered mentally ill.

Although there may be biological predispositions, especially to particular kinds of mental illness, studies of the distribution of mental illness in various societies seem to confirm the fact that the actual expression of mental illness often depends upon specific kinds of life situations encountered by particular individuals. If mental illness can be considered in some degree to represent a last resort for the individual who finds himself in a situation impossible to endure, then the distribution of mental illness can be considered to be dependent upon the kinds of difficult or impossible situations likely to exist in any particular culture and the kinds of alternative ways of dealing with such situations that are available to the individual. In some cases, where such behavior is culturally prescribed, sane individuals may exhibit the symptoms of mental illness as a means of announcing the assumption of some particular role.

Among the Saora, a tribe in India, young men and women, possibly those least attracted to the rather humdrum existence of the ordinary person, very often exhibited extraordinary symptoms.[14] They wept and laughed at strange times, suffered loss of memory, fell to the ground unconscious, and experienced sensations as if ants were biting them all over. In Saora culture these symptoms were recognized as being caused by spirits who sought to "marry" the affected individual. Once a marriage was consummated, the afflicted individual became a shaman and assumed an important and highly responsible role in the curing of the sick. In Saora belief virtually all illness was caused by spirit attack. Illness was cured through the activity of a shaman who entered a trance state in which he was possessed by the disease-causing spirit, who might then demand payment in animals to be sacrificed or beer to be drunk. Once the spirit was bought off in this fashion, the patient was cured. Saora shamans, perhaps because of their extraordinary powers, were not considered to suffer from mental illness by other Saora. In fact they were among the most highly respected and successful members of the tribe. U.S. culture endorses certain prejudices against people who talk with spirits or enter into trance states, and such people are likely to be classified insane and confined in mental institutions. The difference in treatment between U.S. culture and Saora culture lies in the fact that the behavior exhibited is considered highly

[14] Verrier Elwin, *The Religion of an Indian Tribe* (London: Oxford University Press, 1955).

inappropriate in U.S. culture and highly appropriate in Saora culture. The definition of mental illness lies, not in the symptoms or behavior exhibited, but in the appropriateness of the behavior to the cultural setting in which it is exhibited.

The Saora who exhibits the behavior characteristic of a person about to become a shaman is not so much ill as in a perilous state. There are also, however, many cases in which culturally defined illnesses occupy a kind of borderline between physical and mental illness. For example, in many parts of Mexico and Latin America individuals are likely to be afflicted with a disease called *susto*. The symptoms may involve listlessness, depression, timidity, loss of interest, poor appetite, and lack of physical strength. In a study of the incidence of *susto* in two Zapotec Indian communities in Mexico, O'Nell and Selby accepted the idea that *susto* represented a response to stressful or unbearable life situations.[15] They then attempted to determine whether males or females were most likely to encounter such situations. According to their findings women suffered under greater stresses than men and had fewer ways of escaping from them. They therefore predicted that *susto* would afflict women more frequently than men. This turned out to be the case. The cure for *susto* involved elaborate medical procedures involving considerable time and money. O'Nell and Selby hypothesize that the net result is a healing over of the family problems that created the illness. At the risk of massive oversimplification, we could say that women tend to feel unloved or unwanted and hence to develop *susto*. The illness is then cured through demonstrations of concern and affection which tend to be continued as long as other family members sense that there is a risk that the ailment will recur.

Here, *susto* appears, not as a form of mental illness, but as a culturally acceptable strategy by means of which discontented women can effect changes in the way they are treated by their husbands and children. In India new brides, who may be cruelly mistreated by their mothers-in-law, are most frequently the victims of spirit possession. When possessed, they are likely to curse and revile their mothers-in-law and engage in other unseemly behaviors. To prevent recurrence of the illness, mothers-in-law naturally tend to modify their behaviors toward their daughters-in-law.

Saora shamanism, *susto*, and spirit possession all seem to represent culturally approved avenues by means of which individuals can escape from situations that are becoming impossible to bear. There are also a variety of techniques by means of which the individual's friends and relatives contribute to the prevention of mental illness through the application of psychotherapeutic procedures. Among the Eskimo, when the community had offended the spirits and therefore suffered from the effects of bad weather or bad hunting, the shamans gathered community members together and encouraged each one in turn to confess sins and to beg for forgiveness. In Western cultures, such confessions are generally made to priests or psychiatrists. Presumably confession

---

[15] Carl W. O'Nell and Henry A. Selby, "Sex Differences in the Incidence of Susto in Two Azpotec Pueblos: An Analysis of the Relationship Between Sex Role Expectations and Folk Illness," *Ethnology*, 7:95–105 (1968).

serves the purpose of curing depression, anxiety, and loss of self-esteem caused by feelings of guilt and unworthiness or fear of discovery. Among the Hopi of the Southwest, where the thinking of bad thoughts is believed to have very serious consequences, the family pays great attention to any dreams the individual might have. Each dream is discussed and explained and any necessary precautions or actions are carried out. In theory at least, the analysis of dreams serves as a means of identifying developing anxieties and stresses in their early stages of development and of providing suitable assistance to the individual.

The effectiveness of cultural patterns of preventive psychotherapy or of cultural alternatives to mental illness is difficult to measure. Mental illness appears in all cultures with considerable frequency, but the problems of diagnosis and interpretation are such that it is difficult to estimate frequencies comparatively. On a broad scale, rapid cultural change or rapid change in the life expectations of the individual—even where these changes seem to be for the better—are generally considered to increase the incidence of violence, suicide, and mental illness. Cultural differences, as seen in the above examples, have a profound effect upon the symptoms exhibited and upon the kinds of mental illness that develop.

6. Summary

The relationships between culture and the individual can be viewed at two extremes, either as the replication of uniformity or as the organization of diversity. People who share the same cultural tradition have personalities that are quite similar in some respects and quite different in others. Differences in personality within a single culture are guaranteed by biological variation, by differences in the life experience of the individual, and by differences in the behavior expected of people occupying different social statuses. In general a theory about culture is a theory about consistencies in behavior characteristic of a group of members, while a theory about personality is a theory about consistencies in the behavior of the individual. The basic problems involved in the understanding of the relationships between culture and personality have to do with the mechanisms that ensure the replication of uniformity, the organization of diversity, the maintenance of personality, and the transmission of knowledge concerning cultural standards.

Enculturation is the process whereby individuals learn how to perform within their own cultural systems. The influence of culture upon the individual begins before birth and continues throughout life. Although the processes of cultural programming or enculturation may or may not be entirely consistent with the patterns of purely biological development established by the genetic inheritance of the child, it now seems probable that the human genetic potential is sufficiently flexible to accommodate to a wide variety of patterns of child rearing. The older view that specific child-rearing practices such as early weaning or swaddling might in some sense be "unnatural" and therefore inju-

rious to the child has generally been replaced by the view that specific practices have a major impact upon adult practices only when they are a part of an
overall pattern of training which consistently reinforces particular personality
characteristics. Thus the Manus pattern of consistent protection and praise
applied to the development of a wide range of motor skills led to the rapid
development of physical competence. By contrast, the South Indian pattern of
holding and carrying small children led to the rapid development of language
and social skills and to a much later development of motor skills. Although
these and other contrasts among Manus, South India, and the United States
indicate wide variations in the extent to which particular biological potentialities are developed, the extent to which these differences affect the capacity of
individuals reared in different cultures to adapt to changing circumstances is
not clear. The impact of child-rearing practices upon personality and the extent to which individuals having different personalities can learn and adapt in
the face of changing circumstances are important problems affecting our understandings of individual adjustment and of cultural change.

Educational anthropology has to do with the ways in which people teach
and learn. Of particular interest are questions concerning the effectiveness of
particular methods of training. The contrast between the emphasis on punishment by the Chaga and the avoidance of punishment by the Menomini illustrates the problems involved in identifying the goals of different forms of
training and their relative effectiveness. On the whole, most traditional patterns of child training appear to be effective in producing adults capable of
performing culturally assigned tasks. Another aspect of educational anthropology has to do with the existence of discontinuities between patterns of training
characteristic of home and school environments. Thus, although the Menomini home experience appears to present an example of a pattern of home
experience radically in conflict with school experience, it turns out that patterns of conflict between home and school are widespread, affecting not only
the poor, the foreign, or the ethnically different, but middle-class children in
industrialized societies as well. The contrast between the rural Cherokee
Indian who foresaw no benefit from school and who had no influence upon it,
and the South Indians of Namhalli who foresaw great benefits and found the
means of exerting influence illustrates some of the lines along which solutions to the problems of effective education can be found.

Cognitive anthropology has to do with questions about the nature of what
is learned and the ways in which human beings process information. What
people think about and how they think about it presumably is related to the
kinds of experiences they have had as members of a particular culture and
speakers of a particular language. The existence of cultural differences in
ways of perceiving and thinking creates special problems of interpretation. For
the Kpelle, for example, how does one study geometric concepts among people who use the same word to refer to both a circle and an ellipse? Granted
that such problems can be overcome, the problem of knowing what people are
thinking and how they are thinking it remains formidable. In attempting to
solve such problems, cognitive anthropologists have adopted the strategy of
developing models that can be used to generate some aspects of behavior and

attempting to make predictions based upon such models. Where two or more models appear to predict behavior equally well, such techniques as studying patterns of hesitation or error can lead to the selection of models that appear to closely approximate actual cognitive processes. One problem here, illustrated by studies of American kinship terms, is that people may use alternative ways of thinking in different situations or in order to solve somewhat different sorts of problems. Although the study of cognition is in its infancy, progress has been made in a number of fields, among them the manner in which such things as plants and animals are classified.

The anthropological study of mental illness begins with the fact that forms of mental illness tend to vary from one society to another. In identifying particular forms of behavior as symptomatic of mental illness, it is necessary to understand the distinctions characteristic of each culture between forms of behavior that are culturally approved and forms of behavior that are culturally disapproved and considered symptomatic of mental illness. Such distinctions often depend upon the kinds of difficult or impossible situations likely to exist and upon the kinds of alternative ways of dealing with such situations available to the individual. In many cases patterns of behavior that strongly resemble mental illness represent culturally approved strategies for achieving particular sorts of goals. Among the Saora apparent mental illness may simply be a prelude to assumption of the important status of shaman. The definition of mental illness lies in the appropriateness of behavior to the cultural settings in which it is exhibited. Such cultural diseases as *susto* or spirit possession can be interpreted as culturally approved devices by means of which what seem to be symptoms of mental illness are used by sane persons to gain desired ends. Another important aspect of the cross-cultural study of mental illness is the use of such techniques as confession and dream interpretation in the prevention of mental illness. Mental illness tends to be accentuated by rapid cultural change or by sharp dislocations in the lives of individuals, but the symptoms exhibited and the kinds of illness that develop are powerfully affected by cultural differences.

Collateral Reading

Barnouw, Victor. *Culture and Personality,* rev. ed. Homewood, Ill.: Dorsey Press, 1973.
    A good textbook.
Berry, J. W., and Dasen, P. R. (eds.). *Culture and Cognition: Readings in Cross-Cultural Psychology.* London: Methuen & Co., Ltd., 1974. Excellent selection of articles.
Cole, Michael, John Gay, Joseph A. Glick, and Donald W. Sharp. *The Cultural Context of Learning and Thinking: An Exploration in Experimental Anthropology.* New York: Basic Books, Inc., 1971. Makes use of psychological approaches to cognition.
Collier, John. *Alaskan Eskimo Education: A Film Analysis of Cultural Confrontation in the Schools.* New York: Holt, Rinehart and Winston, Inc., 1973. Brilliant use of clues provided by films.

Dennis, Wayne. *The Hopi Child*. New York: Appleton-Century-Crofts, 1940. An early, essentially psychological field study of child rearing outside Western culture.

Gay, J., and M. Cole. *The New Mathematics and an Old Culture: A Study of Learning among the Kpelle of Liberia*. New York: Holt, Rinehart and Winston, Inc., 1967. Cross-cultural problems in education.

Hostetler, J. A., and G. E. Huntington. *Children in Amish Society*. New York: Holt, Rinehart and Winston, Inc., 1971. A unique religious community.

Howard, A. *Learning to be Rotuman*. New York: Holt, Rinehart and Winston, Inc., 1970. Education on a Pacific island.

Hsu, Francis L. K. (ed.). *Psychological Anthropology*, new ed. Cambridge, Mass.: Schenkman Publishing Co., Inc., 1972. Excellent articles.

Leighton, Dorothea, and Clyde Kluckhohn. *Children of the People, Part I*. Cambridge, Mass.: Harvard University Press, 1947. Good field study of child rearing and personality formation.

LeVine, Robert A. *Culture, Behavior and Personality*. Chicago: Aldine Publishing Company, 1973. Good recent textbook.

Lindquist, Harry (ed.). *Education: Readings in the Processes of Cultural Transmission*. Boston: Houghton Mifflin Company, 1970.

Mead, Margaret. *Coming of Age in Samoa*. New York: William Morrow & Co., Inc., 1928. Classical study of adolescence.

Mead, Margaret. *Growing Up in New Guinea*. New York: William Morrow & Co., Inc., 1930. Excellent field study of child development in another culture.

Middleton, John (ed.). *From Child to Adult*. Garden City, N.Y.: The Natural History Press, 1970.

Moore, Alexander. *Life Cycles in Atchalan: The Diverse Careers of Certain Guatemalans*. New York and London: Teachers College Press, 1973. How modes of formal and informal education supply career possibilities to the individual.

Peshkin, Alan. *Kanuri Schoolchildren: Education and Social Mobilization in Nigeria*. New York and London: Holt, Rinehart and Winston, Inc., 1972.

Schneider, David M., and Raymond T. Smith. *Class Differences and Sex Roles in American Kinship and Family Structure*. Englewood Cliffs, N.J.: Prentice-Hall, Inc., 1973.

Segall, M., D. Campbell, and M. Herskovits. *The Influence of Culture on Visual Perception*. Indianapolis: The Bobbs-Merrill Co., Inc., 1966. First study to demonstrate relationships between culture and cognition.

Spindler, George (ed.). *Education and Cultural Processes: Toward an Anthropology of Education*. New York: Holt, Rinehart and Winston, Inc., 1974. Outstanding papers.

Wallace, Anthony F. C. *Culture and Personality*. New York: Random House, Inc., 1961. One of best statements of the field, emphasizing the importance of adequately involving psychological studies.

Wax, Murray L., Stanley Diamond, and Fred O. Gearing (eds.). *Anthropological Perspectives on Education*. New York and London: Basic Books, Inc., 1971.

Whiting, Beatrice B. (ed.). *Six Cultures, Studies of Child Rearing*. New York: John Wiley & Sons, Inc., 1963. Interesting contrasts based on comparable data.

19/Stability and Change in Culture

1. Change as an Aspect of Culture

Although many animals may change their individual or collective modes of behavior in response to changes in environmental circumstances, the primary means of adaptation for most involves the biological processes whereby the genetic code is gradually rewritten. Among the more complicated mammals, and especially among primates and human beings, direct genetic programming of behavior has become relatively less important than behavior developed through experience and learning. Human beings continue to respond to changing environments through changes in genes and gene frequencies, but the primary means of response is through changes in culture. The tiger survives, or did so until recently, partly by virtue of his genetically inherited stripes and claws. The human being, confronted with problems similar to those that produced stripes and claws in the tiger, develops camouflage cloth and knives. The study of change in culture is the study of the means by which human beings develop cultural adaptations to changing external circumstances.

Although the possession and use of cultural traditions mark a dividing line between human beings and other animals in the sense that cultural change is a different kind of change from genetic change, there are many ways in which the development or evolution of culture is essentially similar to the development and evolution of life. In a sense, cultural evolution is simply biological evolution carried out by other means. Where life forms have evolved from simple one-celled organisms through the development of improved means of cooperation and communication between cells, so cultural forms have evolved from simple camps or bands containing a few hundred people to complex civilizations containing millions of people. Similarly life forms have developed increasingly efficient and specialized ways of extracting energy from the environment, and so have cultural forms. Both life forms and cultural forms may undergo changes that have little apparent effect upon their chances of survival, but in the end, both life forms and cultural forms must take form within the limitations of adaptation and survival.

Change in both life forms and cultural forms can be either endogenous or exogenous in origin; that is, change may occur as a result of factors internal to the organism or community that is changing, or it may occur as a result of changes in the environment that alter established patterns of selection. Endogenous, or internal, changes may be the result of simple variation or of inexact transmission of biological or cultural messages. In a sense, changes resulting from simple variation are not changes at all, but simply the working out of different potentialities inherent in the existing form. The processes of mutation and drift which create new genes or modify the frequencies of existing genes have their analogues in the transmission of cultural traditions from one generation to the next. Although both genetic and cultural messages respond to exogenous, or environmental, influences, the means of response are quite different. A genetic response to changing environmental influences can be made only by changes in the frequencies of existing genes or by the sudden, and rather unlikely, appearance of new and adaptive mutations. By contrast, members of a culture may respond to challenge through conscious or unconscious experimentation that may lead to the discovery of new means of cultural adaptation. Although environmental stress is likely to increase the rate of genetic mutation in any species, just as it may increase the rate of invention and innovation in human cultures, the mechanism provides no easy way of directing the thrust of mutation toward a particular problem. Cultural mutations or inventions are much more likely to be directed toward a particular set of circumstances and may even be made purposefully.

Processes of biological evolution can be observed and discussed on a global and all-encompassing scale ranging from general evolution, which deals with all life forms, to specific or microevolution, which deals with the evolution of particular species or even of the genes at a particular locus on the chromosome. In the same way, cultural change can be dealt with on the grand scale in terms of the evolution of all of human culture, or it can be dealt with on a specific scale in terms of the growth and change of individual cultures or of individual ideas or inventions.

In biological evolution significant changes rarely come one at a time. For example, the development of erect posture in human beings had to be accompanied by a wide variety of changes in other aspects of the organism. In the same way, any large change in a cultural system tends to reverberate through the system. An improved method of hunting may cause changes in social organization, in eating habits, and even in religion. A change in religious doctrine might conceivably topple an empire, thereby disrupting the economic life of an entire region. Cultural change, then, is not simply a matter of finding immediate and practical solutions to problems posed by the environment. Each solution creates problems of its own which must be solved if the entire cultural system is to continue to function effectively. In many rural communities, for example, the introduction of a mechanical flour mill may suddenly release the rural housewife from the three to four hours of drudgery previously spent grinding flour by hand. If the women are to be kept busy, drastic changes must then be made in the distribution of work among men, women, and children. Cash crops may have to be raised in order to meet the expense of grinding grain at the mill. The incidence of marital quarrels may change markedly. Children may now receive far more supervision than they are accustomed to. A social class distinction may arise between women who can afford to patronize the mill and those who cannot. Each impact of the mechanical flour mill generates fresh problems to be solved. Ultimately a whole series of adjustments must be made before a state of relative stability can be restored.

Because environments change constantly and so trigger repeated cycles of innovation and change, it follows that all cultural systems are in a constant state of change and that a part of any cultural tradition is a technology for adjusting to the environment and coping with the changes that result.

2. Innovation: Invention and Diffusion

Anything that is new, whether it is a new thing to say, a new object to construct, or a new action to take, is an innovation. Although any human act has an element of newness in the sense that the same person never did the same thing in quite the same way, the concept of newness is generally restricted to things and actions that are sufficiently out of the ordinary to be considered unique or unprecedented. As explained in Chapter 14, human beings constantly exhibit behaviors which in some degree or another violate cultural standards. Not all such behaviors represent innovations. There is likely to be nothing new about such violations of cultural standards as theft or untimely drunkenness. An individual may also engage in new forms of behavior without violating cultural standards; surely no one would object to a straighter arrow or a better way of foretelling the future. Innovation resembles the violation of cultural standards of behavior, however, in that it arises in the same ways as the result of error or as a result of the exposure of the individual to a unique situation. If the individual fails to learn the right way of doing things, he is likely to do them in a new way or a wrong way or both together. Similarly, if the individual is confronted with a situation in which conventional behavior fails to produce results that match his expectations, he is likely to vary his behavior and so to innovate. Such problem-solving behavior may be conscious or unconscious, and the solution itself may involve either the creation or the borrowing of something new.

Every cultural pattern, whether it involves a technique, a mode of behavior toward relatives, a manner of speaking, or a form of religious worship—and every product of these patterns—has its origin in an act of invention performed by someone somewhere. At the same time, almost every item in every known culture can be shown to have been borrowed from some other culture. Such borrowing or diffusion almost always involves invention in the sense that the diffused elements are somewhat modified in the process of diffusion, but, on the whole, a close examination of any innovation tends to show that most of its elements were borrowed. Very often the act of innovation consists merely of combining existing elements in a new way. The successful innovator, the individual who succeeds in persuading others to follow his example, must combine some or all of the following characteristics: (1) he must have access to a wide range of information, preferably new information, (2) he must have the facility for combining such information in unusual ways, (3) he must have the motivation required for the trying out of new things or ideas, and (4) he must be able to secure acceptance of his innovation.

In the South Indian village of Namhalli, located not far from the city of Bangalore, the village headman was a major source of agricultural innovation. He could afford to try new things because he was moderately well-off and could afford the risk of crop failure. Because he was an experienced farmer as well as a comparatively well-educated man, he could make shrewd guesses concerning the requirements of new crop plants. Although he might not have been an agricultural innovator without meeting the two conditions outlined above, his unique qualification lay in the fact that as village headman he had special access to government agencies and a degree of trust in their recommendations. Although it is often argued that political officials and other members of the establishment are unlikely to be innovators because they tend to be reluctant to introduce elements of instability, the village headman also displayed great political creativity. A few years after India gained its independence, he decided that independence meant a return to the old way of doing things. He also remembered, although few other persons in the village except his close relatives shared his memories, that in the old days the village headman was the absolute ruler of the village and that no government official could enter the village without his permission. He attempted to apply this innovation to a subinspector of police, with the ultimate result that the headman was dismissed from office. In this case his lack of success could be attributed directly to his inability to secure acceptance of his innovation.

The headman's feeling that he lacked the power that he should have had stemmed directly from some unusual aspects of his background. For several generations the family of the village headman had failed to produce male heirs to the headman position. Consequently the headmanship had to be handed down in the female line. Thus the headman was the son of a former headman's daughter's husband. It seems reasonable to suppose that the headman's insecurities concerning his title to the position of headman were what led him to develop the concept of the absolute authority of the headman.

Because Namhalli was a rapidly modernizing village, it contained numerous innovators besides its headman. Most of the innovation consisted, however, of borrowing ideas from the city or from other villages. The overall process was one of adjusting other people's inventions to the village setting by making minor changes in them. Although this kind of diffusion–invention seems far less significant than the development of such breakthrough inventions as agriculture or parliamentary democracy, the dramatic character of the breakthrough invention may derive simply from the fact that we have forgotten the intervening stages in its development. The changes required to produce a viable form of agriculture or a successful form of parliamentary democracy may have been no greater than the changes involved in discovering a way to grow tomatoes in Namhalli.

The difference between an "important" invention and a minor improvement may simply rest in the extent to which it successfully triggers other inventions. The unknown cook who first discovered that a fire would burn hotter if blown upon is responsible for all metallurgical inventions, and yet the discovery itself is a trivial one that can be made by almost anyone who lights a fire. Such ideas as using charcoal instead of wood, enclosing the fire, and producing a draft mechanically through the use of bellows create a pattern or paradigm (a forge) within which a host of discoveries and inventions can be made. A lot of interesting things happen when you heat things up. Recognition of this general principle is a much more fundamental innovation than the discovery that heated water boils or that heated metals turn liquid. Thus there is a difference between the invention of a new general principle and inventions that simply derive from repeated applications of the principle.

A. L. Kroeber[1] interpreted human thought as involving a series of patterns ranging in scale from universal patterns, characteristic of all human beings, through total-culture patterns down to patterns as simple as that of a chair. A pattern is essentially an organization of ideas that set limits upon behavior. For something to be a chair it must possess the basic attributes that define a chair. Variation must take place within the limits of "chairness"; otherwise the object created ceases to be a chair. It is possible to redefine the pattern or paradigm so that the definition of "chairness" is altered, but as long as the basic pattern remains unchanged it is impossible to invent a chair except within the limits imposed by the pattern. In Kroeber's view, once a pattern has been created, it is likely to undergo a period of growth or development leading either to stabilization or to a process of bloom, pattern exhaustion, and decay. In other words, once people are satisfied with existing chairs, they will lose interest in any further improvements. The design of chairs will stabilize except for minor "stylistic" variations. In other sorts of patterns, following the period of growth and bloom, people, as it were, become dissatisfied with the same old thing and begin to introduce new and unusual elements into the pattern. The

---

[1] Alfred L. Kroeber, *Anthropology: Race, Language, Culture, Psychology, Prehistory.* New Edition, Revised (New York: Harcourt Brace Jovanovich, 1948); Thomas S. Kuhn, in *The Structure of Scientific Revolutions* (Chicago: University of Chicago Press, 1962), has made use of the term *paradigm* in much the sense that Kroeber used the term *pattern.* We believe that Kroeber's concepts are more generally useful than those of Kuhn.

result is the breakdown of the pattern and the eventual emergence of one or several new patterns.

The discovery of new principles or of new ways of doing things may, of course, diffuse throughout a cultural setting causing modifications to occur in a variety of patterns. For example, the idea of systematic experimentation developed in the physical sciences and then spread to the biological sciences and is now influencing the social sciences. As the idea of experimentation spread, it created dramatic changes in the patterns of research characteristic of each of the sciences it affected. The interactions between patterns can be of the utmost complexity, and in times of extremely rapid or revolutionary change there may be wholesale revision of almost all existing patterns. When a pattern diffuses from one academic discipline to another or from one culture to another, it is likely to be modified in order to fit the "total cultural pattern" of that discipline or culture. One major cause of invention, then, is the modification of patterns in order to maintain more consistent total or overall patterns. When the pattern of a heavy moldboard plow was transferred from the United States to South India, it had to be modified in order to be accommodated to such local conditions as the need to carry the plow to the field, the need to be able to repair it cheaply, and the need to adjust its size to the relatively limited strength of a pair of bullocks. The moldboard plow used in South India is lighter, smaller, and cheaper than the American plow originally introduced, and its construction has been simplified so that village blacksmiths working with traditional technology could build and repair it. On the other hand, the plow could not be modified so as to have no effect on existing patterns. To use the moldboard plow, the Indian farmer must lean upon its two handles rather than simply walking along behind it as he did with the old single-handled plow. The moldboard plow, however, plows twice as fast as the old plow and twice as effectively. The new pattern had awesome implications for relationships between parents and children because young children were too small to use the new plow; for land tenure, because more land could be plowed by a single man; and for caste ranking, because the blacksmith could earn much more money making moldboard plows than he could making wooden plows with iron-tipped blades. A new pattern, even one so trivial as a new kind of plow, is likely to have ramifying effects, even after it has been modified so as to accommodate some existing patterns.

Both in archaeology and ethnography, one of the key problems involved in the study of patterns has been the difficulty of arriving at a description of the precise elements involved in any particular pattern. Research on change and modification in pattern has often foundered on the inability of scholars to agree on the characteristics of any particular pattern. Recent advances in cognitive anthropology (Chapter 18 , §4) seem to be leading to the development of methodologies which will permit the more precise description of patterns and the analysis of changes in them. For the present we are left with the not insignificant facts that patterns change through time, often in predictable ways, that they interact with other patterns, and that they tend to be altered or abandoned when they cease to meet the needs they originally fulfilled or when they are displaced by more efficient or better-adapted patterns.

The survival of any pattern, whether it is a new way of doing science, a new joke, or an entire way of life, depends upon its diffusion from individual to individual within and between cultural systems. Early studies of diffusion in anthropology dealt primarily with the question of the movement of isolated traits from culture to culture. Diffusion was usually studied by mapping the distribution of particular traits across a geographical region and then attempting to reconstruct the history of the traits by interpreting the distribution in terms of a movement from the simple to the complex or in terms of the distance of each trait from an imaginary center. One might imagine, for example, that two-wheeled carts are older than four-wheeled carts because two-wheeled carts are simpler. If four-wheeled carts are found in continuous distribution on the map, whereas two-wheeled carts are found scattered sporadically around the edges of the map, the marginal distribution of two-wheeled carts would strengthen the supposition that they were older.

Although the historical spread of a particular trait or pattern can sometimes be reconstructed through the application of such simple principles as these, the situation tends to be much more complicated in real life. It is not always easy to define simplicity. The bicycle is a two-wheeled vehicle that developed predictably from a one-wheeled vehicle, yet both the unicycle and the bicycle developed long after four-wheeled vehicles. Perhaps, in fact, the bicycle and unicycle should be regarded as more complex than animal-drawn carts because they involve complicated problems of balancing and steering. The geographical distribution of traits and patterns is affected by patterns of communication between peoples and by the existence of natural barriers which make communication difficult. In addition different traits might spread at different speeds or along different channels of communication. They might also accommodate more easily to some situations than to others and thus have a leapfrogging distribution.

Early students of diffusion found these problems to be insolvable, and the study of diffusion was virtually abandoned following heavy criticism of its findings. The study of diffusion probably represents a scientific paradigm or pattern that was introduced prematurely before the technology required for its success had been developed. Today, with advances in computer technology and communication theory, the resurrection of diffusion studies seems inevitable. In other fields the study of the diffusion of scientific ideas through the analysis of bibliographic citations or the examination of social networks has proved successful, and it may be, such being the nature of diffusion, that modern anthropologists will rediscover the study of diffusion by reading the researches of sociologists and social psychologists who originally learned about diffusion from anthropologists.

3. Cultural Evolution: Main Sequence

The beginnings of anthropology as a discipline rest upon attempts to organize increasing information about the variety of human cultures in a systematic way. In particular, nineteenth-century anthropologists sought to demonstrate the idea of progress; namely that there was a worldwide pattern of improvement in the human condition. The thrust of these early investigations was to establish what might be called a main sequence or general pattern of human evolution and then to locate the different cultures of the world within it. Unlike the Darwinian biologists who saw evolution as a process by means of which new species originated as a result of natural selection within particular environments, the classical evolutionists in anthropology interpreted evolution as a consistent movement toward a single perfect state of civilization. Applying essentially technological criteria, the classical evolutionists realized correctly from the beginning that human general evolution involved a progression from hunting through agriculture to industrial civilization. Although Darwinian biologists made distinctions between lower and higher or more advanced animals, they never argued that all species would eventually evolve into human beings (the "highest" form of life) or that human beings would eventually replace all other species. The classical evolutionists in anthropology, however, argued that because all human beings belonged to the same species and were essentially similar, they would all eventually develop modern industrialized civilizations. The "white man's burden" was precisely the burden of caring for less advanced cousins until their biological and cultural development led them into full partnership. In this general model there was room for disagreement on the possible impact of diffusion or the possibility of skipping stages in evolutionary development, but the overall process of progressive attainment of civilization was preprogrammed, possibly by the divine will. The classical evolutionists did not foresee the imposition of industrial civilization upon all other peoples; rather they anticipated that all other peoples would automatically attain to industrial civilization with the passage of time.

One of the more elaborate sequences of cultural evolution was outlined by Lewis H. Morgan,[2] who saw culture beginning in a lower status of savagery—essentially similar to the foraging stage postulated by modern anthropologist and progressing from there through middle and upper stages of savagery, and on through three stages of barbarism to a seventh stage of civilization. Civilization began with the invention of phonetic writing and the beginnings of nineteenth-century European culture. In connection with each stage, Morgan postulated the existence of particular technologies, particular forms of social organization, and particular forms of art and religion. Morgan, like modern anthropologists, found no living analogues to the lowest stage of development, but was able to confidently place living cultures within the remaining stages. Thus the aboriginal Australians were classified as representing the middle status of savagery, whereas the Polynesians (an agricultural people) were placed in the upper status of savagery because they lacked the bow and arrow. The Iroquois were placed in the lower status of barbarism, the Pueblo Indians in the middle, and the Homeric Greeks in the upper status of barbarism.

One of the deficiencies in Morgan's scheme lies in the problem of dis-

[2] Lewis Henry Morgan, *Ancient Society* (New York: Holt, Rinehart and Winston, 1877).

covering logical order, such as a movement from simple to complex, in the grand pattern of evolution. Even where Morgan attempted to apply logical criteria, he went wrong. For example, he saw family organization as developing from promiscuity, to group marriage, to matrilineal clans, to patrilineal clans, and, finally, to monogamy. Although there is little evidence to show that any known people has ever adopted the general practices of promiscuity or group marriage, the other forms of society certainly exist. They do not, however, exist in association with particular technological stages, as Morgan hoped they would. The monogamous nuclear family, for example, is virtually universal in human societies, and occurs with special frequency among hunters and gatherers. Because forms of family and household organization have a variety of important roles to play in economic production, in child care, and in the ordering of human relationships, most anthropologists now feel that variation and change in family and household are the result of a complex adaptation to a host of economic and social factors. Evolution in family and household organization, then, proceeds in terms of progressively improved adaptations to particular local situations, rather than in terms of the discovery and worldwide diffusion of new and improved forms.

Following Morgan, severe difficulties were encountered in attempts to trace the evolution of language, religion, art, and philosophy. Scholars such as Franz Boas and A. L. Kroeber became reluctant to consider main sequence evolutionary theories, except as they applied to technological improvements. A sharper ax or a more seaworthy boat represents a sort of improvement upon which any user can agree and which can be fairly readily measured. Although there are obviously environmental influences upon axes and boats, a progressive improvement operating almost regardless of environment could still be readily identified. For axes, the transitions from percussion flaking to pressure flaking to grinding to copper and to iron and steel could be readily identified and arranged in evolutionary sequence. For boats, the overall transitions from manpower to windpower to steam power to atomic power could also be viewed in an evolutionary way. This view of technological evolution is, of course, somewhat naive because it considers only technological efficiency. The idea that bigger, faster, sharper is better has only lately come into question. Systematic investigation of the impact of technology on such things as the environment or the quality of life is a topic of very recent interest and is associated with the decline of "chosen people" doctrines and of the idea of automatic, divinely inspired progress.

The limiting of main sequence evolutionary theory to technological change had the general effect of discouraging the more sweeping sorts of evolutionary theory. Increased knowledge about past and present cultures tended to increase the number of exceptions that could be found to any theory, and this too created discouragement. The first attempt at modern main sequence evolutionary theory is generally attributed to Leslie White.[3] White's approach, developed during the 1940s, differed from all but a few earlier

---

[3] Leslie A. White, *The Evolution of Culture, the Development of Civilization to the Fall of Rome* (New York: McGraw-Hill, 1959).

approaches to evolution in that White attempted to develop systematic measures of evolutionary development. Drawing upon the ecological concept of energy, White envisioned the use of measurements of energy production and utilization together with measures of technological efficiency as a universal means of ranking cultures on a scale of development. In these terms the three principal stages in the development of culture could be seen in a different light: hunters and gatherers possessed only their own energies (body power); agriculturalists possessed, in addition, the energy made available by cultivated plants and domesticated animals; and industrialized peoples had access to the energy made available in fossil fuels. One of the criticisms of White's approach is that he did not actually measure either energy or technological efficiency, but utilized the traditional qualitative categories of previous evolutionary theory. In fact efficient hunters and gatherers working in a favorable environment, such as the Northwest Coast of North America, may capture and utilize much more energy than agriculturists working under harsh conditions.

The construction of main sequence evolutionary theories based upon systematic measurement did not begin until the 1950s when the Human Relations Area Files, assembled during the 1940s, came into general use. By drawing samples from the large number of cultures included in the files and attempting to score each culture on several different variables, scholars were able to discover correlations suggestive of main sequence evolutionary developments. There are many problems inherent in such cross-cultural correlational approaches: it is difficult to identify cultures that are comparable units; it is difficult for different raters to agree on appropriate scores for any particular culture; it is difficult to select an appropriate sample; and the expense of the procedure often precludes examination of more than two or three variables at one time. These and other limitations upon the method have resulted in a general failure to reach very high correlations or to produce generally convincing results.

Nevertheless certain relationships both plausible and supported by numerous studies, have developed and been summarized by Raoul Naroll.[4] There has been a general increase in the production and control of energy and in the technological efficiency of tools. This has been accompanied by a general tendency for increasing population density and an increase in the amount produced per capita. Specialization of labor has accompanied these changes, perhaps, in fact, increasing more rapidly than population and technological development. With specialization of labor, there has been a corresponding increase in the apparent amount of knowledge and information contained within the cultural tradition. This has probably gone hand in hand with increases in vocabulary. Despite its general acceptance, the belief that kinship becomes less important with technological development has not been supported. There is a general pattern of increasing complexity in social structure. Thus the more recently developed types of societies have more hierarchical

[4] Raoul Naroll, "What Have We Learned from Cross-Cultural Surveys?" *American Anthropologist*, **72**:1227–1289, Nos. 4–6 (August–December 1960).

levels and more groups within them. There has also been a general movement from village to town to city and an increase in the size of the largest settlement in any society or nation. Less firmly, there appears to be a steady tendency toward increasing concentrations of wealth and toward the centralization of authority. This may even be reflected in emphasis on obedience and responsibility training for children. The rise of formal legal systems has also been documented and found to be related to a corresponding decline in the frequency of witchcraft accusations.

Art styles, games, and song and dance styles also seem to reflect in some degree such features as increasing social complexity and specialization of labor. A number of changes in child-rearing practices, adult personality, and value orientations have also been found to be associated in some degree with such factors as increased population density and increased social complexity.

Granted the difficulties involved in the actual measurement of such things as energy production and technological efficiency, it has become obvious that numbers of people and the manner in which they are related to each other in society is often the key variable in cultural evolution. As a village changes to a town and then to a city, a wide range of changes must occur ranging from specialization to increased yield per acre to an increased capacity for organizing and training large numbers of people. As Ralph Linton has pointed out, nonindustrialized cities have almost always had to be constructed in close proximity to large bodies of water because the large quantities of grain required for urban consumption could be transported only by boat.[5] In considering matters of this sort, many anthropologists have involved themselves in chicken and egg controversies concerning the sort of priority that should be given to technological, sociological, and ideological changes accompanying evolution. You cannot have a city containing a million people unless you have a means of feeding those people, and for this reason there has been a tendency, most recently illustrated in the work of Marvin Harris,[6] to insist that technological changes such as increased food production must precede sociological and ideological changes. On the other hand, a city of one million people which lacked a division of labor and a division of the population into organized and hierarchically ordered groups could not possibly exist. As recent history has shown repeatedly, cities composed of groups with antagonistic ideologies may also encounter survival difficulties. The best guess, then, is that different aspects of culture tend to evolve together, with changes in any one aspect of culture automatically triggering changes in other aspects. The construction of progressively larger cities involves so many small, interrelated changes in technology, social organization, and ideology that it is fruitless to attempt to identify the first, and presumably causal, change.

Even under circumstances of the planned and deliberate introduction of change, it is not easy to separate technology from social organization and ideology. One classic article by Lauriston Sharp traces the consequences of

---

[5] Ralph Linton, *The Tree of Culture* (New York: Knopf, 1956), p. 119.

[6] Marvin Harris, "Introduction," *The Rise of Anthropological Theory* (New York: T. Y. Crowell, 1968), pp. 1–7.

the introduction of steel axes among Australian aborigines and depicts a number of changes in social organization that were presumably caused by this single change.[7] In view of the fact that the steel axes were introduced by Christian missionaries, it is hard to believe that the steel axes, as they were traded to increasingly distant groups, did not, as it were, carry with them an ideological stain. People can, but rarely do, transmit items of technology without engaging in conversation and, very often — not perhaps in the case of a simple substitution of steel axes for stone — items of technology cannot be used until organizational changes have been made. Irrigation theorists, deriving their ideas from Karl Wittfogel,[8] have argued that the introduction of irrigated agriculture leads to a need for a social system capable of exerting absolute control oven an entire river valley. Although this seems to be a clear case of technological innovation preceding sociological innovation, it is necessary to wonder how irrigation dams and water distribution systems were built without the development of social organizations to build them. Indeed, a large irrigation system built on the scene by local residents could only develop through gradual increments in which a small group built the first small irrigation work and then, later, through organizational innovation, developed the capacity to organize a larger group to build a larger irrigation work. The organization of larger groups to build ever larger irrigation works could hardly succeed without the development of an ideology that somehow rationalized the combination of previously independent social groupings. The archaeologist V. Gordon Chile connects the development of large-scale irrigation and urbanization in Mesopotamia to the emergence of divinely descended rulers.[9]

4. Cultural Evolution: Local Adaptation

Although the period from 1900 to 1940 was dominated by increasing skepticism about grand evolutionary theories and other sorts of historical reconstructions, the study of cultural evolution on a small scale continued. Even before 1900 Franz Boas, regarded by Leslie White as an archenemy of evolutionary theory, was publicly advocating what amounted to the study of local evolution. In an article published in 1895 entitled "The Growth of the Secret Societies of the Kwakiutl," Boas attempts to trace the changes secret societies must have undergone and suggests that they originated out of the pattern of warfare. Boas does not, however, as a main sequence evolutionist would be impelled to do, imply that secret societies represent a universal response to a particular method of warfare.[10]

---

[7] (Richard) Lauriston Sharp, "Steel Axes for Stone Age Australians," in *Human Problems in Technological Change* (ed.) Edward H. Spicer (New York: Russell Sage Foundation, 1952), pp. 69–90.

[8] Karl Wittfogel, *Oriental Despotism* (New Haven: Yale University Press, 1957).

[9] V Gordon Childe, *What Happened in History* (Hammondsworth, Middlesex, England: Penguin Books, 1942).

[10] Franz Boas, *Race, Language and Culture* (New York: Macmillan, Inc., 1948), pp. 379–383.

Writing in 1927 in the Preface to his classic work on art, Boas[11] states clearly the theoretical principles which he held consistently for thirty years. First, each culture is to be understood as "an historical growth determined by the social and geographical environment in which each people is placed and by the way in which it develops the cultural material that comes into its possession from the outside or through its own creativeness." Second, research has disproved "the existence of far-reaching homologies which would permit us to arrange all the manifold cultural lines in an ascending scale in which to each can be assigned its proper place." Third, "dynamic conditions exist, based on environment, physiological, psychological, and social factors, that may bring forth similar cultural processes in different parts of the world, so that it is probable that some of the historical happenings may be viewed under more general dynamic viewpoints."

Although in practice the evolutionism of Boas was confined to the interplay of diffusion and invention, his overall approach involved the explanation of change in terms of a complex interplay among evironment, diffused influences, and internal characteristics of the culture studied. He did not, however, emphasize the role of adaptation and selection in influencing change. As noted earlier in discussing invention and diffusion, Boas' student, A. L. Kroeber, interpreted cultural evolution as a result of the growth and decay of cultural patterns. His *Configurations of Culture Growth*[12] involved elaborate attempts to trace the rise and fall of historical civilizations in terms of such pattern growth and decay. Working, as did Boas, without the assistance of the concept of adaptation, Kroeber found himself unable to arrive at any general principles that would explain the rise and fall of civilizations.

Working with the sociologists Park and Burgess, Robert Redfield,[13] another student of Franz Boas, developed a general theory of urbanization on the basis of intensive study carried out in Yucatán. Working along lines suggested by diffusion theory, he organized a study of four communities—a city, a town, a village, and a tribe—located along a geographical line thought to represent increasing marginality and isolation. Although the data collected from each of the four communities can be said to represent a study of local adaptation and change, the general principles derived represent a main sequence theory of development. Thus the city is less isolated, more heterogeneous, more dependent upon a cash economy, has more professional specialists, places less emphasis on kinship institutions, relies more on impersonal institutions, is less religious, and allows greater freedom of action and choice to the individual. These differences of degree extend downward through all four communities, so that there is a gradual increase in urban characteristics in moving from the tribe to the city. A theory of this kind, like other main sequence theories, does not explain similarities and differences among groups of the same population size or same degree of technological development. Redfield's

[11] Franz Boas, *Primitive Art* (New York: Dover, 1955; first edition published 1927).

[12] Alfred L. Kroeber, *Configurations of Culture Growth* (Berkeley: University of California Press, 1944).

[13] Robert Redfield, *The Folk Culture of Yucatán* (Chicago and London: University of Chicago Press, 1941).

work, like that of Boas and Kroeber, also fails to provide a mechanism, such as adaptation, which would explain why cities should exhibit particular characteristic features.

Writing in the 1930s, somewhat before Leslie White made use of the concept of energy, Julian Steward is generally credited with the introduction of concepts of ecology and adaptation into theories of cultural evolution.[14] Steward's approach, which he labeled "multilinear evolution," involves attempting to discover meaningful similarities between any set of two or more cultures. Where such similarities can be identified, it may be possible to determine the causal factors that led to their development. If two or more societies can be shown to operate under similar ecological and technological restrictions — if they are adapting to the same conditions — then convergent evolution is likely to take place. Steward hypothesized, for example, that the organization of patrilineal bands was dependent upon the presence of a series of interrelated environmental circumstances, especially those connected with the hunting of large game animals. This idea was later picked up by one of White's students, Elman Service,[15] who attempted to transform it into a main sequence evolutionary theory in which a connection was implied between environmental circumstances and a progressive transition from patrilineal band through chiefdom and state. A similar formulation of the growth of agricultural civilizations by Steward has not been enthusiastically accepted. Ideally the methodology suggested by Steward in connection with the study of patrilineal bands suggests, in strong contrast to main sequence evolutionary theory, a division of hunter-gatherer peoples into a variety of evolutionary types, each representing a particular sort of adaptation. According to biological theories of evolution, one and only one of these types would contribute to the main sequence of evolution. This is true only because biological species cannot exchange information in the way that human beings can. In speaking of cultural evolution, it is possible to argue that all or many of the different evolutionary types of hunter-gatherers might have contributed in one way or the other to such agricultural civilizations as superseded them in many parts of the world. Thus the tree of culture depicted in Kroeber's *Anthropology* has intertwining branches, whereas the tree of life does not.

5. Acculturation and Modernization

Although studies of local adaptation and cultural change could be based upon archaeological evidence or historical reconstruction through the study of trait distributions, it became increasingly evident during the 1930s that much cultural change in existing societies reflected the worldwide impact of processes of modernization and subsequent colonization by west European nations.

---

[14] Julian Steward, *Theory of Culture Change* (Urbana: University of Illinois Press, 1955).

[15] Elman R. Service, *Primitive Social Organization: An Evolutionary Perspective* (New York: Random House, 1971).

Early periods characterized by similar phenomena were also recognized, such as the penetration of Hellenistic cultures in Asia, the spread of Buddhism from India to China and Southeast Asia, or the Romanization of western Asia, northern Africa, and Europe. Such events marked the massive confrontation of markedly different cultures, often with coercive intervention by more powerful societies, leading to rapid cultural changes and readaptations in one or both of the societies involved.

Because European or Western cultures were among the first to be affected by the sweeping influences of industrialization and urbanization, subsequent changes in other parts of the world were often interpreted, especially by nonanthropologists, as a process of Westernization, or even Americanization. Although the concept of a one-way spread of ideas from Europe to all other places is consistent with a concept of unilineal evolution, in which the European cultures are regarded as standing at a pinnacle of advancement, the concepts of Westernization and Americanization make no adequate provision for the rather substantial contributions to the industrial revolution made by non-Western cultures.

The term *acculturation* developed out of an attempt to find a value-free term that could be applied to all situations in which culture change resulted from massive and prolonged contact between different cultures. Initially a number of anthropologists rejected the term; British anthropologists still prefer the more general term *culture contact*. One editor of the *American Anthropologist* rejected articles on acculturation on the grounds that contemporary short-run changes were not a proper concern for anthropology. Such a view, had it been maintained, would have relegated anthropology to the study of dead cultures and past events, and it was ultimately rejected. Acculturation studies proliferated rapidly during the 1930s, and serious efforts were made to define the major problems involved and to set up criteria useful for defining the nature of the contact between cultures, measuring the scale or size of the societies involved, or describing possible alternative outcomes.

Although, theoretically, acculturation could occur as a result of contact between two relatively simple but significantly different cultures, it soon became evident that most available examples of acculturation involved the impact of colonizing or industrializing societies upon smaller, less industrialized, or "traditional" societies. Such types of acculturation are often referred to as modernization. Although, strictly speaking, *modernization* might properly be used to refer to any current changes in any society, it has often been used as synonymous with Westernization and Americanization. A more acceptable use of the term is in reference to current worldwide patterns in which local cultures and communities undergo rapid cultural change in response to a variety of overwhelming pressures generated by larger national cultures. In this view, local or traditional cultures may exert influence upon the larger culture that engulfs them, but their relative impact upon the larger culture tends to be small in comparison to the impact of the larger culture upon them. In this sense, modernization can be used to describe the inevitable interplay between national societies and the many subcultures and alternative life styles exhibited by the smaller groups out of which they are composed. Used cautiously, *modernization* can also refer to the worldwide spread of new ideas and new ways of doing things, provided the process is seen as something more complicated than simply making "them" more like "us." Although the realization that most of the world is not Americanizing or Westernizing, and does not wish to do so, has spread slowly, the examples of Japan, China, and many newly independent countries have gradually provided convincing evidence that high levels of industrialization can be achieved in the comparative ab-

Portrait of "She Likes to Move the Camp," a Crow Indian Woman. Steel axes, woven blankets, cloth, and shoes can be taken as evidence of acculturation. To obtain such goods it is usually necessary to find a source of cash income permitting participation in an urban economy. Such goods may also be obtained through conversion to Christianity. Photograph by Father P. P. Prando. (Courtesy of Smithsonian Institution, National Anthropological Archives.)

sence of Westernization or Americanization. Especially in the newly independent countries that have rejected colonial status, there is often a conscious attempt to develop indigenous versions of modernity which can be interpreted as growth and development of national culture rather than as the substitution of Western culture for traditional culture. For this reason the term *development* is increasingly preferred in descriptions of recent cultural change in modern nations.

By extension, words like *acculturation* and *modernization* have also come to be applied to individuals. In this usage an individual who has abandoned traditional cultural practices in favor of modern cultural practices is considered acculturated or modernized. The same can be said of an individual who retains the ability to play roles in both traditional and modern culture. Individuals who have adapted more readily to changes taking place in their own culture, and individuals who have migrated from one society to another and adapted to the new society, are also sometimes described as acculturated or modernized. This usage confuses changes in the individual and changes in cultural systems, but it is probably too well entrenched to be discarded. A similar confusing usage occurs in connection with urbanization. A traditional culture becomes urbanized only if it develops a city. If it is merely influenced by urban ways, it is modernized or acculturated to an urban tradition.

Systematic research on acculturation and modernization in the United States can be dated from the time of Mooney's classic study of the Ghost Dance, and in Russia from Bogoraz's equally important study of the Chuckchee of Siberia.[16] Acculturation was not, however, recognized as an academic specialization until the 1930s, when attempts were made to define the term in a formal way and to develop ways of describing cultural systems engaged in change over a period of time. Subsequently some anthropologists, despite warnings about the importance of maintaining a distinction between assimilation (the absorption of one culture by another) and acculturation (the contact between two cultures), interpreted the study of acculturation essentially in terms suggestive of main sequence evolutionary theory. In these terms acculturation was essentially the assimilation of traditional cultures into modern cultures viewed as essentially Western in character. The process of acculturation was considered a primarily linear development closely parallel to the folk-urban continuum described by Redfield in his studies of Yucatán (see Chapter 9, § 2). Although Redfield actually was examining folk-urban relationships within a single setting, the Peninsula of Yucatán, many persons in and out of anthropology generalized his findings far beyond this region, adopting a much more restricted view of acculturation. Folk cultures and their members, it was believed, were faced with the alternatives of assimilation or extermination. Although this was true in many cases, there were also many cases where viable alternatives to assimilation or extermination were found.

---

[16] James Mooney, *The Ghost Dance Religion and the Sioux Outbreak of 1890*. 14th Annual Report of the Bureau of Ethnology to the Secretary of the Smithsonian Institution, 1892–3. (Washington, D.C.: U.S. Government Printing Office, 1896); Vladimir G. Bogoraz, *The Chukchee*. Reprint of 1909 ed. (New York: Johnson Reprint Corp.).

For those who saw acculturation as simply a step along the road to assimilation, the main value of a theory of acculturation was the provision of a practical means of easing the "inevitable" transition from folk to urban, or from "savage" to "civilized." As studies of acculturation proliferated during the 1930s and 1940s, those who originally saw a sharp distinction between acculturation and assimilation were vindicated. The realization that there are alternative ways of modernizing, that modernization can be carried out without the loss of cultural identity, and that alternatives to total modernization can be found is now quite general. Further, perhaps as concepts of progress and national superiority have been called increasingly into question, studies of acculturation have given more and more attention to all of the cultures involved in an acculturation situation, rather than just to the study of what might be called the victims of such a situation. In studies having an assimilationist orientation, emphasis was often placed on the victims rather than on the perpetrators, and the anthropologist's idealized view of modern culture was all too often substituted for serious study of the actual configuration of modern influences affecting any particular traditional society. Thus, from an assimilationist point of view, the Hopi Indians, despite their highly successful adaptation to their present modern circumstances, could be viewed as resistant to change, or "unacculturated," because they continued to speak Hopi and to maintain certain traditional Hopi practices. In the broader view, in which assimilation is no longer regarded as inevitable or even desirable, the Hopi can be seen as an example of a group that has found a specialized niche within modern society which has permitted them to maintain many traditional beliefs and practices and to exercise a selective control over the processes of modernization which are affecting them as well as everyone else. Another example of the importance of a distinction between acculturation and assimilation is given in the following section.

6. Acculturation in Mexico

As we have previously noted, the first Spanish expedition under Cortes reached Mexico when it was dominated by the Aztecs of Tenochtitlán, a capital built on the present site of Mexico City. The Aztecs and their neighbors throughout central and southern Mexico lived in an urban society; that is, one characterized by relatively large cities supported by a highly developed system of garden cultivation, and having as well a high degree of occupational specialization, extensive commerce, and well-developed socioeconomic classes. The government at Tenochtitlán had, in the two centuries preceding the coming of Cortes, expanded its control over many other peoples through a systematic and ruthless program of military conquests. Conquered peoples were not, however, drawn into a closely knit political system, but retained considerable freedom and local autonomy as long as they remained at peace with Tenochtitlán and continued to pay that city a fixed annual tribute.

When the Spanish arrived, they found many groups restive under Aztec domination, and some of these gave them a friendly reception. By organizing native disaffection, the small unit of Spaniards, who were never more than 2,500 in number, raised a large native army and destroyed Tenochtitlán. After the fall of Tenochtitlán, many of the peoples formerly dominated by the Aztecs, and who had taken no part in the revolt, peaceably accepted the Spaniards as the successors to the Aztecs and continued paying tribute.

Even more remarkable than the conquest of a region of some 5 to 10 million people by 2,500 Spaniards is the fact that the Spaniards were able to keep control; after eighty years (at the end of the sixteenth century) there still were only about 20,000 Spaniards in the country. An examination of the record shows that this was the result of several processes. In the first place, the Spaniards simply moved into the position in the existing social structure that had previously been occupied by the Aztec upper class. Native rulers friendly to the new regime were allowed to keep their positions; many became rapidly and thoroughly Hispanicized. Intermarriage was frequent. The native religion had been closely bound up with the power of the dominant Aztec group, and when it was defeated, it lost much prestige. Christianity thus found easy acceptance among peoples who were already hospitable toward new religious ideas. For large segments of the population the Spanish Conquest made little change in political participation or economic life; they continued to cultivate their ancestral lands in much the same fashion as before and paid the same tribute to the government, now Spanish rather than Indian. Although public religious performances changed radically, in many regions the "common man" continued to perform his household and agricultural rituals in the old, traditional form.

All evidence points to a period after the Conquest in which the Indians tended to accept European culture with considerable eagerness and rapidity. In addition, the Spanish undertook to produce directional change; that is, official policy was to convert the Indian into a Christian subject of the Spanish crown. For a period of time the existing native class structure was assimilated to the Spanish class structure. Not only did intermarriage occur at higher levels in Mexico, but some of the native nobility migrated to Spain and were assimilated into appropriate levels of the Spanish nobility. Techniques of indirect rule, later to be used in this century by Dutch and British colonists, saw retention of local leaders in positions of authority. Cultural pluralism was also envisaged and many Indian groups were constituted into "Indian republics" in contrast with the "Spanish republics" of the urban centers.

Some Indians became *Ladinos* (literally, "neighbors"); they lived in Spanish-dominated towns, although often in separate districts, and adopted Spanish dress and lifeways. (This early usage of the term *Ladino*, it should be noted, differs from the contemporary usage of the word in the state of Chiapas, Mexico, and in Guatemala, where it refers to mestizos.) In areas where the Spanish became large landholders, the Indians were gradually brought under greater exploitation and control. Their work habits were modified, the non-Christian elements of their religion were eliminated, their dress was changed, and often their language was lost. On the other hand, many food habits and techniques remained, and in considerable part these were adopted by the Spanish conqueror. In short, except for the Spaniards of the cities, who were in constant contact with the Old World, the distinction in culture between Indians and Spaniards tended to disappear, except as the latter maintained their distinctiveness as members of the upper class. Substitutive and additive processes were dominant.

In other regions Indians were put under the administration of missionary orders, which attempted to prevent Indians from learning Spanish in order to protect them from the bad example of the Spanish. Self-governing Indian communities were formed, and Indian titles to land were maintained. These missionaries introduced many elements of European culture, carefully selected, which the Indians accepted either through force, persuasion, or interest, without at the same time losing all their Indian ways. When the missionaries were removed in the eighteenth century, the Indian societies still retained some cohesiveness, although they were not the same as in aboriginal times. The Indians could not speak Spanish, and the secular priests who succeeded the missionaries did not learn Indian languages. The Indians were heavily exploited and disillusioned by their inferior role in the new Spanish-American society. Consequently, they withdrew when they could to avoid all possible contact with the Spaniards. Definite movements to revive old ways developed in many areas, and new European elements were frequently rejected. But because many of the old ways had been forgotten, attempts at revival were often unsuccessful, and the new stable culture that emerged was an amalgam of Indian and European elements.

Today, then, Mexico is a region of many distinctive cultures, roughly to be divided, perhaps, into two main groups. The first of these includes the so-called Mestizo cultures, in many regional variants. The bearers of these cultures are Spanish-speaking and the descendants of those who, under the direct control of the conquerors, took over new ways of living, retaining only a very few elements of their aboriginal and pre-Conquest cultures. The second are the Indian cultures, which differ markedly not only from the cultures of the Mestizos, but also from each other. Bearers of these cultures speak Indian languages in the main and know little Spanish. Except in respect to language, the Indian cultures, especially in their distinctive features, are mainly the result not of the retention and development of pre-Conquest elements, but rather of the retention and readaptation of sixteenth- and seventeenth-century Spanish cultural traits, which have long disappeared from the non-Indian cultures of Mexico. In the Indian cultures these elements, modified and reworked, have been so integrated with aboriginal cultural patterns as to result in completely new cultural wholes, which are amalgams, not simple mixtures, of Spanish and Indian traits. The modern "Indian" cultures of Mexico are, then, certainly not Indian in the pre-Conquest sense, nor are they Spanish; they are, rather, new creations that have emerged from a fusion of both the Spanish and the Indian traditions. They form plural societies.

The concept of Mexico as a plural society that is likely to remain a plural society runs directly counter to the view of acculturation as a process leading to the emergence of a single uniform modern national culture. Although the time may come when all citizens of Mexico speak a single national language and participate equally in a nationwide political and economic order, there is little indication that this necessarily implies the loss of separate ethnic or regional identities.

7. Acculturation in Melanesia

A rather different acculturative situation is reported by Margaret Mead for Manus in Melanesia.[17] When first studied by Mead, Manus culture was only slightly affected by contacts with Europeans. During World War II Manus became a major staging area for the war in the western Pacific. Not only was a huge base constructed, but hundreds of thousands of American troops passed through it, often staying for weeks or months. The people of Manus did not see all of Western culture, but they observed an awesome display of technological developments and had opportunities to observe other ways of life and to know many Americans in various capacities.

Following the war the people of Manus quite consciously decided that their culture was unsatisfactory and set out rationally to change it in almost every respect. At the time of Mead's revisit to Manus they had made great strides in this process. Although Mead still had doubts about the permanence or viability of many of the changes, she found them so impressive that she suggested that very possibly efforts at directed culture change might be more effective if they simultaneously undertook a complete revision of all aspects of culture rather than the piecemeal approach used by most efforts at culture change and development.

Plausibility is lent to this approach by the complexity of culture change as it increasingly is revealed by acculturation studies. The functionalists had already insisted on the interrelationships of various aspects of culture. Acculturation studies show that even small modification, particularly when introduced by force or under pressure, may have far-reaching effects, give rise to profound psychological conflicts, and enforce major reorientations of ideas and values. Not infrequently, acculturative processes result in considerable social disturbances and in much individual neurotic behavior.

8. Summary

Cultural change is the primary means of human adaptation to changing environmental circumstances. Although cultural change differs in many ways from adaptation by means of biological evolution, it may also be regarded as a kind of extension of biological evolution. Cultural evolution resembles biological evolution in that change can be either endogenous or exogenous in origin,

---

[17] Margaret Mead, *New Lives for Old* (New York: Dell, 1968).

it can be examined at either a general or a specific level, and each change is likely to trigger further changes. It differs in that cultural change can be relatively more purposeful, changes can be transmitted from one culture to another by diffusion, and changes can occur during the lifetime of the individual.

Change in culture involves processes of innovation which may result from error, from problem-solving behavior, or from a combination of both. The successful innovator generally has access to new information, ways of combining such information in new ways, motivation for trying new things, and an ability to convince others of the desirability of the innovation. The examples of innovation in Namhalli illustrate some of the problems involved in identifying innovators and in determining whether or not a particular innovation represents invention or diffusion. Because things always change when they diffuse, the problem of distinguishing between major inventions and minor improving changes is difficult to solve. In many cases dramatic breakthroughs may appear dramatic simply because no record exists of the minor developments that led to the breakthrough. Perhaps the most important way of distinguishing between major and minor inventions is in terms of the extent to which one invention triggers others. Thus the trivial discovery that interesting things happen when substances are heated turns out to be a major principle underlying a host of subsequent inventions.

Kroeber's concept of pattern and Kuhn's concept of paradigm provide convenient ways of handling progressive changes within particular domains. Although concepts of stylistic variation and of the bloom, exhaustion, and decay of patterns are useful, there are still problems involved in the precise definition of particular patterns or paradigms. The case of the moldboard plow in South India serves to illustrate processes of diffusion in which a particular innovation is modified in order to maintain the consistency of a total cultural pattern. It also illustrates the ramifying effects that may derive from the introduction of a single new element. The survival of any cultural pattern, whether large or small, depends upon its diffusion or spread from individual to individual or from culture to culture. Traditional studies of diffusion had as their main goal the reconstruction of history. Although such reconstructions often proved unsuccessful, the current success of diffusion studies in other disciplines and the development of improved methods for the study of diffusion are leading to a revival of interest in diffusion studies in anthropology.

Studies of the general evolution of human culture began with the classical evolutionists of the nineteenth century. The idea of an inevitable progression of all cultures through a series of stages of development is illustrated by the work of Lewis Henry Morgan. Later scholars, although they granted the possibilities of technological evolution, encountered difficulties in tracing the evolution of such aspects of culture as language, religion, art, and philosophy. Historical reconstructions and grand evolutionary schemes fell into general disrepute until they were revived during the 1940s by Leslie White and others. More recently, use of the Human Relations Area Files has led to comparatively sophisticated analyses and permitted agreement on at least some aspects of a main sequence theory of cultural evolution. Although many scholars feel that technological changes always precede changes in social organization or ideology, the prevaling view seems to be that changes in all aspects of culture tend to proceed hand in hand.

Although general evolutionary theories now have an important place among theories of cultural change, most anthropologists continue to feel more comfortable with smaller-scale theories of the kind advocated by Franz Boas. Although Boas and such students of his as Kroeber and Redfield made substantial progress toward evolutionary explanations of selected aspects of cultural change, they made sparing use of the biological concepts of adaptation and ecology. The popularization of these concepts, which have tended to emphasize parallels between biological and cultural evolution, is generally attributed to Julian Steward.

Throughout the rise and fall of theories of general and specific cultural evolution, actual research on cultural change has tended to focus on the processes of acculturation and modernization. Acculturation was recognized as a major focus of American anthropology during the 1930s, and systematic research on interactions between cultures in contact has remained important. The example of Mexico indicates how processes of modernization can lead to the development of plural societies, while the example of Melanesia indicates that acculturation need not be a painful or involuntary process.

Collateral Reading

Barnett, Homer G. *Innovation: The Basis of Cultural Change*. New York: McGraw-Hill Book Company, 1953. The nature of innovations and the character of the innovator are examined.

Childe, V. Gordon. *Social Evolution*. London and New York: H. Schuman, 1951. A fairly classical evolutionary and somewhat Marxist view of social and cultural change.

Eggan, Fred. *The American Indian: Perspectives for the Study of Social Change*. Chicago: Aldine Publishing Company, 1964. A thoughtful and important book, theoretically oriented case studies.

Herskovits, Melville J. "The Process of Cultural Change," *The Science of Man in the World Crisis*, (ed.) Ralph Linton. New York: Columbia University Press, 1945, pp. 143–170. A general theoretical statement, still with more than historical interest.

Kroeber, A. L., et al. (eds.). *Anthropology Today*. Chicago: University of Chicago Press, 1953. See especially "Evolution and Progress," by Julian H. Steward; "Universal Categories of Culture," by Clyde Kluckhohn; "Social Structure," by Claude Lévi-Strauss; "The Relation of Language to Culture," by Harry Hoijer. Good reviews of the subject as of the date published.

Mooney, James. *The Ghost Dance Religion and the Sioux Outbreak of 1890*, edited and abridged by Anthony F. C. Wallace. Chicago: University of Chicago Press, 1965. The first major attempt to study a nativistic movement in detail.

Morgan, Lewis H. *Ancient Society*. New York: Holt, Rinehart and Winston, Inc., 1877. The classic early evolutionist statement.

Sahlins, Marshall D., and Elman R. Service. *Evolution and Culture*. Ann Arbor: University of Michigan Press, 1960. A neo-evolutionist study.

Smith, Anthony D. *The Concept of Social Change: A Critique of the Functionalist Theory of Social Change.* Monographs in Social Theory. London and Boston: Routledge & Kegan Paul, Ltd., 1973.

Steward, Julian H. *Theory of Culture Change.* Urbana: University of Illinois Press, 1955. Contains author's views on multilinear evolution.

Tylor, Edward B. *Primitive Culture.* Boston: Estes and Lauriat, 1874. Vol. I, Chapters I–IV. A foundation stone of anthropology of historical interest.

White, Leslie. *The Science of Culture.* New York: Farrar, Straus & Giroux, Inc., 1949. The leading neo-evolutionist expounds his views on energy and society.

Wissler, Clark. *Man and Culture.* New York: Thomas Y. Crowell Company, 1923. Presents the diffusionist and culture area points of view.

20/Applied Anthropology and Development

1. Applied Science and Anthropology

Whether or not deliberately engaged in the study of acculturation, the anthropological fieldworker automatically acquires knowledge about the kinds of changes that are taking place within the group studied. One of the earliest practical applications of anthropology has consisted simply in informing government officials, the general public, or anyone else who would listen about the lifeways and problems of some particular people or group. Although the collection and distribution of information about people remain the chief practical function of anthropology, applied anthropology proper involves the deliberate use of anthropological knowledge in order to produce change.

Under ideal circumstances the applied anthropologist would be employed by a group of people who sought to change their way of life. The anthropologist would assist them in defining their goals; outline the possible consequences of alternative courses of action; aid them in reaching a decision on what is to be done; help them to overcome any obstacles that develop; and evaluate the consequences of each attempt at change. In practice, these ideal conditions can rarely be met. The applied anthropologist tends to be employed by an outside agency that may seek to manipulate the "target population" either for their own good or in order to meet specific goals of the outside agency. Very often the membership of the group to be changed finds it impossible to agree upon goals, has difficulty in comprehending the costs and benefits of different alternative courses of action, and has difficulty arriving at unanimous decisions. In the end, the goals sought may not be attainable and, because anthropology is not an exact science and social situations are extraordinarily complicated, the anthropologist may turn out to be wrong.

Although the problems involved in the development of a workable applied anthropology have led many to doubt its value, the fact remains that in many situations conscientious anthropologists have little choice but to attempt to apply their knowledge. For example, when the island of Bikini was selected by the United States government for an atomic test, the military governor of the Marshall Islands explained the situation to the Bikinians and secured their agreement to removal from the island. The Bikinians were resettled on the island of Rongerik, which had limited resources, produced inferior coconuts, and was regarded as the former home of a dangerous female spirit whose malign influence still lingered. The lack of resources on Rongerik and the lack of will to struggle against what appeared to be a hopeless situation soon brought the Bikinians to the verge of starvation. It was at this point that the anthropologist Leonard Mason of the University of Hawaii arrived on the scene. After he had uncovered the underlying causes of the difficulties and the unanimous wish of the Bikinians to move almost anywhere else, the military government flew in emergency food rations and arranged for the Bikinians to move to another island of their own selection. As of 1976 the Bikinians are still unhappy and still unable to understand the existence of dangerous radio-activity which continues to make their home island uninhabitable. The United States government, for its part, continues to consider ways and means of returning the Bikinians to their homeland. In this case, although the outcome remains far from ideal, the survival of the Bikinians can be seen to be directly related to the deliberate and unsought intervention of an applied anthropologist.

While it is plainly unethical for the applied anthropologist to assist powerful outside agencies in doing things that should not be done, the situation very often is one in which policies are already decided upon and anthropologists have no choice but to attempt to ameliorate the situation to the best of their ability. In some cases, hardly distinguishable from the above, the responsibility of the applied anthropologist is to refuse cooperation with outside agencies and to do everything possible to frustrate their policies. The choice between attempting to work with an outside agency in order to soften the effects of a manipulative policy and organizing direct resistance to the agency and its policies is difficult. Either amelioration or resistance may fail, with disastrous consequences for the people the anthropologist is trying to help. In most cases the choice between amelioration and resistance is not one that the anthropologist should make unaided. In fact, the ability to assist any particular group of people depends upon the anthropologist's success in presenting himself or herself to them and in explaining the options available. It is unethical for anthropologists to use their knowledge of a particular culture and their special position as a means of persuading others to do something that they do not want to do or that is not in their best interests. Although in the past some anthropologists, particularly those working for colonial governments, have justified policies of manipulation on the grounds that "those people" did not know what was best for themselves, the prevailing view today is that applied anthropology is justified only when change is desired by the people themselves or where change is in the process of being imposed by force. In either case the role of the applied anthropologist is not to make policy but rather to explain options and, if possible, to mediate conflicts and correct misunderstandings.

Policies usually are political decisions, involving establishing priorities, weighing competing demands for scarce resources, and deciding between conflicting goals. The anthropologist who enters this realm is apt to become a politician rather than a scientist.

On the other hand, the anthropologist (and these remarks apply to all social scientists) should be involved with policy decisions at many levels. Among the things the anthropologist is in a position to do are:

(1) Assemble and organize the data needed to make informed decisions and, if necessary, provide new data through research. Here the anthropologist should have a major voice in policy in the sense of deciding what research is needed and how it should be carried out.

(2) Estimate the probable social consequences of alternative decisions. It should be pointed out that there always are at least two alternatives, to act or not to act; usually there also are two or more alternatives for action. A thorough analysis will also estimate what future courses of action may be foreclosed or made possible by a policy decision.

(3) Should have a major, although not necessarily final, voice concerning the ways policies should be implemented. If research is needed, again the anthropologist should have a major and perhaps final voice in the formulation of research projects and the methods to be used in carrying them out.

(4) Evaluate the effectiveness of projects or programs in achieving stated goals.

These rules are predicated on the assumption that applied anthropology is needed and desirable. Items (3) and (4) of course assume that the anthropologist accepts the policies finally adopted. As a sociologist has indicated succinctly, if a scientist objects to the policy of an agency, she or he should not take its money. Whether or not an anthropologist is taking money from an agency, a primary ethical and professional responsibility is to make sure that politicians and administrators are aware of the human consequences of their decisions. Finally, anthropologists overwhelmingly agree that their first responsibility is to the welfare of the people they study; this applies with special force to the applied anthropologist.

Many people, including some anthropologists, look with disfavor on attempts to control culture. Some anthropologists feel that such work impairs the scientific points of view of the anthropologists and that they become mere agents of expediency in carrying out administrative policies. Others feel that our knowledge of culture is still not sufficient; we are apt to forget that we do not have all the answers and hence to cease to do the fundamental research that is still necessary. Some anthropologists feel that they should never indicate practical values for their research. A few have gone so far as to say that research should never be published because it might be misapplied, for example, in carrying out warfare or to facilitate exploitation or discrimination. Others assert that science is neutral; whether it is used for good or evil ends depends upon people. The scientists, hence, are not responsible for the uses made of their results. At least a partial answer is that scientists should be concerned about the application of their results. Whether engaged in an applied program or not, many feel that anthropologists concerned about the use to which their results may be put are obligated to specify the proper practical uses. In any case, there is much to be said for the professional responsibility of all anthropologists, whether specifically in the applied field or not, to lose no opportunity to point out the social consequences of public policy and both public and private acts. In so doing, a distinction should be made between the role of citizen expressing personal beliefs and values and the role of scientist working on the basis of established scientific principles and knowledge.

Attempts to control culture involve the lives and futures of many human beings. Serious responsibilities are assumed by those who would undertake such a task. Anthropologists and administrators must decide on objectives and determine values in many cases, although in a democratic society machinery exists for the determination of goals by the members of the group. Such techniques should be improved. Our knowledge is still so limited that mistakes are certain to be made. Control techniques may be used for nefarious purposes, as was done in Nazi Germany.

Perhaps it should be pointed out that much the same arguments were used when science began to show us how to control nature. Many people felt that interference with nature was sacrilegious, overlooking the fact that by mere possession of culture human beings constantly interfered with and controlled nature. Science still has not found ways to control more than a limited part of nature. Moreover, applied science has made many mistakes. For example, during World War I, applied science made possible a great extension of farming in the drier regions of our own Middle West. The unforeseen results were serious erosion, more severe and devastating floods, and the so-called dustbowl conditions of the early 1930s. Nevertheless few people today would have us give up our scientific control of nature. The answer is not abandonment of science but the development of more and better science, and improvement of our understanding of culture and the development of better informed ways of reaching decisions.

2. The Development of Applications

The earliest systematic use of anthropologists by the government in the United States was by the Bureau of Indian Affairs, the Department of Agriculture, and the Soil Conservation Service, then an independent agency beginning in the 1930s. For the most part the anthropologists employed were engaged either in descriptive studies to discover the condition of various social groups or why programs undertaken by these agencies encountered difficulties or failed. Anthropologists had no voice in establishing policy, in determining what research was desirable, or what use was made of their results.

In some cases research results were suppressed. For example, a study by a competent anthropologist established the fact that many of the difficulties of the Ute Indians of southern Utah stemmed from their exploitation by whites in the area. According to the anthropologist, the report was suppressed when a senator from that state threatened to oppose the next appropriation for the Bureau of Indian Affairs. In another rather famous case, Walter Goldschmidt, working for the Department of Agriculture, studied the communities of Arvin and Dinuba in California to discover the effects of large-scale agriculture versus relatively small farm agriculture. In this case the report was published by a Congressional committee, but it aroused great opposition on the part of large agricultural interests and probably contributed to the fact that the Department of Agriculture no longer employs anthropologists.[1]

Somewhat earlier, anthropologists were included in the so-called Hawthorne Studies, carried on at a plant of the Western Electric Company.[2] This was followed by further studies of industrial relations and the organization of such institutions as hospitals and research laboratories. These led to the formation of the Society for Applied Anthropology in 1941. Participation of anthropologists in industrial and organizational studies has continued on a small scale.

During World War II anthropologists were in great demand, partly because of their intimate familiarity with foreign areas. They were called on to prepare manuals for troops in various areas, to interpret the cultures of other nations and regions for a wide variety of agencies, and to participate in formulating policies for occupied areas. Perhaps the best-known by-product of some of these applied activities was Ruth Benedict's *The Chrysanthemum and the Sword,* an interpretation of Japanese culture and personality. Following World War II much of the activity in applied anthropology was centered in the technical assistance programs by United States and international agencies, both public and private.

Those anthropologists connected with the Society for Applied Anthropology recognized that in many cases the problems they dealt with involved other social scientists and raised a number of problems not faced at that time by other anthropologists. In the main this group operated initially with equilibrium models. In brief, they saw a properly functioning society as composed of individuals or groups who have worked out an adjustment to each other so that their relationships may be considered to be in a state of equilibrium. This

---

[1] Walter R. Goldschmidt, *Small Business and the Community: A Study in California on Effects of Scale in Farm Operations* (Washington, D.C.: Government Printing Office, 1946); *As You Sow* (New York: Harcourt Brace Jovanovich, 1947).

[2] F. J. Roethlisberger and W. J. Dickson, *Management and the Worker: An Account of a Research Program Conducted in the Western Electric Company,* Hawthorne Works (Cambridge, Mass.: Harvard University Press, 1939). (Paperback edition, New York, Wiley, 1969.)

state of equilibrium may not be static, but so long as the various parts change harmoniously, the state of equilibrium continues. From time to time, either through internal developments or outside influences, this state of equilibrium is disturbed. In industrial situations this may take the form of strikes, lock-outs, growing grievances, slowdowns, and various other evidences of conflict, including growth of individual tensions and insecurities.

Within such a situation the role of the applied anthropologist is seen as restoring a state of equilibrium satisfactory to those involved. The last phrase is regarded as important, for it is insisted that the applied anthropologist occupy a neutral and impartial role. It is necessary to find the causes of grievances, tensions, and strained interpersonal relationships and seek the reorganization of institutional and interpersonal relationships.

Applied anthropologists working outside the United States are mostly involved in programs designed to improve technical skills and raise living standards, mainly involving improvements in farming and other productive activi-

Andean (South American) peasant house built of rammed earth and mud bricks. It lacks doors, windows, electricity, running water, beds, and indoor toilets. One of the problems of applied anthropology is to find ways of helping people without destroying the things that make their life meaningful and coherent. (Courtesy of the United Nations.)

ties, health, education, and community improvement. Such work most frequently involves employment by or contract relationships with government agencies; only a few years ago the U.S. Administration for International Development was the largest employer of anthropologists in the world. This situation has changed drastically, for reasons that merit some examination.

Two major problems exist in the application of anthropology outside the United States. One is the change in context of applied anthropology in the last two decades, with the termination of colonial rule in much of the world and the emergence of new nations. Along with this is new recognition of the problem of development. A second problem, equally applicable to many applied studies in the United States, is the question of goals and the proper role of the anthropologist.

As we have seen, the early applied anthropologists saw their role primarily in the resolution of disturbances in social relationships. Technical assistance programs, however, usually are set to achieve specific goals. The question of who sets the goals or policies and what the anthropologist is supposed to do then become paramount. Any analysis of applied anthropology activities soon reveals the fact that the anthropologist rarely is asked about the feasibility of goals or the projects planned to implement them. At best the anthropologist is usually asked either to contribute knowledge or information to facilitate the execution of projects or to discover why a project is running into difficulties. As a result the record of anthropology shows few successful applications but is full of analyses of why projects failed because of inadequate attention to cultural and social problems. Frequently the anthropologist is viewed as a technician who has a store of knowledge or a bundle of tricks which can immediately be applied in any situation.

In general terms this view has some truth, although the store of knowledge is still woefully incomplete. The anthropologist, for example, can affirm that any project of technological change must

(1) Have evident advantages understandable to the people affected. The increased yield of hybrid corns appears to offer obvious advantages to Mexican peasants. However, the seed must be purchased, which often involves an impossible cash outlay. Moreover, hybrid corns are more difficult to make into tortillas, the mainstay of peasant diet, and produce a less palatable product.
(2) Be introduced through proper channels. If the influence and prestige of local leaders is bypassed or endangered, they will organize opposition to any innovation.
(3) Utilize existing motivations or establish new motivations.
(4) Be accompanied by adequate education or demonstration. Commercial fertilizers may be used so sparingly that they have no perceptible result or so lavishly that they burn up the crop.

These are but a few of the generalizations that are possible. No anthropologist, however, can tell immediately, or even within a brief period of study, how precisely these conditions can be met. The true leaders of a community are not to be discovered immediately. A chief or an elected mayor may appear to be the obvious persons to deal with; actually an informal council of elders or a priest may be the decisive personalities. Increased monetary rewards or material goods may offer little inducement to change in some societies if they cannot be translated into social prestige through sharing. A member of an extended or joint family organized as a producing and consuming unit will not adopt innovations by himself; the head of the family must first be convinced and the group must operate as a unit. In short, although many principles can be adduced, their implementation differs from culture to culture. From what we have said in preceding chapters, it should be obvious that even the simplest technological change may involve changes through many other aspects of the culture.

Where the anthropologist has had adequate opportunities, applied anthropology has often been helpful. An institute conducting various action experiments to increase food production found an advance study of an Indonesian community by an economic anthropologist to be invaluable. They complained, however, that the study had taken at least a year. Convinced of the utility of anthropological studies, they felt that they could not afford either the time or money for each of their experiments and asked if shortcuts could not be found to produce quicker and less costly results. The answer at the present time is No.

Even in situations where use of anthropological knowledge is accepted to some extent, there is little appreciation of what is involved. A group of engineers with an interesting and otherwise sensibly designed program for small industrial development in a Northeastern Brazilian state asked if two or three anthropology graduate students could be found to spend a summer in the state and tell the planners about the social structure of the area. Again the answer had to be no, especially given the fact that no prior studies of the state existed. In fact one student spent eighteen months in the state and came up with some important data. By this time projects were already so far along that only minor modifications could be introduced.

The basic difficulty is the failure outside of anthropology or the social sciences to appreciate the problems of determining not only the problems of change but the social costs of projects. Engineers may spend hundreds of thousands of dollars and sometimes several years making feasibility and cost studies of a major undertaking such as an irrigation project. Because they are more difficult to put into quantitative or dollar values, little, and more commonly, no attention is paid to determining social costs and balancing them against social benefits.

3. The Anthropology of Development

The anthropology of development arises more or less directly out of anthropological studies of acculturation. Its goals are to assist those nations or groups that seek to, or are being compelled to, industrialize or modernize to make the necessary changes as rapidly as possible and with a minimum of disruptive

Elephants on United States-built highway between Pnompenh and Sihanoukville in Cambodia. Because development projects are often imposed from outside or from above, local residents must often use ingenuity in order to benefit from them. (Courtesy of the United Nations.)

side effects. Most of the early efforts at stimulating the development process focused on technological and economic factors. In his first announcement of the Point IV program in the United States, President Truman spoke of helping people realize their "aspirations for a better life" through making available the United States' "store of technical knowledge." The assumption was that all people shared the idea of progress as understood in the United States and shared in our aspirations. The ideal of progress (which must be distinguished from belief in the perfectibility of humanity, often associated with religious or philosophical doctrines) is a unique idea that arose very recently in Western nations. It has evolutionary undertones, and perhaps reached its peak of acceptance in the last century. The inevitability of progress was questioned in Euro-American societies as early as the 1920s. It is perhaps ironic that it should be spread to other countries at a time when it is being increasingly doubted in the countries of its origin.

Technical aid programs also assumed that knowledge of better technical methods would lead automatically to their adoption and that increased production or material gain would automatically improve the lot of the people involved. Although many of the peoples of the world are satisfied with things as they are and do not seek change in their technologies, new aspirations have appeared in many cultures, especially where colonial powers introduced new educational systems and the people were brought into the increasingly effective worldwide network of communications. Once aware of alternative ways of life, especially when made aware of their own comparative poverty and powerlessness, many peoples actively seek change and modernization. The Manus, and many other peoples, represent cultures that sought not only to change but, specifically, to Americanize.

The early attempts made by the United States to initiate or encourage the development process were nevertheless marred by the fact that most participants from the United States carried with them U.S. basic cultural assumptions and the belief, often unconscious, that the goal of development was to implant the culture of the United States. In some cases teaching people to play baseball rather than cricket appears to have received a higher priority than almost anything else. Very often technical aid personnel from the United States, and from other countries as well, lived in splendid isolation from the people, showing little or no appreciation of their language and culture. The description of other peoples as "underdeveloped" carries the connotation of inferior development in every sphere of life. A descriptive phrase, such as "less industrialized," would often be more appropriate.

An example of the general attitude of some United States officials is given in the following report, written by an anthropologist after attending a meeting of the American Council on Education (1950) devoted to problems of education in occupied countries. The report says, in part:

> The report of Colonel | | on Japan was very discouraging because of the attitude and point of view. He painted a glowing picture in which everything is going beautifully in Japan and there are no problems. As a result of the United States program, Japanese character, personality, and culture have been entirely changed during the past five years and they are well on the road to American democracy. The ethnocentric approach on the part of most delegates and officials toward all of the occupied countries was almost unbelievable. Nearly every discussion and comment was predicated on the assumption that American institutions are perfect and that success in the occupied countries consists only in recasting them more nearly in our own image. It was implied that what is wrong with Japanese culture is that it is so unlike American culture. . . . Japanese universities were thoroughly excoriated because they were copied after the European pattern and not the American pattern. Unquestionably, foreign nationals representing the occupied areas must have felt that most of the discussion was an unvarnished insult to their national cultures.[3]

Anthropological points of view become even more important in the various programs to raise the living standards of countries outside our general cultural

[3] George Foster, "Reports of Committees and Representatives," *American Antropologist*, 53:447–460 (1951).

heritage. These technical-assistance programs, such as our own government's Point IV program or the technical-aid program of UNESCO, are too often predicated on the view that if people only can be brought to live exactly like ourselves, their problems will be solved. Citizens of the United States particularly tend to have a missionary zeal to make the world over in our own image. Such an assumption of the rightness of our own way of behaving often is highly offensive to others and may seriously interfere with the success of technical-aid missions.

Most Americans, even if they do not have such strongly self-righteous feelings about the superiority of their own ways of life, nevertheless find it very difficult to understand the complexities involved in dealing with another culture. Most common is the attitude that people are very much alike underneath when one gets to know them. As Hall has pointed out, the operative words here are what is meant by *people* and what is required if one is truly to know them.

In most countries—and Americans are probably no worse than other nationality groups in this respect—certain human beings are not classed as people by some and hence do not have to be considered. The attitudes of some Japanese toward the Eta, of some Brahmans toward certain untouchables, of some Peruvians toward Indians, of some Americans toward Blacks, of some English toward foreigners are all examples of these attitudes. In addition, few Americans will admit that it is necessary to know anything of the language and the range of cultural patterns to understand "people."

Many of these attitudes stem from a belief in the commonness of experience. The idea that people who are basically the same may view and interpret experiences common to all mankind in widely divergent ways, conditioned by the categories and perceptions imposed by language and by culturally imposed patterns of behavior, is difficult for the average American to accept. The view that unexpected behavior is crazy or psychotic is widespread among Americans faced with the realities of a different culture.

Yet persons with long experience abroad often do acquire insight and understanding even without the aid of anthropological concepts and training. Unfortunately it often takes distressingly long. In Brazil, a culture fairly similar to our own, it is estimated that the average diplomat or businessperson does not begin to "catch on" for seven years; for the Middle East ten to seventeen years have been estimated; for China one missionary told Hall it required twenty-five years if one learned the language, otherwise "never." Pointing out that in the Middle East at first nothing seems to make sense, one diplomat told Hall: "Later you learn it's like a merry-go-round—the white horse always follows the gray horse—but you have to see it go around a few times until you learn that."[4]

Unfortunately throughout our history—and recent times afford few exceptions—our official and unofficial relations with other countries have usually been characterized by what might be called self-righteous ignorance. Attempts

---

[4] Edward T. Hall, Jr., "Orientation and Training in Government for Work Overseas," *Human Organization*, 15:4–10, No. 1 (New York: Society for Applied Anthropology, 1956).

at preparing our people for activities abroad have been sporadic, insufficient, and have often been viewed with suspicion.

Even on a very simple level, knowledge of the total cultural situation is basic to success. Often our technical methods are dependent upon very complexly interrelated factors, such as widespread literacy and mechanical knowledge, specialized production facilities, laboratories, land systems, and economic conditions. These are rarely duplicated in other countries. It should be obvious that teaching people to farm with tractors will not be successful if their economy will not support the purchase or maintenance of machines, if their landholding system is based on small plots farmed by gardening techniques, and if their social system in part revolves about the mutual exchange of labor. In such cases, improvement of agricultural techniques must begin on a nonmechanized basis. The introduction of new plants or of new techniques of tillage, fitted into what the people already know and so presented as not to dislocate existing patterns of interpersonal relations, may be entirely feasible, and may produce far more useful results than premature attempts at mechanization.

Frequently technical-aid programs also bypass recognized local leaders and social groupings, or ignore economic and ideological differences. Efforts to improve the care of children may founder upon economic considerations; people often do not have the money to buy the things the medical men think desirable. A number of years ago the Mexican government attempted to suppress the use by the Otomi Indians of *pulque*, a mildly alcoholic drink fermented from the juice of the agave or century plant. It was soon discovered that many of these Indians not only were totally lacking in any water supply and hence had no other source of liquid, but, even when water was available, *pulque* was almost the only source of certain vitamins and minerals especially essential to the growing child. Efforts to introduce modern medicine often fail when, as among the Navajo Indians, there is a belief that disease is caused by supernatural forces, or, as in much of Latin America, there is no conception of microorganisms as a cause of disease. Efforts to introduce a model public health program in a Latin American country failed because the directors from the United States were totally unaware of the existing class structure and ignored the only group of people who could have led the community to acceptance of the new ideas. In other cases, where a people were ridiculed for their folk concepts of disease, there was again failure to introduce and properly integrate into the culture badly needed medical practices. Examples like these may be recited endlessly.

Although most people would probably agree that there should be some way in which all peoples could have access to important ideas or important new technological developments, there is little agreement on how such developments should be spread. Under colonial regimes it was commonly assumed that the dominating power could and should manipulate colonialized peoples in order to direct them upon the pathways of modernization. As ideas of cultural superiority faded and colonial administrations were supplanted by independent governments, the efforts of modernized nations to transmit aspects of their culture to newly liberated nations were received with increasing suspicion. In many cases, in fact, so-called technical-aid programs were little more than an attempt to buy political alliances with the new nations or to involve them in trade agreements which were in the long run more beneficial to the industrialized nation than to the nation supposedly receiving aid. Obviously it makes a difference whether foreign aid is viewed as an altruistic attempt to help others, as reparations for past colonialist misdeeds, or as an attempt to bind other nations into the sphere of influence of an industrialized nation.

4. Community Development

Anthropologists began to provide important data for development programs when they turned to community studies. In the early period, beginning in the 1920s, the development problem was not widely recognized and most anthropologists were attracted to community studies primarily because the peasant community was seen as a relatively closed system small enough to be studied intensively as a whole. Such was not in fact the case, but to a considerable degree the involvement of such communities in national institutions could be slighted or ignored.

Nevertheless the first community study was in fact undertaken to contribute to a development program in Mexico, the first traditional country to undertake a conscious program of modernization following the revolution of 1910–1920. This was the study of the valley of Teotihuacán, undertaken by the Mexican anthropologist Manuel Gamio.[5] Gamio, with José Vasconcelos and Moises Saenz, was one of the principal architects of the Mexican federal rural school system and the intensive study of the community of Teotihuacán, and its environs had the very practical objective of providing information for formulating new educational programs more suited to the realities of rural Mexican life.

Gamio's pioneering study was followed by numerous village or community studies by North American scholars in Mexico and Guatemala and later in South America and south and southeast Asia. Chinese scholars and others produced studies of Chinese villages. More recent are studies of peasant villages in the Middle East, India, and Europe. The community approach seems less evident in Africa, where interest has focused on social and political systems involving larger areas of tribal groups. All these studies provided data relevant to development problems, although this terminology was not yet in use, and the researchers often had many insights beyond the data in their published reports; its influence, however, was quite limited for a number of reasons. To a considerable extent engineers, economists, and government officials most concerned with development problems either did not know of or ignored the body of anthropological information. Anthropologists frequently were interested primarily in theoretical problems rather than in development

---

[5] Manuel Gamio, *La Población de la Valle de Teotihuacán* (Mexico, 1922). 3 vols. An abbreviated version in English was published by the Columbia University Press.

and often did not report the practical implications of their data. In any event, many of the community studies were done by foreigners; most anthropologists felt it would be improper for them to criticize or suggest policies to a host government unless they were asked to do so.

There were, of course, many exceptions. In 1933 Manuel Gamio asked one of the authors, Ralph Beals, to report on what the Mixe Indians, then almost unknown either to anthropologists or to government, would like the government to do for them. The report made to Gamio was unpalatable; most of the Mixe questioned felt the government had already foisted upon them unwanted schools, and what they wanted most was to be left alone. Some years later the author was asked to investigate the capacity of the Tarascan people of Cherán to finance or contribute to the financing of improved water supply and distribution system, electricity, and other public improvements. Here the answer was that they clearly could contribute adequately and that existing machinery for collecting funds for public religious festivals could be adapted to this purpose. The real obstacle to self-development of the public facilities lay in the

Health clinic worker in Deoli, India, discusses family-planning methods. India's birth rate is not exceptionally high, but substantial reductions in the death rate have produced a rapid net increase in population. (Courtesy of the United Nations.)

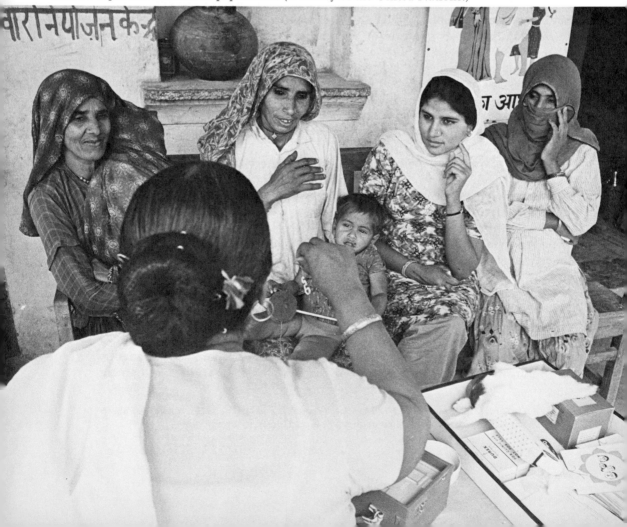

strongly held attitude that these were things that the state or federal government should do for the community. Whether this report had any influence or not is unknown, but at present the Mexican government agencies promoting rural electrification and improved water supplies have developed techniques for pressuring local communities to contribute to the costs and using the collection machinery suggested. This of course involves external intervention in community affairs and promotes internal conflicts between those favoring and opposing change.

In collaboration with Pedro Carrasco and T. H. McCorkle, Beals also published an experimental monograph on Cherán, in which he attempted to combine an anthropological analysis of houses and house use among the Cherán Tarascans with an evaluation of various improvements which might be promoted by government development agencies. Various related problems and the probable consequences of alternative programs were pointed out.[6] As far as is known, no one paid any attention at all to the monograph. Many anthropologists in conversation can recount similar experiences but they rarely get into print.

Community studies by anthropologists have considerable relevance to that aspect of development programs known as community development. This approach has been extensively used by both foreign and international aid programs, by domestic governments, and by some private volunteer organizations. Many community development programs are predicated on the belief that most peasant communities have reserves of labor and sometimes money which they now do not use but which can be organized to increase production of farm products or cottage manufacturers and better the quality of community life by improving interpersonal relations and providing such amenities as better water supplies, schools, and communications with a minimum of outside guidance, stimulation, and inputs of money. Some programs assume that such grass roots improvements will have a cumulative effect, stimulating the national economy. Others have seen such programs as a way of bringing some of the benefits of development immediately to the rural populations with a minimum of expenditure. Many community-oriented programs have been essentially welfare projects with little understanding of their relationship to the developmental process.

Community development programs have an extremely varied history. Frequently they have operated according to preconceived ideas and with little or no anthropological guidance. Very often the community development agent has very definite ideas of what improvements should be made and how to go about them. Unless the agent is successful in convincing the community membership that these are valid, the program may easily fail. For this reason community development manuals often stress the importance of identifying "felt needs" of the community and concentrating on these. It may be, however, as reported for the Mixe, that the community has no "felt needs" or that

[6] Ralph L. Beals, Pedro Carrasco, and Thomas McCorkle, *House and House Use of the Sierra Tarascans*, Smithsonian Institution, Institute of Social Anthropology, Publication No. 1 (Washington, D.C.: Government Printing Office, 1944).

these are trivial or are regarded by the outside worker as nonproductive. What people may want most may be bigger and better fiestas, improvements to the central plaza, or a new façade on the church.

The Vicos project represents one of the few cases of directed culture change planned and conducted by anthropologists.[7] The project was experimental, a combination of research into problems of culture change and an effort to manipulate or move a group of people toward goals established in the first instance by the anthropologists. In 1952 Cornell University leased the traditional hacienda of Vicos in Peru and by an approach called participant intervention undertook to modernize the culture of the residents on the hacienda by inducing change toward a set of predetermined goals.

Prior to the Cornell project, the leaseholder had complete control over the hacienda and almost unlimited control over its population. As the experiment neared its end, the Vicosinos formed a self-governing landowning community with an appreciably higher standard of living. In accomplishing this change, the project directors established a large number of policies and guidelines, some in cooperation with the Vicosinos, others independently. In effect, the anthropologists made a set of initial assumptions, set the goals, and established the policies by which the goals would be realized.

Both the assumptions and goals of the anthropologists involved were clearly influenced by their participation in a society with democratic and egalitarian values and goals. Among the assumptions was that the best kind of community in which to live is just, peaceful, and progressive, both morally and intellectually, and composed of responsible people. The goal, broadly defined, was to permit realization of basic human dignity for all members of the community which requires the broad sharing of power, wealth, knowledge, and skills, health, respect, and affection. These broad goals were broken down into about 130 specific lines of intervention, each oriented toward a specific developmental goal. Various possibilities and strategies were then outlined. As the project continued, each line of operation was continuously reappraised and evaluated. The project made as much use of local personnel as it could and strove to keep external personnel to a minimum. It was able to secure as director a competent person who already was known and respected by Vicosinos. Each step was explained to the local people and they were encouraged at every point to express opinions, to participate in decisions, and to take increasing responsibility for their implementation.

Several important points emerge from the history of the Vicos project. Perhaps most important is the fact that despite its name it was a program rather than a specific project. This was also true of the various operations undertaken. Through the process of constant appraisal and consultation, the

---

[7] A large literature exists on the Vicos project. The main features can be found in the following: Allan Holmberg, "The Research and Development Approach to the Study of Change," *Human Organization,* **21**:107–109 (1962), Allan Holmberg and W. F. Whyte, "From Paternalism "Methods for the Analysis of Culture Change," *Anthropological Quarterly,* **34**:37–46 (1961); Allan Holmberg and Henry F. Dobyns, "The Process of Accelerating Community Change," *Human Organization,* **21**:107–109 (1962), Allan Holmberg and W. F. Whyte, "From Paternalism to Democracy," *Human Organization,* **15**:15–18 (1956).

planned operations were continuously modified. The program also involved the total culture rather than just the alteration of some specific segment of it. In contrast, most development programs are limited in objectives and are set up as fairly rigid and carefully budgeted projects. Modifications in the course of the project often are impossible. An anthropologist may be called in for advice on how to manipulate the situation to gain acceptance of the program or to advise why the project is having difficulties; as a result, the project may be reformulated, but essentially as a new project. There is little flexibility possible if the project turns out not to be meeting programmed goals.

The Vicos project has been both praised and criticized. Some Peruvians have resented the fact that it was limited to a single community and have urged a countrywide approach. Others have objected because it raised expectations which could not be satisfied throughout the country without an enormous expenditure of money which Peru does not have. On the other hand, Vicos has provided a model toward which other communities have begun to strive; the Vicosinos in fact are beginning to give "technical assistance" to other Indian communities.

The success of the Vicos project depended in part on the tolerance and to some extent cooperation of the Peruvian government and the fact that the national economy and society were modernizing and democratizing. It is doubtful if Vicos could have succeeded in the face of governmental hostility or a static economy. How the community will fare should there be a return toward authoritarian government with diminished local autonomy is an open question. Many mestizos regard the Vicosinos as now being the most difficult and disagreeable Indians in Peru, an interpretation based on the fact that they no longer are subservient or "know their place."

The Vicos project describes a highly successful program of community development but one which involved great cost. Less costly approaches can produce some results, such as improving local streets, roads, trails, and other means of communication; improving the appearance of the community; bettering water supplies and drainage or irrigation works; providing more adequate school buildings; and developing more cooperative and pleasant relationships between village members. In accomplishing these and other ends, adequate anthropological training of development agents can improve judgment and facilitate rapid understanding of the local social structure, the identification of leadership, and various cultural obstacles to change.

One deficiency of anthropology in the community development field is the lack of adequate theoretical formulations about the nature of peasant communities. Such formulations as have been made often may be of limited regional applicability. As an example, George M. Foster,[8] an anthropologist with wide experience in development programs of various sorts who also has made intensive studies of peasant communities in Latin America, suggested that many (he is careful not to say all) peasant communities are dominated by the "image of limited good." This means that the peasant sees all good things,

[8] George M. Foster, "Peasant Societies and the Image of Limited Good," *American Anthropologist,* **67**:293–315 (1965).

not only land and wealth, but such things as love, respect, health, and honor, to exist in fixed amounts and in short supply. The individual who gains more of any of these things is believed to do so at the expense of his fellow villagers. This view is accompanied by envy, distrust, and factionalism which inhibit participation in development programs. Fearing envy, individuals do not take opportunities to gain wealth or take positions of leadership, while cooperative undertakings founder on the shoals of suspicion and factionalism.

Various critiques of this concept have been published. Brokensha and Erasmus[9] suggest that Foster fails to give sufficient attention to social stratification and the distribution of power within the larger society. Within the traditional societies of Latin America there is a long history of powerlessness for the peasants, strong dependency relationships and sentiments of superiority–inferiority as between upper and lower strata of society. Latin American peasants are realistically responding to a social system in which as a class they have limited or rationed access to the desirable things of life. They suffer from an *encogido* (trapped) syndrome which makes them unresponsive to development programs. Clearly not all Latin American rural communities share this, for there are examples of successful "self-help" programs.

In numerous communities Brokensha and Erasmus studied in Ghana and Uganda the *encogido* syndrome does not appear. Jealousies exist, as they do in perhaps all communities, but they are not based on differences in economic status. The people lack strong feelings of inferiority–superiority; rather they are outspoken and independent. There has been no confrontation between "peasant" cultivators and land-controlling elites. There is individual rank in these societies but few sanctions against social mobility and rising standards of consumption. Community development projects are more readily embraced, often spontaneous in origin, and increasingly supported by monetary taxes rather than by labor contributions. In Ghana and Uganda, and apparently in some other parts of Africa, development programs seem to be relatively successful, are accepted or even initiated by local communities, and are supported by new national governments.

Anthropology clearly can play a significant role in community development programs in two ways. The use of anthropological knowledge of social and cultural phenomena and techniques of information gathering can improve the implementation of such programs. In addition there are still important basic research tasks to be done on local cultures and their relation to problems of change, whether spontaneous or induced. In addition anthropologists need to examine the relations of communities to their larger societies. Many basic community problems of raising living standards—that is, more food, more money, and improved health and educational services—almost always depend on whether the nation itself is making progress toward modernization. Sometimes marketing or consumers' cooperatives may be useful but even these often must depend upon more capital or credit resources than the community

[9] David Brokensha and Charles Erasmus, "African 'Peasants' and Community Development," in David Brokensha and Marion Pearsall (eds.), *The Anthropology of Development in Sub-Saharan Africa,* The Society for Applied Anthropology, Monograph No. 10 (1959).

can supply initially, and more costly organizational and management advice than the village can afford. The village cannot usually initiate changes in land tenure, provide new markets and credit facilities, supply electricity, reform education, or develop new agricultural technology. Perhaps the most fruitful use of the community development approach is to aid communities to take advantage of the modernizing forces and agencies in a developing nation.

5. Anthropological Studies of Development Problems

In a significant early study, Monica Hunter pointed out the effects of introducing systematic dipping of native cattle in South Africa.[10] As a result, disease was suppressed and cattle herds increased in size. Overgrazing resulted, damaging the range and initiating serious soil erosion. Instead of improving the economic position of the Africans involved, in the long run they became much worse off. This unexpected consequence resulted from the fact that among these tribes (as among many other livestock-raising peoples not only in Africa, but in Asia, or among the Navajo of North America) status and prestige depend upon the number of livestock owned. Numbers of cattle are more important than their quality or their use either as food or as a source

[10] Monica Hunter, *Reaction to Conquest* (New York: Oxford University Press, 1936).

The introduction of factorylike production techniques and wage labor are aspects of modernization. So is the presence of a supervisor (center). Ceylon. (Courtesy of the United Nations.)

of cash income. This early and well-known study should have been a warning beacon for the various programs of technical assistance or national development. It dramatically illustrated the necessity of viewing programs of economic or technological improvement within a total cultural context. The study also illuminates another anthropological viewpoint: traditional cultures usually have come to terms with their environments; that is, they have worked out stable ecological adaptations to them. Development programs which disturb this adaptation may have disastrous effects.

In another early study Manning Nash examined the effects of a textile factory established in 1876 in the Maya-speaking farming community of Cantel in Guatemala.[11] Contrary to widely held belief, supported by numerous examples, the industrial enterprise has not violently disrupted the community way of life. The reason seems to be that the managers of the enterprise to some extent adapted their production schedules, factory hours, and shift arrangements to the fact that their workers came from farming families and that women workers still had household duties to perform. The type of maize farming practiced in Cantel requires only relatively short periods of intensive labor; most of the tasks, such as cultivating and weeding, can be spread out in time. Arrangement of shift hours in the mill to allow several hours a day in the field made it possible to combine mill work with the maintenance of farm activities through most of the year. The higher income and the presence of alternative occupations in time caused changes in Cantel, but they came in the form of gradual readjustments. This situation did not develop, however, until threats and coercion of the Indians to work in the factory were abandoned. Once the Indians were able to make their own choices and were permitted to remain traditional Quiche villagers in other respects, the mill became an acceptable means of livelihood. In this case people lived better without living very differently, although change over time certainly occurred.

The Cantel situation relates to the underemployment of people in traditional farming; that is, their farming activities are highly seasonal. If they do not have alternative occupations, they may be relatively inactive, often for more than half a year. This situation has led some developmental theorists to believe that there is a large potential pool of manpower which can be drawn from the farm for employment in industry without disruptive effects.

That this may not be so is suggested by an unpublished study by Theodore Downing. The Oaxaca, Mexico, village of Diaz Ordaz normally produces a surplus of maize for sale. Most of the larger producers depend at some seasons upon wage labor supplied by villagers with no land or with insufficient land. In recent years better communications and new opportunities have caused a migration to the cities. As a result, labor is scarce and wages have doubled or tripled. Because of this, farmers have ceased cultivating distant or marginal lands and Diaz Ordaz maize production has declined, con-

---

[11] Manning Nash, *Machine Age Maya: The Industrialization of a Guatemalan Community* (New York: Free Press, 1958). (Originally published as American Anthropological Association Memoir, No. 87, 1950.)

trary to national development policy to stimulate agricultural production. This example underscores the fact that a surplus of farm labor is to be measured, not in terms of periods of partial or underemployment, but in terms of the minimum numbers of workers needed at planting, harvest, or other crucial points in the farm cycle. An answer might be in increased mechanization, but at present this is not possible for the farmers of Diaz Ordaz because of size of operations and lack of capital.

A similar dilemma developed in northeast Brazil in connection with a small-scale industrial development project. The major building materials in this region are fired brick and ceramic roof tile. These were produced in a number of small, inefficient, and high-cost plants depending upon hand labor. Supplies of brick and tile were perennially inadequate and high in cost. Engineers showed that a few mechanized brick and tile plants could produce more and better brick and tile at a lower cost. Unpublished studies by an anthropologist, John Davis, showed that several thousand migratory farm workers depended upon seasonal employment in the brick and tile plants to survive through the year. The project for mechanized plants had gone too far to stop, but it was decided that they should not go into full production immediately so that there could be a transition period in which the farm laborers, it was hoped, would find alternative occupations. Development planning here clearly was defective; not only should the facts have been known earlier, but the alternative occupations should have been discovered in advance. Ironically, the region has long been noted for its decorative floor and wall tiles. The new plants with lower costs discovered that they could more profitably produce decorative tile for shipment elsewhere and they reduced or abandoned brick and roofing tile production. Construction in the areas is now back very largely to dependence upon the old high-cost, low-quality handmade brick and tile plants.

Development planners often complain that traditional farmers will not cultivate needed cash crops. In the Philippines farmers were induced to cultivate abaca, a fiber-producing plant, in addition to their subsistence crops. Within a short time most farmers abandoned the new crop. Investigation showed the farmers were not lazy or averse to a cash income, but that they had not profited from the new crop. No credit or marketing facilities had been arranged by the development planners. As a result the not inconsiderable profits were all going to middlemen, who advanced high-cost loans and marketed the crop. The study illustrates clearly that even if people can be persuaded to undertake an innovation, they must share significantly in the rewards for the enterprise and that farming innovation is more than introducing new technologies or crops.

Failures, such as the Philippine abaca project, are often attributed by planners to the lack of entrepreneurial or risk-taking spirit among traditional peasants. Others attribute lack of ambition or "conservatism" to peasants. Elaborate theories about peasant personality have been developed by economists and other planners to account for failures. Numerous studies show that with proper motivations and opportunities peasants may show a lively entrepreneurial spirit. Polly Hill, an economist, has made an essentially anthro-

Demonstrating a device to scutch flax (break up the outer shell to remove the fibers). Some believe that the introduction of simple, "intermediate technology" is the most effective means of accelerating development without destroying local environments or cultures. Ethiopia. (Courtesy of the United Nations.)

pological study of cacao farmers in Ghana which refutes many of the myths held by economists about peasants.[12] In western Ghana undeveloped lands suitable for cacao growing existed and were easy to secure and develop at a time when world markets and prices were good. With little external stimulus or help, farmers from eastern Ghana migrated into the area and developed it. In so doing they faced significant risks, not all of them economic; they suc-

[12] Polly Hill, *The Migrant Cacao Farmers of Ghana* (New York: Cambridge University Press, 1963).

ceeded and often expanded their undertaking by making considerable investment and exercising individual foresight and shrewdness. Many failures in development programs stem from the fact that they were not conceived within an adequate planning framework, but were isolated and externally imposed applied projects such as those described earlier.

6. The Costs of Development

The several brief examples given deal mainly with specific changes in the agricultural process. What does happen to agriculture in successful national development with industrialization? The answer generally appears to be that usually farmers fare poorly. Geertz, in a brilliant study of Indonesian farming under three centuries of colonial rule, has shown that the introduction of cash crops, such as sugar cane, rubber, and other export commodities, under Dutch colonial rule resulted in agricultural involution (the intensified use of traditional techniques).[13] The benefits of the cash crops accrued to the colonial power, but more important, they upset the ecological balance previously existing between types of farming, the environment, and the population. The cultivation of noncash crops, especially rice, underwent elaboration but remained increasingly labor intensive; that is, any increases in productivity were through greater expenditure of labor using more intricate techniques and converting more and more of the forest into irrigated rice fields. At the same time, prior population controls were relaxed, especially with the introduction of modern medicine. The result, basically, was more and more Indonesians working smaller plots of land with a greater expenditure of labor and eating less.

It is popular to assume that a shift from a colonial situation to independence automatically corrects the situation and opens the door to modernization. But one characteristic of all modernization programs is that they require capital; that is, investment in infrastructures and to increase production, not only in new industries but in agriculture itself. The crucial question is where this money is to come from. In an agricultural country there are only two alternatives. One is to borrow the money, with the expectation that increased productivity will more than pay for the costs of borrowing. The other is to make the farmer pay for industrialization through price and export controls. Gifts and free assistance or expropriation of the estates of the wealthy or properties of foreign investors may help briefly but cannot form a major continuing part of development. In almost any case, in early stages, the farmer must carry the major burden of modernization.

A newly independent country or a traditional country embarking on modernization faces the problem of how to initiate increases in productivity large

---

[13] Clifford Geertz, *Agricultural Involution: The Process of Ecological Change in Indonesia,* Association of Asian Studies, Monographs and Papers, No. XI (Berkeley: University of California Press, 1963).

Teak logs awaiting shipment in Burma. The State Timber Board employs about 100,000 men and 1,300 elephants. Such projects may provide the cash required for development, but the long-term results may be costly. (Courtesy of the United Nations.)

enough to outstrip population growth and to generate capital investment sufficient to produce continuing economic growth. Most traditional countries are also faced with the need to strengthen national institutions and to create a sense of nationality among groups with only regional loyalties and often with cultural diversity. The need to transform the state into an integrated nation is often accompanied by exaggerated nationalism, and development decisions frequently are made on this basis rather than upon effectiveness in promoting development in other sectors.

Charles Erasmus provides an example of goals affecting the evaluation of alternate courses of development on a subnational scale.[14] In southern Sonora in northwest Mexico Erasmus studied the effects of different land distribution policies on the Yaqui and Mayo Indians, two neighboring groups with very similar languages and formerly very similar cultures. In a Mayo River *comunidad* Indians were forced to participate with mestizos in competition for lands and in their use and administration. On the Yaqui River, on the other hand, land was granted to Indian communes. Access to the land was limited to Indians, who administered commune affairs. Using a cost-benefit type of analysis, Erasmus points out that the costs of remaining a Mayo Indian were greater than the benefits to be obtained by merging into the mestizo culture. Failure to remain in the Indian pattern for the Yaqui meant leaving the community and foregoing Indian benefits available from the use of commune lands. Erasmus concludes that the policies used with the Mayo are more effective in achieving overall development goals.

Erasmus's conclusion as to policy accepts a more nationalistic version of Mexican development policy, a version which looks toward the elimination of the Indian as a separate entity in Mexican society. Alternative policies which would seek to preserve the values of the various Indian societies while making it possible for them to raise living standards and achieve a greater participation in national life have considerable support in Mexico; on this basis, the approach used with the Yaqui Indians would be preferred.

The intrusion of nationalistic goals is also seen in the operation of the Mexican rural education system. Earlier we pointed out the use of anthropology in formulating the Mexican federal rural school program in the 1920s. The initial assumption that a study of a central highland community could provide a model for the entire country was clearly at fault. This was recognized and partially rectified after a number of years by establishing regional teacher-training centers with curricula to some extent oriented more toward local conditions. Basically, however, the rural school program was and continues to be strongly influenced by nationalistic assumptions and goals. From the earliest grades the curricula of the rural schools were oriented toward establishing the use of the national language, despite some use of instruction in local languages in the earliest grades of some schools. Great emphasis was also placed on making the child aware of its citizenship in the Mexican na-

[14] Charles Erasmus, "Culture Change in Northwest Mexico," in Julian Steward (ed.), *Contemporary Change in Traditional Societies*, 3 vols. (Urbana: University of Illinois Press, 1967), Vol. 3, pp. 1–131.

Urbanizing and industrializing societies must often find new means of social control. Constabulary in the Australian Trust Territory of New Guinea. (From the Australian Government. Courtesy of the United Nations.)

tion. Although they might learn something of the aboriginal high cultures of Yucatán and the Valley of Mexico, Mexican children learned nothing about their own village or its way of life. In a much-quoted passage, Beals concluded that in the Tarascan village of Cherán the curriculum of the six grades taught in the local school did little to prepare the child to live a better life as a farmer in Cherán; rather, it was a preparation for migration to the cities.[15] This appears to remain true of most Mexican rural schools, although some modifications have been made in schools affected by programs of the National Indian Institute. Confronted by overpopulation in most rural areas and with expanding industrial urban centers, this type of program may be realistic. It was not arrived at, however, on the basis of development assumptions but rather through concern with nationalism. In any case the anthropological knowledge and insights were not used to set policies but to find ways to achieve policy goals in Indian communities.

The opening paragraphs of this section mention the costs of capital formation. But these are far from all the costs. Any development program involves manipulation of the lives of people and efforts to change their values, attitudes, and motivation, together with alterations of social relationships as well as technological processes. In the process, status and prestige relationships change; not all individuals are benefited equally, and some may lose; integrated and harmonious social relationships may be replaced by factions and conflict; and some individuals may be alienated permanently from the society. The Mayo finds it too costly to maintain "Mayo-ness." The Mayo Indian

[15] Ralph L. Beals, *Cherán: A Sierra Tarascan Village*, Smithsonian Institution, Institute of Social Anthropology, Publication No. 2 (Washington, D.C.: Government Printing Office, 1946).

must, therefore, abandon a ceremonial system which may have given emotional security and reassurance of social and supernatural support and provides nothing in its place. A Yaqui Indian, on the other hand, who finds the traditional system intolerably confining must pay a high price to move into Mestizo culture. In these and many other ways social costs exist in development programs and they should be identified and evaluated to a much greater extent than is normally the case. Anthropologists are often especially well qualified to undertake social-cost evaluations, but little recognition has so far been given to the criteria which should be met to justify manipulation of the lives and social arrangements of human beings.

7. Anthropology in the Development Process

The examples given thus far indicate that anthropology has played a relatively limited role in programs of development. This is likely to continue. Only specific local projects, such as that of Vicos, have been planned and directed by

Improved transportation raises incomes through increased trade and provides access to medical care and markets. It also facilitates economic assistance and political control. Bus stop on international Asian Highway 1 in Afghanistan. (Courtesy of the United Nations.)

anthropologists, and these of course have required the cooperation of specialists in other fields. In a few cases the anthropologists play a leading role in those parts of development programs concerned with local ethnic or village groups. The most extensive example is the National Indian Institute of Mexico, in which anthropologists have played a leading role both in formulating and administering programs. In most cases, however, the role of the anthropologist in development programs is apt to remain that of a participant in a multidisciplined problem.

Certain anthropological viewpoints are nevertheless gaining wider application. Development increasingly is seen as a process involving the total sociocultural system. This is true of any national program of development as well as local projects or programs. At the local level anthropologists have contributed a great deal to understanding of the problems of acceptance or rejection of change, and to some extent to planning, implementation, and evaluation processes. Operating essentially as applied anthropologists, they have helped in many projects to identify or develop local leadership, facilitate adaptations in social institutions, and identify the points of resistance to change. Certainly an important continuing activity will be community studies with focus on culture change and development problems. As Sanford Mosk, an economist, has pointed out, the real measure of the success of any development process is what happens to people in villages. The role of anthropology too often either is to facilitate programs or discover the causes of their failure. Evaluative studies, few as they are, often are seen as political rather than as scientific.

Anthropologists have important research still to do before they can contribute firmer and more widely applicable general principles and play a larger role in development. Is development simply to provide better exploitation of resources to support more people or should it focus on improving the quality of life for limited numbers? How are people to determine what they mean by the quality of life? The processes of development involve more extensive and intensive utilization of natural resources. How much damage or alteration of the environment will be done and can be tolerated?

The concern of anthropology with cultural values should be of aid to people in reaching informed decisions on goals. Anthropology has demonstrated that stable cultures in the past have always achieved a relative equilibrium between population size, technology, and resources. It also has shown that human beings in the past have upset the ecology. The Pleistocene saw the extinction of many species of mammals; it is possible that human beings were at least partly responsible. Certainly in the past they have converted forests into grassland in many parts of the world, have extended the deserts of Africa and the Near East through overgrazing and deforestation, and have turned extensive areas of the loess lands of north China into badlands. In three important areas related to development anthropology, anthropologists should contribute significantly: population control, the establishment of goals, and the limiting of ecological imbalance. Finally, if anthropologists do not contribute to the developmental problems of new nations, they may find themselves excluded from them as irrelevant. More will be said on this point in the final chapter.

Applied anthropology involves the deliberate use of anthropological knowledge in order to produce change. Although there are many moral and technical problems involved in the development of a satisfactory applied anthropology, there are nevertheless many situations, such as that on Bikini, where the anthropologist can render important services to all parties involved in a changing situation. In general, applied anthropologists should enter into a situation only if they are convinced that the rights of the people concerned will be protected and only if there is a strong probability that their services will be beneficial. While applied anthropologists should generally offer advice rather than attempt to influence events, they must retain an important role in determining how research is to be carried out and how the results of such research are to be used. As is the case with other professionals, applied anthropologists are primarily responsible to the people they work with rather than to the people who employ them.

Within the United States, applied anthropologists have worked with a number of private and government agencies, often attempting to find ways of restoring equilibrium in situations in which antagonisms between opposed groups have made normal ways of doing things unworkable. Outside the United States, applied anthropologists have often been involved in various kinds of development projects. Very often administrators of development programs seek quick and easy solutions and are therefore unwilling to invest the time and money required for adequate foreknowledge of the situation. Even where adequate research is carried out, applied anthropologists often encounter difficulties in effecting the course of programs designed by outsiders who have little time or inclination to become involved in the problems of the people they hope to change. Consequently, much of the energy of applied anthropologists has gone into the development of explanations for projects that have failed rather than into the design of projects that won't fail.

Particularly in connection with development programs sponsored by the United States, an undue emphasis has been placed upon technological improvements rather than upon improvements in the quality of life. In all nations, those concerned with improving the lives of others have often assumed that the secret of development was to make "those people" just like "us." Because this often involves the obliteration of traditional cultures, it has often been assumed that knowledge of other cultures or languages is a superfluous luxury in the development process. The apparent success of the Vicos project and of other anthropological attempts at community development suggests that many of the problems outlined above can be solved. Anthropological studies of the problems involved in the failure of a wide variety of development programs tend to show that although failures are generally attributed to the "stubborness" or "conservatism" of those who refuse to change, the truth is often that projects have been poorly planned without much awareness of local situations.

Even where development programs are technically successful, the costs of development in terms of the quality of life may be high. For example, the successful introduction of cash crops in Indonesia resulted in decreased food supply for the ordinary farmer. Very often the costs of modernization are borne by poor farmers who end up paying out much more than they receive from community development projects. In newly independent countries, nationalistic emphases may lead to the emergence of development goals more oriented to national prestige than to the development of communities. Some of these problems are illustrated by references to patterns of development in Mexico. Although applied anthropology, along with development programs in general, has often been marked by failure rather than success, there is reason to believe that anthropology can now contribute importantly to population control, the definition of goals, and the limiting of ecological imbalances.

Collateral Reading

Beals, Ralph L. *Politics of Social Research.* Chicago: Aldine Publishing Company, 1969. Surveys government involvement in research and the ethics of research, especially overseas.

Brokensha, David. *Community Development: An Interpretation.* Scranton, Pa.: Chandler Publishing Company, 1969. Strengths and weaknesses of community development illustrated in a variety of situations.

Clifton, James A. (ed.). *Applied Anthropology: Readings in the Uses of the Science of Man.* Boston: Houghton Mifflin Company, 1970. Good, recent reader.

Edgerton, Robert B. *The Individual in Cultural Adaptation: A Study of Four East African Peoples.* Studies in Culture and Ecology in East Africa. Berkeley and London: University of California Press, 1971. Attempt to relate social psychological variables to cultural and ecological conditions.

Erasmus, Charles. *Man Takes Control: Cultural Development and American Aid.* Minneapolis: University of Minnesota, 1961. An analysis of the problems of controlled cultural development.

Fabrega, Horacio, Jr. "The Need for an Ethnomedical Science," *Science,* **189**:969–975 (September 1975). Why doctors need anthropological treatment.

Foster, George M. *Applied Anthropology.* Boston: Little, Brown and Company, 1969. Problems and examples for the student.

Foster, George M. *Traditional Societies and Technological Change,* 2d ed. New York and London: Harper & Row, Inc., 1973. Text for anthropology students on planned social and economic change.

Geertz, Clifford. *Agricultural Involution: The Process of Ecological Change in Indonesia.* Association of Asian Studies Monographs and Papers, No. XI. Berkeley: University of California Press, 1963. An unusual study of the antidevelopment effects of colonial policies.

Geertz, Clifford. *Peddlers and Princes: Social Change and Economic Modernization in Two Indonesian Towns.* Chicago: University of Chicago Press, 1963. Examines two routes toward increasing modernization.

Goltung, Johan. *Members of Two Worlds: A Development Study of Three Villages in Western Sicily.* New York and London: Columbia University Press, 1972.

Herskovits, Melville J. *Acculturation, the Study of Culture Contact.* New York: J. J. Augustin, 1938. One of the first systematic statements.

Hill, A. David. *The Changing Landscape of a Mexican Municipio: Villa Las Rosas, Chiapas*. Chicago: University of Chicago Press, 1964. A geographer's view of the effect of development programs and policies.

Hill, Polly. *The Migrant Cocoa Farmers of Ghana*. New York: Cambridge University Press, 1963. An economist examines development without planners or subsidies.

Hunter, Monica. *Reaction to Conquest*. Oxford: Oxford University Press, 1936. A classical example of a field study of acculturation.

Linton, Ralph (ed.). *Acculturation in Seven American Indian Tribes*. New York: Appleton-Century-Crofts, 1940. A series of case studies.

Linton, Ralph. "Present World Conditions in Cultural Perspective," *The Science of Man in the World Crisis* (ed.) Ralph Linton. New York: Columbia University Press, 1945, pp. 201–221. Applied anthropology seen as a need for a world in crisis then as now.

Mead, Margaret. *New Lives for Old*. New York: Dell Publishing Co., Inc., 1968. Study of purposive self-development programs by a tribal group.

Middleton, John (ed.). *Black Africa: Its Peoples and Cultures Today*. New York: Macmillan Publishing Co., Inc., 1970. A collection of papers focused on problems related to development and change.

Nash, Manning. *Machine Age Maya: The Industrialization of a Guatemalan Community*. Chicago: University of Chicago Press, 1967. (Reprint.) Industrialization of a rural area without disruption.

Niehoff, Arthur. *A Case Book of Social Change*. Chicago: Aldine Publishing Company, 1966.

Scott, Robert E. (ed.). *Latin American Modernization Problems: Case Studies in the Crises of Change*. Urbana: University of Illinois Press, 1973.

Spicer, Edward H. *Human Problems in Technological Change*. New York: Russell Sage Foundation, 1957. Examination of social aspects of efforts to induce technological change.

Spicer, Edward H. *Cycles of Conquest: The Impact of Spain, Mexico and the United States on the Indians of the Southwest, 1533–1960*. Tucson: University of Arizona Press, 1962. The effect of different national cultures on the course of acculturation.

Tax, Sol (ed.). *Acculturation in the Americas*. Chicago: University of Chicago Press, 1952. An extensive series of papers presented at an international congress.

Tax, Sol (ed.). *Heritage of Conquest: The Ethnology of Middle America*. New York: The Free Press, 1952. Includes papers on acculturation problems.

Tessler, Mark A., William M. O'Barr, and David H. Spain. *Tradition and Identity in Changing Africa*. New York and London: Harper & Row, Inc., 1973. The personal effects of the clash between tradition and modernity.

Titiev, Mischa. *The Hopi Indians of Old Oraibi: Change and Continuity*. Ann Arbor: University of Michigan Press, 1972. Change in a conservative community.

21/Urban Anthropology

1. Anthropologists and Urban Research

Recent years have seen a rapid growth in anthropological research on urban problems in the United States. Much of this research is in progress or has as yet been reported only in scattered journals. Consequently, this chapter deals primarily with potentialities rather than presenting a comprehensive survey of the field.

Anthropologists have long had an interest in the origins of urbanism, as indicated in Chapter 9. Such concern with origins uses mainly archaeological data or forms part of general theoretical formulations about culture change, often with a strongly evolutionary viewpoint. In the past decade interest in the study of urbanism and complex societies has expanded rapidly. Some anthropological urban studies, however, began in the 1920s, and there has been a small but steadily growing series of anthropological studies since then. Indeed, in the 1890s the Society of Women Anthropologists in Washington, D.C., participated in a local housing survey and the organization of perhaps the first privately financed low-cost housing project in the United States.

Some of the earliest urban studies by anthropologists were in Africa. In 1940 Horace Miner studied Timbuctoo in what is now the republic of Mali.[1] An important purpose of Miner's study was to test Robert Redfield's Folk-Urban hypothesis in the context of an old precolonial city in which European influence was so recent that its effects could be identified. Except for the introduction and a final chapter of theoretical discussion, the remainder of the book is essentially a descriptive ethnography with conventional subject headings.

Following Miner, other anthropologists became concerned with urban problems in the cities of West and East Africa. Many of these studies deal with special features of the cities, such as adjustment of migrants, voluntary associations, family and kinship, or political participation. Similar studies have been made in East Africa. In the central and southern part of Africa many of the studies have dealt primarily with the effects of migration to mines or cities to seek employment. Efforts to generalize about African cities meet with some difficulties because the differences between indigenous cities and those established as European administrative, commercial, or industrial centers are not yet well established.

Urban studies by anthropologists in Latin America are also relatively recent. In this region, much attention has been paid to slum or ghetto areas or to squatter settlements under such names as *barrios, barriadas, vecindades, favelas, callejones*, and similar terms. The main emphasis again has been on special characteristics such as associations, politicalization, or some facet of the urbanization process. In most cases a major concern has been the adjustment of rural migrants to the city. Some sociologists have worked in Latin America, but because of the lack of good statistical data, their work is difficult to differentiate from that of anthropologists.

In the United States an early landmark was the Lynds' study of Middletown (a pseudonym for a Midwestern town).[2] Although the Lynds were sociologists, they considered this an anthropological study for two reasons: (1) they attempted to deal with the total culture and social structure of a community, and (2) they used ethnographic methods extensively (that is, long-term residence and participant observation together with intensive interview techniques). These were supplemented by using such published and statistical information as was available. Appropriately, the preface was written by an anthropologist, Clark Wissler. The study applied to a sizable community much the same approaches as anthropologists were beginning to use in community studies in Latin America. In the first book they sought to identify the formal and informal structure of the town society, economic and social roles, status and prestige mechanisms, nature of the power structure, organization and organizational participation, and range of attitudes and values. The first study was conducted at a time of stability accompanied by growing economic prosperity when the community showed a good deal of cultural homogeneity.

---

[1] Horace Miner, *The Primitive City of Timbuctoo*, American Philosophical Society Memoir 32 (Princeton, N.J.: Princeton University Press, 1953).

[2] Robert S. Lynd and Helen M. Lynd, *Middletown: A Study in American Culture* (New York: Harcourt Brace Jovanovich, 1929); *Middletown in Transition: A Study in Cultural Conflict* (New York: Harcourt Brace Jovanovich, 1937).

The second study examined the effects of the Great Depression of the 1930s, when insecurity, poverty, and shifting values were creating conflict.

A second pioneer among American anthropologists studying the United States urban scene was W. Lloyd Warner. Warner initially undertook a massive study of an old New England community which he labeled "Yankee City" in his publications. His previous field experience had been with Murngin of northern Australia under the sponsorship of Radcliffe-Brown, an experience Warner claimed was invaluable preparation for his urban studies. With a group of associates, Warner undertook a massive ethnographic study of the community he selected, supplementing statistical and printed sources with extensive interviewing in depth. A major purpose of the study was to test the assumption, common in the early part of this century, that the United States was a relatively classless society as compared with European societies. Warner identified three major classes, each with an upper and lower component, resulting in the somewhat awkward terminology of Upper Upper, Lower Upper, Upper Middle, Lower Middle, Upper Lower, and Lower Lower. Warner rejected exclusive reliance on economic and occupational criteria for class membership and used such things as self-evaluation, evaluation by others, and various status measures.

Early stages of a city, Santa Cruz, eastern Bolivia, center of large lowland region beginning to develop. (Courtesy of the United Nations.)

The Warner studies evoked varied criticisms. The definitions of class are often considered unsatisfactory, especially by scholars who prefer Marxist class theories. Others object that he has confused class and status. On the other hand, the wealth of empirical data accumulated makes it impossible to consider class in the United States without reference to his work and firmly established class as an important component of United States social structure, even though Warner's particular contributions may have been overextended in his efforts to apply the study of one community to the social structure of the country as a whole. But Warner, those associated with him, and others stimulated by his work, extended their use of anthropological methods to the study of ethnic groups, the problems of education, and other specialized institutions, as well as undertaking studies of a variety of communities in this country.[3]

2. The Role of Anthropology in Urban Studies

The study of complex contemporary urban phenomena clearly calls for the skills of a number of disciplines. It is a fair question to ask whether anthropology has a contribution to make apart from those of political scientists, economists, and especially sociologists. Opinions differ about this but an increasing number of anthropologists believe that they can and should do research on urban or urban-related problems. The justification for this point of view must be found in the fact that anthropologists bring a different point of view to urban problems, that they ask different kinds of questions, or that they use different kinds of methods. Unless special roles can be defined there is danger that anthropologists in the urban scene may find themselves acting as economists or political scientists or sociologists, asking the same kinds of questions and using the same kinds of methods, for which they often lack adequate training. Urban anthropologists must learn to use and augment the studies of others. In this section we will discuss some of these problems in general terms. In later sections we will examine some selected examples of urban research by anthropologists.

One contribution of anthropologists is the view that specific cultures and societies are structured and form interacting systems. The contribution of Warner's studies of the Murngin in Australia was less in any specific approach than in the vision it gave him of how societies and their cultures are structured and organized into wholes. The Lynds also attempted to look at Middletown as a whole and to seek underlying structure. Numerous other studies by anthropologists and sociologists have utilized a similar approach, and, as we shall see, failure to make sufficient use of this approach is a major criticism of some anthropological studies in the urban setting. It must also be admitted

[3] Of the six volumes in the Yankee City series, the most pertinent here is perhaps W. Lloyd Warner and Paul S. Lunt, *The Social Life of a Modern Community* (New Haven: Yale University Press, 1945); and W. Lloyd Warner and Leo Srole, *The Social Systems of American Ethnic Groups* (New Haven: Yale University Press, 1945). For related studies see the collateral readings listed at the end of this chapter.

that such holistic studies have been limited to relatively small cities. No one has yet successfully attempted to present the total structure of a megalopolis like New York or Los Angeles. Some town planners have perhaps come nearest to such a view, but their analyses often are sketchy or marred by uncritical subjective value judgments as to what constitutes a good life in a city or why people choose to live in cities.

Unfortunately many anthropologists doing urban studies have failed to consider the city as an entity or as a special sociocultural form. One class of studies by anthropologists involves the examination within a city of some problem, such as kinship, family, or associations, which anthropologists have long studied among tribal or village societies. According to Leeds, most of these studies have asked the question, "How does kinship (or another phenomenon) function in this city?" rather than "What is the effect of cityness on kinship?" In other words, they are studies of kinship, not studies of urban phenomena. Such studies usually do not lead to generalizations or generate "broader theory as to cities, urban society, or the social evolution of urbanized societies." [4]

In another class of studies, anthropologists have studied ethnic enclaves, slum areas, or squatter settlements as if they were autonomous communities. In so doing they are simply transferring the techniques of tribal or community studies to an urban environment, including the frequent failure to relate these to the larger context. Methodologically, it may be permissible to abstract a structure such as a community from its context for particular research purposes. Such a procedure, however, carries with it certain dangers and limitations, the most important of which is that variables external to the structure isolated must be identified and their operation taken into account. Put another way, any community or structure examined may be autonomous, but this can never be taken for granted. The significant characteristics of whatever limited entity or structure is investigated may not be the product of internal forces or development but may be the product of the total urban culture in which it is embedded.

A study of such a phenomenon as kinship conducted within a city may, as Leeds observed, contribute to the understanding of kinship but it is not necessarily urban anthropology. To be the latter it must focus on the relation between cityness and kinship. Further, the investigator must not only ask "What are the effects in this place and time?" but "What will this study tell us about urbanism?" One cannot treat kinship as something accidentally occurring in the city, but must focus on investigating the effect of the city on the particular manifestation of kinship encountered in a particular kind of city.

In part these shortcomings of many anthropological studies conducted in cities are common to many urban studies by other social scientists as well. Most students of urbanism until recently have assumed that any city characteristic they discover is common to cities in all times and places. The existence

[4] Anthony Leeds, "The Anthropology of Cities: Some Methodological Issues," in Elizabeth M. Eddy (ed.), *Urban Anthropology: Research Perspectives and Strageties*, Southern Anthropological Society Proceedings, No. 2 (Athens: University of Georgia Press, 1968).

of preindustrial cities suggests that the contemporary relation between industrialization and urbanism is a recent one. But neither are all contemporary cities industrial centers. Indeed, the first major industrial center in Britain, often regarded as the cradle of the industrial revolution, did not develop in cities but about mine-heads in the then nonurban Midlands. A second assumption often made is that what is true of cities in one culture is also true of cities in different cultures. The comparative viewpoint is then an important contribution an anthropologist can make. A few attempts in this direction have been made by anthropologists.

One early attempt in this direction is a series of studies of cities in Oceania edited by Alexander Spoehr (cited in Collateral Reading). The studies make it clear that these cities represent derived urbanism and were initially established as colonial administrative and commercial centers. In a few respects they reflect some of the special urban patterns characteristic of countries of the administering colonial power, especially in physical plan and administrative machinery. In other respects they show many similarities, not only to each other but to urban centers elsewhere, especially in developing countries. Population growth is primarily the result of rural–urban migration but there are important special ethnic groups such as Chinese or Indians. Although some new adaptive social forms appear, generally adequate social controls and social forms have failed to develop. Other studies deal with special problems such as the role of kinship or the character of the urban household. In a number of cases some incipient industrialization to serve local or regional needs has appeared; because of lack of local capital and knowledge, much of this is initiated, financed, and managed by outside organizations.

Other anthropological studies have focused on the comparison of rural and urban life, often simply treating immigrants as peasants or rural people transplanted to the city. Others, more fruitfully, deal with the processes of transition among migrants from the country to the city. The studies are valid and important but the development of urban anthropology calls for more focus on the comparison of cities.

Among the questions which might be investigated are whether artificial capital cities such as Canberra in Australia, Brasilia in Brazil, New Delhi in India, or Washington, D.C., have any common characteristics? Are these due to their similar history? Or are they due to their common function, in which case the same characteristics may in part be identifiable in older traditional capitals. If differences between cities of similar function are found, are these possibly because of differences in the cultures in which they are embedded? Are any similarities the result of urbanism per se? Answers to some of these questions may be of great practical importance. Is it true, for example, that urbanism is accompanied by declining birth rates? Some distinguished demographers have made this assumption in the past, but the evidence is derived almost wholly from the history of Western cities. Nevertheless, it has been suggested that the current explosive increase in population in developing nations will more or less automatically level off once urbanization reaches a comparable level to that in the West. If such an assumption is incorrect, the results could be tragic. Actually, of course, many demographers and others now feel that even if true, time will run out before population will be stabilized through the effects of urbanization. Indeed, many of the most industrialized nations have not achieved population stability. In sum, the comparative point of view suggests that we must not assume without evidence that what is true of one city is true of another, that what is true of one type of city is true of other types, or that what is true of cities in one culture is true of cities in another.

The holistic and comparative approaches are obviously no monopoly of anthropologists but may be used by others with profit. Are there any other kinds of research which anthropologists are particularly equipped to do? In general terms anthropologists are best equipped to do studies oriented toward culture, emphasizing such field methods as depth interviews and participant observation that require relatively close involvement with subjects. Concern with ecological problems, adaptive processes, sociocultural change and stability, life styles, and value systems clearly can be transferred to the urban setting.

The anthropological contribution to urban studies, then, may be considered in part to be the application of ethnographic methods to the urban setting. Nevertheless, it is particularly important to remember that even in contemporary tribal or peasant studies, anthropologists have become increasingly sophisticated in the use of statistics and the collection and use of quantitative data. Anthropologists have begun to make new applications of mathematical methods to qualitative data as well. Urban anthropologists must be particularly sophisticated in these methods. They also must be able to work within interdisciplinary frameworks, either actively collaborating with members of other disciplines, or making the fullest use of the research done by others.

Among the uses of anthropological research methods is the identification and analysis of informal structures or organizational frameworks. For Africa, Epstein recently has classified these as "network" relations, categorical relations, and formal or associational relations.[5] The first involve the networks of social relations with neighbors, work mates, friends, and acquaintances. The core of such networks, he suggests, is comprised of kinship networks or common tribal origins. These concepts are not without relevance in the United States; a recent unpublished study of a medium-sized industrial plant disclosed that 40 percent of the work force came from a single town in Mexico. Categorical relations involve those based on some method of classifying groups. In Africa this also may be common tribal origin. Classifications may be based on such things as ethnicity, residence, or occupation. The third class of relations, the formal or associational, has been investigated by a number of anthropologists, both in Africa and in some cities of Latin America. Such formal associations based upon common village, tribal, or regional origin have been found in many cities. Many associations are not formal and are revealed only by indirect means. The *panalinha* of Brazil, in-

[5] A. L. Epstein, "Urbanization and Social Change in Africa," *Current Anthropology* 8:275–296 (1967).

formal groups used to secure power and influence, are not referred to either in dictionaries or literature about the country.[6] The term and the reality and importance of the informal institution were disclosed by the career biographies collected by Leeds. Similarly, the question of leadership or influence is not always revealed immediately. In a Mexican-American *barrio*, for example, the pattern of respect may be demonstrated by discovering those individuals addressed by the honorific title of *Don or Doña*. But in at least one *barrio*, when people were asked whom they turned to in times of trouble (dealing with police, finding a job), the key person turned out to be the operator of a local pool hall, a man of great influence in the community but who received no respect at all.

Banton has dealt at length with the problems of conceptualization, the identification of structures, units of study, and levels of analysis in urban anthropology. He also has pointed out the problems of relating substructures to larger units or structures in the society.[7] An important additional problem is discovering what it means to the individual to belong to a group or to participate in a particular substructure. Indeed, this may be preliminary to discovering many of the informal structures in the urban environment.

3. The Nature of Poverty

The literature on poverty is vast. In this section we will discuss only a few of the anthropological contributions and suggest some anthropological approaches. A recently popularized view is that there is a distinct culture of poverty with common attributes regardless of the nation involved. This idea owes much to the work of Oscar Lewis, first in Mexico City *vecindades* (a type of slum), later in Puerto Rico, and among Puerto Ricans in New York. The first of his books presented an ordinary day in the life of each of five families of Mexico City, tracing in considerable detail both the group activities and interactions and activities of individuals outside the home. The families differed somewhat in degree of poverty and in backgrounds, and included one possibly nontypical middle-class family.

The ideas of the culture of poverty were first fully developed in *The Children of Sanchez*, which dealt in detail with one of the five families over a period of time and later developed in *La Vida*, a book about Puerto Ricans at home and in New York. In these books Lewis suggests that poverty creates its own culture, with elements common to the poor everywhere. This culture is self-generating; that is, its characteristics are transmitted down the generations.[8] It is a separate way of life with common characteristics wherever found

---

[6] Anthony Leeds, "Brazilian Careers and Social Structure: An Evolutionary Model and a Case History," *American Anthropologist*, **66**:1321–1347 (1964).

[7] Michael Banton, *The Anthropology of Complex Societies* (New York: Praeger, 1966).

[8] Oscar Lewis, *Five Families* (New York: Basic Books, 1959); *The Children of Sanchez* (New York: Random House and Knopf, 1961); *La Vida* (New York: Random House, 1966); *A Study of Slum Cultures: Background for La Vida* (New York: Random House, 1968).

but also forming a subculture within whatever larger cultural context it may occur.

The books by Lewis have aroused a good deal of interest and an equal amount of controversy. The method used was to establish close relationships with the families and tape-record both conversations between family members and descriptions by them of their lives and various incidents in them. Formal interviewing was apparently used mainly to fill in details and provide a framework for the actual life events recounted. A good deal of the material is presented in verbatim accounts. This is particularly true in *The Children of Sanchez,* in which each member of the family presents his autobiography essentially in his own words. These words are sometimes coarse and vulgar, a fact which caused some Mexicans of higher class to denounce the book as a fraud intended to denigrate Mexico because a Mexican would never use such language or express some of the ideas recorded. This reaction of course simply measured the degree to which people in one level of a complex culture anywhere are woefully ignorant of many aspects of their own country.

Some have criticized *The Children of Sanchez* as essentially literary, that it may not be representative, and some have questioned its authenticity. On the latter point, anyone who has lived with or associated closely with the poor in Mexico can affirm that the lives portrayed are believable and the incidents recounted are authentic. This does not, of course, tell us how many people have experienced the same kind of lives or undergone the same incidents. Lewis, if one reads his introduction and his other writings, does make certain limitations clear. The Sanchez family and the other members of the *vecindad* in which they live are not at the poorest level to be found in Mexico. Lewis presents some statistical data on the *vecindad* inhabitants and some comparison with other *vecindades*. The importance of the book lies in the moving and convincing picture of what the lives of some of the poor in Mexico City are like and in the many questions it raises for more thorough investigation.

Lewis suggests that the culture of poverty includes people with relatively high death rates and low life expectancy; low levels of education; low participation in organizations, such as labor unions or political parties; no participation in medical care or other welfare programs; little utilization of city facilities, such as stores, museums, or banks; low wages and little employment security; low skill levels; lack of savings or access to credit; and no food reserves in the house. Life lacks privacy; violence is frequent, including child beating; marriage is often consensual; child and wife abandonment is frequent; families are mother-centered; and authoritarianism in the family is marked. Common are a sense of resignation or fatalism, the importance of the *machismo* (hypermasculinity) complex among men, and the martyr complex among women.

These and other characteristics of the poor listed by Lewis have been reported in other studies. *The Children of Sanchez* illustrates how they operate in individual and family lives and underlines the need for more quantitative studies of many of them. One point that needs investigation is the extent to which some of these characteristics are marks of the poor, how many are shared values with other strata of society. In Latin America the mother-centered family, for example, is not unique to the poor; neither are the manifestations of *machismo*. Both may be manifested differently in various social strata. The mother-centered family is general, but among the poor its importance may be reinforced by the fact women often are household heads because of the high rate of family abandonment by males.

The idea of the self-perpetuating culture of poverty has been rather widely accepted. Although Lewis has repeatedly said he used the term only for a book of expected wide circulation and that what he really meant was the subculture of poverty, he must bear part of the responsibility for its currency today. The point is of more than theoretical importance. If the poor behave as they do and remain poor because they have grown up in a culture with different values from those of the rest of the society, then it is but a step to saying the poor perpetuate their poverty and are therefore responsible for it. The final step is, of course, the essentially racist argument, whether applied to ghetto or Appalachian poor, that the poor are poor because they are inherently inferior.

There appears to be room for a good deal more research on the nature and meaning of poverty. Another anthropologist, Thomas Gladwin, in *Poverty U.S.A.* suggests that poverty in the United States is not only being poor (that is, with low income), but being despised, incompetent (lacking skills), and powerless.[9] These attributes, he suggests, are not the product of a self-perpetuating culture or subculture, but are reflections of aspects of the dominant culture. He suggests that public policy toward poverty, which he considers a failure, has been based on the assumption of a self-perpetuating culture. Consequently the poor remain unskilled, despised, and powerless. Local and national power structures remain unaltered and there is no change in the distribution of material and psychic resources. But perhaps Gladwin's most challenging assertion is that the poor do not have different goals, values, and attitudes from those of the major culture; rather they are frustrated and prevented from realizing these goals. Consequently they seek satisfying alternatives which may not be understood or approved by the majority culture.

A somewhat similar approach is taken by Valentine in a more polemical book, *Culture and Poverty*.[10] He suggests that the poor in the United States represent a heterogeneous series of subsocieties with variable and adaptable subcultures that are only partially and relatively distinct from the dominant national culture. The chief deprivations of the poor and their structural position in the social system, he believes, result from the actions and attitudes of the nonpoor. His remedies include positive discrimination in favor of the poor in jobs and education, a "radical egalitarianism."

There is little doubt that to attribute all the characteristics of the poor to a subculture of poverty is an inadequate explanation. On the other hand even Valentine, by his own use of the term *subculture*, implies the cultural transmission of some attitudes and behaviors among established groups who

---

[9] Thomas Gladwin, *Poverty, U.S.A.* (Boston: Little, Brown, 1967).

[10] Charles A Valentine, *Culture and Poverty: Critique and Counter Proposals* (Chicago: University of Chicago Press, 1968). For an extended discussion of this work see *Current Anthropology*, **10**:181–201 (1969).

Cities grow as rural poor move to city in search of economic benefits. Making adobe bricks, La Paz, Bolivia. (Courtesy of the United Nations.)

happen to be poor. The need for far more ethnographic research making a more sophisticated approach to the concepts of culture, ecology, and adaptation is clearly needed.

At present a good deal of research on poverty centers upon the ghetto and the two principal ethnic groups, Black Americans and the Spanish-speaking Puerto Ricans and Mexican-Americans. As a result there is some confusion between problems of poverty and the problems of ethnicity. If poverty is the focus of research, it should be remembered that there are more poor whites in the United States than poor blacks. The two problems obviously cannot be entirely divorced. More ethnographic research is needed on the basic question of what it means to be poor. But it also is important to know what it means to be poor and black (or Puerto Rican or American Indian).

Research on poverty, oriented at the same time toward ethnic problems, must go beyond the behaviors, attitudes, and values of the poor. In terms of some contemporary issues, do blacks in the U.S. today want integration or segregation? The first implies they share the aspirations, values, and goals of the dominant society, the second implies either they do or do not have a naive view of social reality in believing they can achieve the same goals in a separate or parallel society. Whether blacks in the United States have an autonomous culture or that it has any significant African roots are still open questions. But such anthropological research as has been done suggests that African roots are minimal and that much of so-called Black culture arises out of shared reactions to the dominant culture much as does the culture of poverty. In the United States today poverty is defined in terms of income below a certain level. This tells us little about what poverty means to those who are poor. Moreover, poverty may also be defined in terms of deprivation or frustration. In comparison to a very large part of the world, the poor in the United States are relatively affluent. Within the United States, an income of $6,000 per annum, or whatever other level is the current definition of poverty, may mean something very different to a dweller in Harlem, Watts, or Montgomery, Alabama, a Spanish-American farmer of the upper Pecos Valley, or a Navajo of the Navajo mountain area who has perhaps never even seen Tuba City. They differ markedly in what they consider a satisfactory life and in their knowledge of alternative lifeways.

Poverty research clearly relates to several basic national policy issues. The welfare approach to the problem of poverty is primarily based upon the assumption that there is a subculture of poverty and that the problems will be solved if the poor will adopt current middle-class values. It clearly has failed. Modern research suggests structural changes in the dominant society and its culture are needed. Moreover, contemporary ethnic group aspirations suggest that the "melting pot" view of American society also is fallacious. Ethnic subcultures have special and positive values which people want to maintain. Research might suggest ways to extend the pluralistic nature of United States culture to allow for these divergent values.

4. Squatter's Towns, Ghettos, and Ethnicity

As this heading implies, several phenomena are related on the one hand to poverty, on the other to special locations within urban areas. Squatter's towns refer to settlements of substandard housing, often without clear land titles, within or on the margins of cities. Ghettos usually have an ethnic component to them; the term originated in Italy for urban neighborhoods where Jews were forced to live. Only fairly recently has it been extended to slum areas occupied by other immigrant or ethnic groups because of poverty and discrimination. In modern Africa "stranger's" towns often exist consisting of people of different tribal or religious origin. Kano, Nigeria, for example, consists of four towns physically separated from one another: the old walled city, predominantly Hausa; the Christian city (this must have been heavily Ibo and may have been essentially destroyed in the pogroms preceding the Biafran seces-

Latin American barriada in Venezuela. Such urban slums often involve more organization and less destitution than is apparent to the casual outsider. (Photo by Manuel Antonio Lujo. Courtesy of UNICEF.)

sion); the Stranger's city, inhabited by pagans; and the modern Administrative city, with government offices, hotels, airline offices, modern commercial establishments, and the residences of those who run them.

The squatter's town *barriadas* of Lima, Peru, have been studied by several anthropologists and others. These are squatter's towns on the outskirts of the city and the inhabitants are mainly migrants from the mountains. Investigation has shown that these towns are not the result of random individual settlements. Most *barriadas* began when a people living in a central city slum area organized and moved as a group to some piece of unoccupied land, sometimes owned by the government, sometimes by private individuals. Overnight the squatters would appear, divide the land into parcels, and put up some type of shelter, usually made of impermanent materials. In the Lima environment, owing to the almost complete lack of rain, the main requirements are some midday shade and shelter from the winds. This could be provided by a single north–south wall and a small shade for the middle of the day. In the morning people live on the west side of the wall, in the afternoon on the east.

Usually such new communities have some minimal organization to provide spokesmen for dealing with authorities or landowners. Usually some internal policing is provided and often newcomers must gain permission before joining the squatter's community. Such settlements often have no water supply, except at some distance, and lack sanitation, electricity, or other urban amenities. A function of the *barriada* organization is to attempt to get these improvements from a reluctant and impoverished municipal government. Efforts also are made to gain *de facto* recognition of rights to the land. Once the city makes the concession of establishing streets or street lines, this often is taken as *de facto* recognition of rights and the inhabitants begin to build more permanent structures, usually of adobe bricks. In time *barriada* leaders lose political influence as the area becomes merged into the city.

Another important aspect of the *barriadas* is the formation of associations or clubs composed of people from a particular village or *municipio,* or from a region. These provide meeting places and often recreational facilities and are supplemented by sports clubs. These provide a degree of social and emotional security. Often older and more successful members, who may not live in the *barriada,* help others with their problems of adjusting to the city. These organizations are a good place to learn about jobs or to find a lawyer or doctor. Newcomers who lack relatives may learn here how to dress, how to cut their hair, and how to comport themselves to get jobs.[11]

It is a popular belief, shared by many social scientists, that migration into the city is accompanied by social and personal disorganization. The study of the Lima *barriada* indicates considerable organization of life in the *barriada.* Lewis some years ago documented a case of immigrants to Mexico City from one town in Mexico who similarly made the transition without social break-

[11] William Mangin, "The Role of Regional Associations in the Adaptation of Rural Migrants to Cities in Peru," in Dwight B. Health and Richard N. Adams (eds.), *Contemporary Cultures and Societies of Latin America: A Reader in Social Anthropology of Middle and South America and the Caribbean* (New York: Random House, 1965).

Improved housing in Santiago, Chile. The housing is built by residents under a community development program. The municipality has provided sidewalks, gutters, graded streets, electricity, and other services. (Courtesy of the United Nations.)

down.[12] Evidence is accumulating that this is a frequent pattern in Mexico, although detailed studies have not been made. Information from other parts of Latin America as well as Africa indicated that few people move into the city without knowing either a kinsman, friend, or fellow townsman there. These contacts provide an introduction to the city and the majority of newcomers do not have to develop their own adaptation to urban life but can learn from prior immigrants. There is no doubt that this facilitates the move to the city, but it is also possible that the adjustment made by previous immigrants may be defective in many ways. The way of the newcomer may be eased but perhaps by learning an unsatisfactory adjustment.

Studies in the United States about movement to the city are on the whole unsatisfactory. There is some evidence that not only Puerto Ricans, Mexicans, and rural blacks moving into urban areas, but middle-class whites as well often know people in the city to which they move. Often these are relatives. In some cities particular areas are known to be "ports of entry" for most newcomers. Few studies exist of how these ports of entry function. How do new migrants know of them? To what extent do the ports of entry serve to adjust the newcomer to the city and how long do people remain in them? Answers to these questions are not satisfactorily known.

Leeds, who has studied some of the approximately 300 *favelas* or slums of Rio de Janeiro, points out that most studies treat the residents as rural migrants who have settled in but not become a part of the city. Some of these settlements actually are of some age and involve investments by *favela* dwellers of millions of dollars. To understand them, Leeds suggests that it is necessary

[12] Oscar Lewis, "Urbanization Without Breakdown," *Scientific American,* 75:3–41 (1952).

to know something about the mechanics of migration but that more important is relating conditions in the *favela* to land tenure and rent patterns, labor market conditions, wage structures, alternate types of cheap housing, the transportation system and its costs, discrimination by employers against *favela* dwellers (not based on ethnicity, be it noted), the nature of internal social relationships and organizations such as the Samba Schools, the services and business support provided to the larger community by *favela* dwellers, and their contribution to the labor force. For example, Leeds and his associates have shown that if the *favelas* were to be leveled and the *favela* dwellers moved to new housing in the outskirts of the city, not only would many be unable to pay the higher rents such new housing probably would require, but the cost of transportation to their jobs would take a very high percentage of their income. A shortage of labor, at least at present wage levels, would probably seriously affect part of the city economy. The need to study the *favela* systematically in relation to other aspects of the culture is clearly indicated. The same is probably true of studies of the urban ghetto in the United States.

Until recently few anthropological studies of United States slums and ghettos existed. Whyte early showed that ethnographic methods could be applied to the study of youth gangs and associations, demonstrating the social functions of such organizations to their members and that, contrary to popular belief, ghetto and slum life are highly structured. Recent studies of gangs support Whyte's early research. Other new approaches are a reexamination of the social functions of the matrifocal family, the nature of ghetto dialects, and other special types of groups or institutions. As an example of the latter, a recent study examines males repeatedly arrested for drunkenness and shows how public attitudes and the operation of police and the jails serve to create a subgroup with special cultural characteristics. Other studies deal with special problem areas such as public health or education (discussed more fully in §5). All these studies suggest large and highly relevant areas for further research.[13]

One difficulty with much of the published and contemporary research is the confusion that still exists between the study of ghettos or slums and ethnic research. The two obviously are very closely related but are not always clearly distinguished. Studies of the ghetto or the slum as a social form are generally limited. The same is true of ethnic studies: there are few studies of ethnic populations as a whole. Rather, ethnic studies tend to deal with limited groups. Even studies of the ethnic population of a city of the scope of the earlier work, *Black Metropolis*,[14] a study of the black population of Chicago, are lacking.

Many of the relevant works on ethnic groups have been limited to specific problems such as ethnicity, assimilation, or cultural change and upon some

---

[13] William A. Whyte, *Street Corner Society* (Chicago: University of Chicago Press, 1943); James F. Spradley, *You Owe Yourself a Drunk: Ethnography of Urban Nomads* (Boston: Little, Brown, 1970).

[14] St. Clair Drake and Horace R. Cayton, *Black Metropolis: A Study of Negro Life in a Northern City* (New York: Harcourt Brace Jovanovich, 1945).

A low-cost government housing development of 1,000 houses in Nicaragua. Many such housing developments are constructed without regard to the needs of their intended occupants and are often located far away from factories and job opportunities. (Courtesy of the United Nations.)

limited aspect of culture such as family and kinship, folk medicine, or leadership in which the ethnic group is supposed to show unique characteristics. The slum or ghetto has merely provided convenient limited settings for such research rather than being itself the point of main interest. Just as we need to know more about the meaning of poverty beyond a simple income measure, we also need to know more about the ghetto or the *barrio*. It seems clear that although external forces—such as housing discrimination or absence of inexpensive housing alternatives, educational and skill levels, and external pressures of various sorts—contribute to the formation of the ghetto or the *barrio,* these residential groupings may also offer their members some securities and rewards through association with people of similar speech and behavior.

On the whole, however, it is clear that anthropology has contributed more to the study of urban problems in Africa and Latin America than it has so far in the United States. This may in part be due to a certain romanticism among anthropologists and anthropology students, who tend to find distant and exotic settings more interesting. It also is probably true that it is easier for an anthropologist to get financial assistance to study the problem of rural migrants to Lima than it is to get assistance for studying migrants to Detroit.

5. Urban Education and Health

In Chapter 18, §3 we mentioned the work of the anthropologist, Spindler, on the effect of class differences between teacher and student. More recently, others such as Eleanor Leacock have followed these leads.[15] The effects of sub-cultural differences and child-rearing practices on educational receptivity and performance are being studied by anthropologists. Anthropological studies of the nature and operation of peer-group cultures in school settings are also badly needed.

A number of studies of health concepts have been made by anthropologists, especially among Mexican-Americans. As most Mexican-Americans who migrated to the United States were from rural or marginal lower-class groups in towns or small cities, it was apparent that they brought with them both different attitudes toward sickness and many folk medical beliefs and practices. Not only is illness differently defined but it has different social implications, for it is a family matter rather than an individual one. Once illness is recognized there is a readjustment of relationships within the extended family and neighbors; family duties and responsibilities must be redistributed in the case of an adult; the sick person becomes the focus of family attention and part of the treatment, in effect, is the reintegration of the individual into the family. Not only is the hospital feared, because it is unknown, with strange, unpalatable and even harmful foods, but the sense of isolation is very strong. Some diseases are believed to be caused magically and to result from witchcraft, punishment for sin, *susto* (fright), loss of the soul, and the evil eye. Other diseases are the result of wrong foods or wrong combinations of foods, sometimes in relation to particular circumstances, and there is belief in the efficacy of many herbal remedies. In this category fall many ideas which are folk interpretations of what once was standard practice in Galenic medicine common in Western countries before the beginnings of scientific medicine little more than a century ago. These and related beliefs and attitudes can be documented among many Mexican-Americans, and there is a tendency to assume that they are common.

One major study, *Health in the Mexican-American Culture*, investigated a small *barrio* outside the city of San Jose, California.[16] Over 80 percent of the population was born in the United States, a figure not significantly different from that for Mexican-Americans elsewhere. A number of heads of households had been born in Mexico but the average length of residence in the United States of household heads born in Mexico was 33.6 years. None had lived in Mexico in the previous five years; only 10 percent had lived in Mexico in the previous ten years. Educational and income levels are low. Rents are low; virtually all housing is substandard and some homes are little better than

---

[15] Eleanor Leacock, *Class and Color in City Schools: A Comparative Study* (New York: Basic Books, 1969).

[16] Margaret Clark, *Health in the Mexican-American Culture* (Berkeley: University of California Press, 1959).

shacks. On the other hand, a significant number of families could afford better housing elsewhere; they do not leave because they would feel insecure and uncomfortable in Anglo neighborhoods or among strangers. Old people, especially, prefer an environment with Spanish-speaking neighbors and store-keepers.

The *barrio* inhabitants are believed to make less use of hospitals, clinics, and doctors than members of other groups. The reasons given are several: medical doctors do not understand Mexican diseases; they are cold and frighteningly impersonal; they do not allow other family members to be present at consultations or examinations; they will not allow children to accompany mothers and they have no one to leave them with; the hospitals are very lonely, with restricted visiting hours; hospital food is either tasteless and inedible or is injurious to the patient.

Similar ideas about health have been amply reported for Latin America and for Mexican-Americans in New Mexico and Texas. Does this mean that Mexican-Americans do not resort to hospitals and modern medicine? Anthropologists and some medical and public health personnel believe this to be the case. An as yet unpublished study of hospital usage in Los Angeles, however, casts doubt on these assumptions for urban areas. Although practically all births in Los Angeles County now occur in hospitals, a small percentage still do not. Mexican-American mothers account for a disproportionate number of these. A similar situation prevails with respect to prenatal care and the use of hospitals for serious terminal illnesses. At first sight this seems to bear out the cultural basis for failure to use medical facilities. The investigator went a step further. He compared Mexican-Americans with blacks and whites initially. He then broke down these groups in terms of income and educational levels. When groups of the same income and educational levels were compared there were no significant differences between Mexican-Americans, blacks, and whites. The apparent differences, then, are the result of poverty and lack of education, not the result of "Mexicanness," except in the sense that compared with the other groups Mexican-Americans are poorer and have less schooling. The one significant exception to these conclusions is that individuals fairly recently arrived from Mexico make less use of medical facilities than do long-term residents or native-born Mexican-Americans.

The example cited shows that anthropologists can identify specific characteristics of ethnic groups in ways relevant to urban problems. It also suggests that anthropological studies may have shortcomings when they forget that even ethnic groups are parts of larger cultural settings and do not use their own holistic approach.

A similar point is made by Thomas Gladwin in a review of a study of the mentally retarded conducted by Robert Edgerton, an anthropologist.[17] Edgerton studied the ways mentally retarded individuals behave in the larger society after their release from institutions. Edgerton found many similarities in the ways these mentally retarded behave and suggested they possess a sub-

---

[17] Thomas Gladwin, "Review of Robert Edgerton's *The Cloak of Competence: Stigma in the Lives of the Mentally Retarded*," *The American Anthropologist*, **70**:618–620 (1968).

Training in the servicing and repair of scientific instruments. Highly specialized urban work sometimes appears to separate the individual from the broad understandings of nature and society possessed by rural people. (Courtesy of the United Nations.)

culture. Gladwin asks, however, whether any group of people, simply because they can be given a distinctive label and share distinctive behaviors, necessarily share a subculture. The mentally retarded who have managed to make their way outside of institutions carefully isolate themselves from one another; they can in no sense be transmitting "cultural behaviors" to one another. On the other hand, several studies show that institutions for the mentally retarded do have special subcultures. The dominant culture also has a patterned set of attitudes and reactions toward the mentally retarded. The origin of shared behaviors among the mentally retarded is to be found, then, first in the institutions from which they came, and secondly in common necessary responses to the expectations of the larger culture which will not permit anything else. Gladwin illustrates his point further by references to the so-called Pan-Indian culture of American Indians. The idea that the Indians of the United States, let alone the continent or hemisphere, all shared common cultural characteristics before the coming of Europeans is manifest nonsense. The basis of Pan-Indian movements and any common behaviors of Indians today is simply a set of similar responses to policies, attitudes, and actions of the dominant culture. Gladwin also has made the same point with respect to the culture of poverty (see §3 of this chapter). He suggests not that anthropologists have not made important contributions, but that they have not always made full use of their basic concept of culture. Behaviors that are similar responses of members of the same culture to the same situational factors may look like a subculture.

They may in time be learned and become part of culture, but they cannot be considered cultural behaviors unless the transmission mechanisms can be identified. This is an issue of major importance if one is examining either the behavior of the poor or some such group as the blacks, who for generations have lived within United States culture. To what extent is their current behavior learned through membership in a subcultural group and to what extent does it represent recurrent individual reactions to the dominant culture?

6. Summary

Anthropologists have conducted studies of urban communities in Africa and Latin America. Many of these studies have dealt with special aspects of culture and society, such as rural–urban migration and the processes of adaptation to urban life. Often special structures, such as voluntary organization, or locality groupings, such as squatter or slum communities, have been abstracted from the urban setting for special analysis. A frequent fault of such studies has been their failure to relate them adequately to the total urban structure or to general theories of urbanism. Although some early studies in the United States, such as those of Middletown and Yankee City, were attempts at holistic analysis, most anthropological studies conducted in United States cities have also involved special topics, such as health or education or the isolation of a subcommunity.

The major contributions anthropology can make to the complex problem of urbanism are structural types of analysis directed at the total urban structure and types of studies which lend themselves especially to ethnographic methods of investigation, bearing in mind that other disciplines can more effectively study some kinds of problems. Among the more promising areas of investigation are certain aspects of education, poverty, and ethnicity, where ethnographic methods may delineate life styles and isolate the important questions for detailed and quantitative research. Anthropologists have contributed significantly to problems of the influence of class-determined subcultures and ethnic background in education and health and to understanding of the problems of poverty. The shortcomings of some of these studies appear to lie not in their anthropological points of view and methods, but in failure to use the concept of culture more effectively and to utilize fully the holistic and comparative points of view. Whether there is a self-perpetuating subculture of poverty in the true sense or a set of common responses of the poor and deprived to characteristics of the dominant culture is important theoretically but also has major significance for public policy.

Collateral Reading

Agar, Michael. *Ripping and Running: A Formal Ethnography of the Urban Heroin Addict*. Language, Thought, and Culture: Advances in the Study of Cognition.

New York and London: Seminar Press, 1973. Pioneering use of new methodology.

Banton, Michael (ed.). *The Social Anthropology of Complex Societies.* New York and Washington, D.C.: Frederick A. Praeger, Inc., 1966. One of few attempts at a total review of problems of studying complex societies including urbanism.

Banton, Michael (ed.). *Cities: Their Origin, Growth, and Human Impact.* Readings from *Scientific American.* San Francisco: W. H. Freeman and Co., 1973. Relatively popular articles representing several disciplines.

Eddy, Elizabeth M. (ed.). *Urban Anthropology.* Southern Anthropological Society Proceedings, No. 2, 1969. A collection of recent papers by anthropologists on urban research.

Epstein, A. L. "Urbanization and Social Change in Africa." *Current Anthropology,* 8:275–295 (1967). Reviews studies in areas anthropologists first studied urbanism and finds regional differences.

Foster, George M., and Robert V. Kemper (eds.). *Anthropologists in Cities.* Boston: Little, Brown and Company, 1974. Good collected articles.

Gans, Herbert J. *The Urban Villagers.* New York: The Free Press, 1962. A follow-up on Whyte's *Street Corner Society.*

Gladwin, Thomas. *Poverty U.S.A.* Boston: Little, Brown and Company, 1967. An anthropologist examines what poverty is in the U.S.A. and questions the culture of poverty concept.

Gulick, John. *Tripoli: A Modern Arab City.* Cambridge, Mass.: Harvard University Press, 1967.

Jesús, Carolina Maria de. *Child of the Dark: The Diary of Carolina Maria de Jesus.* New York: The New American Library, Inc., 1964. Autobiographical account of life in a Rio slum.

Leacock, Eleanor. *Class and Color in City Schools: A Comparative Study.* New York: Basic Books, Inc., 1969. An anthropological study of education, class, and color.

Lewis, Oscar. *The Children of Sanchez.* New York: Random House, Inc., and Alfred A. Knopf, Inc., 1961. The most widely known of several works by this author dealing with the "culture of poverty" idea.

Little, Kenneth. *West African Urbanization.* Cambridge: Cambridge University Press, 1965. A good example of anthropological studies of urbanism in Africa.

Mangin, William (ed.). *Peasants in Cities: Readings in Anthropology of Urbanization.* Boston: Houghton Mifflin Company, 1970. An excellent collection of articles.

Matthews, Elmora Messer. *Neighbor and Kin: Life in a Tennessee Ridge Community.* Nashville: Vanderbilt University Press, 1965.

Peattie, Lisa Redfield. *The View from the Barrio.* Ann Arbor: University of Michigan, 1968. Study of slums in a new Venezuelan Industrial city.

Powdermaker, Hortense. *Copper Town: Changing Africa.* New York: Harper & Row, Inc., 1962.

Rubel, Arthur J. *Across the Tracks: Mexican-Americans in a Texas City.* Austin and London: University of Texas Press, 1966. One of the best studies of a "brown" community in a small Texas city.

Safa, Helen I. *The Urban Poor of Puerto Rico: A Study in Development and Inequality.* New York: Holt, Rinehart and Winston, Inc., 1974.

Southall, Aidan (ed.). *Urban Anthropology: Cross-Cultural Studies of Urbanization.* New York: Oxford University Press, 1973. Collected articles.

Spindler, George, et al. *Burgbach: Urbanization and Identity in a German Town.* New York: Holt, Rinehart and Winston, Inc., 1973. A good field study.

Spoehr, Alexander (ed.). *Pacific Port Towns and Cities.* Honolulu: Bishop Museum Press, 1963. A comparison of a special urban type.

Spradley, James P. *You Owe Yourself a Drunk: An Ethnography of Urban Nomads.* Little, Brown and Company, 1970. Pioneering research in the United States.

Spradley, James P., and David W. McCurdy. *The Cultural Experience: Ethnography in Complex Society.* Chicago: Science Research Associates, Inc., 1972. Examples of fieldwork by undergraduates.

Whitten, Norman E., Jr., and John W. Szwed (eds.). *Afro-American Anthropology.* New York: The Free Press, 1970. Most recent studies on the cultures of the Afro-American from Brazil to the United States, from rural to ghetto life.

Whyte, William F. *Street Corner Society: The Social Structure of an Italian Slum,* 2d ed., enlarged. Chicago: University of Chicago Press, 1961. A classic application of ethnographic technique by a sociologist in an urban setting.

Valentine, Charles A. *Culture and Poverty.* Chicago: University of Chicago Press, 1968. A controversial and polemic book about the nature of poverty and what should be done about it.

Young, M., and P. Willmot. *Family and Kinship in East London.* London; Routledge & Kegan Paul, Ltd., 1957. One of the few extensive studies of kinship and the family in an urban setting.

22/Anthropology and the Modern World

1. Contributions of Anthropology to Modern Thought

The relation of anthropology to the contemporary world is varied. It includes the influence of anthropology on the way people think about themselves, their fellows, and the natural and social world in which they live. Related to this are the ways anthropologists, by virtue of their experiences and the findings of their discipline, interpret their own and other cultures. Another set of problems involves the ways anthropologists direct their research toward contemporary problems or involve themselves in action programs to solve them. Yet another set of relationships involves the present and future status of the discipline, relationships that may affect its possible contributions to human welfare. Only a few of these problems can be considered in this final chapter.

The most pervasive influence of anthropology is perhaps its contribution to changing views of the nature of humanity. Particularly in Western thought, the universe commonly was seen as created for human pleasure and use. The contrasting view that humanity is an integral part of nature and must live in harmony with it is increasingly influential and forms part of the abstract philosophical basis for the current concern with ecology. An important influence on these changing views is the anthropological concept of culture, a concept generally accepted today as a commonplace by most social scientists and becoming increasingly familiar to others. Using the concept of culture, anthropology, as Kluckhohn put it, holds up a mirror to humanity that gives people a clearer view of themselves and others. Anthropology contributes to understanding the origins, nature, and functions of society and its institutions, and illuminates the motivations and behaviors of ourselves and others. Its influence is increasingly visible in the realms of philosophy, literature, and politics.

More concrete results of anthropology have been less influential. Anthropology makes clear the essential unity of humanity and anthropologists have emphasized the fallacies and social dangers of racism in their research and teaching, and in repeated public statements. Cross-cultural research makes it clear that although human beings share common problems, the cultural solutions to these problems are diverse. Anthropologists have insisted on the integrity and validity of different cultural systems and have argued for understanding and tolerance. Despite some successes, racial bigotry and contempt for the cultures of other peoples clearly persist, constituting a threat to international peace and the internal tranquillity of nations.

One reason for the partial failure of anthropology to affect the thinking of many people in the United States, as well as to be used in the solution of current problems, is due to the recency of the use of scientific methods in the study of social and cultural phenomena. In many parts of the world the possibility of such application is not known or is rejected. This is also true of many people in our own society. Even some natural scientists, especially those who confuse laboratory and experimental techniques with scientific method, tend to be skeptical. The development of the social sciences became possible only when it was recognized that the scientific method is not limited to laboratory experiment or to any other specialized type of observation. Rather, the scientific method is a process of formulating hypotheses to explain known facts and of continuously subjecting these hypotheses to verification or reformulation by further and extended observations.

Despite advances in the social sciences, including anthropology, many basic decisions about human affairs still are made by polling the opinions of community leaders, whether or not they have the necessary competence or knowledge. This process, called a type of magic by Clyde Kluckhohn, is illustrated by the following incident. Several years ago, a scientist asked a considerable group of people in a university town how they would go about solving a problem confronting the public schools of the community. The group was presented with ten ways of making a decision. The first substantially was, "Find out what leading business men, educators, ministers and other community leaders think, and follow their opinion." The last was, in effect, "Hire an experienced investigator to ascertain all the facts and then form an opinion." The majority of the people questioned chose the first method; none chose the last. In other words, even the most elementary steps of scientific method were rejected in favor of relying upon "leaders," who are supposed by some occult means to discover the right answer.

This approach to social problems is related to the persistence of racism among large sectors of the middle and working classes revealed in recent reactions to integration and the reverse racism that has emerged among some black populations. In the United States there are many complex and difficult problems involved in achieving equality of educational and economic opportunity. The very considerable extent to which proposed solutions are evaluated in overt or covert racist terms while most social science findings are ignored, is a measure of the failure of anthropologists to communicate the results of their research. More and more anthropologists are taking the view that it is not enough to do research but that they have a responsibility to try to see that their research is understood and used.

Knowledge of the processes of culture improves understanding of the behavior of other peoples and helps us to so conduct ourselves that we have better relations with them. Particularly important is the concept of cultural relativity; namely, the recognition that when other peoples react differently they do not do so from stupidity or maliciousness. Basically, as we have seen, human beings everywhere confront similar kinds of problems, for which they have, through many thousands of years, developed solutions different from our own. These historically determined patterns of behavior are closely integrated to form a cultural whole that to its bearers justifies and makes reasonable their actions, ideas, and beliefs. What seems immoral to us may seem right and proper to them; conversely, much that we consider right and proper may appear positively immoral to others. Thus, for example, a woman delegate from Pakistan eloquently and successfully opposed a proposal in the United Nations to condemn polygyny. Millions who live in India believe that the killing of animals of any sort, let alone the eating of their flesh, is sinful. The chief of an African tribe once said that Europeans must be the wickedest people alive to kill millions of men in warfare without even the intention of using their flesh for food. To many other nonliterate peoples it is incredible that people in our society do without while others enjoy abundance. No amount of justification on our part will convince these people that they are wrong, and conversely, many of us probably find it difficult, if not impossible, to accept cannibalism, or even polygyny.

The most ambitious attempts by anthropologists to contribute to widespread understanding of other cultures took place during and following World War II in what are usually referred to as studies of national character. The best known and perhaps most successful was Ruth Benedict's *The Chrysanthemum and the Sword,* a study of the Japanese.[1] Similar studies were also made of the United States; for example, Margaret Mead's *And Keep Your Powder Dry.*[2] Most of these works had a strong psychodynamic orientation. Today many anthropologists regard such studies as a rather embarrassing interlude, but they have not found other means of making anthropological thought widely known.

Whether we consider the opinions probably held by the majority of people in the United States (or for that matter, the majority opinions in most other countries) about other cultures, or the behaviors and attitudes of many United

[1] Ruth Benedict, *The Chrysanthemum and the Sword* (Boston: Houghton Mifflin, 1946).

[2] Margaret Mead, *And Keep Your Powder Dry* (New York: Morrow, 1942; new ed., 1965).

States citizens abroad, it is clear that understanding and tolerance of other ways of life have not been widely communicated. This is particularly evident in United States foreign policy and in the conduct of programs for economic and technical aid. Other countries are judged and dealt with very largely in terms of how closely they conform to United States institutions and values and most aid programs assume that the transplantation of United States culture is the ultimate goal.

Anthropology has an important role in developing respect for the cultural values of others as well as in aiding them in making adjustments to the modern industrial world on their own terms rather than on ours. Cultural relativity makes it clear that many customs we may reject for ourselves represent values in another culture that must be respected. Just as we have accepted the right of people to their own religious beliefs, we must be prepared to accept the right of people to their own culture. Many anthropologists today feel that they should be more active and vocal in making these points of view known. They also are turning to new kinds of research, some of which are mentioned later in this chapter.

The concept of cultural relativity is sometimes misunderstood or misapplied in dealing with our own culture. The shock of discovering that behavior we consider bad may be condoned or even approved in other cultures sometimes leads uncritical students to believe they can abandon all behavior rules. Such a point of view is quite unjustified, for all cultures have moral rules with deep historical roots and there are often functional reasons for their existence within the given culture. What is bad in one culture may be good in another, and vice versa, for precisely the same reasons — the rules are necessary to the proper functioning of the culture and to the adequate adjustment of the individual to one's own environment. To respect the customs of others does not mean that these customs are equally to be practiced in our culture.

The culture of the Euro-American peoples is deeply embedded in Judeo-Greco-Christian backgrounds. Although the values of this background have undergone slow change through the centuries, they cannot be ignored by a member of our culture. It may be that not all our values are of universal validity for other cultures, or that the values of other cultures may in some degree be better than our own, but until some scientific method of studying values can be developed, we must for the most part insist merely upon their validity within a given culture. To respect the validity of another culture is not to deny the validity of our own; when we recognize that a Moslem is bound to Islamic culture, we should likewise recognize that we are bound to ours. At the same time we must not fail to recognize that values, like all the rest of culture, are subject to change, and that the values of an earlier period in our history need not necessarily be of equal importance today.

Anthropology in the modern world, then, has the important function of helping us to understand ourselves and our culture. Through intensive studies of many cultures, we learn that although all peoples have broadly similar capacities and face the same problems of living, they are subject in each society to differing natural conditions and, hence, have developed diverse ways of meeting their problems. These ways of living are complexly integrated into a cultural totality—a set of techniques, habits, customs, beliefs, and institutions, each set characteristic of a given people. Through this understanding we learn as well that our own behavior is similarly conditioned by a culture, one among many others. As we learn more about culture—how it is integrated, its historical and evolutionary development, the processes of cultural change, and the complex relation between culture and individual behavior—anthropology becomes increasingly useful in the understanding and direction of human affairs.

Anthropology is, of course, not the only social science that deals with human behavior, nor does it supply answers to all social problems. Rather it offers, through its central concept of culture and its intensive comparisons of many diverse cultures, an integrative framework that aids all social science in the analysis and understanding of our own very complex civilization. As such it may contribute heavily to the ultimate goal of gaining the same scientific controls over social and cultural phenomena that we now possess in the field of the natural sciences, and, even more important, to the solution of the problem of using such controls for the benefit of all human beings.

2. New Directions in Research

Today the subject matter of anthropological research is undergoing many changes. Some of these have been dealt with in Chapters 20, 21, and 22. Here we will mention a few others, not dealt with in detail, for it is perhaps too soon to be certain how important a part of anthropology they will become. Many changes in research are being undertaken by anthropologists who are dissatisfied with the failure of the discipline to have more impact on contemporary thought and national policy. One reason for this failure is believed to be the failure of past research to focus on issues or situations of relevance to current social problems. Some interpret this as requiring anthropologists to become actively involved in programs of social and cultural change. It is not always clear whether some activists are interested primarily in using organized anthropology to promote their political ends rather than to expand our knowledge of human behavior. In any case the emergence of a radical caucus at anthropology meetings, as well as other special-interest groups such as that concerned with women's position in anthropology, are responsible for a critical reexamination of the nature of anthropological research and for stimulating a number of research trends which had already begun in a minor way.

The major event precipitating critical discussion of anthropological research and the uses to which it may be put was Project Camelot, a vast plan of social science research, sponsored by the United States Department of Defense to investigate the causes of social unrest leading to armed insurgency, and to identify the best ways of either averting the outbreak of violence or suppressing it when it occurs. Disputes, factionalism, conflict, revolution, and war have long been the subject of social science research and the Department of Defense had supported research on past revolutions without arousing any particular objections. What distinguished Project Camelot was its scope, its proposed research in other countries to try to develop methods to identify potential revolutions before they happened, and the use by the Department of Defense of the terms *insurgency* and *counterinsurgency*. The implication also seemed clear to many people that the Department of Defense anticipated active involvement in dealing with insurgency movements in many countries.

The scope of Project Camelot was so vast that to carry it out would have required the participation of very large numbers of social scientists in the United States as well as the cooperation of social scientists in the countries selected for the initial studies. It was the latter fact that first led the project into trouble. An anthropologist going to Chile for other reasons was asked to explore informally with social scientists in that country whether they would be interested in participating should Chile be selected as a location for part of the research. Although the project had never been secret, Chileans for the first time became aware of it. The use of the terms *insurgency* and *counterinsurgency*, the sponsorship of the Department of Defense, and some of the proposed research into such matters as the loyalties of the armed forces aroused violent condemnation in Chile and elsewhere. Project Camelot was investigated by a select committee of the Chilean Chamber of Deputies and by committees of the United States Congress. The project was speedily canceled by the Department of Defense while still in the planning phase. In Chile and in other countries there were proposals, and in some cases actions, to restrict social science research by foreign scientists and often local social science research came under suspicion and attack. The United States government set up strict controls on social science research abroad sponsored by government agencies.

The design of Project Camelot was primarily the product of sociologists and social psychologists and few anthropologists were involved in its planning. Nevertheless, anthropologists reacted more sharply to the events in Chile than did other social scientists. In part this was a reaction to the threat to foreign research which has formed such an important part of anthropological research since the 1920s. Many anthropologists for the first time became fully aware of the potentialities for use of their research for purposes which they did not approve. A major concern also was for possible injury to the people studied by anthropologists. The American Anthropological Association initiated a study of research problems and the ethical responsibilities of anthropologists, with special attention to research in other countries and the relations between anthropology and government. The major results of this study are reported by Ralph Beals in *Politics of Social Research*. The results of a parallel study by the National Research Council are reported by Gene Lyons.[3]

Many anthropologists objected especially to Project Camelot because it implied a United States policy of widespread military intervention in countries experiencing insurgency. The close involvement of most anthropologists

---

[3] Ralph L. Beals, *Politics of Social Research* (Chicago: Aldine, 1968); Gene M. Lyons, *The Uneasy Partnership* (New York: Russell Sage Foundation, 1969).

with the people they study makes them very sensitive to economic and social injustices, and the fact that development and modernization so often seem only to perpetuate old injustices and provide new patterns of exploitation. The proper clients, many feel, are the people studied. Frequently, it appears that only through insurgency and revolution can tribal peoples, the peasants, or the poor terminate long-standing injustices and break the control of exploitative and traditional elites. Thus Eric R. Wolf, an anthropologist long dedicated to the study of peasants and their problems, published a book, *Peasant Wars of the Twentieth Century*, which reviews the participation of peasants in six of the major revolutions of our time, in Mexico, Russia, China, Viet Nam, Algeria, and Cuba.[4]

Wolf points out that the United States, for a variety of reasons, including its isolation and prosperity, is ill-prepared to understand the upheavals in many of the poor nations of the world. Wolf feels the anthropologist, with his interest in microsociology, is especially well-equipped to analyze these movements. Peasants, he points out, differ very much among themselves and in the kinds of relationships they have with the larger society; especially, they usually lack power as compared with other segments of their society. Their participation in revolts stems from different motivations and ideological involvements. The revolutions he discusses vary in the degree to which peasant ways of life have been changed and in the extent to which peasant unrest has been utilized by power-seeking groups mobilizing their support to overturn and replace existing power groups. It is perhaps ironical that Wolf explores many of the same problems that Project Camelot proposed to examine, but in a much less intensive and systematic manner, and his work can be used in the same ways to identify and eliminate causes of unrest through civic action or to suppress insurgency when it occurs. It may also be used as a handbook of revolution, a criticism also leveled against Project Camelot by one member of the United States Congress.

Reactions to Project Camelot are not the sole cause of greater interest in research in contemporary social problems, whether in this country or in developing nations. In Chapter 20 we discussed the growing field of development and, in Chapter 21, some aspects of urban anthropology. A good deal of contemporary research in these fields, much of it as yet unpublished or reported only in preliminary articles, is oriented toward the needs of the groups studied and is motivated by a belief in the importance of finding better solutions to many current social problems. Trends in the study of the American Indian offer one example. Until the 1930s most studies of the American Indian in the United States sought to recover data on aboriginal cultures. In the 1930s anthropologists turned their attention to problems of acculturation or applied anthropology projects, often working for the Bureau of Indian Affairs. More recently anthropologists increasingly have studied problems arising out of the Indian community itself and some have been employed by Indian groups. Theodore Graves and his associates, as one example, have studied the Indians of Colorado and New Mexico in urban or nonreservation

---

[4] Eric R. Wolf, *Peasant Wars of the Twentieth Century* (New York: Harper & Row, 1969).

settings.[5] Special studies have included such problems as alcoholism, but few of his studies have been published as yet. Preliminary studies of Indians have been made in other urban areas but much remains to be done. A few papers exist on the Pan-Indian movement but a serious study is yet to be published. Other studies have been made of contemporary reservation problems such as factionalism, political organization, or relations with whites. The need for further studies of the actual conditions of American Indian life is great. Such studies may contribute to the solution of problems of the Indians as well as to changing attitudes and policies of the dominant white society. In so doing they may also illuminate more general and theoretical problems of anthropology.

In Chapter 21 we mentioned studies of poverty and the problems of the ghetto. Both here and in the dominant society there are obvious areas of research, only some of which are beginning to be explored. The anthropological study of special groupings and movements is in its infancy. Shortly before his death, Ralph Linton, who first provided a systematic framework for the study of nativistic and revivalistic or millennial movements, suggested that the then active Great Crusade, which led to the election of President Dwight D. Eisenhower, had many of the characteristics of a nativistic movement and deserved study in these terms. More recently, Anthony F. C. Wallace has used the term *religious revitalization movements* for those nativistic movements involving deliberate attempts by some or all members of a society to create a more satisfying moral order. Many such movements in the past have been responses of oppressed people to their situation, often the domination of an alien culture. They have been a frequent response to the spread of colonialism. Anthropologists have studied some of these such as the Cargo Cults of Melanesia or the Ghost Dance and Handsome Lake movements among the American Indians. The Black Muslim movement also falls in this category. In most similar cases a reorganization of the supernatural world and one's relations to it have been involved. Wallace suggests that most new religions emerging now or in the past have had their origin in such movements, although some, for example, Buddhism, did not begin among dominated peoples.

Although Wallace considers all revitalization movements to be religious, in his discussion of Communism he suggests that belief in supernatural beings is not essential to a religious movement. In such cases individuals or the state may attain the respect once demanded by supernatural beings. If this is accepted, then many phenomena of contemporary society may be analyzed in the same framework. All seek to reform society, to give a new sense of moral worth, and a new sense of identity. As Wallace remarks, "And no lesson of human experience is more fully proven than that men will do anything, including killing themselves and their fellows, to preserve or to regain a sense of moral worth."[6] The understanding of such contemporary movements may

---

[5] Theodore Graves, with Minor Van Arsdale, "Values, Expectations and Relocation: The Navaho Indian Migrant to Denver," *Human Organization,* 25:300–307 (1966).

[6] Anthony F. C. Wallace, "Religious Revitalization: A Function of Religion in Human History and Evolution," in Eugene A. Hammel and William S. Simmons (eds.), *Man Makes Sense* (Boston: Little, Brown, 1970).

determine whether large pluralistic societies such as the United States may
survive through a common consensus among diverse groups or may survive
only by the use of centralized force. These and similar studies also may determine the survival of a fragmented world order capable of destroying life
itself through misuse of natural forces either through nuclear warfare or
the destruction of the ecological balance necessary for human survival.

3. Anthropology and Public Policy

The preceding section makes clear the many ways in which anthropologists
may contribute to greater understanding of critical social problems. There
remains the question of how this knowledge may be translated into effective
changes in human culture and society. Certainly, one way is through bringing
this knowledge to bear upon the formation and implementation of public policy. A significant number of anthropologists today, as in the past, have rejected
working through existing governmental forms, finding them too bound to
outworn solutions. To many, however, it seems clear that even if the existing
political order is destroyed, it will be replaced by a new political order which
must somehow be brought to use the findings of anthropology and the other
social sciences if these are to be useful for human welfare. In this section we
discuss some of the problems of making social science more influential within
the existing political order with special reference to the United States.

Anthropologists as a group have always expressed a belief that their findings ultimately should be of service to human welfare. The "Statement on
Problems of Anthropological Research and Ethics" adopted overwhelmingly
by the Fellows of the American Anthropological Association in March of 1967
refers to conditions which might threaten the "contribution anthropology
might make to our own society and to the general interests of human welfare."[7] Despite these sentiments most anthropologists have felt their contribution was best made through basic research to develop understanding of human
behavior in the context of culture and society. A good many anthropologists
felt uncomfortable about the beginnings of applied anthropology or any direct
connection between anthropology and public policy.

Actually, policy involvements have long existed, perhaps most obviously in
the use of anthropology in the formulation of administrative policy in colonial
or trusteeship areas. In the United States one important argument advanced
for the establishment a century ago of the Bureau of American Ethnology
within the Smithsonian Institution rather than within an operating agency
was that it would provide information for the administration of American
Indian groups. The fact that it was located in an independent research agency
rather than in an operating agency is relevant to the entire problem of policy
research to be discussed here. So too is the fact that for more than half a century neither the Congress nor administrative operating agencies made any use

[7] *American Anthropologist,* **69**:318–322 (1967).

of the Bureau for policy or administration. The more recent uses of applied anthropology, development and urban studies, have been detailed in the previous chapters. What has disturbed many anthropologists is the realization that many government operating departments and agencies today, from the Department of Defense to the Department of Urban Affairs, are using anthropology and other social sciences in connection with policy matters and administration. Economists and political scientists have long assumed that their disciplines were policy sciences; that is, that their results would be employed in the formation and execution of public policy. To a lesser degree sociologists have also assumed that their discipline was a policy science, but for a good many anthropologists this is a new idea, and some do not like it. They often are especially disturbed by the realization that even the most theoretical or "basic" study involving ethnography can be used as a basis for policy formation or as a means of justifying policy administration.

If anthropologists really believe that their discipline ultimately will be of service to human welfare, they should welcome the increased interest of policy makers. Anthropology in the past has probably improved the human lot to some extent through the increasingly wider understanding of the nature of culture, the fallacies of racism, and the exploding of myths about human behavior. But a good deal of the implementation of knowledge about man, for or against his own benefit, must come through the operations of government and related institutions. In the past administrators and bureaucrats have found social science threatening to them. Administrators often relied basically on popular knowledge, experience, and intuition. The possibility that popular knowledge can be wrong, experience inadequate, and intuition wrong has made them very suspicious and often hostile to social science, for it threatens their presumed special competence.

Even today social science is used very unevenly both in industry and government. Many administrators still do not understand it and view it with suspicion; others attempt to manipulate research in social sciences for their own ends. Social science advice or information often is not sought as an aid in arriving at policy decisions. Instead, not infrequently there are attempts to hire or contract with some "tame" social scientists to justify decisions already made or, less venal perhaps, to find the best ways of implementing or gaining acceptance of policy decisions already made. If anthropologists want their research ultimately to benefit the human condition, they must be concerned with the role of social science in government.

At present there is no systematic relationship between most social sciences and government. The one exception is the President's Council of Economic Advisors. Even in this case, where rather important divisions of opinion exist among economists, there is no assurance that the President will have the benefit of divergent viewpoints. On the other hand, the influence of the Council has led to an improvement in the collection of economic information by the government. The physical and biological sciences are also represented by a presidential science advisor and an advisory group. Bills have been introduced in Congress in recent years to establish similar advisory machinery for the social sciences, but none has been passed.

As we have indicated, many departments and agencies of the United States government do make use of social science in various ways. Presidents have sought the advice of anthropologists since the time of Woodrow Wilson. Special advisory panels have been convened by most Presidents or their executive staffs in recent decades. The need for such panels, the selection of their personnel, or the decisions to sponsor research have, however, been essentially dependent upon individual and personal contacts. The same has been true of occasional Congressional hearings summoning social scientists. If government decisions are to be based on the best available social science advice and if the results of social science research are not to be misused, then advisory machinery should be devised and professional organizations must develop more concern about government actions.

Government conduct of social science research through employment of social scientists or through contract arrangements carries with it certain dangers. The methods employed or the scope of the research may be limited to predetermine the results, publication may be prohibited, or secrecy may be invoked if results are unpalatable to an administrator or political official. Many people in government have recognized this danger and the establishment of autonomous research groups, somewhat along the lines of the former Bureau of American Ethnology, has received some Congressional consideration. At the same time such agencies as the National Science Foundation and the National Institute of Health have been so organized as to support basic research in a relatively autonomous fashion, although dollar support, especially for the social sciences, is believed by many scientists to be inadequate. Moreover basic research, especially in the social sciences, often becomes unexpectedly relevant to current problems or controversies and hence comes under attack by people with preconceived notions or representing special interests.

In the United States, fortunately, research in the past has not been dependent upon government support. The varied and independent nature of United States universities and the large number of private educational foundations have permitted researchers great freedom in selecting their research problems, experimenting with methods, and publishing results. In most of the world this is not the case. Universities are commonly supported by national governments, which often dictate policies. Support is available only for research understood or approved by government-related agencies, and publication often depends upon the favors of government officials. The locally controlled or private university and the educational and charitable foundation are very rare outside the United States.

In the United States several factors already are changing the previous situation. We have noted the greater need and demand by government for social science research and that such research is less free than independent research. In addition, the period since World War II has seen the rise of large-scale research. As social science knowledge and skills have improved, many new problems have been identified which require large funds and sizable staffs if they are to be investigated properly. Anthropology has been more fortunate than most of the social sciences in the fact that much of its research has been small scale; anthropologists required only time and minimal travel and subsistence money to do their work. But this is changing in anthropology as well. The small research budgets of universities have long become inadequate. Foundations too are unable to meet all needs and are being placed under increasing government control and limitations. Today the largest single sources of basic anthropological research funds in the United States are probably the National Science Foundation and the National Institute of Health.

So long as it is possible for some anthropologists to undertake independent and critical research, the basic studies necessary to improve and expand theory can continue. Anthropologists and other social scientists can remain free to bring home to administrative and political figures the human consequences of their decisions and give independent evaluations of the potential results of alternative decisions and courses of action. This freedom is threatened, however, as the character of government changes and research becomes increasingly dependent upon government financing.

Perhaps a greater threat to continuing development of social science lies in the very rapid trend toward development of the welfare state within modern nations and, as yet less realistically, in most of the developing nations. No anthropologist concerned with improving the human condition can be antagonistic to the general aims of the welfare state. But the setting of goals, the definition of human welfare, the establishment of policies, and the implementation of programs allow for considerable divergence of opinion and may produce unforeseen results. The pressures on anthropology will be either to do research justifying policies and programs or to focus on research with immediate practical applications. A national commitment to the abolition of poverty may turn out to be very impatient of research not directed at facilitating particular programs. The question of the nature and causes of poverty, of its meaning within alternate goal patterns, or of whether it represents a self-perpetuating subculture may be regarded as irrelevant and unworthy of support. Already this tendency is apparent in recent Congressional action authorizing the National Science Foundation to expand research with immediate practical application; a next step may be to require that it spend all or a specified portion of its funds for this purpose. Precisely at a time when more and better research aimed at improving theories of human behavior and the methods of studying it is most needed, we may see action programs frozen into patterns based on faulty data, misleading theoretical conclusions, and inadequate methods. Similarly the polarization of opinions about integration or about human ecology may lead to dogmatic and intolerant positions and foreclose the research necessary to find adequate solutions.

The problems of culture, involving as they do, millions of individual human beings, are among the most complex problems we face. Vastly more research is needed before we can achieve relatively good controls over culture. Unless we wish to continue to be the unwitting pawns of cultural forces, we must have vastly more science rather than less. University budgets for research into society and culture—that is, for the social sciences as a whole—must be greatly increased. Great research centers must be developed, similar to those existing for research in the physical sciences. Freedom of inquiry and discussion must be maintained. As Linton has said, the Greek scholars forged a key to the door to the natural sciences but were prevented from opening the door by the rise of dogmatism and intolerance. Not until modern times did conditions come about that permitted the use of the Greek key to open the door to the control of nature. The social sciences, Linton believes, are today in the position of the Greek natural sciences. The social sciences have forged a key to open the door to the understanding of society and culture. The threatening rise of dogmatism and intolerance would end, perhaps for centuries, any possibility of using the key that has been created.

Collateral Reading

Beals, Ralph L. *Politics of Social Research*. Chicago: Aldine Publishing Company, 1968. Reviews problems of research and the responsibilities of social scientists abroad in relation to government.

Boas, Franz. *Anthropology and Modern Life*. New York: W. W. Norton & Company, Inc., 1962. One of the founders of anthropology reviews its significance to the problems of his day.

Frantz, Charles. *The Student Anthropologist's Handbook*. Cambridge, Mass.: Schenkman Publishing Co., Inc., 1972.

Fried, Morton H. *The Study of Anthropology*. New York: Thomas Y. Crowell Company, 1972.

Hymes, Dell (ed.). *Reinventing Anthropology*. New York: Random House, Inc., 1972. Articles raising questions about the role of anthropology.

Lyon, Gene M. *The Uneasy Partnership: Social Science and the Federal Government*. New York: Russell Sage Foundation, 1969.

Oswalt, Wendell. *Understanding Our Culture: An Anthropological View*. New York: Holt, Rinehart and Winston, Inc., 1970. An application of anthropological concepts to common questions about ourselves and our culture.

Warner, W. Lloyd. *American Life: Dream and Reality*. Chicago: University of Chicago Press, 1962. (rev. ed.: first published as *The Structure of American Life*.)

Weaver, Thomas (ed.). *To See Ourselves: Anthropology and Modern Social Issues*. Glenview, Ill.: Scott, Foresman and Company, 1973. Articles on different aspects of anthropological involvement.

Glossary

ABO — a system of blood hemoglobins in man varying according to presence or absence of a number of alleles at a single gene locus.

acculturation — culture change occurring under conditions of close and prolonged contact between two cultures, not necessarily leading to assimilation.

Acheulian — same as the biface tradition characteristic of many Early Paleolithic sites.

achieved status — a status that must be earned through the demonstration of ability.

actual or *real pattern* — what people actually do.

adaptation — continuing adjustment to environmental conditions in such a way as to permit the survival of the individual, population, species, or cultural system.

adaptive radiation — the spread of a species from its point of origin through adaptation to new environments.

adolescence — the period of life between puberty and adulthood (usually as defined in each culture).

affinal — kin or relatives by marriage.

Africanus — a highly variable species of the genus *Australopithecus* regarded by most authorities as in the direct line of human evolution; that is, as a hominid.

age area — the concept that there is a relation between the extent of the distribution of a culture element and its age relative to similar elements.

agriculture — the production of vegetable food through systematic cultivation; used in contrast to horticulture to refer to the use of the plow in cultivation.

albinism — a genetically caused reduction or absence of pigment, especially in skin, hair, and eyes.

alleles — genes with contrastive effects that occur at the same locus on a chromosome.

ambilateral — recognizing equally kin related through both the father and mother.

ambilocal — residence where a married couple shift back and forth between the husband's and the wife's group.

analogous structures — (biology) organs with similar functions or external appearance but of different derivation or internal structure; for example, wings of birds and bats.

Anasazi — the prehistoric Pueblo Indian cultures of Southwestern United States.

700

Andean Region — the highland Andes in South America and adjoining coastal area from Colombia to northern Chile.

angakok — term for shaman used by the Polar Eskimo.

animatism — the belief that inanimate objects are capable of sentient action and movement.

animism — belief that events in the material world are affected or controlled by supernatural entities, such as ghosts, spirits, or witches.

Anthropoidea — a suborder of the Primates, including monkeys, apes, and man.

anthropological linguistics — the study of language in cross-cultural perspective as an aspect of culture.

anthropology — the study of the origin, development, and nature of the human species.

apes — common name variously applied to the members of the Anthropoidea; in text applied to great apes (gorilla, chimpanzee, and orangutan), gibbons, and baboons.

apollonian — term applied by Benedict to cultures emphasizing order and restraint.

archaeology — branch of anthropology that uses techniques of excavation and historical research to reconstruct the lifeways of vanished peoples.

artifact — any material object (for example, an ax, a canoe) manufactured by human beings.

ascribed status — a position that is acquired by virtue of descent or some other conventional criterion.

atlatl — Aztec name for a spear thrower.

Aurignacian — culture period of Upper Paleolithic.

australopithecines — various members of the genus *Australopithecus*.

Australopithecus (Australopithicinae) — a fossil genus of the *Hominidae;* most commonly divided into two species, *Africanus* and *Robustus,* although some writers recognize other species.

Avoidance — a set of rules that define or restrict the behavior of certain relatives (usually in-laws) toward each other.

baboon — large ground-dwelling ape of genus *Papio.*

band — a small and loosely organized group of families who usually occupy an identifiable territory.

behavioral patterns — the actual behavior patterns of members of a society (as contrasted with their ideal patterns of behavior).

behavioral standards — the rules and culturally induced expectations concerning proper or acceptable behavior.

bifaces — simple tools made from nodules of flint or similar stone by percussion flaking of both faces.

bilateral — (kinship) a system of descent reckoned equally through both parents.

bilocal — residence of a married couple with either the husband's group or the wife's group.

biochemistry — the chemistry of living organisms.

biogram — term used to refer to biological programming of characteristics which typify living organisms; e.g., Primates.

biological anthropology — branch of anthropology using the techniques of the biological sciences to study fossil and living human beings.

bipedal progression — travel on two feet (in contrast to quadrupedal, or four-footed, movement).

blade tools — made from long flakes, prismatic in cross section, produced by a special striking technique from a prepared core.

blood-group M—a blood hemoglobin whose presence is determined by a single gene allele.

blowgun—a long tube through which darts or pellets are propelled with the breath.

bola—a device consisting of two or three weights connected by cords and thrown to entangle an animal.

boomerang—a throwing stick. Some Australian boomerangs will return to the thrower if they fail to strike the target.

boreal forests—forests within or near the Arctic Circle.

breeding population—see *population*.

bride price—the payment made to a bride's relatives by the groom or his relatives as part of a marriage arrangement.

burin—a stone blade tool with one chisel-like edge.

California area—a culture area including most of the coastal area and central valleys of the state.

calpulli—a landowning group among the Aztec of Mexico composed of several primary families said to be related in the paternal line.

Capsian—Late or post-Paleolithic of North Africa and southern Spain characterized by microliths.

carbon 14 (^{14}C)—a radioactive isotope of carbon useful in dating organic remains of late Pleistocene and Recent periods.

cargos—a system of political and religious offices in Latin America. Service in the religious offices is often expensive and a prerequisite to service in the powerful political offices.

caste—a division of a society often characterized by endogamy, occupational or ritual specialization, and rank within a hierarchy of castes.

Caucasoid—persons of European ancestry, or resembling persons of such ancestry; "whites." (Term arose through old [and erroneous] theory that place of origin of all "whites" was in the Caucasus of western Asia.)

Ceboidea—the New World monkeys, a superfamily of the Anthropoidea.

cell—the basic unit of most living things, consisting of a semipermeable membrane enclosing one or more nuclei and other living matter and its by-products, and capable alone or with other cells of sustaining life functions.

celt—a polished stone blade, usually ovoid in outline.

Cercopithecoidea—the Old World monkeys, a super family of Anthropoidea.

chopper—*chopping tool tradition*—south and east Asian tool complex based on use of pebbles.

chordata—refers to the phylum of animals whose nervous systems are organized by a long chord running lengthwise.

Choukoutenian tradition—a chopper-chopping tool tradition of China.

chromosome—common term for the chains or polymers of DNA molecules transmitting hereditary information.

churinga—sacred objects of many Australian local groups.

cire perdu—casting in a mold formed around a wax model which is drawn off by melting the wax.

civilization—a complex culture usually possessing advanced technology, many specialized roles, and urban settlements.

Clactonian—an early tool tradition involving striking large flakes from an unprepared core.

clan — a unilineal corporate descent group based on real or, more commonly, fictive kinship.

class — any set of things sharing one or more common characteristics; (biological) a subdivision of a phylum or subphylum; (social) a set of similar people or, more narrowly defined, one of several hierarchically arranged sets.

classic — the archaeological periods of major urban development in Middle America and Andean regions; in the Old World, the period of great development of Greek culture.

classical evolutionism — the doctrine that all cultures inevitably pass through the same sequence of development, although at differing rates of speed.

cline — in population genetics, a line of increasing or decreasing incidence of a gene from one population to the next.

collateral — relatives or kin sharing a common ancestor but in different descent lines.

collecting — as used in this text, systematic search for and use of plants with special technological aids.

collectors — peoples that use a specialized technology and depend for food primarily on a small number of plant species.

compadrazgo — a system of ritual kinship widespread in Latin America.

competition — socially approved conflict involving status or position.

confederacy — a loosely organized grouping of tribes, tribelets, or settlements for common action.

conflict — the exchange of verbal and nonverbal behaviors symbolizing opposition.

consanguineal — relatives traced through descent from a common ancestor.

contrasting characters — (biology), phenotypic characteristics produced by different alleles at same gene locus.

Copper-Bronze Age — refers to a traditional division of Old World culture history based upon technology (see also Paleolithic, Neolithic, and Iron Ages).

corporate group — a true or organized group; may also refer to a group capable of persisting through recruitment despite the death of members.

coup — among the Plains Indians, it referred to a brave or victorious act. A coup was granted for scalping or killing an enemy, or for being the first to strike the enemy.

coup, counting — among certain Plains Indians, the system whereby status and prestige were conferred for performing certain feats; e.g., touching an enemy or an object belonging to the enemy.

coup-de-poing — a biface stone tool.

couvade — institutionalized restrictions on the activities of a father after birth of a child.

cranial capacity — the volume of the cranial cavity, usually determined by filling with millet seed or shot.

cross-cousins — offspring of father's sister or mother's brother.

cult — group organized about special religious beliefs or practices.

cultural anthropology, cultural-social anthropology — branch of anthropology that uses techniques of historical research, observation, and interview in the study of the verbal and nonverbal behavior of groups of human beings.

cultural ecology — relationships of a cultural system to its environment; used by some to refer to perceptions of the environment characteristic of the members of a cultural system.

cultural integration — the manner in which each aspect of a cultural system is connected to other aspects.

cultural patterns — the socially recognized limits within which individual variation in verbal and nonverbal behavior properly takes place; the rules of the cultural game.

cultural pluralism — the maintenance of diverse cultural traditions within a large society or nation.

cultural system or *sociocultural system* — a complex whole formed by people interacting within an environment in terms of a cultural tradition and using a material culture to facilitate characteristic activities and behaviors.

cultural tradition — the rules, beliefs, knowledge, understandings, and instructions that form the basis for decision making and activity within a cultural system; what people learn as members of a group or society.

culture — a set of learned ways of thinking and acting that characterizes any decision making human group; defined by Tylor as "that complex whole which includes knowledge, belief, art, law, morals, custom, and any other capabilities and habits acquired by man as a member of society"; also used as a synonym for society, sociocultural system, nation, tribe, or cultural system.

culture area — a region within which a number of societies share many similar elements of culture when compared within the cultures of other regions.

culture as an abstraction — statements about a group of people that are useful in predicting some aspects of their behavior; the general statements made by an anthropologist or social scientists about the characteristic behavior and ways of thinking of a particular group of people.

culture shock — the psychological effects on an individual of contact with a different culture.

curaca — officials and minor nobility of the Inca or Quechua nation.

cytology — study of cells.

deme — endogamous local community.

dendrochronology — dating based on growth rings of trees.

derived needs — needs believed to be essential to well-being as the result of cultural conditioning.

descent — a genealogical term referring to the relationship of parent and child.

diachronic — the study of a culture or set of cultures through time; (linguistics) the study of a language or set of languages through time.

dialect — a local or class variant of a language.

dialect tribe — a group of individuals speaking the same dialect of the same language.

diffusion — the spread of culture elements from one society to another; less commonly, the spread of an innovation from an inventor or innovator to other individuals.

Dionysian — term applied by Benedict to culture emphasizing emotional and sensory experience.

distribution — the way in which goods and services are allocated to different individuals and subgroups within a group.

division of labor — where different individuals or subgroups perform different tasks.

DNA — deoxyribonucleic acid (variations in its molecular structure play a major part in biological heredity).

dominance — when one gene of a pair prevents the expression of the other.

double descent — coexistence in the same group of patrilineal and matrilineal corporate descent groups or clans.

dowry — payment of wealth or property made by the bride's family to the husband at marriage.

Dryopithecus—a genus of fossil anthropoids of the Miocene.

dysfunctional—when part of a culture impedes the functioning of the whole culture or some important part thereof.

ecological niche—a habitat supplying the factors necessary for the existence of an organism or species.

ecology—the systematic relationships between organisms and their environment, including other organisms; the systematic relationships of cultural systems to their environment including other cultural systems.

Eem—interglacial, or glacial retreat resulting in warmer period, between Saale and Weichsel glaciations during the Pleistocene.

elites—groups in a society claiming or accorded special status and functions of leadership.

Elster—major glacial period in Europe during the Pleistocene.

enculturation—the process by which children acquire and internalize their culture.

endogamy—marrying inside a specified group (compare *exogamy*).

environment—the natural, biological, and social setting within which the members of a cultural system carry on their activities.

equilibrium—the harmonious steady relationship between parts of a culture.

equilibrium models—static models of culture in which all parts function harmoniously and adjust to any change without altering functional harmony.

estrous period—the period in females when conception is possible.

ethnic—related to groups with different cultural backgrounds and values.

ethnography—study and descriptive recording of existing cultures.

ethnohistory—recovery of ethnographic information on past cultures from study of written records.

ethnology—see *cultural anthropology*.

ethnoscience—a special systematic method of organizing and analyzing ethnographic data.

ethology—study of animal behavior.

eutheria—mammals possessing a placenta, an internal structure to nourish the fetus between conception and birth.

evolution—(biological) change over time in frequencies of genetically determined characteristics; (cultural) change over time in culturally determined characteristics. See also *classical evolutionism*.

exogamy—marriage outside a specified group.

faction—a group or clique usually organized about a personality or issue and involved in conflict with similar groups.

family—(biological) a subdivision of an order or suborder; (cultural) established group comprising one or more adults of each sex, together with any offspring.

family, augmented—a family group that includes a variety of distant relatives.

family, extended—a family including other near relatives besides the nuclear family group, not necessarily forming a single household.

family, joint—two or more nuclear families linked through paternal or maternal lines, usually with common residence or other close ties.

fetus—unborn young after attaining basic structure of its species; in humans, usually about three months after conception.

fishers—people who use a specialized technology to obtain fish as a primary source of food.

folk categories—distinctions and classifications made by the membership of a particular group in contrast to distinctions made by an outside observer or scientist.

Folsom point—a fluted stone projectile point characteristic of early hunters in North America.

foraging—an environmental adaptation characteristic of many primates which involves daily collection of a wide variety of foods and periodic movement of the group from one campsite to another.

foramen—an opening or orifice.

Formative—pre-Classic period in Middle America and Andean region with beginnings of urbanism and large ceremonial centers.

fossil—the preserved evidence of prehistoric life forms; most commonly refers to bony structures preserved through mineralization.

founder effect (founder principle)—establishment of a population by a few original migrants or founders whose genetic makeup may be an aberrant sample of the gene pool of the larger population from which it migrated.

fraternity—a club with voluntary membership, often with ritual or ceremonial functions.

function—what each aspect of a cultural system contributes to the maintenance of the whole.

gene—an independent unit of hereditary information thought to consist of a single DNA molecule.

gene flow—the transmission of genes from one population to another through interbreeding; that is, mating of individuals from different populations.

generalized species—species that adopt the strategy of occupying a number of environments and/or using resources in a variety of ways.

genetic drift—changes in the composition of a gene pool through sampling errors in reproduction.

genetics—study of the processes and mechanisms of biological heredity.

genotype—the genetic constitution of an individual which reacts with the environment to produce the phenotype.

genus (pl. *genera*)—a subdivision of a family (in a biological classification).

ghetto—originally, in Italy, name for an urban quarter in which Jews were forced to live; now usually a slum area in which people are forced to live through discrimination or poverty.

ghost dance—a religious movement among Indians of the western United States in the nineteenth century.

ghosts—spirits of the dead.

glottochronology—a method of dating splits of speech communities that result in divergent but related languages.

go-between—an individual who conducts negotiations, primarily in respect to marriage, between other people.

gods—personalized supernatural beings of great power.

gorilla—a genus of the Pongidae found in parts of Africa; one of the great apes.

grade—basic division of animal forms into protozoa and metazoa.

grammar—a set of rules that govern the arrangement of words and morphemes in a particular language.

Great Basin—an arid or semiarid region of western North America between the Sierra Nevada and the Rocky mountains.

group—a set of individuals or members who participate in or are affected by decisions concerning the relevance or appropriateness of particular behavior; a set of individuals who exchange interactions or communications with each other.

group marriage — marriage of a group of men to a group of women with sharing of conjugal rights.

hacienda — term commonly used in Spanish-speaking America for a type of large landed estate.

headman — the recognized leader of a band, village, council or other small social unit, usually with limited authority.

heterozygous — possessing different alleles at the same gene location on each of a pair of chromosomes.

Hohokam — prehistoric cultures of lowland Arizona.

holism — the attempt to study cultural and ecological systems as wholes.

Holocene — the second division of the Quarternary or Recent geological period, approximately from 10,000 years ago to present.

Holstein — interglacial or glacial retreat resulting in warmer period, between Elster and Saale glaciations during the Pleistocene.

hominid — ground-dwelling, bipedal, tool-using primate; used in reference to species of Homo and their probable fossil predecessors.

Homo — the genus of the family *Hominidae* to which all modern and some fossil men belong.

Homo erectus — a widespread extinct species of the genus Homo; originally classified as *Pithecanthropus erectus,* or ape-man.

Homo habilis — a fossil form from East Africa regarded as representing either the first of the human beings or the last of the australopithecines.

Homo heidelbergensis — a species based on a massive fossil jaw from Germany now consider to belong to *Homo erectus.*

Homo neandertalensis (Homo sapiens neandertalensis) — a type of *Homo sapiens* occurring in relatively late Pleistocene times.

Homo sapiens — the genus and species to which all modern humans and some fossil humans belong.

Hominidae — a family of the superfamily Hominoidea including all living and extinct humans and some humanlike forms.

Hominoidea — a superfamily of the Anthropoidea, including humans and the apes.

homologous structures — organs of different function or appearance but of similar origin or internal structure; for example, flippers of seals and forelimbs of most land mammals.

homozygous — possessing identical genes or alleles at the same gene locus on each of a pair of chromosomes.

horticulture — cultivation by gardening techniques without use of plow or draft animals.

household — a common living group of one or several nuclear families or other attached individuals.

hunter-gatherers — people with an environmental adaptation similar to foraging, but involving the use of tools and technology to obtain food.

ideal pattern — what people ought to do when things are the way they're supposed to be.

Illinoisan — one of the major glacial periods that occurred in North America during the Pleistocene.

Incas — the aristocratic class of the Quechua or Inca Empire.

incest — sexual relations between socially forbidden categories of real or putative kin.

Indo-European languages — a family of languages found over most of Europe and parts of the Middle East and India.

infrastructure — (economics) the basic structure necessary for increasing economic activity, such as education, health, and communications.

inheritance — (cultural) the procedure for the transmission of property, rights, or status to others after death.

interculture — see *polyculture*.

interglacial — a period between two major glaciations.

internalizing — establishing habitual and often unconscious patterns of response or behavior.

interstadials — periods of temporary retreat of glaciers in a major glacial period.

Iron Age — refers to a traditional division of Old World culture history based upon technology (see also *Paleolithic, Neolithic,* and *Copper-Bronze Age*).

kachinas — a class of supernatural beings among most village Indians of the Southwestern United States.

Kansan — one of the major glacial periods that occurred in North America during the Pleistocene.

kin — those who are, or are supposed to be, relatives.

kin term — words used to designate one's kin — mother, uncle, cousin, etc.

kin type — genealogical positions such as Fa, MoBr, FaBr.

kinship — a system of categorizing or classifying persons primarily on the basis of relationship through descent and marriage but often including others.

kinship, fictive — the recognition of some unrelated individuals as kinfolk, usually involving a formal ritual.

kinship, ritual — see *kinship, fictive*.

kiva — rooms or chambers for ceremonial use among village Indians of the Southwestern United States.

kula ring — a system of ritualized exchange in Melanesia.

Laurel-leaf-blades — finely flaked blades of laurel-leaf shape characteristic of Solutrean culture.

laws — behavioral standards for which there exist special measures designed to ensure conformity.

legal systems — those relatively formal arrangements by which reported violations of laws are investigated, miscreants identified, disputes resolved, and corrective measures taken.

legislation — the various processes by means of which behavioral standards come into being.

lemurs — a number of related genera belonging to the *Prosimii*, a suborder of the Primates.

Levalloisian — a widespread flake-tool tradition involving preparation of a core in a distinctive manner.

levirate — marriage with the wife or wives of a deceased brother.

lineage — a unilineal kinship group larger than the family that traces its descent from a common ancestor.

lineal relatives — relatives in an individual's direct line of descent.

linguistics — see *anthropological linguistics*.

local group — segment of a band associated by common residence or economic activities.

locus — the site or location of a single gene or its alleles in a chromosome.

logographic — denoting a system of written symbols, each of which represents a word in a language.

lost-wax method — see *cire perdu*.

macroevolution — the major changes in evolution, such as emergence of species and genera.

magic — performance of rites and recitations of spells believed to produce specific supernatural results.

magic, contagious — belief that treatment of a part of an associated object may affect an individual.

magic, imitative — belief that imitating a desired result with proper procedures will cause it to occur.

magician — one believed to influence supernatural powers through performance of rites and spells.

Magdalenian — culture type of Late Paleolithic.

Maglemosean — a Late Mesolithic culture of northwestern Europe.

maize — corn in most dialects of American English.

mammalia, mammals — a class of vertebrate animals with mammary glands producing milk for suckling the young (as well as other special features).

mana — impersonal and pervasive supernatural power.

manitou — Algonkin term for impersonal pervasive supernatural power.

manor — a type of landed estate common in feudal Europe usually dependent on labor of serfs attached to the land.

market — a situation in which there exists a demand for a transaction of a certain type.

marketplace — an established place where goods are regularly bought and sold.

marriage — a socially recognized union of man and woman.

material culture — the equipment and artifacts used by the membership of a cultural system including the permanent and tangible effects that past and present memberships have had upon the environment.

mating — the joining of individuals of opposite sex for coitus.

matrilateral — all recognized kin on the mother's side of the family.

matrilineal — tracing kinship through the female line only.

matrilocal — residence of a married couple in or near the home of the wife's relatives.

matrisib — a matrilineal nonlocalized descent group.

maximization — (economics) the effort to get the largest possible returns or benefits from an economic activity.

mayordomias — a system of religious offices in Latin America organized to celebrate various Saints' days. See *cargos*.

meiosis — refers to the process by which sex cells divide and replicate through reduction division which results in only 23 chromosomes in the sex cells.

Melanesia — a culture area of the South Pacific.

melanin — pigmentation occurring in varying quantity and distribution in all normal humans.

Mesoamerica — see *Middle America*.

Mesolithic — a transitional period between the Upper Paleolithic and Neolithic; sometimes classed as Terminal Paleolithic.

metazoa — many-celled animals.

microevolution — genetic changes within a single species.

microliths — very small flaked-stone tools probably set in handles.

Middle America — the area of urban civilization including most of Mexico and Central America.

middle class — an intermediate group in a class society. (Differently defined in various societies.)

minimal family — a woman and her offspring, the smallest unit required for reproduction and child care.

mitosis — refers to the process by which cells divide and replicate.

Mogollon — a prehistoric culture of the American Southwest.

moiety — one of two divisions (usually based on kinship) found in a society.

molecular biology — study of the molecular structure of living matter.

monkeys — popular term for many small members of the Anthropoidea, a suborder of the Primates.

monoculture — planting of only one type of crop plant in a field (contrast with *polyculture*).

monogamy — marriage to a single spouse.

morpheme — a unit of a language which conveys a meaning and which cannot be divided into separate elements each of which has meaning.

morphology — in linguistics, the study of morphemes.

Mousterian — Middle Paleolithic culture.

mutations — changes in the chemical structure and effects of a gene.

natural selection — see *selection*.

Neanderthal — a human type of late Pleistocene: *Homo sapiens neandertalensis*.

neolocal residence — where a married couple live apart from the parents of either husband or wife.

Negrito — a term for short-statured peoples who dwell in isolated groups in Southeast Asia, and the southwestern Pacific from the Andaman Islands to New Guinea.

Neolithic — denoting New Stone Age, based on an imagined correlation between polished stone tools and agriculture.

Northwest Coast area — a culture area extending along the Pacific coast of North America from northern California to southern Alaska.

nuclear family — a married couple and their children.

oasis — a relatively well-watered area in a predominantly arid or desert region.

obsidian — volcanic glass.

Oldowan — name for tool tradition excavated from Olduvai Gorge, East Africa, which first appears during the Early Pleistocene.

opposable thumb — a thumb which can push against the tips of the other digits or fingers (characteristic of humans but only weakly developed, if present at all, among other Primates).

orangutan — a genus of the Pongidae found principally in Borneo (one of the great apes).

order — (biological) a subdivision of a class or subclass in the classification of living beings.

ovum (pl. *ova*) — egg or sex cell produced by females, consisting of only 23 chromosomes.

Paleo-Indians — earliest American Indians.

Paleolithic — denoting Old Stone Age, before the development of agriculture.

parallel cousins — offspring of father's brother or mother's sister.

pastoralists — social groups who live primarily by herding domestic animals.

patrilateral — all recognized kin related through an individual's father.

patrilineal — tracing kinship through the male line only.

patrilocal residence — residence by a married couple in or near the home of the husband's family.

patrisib — a patrilineal nonlocalized descent group.

peasants — food-producing segments of urbanized societies, usually forming partially autonomous settlements.

pebble tools — stone pebbles with cutting edges produced by striking with another stone.

percussion flaking — striking flakes from stone cores with a hammer stone.

Perigordian — a local culture of the early late Paleolithic of France and Spain.

phenotype — the structural or external bodily form of an organism.

phonemes — the basic or significant sound units of a language.

phonology — the study of the rules for combining phonemes.

photosynthesis — synthesis of chemical compounds with the aid of light, especially in chlorophyll-containing cells of green plants.

phratry — a group, usually exogamous, that includes two or more clans.

phylum (pl. *phyla*) — a major division in the classification of living things.

Pithecanthropus — an older name for the fossil now included in the genus *Homo* and the species *erectus*.

placenta — a platelike structure in most female mammals to nourish the fetus after conception.

Plains culture — those culture patterns and elements shared by most Indian tribes of the United States Plains.

Plasmodium falciparum — a type of malaria.

Pleistocene — the geological epoch preceding the Present or Holocene from approximately L5 m. to 10,000 years ago.

Pliocene — the geological epoch preceding the Pleistocene.

pluvial — a period of heavy rainfall relative to the present.

political process — those aspects of social behavior that have to do with the establishment and enforcement of behavioral standards and with the circulation of individuals from status to status.

polyandry — marriage of one woman to two or more husbands.

polyculture — planting of more than one crop plant in the same field (contrast with *monoculture*).

polygamy — a recognized system of multiple spouses.

polygenes — groups of genes, each member of which may influence a particular phenotypic characteristic.

polygenic — a biological trait or characteristic that is influenced by more than one gene or allele at several loci.

polygyny — marriage of one man to two or more wives.

polymorphic species — species characterized by a high degree of individual variation within its different breeding populations.

Pongidae; Pongids — a family of the superfamily Hominoidea that includes the orangutan, gorilla, and chimpanzee.

population — (biological) the interbreeding members of a species or variety, usually within a specific geographical range; (cultural) the totality of a group defined geographically or by national or other sociocultural boundaries.

post-Classic — the archaeological period of relatively late local cultures in Middle America and Andean America.

potlatch — a hierarchical ranking system in which individuals exchange wealth for prestige and power among the American Indians of the Northwest Coast of North America.

predators — animals that live by hunting and eating other animals.

preferential marriage — a type of marriage in which marriage with certain individuals receives special approval.

pressure flaking — removing flakes from stones by controlled application of pressure.

priest — a functionary of a standardized cult or religion.

primary group — a group where all, or nearly all, of the members interact directly with each other.

Primates — an order of the subclass Eutheria (placental mammals) including the tree shrews, tarsiers, lemurs, monkeys, apes, and man.

primatology — the comparative study of primate species including human beings; the study of nonhuman Primates.

production — the process of obtaining goods from the natural environment.

proletariat — a term often applied to low-income workers in a highly industrialized society.

Prosimii — a suborder of the order Primates.

protohominids — early fossil forms that presumably antedated *Homo,* and who may have been directly ancestral to *Homo.*

protozoa — single-celled animals.

psychic unity — belief that the human mind is everywhere essentially similar.

psychological anthropology — the study of the interrelationships between psychological processes and culture.

puberty rituals — observances related to the attainment of sexual maturity in the young.

Pueblo Indians — term for modern and prehistoric village-dwelling farmers of the Southwestern United States.

purics — commoners in Quechua or Inca society.

pygmies — short-statured peoples of the African forest.

Quarternary — the last major geological epoch.

Ramapithecus — a late fossil form of *Dryopithecus* believed ancestral to humanity.

recessive gene or *allele* — one that has no detectable effect when paired with another, dominant gene.

reciprocity — exchange of goods or services based on equivalent returns other than money.

redistribution — social mechanisms to reduce accumulations of goods.

reincarnation — belief that the spirit or essence of the dead is reborn in a child or other life form.

relativism, cultural — belief that cultures are unique and that cultural behavior must be understood in the cultural context in which it occurs.

religious ritual — patterned activities, usually symbolic rather than practical in character, and having to do with supernatural figures and other religious phenomena.

reproductive isolation — when a population is separated from other populations so that interbreeding does not take place between them.

role — a special pattern of behavior associated with a particular status in society.

Rorschach — a projective test used by psychologists involving the interpretation of responses to standardized ink blots.

Saale — major glacial period in Europe during the Pleistocene.

sanction — social means of inducing conformity to approved social norms through punishment or rewards.

Sangamon—interglacial, or glacial retreat resulting in warmer period, between Illinoisan and Wisconsin during the Pleistocene.

sapiens—the species to which all living and some extinct human forms belong.

secondary group—a group composed of interacting groups.

segregation—(biological) the separation of paired genes in the process of reproduction.

selection—the process whereby environmental and cultural factors permit some individuals to survive and reproduce while others do not, used broadly to refer to environmental influences upon the comparative rates of survival of cultural systems, ideas, or ways of acting.

shaman—individual with powers derived from direct contact with supernatural.

Shanidar Cave—an important site in Iraq producing fossils of Neanderthal.

sib—see *clan*.

Sibelian—terminal Late Paleolithic culture of Egypt.

siblings—one's brothers and sisters regardless of sex.

sickle-cell anemia or *sicklemia*—a genetically produced malformation of red blood cells causing a usually fatal anemia, occurs when individual is homozygous for the sickle-cell gene.

sign—an object with a learned arbitrary meaning.

Sinanthropus pekinensis—term for fossil finds in China later merged with *Pithecanthropus erectus* of Java and now considered a local variety of *Homo erectus*.

smelting—removal of metal from ores involving application of heat and sometimes mixture with other substances.

Soan—a chopper; chopping tool tradition of India.

social control—the means by which the members of society are encouraged to conform to behavioral standards.

social process—the culturally significant behaviors by means of which a cultural system is maintained.

social organization—the way in which relationships among the members of a cultural system are organized to facilitate the carrying out of characteristic activities.

social structure—a set of positions or statuses arranged in terms of principles of relationship such as kinship or rank.

socialization—the process by which children learn and internalize the social behaviors appropriate to their society.

society—a cultural system that is politically independent and largely self-sufficient.

Solutrean—a culture period of European Upper Paleolithic.

sororate—marriage to the husband of a sister.

spear thrower—a device for throwing spears or darts.

specialization in production—where different individuals or subgroups in a society produce different goods and services that are then exchanged.

specialized hunters—hunters who use a specialized technology and depend for food primarily upon a small number of animal species.

specialized species—species that adopt the strategy of occupying a single environment and/or using its resources in a limited way.

species—a subdivision of a genus; usually members are capable of interbreeding and producing offspring.

species-specific—refers to genetic traits that are characteristic of a species.

sperm; spermatozoan (pl. *spermatozoa*)—sex cell produced by males, consisting of only 23 chromosomes.

spirits—minor supernatural beings, usually with specific and limited powers.

squatter's towns — settlements of substandard housing, often on land appropriated by the settlers, common on outskirts of many cities.

state — a loosely organized group of people or peoples with some degree of central control.

status — an identifiable position within a society.

steppes — cold or semiarid unforested regions.

stone boiling — boiling liquid by dropping hot stone in it.

strains — the various factors that produce situations in which individuals or groups are likely to display behaviors that are interpreted as symbols of opposition.

stratigraphy — the vertical distribution of objects or layers of material deposited on the earth's surface.

subsistence economy — economy of a society producing little for export or providing most of its own food, shelter, and implements.

supply and demand — (economic theory) the amount of something and the demand for it, which together determine price.

swidden agriculture — a widespread system of forest agriculture in which clearings are made, used for a few years, and then abandoned until secondary forest reappears; also known as slash burn or shifting agriculture.

syllabary — a system of written symbols, each of which represents a syllable in a language.

symbiosis — groups or organisms living in a state of interdependence.

symbol — an object, sign, or sound to which an arbitrary shared meaning is attached.

sympatric — species occupying same area (often refers to very similar species competing for same resources).

synchronic — (anthropology) the study of a culture or cultures at one point in time.

syntax — see *grammar*.

taboo (tabu) — a supernaturally supported prohibition.

talking chief — in Polynesia, a spokesman for the paramount chief who is too sacred for direct contact with his subjects.

tarsiers — a number of related genera belonging to the Prosimii, a suborder of the Primates.

technology — the specific methods of getting things done that are given within the cultural tradition; the items of material culture used in the process of getting things done.

temporal species — species whose total membership has undergone significant change through time (as opposed to new species developing through divergent changes from an ancestral form).

Thematic Apperception Test — a test involving responses of subjects to standardized sets of pictures.

theme — set of interrelated ideas and practices that are considered to be of great importance by the members of a cultural system.

tipi — a conical skin-covered structure of poles characteristic of the Indians of the United States Plains.

totem — an animal, or less often, a plant with special significance for individuals or groups.

totemism — any systematic beliefs or institutionalized behaviors relating to totems.

trade — transaction in which goods are directly exchanged for each other or for money.

trained incapacity — inability to learn some skill because of early training.

trait, culture — refers to the basic unit into which a culture can be analyzed; a specific entity within the culture. A combination of traits is a culture complex.

transvestite — persons who dress as members of the opposite sex (not necessarily homosexual).

travois — a kind of land sledge with one end supported by a draft animal; common among but not unique to United States Plains Indians.

tree ring dating — see *dendrochronology*.

tree shrews — a number of related genera of the Prosimii, a suborder of the Primates.

tribe — politically independent group usually claiming a definite territory and often with a distinctive dialect and culture.

tundra — a vegetation complex found in regions of permanently frozen subsoil.

turtle-shaped cores — the distinctive stone cores of the levalloisian tradition.

umiak — large Eskimo boat made of skins over a wooden frame.

unilineal organizations — groups with membership based on descent through a single parental line.

urbanism — way of life involving relatively large settlements with dense populations, many members of which are not food producers.

uxorilocal — residence of a married couple with the wife's group.

value — (anthropology) a widely held explicit or implicit norm that controls decisions when individuals must choose a course of behavior or must approve or disapprove of the behavior of others.

variations — (biology) differences between individuals of the same species or population.

vertebrata, vertebrates — animals with a spinal chord with an articulated bony covering or vertebrae.

virilocal — residence of a married couple with the husband's group.

warp — (weaving) stiff or fixed longitudinal elements.

weft — (weaving) flexible element interwoven with fixed or inflexible warps.

Weichsel — major glacial period in Europe during the Pleistocene.

wickiup — a dome-shaped, bark-covered shelter of Algonkin Indians of northeastern North America; (by extension) similarly shaped bark- or brush-covered structures found elsewhere.

Wisconsin — one of the major glacial periods that occurred in North America during the Pleistocene.

witchcraft — ability or knowledge to influence, harm, or protect others through magic.

world view — fundamental and important ideas about the nature of things.

Yarmouth — interglacial, or glacial, retreat resulting in warmer period, between Kansan and Illinoisan during the Pleistocene.

zygote — result of fertilization of the ovum by a sperm.

Ethnographic
Bibliography

Anderson, Eugene Newton. *The Chumash Indians of Southern California.* Banning, Calif.: Malki Museum Press, 1968.

Balikci, Asen. *The Netsilik Eskimo.* Garden City, N.Y.: The Natural History Press, 1970.

Basso, Keith H. *The Cibecue Apache.* New York: Holt, Rinehart and Winston, 1970.

Beals, Alan R. *Gopalpur: A South Indian Village.* New York: Holt, Rinehart and Winston, Inc., 1962.

Beals, Ralph L. "Ethnology of the Nisenan," *University of California Publications in American Archaeology and Ethnology,* **31**:335–414 (1933). Berkeley: University of California Press.

Beals, Ralph L. "Ethnology of the Western Mixe." *University of California Publications in American Archaeology and Ethnology,* **42**, No. 1 (1945). Berkeley: University of California Press, 1945.

Beals, Ralph L. *Cheran: A Sierra Tarascan Village,* Smithsonian Institution Institute of Social Anthropology Pub. No. 2. Washington, D.C.: United States Government Printing Office, 1946.

Beals, Ralph L. *Community in Transition: Nayon-Ecuador.* Latin American Studies, Vol. 2. Los Angeles: Latin American Center, University of California, 1966.

Beals, Ralph L. *The Peasant Marketing System of Oaxaca, Mexico.* Berkeley: University of California Press, 1975.

Berndt, Ronald Murray (ed.). *Australian Aboriginal Anthropology: Modern Studies in the Social Anthropology of the Australian Aborigines.* Nedlands: Published for the Australian Institute of Aboriginal Studies by the University of Western Australia Press, 1970.

Birket-Smith, K. *The Eskimos.* New York: E. P. Dutton & Co., Inc., 1936.

Briggs, Jean L. *Never in Anger: Portrait of an Eskimo Family.* Cambridge: Harvard University Press, 1970.

Caso, Alfonso. *The Religion of the Aztecs.* Mexico City: Central News Co., 1937.

Castro, Josue de. *Death in the Northeast* (1. ed.) New York: Random House, Inc. (Trans. from the Portuguese: Sete palmos de terra e um caixao; ensaio sobre Nordeste, area explosiva, 1965), 1966.

Chance, Norman A. *The Eskimo of North Alaska.* New York: Holt, Rinehart and Winston, Inc., 1966.

Coon, Carleton S. *A Reader in General Anthropology.* New York: Holt, Rinehart and Winston, Inc., 1948.

Dentan, Robert Knox. *The Semai: a Nonviolent People of Malaya.* New York: Holt, Rinehart and Winston, Inc., 1968.

Dozier, Edward P. *The Pueblo Indians of North America.* New York: Holt, Rinehart and Winston, Inc., 1970.

Eggan, Fred. *Social Organization of the Western Pueblos.* Chicago: University of Chicago Press, 1950.

Ekvall, Robert B. *Fields on the Hoof: Nexus of Tibetan Nomadic Pastoralism.* New York: Holt, Rinehart and Winston, Inc., 1968.

Embree, John F. *Suye Mura: A Japanese Village.* Chicago: University of Chicago Press, 1964. (First published 1939.)

Evans-Pritchard, Edward E. *Witchcraft, Oracles and Magic Among the Azande.* London: Oxford University Press, 1937.

Evans-Pritchard, Edward E. *The Nuer: A Description of the Modes of Livelihood and Political Institutions of a Neolithic People.* Oxford: Clarendon Press, 1940.

Evans-Pritchard, Edward E. *The Azande: History and Political Institutions.* Oxford: Clarendon Press, 1971.

Forde, C. Daryll. *Habitat, Society and Economy.* New York: E. P. Dutton & Co., Inc., 1950.

Gero, F. *Death Among the Azande of the Sudan* (beliefs, rites, and cult) (Translated from the Italian by W. H. Paxman). Bologna: Editrice, Nigrizia, 1968.

Goldschmidt, Walter. *Nomlaki Ethnography.* Berkeley: University of California Press, 1951.

Handy, E. S. C. *The Native Culture in the Marquesas.* Honolulu: B. P. Bishop Museum Bulletin, No. 9, 1923.

Hanley, Gerald. Warriors and Strangers. London, Hamilton, 1971.

Hart, Charles W., and Arnold R. Pilling. *The Tiwi of North Australia.* New York: Holt, Rinehart and Winston, Inc., 1960.

Hill, Polly. *The Migrant Cocoa-Farmers of Southern Ghana: A Study in Rural Capitalism.* Cambridge University Press, 1963.

Hill, Polly. *Studies in Rural Capitalism in West Africa.* Cambridge University Press, 1970a.

Hill, Polly. *The Occupations of Migrants in Ghana.* Ann Arbor: University of Michigan, Museum of Anthropology, Anthropological Papers, #42, 1970b.

Hollis, A. C. *The Masai.* Oxford: Clarendon Press, 1905.

Holmes, Lowell D. *Ta'u: Stability and Change in a Samoan Village.* Wellington: Polynesian Society (Reprint of Polynesian Society, No. 7), 1958.

Johnson, Allen W. *Sharecroppers of the Sertao: Economics and Dependence on a Brazilian Plantation.* Stanford, Calif.: Stanford University Press, 1971.

Kaberry, Phyllis Mary. *Aboriginal Woman, Sacred and Profane.* Farnborough, Eng.: Gregg International Publishers, 1970.

Kagwa, Sir Apolo. *The Customs of the Baganda.* (Trans. by Ernest B. Kalibala) N.Y.: Columbia-University Press, 1934.

Keiser, R. Lincoln. *Vice Lords: Warriors of the Streets.* New York: Holt, Rinehart and Winston, Inc., 1969.

Kelly, Isabel. *Southern Paiute Ethnography.* Salt Lake City: University of Utah, Department of Anthropology, 1964.

Kroeber, A. L. *Handbook of the Indians of California.* Washington, D.C.: Bureau of

American Ethnology, Bulletin 78, 1925. (Berkeley: California Book Co., reprint, 1953).

Landberg, Leif C. *The Chumash Indians of Southern California.* Los Angeles, Southwest Museum, 1965.

Lee, Richard B. "What Hunters Do for a Living, or How to Make Out on Scarce Resources," in Lee and DeVore (eds.), *Man the Hunter.* Chicago: Aldine Publishing Company, 1968, pp. 30–48.

Lee, Richard B. "Population Growth and the Beginnings of Sedentary Life Among the !Kung Bushmen," in Brian Spooner (ed.), *Population Growth: Anthropological Implications.* Cambridge, Mass.: Massachusetts Institute of Technology Press, 1972, pp. 329–342.

Liebow, Elliot. *Tally's Corner.* Boston: Little, Brown and Company, 1967.

Linton, Ralph. "Marquesan Culture," *The Individual and His Culture,* by Abram Kardiner. New York: Columbia University Press, 1939, pp. 137–196.

Lowie, Robert H. *The Crow Indians.* New York: Farrar and Rinehart, 1935.

Mead, Margaret. *Coming of Age in Samoa: A Psychological Study in Primitive Youth for Western Civilization.* New York: Blue Ribbon Books, 1928.

Means, Philip A. *Ancient Civilizations of the Andes.* New York: Charles Scribner's Sons, 1931.

Meggitt, M. J. *Desert People: A Study of the Walbiri Aborigines of Central Australia.* Sydney: Angus and Robertson, 1962.

Meillassoux, Claude. *Urbanization of an African Community: Voluntary Associations in Bamako.* Seattle: University of Washington Press, 1969.

Murdock, George P. *Our Primitive Contemporaries.* New York: Macmillan Publishing Co., Inc., 1935.

Oberg, Kalervo. *The Social Economy of the Tlingit Indians.* Seattle: University of Washington Press, 1973.

Opler, Morris E. "An Outline of Chiricahua Apache Social Organization," *Social Anthropology of North American Tribes,* (ed.) Fred Eggan. Chicago: University of Chicago Press, 1937, pp. 173–242.

Opler, Morris E. *An Apache Life-Way.* Chicago: University of Chicago Press, 1941.

Oswalt, Wendell H. *Alaskan Eskimos.* San Francisco: Chandler Publishing Co., 1969.

Ottenberg, Simon. *Double Descent in an African Society: The Afikpo Village-Group.* Seattle: University of Washington Press, 1968.

Pospisil, Leonard. *Kapauku Papuan Economy.* Publications in Anthropology, #62. New Haven: Yale University Press, 1963.

Radcliffe-Brown, A. R. *The Social Organization of Australian Tribes.* Melbourne and London: Macmillan & Co., Ltd., Part 1, 1931.

Rasmussen, Knud. *The People of the Polar North: A Record.* Comp. from the Danish origs. and ed. by G. Herring; illus. by Count Herald Moltke. London: K. Paul, Trench, Trubner & Co., Ltd., 1908.

Rasmussen, Knud. "The Netsilik Eskimo," *Report of the Fifth Thule Expedition, 1921–24,* VIII, Nos. 1–2, Copenhagen: Gyldendal, 1931.

Rivers, W. H. R. *The Todas.* London: Macmillan and Co., Ltd., 1906.

Roscoe, John. *The Baganda.* London: Macmillan and Co., Ltd., 1911.

Soustelle, Jacques. *The Daily Life of the Aztecs, On the Eve of the Spanish Conquest* (Translated from the French by Patrick O'Brien). New York: Macmillan Publishing Co., Inc., 1968 (1961c).

Spencer, Baldwin, and F. G. Gillen. *The Native Tribes of Central Australia.* London: Macmillan and Co., Ltd., 1938 (First published, 1899).

Spencer, Baldwin, and F. G. Gillen. *The Arunta*. Oosterhout, N. B. Netherlands: Anthropological Publications, 1966 (First published, 1927).

Spencer, R. F. *The North Alaskan Eskimo: A Study in Ecology and Society*. Washington, D.C.: Smithsonian Institution Press, 1959.

Steward, Julian H. *Basin-Plateau Aboriginal Socio-Political Groups*. (Bulletin 120, Smithsonian Institution Bureau of Ethnology) Washington, D.C.: U.S. Government Printing Office, 1938.

Suggs, Robert C. *Marquesan Sexual Behavior*. New York: Harcourt Brace Jovanovich, 1966.

Swanton, John R. *Contributions to the Ethnology of the Haida*. Leiden: E. J. Brill, Ltd.; New York: G. E. Stelhert, 1905.

Thomas, Elizabeth Marshall. *The Harmless People*. New York: Alfred A. Knopf, Inc., 1959.

Thompson, John Eric. *Mexico Before Cortez*. New York: Charles Scribner's Sons, 1933.

Tindales, Norman B. "The Pitjandjara," in M. G. Bicchieri (ed.). *Hunters and Gathers Today*. New York: Holt, Rinehart and Winston, Inc., 1972.

Titiev, Mischa. "Old Oraibi, A Study of the Hopi Indians of Third Mesa," *Papers of the Peabody Museum of American Archaeology and Ethnology*, 22:16–301 (1944). Boston: Harvard University.

Titiev, Mischa. *The Hopi Indians of Old Oraibi: Change and Continuity*. Ann Arbor: University of Michigan Press, 1972.

Turnbull, Colin M. *The Forest People: a Study of the Pygmies of the Congo*. New York: Simon & Schuster, Inc., 1961.

Turner, G. *Samoa*. London: Macmillan and Co., Ltd., 1884.

Vaillant, George C. *Aztecs of Mexico*. New York: Garden City, N.Y.: Doubleday & Company, Inc., 1941.

West, James. *Plainville, U.S.A.* New York: Columbia University Press, 1945.

Whyte, William Foote. *Street Corner Society: The Social Structure of an Italian Slum*, 2d ed. Chicago: University of Chicago Press, 1955.

Index

TRIBES

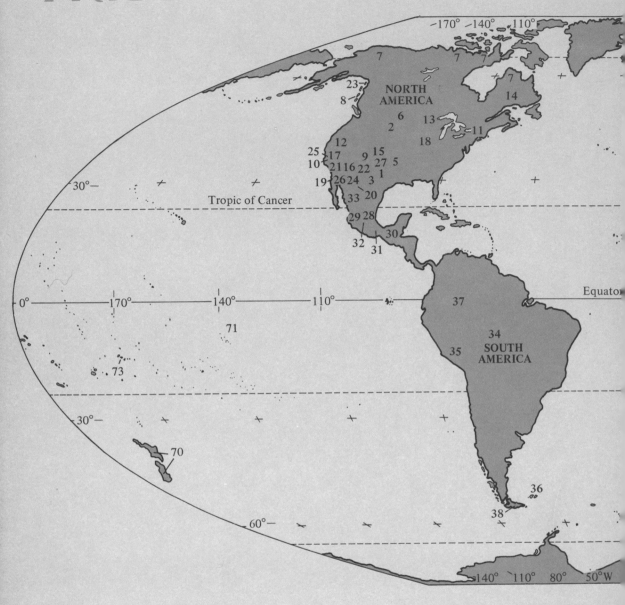

AMERICAS

NORTH

1 ACOMA
2 CHEYENNE
3 CHIRICAHUA APACHE
4 CHUMASH
5 COCHITI
6 CROW
7 ESKIMO
8 HAIDA
9 HOPI
10 HUPA
11 IROQUOIS

12 KAROK
13 MANDAN
14 NASKAPI
15 NAVAJO
16 NISENAN
17 NOMLAKI
18 OMAHA
19 OWENS VALLEY PAIUTE
20 PIMA
21 POMO and NOMLAKI
22 SHOSHONE

23 TLINGIT
24 WESTERN APACHE
25 YUROK
26 YUMA
27 ZUNI

MIDDLE

28 AZTEC
29 HUICHOL
30 MAYA
31 MIXE and ZAPOTEC

32 TARASCAN
33 YAQUI and MAYO

SOUTH

34 CARAJA and TAPIRAPE
35 INCA (QUECHUA)
36 ONA
37 WITOTO and YAGUA
38 YAHGAN